Teaching the Heart of the Old Testament

TRUTHFORTODAY
FROM THE OLD TESTAMENT

Teaching the Heart of the Old Testament

John Ortberg
with Kevin and Sherry Harney

Previously published as *Old Testament Challenge*

ZONDERVAN®

ZONDERVAN.com/
AUTHORTRACKER
follow your favorite authors

ZONDERVAN

Teaching the Heart of the Old Testament

Previously published as *Old Testament Challenge Vol. 1: Creating a New Community Teaching Guide, Old Testament Challenge Vol. 2: Stepping Out in Faith Teaching Guide, Old Testament Challenge Vol. 3: Developing a Heart for God Teaching Guide,* and *Old Testament Challenge Vol. 4: Pursuing Spiritual Authenticity Teaching Guide,* copyright © 2003.

This title is also available as a Zondervan ebook.
Visit www.zondervan.com/ebooks.

Requests for information should be addressed to:

Zondervan, *Grand Rapids, Michigan 49530*

ISBN 978-0-310-32956-5

Cover design: Kirk DouPonce
Interior design: Matthew VanZomeren

Printed in the United States of America

10 11 12 13 14 15 16 /DCI/ 27 26 25 24 23 22 21 20 19 18 17 16 15 14 13 12 11 10 9 8 7 6 5 4 3 2 1

Contents

Part 3: Developing a Heart for God

Life-Changing Lessons from the Wisdom Books

Part 4: Pursuing Spiritual Authenticity

Life-Changing Words from the Prophets

Introduction

Teaching the Heart of the Old Testament is a teaching resource in the *Truth for Today: From the Old Testament* series by John Ortberg that is designed to foster spiritual formation and growth on three distinct levels (congregation-wide, small group, and individual). This book addresses the first level of learning by providing leaders with material they can teach and preach to the full community of God's people. The primary reason these materials were developed was for use in a worship service, but there could also be some application of these materials in a larger class setting.

In addition, while the material in this book is provided to facilitate a stand-alone, thirty-two message preaching series on the Old Testament, it has also been developed to correspond with four small group Bible studies that match the material. These studies are optional, but can be used, along with the weekly messages, to encourage further study of the material. These studies are available for purchase separately. Each of the four small group studies matches one of the four sections of this book and the reading plan included on the DVD-ROM.

This book, *Teaching the Heart of the Old Testament*, is designed to give teachers a wealth of ideas as they prepare to bring a message from God's Word. These materials have been designed to provide a large pool of information on the text and ideas for preaching. From these materials, the teacher can shape and form a message that fits the congregation he or she serves. As you will discover when you begin to dig into the teaching resources, there are far more source materials and ideas than can be incorporated in a normal sermon or teaching session. Each teacher will need to decide what materials best fit their situation, add their own personal illustrations and teaching ideas, and then form a message that fits their congregation and personal teaching style.

These materials have intentionally been developed on two levels. First, John Ortberg wrote the initial messages and preached them at Willow Creek Community Church. John developed these messages to teach them at the New Community Believer's Services. You will find digital audio of his original messages on the included DVD-ROM. You will also notice that there were a few guest preachers who took part in the original teaching at Willow Creek.

Next, the materials and resources from this series were adapted for a second-generation church, Corinth Church in Grand Rapids, Michigan. Kevin Harney continued the process of developing and expanding the materials as he preached the messages in the Sunday morning services at Corinth Church. New illustrations, creative message ideas, PowerPoint presentations, Frequently Asked Questions about the Old Testament, and other study materials were added and the messages were expanded. Although John Ortberg was the primary writer/teacher at Willow Creek and Kevin Harney the primary writer/teacher at Corinth Church, a whole team of teachers, leaders, and editors have partnered together to develop and create this teaching resource.

What makes this teaching resource so unique are the many different tools offered to the teacher. Inside, you will find the following categories of material in various combinations:

- Creative Message Idea
- Heart of the Message
- Heart of the Messenger
- Historical Context
- Illustration
- Interpretive Insight
- Life Application
- Narrative on Life
- Narrative on the Text
- New Testament Connection
- On the Lighter Side
- Pause for Prayer
- Pause for Reflection
- Quotable Quote
- Significant Scripture
- Word Study

It is important to note that some of the teaching resources listed above will appear in every study (for example, The Heart of the Message, The Heart of the Teacher, and Interpretive Insights). Some of the other resources might appear in one message but not in another. The various components of the messages contained in this resource are defined in the pages that follow.

Creative Message Idea

This section will offer a broad variety of ideas a teacher can use to bring a biblical point home with power. This section will include video pieces developed for the original messages. These are on the DVD-ROM included with the book. This section will also include a number of ideas for using props or visual aids to communicate a relevant biblical truth. Some of the creative message ideas will help the teacher move worshipers to respond or interact during the message. We can't begin to cover all the creative ideas that have been developed to bring the message of the Old Testament alive, but if you take a few moments and skim through them, you will begin to get a sense of the kinds of creative ideas that are available for a teacher or preacher. In an effort to make these ideas user friendly, we have listed everything that is needed to naturally incorporate each creative idea into the message. Each of these ideas has been used effectively at Willow Creek, Corinth Church, or both, but we encourage you to decide which ones will connect in your particular context. On the DVD-ROM, you will also find relevant PowerPoint presentations and even a game, "Are You an Old Testament Expert?"

Heart of the Message

This is a brief description of the heartbeat or central theme of *the entire message.* Each message will begin with a short section to help the teacher gain a sense of the core idea or ideas being communicated in each message.

Heart of the Messenger

Teachers and preachers can't communicate with passion and clarity until their hearts have been touched and impacted by the truth of God's Word. This section will give some direction for how each teacher can begin to prepare to study and open their heart to what the Holy Spirit wants to say to them. One of the goals of *Teaching the Heart of the Old Testament* is to help teachers move forward in their own journey of faith. We believe the process of self-examination, deep learning, and personal growth that will be experienced while leading this series can be life-changing! This section will usually include a few questions for personal reflection as the teacher prepares to bring the message.

Historical Context Note

Throughout this resource you will find helpful notes on the historical context of certain passages. There are a number of texts we will study in these messages that make much more sense when we have an understanding of the culture and the world of the Old Testament. The Historical Context Notes are provided to help you teach about this kind of background information. These notes are not designed to be highly academic observations but are intended to help the teacher make natural observations about culture and customs that will bring the message of the Old Testament alive.

Illustration

Jesus was a master storyteller. He used word pictures to illustrate much of what he taught. In this resource we have provided many ideas for illustrating core Old Testament ideas. Sometimes these illustrations can be read just as they are printed. At other times, the teacher will be given ideas or direction on developing an illustration out of their own life or ministry. Each teacher must decide whether an illustration fits for their setting. Even if a particular illustration does not fit in your context, it might spark some ideas for an illustration that does.

Interpretive Insight

A huge part of teaching the Bible is doing interpretive work. We have provided solid biblical interpretation that can function as the backbone of each message. This does not mean that the teacher should not do additional study, but it does offer a great starting point. Major texts being used in each message will have a brief, or sometimes extended, section of biblical interpretation provided in this resource.

Life Application

In the book of James we read these words, "Do not merely listen to the word, and so deceive yourselves. Do what it says" (James 1:22). Any study of God's Word that is going to have life-changing power must include application. In each message you will find ideas for life application. Sometimes these ideas are specific. They will give detailed instruction on concrete ways a congregation can respond to God's Word. At other times these applications will be broad, intended to encourage individual reflection upon a specific area of life. In these cases, the specific application will come as the Holy Spirit speaks to the heart of each person and shows where change needs to take place.

Narrative on Life

Occasionally telling a story from everyday life is the best way to bring a biblical truth home to the listeners. In this resource we have captured some great examples of life narratives that speak powerfully. These can be used as they are found, or you can retell them in your own words.

Narrative on the Text

One of the unique gifts John Ortberg has as a preacher is the ability to tell a familiar biblical story in a fresh narrative form. This retelling of the story, including some natural commentary on the text, brings familiar passages alive. These sections of John's sermons have been captured in a form that can be read by the teacher. Or, they can become a source of ideas as you tell the story in a narrative form that fits your style of communication.

New Testament Connection

There are many places where the Old Testament and New Testament intersect. Because most Christ-followers are more familiar with the New Testament, we have tried to make note of natural connection points between these two parts of the Bible. Sometimes the connection is linguistic, at other times it is thematic, and there are also times when a specific Old Testament passage is used in the New Testament. You will find helpful insights on how the Old Testament passage you are studying relates to familiar portions of the New Testament.

On the Lighter Side

Humor can be one of the greatest tools in a sermon. Jesus used irony and humor in his communication, and we can learn to use it as we teach God's Word. In these portions of the book you will find two specific kinds of humorous insights. First, we will make note of biblical passages or insights that have a humorous aspect to them. Second, we will give you ideas for stories or jokes that might hit a main theme in the message.

Pause for Prayer

Too often a teacher waits until the end of a message to pray with God's people about what is being taught and learned. Sometimes the best time to pause for prayer is right in the middle of a message. If a point has a strong life application or potential for conviction and transformation, you might want to pause right in the midst of the message and take a few moments for prayer. The Pause for Prayer sections give suggestions for when you might want to do this and how to move naturally into prayer at these times.

Pause for Reflection

We live in a hurried world. Often, we preach and teach with the clock in mind. In our busy world, we need to be reminded that teaching God's Word should always include time for personal reflection. We need to make space for the Holy Spirit to speak to our hearts and touch our lives. The Pause for Reflection portions give the teacher ideas for when they might want to pause, right in the middle of the message, and take a moment for silence. These moments can be used to listen, process the lessons that have been learned, and reflect on personal life application goals.

Significant Scripture

Every message in this book is rooted in Scripture. At the beginning of each section of each message is a list of significant Scriptures for that portion. Most of the Scriptures listed are included in the message notes, but some are not. Occasionally we will list a related passage because we believe it would be worth studying as you prepare your message. Most of the time there is exposition of the passages listed in the Significant Scripture part of the study, but some of the time these are simply passages we encourage you to use for reflection as you prepare your message.

Quotable Quote

God has spoken powerfully through many of his people through history. We have collected some great quotes from Christians throughout the ages and included them in this resource.

Word Study

Often the background of a word in the Bible helps a passage come alive and make sense. Any time we feel a word needs explanation, we include a short background piece in a word study. Sometimes these word studies give linguistic background; at other times they simply give a broader meaning for a word that might go unnoticed if not highlighted.

DVD-ROM Resources

Included with this book is a DVD-ROM with some additional, supplemental resources. These include:

Audio Messages: MP3 files containing the original thirty-one messages as they were taught at Willow Creek Community Church as part of the *Old Testament Challenge* series.

Video Segments: There are sixteen creative video segments included with this resource. Some of these cover general topics that can be used anywhere during the series. Others are specific to a certain message, as indicated in the material.

Daily Reading Guide: One of the primary goals of this series is to help followers of Christ see the life-changing relevance of God's Word. The best way to do this is to help them dig into the Bible on a regular basis. In an effort to accomplish this, we have laid out the entire Old Testament in forty weeks of reading. Individuals who decide to read the entire Old Testament will have a tool you can make available to them. For those who feel they cannot commit to the entire forty weeks, a "fast-track" thirty-two-week study guide is also included, with each week's lesson corresponding to the messages that are preached (and the optional small group materials). This can be uploaded to your website, distributed electronically, or printed and distributed to the congregation.

Frequently Asked Questions: There are forty two-page documents included on the resource disk that answer frequently asked questions (FAQs) about the Old Testament. Each FAQ corresponds to a week of the complete (forty-week) daily reading guide. These can be uploaded to your website, distributed electronically, or printed and distributed each week before or after the service.

PowerPoint Presentations: A PowerPoint presentation is included for every message for a total of thirty-two presentations.

Interactive Games: An interactive "Are You an Old Testament Expert?" game in Adobe Flash format (.SWF) is provided for several of the reading weeks. These games can be used by participants to test their knowledge of that week's reading, and they correspond to the complete, forty-week reading plan. These can be used in a worship service or a teaching setting, placed on your church's website, or you may find another creative use for these materials.

Small Group Resources

Teaching the Heart of the Old Testament is a comprehensive resource for leading your congregation through a thirty-two-week study of the Old Testament. In addition to the resources provided in this book and on the included DVD-ROM (for congregational and individual use), there are optional small group studies that correspond to the teaching materials.

Each of the four studies matches a section of this book, and each session has Scripture readings, small-group questions, and written pieces to spark meaningful discussion. At the end of each study booklet is a collection of leader's notes to help both participants and leaders as they prepare for their small-group gathering. These small-group studies also include occasional word studies and quotes to help participants go deeper into the topic of the study.

The *Truth for Today: From the Old Testament* series includes the following four small-group Bible studies:

Creating a New Community

Life-Changing Stories from Genesis to Deuteronomy (9 sessions)

Guiding you through the five books of Moses, this volume reveals God's passionate desire for intimacy with his people and among his people.

Stepping Out in Faith

Life-Changing Examples from the History of Israel (7 sessions)

This volume guides you through the history of Israel, revealing God's presence and unyielding commitment to show his children how to follow him in good times as well as difficult times.

Developing a Heart for God

Life-Changing Lessons from the Wisdom Books (8 sessions)

This volume takes you through the wisdom books of the Old Testament and unveils truths that will help you grow in your love for God and those around you.

Pursuing Spiritual Authenticity

Life-Changing Words from the Prophets (8 sessions)

This volume unpacks the words of the prophets to help lead you to new levels of spiritual maturity. The prophets' words trumpet across the centuries, calling all Christ-followers to authentic spiritual lives.

Part 1

Creating a New Community

Life-Changing Stories from Genesis to Deuteronomy

Message 1

God's Greatest Dream

Genesis 1–2

THE HEART OF THE Message

Infants who receive no love, touch, or words of affection can be damaged for life. Some even die. Before they can ever express their need in words, the smallest of babies cry out for the community and tender touch of other human beings. Children and teens long for acceptance and will do almost anything to have a sense that they fit in and belong to some group, club, team, or even a gang—if that's what it takes to satisfy their hunger for community.

This need does not go away as we become adults. There seems to be some deep and unyielding cry of the heart that says, "I don't want to be alone. I need to love and be loved. My heart is crying out for a place where I can be accepted and belong."

From the beginning to the end of our lives, we hunger and long for community. We were not made to be alone, but in loving and life-giving relationship with God and each other. God, who exists in eternal community as Father, Son, and Holy Spirit, invites us into the beauty and wonder of fellowship with him. He also makes it possible for us to connect heart-to-heart with each other. This journey toward authentic community begins in the first verses of Genesis and finds its culmination in the final verses of Revelation. We were made for community, and it is God's plan to bring us into life-giving relationship with him and with each other. The longing of our heart can only be satisfied when we enter God's plan for community.

BRIEF MESSAGE OUTLINE

1. God created the heavens and the earth and everything in them.
2. God wanted his community to have a wonderful place to live.
3. The climax of creation is men and women in life-giving community with God and each other.

THE HEART OF THE Messenger

As you prepare to teach this message, take time to do a heart check. Do you live with an increasing awareness that God loves you? Are you overwhelmed with the reality that God loves each person you will encounter today? Are you stunned by the fact that God longs to invite you into deeper and deeper places of community with him and with others?

Ask God to remind you of the simple, yet life-changing truth that you are God's beloved child! Pray for your heart to be expanded with God's love so that as you teach this message, you speak from a place of joy-filled amazement over God's passion and affection for you! As you prepare to lead, ask God to remind you that your need for community is just as deep in those you will be teaching.

SIGNIFICANT SCRIPTURE

Genesis 1:1

Introduction

The chair illustration (bottom of page 21) is a powerful way to help people form a mental picture of the community experienced by the Trinity and also a picture of the human need for community.

INTERPRETIVE INSIGHT | *Challenging the Prevailing Worldview*

It is fair to say that the first sentence of the Bible is the single most controversial and important sentence that has ever been written. It is hard for us to imagine how the opening words of the Bible challenged and shattered the prevailing worldview.

CREATIVE MESSAGE IDEA | *Art That Reflects the Artist*

A strong theme in this portion of Scripture and this message is that the created world reflects the heart, character, and attributes of the creator (the artist). You might want to have a number of people from your congregation (2–6 people) bring a piece of art they have created (from children to adults) and have it on display in the entry area of the church or on the teaching platform. Allow people to begin thinking about how art reflects the artist. Use this as a visual tool to lock in on this aspect of the message. These people could bring paintings, drawings, sculptures, or any other visual art form. It might be helpful to have them stand by their piece of art after the service and tell people how their art expresses something unique about themselves as an artist.

You Will Need

- Someone who can contact 2–6 people in your congregation who have an artistic background to see if they can bring a piece of art that expresses something about who they are as a person
- Space in the entry area of your church or on the platform for these pieces of art to be displayed
- Stands for pictures and small tables for sculptures (as many as are needed for those who will be bringing their art work)
- If you have a digital camera and video projection capability, you might want to have someone take pictures of these pieces of art from varied angles and project these on the screen in your sanctuary before the worship service or during your message

CREATIVE MESSAGE IDEA *Video of Nature's Beauty*

The DVD-ROM included with this book has a visual/music montage that beautifully illustrates the creation story. This video includes music, pictures of creation, and texts from Genesis. The video runs three minutes and twenty seconds and can be used during the worship service, at the start of the message, or in the midst of the message.

You Will Need

- Video projection capability in your worship center
- Someone to run the video during the service

CREATIVE MESSAGE IDEA *A Picture of the Trinity in Community ... The Three Chairs*

Set three chairs on the stage (before the service begins, if possible). Have the chairs facing each other as if three people were sitting in them in intimate conversation. As you begin your message, you might want to invite three people to come and sit in these chairs as a picture of the community. You might also have a fourth chair off to the side, out of community with God. A person in this chair could represent people who are not in intimate relationship with God. These chairs and people can be used to paint a picture of community as you begin your message.

They can be used as you describe the Trinity and how God exists in eternal community. They can be used as you describe the community that God longed to forge with Adam and Eve, his children. As you work on this imagery, you can move in other directions as well. When you look at how community is broken through sin, you can move a chair away to portray separation from God or from community with other people.

This illustration is a simple visual that can be used in this message and possibly carried into a future message as well. It is a strong way to begin your message. Once you have painted this picture of God's eternal community and his longing to invite us into this wonderful place of fellowship, you can have your volunteers return to their seats (with a big "thank you" for helping out with the message). The chairs can remain where they are so that you can refer back to them as you walk through the message.

You Will Need

- Three chairs facing each other
- One additional chair off to the side

Use the image of the three chairs and reflect on how God exists in eternal community. He did not create us because he was bored or so that we could do the chores he did not want to do. God's creation of man and woman reflects his very nature; he is a God who exists in eternal community: Father, Son, and Holy Spirit. At this time you might want to add another chair to the circle of three you have on the stage. Let people know that the fellowship of the Father, Son, and Holy Spirit is not closed, but open! God has placed a chair and invites you to come and join this community.

Reflect on how these words rivaled the conventional wisdom taught in the creation stories of that day. To get a sense for how these words would have hit people in the Old Testament world, you need to use your imagination. Imagine for a moment that you lived in the days the book of Genesis was written and that you have never heard that there is a personal God who created all things and who promises life in heaven. This idea has never entered your thinking.

Rather, since you have grown up in the ancient Near East, you have heard a number of stories about how creation took place. None of these myths involve a loving and personal creator. These myths embrace a belief that the universe is filled with many gods, and all these gods are limited in power and morally fallible. The gods are petty and jealous of one another.

As a result of this worldview, you live in fear and are ruled by superstition. You are in a world with fertility cults that encourage gross sexual immorality. The people around you worship objects like the sun and the moon and even small stone statues. The common belief is that heavenly bodies, like stars, actually have influence over the affairs of human beings.

You are familiar with practices such as human sacrifice, used in an effort to manipulate the gods and to gain their favor. You are profoundly aware that the view of human beings is low and that the common belief system says that people were created to do the work that the gods didn't want to do. Life is a cycle of conflict between people and the gods, and, in turn, between fellow human beings. Life is not about servanthood; rather, it is a fight for dominance. Immense violence, elimination of the weak, and infanticide are common and acceptable practices.

The central belief is that life is just an endless cycle. Life is, in the words of the scholars, "a wheel of life that rotates around the hub of death." One generation is born, grows old, dies, another one comes along, and so it goes without any meaning or purpose.

Into this horribly destructive belief system these words are spoken: "In the beginning God"—a transcendent, all-powerful, eternal, personal being—"created the heavens and the earth." These words were written, and the world has never been the same.

> Our culture, civilization, has been so shaped by the Old Testament that it's almost impossible to conceive how these words changed the world.
>
> *Thomas Cahill, in* The Gift of the Jews

SIGNIFICANT SCRIPTURE

Genesis 1:1–3
James 1:17
John 1:1, 14; 17:21

1. God Created the Heavens and the Earth and Everything in Them

It is the first question asked by countless children. As we grow up, we ask it over and over again. It is a good question, a fair question. And it is just one word: "Why?"

We all have a desire to know why things are the way they are. Why am I here? Why is anyone here? In this portion of the message we will address why God created the heavens and the earth. Ultimately, we will answer the question: Why are we here?

> "Why does something exist rather than nothing?" It's a great question!
> *Richard Swinburne, a great twentieth-century philosopher*

INTERPRETIVE INSIGHT | *Community from the Beginning*

Highlight the presence of the Trinity from the very beginning of creation. Make note of the community that existed even in the creation of the world:

- In verse 1 we *see* the **Father** creating. In James 1:17 this Creator is called "the Father of the heavenly lights," who sends us every good and perfect gift from above.
- In verse 2 the **Spirit** of God is hovering over the waters. Similar language is used to describe the Spirit of God hovering over Jesus at his baptism.
- In verse 3 God creates by speaking his word. In the beginning of the gospel of John we learn that "the Word" through whom all things are created is none other than Jesus Christ, the **Son of God** (John 1:1, 14).

Out of this community, this Trinitarian joy and delight, God creates. He does not do this because he is bored or because he is lonely. God does not create us so that he will have little servants to do the chores he does not want to do. Rather, out of the magnificent richness of the eternal community experienced by the Trinity, God decides to broaden the circle. He longs to invite us to live in his love. This invitation is not for us to become little gods, but it is for us to bask in the glorious fellowship of the Trinity. This is the first open chair in all time. We sit in that chair, and God invites us to enter his circle, to pull up to his table, to join the community of the Father, Son, and Holy Spirit.

> God's aim in history is the creation of an inclusive community of loving persons, with himself included as its primary sustainer and most glorious inhabitant.
> *Dallas Willard*

NEW TESTAMENT CONNECTION

The Heartbeat of God

John 17:21 captures the heartbeat of the Father and the Son who long to invite us into intimate fellowship. The community of the Trinity is so rich; they long to invite us in to share in the feast. The community God longs to have with his people all the way back in the first chapters of Genesis is still something God desires.

PAUSE FOR PRAYER

You might want to pause right here, in the middle of your message, and invite the congregation to pray for the ability to hear and receive God's invitation to enter into the rich and eternal fellowship of the Father, Son, and Holy Spirit.

2. God Wanted His Community to Have a Wonderful Place to Live!

SIGNIFICANT SCRIPTURE

Isaiah 55:1–2
Ephesians 2:8–9

We get confused. All of us do, sometimes. We forget that only the Creator is to be worshiped, never the creation. At the time Genesis was written, people worshiped the sun, moon, stars, and even little stone idols. Thankfully, we have moved well beyond that kind of adoration of material things ... or have we?

> You can't buy happiness, but now you can lease it!
>
> *Magazine ad for a car company*

Many people have become entangled in new forms of idolatry. Let some of these words float through your mind for a moment: Lexus, Beemer, my portfolio, the summer cottage, or my horoscope, just to name a few. Material things still cry out for our worship, and we need to get a proper perspective on the stuff of this world. We need to remember who made it all, who sustains it all, and who truly deserves our worship and adoration.

ILLUSTRATION | *My Story*

You might want to tell a story about a time you were in God's creation and learned about his character and beautiful creativity as you looked at all he has made. We need

NEW TESTAMENT CONNECTION | *Celebrating the Creator and His Creation*

God created a place where we could enter into community with him and with each other, but we need to live with a deep awareness that the Creator and the creation are infinitely different. Though the creation can reveal things about the nature and character of the Creator, the creation is never to be worshiped. There is a human tendency to get this confused! In the New Testament, the apostle Paul put it this way, "They exchanged the truth of God for a lie, and worshiped and served created things rather than the Creator—who is forever praised. Amen" (Romans 1:25).

Look at the order of creation and how God made the sun, the moon, and the stars. In the order of creation, the sun and moon were not spoken into existence until the fourth day. This truth spoke volumes to people who worshiped the heavenly bodies. Genesis teaches that the sun and moon are not divine; they are created objects. They were made by the one God who spoke heaven and earth into existence. Not only does the Bible teach that they have a beginning but also that they will have an end (Revelation 21:23).

A healthy understanding of creation will give us a balanced perspective on material things. We should not be captivated by the stuff of this world; rather, we should worship the One who made it all. Too often in this life we become enamored by material things instead of the Creator. Genesis gives us a true perspective on happiness. We can't buy it, we can't lease it, but God invites us to receive freely what we could never afford.

to celebrate the wonder of his creation, but let this celebration turn our eyes beyond the creation to the Creator.

> **WORD STUDY**
>
> *Ex Nihilo*
>
> The following is a phrase taken from the Latin language: *ex nihilo*. Literally it means, "out of nothing." We can create things from the stuff God has already made (wood, metal, clay, etc.). But only God can create *ex nihilo*.

ILLUSTRATION | *"We Don't Have the Power!"*

Seven times we read that God spoke and things came into existence. We are so limited in power, but God can speak and the universe comes into being. In the *Star Trek* series, Captain Kirk often barked out a command, "I need more power!" Often he would hear back from Scottie, "I can't do it, Captain." With all the resources of the Enterprise and all the futuristic instruments they had, there were times when the captain's commands were met with a panicked, "We don't have the power!" When we speak, we see limited results; when God speaks, there is always enough power!

INTERPRETIVE INSIGHT | *Good Stuff*

Another theme in creation we need to notice is that God kept giving a running commentary on his creation. Do you notice how he describes it, over and over again? He says, "It is good." God takes endless delight in his creation.

ILLUSTRATION | *A Glimpse of God's Love*

Many people have a deep love for animals. They have a pet that means so much to them. There is a true story about a guy who chartered a plane and flew his dog across three states just so they could be together. It was just the pilot and the dog on the trip ... a private plane ride. It might seem strange to some people, but those who really love their pets can understand this story. Now, take the love that guy had for his pet dog and multiply it over and over, and you might get a glimpse of how God feels about his creation.

As a teacher, you can tell this story, or tell a story from your own life about someone you know who did something extraordinary because he or she loved a pet. The key is helping people see that God's love for his creation is so much greater than our love.

> God has boundless delight in what he creates.
>
> *G. K. Chesterton*

Because children have abounding vitality and because they are fierce and free in spirit, they want things repeated and unchanged. They always say, "Do it again," and the grown-up person does it again until he is nearly dead—for grown-up people are not strong enough to exult in monotony. But perhaps God is strong enough to exult in monotony. It is possible that God says every morning, "Do it again," to the sun; and every evening, "Do it again," to the moon. It may not be automatic necessity that makes all daisies alike; it may be that God makes every daisy separately but never gets tired of making them. It may be that he has the eternal appetite of infancy; for we have sinned and grown old, and our Father is younger than we.

LIFE APPLICATION | *Take Time to Notice*

When we celebrate the wonder of creation and this celebration leads us to authentic worship of the Creator, we discover joy. Take time this week to drink in the wonder of God's creation. Go to a forest preserve, the oceanside, the lakeside, or a large park, or just take a long drive. Notice the colors, the birds, the plants, the color of the sky, and whatever else you see. Take time to praise the Creator for the beauty of his handiwork. Tell him, "You know, Lord, you are right! This really is good."

3. The Climax of Creation: Human Beings in Community with God and Each Other

As human beings, we live with the risk of forgetting who we are. We live between two radically different extremes. On the one hand, we can become prideful and believe we deserve a place equal to God. Sadly, this happened early in human history, and it still happens today. On the other end of the continuum is an attitude that degrades human beings and treats them as some coincidental result of a random Big Bang or cosmic accident.

Between these poles lies the truth. We are God's creation. Human beings are the apex, the pinnacle of God's creative work. Yet, we are not God, we are his children. We are valuable because of who made us, and we are significant because of how he made us, in his image! Yet we must never forget that he is the Creator and we are his creation.

WORD STUDY

Imago Dei

It's time for another brief Latin lesson. Here is a great phrase that has been used for centuries by scholars and theologians: *imago Dei*. It means "the image of God." In Genesis 1:27 we are told that we were created in the image of God. We have the *imago Dei* within us. For example, we have a capacity for community. We don't know all of what it means to be created in the image of God, but our capacity for community is certainly part of it.

INTERPRETIVE INSIGHT | *A Healthy Perspective*

The first thing we need to notice when we read of the creation of human beings is that we are finite, limited, and fragile. We are not gods. We are made of dust. It is important to note that everything else in creation was spoken into existence. We are told, from the very beginning, something that gives us perspective on life. Genesis 3:19 teaches us that we came from dust and will return to dust.

> Big deal, I'm used to dust.
> *Erma Bombeck*

INTERPRETIVE INSIGHT | *More Than Dust*

The dominant scientific worldview today says we are simply highly evolved apes without tails. We are just the next step in the evolutionary chain of events. But Genesis tells a different story. We might be made of dust, but we are still the apex of God's creation. The crescendo at the end of this symphony is the creation of men and women, made in the image of God.

INTERPRETIVE INSIGHT | *God Loves His Creation*

Focus on how God relates with his creation and how he continues to build relationship with us:

- God blesses his people and gives abundant life (Genesis 1:28).
- God provides for his people (Genesis 1:29).
- God calls us to meaningful and rich experiences of work (2:15). It is important to note that work is not a result of the Fall, but was a gift given before the Fall. After the Fall work became painful, but before, it was a gift from the hand of the Father. God actually left some things undone and invited us into the joy of being coworkers with him.

ON THE LIGHTER SIDE | *Woman*

Genesis records a charming story about a parade of animals that are brought before Adam to see if any of them might be his type. They are all brought to him, and Adam gives them each a name. It seems Adam is an excellent namer. Naming has to do with studying these creatures and perceiving their natures. Adam is beginning to learn and to work and to add value to the world around him.

Adam looks at each of the animals and says, "Oh, I like it, great job, God. But, to tell you the truth, it's not really my type." So, God creates a woman, and Adam immediately decides she *is* his type. His response is sheer poetry (Genesis 2:23). It really is Hebrew poetry. There's a kind of playfulness to this text. It's hard to translate into English.

In effect, what Adam says is, "She shall be called *'ishsha*, for she was taken out of *'ish*." These words are somewhat like the words for *man* and *wo-man* in English. In fact, that's where the old line comes from that Adam sees Eve for the first time and says, "**Whoa, man**—yeah, that's it: **Woman**." This play on words in English is similar to the play on words in Hebrew. This kind of wordplay is quite common in Hebrew.

Closing Reflections and Challenges

1. *Invitation to participate in this series.* Give a strong exhortation to commit to daily study as well as small group gatherings (if you are a part of these). This might be a good time to remind people about the idea of keeping notes in their Bible and add the four symbols to help them remember what struck them as they studied:

   ? What's up with that?
   ! Pay attention to this command!
   ♥ My heart burned within me. This marks a prompting of the Holy Spirit for life change.
   △ Lessons about the character of God.

2. *Reissue the challenge to take time in creation and celebrate the Creator and all he has made.* Sound the call to slow down, notice, appreciate, and celebrate God's creation, but also to keep a proper perspective. Praise and worship belong to the Creator, never the creation!
3. *Pray.* Thank God for his amazing invitation into community with him and the people he has created.

Message 2

Community Busters

Genesis 3–11

THE HEART OF THE Message

God's plan was for community. His desire was for human beings to live in harmonious and loving relationship with him and with each other. God did his part. He made us and gave us a wonderful place to meet with him and enter into rich and life-giving relationship with each other.

Sometimes the best of plans go bad. In Genesis 3–11 we see the downward spiral of sin in four distinct scenes: Adam and Eve, the story of Cain and Abel, the Flood, and the Tower of Babel. As we watch the drama unfold, we see things go from bad to worse. Sin goes deep and spreads wider. We also learn from God's response to the sinful choices made by his children.

In this message we will look into the mirror of God's Word and see ourselves. We will face the reality of our sin and be reminded of the depth of God's grace for his beloved children.

BRIEF MESSAGE OUTLINE

1. Adam and Eve
2. Cain and Abel
3. The days of Noah
4. The Tower of Babel

THE HEART OF THE Messenger

This is a message that will invite the Holy Spirit to come and lay every heart bare before the Father. We will look deeply into Scripture and also intently into the mirror to see ourselves as God sees us. The reflection we see is not always attractive!

As a teacher, take time to search your own heart and ask God to show you where there is hidden sin. Take time to read and reflect on Psalm 51 (a prayer of confession David lifted to God after a time of brazen sin and deep brokenness). Ask for God to prepare your heart to teach on a very important but difficult subject.

Introduction

INTERPRETIVE INSIGHT | *The Authorship of the Pentateuch*

Scholars believe Moses wrote most of the Pentateuch, but they are pretty confident that he didn't write every word. Because Deuteronomy records the story of the death of Moses, we can be confident he did not write that section. In Numbers 12:3 we read the statement, "Now Moses was a very humble man, more humble than anyone else on the face of the earth." It is difficult to imagine Moses writing, "I was a very humble man, more humble than anyone." The Pentateuch is closely associated with Moses, but there may be some sections that were not written by him.

LIFE APPLICATION | *Old Testament Bible Study*

You may want to take a brief moment and make a clarifying comment about studying the Bible in this series. There are thirty-two messages in the full series. If you are walking through the entire Old Testament study with your church, here are a couple of points of clarification that will be helpful for those who are participating:

- Walking through the series (including the individual reading and small group studies) will give your church members a chance to get strongly grounded in the Old Testament. But, because this is an overview study, there is not enough time to look at every individual chapter of each book in the Old Testament.
- In this study you will spend more time in some books, such as Genesis, than in other books, because Genesis has more foundational material.
- Each message will not correspond with the exact passage that you are reading each week if you are doing the full reading guide. However, the message will line up exactly with the abbreviated reading guide provided.
- Encourage participants to commit to this series regardless of how much of the Old Testament they decide to read along the way.

WORD STUDY

Pentateuch

The first five books of the Bible are called the Pentateuch. The word *Pentateuch* comes from two words: *penta*, which means "five" (as in "pentagon"), and *teuch*, which means "scroll." The word Pentateuch means the five scrolls, because these are the first five books of the Old Testament. The Jews called these books the "Torah," and in the New Testament they are called the "Law." When you read the phrase "the Law and the Prophets," "the Law" refers to these first five books and "the Prophets" refers to the other historical books as well as the prophetic books of the Old Testament. The Pentateuch is essentially the work of Moses. When we look at this portion of the Bible, it is best to see it as one book with five sections.

1. Adam and Eve

Adam and Eve had everything they needed. God had provided a paradise beyond what any one of us could imagine. They had access to all the fruit of the garden ... with one explicit exception.

What follows is tragic. Rather than celebrating what they had, they fixated on what they did not have. Rather than enjoying what was in-bounds, they wanted what was out-of-bounds. What follows is an account of the temptation they faced, how they fell, and the staggering consequences of this rebellion. Along with the unveiling of the tempting tactics of the devil, we see the relentless love of God for his children. Among the dissonant notes of sin, we hear the strains of grace begin to echo through history.

SIGNIFICANT SCRIPTURE

Genesis 2:16–17

INTERPRETIVE INSIGHT | *The Nature of Sin*

Sometimes people wonder, "Why did God give this command? If God had not given any commands at all, human beings wouldn't have sinned and everything would have

CREATIVE MESSAGE IDEA | *The Three Chairs*

Again, use the three chairs to represent the Trinity in perfect community. Set another chair in the middle of them to represent people who are invited into community and intimate relationship with God.

As you look at each of the four scenes that reflect sin and broken community, move the chair in the middle farther and farther from the other three chairs. Let this be a visual reminder, as you teach, of how sin breaks community and creates greater distance from God.

You Will Need

- Three chairs facing each other
- One additional chair in the middle of the three chairs (it might be helpful to have this chair look different from the other three)

CREATIVE MESSAGE IDEA | *Picture the Downward Spiral of Sin*

As you talk about each of the four scenes of how sin impacts our lives and our community with God and each other, add the names of the key people and then draw a downward spiral showing how sin becomes a powerful cycle pushing us further and further from God (see the diagram). This simple visual tool paints a picture in the minds of listeners.

You Will Need

- A large flip chart or a large, dry-erase marker board
- An easel to hold up the board
- Large, wide-tipped markers

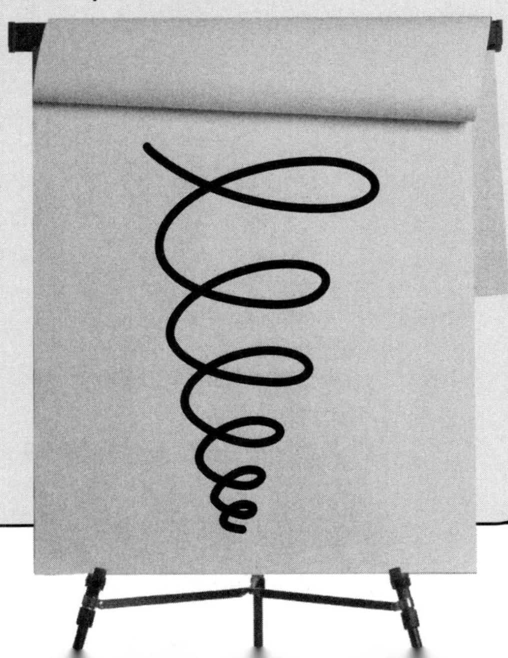

been OK." And people wonder, "Why doesn't God want Adam and Eve to know the difference between good and evil?"

The point of this command is *not* that Adam and Eve will gain moral discernment if they eat from the tree. Moral discernment is a good thing. The idea is that in eating from the tree, they will be declaring, "Now we can decide what is good and evil quite apart from God or anybody else. Now we can be our own God." God is allowing them to choose to be in community with him or to reject community.

SIGNIFICANT SCRIPTURE

Genesis 3:1–6

NARRATIVE ON THE TEXT | *The Tactics of the Enemy*

The enemy comes into the picture early in human history! He is not called Satan in this story, but the Christian church came to identify the serpent with the evil one. What follows is an absolutely brilliant exposition of how temptation works. This was true at the beginning of time, and it is just as true today!

Tactic of the Enemy 1: He twists the truth.

Satan begins with a lie! He twists the truth and misquotes God. Did God say Adam and Eve could not eat from any tree at all? No. God said they could eat from *every tree except one*. In Genesis 2:9 we're told that there were all sorts of trees that were beautiful to see and the fruit was delicious to eat. Adam and Eve were invited to feast on the fruit of all of them! They could eat from any tree *except one*. But the serpent taunts them by saying that God would not let them eat from any tree at all!

This is a misquote of litigious proportions. What is the serpent up to here? He wants to plant a doubt in the woman's mind. He wants her to doubt the goodness of God. He wants her to think, "I can't trust that God has my best interests at heart. I think if I really obey God fully, I will miss out on something good, so I guess I will have to watch out for myself in this world. I guess I better be prepared to set aside what God says if it's really necessary." The decision to sin always involves these kinds of thoughts. Satan sows seeds of doubt concerning God's goodness, and we have to decide if we are going to entertain those thoughts.

Tactic of the Enemy 2: He wants us to see God as more severe than he is.

In Genesis 3:2 we see a second tactic of the enemy. Eve begins to make God more severe than he really is. The woman corrects the serpent when he speaks deceptive words, but notice one inaccuracy in her account of what God says. Did you catch it? When speaking of the forbidden fruit Eve adds the words, "and you must not touch it." God never said, "You must not touch it." But, in Eve's mind she's making God a little more severe than he really is. She's making him a little unreasonable so that disobeying him becomes a more justifiable act.

Tactic of the Enemy 3: He attacks our vulnerable spots and isolates us.

Another tactic of the enemy is that he will always strike at people's vulnerable points. In Genesis 2:16, when God originally gave the command concerning the forbidden fruit, who was present? It was just the man. So, presumably, where does the woman get her information about what God said? From the man. She gets it secondhand!

Notice something else. As she is engaged in this process of deliberation and dealing with temptation, she does not involve the man. When we play with temptation and do it in isolation, we are in grave danger. The enemy wants us to keep it to ourselves—to keep things hidden in the darkness of our own heart. But, when we don't tell anybody else about our struggle and temptation, we make ourselves infinitely more vulnerable.

That is exactly what Eve did and what we do so often. She didn't talk with God about it. She didn't talk with Adam. She stayed in isolation and dealt with it on her own.

NEW TESTAMENT CONNECTION

The Father of Lies

In John 8:44 we read these words spoken by Jesus about the devil: "He was a murderer from the beginning, not holding to the truth, for there is no truth in him. When he lies, he speaks his native language, for he is a liar and the father of lies." What a powerful reminder that, from the beginning of creation, the tactics and the strategies of the devil have not changed.

Tactic of the Enemy 4: He wants us to fixate on sin.

Read Genesis 3:6 closely and notice what happens. The implication of this verse is that Eve's mind becomes obsessed with the fruit she is not to eat. She keeps thinking about what she'd miss if she didn't eat it. She keeps looking at it, obsessing over it without God or another person to challenge her thinking. When she does that, the next step becomes inevitable. It's just inevitable that she'll eat it.

Tactic of the Enemy 5: He entices us to invite others into our sin.

When we read the account of sin entering the world, we simply read that Eve gave Adam the fruit, and he ate. Have you ever noticed that sin loves company? So often, when a person enters into sin, they want others to join with them. It is as if we think we will feel better if others are engaged in the same activity.

Does it strike you that the man is a little passive when Eve offers him the fruit? She offer; he takes; he eats! It seems as if Adam did not even think about his actions or the implications. You know what? Sin is often like that. If you ask a child why they do something foolish or destructive, what do they say? "I don't know."

> One reason sin flourishes is that it is treated like a cream puff instead of a rattlesnake.
>
> *Billy Sunday*

If you were to ask Adam, "Adam, why? You had the whole garden with all these wonderful things to eat. God told you not to eat from this one tree. Why did you eat the fruit?" What do you think Adam would say? "I don't know. It seemed like a good idea at the time." Sin really does involve that kind of thoughtlessness.

NARRATIVE ON THE TEXT | *The Consequences of Sin*

Consequence of Sin 1: The *imago Dei* is marred.

Now immediately we see the consequences. Their eyes were opened. That's what they had been hoping would happen. That's what the serpent promised. But what a nightmare they saw. They looked at each other, and the beauty of the image of God that we talked about last week—the *imago Dei*—had been horribly twisted and marred.

SIGNIFICANT SCRIPTURE

Genesis 3:7–24

Consequence of Sin 2: Shame

This man and woman, who had never known shame, looked at each other, and shame filled their hearts. They saw a stranger. They wanted to hide. Something happened to human nature in that moment that we need to be very clear about: Sin entered in. Theologians coined this moment "the Fall."

Consequence of Sin 3: Alienation

The consequences of sin were horrific. Adam and Eve were alienated from themselves, alienated from each other, alienated from their God, alienated from their work, and alienated from creation. Before, they had walked with God in the cool of the garden. Now, when he came to walk with them, they ran away! Alienation had entered the human experience.

Consequence of Sin 4: Fear

When God asks Adam where he is, Adam makes an amazing statement. He tells God that he was afraid and was hiding. Wow! This is the first mention of fear in the Bible. Sin creates fear in our hearts and drives us away from the very one, the only one, who can remove the pain and consequences of our sin.

Consequence of Sin 5: Blame

God confronts Adam and asks him if he has broken God's commandment and eaten fruit from the tree that was clearly off-limits. When facing this direct and incriminating question, Adam carefully reflects on the importance of taking personal responsibility for his actions. He summons up all of his courage and says, "The woman *you* put with me—she wasn't my idea. She is at fault!" Adam is not giving any more of that "bone of my bone" stuff. Not anymore. You can almost hear Adam saying, "When it was just me and the animals, everything was OK. But that woman, she sure has gotten

ON THE LIGHTER SIDE *How Men Communicate*

A couple of questions here just for women. How many of you have ever known a man? How many of you have ever known a man to have any kind of communication difficulties? How many of you have known a man who did not always give fully detailed accounts of his conversations and activities? Remember, God gave his instructions to Adam, and Adam had to pass this information on to Eve. Now the enemy is after the one who was not directly present to hear what God said.

us into a lot of trouble!" At this moment, blaming enters human history. Do you think they'll be the last married couple to blame each other?

Consequence of Sin 6: Pain

One of the greatest lies the enemy has ever told is when he said, "You will not surely die." The moment Adam and Eve disobeyed God and ate the fruit, death began to set in all around them. Certainly physical death began, but the consequences of sin were deeper and wider. The *imago Dei* ("image of God") was marred, shame filled their hearts, relational death began, alienation took hold, fear consumed them, and the blame game started. On top of all of this, Adam and Eve faced a new reality—pain!

The woman is told she will face pain (labor) in her delivery of children. The man is told he will experience pain (labor) in his work. In the Hebrew, the language gives the sense that the curse is similar for both the man and the woman—pain has entered into the human experience. They will also face the relational pain that grows out of all the consequences already listed.

The battle and strife between men and women goes on to this day as a result of the Fall. The wonderful oneness we saw in Genesis 1 and 2 has been shattered. Spiritual death began on that day, and physical death as well.

> Depravity is a spiritual condition that involves our readiness to harm others or at least let harm come to them if that will help us reach our goals of security, ego-gratification, or the satisfaction of our deep desires. Depravity is this: We would like to do what's right, but we're prepared to do what's wrong if we feel it's necessary for our survival or well-being.
>
> *Paraphrase of Dallas Willard in* The Spirit of the Disciplines

ILLUSTRATION | *Will You Share? No*

There are all kinds of examples of depravity. We just need to look at our lives and the lives of those around us, and we can find signs of this spiritual reality everywhere. Think for a moment about a two-year-old child. What are the odds that if you make a two-year-old share a toy that he's been hogging, he'll say, "I'm so glad it brings you joy. Would you like to use my blankey as well?" Think about it. Do you need to

WORD STUDY

Depravity

The old theological language for the human condition after sin entered in is *depravity*. This is the birth of shame and guilt. People in our day often speak about believing in the basic goodness of human beings. As Christians, we believe it is very good that God made human beings. We matter to him immensely, and we were made in God's image. It is also true that human beings often do good things. But followers of Christ understand that because of the Fall, human beings are not simply neutral, moral agents who can always choose to do good if we just try hard enough.

Here is the truth: As glass is predisposed to shatter and nitroglycerin is predisposed to explode, we are predisposed to do wrong when the conditions are right. Theologically, that human predisposition is called depravity. In the days of the Reformation, great Christian thinkers even talked about total depravity. The primary idea is that depravity affects all of us—not just our behavior but also our thoughts and our feelings. God's Word is clear that we cannot fix this problem on our own. We need God's help.

teach a child to be selfish? No! This comes quite naturally. What we have to teach is generosity and selflessness! This is just one sign of depravity.

WORD STUDY

Walking

In the Old Testament, walking with God is a picture of intimate communion. Sin destroyed Adam and Eve's desire for this intimacy, but God still wanted it. They were ready to run away, but God wanted to walk with them. This word "walking," when used in the context of walking with God, is powerful. It is a sign that God longs for close friendship with the people he has created. Here is an encouraging reminder: God still wants to walk with us today!

INTERPRETIVE INSIGHT | *Why God Asks Questions*

Through the whole Bible, God often asks questions. In Genesis 3:9 we hear God say to Adam, "Where are you?" It is important for us to note that God is not asking because he can't find Adam. God knows exactly where Adam is (physically and spiritually). What God is doing is giving Adam a chance to show himself and confess. This question is a great sign of God's amazing grace. Each time you hear God ask a question in the Bible, stop and reflect. If God already knows the answer, why is he asking the question?

INTERPRETIVE INSIGHT | *Who's in Charge Here?*

Many people believe that a husband's ruling over his wife was part of God's original plan. To some people, this might even seem like a good idea. But as we study the Bible, it becomes clear that this was one of the results of the Fall. This is part of the curse. Here is the good news: God has come to set us free from the power of sin and the curse. God's plan is for husbands and wives to walk together in harmony and find the place of oneness that existed before the Fall.

INTERPRETIVE INSIGHT | *Grace Notes*

As we study Genesis 3, it is not all bad news. Tucked right in this section about sin, depravity, and the Fall are two hope-filled notes of grace. First, God tells the serpent (verse 15) that there will be enmity between him and the woman (including her offspring). We also learn that the serpent will strike at his heel, but the woman's offspring will crush the serpent's head. This passage is talking about Jesus Christ. Right after sin enters in, God is already giving a promise of salvation. Jesus will crush the enemy and destroy the power of sin. This is the first prophetic mention of the coming of the Messiah in all of Scripture. It comes in response to the first sin.

Another grace note in this passage is seen when God made garments of skin for Adam and Eve. At this point Adam and Eve were running around in stitched fig leaves, and they looked severely fashion-challenged. So God became a tailor, and he clothed them so they could come into his presence without being overwhelmed by shame. What a picture of God's grace and love!

If we look closely, we see that there is even more going on here. Because these coverings were made of skin, we know a sacrifice had been made. For the first time in history, innocent blood is shed so that human shame might be covered and human fellowship with God be restored. God is setting the stage for the Passover, and later for the death of Jesus as the sacrifice for our sins. What a powerful reminder of God's grace in these opening pages of the Bible.

2. Cain and Abel

SIGNIFICANT SCRIPTURE

Genesis 4

After the Fall Adam and Eve must have wondered: Would God still continue his plan to fill the earth with human beings, now that they had sinned? Or would it be only the two of them until death? Was this the end of the story, or would there be another chapter? The story of Cain and Abel begins with hope, but soon sin enters in again.

As you look at the story of Adam and Eve and then the story of Cain, you will notice some profound differences in how sin enters in and impacts human community. Eve had to be persuaded by an external tempter to do wrong; Cain had no one tempting him — just his own sinful heart. Adam and Eve's sin was to eat fruit; Cain committed the murder of his brother. Adam and Eve accept their judgment from God without protest; Cain complained that God was being too harsh. This time, the stain of sin went deeper into the fabric of God's beautiful tapestry of community.

INTERPRETIVE INSIGHT | *The Law of Firstfruits*

Every time Adam and Eve look at Cain, they are reminded of God's grace. God did not let their sin kill his dream. Then Abel comes along — another gift from God. He is another reminder that God still has plans for the human race.

As time passes, both Cain and Abel bring sacrifices to God. Cain is a farmer, so he brings produce. Abel is a rancher, so he brings an animal sacrifice. God looks with

ON THE LIGHTER SIDE | *What's Happening to Eve?*

Try to imagine what it must have been like when Eve became pregnant. There was no precedent. This was all new territory. One day, something happens to Eve. She feels a little nauseous. She starts to get a little moody. She has strange cravings. This has never happened before. There are no books for Eve to read to explain what is happening to her.

One day Adam makes an innocent little observation. "Hey, Eve, you're putting on a little weight there. Your old garments don't fit so well. We'll have to get you a new skin — from a much larger animal this time — like a buffalo or something."

About nine months later a new life enters the world. Here we see again how important names are to the story of the Old Testament. Eve gives this baby the name "Cain." Then she says, "With the help of the Lord I have brought forth a man."

This is typical of women to this day. When they give birth, they mention God a lot and don't express much appreciation to their husbands.

favor on Abel's sacrifice but not on Cain's. People wonder why. Some think that Abel's sacrifice was accepted because it was a blood sacrifice, but I don't think that is what is going on here. I think the best explanation for this lies in a close look at the language. Abel's offering came from the *firstborn* in his flock.

There is a principle in Scripture that the firstborn belongs to God. There's something called the "law of the firstfruits." The idea is that when the very first returns appear—the firstfruits of the tree, the first calf to be born, the first of the harvest brought in—this is to be given to God as an act of trust that he will continue to provide. Abel was living by this principle. He brought what came first, that which was a sacrifice to give. Abel's offering cost him something and required trust!

By contrast, Cain's offering appears to be quite casual. God sees this. He doesn't say he rejects Cain, nor does he even say he is angry. He just sees when a heart is devoted to him and when a heart is going through the motions. At this point, Cain could have done a heart check and recognized his own apathy. This could have been a wake-up call. Instead, he broods, resents, and begins to envy his brother.

HISTORICAL CONTEXT

Good Fat

Notice that Abel gives "fat portions from some of the firstborn of his flock." In our day, fat has negative connotations. We figure Lean Cuisine is much more spiritual. But in their day, the battle was against starvation. The fat was the most desirable part, the most life-giving part. Abel chose to give what cost him most and required the greatest trust.

LIFE APPLICATION | *The Firstfruits*

In a world of scarcity we declare that we won't wait until it's easy to give back to God. We will give the firstfruits as an act of trust that God is going to provide for our future. That's what Abel did. That's what Cain refused to do. That's what we're called to do every time the offering plate gets passed. The law of the firstfruits is still in effect today. The question is: Are we living with a faith that produces deep trust that God will provide?

You might want to challenge people to look closely at their giving patterns and ask themselves if they are giving God from their firstfruits or simply tossing God the leftovers.

LIFE APPLICATION | *Beware of Envy*

Notice that Cain doesn't envy Abel's wealth or success. What does he envy? Cain envies his brother's *spiritual status*. Envy can strike anywhere and anyone! Even spiritual people are susceptible. You might even say that spiritual people are especially susceptible to envy! This should be a clear warning for teachers, small-group leaders, pastors, church-board members, and anyone who serves God. Read Genesis 4:6–7 slowly and carefully: "Why are you angry? Why is your face downcast? If you do what is right, will you not be accepted? But if you do not do what is right, sin is crouching at your door; it desires to have you, but you must master it." These words of warning need to be heard with great clarity today!

INTERPRETIVE INSIGHT | *An Invitation to the Light*

Notice that God asks another question in Genesis 4:9. What's happening here? Is God unaware of what has happened? Is God looking for Cain because he can't find him? No!

God is graciously playing counselor. He is inviting Cain to come into the light, to acknowledge the condition of his heart, to make this right. God is inviting Cain to come clean and confess. There is this warning, "Sin is crouching at your door," like a beast in you; it will consume you if you let it.

What do we learn as we read on? Cain prefers the darkness. Look at verse 8 and notice how the writer keeps repeating the word "brother" to underscore the tragedy. God is calling Cain to a place of repentance over the murder of his brother. Cain is fighting to stay in the darkness. He says, "Am I my brother's keeper?" Notice that Cain is distorting God's words. "What? Do you expect me to watch him every second?" This is Cain's way of pushing aside God's intent: "Cain, come clean." So God has to pronounce judgment yet again.

INTERPRETIVE INSIGHT | *A Severe Mercy*

God tells Cain that he will be driven from community and become a restless wanderer. God knows that if Cain stays in community, he will bring more destruction to God's creation. Cain has broken community and lost sight of God's great dream. But God again offers a kind of severe mercy. Cain complains that someone will kill him in revenge, so God places a mark on him. This is the mark of Cain. It's a reminder of Cain's sin, but it's also a mark of divine protection, a pronouncement that his life is not to be taken. Isn't it amazing to see how quickly God follows judgment with grace?

3. The Days of Noah

SIGNIFICANT SCRIPTURE

Genesis 6

There are a few exceptions, but as we move through Genesis the world seems to go from bad to worse. Just read Genesis 6:5: "The Lord saw how great [human] wickedness on the earth had become, and that every inclination of the thoughts of his heart was only evil all the time." And Genesis 6:11 – 12: "Now the earth was corrupt in God's sight and was full of violence. God saw how corrupt the earth had become, for all the people on earth had corrupted their ways." When we read the story of Cain, we saw how sin went deeper. As we study the days of Noah, we see how sin goes wider.

INTERPRETIVE INSIGHT | *"And God Saw"*

When we read, "And God saw" in Genesis 6:12, it's the first time this phrase has been used since Genesis 1. Back in Genesis 1 the phrase is followed, over and over again, by, "It was good." Now there is a dramatic shift. The phrase appears again, but this time it is followed by the words, "It was ruined!" There is a clear sense that this contrast shows that God's good plan has been corrupted.

INTERPRETIVE INSIGHT | *One Bright Spot*

There's one bright spot left on the earth. His name is Noah! It is as if God says, "The only way this dream can be kept alive is to start over again. The level of corruption is so high there is no other way." So we learn that God is going to send a flood. He gives Noah some instructions. Noah goes to the local hardware store, places a really big order, and the rain begins to fall forty days and forty nights (Genesis 7). Noah obeys God, and God begins his dream again. God says to Noah, in a sense, "I will establish my covenant with you." And God gives Noah a sign to seal this covenant agreement: the rainbow.

SIGNIFICANT SCRIPTURE

Genesis 11:1–9

4. The Tower of Babel

The story of Babel and the sin of the people is almost a satire on the folly of human arrogance. It is not a commentary on architecture but on the heart of human beings. The people decide to build a tower up to God. This is the same old story of human sin. "We can become like God. We can build something that reaches to the heavens—the place where God lives. Our ultimate devotion will be to ourselves and to the accumulation of power, wealth, and fame." The story of Babel is a reminder of the cycle of sin that human community can fall into. We need to remember that God has called them to multiply and fill up the earth. Instead, they decide to defy God's command and stay centrally located—all in one place. This is just another example of human defiance!

NEW TESTAMENT CONNECTION

"If" We Confess

Since the garden of Eden, the need for human beings to confess their sin has always been profound. Fortunately, we serve a God who invites us to come to him with broken hearts and to seek his grace. In 1 John 2:9 we read, "If we confess our sins, he is faithful and just and will forgive us our sins and purify us from all unrighteousness."

INTERPRETIVE INSIGHT | *Looking Down*

Now in Genesis 11:5, where does the Lord come to see the Tower of Babel? What direction does he move? Down. Again, this is irony. Where were they going to build their tower? Up to the heavens. God sits in the heavens and looks down and says, "Look at that little tiny bump down there. I guess I'll have to go down to get a closer look."

INTERPRETIVE INSIGHT | *Moving East*

Be sure to take notice of where Babel was located. Also take note of which direction the people moved when they left Eden. It was eastward. Ever since the Fall there has been a movement east—farther and farther from paradise.

For the Israelites, the Mediterranean Sea was on their west. The east was the place of danger, hostility, enemies, and the loss of community. They did not want to move east anymore. East of Eden becomes this picture of the loss of God's precious dream.

PAUSE FOR REFLECTION

A Time to Confess

Take time as a leader to invite people to come before God with humility, to come out of hiding, to do what Cain would not do. Invite people to take a few moments to reflect on any temptation or sin they need to confess to God. Ask them to close their eyes. Invite the Holy Spirit to search their hearts. Call God's people to a place of humble repentance.

ILLUSTRATION | *The Downward Spiral of Sin*

Either use PowerPoint or make a drawing of how people kept spiraling deeper and deeper into sin and farther from God. Show how this movement can be symbolized as a movement east and away from God's plan for paradise in human community.

LIFE APPLICATION | *Facing Sin Head-On*

In Genesis 6 we learn that God's heart is filled with pain because of human sin. This is not trivial. Even though sin has been trivialized in our society, it still matters to God. Just think about it. Outside the church, the only place where you see the word "sin" is on dessert menus in restaurants. It is time for followers of Christ to take a personal inventory and be sure they are taking sin seriously.

The enemy, who was in the garden, whispers to you and to me just as he did to the people back in Genesis. Sin still crouches at the door of the human heart. We might be tempted to gloss over it, deny it, blame it on someone else, or compare ourselves to somebody we think is worse, but we need to face sin head-on.

To yield and give in to our sinful desires is the lowest form of slavery. To rule over such desires is the only true freedom.

Justin Martyr (second century)

ON THE LIGHTER SIDE | *An Investment in Eight-Track Tapes*

When we look at Genesis 11:3, we see that the writer is ridiculing human arrogance. He points out that the people of Babel are building with bricks instead of stones! Historically we know that in Babylon, home of Babel, they actually did build with bricks. In Israel they used stone.

Which lasts longer? Stone or brick?

The answer is stone ... by many times over.

The writer is saying, with some irony and humor, "They think they're building like gods, and they don't even know enough to build with stone rather than bricks. They don't even know the latest technology."

In our day, it would be a bit like saying, "I have a great idea, I am going to invest all of my money in eight-track tapes! I think they are going to make a real comeback. If that goes well, I'll sink my profits into record albums."

ON THE LIGHTER SIDE | *No Hablo Inglés*

Something happens at Babel that is rather funny if you think about it. Up to this point, all people have spoken the same language. Now, all of a sudden, one guy says to the other, "Can I borrow a hammer?" And the guy next to him says, "*No hablo Inglés*." Up to this point, they used to just speak Swedish (or the language of your choice for your context) – the language of heaven. Now their languages are confused, and they are scattered across the earth.

Message 3

It's Time to DTR (Define the Relationship)

Genesis 12–22

THE HEART OF THE Message

We have all experienced what it is like to hit the pivotal moment in life when we need to do a DTR: "Define The Relationship!"

A couple has been dating for a number of months, things are going well, and everyone seems happy with how things are proceeding. Then things begin to get a little more serious. Both parties involved are wondering, "Is this the real deal?" One, the other, or both sense the need to sit down and ask the big questions, "What are we doing here? Where are we going? What comes next in this relationship? Is this the one for me?" This is a DTR! It is one of those tipping points where things can go one way or the other. A DTR is when we have to ask ourselves, "Am I going to take the next step forward in this relationship and take things to the next level?"

Abraham discovered that DTR moments happen with God all through life if we are paying attention and are ready to respond. Over and over God invited Abraham to a new place of intimacy, a new level of commitment, and a deeper place of community. In each case, Abraham moved out of the DTR moment into a new place of faith. In the same way, God invites us to keep taking steps of faith as we walk with him. He wants us to tune in and recognize when we have DTR moments so that we can respond and go to deeper places of faith and love.

THE HEART OF THE Messenger

The God of Abraham is the same God we worship today! He still speaks to, prompts, and leads his children. He still wants to have profound moments when he can do a DTR with each one of us. As you prepare your heart to teach this message, invite God to do a DTR. Ask the Holy Spirit to search you and open your eyes to see areas in which you hunger for deeper places of faith and love.

BRIEF MESSAGE OUTLINE

Four defining moments in the life of Abraham:

1. The call to leave
2. The cutting of a covenant
3. The call to hope
4. A call to deeper faith

Take time to read Psalm 139:23–24 and Psalm 103:1–5. Then wait in silence and invite the Spirit to challenge, convict, encourage, bless, or do whatever he wants to do in your heart. As you prepare to teach about DTR moments in the spiritual life of a follower of Christ, be sure you give God space to have a DTR moment with you!

Introduction

CREATIVE MESSAGE IDEA | *Bendable People*

At the very beginning of the message, invite a couple from the congregation to volunteer to help you present a brief visual picture of some DTR moments in human relationships. You might want to ask a couple before the service and be sure you get a married couple who really loves each other and who have some warmth and energy. Use three or more scenarios and comment briefly after each one that these are defining moments in life.

With each scenario, tell the couple where to stand, how to posture themselves, and how to look at each other. Then, read a statement (provided below) and ask for the appropriate person of the couple to respond both physically and in their facial expressions.

Scenario 1: He stands facing the congregation with his hand to the side of his head as if he is holding a phone receiver. She stands off to the side, also holding a receiver to her ear. Then you read the following statement and ask *him* to respond.

They have gone out on a first date and he is crazy about her. He is waiting to hear what she thinks about him. She calls and says these words to him, "I think you have a really nice personality, but I just don't feel any spark. I'm sorry ... goodbye."

Scenario 2: She stands facing the congregation with her hands in front of her as if she is holding and reading a letter. He stands off to the side with one palm turned up and the other hand set as if he is writing a letter to her on paper held in his hand. Then you read the following words and ask *her* to respond.

CREATIVE MESSAGE IDEA | *Deb Poling Video Testimony*

One of the videos provided with the DVD-ROM materials has a testimony that can be used well in connection with this message or worship service. You can use this here in week 3 (or even in week 2 if you feel it fits better there). The goal of the Deb Poling testimony is to inspire people to begin a committed study of the Old Testament by engaging in the reading early on in the process.

You Will Need

- Video projection capability in your worship center
- Someone to run the video during the service

They have been dating for a time and she has written him her first love note. She has bared her soul and heart. She has taken a risk and signed the letter, "With all my love." She is now reading his letter of response. It is a kind letter, it is a polite letter, it is a cordial letter, and it is signed, "Your brother in Christ."

Scenario 3: They stand facing each other and holding hands, looking eye to eye. You read the following words and ask *him* to respond.

They have been dating for six months. He thinks she is the one! They are out on a date. She looks into his eyes, swallows hard, and says, "I really like you. You are a very special person! But . . . I think it would be best for both of us if we were just . . . (pause here) friends!"

Scenario 4: Again they stand facing each other, looking eye to eye. They have been dating for two years, they are very serious, and both feel they are in love. Tell them that this time *both of them* are invited to respond.

He says to her, "It's been two years since we started dating, I am in love with you, you are the one for me, my heart is bursting, my passion is great, I think we are finally ready for our first kiss!"

Then shout . . . *"Action!"*

(This can be a fun moment, but be sure you know the couple won't be embarrassed.)

Scenario 5: He kneels on one knee and looks up into her eyes. She holds his hands and looks down longingly. Be sure to encourage sincere, longing looks! Read the following words and ask *her* to respond.

He looks into her eyes, thinking of the years of their friendship and growing love. He clears his throat, swallows, and chokes out the words, "Will you marry me?"

HISTORICAL CONTEXT | *Covenant*

A covenant is "a means to establish a binding relationship where none existed before, based on faithfulness to a solemn vow." Faithfulness is the core virtue of covenant behavior. There were different kinds of covenants back in ancient days. Sometimes they were *unilateral*—a covenant between unequal partners. An example of a unilateral covenant would be between a king and his subjects. There were also *bilateral* covenants, which were established between equals. An example of this would be a covenant between friends.

In the Old Testament we find references to "covenant" 285 times. As you read the Old Testament, you can't help but note that God is the God of the covenant; he is characterized by covenantal love. Sometimes this is referred to as "steadfast love." The covenant term "steadfast love" reminds us that God is the One who makes promises out of the depth of his love. He is also the One who always keeps his promises.

WORD STUDY

Abram and Abraham

As we have been learning, names were very important in the Old Testament. Most names had significant meaning. This was certainly true for Abraham. When we first meet him, we discover his name is Abram, which means "exalted father." Later, God gives him the name Abraham; this means "father of many nations." As you study Genesis, you will discover the importance of this name change.

Scenario 6: They are standing at the door of their home holding hands as the last guest leaves their fiftieth wedding anniversary party. With their free hands they both wave good-bye. As they stand side-by-side, holding hands, you read the following words and invite both of them to respond.

She leans over to him and whispers in his ear, "I love you more today than I did fifty years ago! How 'bout another fifty?"

INTERPRETIVE INSIGHT | *God's Plan*

As we continue in this study of Genesis we might wonder, will God run out of patience? Is his dream of community broken beyond repair? When we get to Genesis 12, we discover that God still has plans for his children. God will begin again, but this time with a new strategy. He'll work with one man. His name is Abram. God will rename him Abraham, and he will be the father of many nations. God will call Abraham to a series of DTRs as we watch on. In this section of Scripture, Abraham discovers the ultimate DTR: a covenant.

Through Abraham something remarkable is happening. God, who created the heavens and the earth, is entering into a relationship with an ordinary human being. God is promising himself to fallen people. As we look at Abraham's life we discover four dramatic encounters he had with God that kept clarifying their relationship.

ON THE LIGHTER SIDE | *Traveling Without a Map*

God tells Abraham, "Leave your country, your people and your father's household and go!" Go where? "Go to the land I will show you." Let's be honest, these instructions are a little vague! There is not much here for Abraham to tell Sarah. And, as many of us know, wives like to have details about these sorts of things.

Imagine the conversation they must have had. And remember, these are real people. Just think of what this interaction would have sounded like: "Sarah, pack up all our belongings. We're moving away from everyone and everything familiar to us."

"Where are we going?"

"I don't know exactly. I'll know it when I see it."

You have to believe that Sarah would have asked what any wife would ask: "How will we know if we get lost? Whom will we ask for directions?"

Abraham replies, "We won't get lost. God will tell me when we get there."

"God who?" Remember, Sarah didn't know this God.

"I didn't catch his last name."

This would be the only trip in human history when a wife would say, "Where in the world are we?" and her husband would say, "God only knows," and he'd be speaking literal truth!

DTR 1: The Call to Leave

God has a single command for Abraham: Leave! Leave your country, your people, your tribe, and your father's household — everything safe and familiar. Implied in this is also the call to leave his old gods. Abraham did not know this God who was calling him to this radical step of faith. In Joshua 24:2, Joshua is talking to the Israelites: "Long ago your forefathers, including Terah the father of Abraham and Nahor, lived beyond the River and worshiped other gods." Yet here is Abraham, faced with an epic DTR moment. Will he stay, or will he leave and follow this God who is calling him?

There's an Old Testament principle here. It might be called the "Principle of Separation." God says, "Be separate from other gods — old values, old priorities — and be separate for the one true God." This principle was in effect for Abraham, and it is still in effect for us today.

SIGNIFICANT SCRIPTURE

Genesis 11:31 – 12:4

> The history of all the great characters of the Bible is summed up in this one sentence: They acquainted themselves with God, and acquiesced to his will in all things.
>
> *Richard Cecil*

INTERPRETIVE INSIGHT | *Abraham's Home*

We have to understand the choice that Abraham is facing. Abraham is not some uncouth nomad with nothing to lose. He is a prosperous merchant. In verse 5 we read that he has accumulated many possessions, enough to have a whole retinue of servants and slaves. He lives in an urban setting in civilized Mesopotamia.

Haran, where Abraham's family came from, was located far in the northwest part of Mesopotamia. It is listed in Ezekiel 27:23 as one of the great commercial centers of the ancient world. It's on the Euphrates River. In that metropolitan center Abraham is known, respected, and secure. It is a place of safety and familiarity.

Yet Abraham is told to leave for a wilderness where he has no lands, no networks, no connections, and no prospects. This move, humanly speaking, is financial, vocational, and maybe literal suicide. What kind of a person would follow a call like that?

> Our heavenly Father never takes anything from his children unless he means to give them something better.
>
> *George Mueller*

WORD STUDY

Bless

God gave Abraham a promise. It involved something bigger than he could have imagined. The essence of the promise was one word.

As we read through Scripture, it is always important to look for words that are repeated numerous times in a passage. When this happens, they often carry a lot of weight. Notice in this passage what word is repeated over and over. (You might want to pause as people look at their Bibles to discover this word for themselves.)

The word is simple, yet powerful: *bless*.

The word "bless" or "blessing" or "blessed" is repeated five times in this passage. God says, "I will make you into a great nation." We already know that Abraham and Sarah were childless. Yet God says, "I will make your name great."

LIFE APPLICATION | *What Can I Leave Behind?*

Is God asking you to leave anything? Is he calling you to walk away from some idol, any sin, or some fear? Is God calling you to go someplace, to take a step of faith, to risk for him, or to start serving in some new area of ministry? Do you ever trust God as Abraham did? This is not to say that Abraham was a pillar of spiritual perfection. He had his flaws — and so do we — but he stepped out in faith, and God calls us to do the same.

SIGNIFICANT SCRIPTURE

Genesis 14:8–24; 15:9–19; 17:1–14

DTR 2: The Cutting of a Covenant

Some things in life make sense and some things just seem to baffle us! God's desire to enter a covenant with Abraham (and with us) is one of those things that seems almost beyond comprehension. He has everything and we have so little (and what we have has been given by him!). Yet, God initiates an agreement with Abraham, and through him with us. This agreement or covenant reveals the depth of love God has for us as his children. When we enter a covenant relationship with the living God, we face the most significant DTR moment of our lives.

INTERPRETIVE INSIGHT | *God's Covenant with Abraham*

As noted on page 45, the ancient world saw bilateral covenants (between two equal partners) and unilateral covenants (between a stronger and a weaker partner). The covenant between God and Abraham was clearly unilateral.

Generally speaking, in unilateral covenants the stronger partner always had an agenda. The covenant was based on the idea that there was something the stronger partner could gain from the weaker partner. In Abraham's day, the stronger partner in a covenant was usually after water rights, land to graze his herds on, or something else that would benefit the stronger party in the agreement. Here is the key question we need to ask: "What is God going to get out of this deal? He knows the human race. He knows he will be facing heartache, ingratitude, folly, and sin. So what does he get out of this covenant?"

He gets someone to bless! He gets someone on whom to pour out all of the affection and warmth and mercy and love of his heart, even though it's going to break his heart. This is why the Old Testament writers are staggered by the fact that the God who created the heavens and the earth would choose to enter into a covenant with fallen human beings.

PAUSE FOR REFLECTION

A Step of Faith

Take time to pray and reflect on what you might leave behind so you can follow God with a deeper level of commitment. Allow a few moments of silence during the message and challenge people to do business with God then and there.

INTERPRETIVE INSIGHT | *God's Chosen People*

It is important for us to understand what the Old Testament means when it calls Abraham, or Israel, the "chosen people." Some take this to mean that these people are chosen as God's favorites or that they have an inside track to getting into heaven. Because of this perspective, others find this arrangement unfair or arbitrary on God's part.

But when the Bible talks of God's chosen people, it means that Abraham and his descendants were chosen by God to be a kind of model community. This is not for their sake alone, but for the sake of the whole world. The privilege of this calling is the call to serve.

You could put it like this: God so loved the world that he made a covenant with Abraham that all the peoples of the world should be blessed through him. Look at what Paul writes to the Galatians in Galatians 3:8: "The Scripture announced the gospel [or good news] in advance to Abraham when it said: 'All nations will be blessed through you.'"

INTERPRETIVE INSIGHT | *The Sign of the Covenant*

The sign of Abraham's covenant was circumcision. One of the aspects of circumcision, obviously, is that it's a very physical reminder of the covenant. The physical sign was for males only. It was not done to females, but it did include everybody in a corporate sense. This sign of the covenant was also available to people who were not Hebrews. They too could be a part of the circumcised covenant people. One important element to note is that when God called Abraham to institute circumcision, he obeyed *that very day.*

LIFE APPLICATION | *The Beginning of Evangelism*

Evangelism in the Bible doesn't really start with the Great Commission. Evangelism starts in Genesis 12:3. God wants to bless the whole earth. He wants to do it through Abraham and this model community, but his desire is not to bless Israel for Israel's sake. It's to bless his people, and then, through his people, to bless everybody on earth. That's God's heart from the very beginning. God doesn't want to leave anybody out.

ON THE LIGHTER SIDE | *Noah Got a Rainbow*

Imagine that you are Abraham. God comes to you and says, "There's going to be a sign for our covenant." (Covenants often had signs that functioned as a constant reminder of the agreement that had been established.) Then God continues, "This is the sign for our covenant: I want you to be *circumcised*." Now, imagine you, as Abraham, have just received the news. Don't you feel a bit like saying, "Hey! Noah got a rainbow. It doesn't seem quite fair. Couldn't we make our sign something a little more gentle, like a cloud, a secret handshake, a decoder ring, or something like that?"

This should be a clear reminder to each person who knows what it is to be called a child of God and one of his chosen people. We are blessed to be a blessing, and we are called to invite others into his family. Invite each person present in your audience to identify one person who is outside of the family. Challenge them to identify one practical way God might use them to be a blessing to this person in the coming week.

NARRATIVE ON THE TEXT | *Abraham's Ups and Downs*

The very first words of Abraham ever recorded in Scripture are, "As he was about to enter Egypt, he said to his wife Sarai, 'I know what a beautiful woman you are. When the Egyptians see you, they will say, "This is his wife." Then they will kill me but let you live. Say you are my sister, so that I will be treated well for your sake and my life will be spared because of you.' "

This is not a great moment in the history of husbanding. Sarah ends up getting stuck in Pharaoh's harem, and God has to intervene. Pharaoh ends up giving Abraham a lesson on integrity, which apparently doesn't strike a real deep chord, because in Genesis 20 Abraham uses the same lie on another king named Abimelech. Let's be honest: Abraham was not a pillar of spiritual perfection.

> What reality is there in your Christianity if you look at men struggling in darkness and you are content to congratulate yourselves that you are in the light?
>
> *Frederick William Robertson*

However, in chapters 13 and 14 he gets some things right, especially as they relate to possessions. In chapter 13 there's a conflict between Abraham's staff and the employees of his nephew Lot over grazing rights. Abraham deliberately gives Lot first choice of whatever land he wants. As the older uncle, Abraham could have insisted on getting his own way, but he is both humble and generous. Because he does this, Abraham experiences the blessing of his generous God.

In chapter 14, Lot is captured in a battle that involves some local chieftains. A coalition from the East comes and defeats a local coalition. Abraham has 318 trained soldiers on his staff (a clear sign of his prominence), and he takes them as he rescues his nephew Lot.

The two kings Abraham interacts with in chapter 14 represent two different ways of dealing with possessions. One of them, the king of Sodom, offers to allow Abraham to keep the spoils of war. He says, "You can keep your stuff," but with the implicit condition that Abraham will now owe allegiance to him. The message of this king is that powerful men are allowed to grab and keep whatever they can. He invites Abraham to be part of his coalition, and Abraham, at great cost to himself, says, "No! I won't keep the spoils. I won't be part of your coalition. I won't be that kind of man."

The other king, Melchizedek, is an intriguing character. He is mentioned only briefly. He is also called the priest of the Most High God. In other words, Abraham finds God at work in people from places he didn't even know about. In Genesis 14:18 we read that Melchizedek blessed Abram. Melchizedek let Abraham know that his victories and possessions were gifts from God and that they really didn't belong to Abraham.

WORD STUDY

Theophany

The Old Testament is full of theophanies. These are manifestations of God's presence in a form that people can see and recognize. The burning bush is a great example. We need to note that in the Pentateuch, smoke and fire often symbolize the presence of God. So when the text says, "The fire and the torch passed between the pieces," we need to recognize that this is a picture of God. This visual appearance is what theologians call a *theophany*.

LIFE APPLICATION | *Tithing*

We find an important biblical teaching introduced through the life of Abraham when we read, "Then Abram gave him a tenth of everything." The lesson of tithing (giving our first tenth) is significant because when we give, when we tithe, we are living in covenant relationship with the God who provides for his children. We declare boldly that we trust God to bless us, and we long for him to use us to be a blessing to others. That's what Abraham does here. He sets a standard we should all embrace.

INTERPRETIVE INSIGHT | *Covenant Breakers and the Covenant Keeper*

In Abraham's day, when somebody violated a covenant, it was not voided. It was not ripped up. When somebody violated a covenant, there were specific consequences. When this happened, things became very unpleasant for the violator. In most cases, blood was shed!

HISTORICAL CONTEXT | *Cutting a Covenant*

In most translations we read, "The LORD made a covenant." But in the Hebrew it literally says, "The LORD cut a covenant." The reason this term was used is both shocking and powerful!

In those days, when people made a covenant, they would take animals and literally cut them in two pieces and set the two pieces next to each other, side by side. Then they would go for a covenant walk. They would pass between the pieces of the animal, and the symbolic meaning of this walk was, "May this be my fate if I don't live up to the covenant, if I don't honor the covenant, if I am not faithful." Jeremiah 34:18 says, "Those who have violated my covenant, I will treat like the calf they cut in two and then walked between its pieces." When people cut a covenant, blood was shed. It was a way of saying, "I take this very seriously."

As we study God's covenant with Abraham, we need to notice who makes the covenant walk (Genesis 15:17). It is God! God is the one who passes between the dead carcasses of the animals – as if to say, "I will keep my agreement with you, and if I don't, may I be like these animals!" That's unbelievable! God condescends to take an oath. "Abram, I want so much for you to trust me, I'll take the covenant walk. May it be so with me if I don't keep my word to you." This is truly amazing!

When we understand the cost of broken covenants in the Old Testament, we discover the power of Jesus' words when he said, "This cup is the new covenant *in my blood*." The old covenant had been broken by sinful human beings. The covenant was violated. Somebody had to pay. Jesus said, "I'll pay. I'll suffer. I will pay the price that my children deserve, and then I will cut a new, unforgettable, and unshakable covenant with my blood. I will be cut. I will cut a covenant with my body." When we have this picture in our minds, coming to the communion table takes on a whole new level of significance. We realize that the punishment we deserve was paid by Jesus.

SIGNIFICANT SCRIPTURE

Genesis 16;
17:15–22;
18:9–15;
21:1–7

DTR 3: The Call to Hope

God gave Abraham a specific and staggering promise. The promise was that Abraham would have descendants as vast as the stars in the heavens and as numerous as the sand on the seashore. The God who called Abraham to leave everything and to go to a new place had assured him that a new community would be born!

There was just one problem: Abraham had no descendants. He had no kids. What was worse, he was in his eighties, Sarah was in her seventies, and his wife was barren. Abraham and Sarah had a promise—but no children. They had a word from God in their hearts—but no baby in their arms.

Out of this painful and apparently hopeless situation God brings laughter, joy, and hope. As we look at this DTR moment in Abraham's life, we discover that God calls us to cling to hope even when outside circumstances dictate against it.

NARRATIVE ON THE TEXT | *My Way*

In Genesis 16 we discover that Sarah (Sarai) and Abraham know what it feels like to become hopeless. Although they were called to hope, they have grown discouraged. Sarah lets Abraham know that she feels the Lord has kept her from having children, so she is ready to institute her own plan: She will have children through Hagar. She actually tells Abraham to sleep with her servant Hagar and have children with her. Abraham agrees and does as Sarah requests.

ON THE LIGHTER SIDE | *Cross My Heart*

A small reflection of covenantal thinking happens in our day with children. When kids make a serious promise, they'll often say, "I promise. *Cross my heart and hope to die, stick a needle in my eye*." This is a gruesome image, but it makes a point (pun intended). This is the way children say, "I'm really being truthful. I really honor my word. If I am lying, it will cost me!"

This seems a little passive on Abraham's part. He doesn't argue real hard. As you read the passage, it is a little troubling. You can almost hear Abraham say, "Well, OK honey, if you think it's a good idea. I'll do it for you." Abraham follows through on his words, and Hagar conceives a little boy. Some time later, Ishmael is born.

This is a powerful example of trying to accomplish God's plan, but doing it my way!

INTERPRETIVE INSIGHT | *Another Fall*

In his telling the story of Ishmael's conception and birth, we discover that the writer is very artistically crafting this passage by repeating the words from the Fall in the garden of Eden. Back in the garden the writer said, "The woman took some [of the fruit] ... and gave some to her husband." Literally the text says, "And the man listened to the voice of the woman." And here the writer says, "And Abram listened to the voice of Sarai. And Sarai took ... Hagar ... gave her to her husband to be his wife." It's another fall. This is not trusting covenant behavior! This is just another reminder of the reality of the Fall and the power of sin to break the community God wants to establish.

The Christian life that is joyless is a discredit to God and a disgrace to itself.

Maltbie D. Babcock

NARRATIVE ON THE TEXT | *The Birth of Hope and Laughter*

Genesis 18 and 21 are filled with hope and laughter. Visitors come and tell Abraham that Sarah will bear a child and the dream of a new community will be born. But we need to remember that Abraham is just shy of a hundred years old, and Sarah is now almost ninety. The childbearing years have come and gone for this couple ... or so it would seem.

God speaks through three visitors who pay a visit to Abraham and Sarah, and Sarah is in the tent listening as the Lord is talking to Abraham. God promises that in a year Sarah will have a baby, their baby, in her arms. She cannot help herself; she lets out a muffled laugh at the very thought of herself and Abraham experiencing pregnancy and delivery at this stage in their life. Her response is recorded for us: "So Sarah laughed to herself as she thought, 'After I am worn out and my master is old, will I now have this pleasure?' "

Sarah may have been a little ironic in her choice of words. To her, the whole proposal must have sounded absurd. Abraham is ninety-nine years old and Sarah is eighty-nine. Viagra has not yet been invented! How could this be?

God asks Abraham why Sarah laughed. But Sarah lies and claims she did not laugh. In response, God assures her that she did laugh and that he heard her: "Yes, you did. You did too laugh. I heard you laugh." They have a little "did Sarah laugh?" debate right here.

As we move on, we see that Abraham and Sarah are filled with doubt, but they seek to obey God and live in a hope that seems beyond their reach. Finally, one day, a child is born. God tells them to name him Isaac. He is aptly named, because Isaac means, "He laughs."

SIGNIFICANT SCRIPTURE

Genesis 22:1–18

DTR 4: A Call to Deeper Faith

As we look at the life of Abraham, it is clear that God is in the process of shaping a relationship. First he is called to leave everything he knows; this is a huge DTR moment. Next, God cuts a covenant with Abraham; this is a second DTR moment of epic proportions. Third, Abraham and Sarah are called to hope in a promise that has begun to feel hopeless. But as they seek to walk in faith and hope, God gives them a son.

We might wonder, isn't that enough? Haven't they grown to full maturity? Could there possibly be another DTR between God and this elderly couple? But we discover in Genesis 22 that the greatest challenge is still ahead! Just when you wonder if maybe you have grown all you can grow, God says, "Let's take another step of faith." Just when you think God cannot stretch you any more, you discover that it is time for one more DTR!

INTERPRETIVE INSIGHT | *This Is Just a Test!*

Genesis 22:1 is an important first sentence. The writer wants us to know what Abraham does not know, namely, that what he will soon go through is only a test. The writer knows that the strain of this passage will be too intense for readers if they don't understand, in advance, that this is only a test. God is asking Abraham to take a shocking step of faith. "Will you trust me even when you don't understand? Even when it doesn't make sense?" God does not intend Abraham to kill Isaac; this option is never really on the table. But Abraham does not know this.

ON THE LIGHTER SIDE | *Everyone Gets a Laugh!*

Isaac is born, and the laughter continues. "Sarah said, 'God has brought me laughter, and everyone who hears about this will laugh with me.' " She was right! People laughed at a child born in the geriatric ward, with Medicare picking up the tab. They laughed because Sarah is the only woman in the supermarket who's buying Pampers and Depends at the same time. People laugh when Sarah stocks up on strained vegetables for Isaac, Abraham, and herself because nobody in the family has a single tooth.

NARRATIVE ON THE TEXT | *A Hard Walk of Faith*

God calls, "Abraham!" And Abraham says, "Here I am." We need to understand that when Abraham says this, he is not talking about his location. He is saying, "Speak, Lord. Whatever you say I will do. I will obey. Here I am. I am your servant." All of his life, Abraham has heard this voice. He heard it many decades ago when it told him to leave his home ... and he did. He'd heard it when it called him to be in a covenant relationship ... and he accepted. This same God called Abraham to hope and trust for the son that seemed to be an impossible dream. Abraham trusted and God provided.

Now this voice speaks to Abraham one more time. It's the last time he hears God's voice in Scripture. God says, "Take your son, your only son, Isaac, whom you love" and sacrifice him! It is interesting to note that this is the first time the word "love" is used in the Bible. It's used for a father who is willing to sacrifice his beloved son.

We need to also remember that this is not just his son; rather, this son is the promise of a new community. This is the dream. There is nobody else to step in and take the role that has been assigned to Isaac.

Once again, Abraham obeys God's call. He and Isaac begin a three-day journey. The details in this story are almost excruciating. "On the third day Abraham looked up and saw the place in the distance." We read in Genesis 22:6 that he takes wood for the burnt offering and places it on his son Isaac. But Abraham carries the fire and the knife himself. Why does he do this? Because fire and a sharp knife are things that can hurt a young boy. So, instinctively, Abraham carries them to protect his son. What a dramatic contrast! While he is taking his son to a place he will be sacrificed, Abraham is looking out for his safety.

The strain becomes almost unbearable. In verse 7 Isaac says, "Father?"

"Yes, my son?"

"The fire and the wood are here, but where is the lamb for the burnt offering?"

Abraham assures him, "God will provide, my son."

Abraham keeps saying, "My son. My son." You can almost hear the grief in his voice.

Soon they arrive at the place of sacrifice. Abraham builds the altar ... in obedience. He takes the wood off Isaac's back ... in obedience. Now it is time. Abraham takes Isaac, the promise of the new community, the dream of God, and in obedience he prepares for the sacrifice. He ties up his legs and binds his arms so there will be no struggle at

NEW TESTAMENT CONNECTION

Mount Moriah

According to 2 Chronicles 3:1, Mount Moriah is the same mountain on which the temple was built – in essence, the same mountain on which Jesus was crucified, Mount Calvary. Many centuries later, God the Father did exactly as Abraham does here. He took his only Son, whom he loved (note God's words at Jesus' baptism and transfiguration, Mark 1:11; 9:7), put on him the wood (the cross), and, like Abraham, was fully intent on the death of his Son (cf. Acts 2:23, God's set purpose and foreknowledge caused him to be handed over to his enemies for crucifixion). This time, however, there was no substitute ram in the bushes. Jesus shed his own blood for us – the blood of the Son of God. In other words, God sacrificed his Son on Mount Moriah so that we might have life, so that we might be in covenant (the new covenant) with him.

the end. He picks up his son, and he holds the same body that he held on the first day he came from Sarah's womb. This is the little body he used to bathe and rock and tell stories to about a home somewhere far behind him, and a greater home somewhere in the future—a home Abraham would never know, but maybe Isaac would.

He places Isaac on the altar.

As he looks at Isaac, he remembers that this is the little body he would check on at night to make sure it was still breathing. This was the boy named "laughter," whom he had held countless times and chuckled to himself at the sheer impossibility of it all. But right now there was no laughter.

> He asks all, but he gives all.
>
> *Thomas R. Kelly*

Abraham looks at his boy on the altar and realizes that Isaac is the reason he left everything so many years ago. This boy is the one hope for a multitude that will be formed into God's new community. This is his son, his only son, Isaac, whom he loves.

In obedience, Abraham takes the knife and reaches toward heaven as he prepares to destroy, with a single thrust, the life that he has helped to create.

Then God says, "Abraham! Abraham!"

And Abraham replies, "Here I am"—the same words as at the beginning of the story. "Here I am, God. Where else am I going to go? Who else am I going to turn to? Who else would I follow?" And God says, "Don't harm your son. I know now that you fear me, you honor me, you reverence me, and you trust me."

Abraham breathes again. He receives his son back, and the dream of God's new community continues.

INTERPRETIVE INSIGHT | *A Vision of Hope*

Abraham goes on to die a very old man. There's a poignant scene at his grave in Genesis 25:9. As we read about his burial, we see his sons Isaac *and* Ishmael there together. They are together for the first time since they were separated at Isaac's infancy. These

HISTORICAL CONTEXT | *The Value of Life*

Among the many lessons we can learn from the story of Abraham and Isaac is that God does not affirm human sacrifice. In those days, many of the people in that region did offer their children as sacrifices. The Ammonites were known for their devotion to a false god they called Molech. They often sacrificed children to him. But God warned the people of Israel, "Do not give any of your children to be sacrificed to Molech, for you must not profane the name of your God. I am the LORD" (Leviticus 18:21). Unlike the false gods that were worshiped in that region, the God of Abraham would not tolerate human or infant sacrifice. Life is too sacred!

two brothers whom God loved, whom God was with, are now together at their father's grave.

Our world still waits for the children of Isaac and the children of Ishmael to live together like brothers under the covenant of love. The world still waits for the day when bloodshed ends and the peace of God can reign.

PAUSE FOR REFLECTION | *An Invitation*

At the end of the message, before you close in prayer, you might want to pause and invite those present to quiet their heart and reflect on one of the following questions. Take a moment for silence and allow room for the Holy Spirit to speak to the heart of each person.

- What do you need to *leave* behind if you are going to fully follow God?
- Are you walking in *covenant* relationship with God through Jesus? Are there any ways you are breaking the covenant?
- Where do you need to experience new *hope* in your life?
- What *step of faith* might you take today that will help you walk more closely with God?

Message 4

God Is with Us

Genesis 24:1–58; 27–33; 37; 39; 50:19–21

THE HEART OF THE Message

Have you ever noticed that you can be in a crowd of people and still feel very alone? We have all experienced moments of deep loneliness in this life. Even those extroverted people who seem to be the life of the party and always have someone calling them to "do lunch" or "meet for coffee" know what it is to feel alone.

In this session we will discover that God is with us, no matter what we might feel about our human relationships. Through the book of Genesis we see God reminding his people of his presence and care for them. In the moments they feel most alone, abandoned, and fearful, they hear God's persistent reminder that he is with them.

BRIEF MESSAGE OUTLINE

1. God is with Isaac
2. God is with Jacob
3. God is with Joseph

THE HEART OF THE Messenger

As you prepare to bring this message, take time for personal reflection. Identify times you have felt very alone. How did you respond to these feelings? How did you experience the presence of God during these times of your life? It will be important for you to hold these experiences in your heart as you teach. As you speak about God's presence, even in the hardest of times and the strangest of places, be aware of whether you are living with a conviction that God is with you.

Introduction

NARRATIVE ON LIFE *Looking at Genesis*

One of the most ironic remarks people make about the Bible goes something like this: "The Bible is a book of pious, well-meaning advice that is not relevant to, or reflective of, the real world." People who make this kind of comment immediately betray one simple fact: They haven't actually read the Bible. If we are honest, a simple reading of the book of Genesis will show that the Bible pulls no punches and glosses over nothing. It is real life, down to earth, and relevant to the point of being startling.

If you read the book of Genesis, the number of mixed-up families you meet will shock you. Here is a quick overview:

- Cain is jealous of his brother Abel and kills him.
- Lamech introduces polygamy to the world.
- Noah, the most righteous man of his generation, gets drunk and curses his grandson.
- Lot, when his home is surrounded by the residents of Sodom who want to violate his visitors, offers his daughters instead.
- Later on, Lot's daughters get him drunk and get impregnated by him, and we are told that Lot is the "most righteous man in Sodom."
- Abraham plays favorites between his sons Isaac and Ishmael, and they end up estranged from each other.
- Isaac plays favorites between his sons, Jacob and Esau, and they become bitter enemies for twenty years.
- Jacob plays favorites between Joseph and his eleven other sons, and they want to kill him but end up selling him as a slave to travelers from another country.

The marriages in the book of Genesis are filled with disaster.

- Abraham has sex with his wife's servant (at his wife's request) and then he sends her and their son off into the desert.
- Isaac and Rebekah fight over which of their boys is going to get the blessing.
- Jacob marries two wives and ends up in a fertility contest with both his wives and their maids.
- Jacob's firstborn son, Reuben, sleeps with his father's concubine.
- Another one of Jacob's sons, Judah, sleeps with his daughter-in-law (she is disguised as a prostitute and he does not know who she is).

These people are badly messed up. These are not the Waltons! They need Dr. Phil, Dr. Laura, Dr. Ruth, Dr. Spock, Dr. Seuss—they need somebody!

INTERPRETIVE INSIGHT | *Why Be So Honest?*

When we begin reading the Old Testament, we are quickly convinced that these are not a bunch of pious stories that look nothing like real life. The opposite is true. When we begin to read the Bible, we start to wonder why the writer includes so much graphic detail about the sins and real-life struggles of these people. Why is all this shocking material here?

Some of these stories are indeed shocking and horrific. For instance, Genesis 34 tells the story of Jacob's daughter, Dinah. She is raped by a man named Shechem, but her father is passive; he does nothing to vindicate her. However, the sons of Jacob respond by telling the men of Shechem's city that if they get circumcised, they will be welcome to marry the women of Israel. The men of the city agree, and they are all circumcised. While they are in great pain after their surgery (remember, this was done with flint knives and no anesthetic), Levi and Simeon enter the city and murder all of them!

The behavior of all the men in this story is a disgrace, but the writer of Genesis never says, "Here's the bad guy" or "Here's the moral of the story." It can leave the reader wondering, "What's going on?"

To start with, it is critical that we recognize that the author of Genesis is not morally confused. The Pentateuch is the source of the Ten Commandments. These opening five books of the Bible are the most morally influential writings in the history of the world. The Pentateuch is a work of an absolute genius.

What we need to realize is that the writer of Genesis is perfectly capable of saying, "You shall not murder. You shall not steal. You shall not commit adultery." And he does say those things. The Pentateuch is filled with moral absolutes. At the same time, the writer of Genesis tells stories to force us to think. When we read these stories, we have to develop discernment and apply judgment.

These stories are often a kind of moral case-study. They are quite complex, with real people in all of their ambiguity. The story of Dinah's rape and her brothers' revenge demands that the reader of Scripture ask questions like, "When something terrible happens, how do I distinguish between justice, which is good, and vengeance, which is death?" This question, which was relevant in the days of the Old Testament, is just as relevant today. God does not always give us an easy and clear answer, but he often invites us to use the mind he has given us to grapple with hard issues and come to godly conclusions.

INTERPRETIVE INSIGHT | *The Real Hero*

As we read through the opening book of the Bible, we discover that God does not always give us commentary on what we read. The good guys don't have a halo over their head and the bad guys don't have horns. Sometimes the good people make poor choices and enter into sin. At other times, a person who seems like the villain ends up doing something that honors God. In movies and books we can usually figure out fairly quickly who the hero is, but in the Pentateuch it can be hard to tell.

Why is this? Why are so many of the pivotal players such a mixture of strength and weakness? Why are so many of the stories in the Old Testament filled with people who seem so human? The reason is that these people are not to be held up as the heroes in the story. Certainly we can learn a great deal from Abraham and Sarah, but they are not the heroes. There is no question that Joseph's life-lessons are there to teach us about faithfulness and endurance, but he is not to be exalted as the final hero in the story.

The stories recorded in the Bible are there to point us to the real hero — God. God is working with real flesh-and-blood people. God knows that these people are living in a terribly fallen world and that sin does unspeakable damage. So God sheds light on what people are really like, but also on what he is like. At the end of the day, we all need to discover that God is the hero and that each of these stories points us toward him!

SIGNIFICANT SCRIPTURE

Genesis 24:1 – 58

1. God Is with Isaac

It is easy to believe God cares about the big things in the world. International crises, the decisions of presidents, kings and queens, world hunger, and the spread of the gospel — these are the things that must occupy the heart of God. We have no problem being confident that God wants to be involved in the big things that happen in this world.

But what about the little stuff? Is God available to help with my personal needs? For instance, does God care enough to get involved in helping me figure out the right career? Is he concerned about helping me choose healthy friends? Does God care enough to get involved in the process of helping me find the right person to marry? As we look at the life of Isaac, we discover that God not only cares deeply about the details of our lives, but he wants to get intimately involved with us. God is with us in the big things of life, and he is also with us in the little things.

NARRATIVE ON THE TEXT | *God Is with Isaac*

Isaac discovered that God was with him in a unique way. It came through the provision of a wife, through an amazing series of circumstances. Abraham was growing old. He had experienced great blessing and provision from the hand of God. His son Isaac was drawing near the age when he would marry, but Abraham was concerned about who his wife would be. Thus, he called his chief servant in for an important meeting. We know that Eliezer was Abraham's chief servant over all of his affairs, so we can be fairly confident that this was the one who carried out Abraham's plan. When Eliezer

HISTORICAL CONTEXT | *Just Part of the Oath*

In our day and age, we tend to seal an agreement with a handshake. This works quite well for most people. But in Abraham's day, the tradition was different. Placing a hand under a person's thigh was just part of the oath. It would have been as natural as shaking hands in our day. It was a method of promise in the old days, an expression of complete trust. In this oath, Eliezer promises that he will not get a wife for Isaac from the daughters of the Canaanites. Rather, he will find a wife for Isaac among Abraham's own people.

entered the room, Abraham asked him to place his hand under his thigh and swear by the Lord that he would do what Abraham was about to request.

INTERPRETIVE INSIGHT | *What's Wrong with a Canaanite Woman?*

What would have been so bad if Isaac had married a Canaanite woman? What was the big deal? Abraham's concern here is that Isaac will not be tempted into idolatry—into leaving this God of the covenant. Abraham knows the potential lure of love. If Isaac were to marry a pagan, Canaanite woman, he might just end up worshiping her false gods and dishonoring the one true God.

LIFE APPLICATION | *Being Equally Yoked*

The warning we see here in Genesis about the danger of marrying somebody who is not committed to God runs all the way through the whole Old Testament and into the New Testament. In numerous places in the Old Testament, God warns against intermarrying with the pagan nations (for example, see Exodus 34:15–16; Deuteronomy 7:3; Ezra 9–10). Paul talks about the importance of being "equally yoked" (2 Corinthians 6:14). Because God's people are part of a covenant community, they should marry people who are also followers of Christ.

Note to the teacher: It is helpful for you as a teacher/preacher to remind God's people of this important biblical truth. We live in a day when many followers of Christ are asking if it is really a big deal if they marry someone who is not a fully devoted follower of Jesus. The answer is the same today as it was the day Abraham sent Eliezer to find a wife for Isaac.

NARRATIVE ON THE TEXT | *Eliezer on a Mission*

Abraham sends his chief-of-staff, Eliezer, off with a caravan of ten camels loaded down with all sorts of riches and provisions. Anyone who saw this caravan coming would know that someone with great wealth was coming to town.

> The smallest act of kindness is better than the greatest of kind intentions.
>
> *Ken Gire*

We need to understand the difficult nature of this assignment. Eliezer is sent to a part of the world he doesn't know, and there are no maps to show him the way. He has to find Abraham's relatives and talk them into sending one of their women away forever to marry some kid they've never met. From the very beginning, this is a huge challenge.

It is a joy to see what Eliezer does first. He prays, "O Lord, God of my master Abraham, give me success today, and show kindness to my master Abraham" (Genesis 24:12). Eliezer prays. This is only the second prayer recorded in the entire Bible. The first one is when Abraham intercedes on behalf of Sodom and Gomorrah.

Eliezer is not a part of Abraham's lineage, though he is a part of the circumcised covenant community and he does trust God. This servant calls out to the God of Abraham. If you look closely, you will see a detail that some people might miss. While Eliezer is still praying, while he is still on his knees, while he is in the process of asking for the right woman to come along so that Isaac might have a wife, Rebekah walks onto the scene.

Eliezer meets Rebekah, and she exceeds his prayer. She is a relative of Abraham, as he has prayed. This is good news because she'll be less likely to tempt her husband Isaac to worship idols. She's also available to be a wife because she is a virgin; moreover, she is "very beautiful." What more could Isaac (and Abraham) ask for?

LIFE APPLICATION | *The Power of Specific Prayers*

Eliezer discovers the power of prayer in a big way! He has asked the God of Abraham to send along a woman who will be willing to water all ten of his camels after their long and arid trip. In response to his prayer, Rebekah arrives and offers to do exactly what Eliezer prayed.

For Eliezer, a specific prayer leads to a specific answer. Too often we offer up vague prayers. In many cases, our prayers can be so general that we have no idea if they are actually answered. We need to learn to be specific in our prayer requests. There is no guarantee that every prayer we lift up will be answered in the affirmative. But when a prayer is answered, we should be able to recognize it because the request has been specific.

NARRATIVE ON THE TEXT | *Rebekah's Decision*

Rebekah's response and dramatic act of service is even more impressive because we know she doesn't have any idea what's at stake. She doesn't know that her whole future and participation in God's redemptive community is on the line. She is just serving.

HISTORICAL CONTEXT | *Thirsty*

A thirsty camel can drink up to thirty gallons of water. Simple math shows that Rebekah was offering to draw up to three hundred gallons of water, since there were ten camels.

When we think about getting water, we imagine turning a knob and watching the water flow. In those days, the wells were often deep. The water was retrieved by throwing a bucket down the well and pulling it up by hand. To draw three hundred gallons of water by hand was a task that would exhaust most people, then or now. Yet Rebekah gladly offers to do this humble act of service. In this story we learn a couple of things about Rebekah. First, she has a servant's heart. Second, this girl has some serious biceps!

Eliezer recognizes that God is at work in this far country. He sees that this beautiful, servant-hearted woman is the answer to his prayer. Eliezer gives her some expensive jewelry as a gift from Abraham and Isaac, and Rebekah invites him to meet her family. Eliezer knows it is going to take a fair amount of ingenuity and wise persuasion on his part, but he has no question that God is at work.

Eliezer meets Rebekah's brother Laban and quickly discovers what makes him tick. He is a money guy (we will discover this in greater detail in the next message). He is very interested in money, and the costly jewelry Rebekah is wearing gets Laban's attention.

Within a short time, Eliezer clearly expresses why he has come and tells them the whole story of his bold and specific prayer as well as Rebekah's actions that fulfilled his prayer. Eliezer asks if Rebekah can go with him immediately. When she is asked if she is willing to accompany Eliezer back so that she can meet Isaac and become his wife, she responds with one word (in the Hebrew) that simply means, "I will go." Eliezer has accomplished his mission, and he is ready to head home.

LIFE APPLICATION | *Beginning with Prayer and Ending with Praise*

Eliezer began his task with a clear and specific prayer. What a wonderful example for all of us. He was facing a challenge and knew he could never accomplish it on his own, so he prays.

When his task is completed successfully, he bows down again and lifts up a prayer of praise. Note Genesis 24:27: "Then the man bowed down and worshiped the LORD, saying, 'Praise be to the LORD, the God of my master Abraham, who has not abandoned his kindness and faithfulness to my master. As for me, the LORD has led me on the journey to the house of my master's relatives.'"

Eliezer is given a difficult assignment. He begins in prayer. He sees God work. Finally, he ends with worship. This is a God thing every step of the way! Eliezer becomes an example of how we should live our lives: Begin with prayer and end with praise. What a great model for life!

INTERPRETIVE INSIGHT | *A New Vision of God*

The writer of Genesis is saying something unprecedented. This had never been said before to the history of the human race. Genesis is teaching us that the one and only transcendent God, who existed before time, who was in the beginning, who created the heavens and the earth, is also the immanent God who is with us right here, right now. In this story we discover that the transcendent Creator of the

NEW TESTAMENT CONNECTION

Ask, Seek, and Knock!

Jesus was the wisest man who ever lived. Here is what he had to say in Luke 11:9–13 about the Father's desire to hear and answer our prayers:

> "So I say to you: Ask and it will be given to you; seek and you will find; knock and the door will be opened to you. For everyone who asks receives; he who seeks finds; and to him who knocks, the door will be opened.
>
> "Which of you fathers, if your son asks for a fish, will give him a snake instead? Or if he asks for an egg, will give him a scorpion? If you then, though you are evil, know how to give good gifts to your children, how much more will your Father in heaven give the Holy Spirit to those who ask him!"

heavens and earth is concerned about nomads, their kids, and a servant named Eliezer. In this story we see God revealing himself as both transcendent and immanent.

He is the God Immanuel, which means "God with us." He's the God who is next to us every moment of every day. This transcendent God is present and intimately concerned about the little details of our daily lives. Isaac discovered this powerful spiritual reality and lived in it through his whole life, and so can we.

SIGNIFICANT SCRIPTURE

Genesis 27–33

2. God Is with Jacob

There are people in this world who never seem to learn from their mistakes. Because they refuse to learn, they are doomed to repeat the same unhealthy behaviors over and over again. There are also people who *do* learn from their mistakes. These people grow in wisdom and avoid all sorts of pain and struggle. However, there is a group of people who are wisest of all. These are the men and women who learn from the mistakes of others. They watch, listen, and learn. Rather than having to face the consequences of unwise choices and actions, they see the results of these things in the lives of others and avoid them at all costs.

The story of Jacob's life is an example of all three of these kinds of people wrapped into one. Sometimes when we look at Jacob, we see a man who repeats the same mistakes over and over. At other times, Jacob learns from his mistakes and grows in maturity as he discovers that God is with him, even in the hard times. As we walk through Jacob's life, we see him grow in wisdom and come to a place where he is able to learn from the mistakes of others and not have to feel pain before he learns the lessons God wants to teach him. As we study the life of Jacob, we are invited to a place of wisdom where we can discover God's desire to be with us and teach us in every experience of life.

WORD STUDY

Deism and Pantheism

The theologians are right when they say God is transcendent. But if people believe in a God who is *only* transcendent, they end up adopting what's called *deism*. The idea of deism is that God created the world and then decided to have little or nothing to do with it. God got the ball rolling, but now it is up to us. God has no plans to meddle, interfere, or help.

The other extreme is the belief that God is *only* immanent and not transcendent. This leads to something called *pantheism*. This is a belief that God is so immanent that material things are divine. These philosophies and religious systems lead people to worship the earth, the sun, and the moon.

NARRATIVE ON THE TEXT | *Jacob the Deceiver*

Isaac and Rebekah are married and God's plan of community continues. They end up having twin sons, Jacob and Esau. Jacob is a con artist. He is a scammer. Jacob is always looking for an angle, and he's like that right out of the womb.

Genesis 25:24–26 tells the story of the birth of this odd couple. Esau was the firstborn, and this kid had a serious hair problem. The Bible tells us that when he was born, he was like a hairy garment. Jacob came next, and when he came out he was grasping onto his brother's heel.

NARRATIVE ON THE TEXT | *Messed-Up Family Dynamics*

As these two boys grow up, they become two dramatically different people. Esau is a hunter and an outdoorsman. Jacob is a quiet man who likes to stay inside. We read that, again, the parents make the mistake of playing favorites. Isaac dotes over Esau because he is a jock; he's a man's man. This kid might not be the brightest lightbulb on the chandelier, and he might have some serious body hair, but he also has the heart and affection of his father.

Rebekah favors Jacob. She helps Jacob trick his dad into stealing the family blessing from Esau. She teaches her boy how to be Jacob the deceiver. You don't have to look hard to discover that you have some really messed-up family dynamics here. Things get so bad that when Esau realizes he has lost both his birthright and blessing to his younger brother, he plans to kill him.

LIFE APPLICATION | *No Favorites*

All through the book of Genesis we see examples of parents playing favorites. Here is the key observation we need to make: It never works out well. There is never a sense that these actions and attitudes of favoritism bring life and health. They never lead to the edification of the children or the parents. Favoritism brings conflict, tension, and brokenness in each family.

WORD STUDY

Jacob and Esau – What's in a Name?

Both of these boys receive names that fit them. *Esau* simply means "red." One obvious reason for this name is that he was a redhead – and a red everything else. This kid has red hair from head to toe! Also, later in life, he sells his birthright to his brother for a bowl of red stew.

Jacob literally means "he who grasps the heel." Metaphorically his name meant "the deceiver." Jacob's name is a foreshadowing of the kind of character Jacob will have for a good portion of his life. Jacob becomes the one who grasps the heel, the one who trips others up, the deceiver. But with time, God will give him a new name and a new character.

WORD STUDY | *Transcendent, Immanent, and Omnipresence*

For centuries Christian theologians have used three words to describe God. One of them is transcendence. Our God, the God of the Bible, is a transcendent God. The idea behind this word is that God is eternally self-sufficient apart from his creation. He was around way before the world was created. He can live apart from his creation. Isaiah 6:1 gives us a picture of this: "I saw the LORD seated on the throne, high and exalted." God is totally other from us. He is the infinite and holy God.

A second word theologians use to describe God, which is a sort of counterpoint to transcendence, is *immanence*. The idea of immanence is that God is continuously, actively present with us. This theological concept is similar to the idea of the next word, though with a subtle difference. Immanence means God is active everywhere. God sees. God knows. God cares. God works.

Omnipresence is a spatial concept, which teaches us that God is everywhere. The psalmist paints a picture of God's omnipresence with these words: "If I go up to the heavens, you are there; if I make my bed in the depths, you are there" (Psalm 139:8). Wherever I go, God, you are there with me.

PAUSE FOR REFLECTION

Being Aware

Where is the house of God? Where is God present? Everywhere. He is right next to each one of us. So often we are like Jacob and have to say—"Surely the Lord is in this place, and I was not aware of it." Our goal should be to grow in our awareness of God's presence and become people who can say, "Surely the Lord is in this place and I see it. I see him at work."

It could be a very rich experience to take a few moments of silence and invite those gathered to reflect on life situations where God is present, but they are not tuned in to see and hear him. Invite the Holy Spirit to speak to the heart of each person and begin to give them a greater clarity to realize that God is with them, even in the times and places he is hard to recognize.

What a sobering reminder to all those gathered who are parents or hope to be parents. It is also a good warning to grandparents and other family members, like aunts and uncles. Beware of the danger of favoritism. God's Word teaches some good lessons about avoiding favoritism. Many of those gathered have experienced the sting of growing up in a home where they were not "the favorite." God longs that this dysfunction not be passed on to the next generation.

NARRATIVE ON THE TEXT | *Jacob on the Run*

As the story of Jacob and Esau continues, God decides Jacob must go to character school. Life is going to get very hard for Jacob. He will have to travel a long way from home. But God wants Jacob to know he is not abandoned. God is still with him. When we get to Genesis 28, Jacob has left his home and is fleeing from his brother, Esau. Jacob runs for his life, but he has no idea that he is running straight toward the arms of the God who is with him and into the plans God has for him.

While on the run, Jacob has a vision. This is one of the most important visions of the Old Testament. In this vision, Jacob comes to see that God is present with him.

INTERPRETIVE INSIGHT | *Jacob's Ladder*

In Jacob's vision he sees a kind of a staircase with angels of God ascending and descending from heaven. This is the kingdom of heaven intersecting with earth and human life. God is present and is speaking to Jacob. This is one of the most fundamental visions any human being has ever had because it gives a picture of the connectedness of the kingdom of heaven and those who dwell on this earth. In this vision, Jacob is reminded that the transcendent God is also immanent.

Through this vision God is telling Jacob, "I am with you and will watch over you wherever you go, and I will bring you back to this land. I will not leave you until I have done what I have promised" (Genesis 28:15). What a life-changing reminder! When Jacob wakes up from his sleep and the vision is over, he realizes, "Surely the Lord is in this place, and I was not aware of it" (28:16). Jacob realizes something that we all need to discover at some point in our spiritual journey: God can be very present, and we can miss it. We need to pay attention and learn to see how God is with us at all times and in all places.

> All God's giants have been weak people who did great things for God because they reckoned on his being with them.
>
> *J. Hudson Taylor*

NARRATIVE ON THE TEXT | *New Family Ties*

As we continue to study Jacob's life, we see the process of Jacob's transformation. In chapter 29 he goes to Haran, the hometown of his grandfather Abraham. Jacob travels hundreds of miles from Canaan to Haran, and there he meets his Uncle Laban. Jacob does not realize it right away, but when he meets Laban, he has met his match when it comes to deception. Laban is the king of con artists, and Jacob will learn some powerful life lessons as he relates to Laban in the coming years.

When Jacob arrives in Haran, he meets some folks around a well. While he is talking with them, a beautiful shepherdess arrives. In Genesis 29:9 we read, "While he was still talking with them, Rachel came with her father's sheep, for she was a shepherdess. When Jacob saw Rachel daughter of Laban, his mother's brother, and Laban's sheep, he went over and rolled the stone away from the mouth of the well and watered his uncle's sheep."

WORD STUDY

Bethel

Jacob is learning that God is always intersecting with human life. In response, Jacob gets up early in the morning and sets up a pillar, a visual reminder of what he has learned. He pours oil on it and gives that place a new name. Before, it was called Luz. Now it will be called "Bethel." The name Bethel comes from two words: *beth*, which is the Hebrew word meaning "house," and *el*, a Hebrew word for God. This is "the house of God." This is the place where God is present.

NARRATIVE ON THE TEXT | *Leah, Not Rachel*

Laban has two daughters. Leah is the older one, but Jacob is in love with Rachel. He is so crazy over Rachel that he works seven years to earn her hand in marriage. That was the agreement. That was the deal. But we read these words: "They seemed like only a few days to him because of his love for her" (Genesis 29:20). Jacob is one love-sick, desperate guy.

In verse 21 we read, "Then Jacob said to Laban, 'Give me my wife. My time is completed, and I want to lie with her.' " That sounds a little crass. Most fathers would not recommend this as the lead-in line for a man who is ready to marry his daughter. Jacob is messing with the wrong guy, and he is about to discover a whole new level of deception. Jacob had a college degree in deception, but Laban had a doctorate. On his wedding night, into his tent, wrapped in a veil, silent in the darkness, Laban sends in his first daughter, Leah.

HISTORICAL CONTEXT | *Big Rock*

The stones that covered wells in those days were enormous. They weighed hundreds of pounds. They were designed to require several large, burly shepherds to remove them because they were supposed to protect the water supply, which was very precious. The whole idea of covering the well with such a big rock was to make sure that no one could uncover the well until all the shepherds arrived and moved the stone as a group. The sight of seeing one man move this rock would have been shocking.

NARRATIVE ON THE TEXT | *The Deceiver Deceived*

As anyone would guess, Jacob is not happy about his morning surprise. So Jacob says to Laban (verse 25), "What is this you have done to me? I served you for Rachel, didn't I? Why have you [it is important to note the next word] deceived me?" The word he uses is a form of his own name—Jacob. And this is a theme in his story. In a sense, Jacob is asking Laban, "Why have you treated me the way I have treated so many others?"

INTERPRETIVE INSIGHT | *I've Been Jacobed!*

Later on in Genesis 31:7, Jacob says, "Laban deceived me by changing my wages ten times." The writer is telling us, with this kind of code word, that Jacob is now on the receiving end of what he had been dishing out his whole life. He has to learn what it feels like to be deceived. In the Hebrew, Jacob is actually asking Laban, "Why have you Jacobed me?" He has been out-deceived, and Jacob does not like it.

NARRATIVE ON THE TEXT | *A Spiritual Overhaul*

Jacob needs a spiritual overhaul. The road he will take to spiritual maturity will not be an easy one. He needs new eyes, a new mind, and a new heart. And there's no way to

ON THE LIGHTER SIDE | *Love Steroids*

Jacob, you'll remember, was an indoor boy. He was not a jock. He did not have the "Body by Jake." He had a body by Jacob, and it was not real impressive. It was Esau who loved to take off his shirt and flex his hairy biceps. But Jacob is so inspired by Rachel that he wants to show off. It's like he's all of a sudden on love steroids. Jacob, the indoor boy, puts his shoulder against this massive rock and pushes for all he is worth. To the surprise of everyone there, including Jacob, the stone rolls away.

ON THE LIGHTER SIDE | *"It Was Leah"*

What follows in this account is told with some wit, artistic flair, and great economy of words. Jacob shares his night and bed with the veiled woman Laban sends into his tent. Jacob is elated! He has waited for seven years for this night. He believes it is his beloved Rachel. Then the sun rises and we read these words recorded in verse 25, "When morning came, there was Leah!" Oops!

go through that process but the painful, laborious, character-building process of being on the receiving end for a while. Suffering will teach him what nothing else can. So he goes to Laban and asks, "Why have you deceived me?"

Laban informs Jacob of a painful reality, "It is not our custom here to give the younger daughter in marriage before the older one." Laban is getting in a dig. "Around here," he's saying, "we don't allow the grabby, younger child to steal the rights of an older one. You know of any cases where that happened? Maybe it's different where you come from, Jacob. But around here that sort of thing just doesn't fly."

WORD STUDY

Israel

For a long portion of his life, the name of the man we have been studying was Jacob, the deceiver, and he lived out the meaning of his name. Now God gives him a new name, *Israel*. This new name points to his future. His new name means, "he who struggles with God."

NARRATIVE ON LIFE | *The Story of the Unloved Sister*

Think of what the wedding night must have been like for Leah. So often we tend to focus on Jacob and Rachel, but Leah was a real person, with real feelings, who experienced real pain. This is her one and only wedding night, and she's in the tent because her husband thinks she's Rachael. She says nothing. All she had to do was say a word, and it would be over. She says nothing. Why? Maybe she's afraid of her father's anger. Maybe she feels she's unattractive and she'll never be loved. Maybe she's desperately in love with Jacob.

This story of the heartache of the unloved sister is one of the saddest in Scripture. But we read that God hears and God cares. God notices the tears of Leah. God is with Leah in her pain and sorrow. He cares for her and gives her children. What a great reminder that God is not just with the key players in the story; he is with each person at his or her point of need!

NEW TESTAMENT CONNECTION

New Beginnings

In 2 Corinthians 5:17 the apostle Paul reminds us that God still brings new beginnings for each person who has a relationship with him through Jesus. Listen to these words: "Therefore, if anyone is in Christ, he is a new creation; the old has gone, the new has come!" The same God that made Jacob into Israel can give us a new beginning today!

NARRATIVE ON THE TEXT | *A Time of Transformation*

For twenty years Jacob goes to character school. Jacob the deceiver meets Laban and learns about the pain of deception, and he begins to change. God is with him. Then he finally decides to return home and face his brother Esau. This is a courageous decision because Jacob has been a runner and an avoider his whole life. But now he decides to go back and be reconciled to his brother or die trying. It's a courageous thing to do.

Jacob has a life-changing encounter with God on the way. Jacob, the man who had lived in deceit, manipulation, and fear, wrestles all night with a man. Jacob says, "I will not let you go until you bless me" (Genesis 32:26). He discovers he is wrestling with God, and God says, "I'm going to give you a new name."

INTERPRETIVE INSIGHT | *A New Man*

After wrestling with God and receiving a new name, Israel is a different person. Before all this happened, he had devised a strategy to send groups ahead of him to try to meet Esau first and appease him. He had planned to let a series of gifts act as a buffer before he met his brother. Remember, last time these two brothers were together, Esau wanted him dead!

Before, Jacob fled in fear, but now he is Israel. He gathers his family and all he has and walks toward his brother. But instead of sending waves of animals, servants, and gifts ahead of him, we read these words, "He himself went on ahead." He's the fighter. He's going first. He's leading the way. He'll take the risk. He's a new man.

PAUSE FOR REFLECTION

Broken Relationships

In light of this staggering example of reconciliation, this might be a good time to challenge people to identify a relationship where they need reconciliation. Give a word of hope and encouragement that God does have the power to restore even the most broken of relationships. Then allow a time of silence for people to invite the Holy Spirit to help them identify a relationship that needs healing.

LIFE APPLICATION | *The Hope of Reconciliation*

As we read the story, we might expect Esau to come with anger and vengeance. We read that he arrives to meet Jacob with four hundred men! This could have felt very threatening. But here we read some of the most touching words in the Bible: "But Esau ran to meet Jacob and embraced him; he threw his arms around his neck and kissed him. And they wept." And the long, slow, redemptive work of God bears fruit, and the dream of community wins a little bit. Finally, in this sad book, two brothers are reconciled.

HISTORICAL CONTEXT | *Seeing Your Face*

One of the great statements in the Bible is found in Genesis 33:10. This is definitely a verse worth underlining in your Bible. Jacob says to Esau, "If I have found favor in your eyes, accept this gift from me. For to see your face is like seeing the face of God."

Now, "to see the face" in the Hebrew language meant to know someone, to grasp their character. If you think about someone whose back is turned toward you, you can't see his or her character. But when they turn so you can see their face, you get to know their heart. You know what's going on inside of them. You see their face.

Israel is stumbling slowly toward knowing more and more about God. As he grows to know God, it changes the way he sees people. So he says to his brother, Esau, "When you offer mercy, when you desire to reconcile, it reminds me of God. You remind me of God." The image of God begins to be a little more visible in human beings. It's just a beautiful statement: "For to see your face is like seeing the face of God."

3. God Is with Joseph

> **SIGNIFICANT SCRIPTURE**
> Genesis 37; 39; 50:19–21

It is easy to recognize the presence of God in our lives when things are going well. When the sun is shining, there is money in the bank account, and our body feels healthy, there is a sense that God is near. But what about on the cloudy days, when the stock market does poorly, the doctor brings bad news, and relationships seem to be coming apart at the seams? Where is God when pain and sorrow envelop our lives? From Joseph we learn that God is still with us, even in the times of greatest darkness. And, sometimes, we find that God is with us in these times most of all.

INTERPRETIVE INSIGHT | *Not a Perfect Son or Brother*

Some people present Joseph as the perfect son who is treated badly by his brothers with no apparent provocation. But if you read this account carefully, it appears Joseph does not help things very much. The text suggests that he is a pretty spoiled kid and that he doesn't seem to mind it too much.

To get a sense of the family dynamics, we are told in Genesis 37:2, "Joseph, a young man of seventeen, was tending the flocks with his brothers, the sons of Bilhah and the sons of Zilpah, his father's wives, and he brought their father a *bad report* about them." Remember that Joseph is the son of Jacob's favorite wife, Rachel. These other boys are not Jacob's favorites. On top of this, Joseph brings a bad report about his brothers.

HISTORICAL CONTEXT | *A Lot More Than a Robe*

Jacob, the father, gave Joseph a special robe. The adjective to describe it is a little uncertain in Hebrew. The NIV translates it "a robe with long sleeves." In the King James Version, the expression is a "coat of many colors." Though we don't know exactly what the robe looked like, we do have a sense of its significance.

Let's put it this way, Jacob got it from Nordstrom. It was hand-tailored. The rest of the boys got their clothes off the rack from K-Mart when the blue light was flashing. There is no question this coat set young Joseph apart from his brothers in a way that everyone could see. What made this coat explosive was not just that it was more expensive or made of nicer material. The problem was the meaning behind Jacob's giving this coat to his second youngest son (the older son of his favorite wife, Rachel).

There was a ceremony involving such robes in the ancient Near East that marked the recipient as the father's primary heir. Joseph, the eleventh son in the family lineage, takes the rights of the firstborn. Joseph gets the farm. When he receives this special robe, the situation is packed with emotions because the whole family inheritance is at stake. This is a volatile moment because the older boys can clearly see that Joseph has been placed before all of them. This is a recipe for sibling civil war, and that is exactly what happens.

In our day, a kid who tells on his brothers and sisters is called a tattletale. This is actually somewhat worse. The word for "report" or "tale" used here occurs elsewhere in the negative sense of an untrue story. And here it is described by the word "bad" or "evil," which most likely means that Joseph made up bad stuff about his brothers, which was not entirely true, and his father believed him rather than his brothers.

NARRATIVE ON THE TEXT | *A Look at Dreams*

As we move on in the story, Joseph has a pair of dreams. Dreams were generally considered prophetic in those days, though, interestingly, here the writer does not say they are from God. He just leaves it open-ended. You would think Joseph might have the common sense to keep his dreams to himself. His brothers already have real problems with this fancy robe-wearing, inheritance-stealing younger brother.

Instead of having the wisdom to remain quiet, Joseph gathers all of his brothers together to tell them about his dream. Remember, these are the brothers who have no robe, who have been desperately hurt by their father, and who hate Joseph's guts. But he gathers them together and says, "Listen to my dream, brothers. In my dream all of you are little sheaves. And I am a great big sheaf. My sheaf rose up, and it stood tall, and your little sheaves gathered around and bowed down to my sheaf—which means one day I will rule over all of you." You can almost hear Joseph telling them, "I will command and you will submit. You will bow down in humble expression of your obedience to my authority. Isn't that cool? Aren't you happy about this dream? Let's play 'Bow Down Sheaf' now, just to get ready."

Their response is clear. Verse 4 says, "When his brothers saw that their father loved him more than any of them, they hated him and could not speak a kind word to him. Joseph had a dream, and when he told it to his brothers, they hated him all the more." Verse 8: "His brothers said to him, 'Do you intend to reign over us? Will you actually rule us?' And they hated him all the more because of his dream."

One word keeps popping up through this section of Genesis: "hate." In verse 9, Joseph has another dream. You'd think by now he'd learn to keep his dreams to himself. These dreams are not helping the family out. This time there are eleven stars, the sun, and the moon, and they all bow down to Joseph. Again, the brothers get the message loud and clear. This time they are being told that all of them, and their parents, will bow down to Joseph. Now they hate him even more! They hate him so much that they end up secretly selling him as a slave to a band of travelers heading to Egypt, and they tell his father that his favorite son is dead.

INTERPRETIVE INSIGHT | *Character School*

Jacob thinks Joseph is dead, but he is actually on his way to character school down in Egypt. Joseph had dreams of being exalted, but now he is a slave. This young man has gone from being on top of the pile to the bottom of the totem pole. But, even in slavery, betrayed by his brothers and taken against his will to a foreign country, we read these words, "The LORD was with Joseph" (Genesis 39:2).

Joseph arrives in Egypt and becomes a slave in the home of a wealthy leader named Potiphar. Things go pretty well until Mrs. Potiphar makes advances on Joseph and he rejects her. In retaliation, she lies and says he has assaulted her. Joseph ends up in prison because of that lie. All he has done is seek to honor God and remain faithful, and now he is being punished. At this point it would be easy for Joseph to feel he has been completely abandoned by God. But Genesis 39:20–21 says, "Joseph's master took him and put him in prison, the place where the king's prisoners were confined. But while Joseph was there in prison, the LORD was with him."

> God's love is more concerned with the development of a person's character than with the promotion of his or her comfort.
>
> *J. Ireland Hasler*

Joseph, who had been preoccupied with his own little dreams at home, now learns to notice and care for other prisoners. His physical living space has gotten much smaller, but his world has expanded. This moment marks the beginning of Joseph's exaltation. It's an interesting thing that Jacob, who was a deceiver, had to learn what it felt like to be deceived. Joseph, who dreamed of life at the top and spoke about it in grandiose terms, has to experience life at the bottom. It is precisely at the moments of his greatest pain and aloneness that God is with him.

From this place of darkness and imposed humility, God raises Joseph up and uses him to save whole populations in Egypt from starvation during a famine. Joseph is raised up through interpreting a series of dreams, and he becomes the second most powerful man in all of Egypt. Next to Pharaoh, Joseph rules over Egypt. One day, many years later, he is reconciled with his brothers.

INTERPRETIVE INSIGHT | *Trusting God*

Genesis 50:20 is a summary of Joseph's entire life. In a sense, it is a statement about the theology of Genesis. This short verse hits on a key Old Testament theme that helps us understand that God is at work and is with us even when we don't know it. When Joseph's brothers finally realize who he is, they throw themselves before him and tell him, "We'll be your slaves." They are sure he's furious at them. But he says, "Don't be afraid. I'm not angry with you. I'm not going to pronounce judgment on you."

As they tremble in fear, knowing he can speak one word and have them executed for what they did to him so many years before, Joseph speaks these words, "You intended to harm me, but God intended it for good to accomplish what is now being done, the saving of many lives." Joseph realizes that the Lord God has been with him every step of the way!

LIFE APPLICATION | *A God Hunt*

Here's the assignment for all those who want to experience God's presence in deeper ways. We need to go on a God hunt.

David Mains used to talk about this idea on a radio show called "Chapel of the Air." A God hunt is simply learning to look for signs that the God who walked with Adam and Eve, with Enoch and Noah, with Abraham and Isaac and Jacob and Joseph really will be with us. If we learn to do this, it will make a fundamental difference in our lives. We begin to live with a new kind of expectancy.

Invite people to hunt for God in their daily lives. Here are five things they can look for. All of these come from the life experience of the three men we have studied in this session:

1. Concrete answers to specific prayers
2. Leadings or promptings from God
3. Unexpected resources
4. Surprising outcomes
5. God-ordained "demotions"

Each of these can help us see that God is with us, leading and shaping us each and every day.

Message 5

God the Deliverer

Exodus 1–12

THE HEART OF THE Message

Everyone faces moments in life when they need some help. Sometimes we humbly accept a hand from someone else. At other times, we stubbornly insist on doing things ourselves. Like the man or woman driving late at night who is hopelessly lost, we refuse to stop and ask for directions. We would rather stay lost than admit we need help. We have the strangest ability to live in the worst of situations and pretend everything is under control. Life goes so much better when we can admit we need help. All of us face moments when we need a deliverer.

The people of Israel came to this place often. Sometimes they stubbornly refused God's help and lived with the consequences. At other times they would cry out and accept God's delivering hand. All of us can grow to see God as our deliverer. Not only does he have the power to save, but also he longs to deliver his children. He is waiting to act. In this message we will discover how we can walk in the delivering power of God.

BRIEF MESSAGE OUTLINE

1. Clinging to God when things seem hopeless
2. Strength in weakness
3. The God who delivers

THE HEART OF THE Messenger

We all need the deliverance that only God can offer. The starting point is when we come to a place where we realize our sin has us captive and only God can save us through the shed blood of Jesus, the new Passover Lamb. As a leader in Christ's church, you have come to this place of calling on God for deliverance. As you prepare to bring this message, take time to thank God for sending his only Son as your deliverer.

However, God's delivering power and plans don't stop at the cross and the empty tomb. The same God who worked miracles in Egypt and parted the Red Sea is ready to move in your life today. As you are studying and preparing for this message, take time to evaluate your life—your habits, attitudes, and motives—and look for areas you might need God's deliverance. Ask the delivering God of the Israelites to reveal his power and set you free as you speak his truth to the church.

SIGNIFICANT SCRIPTURE

Exodus 1:1–14

1. Clinging to God When Things Seem Hopeless

As we begin Exodus, the Israelites seem to be in an impossible situation. They are strangers in a strange land. They are oppressed. They are powerless. Humanly speaking, there is no way out. Yet God calls them to cling to him, even if their eyes see no hope of relief. In the same way, we need to hold fast to our God when the waters rise around us. No matter how bad the storm and no matter how great the enemy, our hope is in God.

INTERPRETIVE INSIGHT | *Be Fruitful and Multiply*

At the beginning of Exodus we hear a phrase that is becoming a refrain throughout the Pentateuch. We see a theme that is close to the heart of God. It is captured in these words, "Now Joseph and all his brothers and all that generation died, but the Israelites were fruitful and multiplied greatly and became exceedingly numerous, so that the land filled with them." You might remember that in the very first command in the law, Genesis 1:28, God says, "Be fruitful and increase in number." After the flood God repeated these words to Noah and his family, "Be fruitful and increase in number" (Genesis 9:1).

Similarly, God came to Abraham and made a promise: "I will make you fruitful; I will make nations of you" (Genesis 17:6). Abraham actually laughed because he did not think it was likely that he would be fruitful. He and Sarah had reached an age where they didn't even buy green bananas anymore. They did not think it was too likely. But they did finally receive the promised son, and now his descendants have

HISTORICAL CONTEXT | *Hopeless?*

God had promised Abraham that his descendants would be like the sand of the seashore and the stars of the heavens and that they would populate the land of Canaan. Yet as the book of Exodus opens, this great promise seems to be in jeopardy. Abraham, Isaac, Jacob, and Joseph are dead. Their descendants are oppressed slaves in a foreign land. The idea of a great nation living in the Promised Land must have seemed like a distant dream. To the human eye, it seemed as if hope was gone.

ended up in Egypt. Nevertheless, even while they are in this furnace of oppression, they are fruitful and multiply greatly.

Who is at work here? It's God. The Israelites may not recognize it, but we can see it as we read the Bible and look back on what happened. It is no accident that the Israelites are proliferating like this. In the covenant, God promised Abraham that he would have more descendants than stars in the sky. This promise is coming true, even if the people of Israel do not recognize it.

HISTORICAL CONTEXT | *Location, Location, Location!*

Every real estate agent will tell you about the importance of location when it comes to buying a house. The three most important things are location, location, and location. This might be true with houses, but it is also true when it comes to the land occupied by a nation. Israel learned, very early on in their history, that the location of this Promised Land they were to occupy was critical in the world at that time (and in many ways, today as well).

In this part of the world there was something called the Fertile Crescent. This was an area that got enough rain and had enough water to sustain life. At that time in history, in that part of the world, it was all about water. Water is what made life possible, and it was crucial to travel and survival. The Fertile Crescent was one of the few places where water was available.

The Fertile Crescent started down at the Persian Gulf, crossed through the Tigris and the Euphrates rivers, and then ran down the Mediterranean to the Nile. This is

CREATIVE MESSAGE IDEA | *Map Time*

In an effort to help your listeners grow in their understanding of the landscape where this story takes place, have them take out a piece of paper and draw a basic map with you. You can do this on a flip chart, a dry-erase board, or use the PowerPoint map that is provided. You can describe it your own way or use the brief description provided. The PowerPoint slide for this map follows what is written below.

On the left side of your paper, draw three sides of a rectangle (open at the left) – this is the Mediterranean Sea. Then down below the rectangle draw a "Y" that extends on down; this is the Nile River. Then draw what looks kind of like an arm with a hand that's making a victory sign. This is the Red Sea. Then toward the right side here draw a little circle and a line coming down and a little oval. That's the Sea of Galilee, the Jordan River, and the Dead Sea. Finally, all the way to the right draw a kind of amoeba shape (that's the Persian Gulf) with an antenna coming up out of the amoeba that forks off into two branches. Those are the Tigris and Euphrates rivers. The land between the Jordan and the Mediterranean Sea is the Promised Land – that's Canaan. This is the place the people of Israel want to be. With this map you can point out Egypt, the Promised Land, and the desert.

where land was habitable, crops could be grown, and people could survive. That's why it's called the *Fertile* Crescent—because things could be grown. This part of the world is known as the cradle of civilization.

All of the powers of the ancient world lived in the Fertile Crescent. The problem is that they tended to live in the north and south, and the Promised Land was right in the middle. This middle part of the Fertile Crescent became a highway for armies and trade. It was virtually impossible to go down to Egypt or up to Assyria without going through Canaan.

> All I have seen teaches me to trust the Creator for all I have not seen.
>
> *Ralph Waldo Emerson*

As the various superpowers wrestled with each other for dominance of the world, the little strip of land called Canaan (later on it was called Palestine) became crucial for military superiority. If Assyria or Babylonia wanted to dominate the world, they had to go through the Promised Land to get to Egypt. And if Egypt wanted to be a superpower and dominate the world, they had to defeat the Hittites to the north. It is clear to see that their armies met right in the land God had given to the people of Israel.

Not only is the land of Canaan of military importance, but it was also a critical crossroads for trade and finances. During this era, trade began to become important in the ancient world. If caravans were going to move goods, they could not get across the Arabian Desert, for there was no water. They would never make it. They had to go right through Canaan.

It is important for us to see how strategic God was in placing his people right where he did. Financially and militarily, this little piece of land had become the center of the known world. Because this land was so strategic, whatever happened there, the stories of Israel and their God would be able to spread throughout the known world as they would from noplace else. It is no coincidence that God has his people positioned here to be a blessing to all the peoples on earth.

LIFE APPLICATION | *Depending on God*

Once Israel was back in the Promised Land, they would have many opportunities to grow in their trust of God. Because they were surrounded by all these superpowers fighting with each other, Israel would have to live in constant dependence on God because they were a small people with a modest army surrounded by massive nations with military might.

They knew every day they would have to depend on God, because Israel was never a superpower. God's mission for them did not involve that kind of power. They were never a player in the world game like Assyria, Babylonia, or Egypt. They are very rarely mentioned in ancient texts of the Egyptians and the Babylonians. Their very existence is a kind of early example of a basic principle of the kingdom of God: that often the least are the greatest of all, and those who appear to be last will be first.

Followers of Christ today live in a similar situation. In most parts of the world, Christians do not hold the seat of power or control the government. But, like Israel, we are invited to live with utter dependence on God. Our victories don't come by our might or power, but as Zechariah says, by the Spirit of the Lord. God longs to help us identify our life situations and circumstances where we do not feel powerful and in control and to look at these as opportunities to live in a day-by-day dependence on God.

PAUSE FOR PRAYER

Longing to Depend on God

Allow a short time of silence in your message. Invite people to reflect on their lives and identify where they feel powerless. Then encourage them to pray for a deep and profound sense of God's presence, protection, and power.

LIFE APPLICATION | *Facing Pharaoh*

This section of the Bible helps us gain a new perspective in our lives when our circumstances get desperate and we are facing a pharaoh. When we realize that God had the power to deliver his people from the hand of the pharaohs, we have hope that he can deliver us as well, and we know that we do not have to despair. We can stay faithful. We can hang on for God to deliver.

One of the great gifts God gives us in the Bible is reminders. As we look back on these real life stories of God's faithfulness, we can know that the same God is watching over us today. We need to take time to identify the pharaohs we are facing and acknowledge that God is sovereign over them. We don't have to live in fear. We don't have to run and hide. There is no oppression, no fear, no addiction, and no brokenness that is too much for God to conquer.

2. Strength in Weakness

SIGNIFICANT SCRIPTURE

Exodus 1:15 – 7:7

We live in a world where the powerful rule. Yet God has a different vision for how life should work. God turns everything on its head. God exalts humble midwives above the powerful pharaoh. God uses a stammering, runaway shepherd to lead his people to freedom. God blesses an obedient wife who stands in the gap for her husband, who refuses to hold to the covenant God established. In the days of the Old Testament, as in our day, God reveals his strength in our weakness. He still exalts the humble and humbles those who exalt themselves.

INTERPRETIVE INSIGHT | *The Upside-Down Kingdom*

In Exodus 1:15 – 17 we read, "The king of Egypt said to the Hebrew midwives, whose names were Shiphrah and Puah, 'When you help the Hebrew women in childbirth and observe them on the delivery stool, if it is a boy, kill him; but if it is a girl, let her live.' The midwives, however, feared God and did not do what the king of Egypt had told them to do; they let the boys live." These are remarkable women, and it is important that we remember their names. These two women defy a pharaoh and risk their lives in an act of heroism. They will not kill the Israelite boys. The pharaoh calls them in and asks them, "Why do you do this? Why do you let the boys live?" The women do not respond, "It's because we fear God." Rather, they say, "Well, these Hebrew women are vigorous, and their babies pop out before we can get there."

It might be helpful to pause here and address the issue of lying. This passage is not an affirmation of lying. If people ask, "Does this passage affirm lying?" you might want to say, as a short answer, "If you are ever coerced into committing mass murder by a genocidal maniac and the only way you can find to get out of this horrendous act is to deceive the genocidal maniac with a lie, I think God will understand. If, however, you try to use this passage to justify the kind of self-serving deceit that most of us engage in, which breaks community and destroys trust, that's a big mistake. This is not what God is trying to teach us in this passage."

It is interesting to note that the author of Exodus never mentions the pharaoh's name. The text never says which pharaoh Moses faces. In the hierarchy of Egypt, the pharaoh is at the top of the organizational chart and the midwives are at the very bottom. Midwives are the servants to the slaves. They don't count. But in God's organizational chart, the midwives are heroes. They risk their lives to accomplish God's purposes.

Even Abraham didn't do that. He was willing to sacrifice Sarah's well-being just to save his own scalp. Not these two brave women. It is as if God is saying, "These two women, who are nobodies in the eyes of the world, are the ones who go in my book." The first will be last. The humble will be exalted. This is the way God works.

HISTORICAL CONTEXT | *A New King in Town*

As we begin Exodus, things are looking pretty good for the Israelites. They are being very fruitful and they are multiplying. Then in Exodus 1:8, things take a turn for the worse. We read, "Then a new king, who did not know about Joseph, came to power in Egypt." There is going to be tension in Exodus from now on. This tension will become conflict and then grow to full-blown spiritual warfare. Through the first half of Exodus, things seem to get worse and worse. This new pharaoh does not care about history and what Joseph had done for Egypt four hundred years earlier. He sees all these Israelites as a threat and begins to treat them mercilessly.

On the one hand, God makes this promise, "I'm going to give you a land." On the other hand, their circumstances keep getting more and more desperate. The chances of the promise ever being fulfilled become more and more remote. The reason the writer lets us know about this tension is so that when the people of Israel are finally delivered, there will be no question that God gets the credit.

LIFE APPLICATION | *Who Is Great in God's Eyes?*

Sometimes we can feel unimportant, like Shiphrah and Puah. We feel as if we don't matter and nobody notices us. When this happens, God wants us to remember these two courageous women. Faithfulness really does matter! God does care about those whom the world looks right past. God is far more concerned about the condition of our hearts than the balance in our savings account or our appearance in the eyes of others. We need to live in the reality that greatness in the eyes of God is radically different from greatness in the eyes of the world.

Every time we read the names Shiphrah and Puah, we should come back to this basic truth. Over three millennia after they lived, the names of Shiphrah and Puah are still known and celebrated. Pharaoh's name didn't even make it in the book.

> Gratitude is born in hearts that take time to count up past mercies.
> *Charles E. Jefferson*

NEW TESTAMENT CONNECTION

The First and the Last

Jesus had a great deal to say about serving others. He was clear that there is a special place in the heart of God for those who walk humbly and who don't seek to exalt themselves. Jesus put it this way in Matthew 20:25–28:

> Jesus called them together and said, "You know that the rulers of the Gentiles lord it over them, and their high officials exercise authority over them. Not so with you. Instead, whoever wants to become great among you must be your servant, and whoever wants to be first must be your slave—just as the Son of Man did not come to be served, but to serve, and to give his life as a ransom for many."

NARRATIVE ON THE TEXT | *Meeting Moses*

Think about what a precious gift a baby is to a mother and father. Then try to picture the Egyptians throwing boy baby after boy baby into the Nile River. There were dozens, hundreds, perhaps thousands of Hebrew babies being thrown to their death just because Pharaoh spoke the word. You look at the Nile and see the bodies of countless dead babies floating away. The people of Israel would have seen this day after day. It was becoming normative in the land of Egypt.

Out of this unthinkable genocide one baby boy is saved. His mother places him in a little waterproof basket, a custom baby boat, and sets him floating in the reeds of the Nile River. His sister watches from a distance to see what will happen to her baby brother. Will an Egyptian find him and toss him into the river like the rest of the babies?

In an ironic twist, Pharaoh's daughter finds the baby and keeps him as her own. She needs someone to nurse him, and Moses' sister Miriam offers to get a Hebrew woman. Well, guess what? She gets her mother, and baby Moses is placed back into his own home and in the arms of his own mother. On top of that, Pharaoh picks up the bill for child care. Pharaoh's daughter actually pays Moses' mother to raise her own son and places a protective wall around Moses and his family. No one is going to mess with the adopted grandson of the pharaoh.

PAUSE FOR PRAYER

A Time for Thanksgiving

Just as pharaohs still live, so do Shiphras and Puahs. We have all met wonderful people who follow Christ with a deep humility, the heart of a servant, and a passion to faithfully follow the Savior. Take time to offer prayers of thanksgiving for the Shiphrahs and Puahs in the lives of those gathered. In your church it might be most appropriate to do this silently. If it is normative or appropriate to do this out loud, consider doing this as well.

As Moses grows, he finds himself living in two worlds. He's concerned for his people, the Hebrews, but he is educated and trained as an Egyptian. In Exodus 2:11 – 12 we read, "One day, after Moses had grown up, he went out to where his own people were and watched them at their hard labor. He saw an Egyptian beating a Hebrew, one of his own people. Glancing this way and that and seeing no one, he killed the Egyptian and hid him in the sand." Moses had the freedom of an Egyptian, but his heart was still with his own people.

LIFE APPLICATION | *Looking This Way and That*

We read that Moses looks "this way and that." He looks to the right and looks to the left. Which way does he not look? He does not look up. He does not think about God. Moses looks around him to be sure he will not be caught in his act of murdering an Egyptian. When he sees that the coast is clear, he acts on his human impulse to vindicate his people. But Moses does not stop to look up to his God and seek heavenly counsel or wisdom.

We can easily repeat Moses' error. We might not look "this way and that" and then kill someone, but we can be just as guilty of forgetting to look up to God in moments of need. It is the husband who is out of town on business and meets an attractive woman in his travels. He looks this way and that and is certain no one will ever know. He tells himself that what his wife does not know won't hurt her. The coast is clear, but he forgets to look up to God and realize that God sees and cares deeply about the decisions he is about to make. It is the college student who looks this way and that and then decides to cheat, just a little, on her exams, because no one will ever know. It is the businessman who knows the deal is shady, but he can cover his tracks and everyone else is doing it.

Just as Moses was tempted to look around and be sure no one was looking before he acted on his sinful impulses, so we can be tempted to do the same. We need to learn to look upward, into the eyes of the God who sees and cares.

NARRATIVE ON THE TEXT | *Moses in Midian*

Even though Moses looks "this way and that" before he strikes out against the Egyptian, he still gets caught. What a vivid reminder that no matter how hard we look before we sin or try to cover our tracks after we have acted on sinful impulses, it seems someone always finds out. This is true for Moses — and it is true in most of our lives as well. Word of what Moses did hits the street like front-page news, and Pharaoh gets word of it in no time at all. To make things worse, Pharaoh puts a price on his head. So Moses runs for his life and ends up in the land of the Midianites.

When Moses gets to Midian, he is sitting by a well and notices some young women with flocks who are being chased from a well by a group of surly shepherds. Apparently Moses has a passion for justice and cannot stand to see people oppressed, because here he single-handedly comes to the rescue of these women. He ends up marrying one of them, a woman named Zipporah. He has a son, and it looks as if he will spend the rest of his life as a shepherd far away from his own people in Egypt. But there is some backstage action going on in heaven. God is at work, and Moses is about to enter a whole new chapter of his life.

Exodus 2:23–25 says, "During that long period, the king of Egypt died. The Israelites groaned in their slavery and cried out, and their cry for help because of their slavery went up to God. God heard their groaning and he remembered his covenant with Abraham, with Isaac and with Jacob. So God looked on the Israelites and was concerned about them." Moses is busy tending sheep and raising a family, very ordinary things. God is busy preparing a leader to bring his people out of Egypt, something extraordinary. What Moses does not yet know is that he will be this leader.

INTERPRETIVE INSIGHT | *Turning Aside*

Moses was leading a fairly ordinary and uneventful life in Midian. Some might have called it boring. For about forty years he took care of sheep. But one day, everything changes. In Exodus 3:1–3 we read:

> Now Moses was tending the flock of Jethro his father-in-law, the priest of Midian, and he led the flock to the far side of the desert and came to Horeb, the mountain of God. There the angel of the LORD appeared to him in flames of fire from within a bush. Moses saw that though the bush was on fire it did not burn up. So Moses thought, "I will go over and see this strange sight—why the bush does not burn up."

Once again, God shows up in the most unexpected place. When this happens, Moses makes a decision that will change his life. The New Revised Standard Version translation of verse 3 is, "Moses says, 'I must *turn aside* and look at this great sight, and see why the bush does not burn up.'" There is a sense in which everything hinges on Moses' decision to turn aside. He doesn't have to do that. He could have said, "I'm a busy man with much to do. I don't have time to turn aside." He just would have missed his calling. He would have missed the exodus. He would have missed the reason for which he was born.

LIFE APPLICATION | *Being Willing to Stop and Listen*

Pause for a moment and invite your listeners to look at their lives and ask themselves how they are doing at *turning aside*. Remind them of the things you talked about last week at the end of the message about going on a God hunt. How are they doing? Are they slowing down

WORD STUDY

Remembered

In Exodus 2:24 we read, "God heard their groaning and he remembered his covenant with Abraham, with Isaac and with Jacob." When the Bible says "God remembered," it doesn't mean he had forgotten. Anytime you see the expression "God remembered" in the Old Testament, it means God is about to act. Watch out, God is going to do something. When you read about God's remembering something, don't get the idea that he has a short memory; rather, be encouraged that God takes action on behalf of his people.

and noticing God more? Are there burning bushes they need to turn aside and look at? Are there places where God was present, where they've stopped, and where they've met him? Did they hear promptings and follow them? Are there answered prayers they should celebrate?

INTERPRETIVE INSIGHT | *The Heart of God*

Moses did what many of us miss. He turned aside and met with God. In Exodus 3:5 God says to him, "Do not come any closer. Take off your sandals, for the place where you are standing is holy ground." That's the first occurrence of the word "holy" in Scripture.

Then we read in verses 7–8:

> The Lord said, "I have indeed seen the misery of my people. I have heard them crying out because of their slave drivers, and I am concerned about their suffering. So I have come down to rescue them from the hand of the Egyptians and to bring them up out of that land into a good and spacious land, a land flowing with milk and honey."

The heart of God cries out from the far reaches of history and the pages of Scripture. "I love my people! I long for their good. I want to deliver them." God says, "I have seen, I have noticed, I care, I've come down, I want to bring my salvation."

What a God we serve! He loves us as children and wants to lead and guide us. He hears our prayers when we cry to him. He loves to pour out his goodness on his people.

INTERPRETIVE INSIGHT | *Five Objections*

At this point, Moses launches into a series of five objections. He is much like the rest of us. He believes in God's power, but he is not so sure about himself. He does not feel up to the task and worthy of the calling.

ON THE LIGHTER SIDE | *I've Got a Job for You*

There's all this good news: "I've noticed, I've come down. So now, Moses, you go to Pharaoh, the tyrannical dictator of the most powerful nation on earth, who may still have a bounty on your head, and tell him to let his prime labor force go for no reason at all. Remember to check in with me when you're finished. Then I may have a difficult job for you this afternoon."

It is quite humorous when you read the passage. God tells Moses that he has been watching his chosen people and he is very aware of their plight. God has seen, he has heard, he is concerned, and he will rescue them. But then he adds, almost as an afterthought, "and by the way, Moses, you will be the one to accomplish my purposes and deliver the people." Can you imagine the look on Moses' face?

Moses' first objection is, "Who am I?" It is an argument from a feeling of inadequacy. God simply responds by saying, "I will be with you." God wants Moses to understand that his own pedigree or power is not the issue, only God's presence.

Next, Moses asks, "Who are you?" This is an argument of authority. Moses knows he will have to tell others about this God and he needs to know whom he is dealing with. God's response is short and to the point, "I AM WHO I AM." God reveals the great name Yahweh and tells Moses that he is the eternal God who always is.

Moses then presents his third objection: What will he do if the people will not listen to him? Moses is afraid the people will think he has made the whole thing up. His own authority and integrity may be questioned. Again, God is patient. He asks Moses a question, "What is that in your hand?" By now we know that when God starts asking questions, things get interesting. Moses says, "It's a staff." God says, "Throw it on the ground." Moses does so, and the text tells us that it becomes a snake and Moses runs away from it.

Notice a little detail that is often missed. In Exodus 4:4 we read: "Then the LORD said to him, 'Reach out your hand and take it by the tail.'" In the unlikely event that you were going to pick up a dangerous snake, where do you think you'd pick it up? Right behind the head. Definitely not the tail—that's the most vulnerable thing to do. But God is saying, "Moses, trust me. You're going to have to get used to dealing with snakes and other sorts of dangers, so you might as well start now. Go for the tail." God gives Moses a few other miracles, but Moses is still not ready to sign on.

In Exodus 4:10, Moses offers a fourth objection. In effect he says, "Speaking is not one of my core competencies." Moses tells God that he does not feel his public speaking skills are sharp enough for this particular task. But God counters by telling Moses, "Not a problem. I'm in charge of spiritual gifts. I can take care of that. I made your mouth and I can give you all you need to speak to Pharaoh."

Finally Moses is out of formal excuses, so he unloads his fifth and final effort to get out of this calling. He swallows hard and gives God a little advice: "God, please send someone else." God gets stern with Moses at this point and makes Moses an offer he cannot refuse. "You go, and I will send Aaron with you as a partner. He can be your spokesman." Grudgingly Moses says, "All right, I'll do it."

WORD STUDY

Yahweh

The name Yahweh is used almost seven thousand times in the Old Testament. It was so revered by the Jewish people that they wouldn't even pronounce it. We don't even know the exact, correct pronunciation because they wouldn't say it aloud out of reverence.

Its significance here means that God is saying, "I'll make myself known to you." That's what telling someone your name was all about in Bible times. It is as if God is saying, "I'll reveal my character, my identity. I am the God who knows and sees and cares and acts. I am with you."

NARRATIVE ON LIFE | *Heroes in the Pentateuch*

Here is a short note about heroes in the beginning of Exodus. Here is a list of the heroes:

- the two midwives, who save the Israelites
- Moses' mom, who risks her life to save her son

- Moses' sister, who stands guard over him
- Pharaoh's daughter, who defies her father to raise Moses
- Moses' wife, who corrects his disobedience

Notice the one trait these all have in common? They're all women! It is a striking reality that in a highly patriarchal world, God keeps using women to accomplish his purposes.

NARRATIVE ON THE TEXT | *Facing Pharaoh*

Moses goes to the people of Israel, tells them what God says, and shows them the signs God gave him, and they seem to be on board with the whole plan. They accept his words and bow down and worship God. Everything is working according to plan. The last detail is to get Pharaoh's signoff, and then Moses and the people of Israel are home

HISTORICAL CONTEXT | *Blood Kin*

Before Moses goes to Pharaoh, there is a unique episode recorded in Exodus 4:24 – 26. This account of Zipporah circumcising her son, touching Moses' feet with the foreskin, and then calling Moses a "bridegroom of blood" seems very odd. On top of that, we read that God was about to kill Moses and the actions of his quick-thinking wife saved his life. This also seems out of place.

There is a fair amount of consensus among Old Testament scholars that this is a story about the profound importance of circumcision in the covenant. Circumcision was a kind of signature on the part of a person, which meant they wanted to be in a covenant relationship with God. Apparently Moses had not circumcised his son, although he knew he should have. Most likely, he has not been circumcised himself, which means he is deliberately disobeying God. He is holding himself outside of a covenant relationship with the Lord. There is simply no way he can take on God's mission until this is remedied.

So Zipporah, his wife, recognizing what's happening, takes a flint knife – the appropriate instrument – and circumcises their son. Then she touches Moses' feet. The word for feet is often a euphemism in Semitic culture for genitals. She touches him as a kind of temporary, vicarious circumcision of Moses until the time comes when Moses can be properly circumcised.

When Zipporah makes that statement about "you're a bridegroom of blood to me," it might sound like a negative thing to say, like, "What a lot of bloodshed you and your God are causing me." But this is not what she is saying. It was actually a ritual marriage statement that a Hebrew bride would make when her groom had been circumcised before marriage. It's a positive statement: "You are blood kin to me. We're members of one family. We're a covenant people together." What's really happening here is that Moses has been disobedient to God's covenant calling. God is serious about it, and Zipporah's quick insight and actions save the day.

free. So Moses goes to Pharaoh and says, "This is what the LORD, the God of Israel, says: 'Let my people go, so that they may hold a festival to me in the desert'" (Exodus 5:1).

This is a bold way to approach the most powerful man in the world. There is no small talk or preparation. Moses stands and makes God's plan clear. The people of Israel want to pack up and head out into the desert to meet with their God.

But Pharaoh is not ready to see his slave labor take a vacation. So he responds, "Why are you taking these people away from their labor? Get back to work!" (Exodus 5:4). Pharaoh's take on this whole deal is clear: "They are lazy; that's why they are crying out, 'Let us go and sacrifice to our God.' So make them work harder. That way they will keep working and pay no attention to lies." From a human perspective, it seems as if the whole thing has backfired and exploded in Moses' face.

NARRATIVE ON THE TEXT | *A Word of Hope*

Pharaoh asks, "Who is this Yahweh? I am not impressed." Moses looks at how things are proceeding and struggles because this is not what he has signed up for. The Israelites think, "We might as well go to Pharaoh. We're already slaves. It can't get any worse." And then guess what happens? It gets worse. So they complain. "We don't want to make bricks without straw. What have you done to us?" they say to Moses. "You have made us stink to Pharaoh." The people of Israel are not happy with Moses at this point and blame him for how badly things are going.

Moses is left alone — just he and Aaron. But now he is not only pitted against Pharaoh in Egypt, but the people of Israel are angry with him as well. In the midst this turmoil and fear, God offers reassurance. He says in Exodus 6:6–7:

> "Therefore, say to the Israelites: 'I am the LORD, and I will bring you out from the under the yoke of the Egyptians. I will free you from being slaves to them, and I will redeem you with an outstretched arm and with mighty acts of judgment. I will take you as my own people, and I will be your God. Then you will know that I am the LORD your God.'"

Even in times of conflict, pain, and struggle, God speaks a word of hope.

ON THE LIGHTER SIDE | *Servant Leadership*

As we look at Pharaoh, we discover that he is not into servant leadership. He is not a team-empowering, people-building kind of guy. He is not into the inverted pyramids where the top guy is on the bottom and serves others. He is into the original pyramids, where the top guy is on the top. Because he built the original pyramids, he thinks that's a good way to structure things.

LIFE APPLICATION | *Facing Discouragement*

Exodus 6:9 reveals a deep heart problem in the people of Israel. It is a poignant verse, "Moses reported this to the Israelites, but they did not listen to him because of their discouragement and cruel bondage." Discouragement will crush a human spirit. The people of God are deaf to good news from God because they are discouraged. There are times when each one of us needs to be reminded that a discouraged spirit keeps us from hearing and following God's voice. God wants to say to us, "Don't let discouragement have the last word. I am still at work, and I who delivered my people a long time ago, I can deliver you. Keep looking for me. Keep trusting me. Keep waiting. Keep obeying."

Challenge your listeners to resist giving in to discouragement. Remind them that they will face many hard situations in life, but with God in the equation, there is always hope. Invite people to identify where they feel discouraged and to seek God to lift the dark cloud of discouragement and to pray for his light to shine through.

Also challenge those who are feeling strong and encouraged to be a blessing to others around them. If they know someone who is going through the valley of discouragement, challenge them to take a role as an encourager. Challenge them to pray, love, and bless those who are hurting. In this way, they can be used as a messenger of God's encouragement.

SIGNIFICANT SCRIPTURE

Exodus 7:8–12:42

3. The God Who Delivers

Little children love to say, "I can do it myself!" Often, this makes their parents proud. But when it comes to deliverance, God does not want to hear these words from the mouths of his children. We can't do it on our own. The Israelites couldn't, and neither can we. We need God's heavenly power and mighty help. Like the people of Israel, we need to come to a point where we cry out to the one who loves to bring deliverance to his children.

NARRATIVE ON THE TEXT | *The Plagues Begin*

Now the battle starts. God initiates a series of "plagues" or "mighty acts" on Pharaoh and Egypt. In the first one, the Nile River is turned to blood. This would have deep meaning for the Israelites. Remember, the Nile had been filled with the blood of their infants. It would be significant for them to see God bringing justice for the heartless brutality of the Egyptians.

The second plague has quite a different tone to it. God sends frogs, and the writer deliberately paints a picture to ridicule the pretensions of Pharaoh. Notice the detail he gives in Exodus 8:1–4:

> "This is what the LORD says: 'Let my people go so that they can worship me. If you refuse to let them go, I will plague your whole country with frogs. The Nile

> will teem with frogs. They will come up into your palace and your bedroom and onto your bed, into the houses of your officials and on your people, and into your ovens and kneading troughs. The frogs will go up on you and your people and all your officials.' "

The writer is specific about how bad this plague of frogs will be.

PAUSE FOR PRAYER

An Attitude Check

Some people see the cup half full; others see it half empty. There is yet another group of people who see the cup full and overflowing, even if it "looks" half full. Pause for a time of silent listening prayer. Call the people gathered to inspect their hearts. Does a spirit of discouragement rule them? Do they have a negative attitude that hangs over them like a dark cloud? Or do they have a healthy and godly optimism? Do they see the presence of God, even in hard times?

Pray for each person to come to a place of freedom from discouragement. Pray also that they will be released as bearers of God's encouragement and blessing in the lives of those they encounter each day.

INTERPRETIVE INSIGHT | *The Signs of a Hard Heart*

There's a pattern developing with Pharaoh. It starts with a hard-hitting plague, followed by what looks like repentance, then next comes the plea for deliverance, and finally Pharaoh's heart becomes hard again. Plague after plague continues: gnats, flies, dying livestock, boils, hail, locusts, and darkness all come to Egypt. Again and again Pharaoh seems to repent but later ends up with a hard heart.

In Exodus 9:27–28 we see an interesting dynamic of the way sin works. After the plague of the hail Pharaoh calls Moses and confesses. " 'This time I have sinned,' he said to them. 'The LORD is in the right, and I and my people are in the wrong. Pray to the LORD, for we have had enough thunder and hail. I will let you go; you don't have to stay any longer.' "

Every outward indication would give the impression that he is repenting. He even says, "I have sinned." In verse 34 Moses prays, and God stops the plague of hail. Then we read, "When Pharaoh saw that the rain and hail and thunder had stopped, he sinned again: He and his officials hardened their hearts."

When the pain is intense, Pharaoh says, "I have sinned. I will change." When the pain goes away, his repentance goes away too. He never really repents. He is just trying to avoid the pain he is feeling.

This can happen with people who seek to follow Christ. When they are in intense pain, their spiritual sensitivity seems to go up. But when the pain goes away, so does their openness to God. Their willingness to surrender is contingent on the presence of pain. Their willingness to submit and obey evaporates like the morning dew after the pain is over.

LIFE APPLICATION | *True Repentance or Pain Control?*

Pharaoh is never really repentant; he is just trying to do pain control. We can do the same thing. We must learn to ask ourselves a simple question: Am I really repenting right now or am I just trying to do pain control with God? If we see that our repentance is just a way to get quick relief but we have no intention of changing our behavior or attitudes, we are not truly repentant.

Take time for those gathered to reflect on their patterns of repentance. If they are responding only in an effort to avoid personal pain, invite them to look to the heart of God. Seeing God's pain over our sin leads to repentance.

NARRATIVE ON THE TEXT | *The Passover*

The tenth and final plague is the most devastating of all. God sends the angel of death and takes the firstborn in the Egyptian households. The people who committed genocide against the Israelites now lose their firstborn.

Imagine for a moment being in one of the Israelite homes on that night. God tells his people, "This is what the LORD says: 'About midnight I will go throughout Egypt. Every firstborn son in Egypt will die, from the firstborn son of Pharaoh, who sits on the throne, to the firstborn son of the slave girl, who is at her hand mill' " (Exodus 11:4–5). Imagine being in the home of one of the Israelites on that night. God has told you to get ready to leave. God has told you, "Sacrifice a lamb and put the blood of the lamb on the door frames around your home, and I will pass over your home. Death and judgment will pass over you and your family because you're covered by the blood of the lamb." So, in obedience, you slaughter a lamb, put the blood on your doorpost, and wait. It must have been the most awful night of darkness, death, and judgment in history.

You wonder if this is real. Will the angel of death come? Will your children be spared? Will judgment be poured out on the Egyptians? You are hardly able to breathe

ON THE LIGHTER SIDE | *Frogs and Pharaoh*

Do you get the picture? Frogs in your house, frogs in the bedroom, frogs in the bed, frogs everywhere. The frogs are getting real disruptive of daily life. It's hard to get a good night of sleep when the bed is full of frogs. On top of this, there are frogs in the kitchen. There are going to be frogs in the microwave, in the mixing bowls, frogs in the pizza, and frogs on the cereal. The people of Egypt had better get used to the taste of frogs! There will be frogs in the garage getting crunched under the wheels of the royal chariot.

Now, here is where things get humorous. Guess what Pharaoh's magicians do to show their great power? *They make more frogs.* By this time, Pharaoh must be getting a little tired of frogs. He actually says to Moses, "Pray to the LORD to take the frogs away from me and my people" (Exodus 8:8).

An author/comedian named Ken Davis sees great humor in Pharaoh's response. You see, Moses tells Pharaoh to name the time he is ready to be rid of the frogs. When Pharaoh gives a time, Moses will pray and the frogs will be done with. Now, guess what Pharaoh says? "How about tomorrow?" It is as if Pharaoh is saying, "Let me have one more night with the frogs in the bed, one more meal with frogs in my bowl, and one more drive with frogs all over the roads." How strange is that?

all night long. But God is true to his word. He passes over all the houses of Israel, which are covered by the blood of the lamb. This picture of the Passover, the deliverance from death, prefigures the salvation that will belong to all of God's people who are covered with the blood of Jesus Christ, the Lamb of God.

LIFE APPLICATION | *Lord, Deliver Me!*

As you close this message, you might want to ask a personal question of those gathered: *Is there anywhere in your life where you need God the deliverer?*

Invite the people to close their eyes for a moment and talk with God about this. *Is there any sin or temptation that feels like it has got a hold on you? Has hardness of heart taken hold of you as it took hold of Pharaoh? Maybe it is a pattern of sin. It might be a habit that has been there for a long time.*

Invite people to ask God for deliverance and then to do whatever God tells them to do to walk toward freedom.

You might want to give other simple promptings to help people reflect on areas in which they might need deliverance, such as:

Maybe you're in a real difficult situation or a troubling relationship.

Maybe you've made a commitment to God in some area of your life, and it's getting hard.

Maybe you feel trapped in a financial commitment and now things are difficult.

Maybe you made a commitment to read through the Old Testament, and it's just getting hard.

Maybe, like the Israelites, you're just beaten down and discouraged.

After a time of silent reflection, pray for each person to find the deliverance they need in the saving power of the God who set Israel free from Egypt.

Message 6

God the Lawgiver

Exodus 3:1–6; 19–20; Leviticus

THE HEART OF THE Message

God is perfectly holy. We are not. We are an unholy people desperately seeking a way to grow in holiness! How do impure people learn to walk in holiness?

The answer is: We walk with a God who is holy, and he transforms us. First, he makes us holy through his cleansing power and grace. Second, he teaches us to *grow in holiness* as we learn to walk in his ways. The people of Israel learned that growing in holiness is a process that takes a lifetime. As a nation, they learned that the journey toward holiness carries over many generations and centuries.

As we study the book of Leviticus (and other books of the Pentateuch), we discover that God makes us holy as we enter into a living relationship with him through Jesus Christ. Yet, holiness is also something that continues growing in us for a lifetime. In this message we will hear the invitation of God to grow in holiness. We will be called to transformed lives as we hear the living God say:

> "I am the Lord your God; consecrate yourselves and be holy, because I am holy. Do not make yourselves unclean by any creature that moves about on the ground. I am the Lord who brought you up out of Egypt to be your God; therefore be holy, because I am holy." (Leviticus 11:44–45)

BRIEF MESSAGE OUTLINE

1. Understanding the holiness of God
2. Are people saved by obeying laws we read in the Old Testament?
3. Why is there so much detail in these laws?
4. How do we know what laws we are to obey today?

THE HEART OF THE Messenger

The truth revealed in Leviticus peels back the facade of self-righteousness and reveals the true condition of our hearts and lives. We are impure and tainted by sin. The message of Leviticus is both painful and freeing. It is painful because it shows us the depth of our sin. It is freeing because it reveals a God of holiness who has the power to make us more like him than we ever dreamed.

Take time as you prepare to teach this message and meditate on the first half of Leviticus 11:44, "I am the Lord your God; consecrate yourselves and be holy, because I am holy." Ask the Holy Spirit to shine the light of holiness on your life and reveal any areas you need to consecrate to the Lord. Begin praying for holiness to grow in your life.

SIGNIFICANT SCRIPTURE

Exodus 19

1. Understanding the Holiness of God

All things being equal, we prefer purity. If we can have coffee made from beans that are only 9 percent infested with insects, or coffee that is 100 percent free of insects, we prefer the pure stuff. When it comes to our food and beverages, we are all in favor of purity.

But when it comes to our own lives, we give ourselves a fair amount of latitude. "After all, we're only human," we say as we justify our impurity. We're prepared to put up with a lower standard when it comes to us. The FDA tells us what is pure enough when it comes to our food. We try to do the same with our lives. The problem is that we work on a sliding scale. Our idea of purity is a far cry from God's definition. God is holy, and he is committed to seeing us grow in holiness.

ON THE LIGHTER SIDE *What Is Purity?*

Our society has certain standards and laws designed to guard purity. A whole department of our federal government, the Food and Drug Administration, functions as a watchdog for purity. However, their standards of what counts as pure are surprising.

The standards below come directly from the Food and Drug Administration:

Apple butter: If apple butter averages four or more rodent hairs per 100 grams, or if it averages five or more whole insects, not counting mites or aphids (which are OK with the U.S. government), the FDA will pull it from the shelves. Otherwise, it goes right on your bagel.

Mushrooms: When you get 15 grams of mushrooms, they're OK unless they contain an average of 20 or more maggots of any size.

Fig paste: If there are more than 13 insect heads per 100 grams, the FDA will toss it out. Apparently other insect body parts are OK, but we don't want to have to look at their little insect faces.

Coffee beans: All the caffeine addicts can get a little nervous now. Coffee beans are only withdrawn from the market if an average of 10 percent or more of them are insect infested.

Hot dogs: You don't even want to know. If they took all the impurities out of a hot dog, there would be nothing left.

NARRATIVE ON THE TEXT | *Impure People Called to Holiness*

In Exodus 19 we come to the foot of Mount Sinai. Here we see a ragtag group of frightened, grumbling, fugitive slaves. They have no real sense of identity yet, and no clear knowledge of God. They are thoroughly impure. They are ready to run back to Egypt at the first sign of difficulty.

What is amazing is that God is banking his whole hope to redeem the world on these people. How can God possibly get them to appreciate how high the stakes are? What must he do to help them see that their little lives matter so much? God longs to help these people understand that there is another way to live besides the kind of grasping, clutching, grubbing, and grabbing they have grown accustomed to.

In an effort to help the people see the magnitude of his plan, God speaks to Moses in Exodus 19:3–6:

> "This is what you are to say to the house of Jacob and what you are to tell the people of Israel: 'You yourselves have seen what I did to Egypt, and how I carried you on eagles' wings and brought you to myself. Now if you obey me fully and keep my covenant, then out of all nations you will be my treasured possession. Although the whole earth is mine, you will be for me a kingdom of priests and a holy nation.' These are the words you are to speak to the Israelites."

You can almost see this fearful group of wanderers standing in stunned amazement as they begin to realize that God is serious! His plan to impact and reach the whole world with his love will be built on this group of people. And to accomplish this great purpose, this people will need to grow in holiness.

A true and faithful Christian does not make holy living a mere incidental thing. It is his great concern. As the business of the soldier is to fight, so the business of the Christian is to be like Christ.

Jonathan Edwards

LIFE APPLICATION | *Purity of Heart*

The standard for hot dogs, fig paste, and even coffee is not nearly as pure as we think it should be. This is also true of our hearts. It's true of our words. It's true of our minds. It's true of our culture, media, and relationships. We live in an impure world.

Every human being alive convinces himself or herself that, "My little impurities don't really matter. They don't really amount to much. They're really quite tolerable." But add them all up, and you have the tragedy of the world in which we live, the downward spiral of human sin.

Every follower of Christ needs to do a regular heart inventory and see where impurity is creeping in. We need to ask the Holy Spirit to search our hearts and reveal where we need to grow in purity and be purged of impurity (see Psalm 139:23–24).

PAUSE FOR PRAYER

Search Me, O God!

Allow a time for silent prayer. Invite people to listen for the Holy Spirit to begin speaking to them about areas of impurity that need to be cleansed and areas they need to grow in purity. After a time of silent listening, lead in a prayer for each person to grow in purity.

INTERPRETIVE INSIGHT | *The Love of God*

Before God ever gives the Ten Commandments, he reminds Israel of his loving concern for them: "I carried you on eagles' wings" (Exodus 19:4). God describes his intention and vision for their future with three phrases that they will never forget (Exodus 19:5–6).

He says, "*You'll be a treasured possession.*" This little, insignificant, wanna-be nation really matters to God. He also declares, "*You'll be a kingdom of priests.*" Every person can relate directly to God. They will have access to God and be in a relationship with their Creator. Finally, he says, "*You'll be a holy nation.*" God lets them know that they will be a model community set apart to draw all the peoples of the earth to God.

WORD STUDY

Holiness

Originally, at its root, the word "holy" simply meant "set apart." This word pointed to things that were reserved for a special use and were not to be touched or used for anything else. Later the word "holy" began to point to moral purity, but at the root of the word is the idea of something (or someone) that is set apart.

In the Bible many objects are said to be holy. In Exodus 3, when Moses was on this same mountain, God said, "Take off your shoes, because this is holy ground." In this passage the mountain is said to be holy. Sometimes clothing or certain foods are declared holy in the Bible. These things are set apart.

INTERPRETIVE INSIGHT | *Preparing to Meet God*

The people go to great extents as they prepare to meet with God. In Exodus 19:10–11 we read, "And the Lord said to Moses, 'Go to the people and consecrate them today and tomorrow. Have them wash their clothes and be ready by the third day, because on that day the Lord will come down on Mount Sinai in the sight of all the people.'"

Certain limits are placed around the mountain. They are told not to touch the mountain. They are even told to abstain from sexual activity as they prepare their hearts, minds, and bodies to meet with God.

LIFE APPLICATION | *Being Prepared*

Too often we approach God with a casual attitude. There is a place for confidence when we draw near to God, and we know that his arms are wide open to his beloved children. But God is the mighty and holy Creator of heaven and earth. His power is beyond our wildest dreams. Like the people of Israel, we need to learn to prepare to meet with God. This is particularly true as we think about gathering together in corporate worship with the community of God's people.

There are many things we can do to prepare ourselves to gather with God's people and meet with our heavenly Father. Here are just a few ideas:

- Seek to go to worship feeling physically rested. If you go to morning services, be sure to get to bed at a reasonable time.
- If you drive to church services alone or with others, use the time to pray. Pray for the Spirit to move, pray for your heart to be soft, pray for those who will be leading worship, pray for visitors who might come, and pray for anything else that comes to your heart.
- Arrive early enough that you can park, get into the building, visit with those you meet, but still sit down five or ten minutes before the service begins. Use this time to quiet your heart, confess your sins, and tune in to God's still small voice.

ILLUSTRATION | *Holy Cake*

Here is a modern-day example, as told by John Ortberg, of something that was set apart (the meaning of "holy"). You can tell this story or one from your life that communicates a similar message.

> I got home from work on a Friday evening. My daughter had made chocolate cake with homemade frosting. Personally, I think chocolate cake is one of the greatest proofs for the existence of God in the world!
>
> Here was the dilemma: She had made this particular chocolate cake for another group of people. It was not for our family. It was not for me! So, right next to the cake there was a single piece of paper, and on that paper was one single word, "NO!" This word cried out from the paper because it was followed by several exclamation points. This note was intended for me, the father of the family. She knew it, I knew it, and everyone who read the note knew whom the cake-maker was thinking of when she wrote the note.
>
> The message was real clear and echoed with a message that went all the way back to the book of Genesis: "From every other cake in the house you may freely eat, but of this cake, the chocolate cake, you may not eat, for on the day you eat thereof, you shall surely die." This cake was set apart—holy.

INTERPRETIVE INSIGHT | *The Holiness of God*

The objects in the Bible that are declared holy are not holy in themselves. Only God is holy in himself, and only God can make something holy when he touches it. Objects become holy when they are set apart for God's use.

Something unique and important happened in Israel's understanding of holiness as time passed. The holiness that sets God apart came to be understood, above all else, as his moral excellence, his blinding purity, his perfect character. This God was set apart from sin.

Now, here is the problem: This holy God is in relationship with this group of people at the foot of the mountain, and they are steeped in sin. He is also in relationship with us, and we are no less tainted by sin than the people we read about in

Exodus. Since the Fall, every human being who has walked this earth (except Jesus) has been marked by sin, and this leads to a terrible ambivalence toward this holy God. We are drawn to holiness, we hunger for it, but we are afraid of it. We long for it, we know we need it, and yet we fear it will destroy us.

ILLUSTRATION | *Meeting Aslan*

In the first book of C. S. Lewis's Chronicles of Narnia, one of the characters (Lucy) hears a description of the Christ figure, Aslan. It occurs to her that she might be a little nervous if she were to come face-to-face with this magnificent being. Mrs. Beaver (one of the many talking animals in the land of Narnia) says to her, "That you will, dearie, and no mistake. If there's anyone who can appear before Aslan without their knees knocking, they're either braver than most or else just silly."

CREATIVE MESSAGE IDEA | *The Holiness of God*

As you are teaching about the holiness of God, read Exodus 19:16 and then invite people to imagine the power, majesty, and holiness of God while they listen and watch. If you have the technical ability to do this, have a brief light show with trumpet blasts and thunderous sounds! Invite the people to imagine what it might have felt like to have been there with the people of Israel as God descended on the mountain in this earth-shattering theophany.

Read:

> On the morning of the third day there was thunder and lightning, with a thick cloud over the mountain, and a very loud trumpet blast. Everyone in the camp trembled. Then Moses led the people out of the camp to meet with God, and they stood at the foot of the mountain. Mount Sinai was covered with smoke, because the LORD descended on it in fire. The smoke billowed up from it like smoke from a furnace, the whole mountain trembled violently, and the sound of the trumpet grew louder and louder. Then Moses spoke and the voice of God answered him. (Exodus 19:16–19)

After the lights stop and the room quiets, explain that the trumpet blast was associated in Israel with the sound of worship. It meant, "The Lord, Yahweh, is coming." In this passage we read of the trumpets blasting, but there's no human being blowing the trumpet. God is announcing his own arrival. Everyone trembles because they know that God is near.

You Will Need

- The ability to create the appearance of lightning with your lights
- Someone to run the lights and be ready to give the best light show they can
- The ability to make thunderous sounds and trumpet blasts. These can be live or pre-recorded. If you can create a low bass sound that will make the building shake, go for it!
- If you have the capability to safely have smoke billow from the stage down into the congregation, this would add to the effect

"Then he isn't safe?" asks Lucy.

Mr. Beaver answers, "Safe? Don't you hear what Mrs. Beaver tells you? Who said anything about safe? 'Course he isn't safe. But he's good. He's the king, I tell you."

INTERPRETIVE INSIGHT | *A Consuming Fire*

There are many statements in Scripture that teach of the reality of God's holiness. In Deuteronomy 4:24 Moses says, "For the LORD your God is a consuming fire." In Exodus 20:20 we read, "Moses said to the people, 'Do not be afraid. God has come to test you, so that the fear of God will be with you to keep you from sinning.'" Notice the paradox. The people say, "Keep him at a distance from us! He's not safe." Yet at the same time, they long to draw near to God.

> True faith can no more be without holiness than fire without heat.
>
> *John Owen*

It is as if Moses is saying, "Who said anything about safe? He is coming to put the fear of God in you so that you will be done with the folly and destructiveness of sin. Of course he's not safe. But he's good. Don't be afraid." On this mountain God speaks. He gives the Ten Commandments, the cornerstone of ethical guidelines for his people. These teachings have changed the world.

LIFE APPLICATION | *In the Light of His Holiness*

Imagine for a moment what it would be like for an unholy people to come into the presence of a holy God. If you want to know the people's response to this real-life experience, look at Exodus 20:18–19: "When the people saw the thunder and lightning and heard the trumpet and saw the mountain in smoke, they trembled with fear. They stayed at a distance and said to Moses, 'Speak to us yourself and we will listen. But do not have God speak to us or we will die.'"

This is a constant theme in Scripture. When people really encounter a holy God, the first thing that happens is they are overwhelmed and undone by their own sense of sinfulness. In Isaiah 6:5 we read a magnificent vision of God in the greatness of his holiness, and we see Isaiah's response: "Woe to me!... I am ruined! For I am a man of unclean lips, and I live among a people of unclean lips, and my eyes have seen the King, the LORD Almighty." In the New Testament, Peter sees the reality of Jesus' power and holiness, and his response is, "Go away from me, Lord! I am a sinful man" (Luke 5:8).

Each one of us needs to come to the mountain and see God, in all his power and glory. We need to fall on our faces in the radiating light of his holiness and be overwhelmed with the reality of our sin and his purity. We need an Isaiah moment, where we cry out, "Woe is me!" These are the moments that we stop making excuses, stop rationalizing, and stop defending the indefensible.

SIGNIFICANT SCRIPTURE

Exodus 20

2. Are People Saved by Obeying the Law?

Sometimes people read the Old Testament and they say something like this, "You know, I think the God of the Old Testament is all about the law. The old covenant means people got saved by keeping the law. Are you trying to tell me that the God of the Old Testament is a God of grace? No way! He is all about law."

These people, who are often well meaning, have this idea that some people attain salvation by following specific biblical rules and regulations. In this section of the message we must be very clear on this issue. The law, including the Ten Commandments, was never given to people so they could earn God's favor. That was never God's way of dealing with human problems. These laws were given to them after God had already been gracious to them and reached out to them with tender love.

INTERPRETIVE INSIGHT | *Breaking the Law*

When we see the Ten Commandments, they tend to be hung on a wall and they read like a list of do's and don'ts. They feel like a list of rules to be followed. The people of Israel would have looked at them differently. They saw a promise of the presence of

HISTORICAL CONTEXT | *Ancient Covenants*

One of the exciting archaeological discoveries of the last century has been the unearthing of many ancient treaties (covenants) from the Hittite people. These covenants had certain elements that were uniform and very important. They were featured in all covenants back in those days. These elements were:

- *The preamble*: This portion identified the powerful king initiating the covenant and the people who would become his subjects or vassals through the covenant.
- *The historical review*: In this portion the more powerful king listed the many things he had done for the people.
- *Stipulations of the covenant*: These were statements about specific behavior that was expected by each of the two parties in the covenant.
- *Provisions for storage*: In the covenant agreement there were a number of copies of the covenant. This was important so they could be kept and read publicly.
- *Blessings and curses*: Next, associated with the covenant was a list of blessings you could expect if you kept up the covenant and a list of curses for those who broke the covenant.
- *Vow of faithfulness*: This is where people said, "I will be a covenant keeper."

In Exodus, and scattered throughout the whole rest of the Pentateuch, we find every one of these features. God is all about covenant.

What we have to keep in the forefront of our minds is that the laws were never intended to be a list of rules that somebody had to keep to earn salvation. These laws were given after God had redeemed his people from Egypt and called them his beloved children. They were intended to describe *what a covenant relationship with God was supposed to look like*. What would it look like to be a kingdom of priests and a holy nation?

God. They saw God's copy of his covenant with them. The very first line reads, "I am the LORD *your* God." They carried both copies with them as a reminder of God's loving agreement to be in relationship with them. Were they expected to follow these commandments? Yes! But was God's love for them based on perfect obedience to these commands? No, for he had expressed and promised his love before these laws were given.

With all of this in mind, you can begin to get a picture of what it meant when Israel broke the commands of God. They were not just breeching some little agreement or bending some little rule. They were breaking their covenant with the God who loved them so passionately.

When Israel disobeyed God by making and worshiping the golden calf, do you remember how Moses responded? He smashed the tablets. He shattered them. This was not a thoughtless outburst of anger on his part. The tablets were the visible sign of the covenant. Moses was doing symbolically what the people were doing literally—*breaking the covenant.*

LIFE APPLICATION | *The Concern of God's Heart*

God loves us and is deeply concerned about the condition of our hearts and lives. He longs for us to understand that his love for us is not based on our daily performance in keeping every rule and regulation. He wants us to enter into a naturally loving relationship with him.

Sometimes people will think, "I may be living in direct, willful disobedience to God's command, but God owes me a heaven ticket because I walked down the aisle," or, "I prayed a prayer," or, "I signed the card," or "I can pinpoint a date." That's a dangerous road to walk. God is concerned about our heart.

ON THE LIGHTER SIDE | *Love and Marriage*

Think about a marriage covenant. It needs to begin with a loving and grace-filled commitment, and then actions flow naturally. Suppose a man is dating a woman and things are starting to get to that "serious point." What would happen if he looked deeply into her eyes and said, "OK, here's the program. I want you to wash my clothes, fix my meals, darn my socks, and clean my house. If you do these things well enough, and I am happy with your performance, then I'll marry you." How would most women respond to this offer?

But once we're married and there is grace-filled love and concern, do you think those actions would just flow naturally? OK, maybe that's not the perfect example, but here is the point. A healthy marriage begins with mutual love and care, and then the actions flow out of this love. God's covenant with us is like this. It begins with grace. This was as true in the Old Testament as it is in the New Testament. People have always been saved by grace through faith by trusting in a loving and forgiving God. Then, obedience to his law becomes a response of love to God's goodness. Salvation has never been earned by following certain laws; it has always been by grace.

SIGNIFICANT SCRIPTURE

Leviticus 11:29–30; 13:40–41; Deuteronomy 24:19–22

3. Why Is There So Much Detail in the Laws?

Some people read the laws in the Old Testament and wonder, "If God was so concerned about the heart, why did he give so many different laws and why are they so detailed?" The truth is that there are a lot of laws in the Old Testament that can seem very strange to the modern reader. At first glance, someone might think that Moses was an obsessive-compulsive with all these minute details.

But when we look closer, we begin to learn that God had a distinct purpose for every law he gave. Each law, in some way, was a manifestation of God's love and care for his people.

INTERPRETIVE INSIGHT | *Why All These Laws?*

The Old Testament has a number of broad laws that make sense to most people. God said things like, "Don't kill each other"; "Don't steal from one another"; "Don't tell lies." We read these, nod our heads, and say, "That makes sense." But, there are a lot of laws that were given for very specific situations. If you're in a certain life situation, you often need a great deal of detail.

Here are a few examples of different kinds of laws that had details that can be confusing:

A law about food: Leviticus 11:29–31 says, "Of the animals that move about on the ground, these are unclean for you: the weasel, the rat, any kind of great lizard, the gecko, the monitor lizard, the wall lizard, the skink and the chameleon. Of all those that move along the ground, these are unclean for you. Whoever touches them when they are dead will be unclean till evening."

A law about cleanness: Leviticus 13:40–41 says, "When a man has lost his hair and is bald, he is clean. If he has lost his hair from the front of his scalp and has a bald forehead, he is clean."

A law about farming: Deuteronomy 24:19–22 includes these words, "When you beat the olives from your trees, do not go over a second time."

People look through law after law after law and wonder, "Why are these laws so specific?" If you read through the Pentateuch, you find laws about what to do if someone gets gored by an ox, if a slave gets a tooth knocked out, and who to call if you find a spot of mold on the wall of your house. All these laws can start to feel a little overwhelming!

PAUSE FOR REFLECTION

How God Sees My Heart

Take a moment of silence for a heart check. You might want to prompt reflection by asking a few leading questions, such as:

- Are you driven to follow God's commands out of fear and guilt, or out of a deep awareness of his love?
- Are you learning to find joy in following God's commands, or is it always a chore?
- As God looks into your heart today, does he see it full of love for him, partially full, or running dry?

LIFE APPLICATION | *Applying God's Laws*

We need to learn how to read the laws in the Bible and discover which ones are meant to be a general rule of life that can be applied in many contexts. Here are some examples that will help us know how to apply the truth of God's laws in daily situations.

HISTORICAL CONTEXT | *Two Tablets*

Another indicator that the Ten Commandments were given in the context of God's covenantal grace is seen when we understand the way ancient covenants were preserved. There was always a provision for preserving a copy of a covenant. This was done by making two copies of every covenant – one copy to be kept by each party in the covenant. The king would keep one copy in his "files," and the "vassal nation" kept the other one. Without copy machines, it was certainly expensive for two copies to be chiseled onto stone, but that way each party could continually review the covenant they had agreed to, along with its expectations.

When Moses came down from the mountain with the Ten Commandments, how many tablets was he carrying? The answer is, two (Exodus 32:15). Some people think that God ran out of space on the first tablet, so he kept writing on a second one. Others have a picture in their mind of two tablets with five commandments on each of them. But the most likely reason there were two tablets is that God provided a copy for each party, in accordance to the custom of the day. This way, the people of Israel could keep a copy and it could be read and reread publicly. One of the copies belonged to Israel and the other copy belonged to God. But since God lived in the tabernacle in Israel, both copies were kept together.

HISTORICAL CONTEXT | *A Barbaric Age*

When we look at the detail in the Old Testament laws and the specific nature of so many of them, we need to keep in mind what might be called "*the moral baseline of the human race*." At this time in history, there was no moral or social code to lead human beings. The world we live in today can be very dark and sin-filled, but try to imagine turning the clock back over three thousand years, before there was any influence of the Judeo-Christian ethic. We live with the advantage of over three millennia of the civilizing, restraining, and heart-changing influence of the power of the Ten Commandments.

In the time before God began to give his law, the world was barbaric. Although history teaches us that there were some written moral codes in existence by this time (such as the Code of Hammurabi), it is clear that the world was still in a moral dark age. For instance, infanticide was common. Israel lived in a world where people routinely sacrificed newborn children to an idol named Molech.

The Old Testament speaks out against sacrifice to Molech. It was a large, hollow, metal statue. When people wanted something from Molech, they would build a fire inside of it and wait until the statue was glowing with heat. Then they would place their child on the arms of the statue. The baby would be seared and burned to death. This religious practice was actually common when God began to give his law.

Slaves were routinely killed with no accountability. Women were largely treated as slaves and possessions. Pagan religions regularly encouraged temple prostitution. When you understand the historical context, you begin to realize that God had to start where the people were, and they were living in a barbaric time.

WORD STUDY

Paradigmatic Laws

Many of the laws God gave were paradigmatic. This means specific laws gave an example about how to apply a basic life principle. The law may have had a specific application, but a deeper life lesson could touch many more situations than those mentioned in the Bible. In other words, the law was an example, but it was not exhaustive. In our day we try to make laws that will cover virtually every single possible situation. Paradigmatic laws give a general rule that can be applied to countless situations.

Deuteronomy 24:20 speaks of how farmers should deal with their olive harvest. They are told to beat the branches so that olives come down and can be gathered. But they are told not to go back and beat those branches a second time. If there are olives that stay on the tree, just leave them there. Then the text opens our eyes, and hearts, to what God is teaching: "Leave them for the poor so the poor can come through and find something." The principle behind this strange command makes sense to every follower of Christ: Be concerned for the poor; help those in need.

This is the application of a paradigmatic law: "If you're a farmer, be a little sloppy so that the poor can have food." Now, the passage only mentions olive trees. If you had fig trees, you could not say, "Well, the Bible just says olives. It doesn't apply to me because I have fig trees, so I can take down every fig." The judges in Israel would look at the principle involved: "Leave some for the poor." It was a paradigm. It was an example.

The point here is that the law given to Moses by God was never about a narrow, legalistic, nitpicking, rule-keeping mentality. There would be a lot of specific examples so that people would get specific and actually obey God's laws. The laws were meant to transform the hearts of God's people. We need to ask ourselves, "Am I seeking to help those who are poor and outcast?" Or, "Am I living selfishly and providing only for myself? Am I beating the branch twice and leaving nothing for the poor?"

SIGNIFICANT SCRIPTURE

Leviticus 19:18;
Deuteronomy 5:17; 6:5; 14:10;
Mark 7;
Romans 13:1 – 7

4. How Do We Know Which Laws We Are to Obey?

Some people can look at Christians today and wonder if we simply pick and choose which laws we will follow. Are we arbitrary and self-serving as we choose which laws to follow and which ones no longer apply to us? For instance, most followers of Christ break Old Testament dietary laws every day. We eat things that are forbidden. Also, we fail to follow all the laws for ritual cleansing. Are we being disobedient to God? We need to clarify how we can know which laws in the Old Testament still apply to us today.

INTERPRETIVE INSIGHT | *Kinds of Laws: Civil and Ceremonial*

Since Christ, our relationship to the law has fundamentally changed. The Old Testament law can be put into three general categories. These are not always clear-cut, but the formal distinctions go back to the days of John Calvin.

First of all, some of the Old Testament laws can be called *civil law*. Because Israel was a nation, there were certain laws that had to do with the governance of a people. Things like property rights and sentencing guidelines for the courts (eye for an eye, tooth for a tooth) fall into this category. Now, however, God's people are no longer restricted to one nation. We are scattered throughout all the nations. This means the civil laws about the governance of one particular nation no longer apply to us in the same way. As a matter of fact, the New Testament is clear that followers of Christ ought to follow the laws of the country in which they live and to see those in positions of authority as placed there by God (Romans 13:1–7).

Another kind of law can be called "*ritual law*" or "*ceremonial law*." These are mostly laws about worship, the sacrificial system, or cleanness versus uncleanness. The law of circumcision is an example of ritual law.

In the New Testament the whole sacrificial and ritual system was fulfilled in Christ. He was the ultimate sacrifice and made any continued sacrifices meaningless. All the sacrificial laws came to an end when Jesus died on the cross and rose again. In the same way, all of the laws about ritual cleansing became null and void when Jesus paid the price for our sins and offered cleansing through his shed blood. Ritual cleansing only pointed to Christ. The sacrificial system pointed to Christ. Since he has come, the ceremonial laws are now meaningless and do not need to be followed.

PAUSE FOR REFLECTION

How Can This Be?

The topic we are addressing is no small issue. How can we know which laws to follow? Just think about it. Deuteronomy 14:10 teaches us that any creature in the water that doesn't have fins or scales, "you may not eat." Yet, many Christians ignore this and sink their teeth into butter-covered lobster and think nothing of it. At the same time, Deuteronomy 5:17 says, "You shall not murder." We seek to uphold this law tenaciously. Both of these commands come from the same book of the Bible. One is widely ignored and the other is upheld in our lives, the church, and society. How can this be?

LIFE APPLICATION | *Life Lessons for Past Laws*

Often there are important principles that can be learned from some of the laws that we no longer need to follow to the letter. Jesus himself spoke directly about this. In Mark 7, for example, he says, "It's not the food that goes into a man that makes him clean or unclean, it's what comes out of his heart." Mark makes a parenthetical comment in Mark 7:19, "In saying this, Jesus declared all foods clean." In other words, Jesus was saying, and Mark makes it explicit, that these old ritual laws about cleanness and uncleanness no longer apply to us.

More than that, Jesus (and Mark) is showing that the categories of clean and unclean things existed to help people develop clean hearts. That's the point, to establish the category of cleanness and rightness, which ultimately impact our hearts. God is still concerned about our hearts, and we should be as well. We may not have to worry about eating something that is categorized as an "unclean" food. But we should always be concerned about what comes out of us. This includes our words and what they communicate to others. It also includes the attitudes and intentions of our hearts. These things matter a great deal to God, and they should matter to us as well.

CREATIVE MESSAGE IDEA | *Reading of the Ten Commandments*

As a way of honoring God's Word, invite people to stand together and read through the Ten Commandments together. You can make a brief comment after each one or simply have people read them. You can project what they will read onto a screen or have them read out of the Bible, if you provide Bibles that are all the same translation.

Commandment 1: "You shall have no other gods before me."
Comment: God says, "Make following me your top priority above all else."

Commandment 2: "You shall not make for yourself an idol."
Comment: Serve God alone, only God. Don't fixate your eyes or heart on anyone or anything else.

Commandment 3: "You shall not take the name of the LORD your God in vain."
Comment: This commandment applies to profanity, but it is addressing more. It means don't misuse God's name in an oath if you are lying. Don't use spiritual language to cover up a dark heart.

Commandment 4: "Remember the Sabbath day by keeping it holy."
Comment: Honor God by ceasing your constant work and taking time for worship and rest. If God rested on the seventh day, how can we ever hope to press on and never experience Sabbath rest?

Commandment 5: "Honor your father and your mother."
Comment: Even when it's difficult, give them respect, listen to their wisdom, and thank them for all they have done for you.

Commandment 6: "You shall not murder."
Comment: This goes well beyond the prohibition against murdering someone. It means we need to identify and avoid things like tearing people down with our words, hating people in our hearts, and holding grudges. It means we need to learn how to forgive.

Commandment 7: "You shall not commit adultery."
Comment: This includes resisting the temptation to lust and growing in sexual purity.

Commandment 8: "You shall not steal."
Comment: We need to learn to be generous givers and receivers.

Commandment 9: "You shall not bear false witness."
Comment: Be a person of integrity. Let truth flow in every area of your life.

Commandment 10: "You shall not covet."
Comment: Refuse to give in to envy or jealousy. Love people more than their things.

You Will Need
- Someone to lead the congregation in reading the Ten Commandments
- Someone to give a brief word about what these commandments mean to us today after each is read

INTERPRETIVE INSIGHT | *Kinds of Laws: Moral*

God's concern for the heart can be seen most clearly in the third category of Old Testament law, which is called "*moral law*." The Ten Commandments are a great example of moral laws. Deuteronomy 6:5 ("Love the LORD your God with all your heart and with all your soul and with all your strength") and Leviticus 19:18 ("Love your neighbor as yourself") are also moral laws. These laws apply at all times. They are not ritual laws that have become void through Christ. They are not civil laws that are now replaced by our national civil laws. These are God's moral laws, which will always remain.

We obey these, not as a way to earn God's love, but as a sign of a life built on a covenant relationship with our Creator. The great promise of the Old Testament is that one day these laws will be written on our hearts. God says, through the prophet Jeremiah, "I will put my law in their minds and write it on their hearts" (Jeremiah 31:33). The moral laws apply to all of us, in all situations, at all times!

LIFE APPLICATION | *God's Law on Our Hearts*

In Exodus 24, after Moses reads "the Book of the Covenant," the people make a vow of faithfulness. In verse 7 the people say, "We will do everything the LORD has said; we will obey." This was a sign of the great hope that one day God's people would obey his commandments in the same way that they obey the law of gravity. It would be natural and normal. At this time, they would follow his commands out of hearts overflowing with love.

God's vision for hearts fully devoted to him continues today. He longs for us to learn his moral law and joyfully and willingly to obey it. We need to look at our hearts and make sure that God's law is deep inside of us. Where we are living in disobedience to God's law, we must seek to adjust our lives and attitudes to come in line with God's plan for us.

NEW TESTAMENT CONNECTION

Jesus and the Law

Jesus had a lot to say about the law. He set the whole context for his understanding of the law with these words in Matthew 5:17–18:

> "Do not think that I have come to abolish the Law or the Prophets; I have not come to abolish them but to fulfill them. I tell you the truth, until heaven and earth disappear, not the smallest letter, not the least stroke of a pen, will by any means disappear from the Law until everything is accomplished."

Jesus was clear that he was going to uphold the law of God, not break it. At the same time, he gave new definition and tone to how we are to understand the law. The people had become legalistic and narrow in their understanding; Jesus brought them back to the heart of what the law was about. In Matthew 5 Jesus gives extended commentary and rabbinic teaching on the Ten Commandments and other laws.

INTERPRETIVE INSIGHT | *A Developmental Process*

God takes us through this whole developmental process as he seeks to transform our hearts. All the way back in the garden of Eden, God gave his commands orally to Adam and Eve. After the Fall took place, God's commands were written down, chiseled in stone and parchment, for his people.

Later in the history of Israel, God sent the prophets to help clarify his teachings and laws. Even later, God sent Jesus so that we could finally see what a life looks like when somebody follows the law of God out of a true response of love. It was Jesus who spoke the words of Matthew 5:17–18 (see page 109). God was developing his people's understanding of that law and how to follow it. At Pentecost, God sent his Holy Spirit to continue speaking the truth of God's law into our hearts. The Spirit still does this today.

All of this developmental process is for us, so that we can have God's magnificent and beautiful law, the intent of God for human life, written in our hearts. It is not given so that we can walk around trying to keep a bunch of mechanical rules to prove how righteous we are. Instead, it is given as a precious gift that will help us grow in a living and loving relationship with our Creator and with each other.

PAUSE FOR REFLECTION | *What If?*

As you close this message, consider inviting people to imagine what life would be like with the full blessing of God's law. Ask people to close their eyes and imagine what our world would be like if, even for one day, everyone on the earth had the law of God written on their hearts and followed it with joy. What if, for one day:

- No life was ended through random violence.
- There were no acts of terrorism.
- Nobody was killed, struck, or even cursed at in anger.
- Not a single lie was told.
- Everyone spoke the truth to one another.
- Every father and every mother was honored all day long, and the hearts of the parents were turned toward their children, and the hearts of the children were turned toward their parents.
- Nothing was stolen.
- Not one greedy thought or action took place in all the earth.

What would the world be like if God's magnificent law were written on our hearts and we lived them out in our lives? What if we lived the kind of life Jesus did right in our home, our workplace, our school, and our church?

As you close the message, invite people to consider living out that dream in their lives. Pray for each person gathered to begin walking in the dream, because God wants to make it a reality.

Message 7

Lessons from the Wilderness

Exodus 3; 13–16; 32–33;
Numbers 11–13; Deuteronomy 8

THE HEART OF THE Message

The wisest people learn from the example of others. Sometimes the lessons learned show the path to life. At other times, these lessons show us which paths to avoid. As we look at the people of Israel in their wilderness wanderings, we learn from their victories and their failures. In this message, God will invite us to grow in wisdom as we learn from those who have gone before us. Their pitfalls can be avoided. Their victories can be repeated. We can grow as we walk through the wilderness experiences of our lives.

God kept his people in the wilderness because there were certain lessons they needed to learn. The wilderness doesn't provide a lot of distractions. In the wilderness, people are a lot more likely to pay attention to God. It is a furnace where God can refine, melt, purify, and shape his people into who he wants them to be. Throughout the history of the Old Testament many of God's most important people spent time in the wilderness furnace: Moses, David, Elijah, and the entire nation of Israel. God still invites those he loves to his wilderness school.

BRIEF MESSAGE OUTLINE

1. A lesson about God
2. A lesson about remembering
3. A lesson about attitude
4. A lesson about perspective
5. A lesson about manna (provision)
6. A lesson about presence
7. A lesson about humility
8. A lesson about fear and faith

THE HEART OF THE Messenger

In this message you will study eight different life lessons drawn from the wilderness time in the history of Israel. As you prepare to communicate these lessons to God's people, ask the Holy Spirit to speak to your heart about which lessons you need to learn today. Seek to identify one key lesson that really hits home for you. How does this lesson affirm a positive direction you are taking in your journey toward

God? How does it uncover ways you are wandering away from God's plan for your life? What adjustments do you need to make in order to align your life and attitudes with God's plan for you according to what you learn through this wilderness lesson?

Introduction

SIGNIFICANT SCRIPTURE

Exodus 3:7–10; 13:17–18; Deuteronomy 1:2

In the introduction, you can use one or more of several video clips, contained on the DVD-ROM, as creative message ideas.

Wilderness Lesson 1: A Lesson about God

NARRATIVE ON THE TEXT | *Map Time*

(For this section you will need the PowerPoint slides provided on the DVD-ROM.)

To help people get a sense of the travel route the people of Israel took to get from Egypt to the Promised Land, consider using the maps provided in the PowerPoint presentation. You can put the trip in your own words or use the narrative provided below.

The trip the people of Israel were to take was quite a simple one. They were in Egypt and were going to go to Canaan. If you take a look on the screen, you will see the simplest route, called the Way of the Sea. God says, "I've come to bring them out of Egypt into a good and spacious land flowing with milk and honey."

As you look at the map, it looks like a really simple trip from Egypt to the Promised Land. The only bad thing is they have to go through the Sinai Peninsula, which was not pleasant. But it is not a long trip, only about two hundred miles from Goshen in the land of Egypt to where the Israelites are heading in Canaan, and they all know the best route to get there.

Everybody knows the shortest distance between two points is a straight line. There was pretty much a straight road between these two locations in those days. It was an international trade route called the Way of the Philistines. It was a real road. In Isaiah 9:1 it's called the Way of the Sea. It was kind of the scenic route, because it went right

CREATIVE MESSAGE IDEA | *"What's Up" Video Clip*

The video materials on the DVD-ROM include several "What's Up" video pieces. These are a light and often humorous way to help people learn that asking questions is good. You can use one of these video pieces here (or any other week you feel it fits). We have placed it here so that you have a video every other week, but this piece is not bound thematically to any particular week of the study.

You Will Need

- Video projection capability in your worship center
- Someone to run the video during the service

along the Mediterranean Sea. You can see it on the map. The people of Israel knew that this would be the natural and quickest way to go. It would be a short trip—a matter of weeks—not months, but weeks.

But, surprisingly, in Exodus 13:17–18 we are told that God has decided on a different route:

> When Pharaoh let the people go, God did not lead them on the road through the Philistine country, though that was shorter. For God said, "If they face war, they might change their minds and return to Egypt." So God led the people around by the desert road toward the Red Sea. The Israelites went up out of Egypt armed for battle.

The desert road was heavily strategic and heavily fortified. The Egyptians had a large military presence there. God knew the hearts of his people. He knew they were timid and easily frightened. He knew that they did not have much faith. He knew that if they ran into much opposition, they would turn around and go back to Egypt and be slaves again. So he did not send them along the Way of the Sea, even though it was the fastest and most direct route.

There was another road that cut pretty much through the center of the Sinai Peninsula. It ran east and west. It would have been a little more out of the way, but much safer. However, God did not send them on that road either.

There was a third road that went almost directly south, called the Way of the Wilderness. This was the road that God led them down after they crossed the Red Sea. If you look on the map, you will see that this road went all the way down to Mount Sinai.

Nobody knows exactly where Mount Sinai was located, but the general consensus among scholars is that it was located down somewhere in the southern tip of the Sinai Peninsula as pictured on the map. Once they traveled to Mount Sinai, the Israelites were there for about a year. Look at it this way: The first leg of the Israelites' journey was a two-week trip that took them one year.

CREATIVE MESSAGE IDEA | *Drama on Video: "Mysterious Ways"*

This video drama is included with the DVD-ROM materials. It is six minutes and forty-five seconds long and can be used at whatever point in the worship service it fits best. You will want to review it in advance to find the best place it fits, perhaps even in the midst of the message.

You Will Need

- The ability to show a video tape during your service
- Someone to run the video for you

Finally it was time to break camp, and the pillar of cloud and fire was going to lead them onward to the Promised Land. They took a road called the Mount Seir Road, or the Road to Kadesh Barnea. It went from the tip of the Sinai Peninsula to Canaan. We know how long this journey took because Deuteronomy 1:2 says: "It takes eleven days to go from Horeb [Horeb is another name for Mount Sinai] to Kadesh Barnea by the Mount Seir road." This time an eleven-day trip took thirty-nine years!

ON THE LIGHTER SIDE

When Will the Hurrying End?

From our youngest days we begin the frenzied and hurried pace. We push forward and keep crying out, "Are we there yet?" Parents are in a hurry for their little one to take their first step, speak their first word, and catch their first ball. Soon the child learns the hurry game.

"When do I start school? Am I there yet?"
"When will I be grown up? Am I there yet?"
"When will I fall in love? Am I there yet?"
"When will I get out of school? Am I there yet?"
"When can I move out? Am I there yet?"
"When will I get married? Am I there yet?"
"When will I get the perfect job? Am I there yet?"
"When can I retire? Am I there yet?"
"When will I die? Am I there yet?"

If we are not careful, we can rush from the cradle to the grave and forget that God has plans for us today!

ON THE LIGHTER SIDE

A Day and a Thousand Years

We get very anxious about time. God has a different perspective. This humorous story makes the point and gives a lighter look at God and time.

A little boy (or girl) was praying after his Sunday school lesson. He said, "Dear God, I hear that time is very different for you than it is for us. Is that true?"

God said, "Yes, my child, that is very true."

The boy continued, "What is a thousand years like to you?"

"It is like a second," God replied.

"Then what is a second like?" the boy asked.

"It is like a thousand years."

This got the boy thinking. The little wheels in his head really got spinning. "God, what is a million dollars like to you?"

God answered, "It is like a penny."

The boy asked, "Then what is a penny like to you?"

"It is like a million dollars."

The boy paused and then asked his final question, "Dear God, can I please have a penny?"

God answered, "Yes! I'll give you a penny, but you'll have to wait for a second!"

INTERPRETIVE INSIGHT | *God Is Not in a Hurry*

There is a huge spiritual lesson in the travel plans God had for Israel: God is not in a hurry! God's primary concern is not speed. Ours usually is. God knew that *where* the people of Israel were going was not nearly as important as *who* they were becoming. God knew that possessing a land flowing with milk and honey was not nearly as important as having a heart flowing with love, justice, courage, and faith. God's first concern was not how fast his people would be going to the Promised Land. His deepest concern was that they would be the right kind of people once they arrived. If it took forty years to prepare their hearts, then so be it!

ILLUSTRATION | *Are We There Yet?*

Anytime a family goes on vacation and they have little kids in the backseat, the little kids will ask a question. They ask it often. They ask it irritatingly. They sometimes turn it into a chant or a song. The longer the trip is, the sooner they start with the question. And the question, of course, is: "Are we there yet?"

Parents look forward to the day when kids mature and become patient and there's no more silly fighting over space violations, no more arguing over what radio station should get played, no more whining about where or when they're going to stop for lunch. They wait a long time for that day to come because, although most of us grow up, we never get much different.

LIFE APPLICATION | *Still in a Hurry*

As we grow older, we discover that our childlike chant "Are we there yet?" continues with some subtle adjustments. Now it sounds like this:

"God, get me into this job and do it now."

"Get me into this house, I need it soon."

"Get me into this relationship, I can't wait."

"Get me into this financial condition, I can't hold on any longer."

"Are we there yet? Are we there yet? Are we there yet?"

What God knew for the people of Israel, he still knows for us today. Having a portfolio flowing with dollars or a job flowing with power doesn't matter nearly as much as having a character that flows with the fruit of the Spirit. God is still more concerned with who we are becoming than how quickly we get to our desired location.

PAUSE FOR REFLECTION

Time to Slow Down

Allow a time for silence and encourage people to take an honest inventory of their lives. Where are we rushing? What is our destination? Are we rushing to arrive but forgetting to walk with God along the way? How can we slow down to notice God, hear his voice, and respond to his leading in our lives?

Here is a thought for reflection for you as a teacher. As you prepare this message and bring it to God's people, be sure you take time to slow down and meet with God. You might even want to consider prayerfully choosing only selected lessons from this message as you teach. If your time constraints will not allow you to address all eight lessons effectively, teach only those that will connect most closely with the needs of your congregation – and do so slowly.

New Testament Connection – God and Time

We have a certain way of looking at time. Our perspective is limited because we live within the confines of space and time. God has a radically different vantage point. He created time and space, and he is not subject to their limitations. This is why the apostle Peter writes, "But do not forget this one thing, dear friends: With the Lord a day is like a thousand years, and a thousand years are like a day" (2 Peter 3:8). We might be in a hurry, but God has a better view than we do: He created time, so we can trust him to lead us in his timing.

SIGNIFICANT SCRIPTURE

Exodus 15:22–24; Psalm 136

Wilderness Lesson 2: A Lesson about Remembering

INTERPRETIVE INSIGHT | *Being Intentional about Remembering*

We need to be intentional about remembering what God has done and who he is. The Israelites have just been delivered from Pharaoh and his army. They have crossed the Red Sea, and God has given them miraculous redemption. The mighty hand of God has been revealed in power through plagues, a pillar of fire, and deliverance from the hand of the most powerful ruler on the face of the earth! It would seem that this manifestation of God's presence and power would leave a lasting and indelible impression on the people of Israel. It would be natural to think that the impact of these events would stay with them forever. But notice how quickly they forget. In just three days they are discouraged, grumbling, and angry.

It took only three days for the people to forget all that God had done for them. You might think that since God has just delivered them from Egypt, performed the ten plagues, and drowned Pharaoh and his army in the Red Sea that their faith might be unshakable. But just three days later God is at the wheel driving and the kids are in the backseat whining and complaining. They have forgotten. Their short memory is evidence of the fact that they have missed the profound spiritual reality that *God is with them.*

LIFE APPLICATION | *Setting Up Memorials*

All through the Old Testament, God called the people of Israel to remember what he had done for them. One of the practical reminders was setting up a pile of stones as a memorial so that they would see this visible sign and remember what God had done for them (Joshua 4:4–7). We, like the people of Israel, are prone to forget. We need to learn how to set up piles of stones that will remind us of the great things God has done for us.

Maybe we don't actually pile up rocks, but there are ways we can remember God's goodness in our past. Some people keep a list of answered prayers to remind them of God's power and faithfulness. Others make a point of retelling stories of what God has done in their past (Psalm 136). There are people who will capture a great moment of spiritual growth or learning with a photograph they display or in a poem or picture they have drawn. The key concern is not *what* we use as a reminder as much as *that* we remember God's goodness in our lives.

Wilderness Lesson 3: A Lesson about Attitude

SIGNIFICANT SCRIPTURE

Exodus 15:22–24; 16:6–12

INTERPRETIVE INSIGHT | *Prone to Grumble*

We are all prone to grumble, but we must fight against this temptation. When the people of Israel come to Marah and find that the water is bitter, they begin to grumble and complain. They forget God's mighty acts and focus only on their thirst. Even though their attitudes are poor, God miraculously provides. He tells Moses to throw a piece of wood into the water, and when Moses does, the water becomes pure.

Now it would seem that the people of Israel have everything they need. Let's do a quick inventory:

- They have freedom from the oppression of Egypt.
- They have miraculous guidance and direction through God's presence in a pillar of cloud and fire.
- They have supernatural water to drink.

With all of this going for the people of Israel, we would expect to see them faithful to God and content with his provision. But there is one theme, one key word that jumps out of this story over and over again. Read Exodus 16:6–12 and ask those listening to identify the word that seems to come through again and again. It's the word "grumble."

LIFE APPLICATION | *Yes, It Is a Sin!*

Grumbling is a sin! There is no question about it. Although we often don't see it as a big deal, God does. Grumbling causes division and conflict in homes and churches. This is a sin that God wants to be purged from our lives.

We need to look at our own lives and be sure we have not fallen into patterns of grumbling and complaining. It is helpful for every follower of Christ to do an occasional attitude check and make sure a grumbling spirit has not begun to grow in our hearts. If you are the

NEW TESTAMENT CONNECTION

Lesson for Generations to Come

God is so concerned about the sin of grumbling that he lists it alongside idolatry, sexual immorality, and testing God (1 Corinthians 10:6–10) as the sins of God's people while they were in the wilderness. The apostle Paul is clear that the history of Israel in the wilderness serves as a reminder of some things we should *not* do. Paul puts it this way: "Now these things occurred as examples to keep us from setting our hearts on evil things as they did."

courageous type, you might even want to ask a close friend or family member if they see any patterns of grumbling and complaining in your life.

> Always speaking well of the deserving, but never ill of the undeserving, we shall attain to the glory and kingdom of God.
>
> *Irenaeus (second century)*

SIGNIFICANT SCRIPTURE

Exodus 16:1–3

Wilderness Lesson 4: A Lesson about Perspective

INTERPRETIVE INSIGHT | *On Discontent*

Discontent distorts our perspective and twists our view of reality. In Exodus 16 we see how the entire perspective of the Israelites becomes warped. In their discontent, they begin to rewrite their history. Discontent can distort our perspective and play with our mind. We begin to maximize how bad our present condition is, and we look with rose-colored glasses at how things used to be or at how things are for somebody else. That's just human nature. That's what's going on with the people of Israel.

Note Exodus 16:3: "If only we had died by the LORD's hand in Egypt!" These people are raising complaint to an art form. "We're not asking for much," they say, "just death. There in Egypt we sat around pots of meat and ate all the food we wanted."

Think for a moment about what their occupation was in Egypt. They were slaves! They did not sit around having fondue all day long when they were in Egypt. They were in forced servitude; they were being beaten; they were miserable! But now, discontent about their present situation allows them to see their past in a distorted light. That's what discontent can do.

ON THE LIGHTER SIDE | *What Is It?*

This name "manna" becomes kind of an inside joke to the Israelites. In the Hebrew language, *manna* simply means "what is it?" They didn't know exactly what this stuff was, so they called it *manna*. Can you imagine the conversation in the morning? "What do you want for breakfast?" "I'll have a bowl of 'what is it.'"

For a little more information on manna, read Exodus 16:14, "When the dew was gone, thin flakes like frost on the ground appeared on the desert floor." This was the introduction of the first breakfast cereal, Frosted Flakes. When the Israelites first started eating the manna, they thought it was Grrrrrreat! Sadly, after a short time they even complained about this provision from God.

Wilderness Lesson 5: A Lesson about (Manna) Provision

SIGNIFICANT SCRIPTURE

Exodus 16; Deuteronomy 8:1–5

INTERPRETIVE INSIGHT | *Living One Day at a Time*

We are invited into a journey of living one day at a time. The people have grumbled and complained. They have become discontent and have begun to look back on the "glory days" of Egypt. We might expect God to get upset, impatient, or even angry, but he is very gracious. He just keeps providing. God gives the people meat in the form of quail and bread in the form of manna.

God's provision is wonderful. It is exactly what they needed and there is enough for everyone. Every day, one day at a time, God gives what his people need. In an interesting twist, anytime the people gather more than they need and try to stockpile it for the next day, it goes rotten and is filled with maggots. They can only gather what they need for the day. Then, to the amazement of all the people, when they gather twice as much as they need before the Sabbath (as God commands), the manna stays fresh.

> All we want in Christ, we shall find in Christ. If we want little, we shall find little. If we want much, we shall find much; but if, in utter helplessness, we cast our all on Christ, he will be to us the whole treasury of God.
>
> *Henry Benjamin Wipple*

INTERPRETIVE INSIGHT | *All You Need*

What is God trying to teach his people? Moses makes this explicit in Deuteronomy 8:3 when he looks back on this episode decades later. He says, "God humbled you, causing you to hunger and then fed you with manna." God was teaching his people to depend on him, one day at a time. They could not rely on their own strength,

ON THE LIGHTER SIDE | *A Divine Tailor*

God provided more than just food for his children as they wandered in the desert. In Deuteronomy 8:4 we read, "Your clothes did not wear out and your feet did not swell." In other words, shoes and sandals were provided as well. Think of what forty years of constant marching, blazing sun, and howling sandstorms would do to clothes. Do you think they ran into a lot of K-Marts out in the desert? As God provided through divine power, their clothes did not wear out. Moses said, "You didn't get your clothes from Lord and Taylor. The Lord was your tailor." That's the way it worked in the desert. God was saying to his people, "I'll take care of you. I'm enough. Trust me."

their own wisdom, or their own resources. In the desert they learned that all they needed could be found in the hands of the God who had formed them.

PAUSE FOR PRAYER

A Prayer for Manna

Take a moment to pray for each person gathered to begin living by the manna principle. Also, allow a time of silence where they can pray for God to give them a new trust for the daily manna that only God can provide.

You might even want to use the brief prayer provided below:

> God, give me manna for today, just this day. Give me enough wisdom. Give me enough patience. Give me enough courage. Give me enough love to handle this day. And as best I can, God, I'll trust that when I wake up in the morning, you'll be there with me and you'll help me face tomorrow. I'm not going to try to collect more from you than I need. I want to learn to trust you for this day.

LIFE APPLICATION | *The Manna Principle*

Here is the manna principle: *one day at a time.* God will provide for you one day at a time. Trust God for this day right now. Some of the Israelites got anxious. Some got greedy. Some got afraid. Some thought they'd beat the system by gathering tomorrow's manna. God had something important to teach them—and us as well. It is the manna principle by which we are to live. God says, "I want you to live your life trusting me one day at a time—just this day. Learn to trust me for this day. If you start worrying about tomorrow, you are going to worry your whole life long."

We don't need to ask for guarantees about tomorrow. We don't need to ask for answers to questions we are not being asked yet. We don't need to ask for the ability to cross a bridge that we haven't yet reached. We need to learn to pray, "God, I'll trust you for this day, my daily bread, today. When I wake up tomorrow morning, like manna, your mercies will be new once again."

New Testament Connection – Our Daily Bread

Jesus lived with an understanding of the Father's daily provision and called his followers to do the same. When he taught his disciples the essential life prayer (often called the Lord's Prayer), he told them to pray, "Give us today our daily bread" (Matthew 6:11). That's the manna principle. That's the way Jesus lived. That's the way we should live.

Wilderness Lesson 6: A Lesson about Presence

SIGNIFICANT SCRIPTURE

Exodus 17:7; 32:1–21; 33:12–17; Psalm 84:10

INTERPRETIVE INSIGHT | *Life Choices*

We can choose to walk in the real and life-changing presence of God or we can cling to lifeless idols. The people of Israel ask a fundamental question that goes through all of our minds at one point or another in our lives: "Is the LORD among us or not?" (Exodus 17:7).

When we hear the Israelites ask this question, it seems unbelievable. After all God has done—the ten plagues, the parting of the Red Sea, the deliverance from Pharaoh, the destruction of the Egyptian army, the provision of manna and water—they still dare to ask this question: "Is the Lord really among us?"

But before we come down too hard on them, we need to look at our own lives. God is so powerful, he is so present, and yet we dare to wonder if he will continue to be with us. We, like the people of Israel, need to learn that God is with us, even when we are too blind to see him and too hardhearted to feel his presence.

NARRATIVE ON THE TEXT | *Unwilling to Wait*

Even though God's people question his presence, once more he is patient. Once more he provides. He leads them to Mount Sinai, and Moses is called to meet God on the mountain for forty days and forty nights. All the people have to do is wait. That's all they have to do—just wait. They're not hungry; they've got manna. They're not thirsty; they've got water. All they have to do is wait—they just need to have enough faith to wait.

In Exodus 32:1 we read, "When the people saw that Moses was so long in coming down from the mountain, they gathered around Aaron and said, 'Come, make us gods who will go before us. As for this fellow Moses . . .' " Notice the language here. "This fellow" is kind of a distancing thing. "Where's what's-his-name—Moses?" "As for this fellow Moses who brought us up out of Egypt, we don't know what has happened to him."

So the people cry out to Aaron, "Make us gods who will go before us." They don't want to wait. They're not interested in God's timing. They don't understand that God has good reasons for wanting them to be rooted where they are for awhile. They just want to get out of this desert and get to the milk-and-honey place. We can hear their voices crying through history, "Are we there yet?"

INTERPRETIVE INSIGHT | *Commandments Given and Broken*

The people of God are unwilling to wait forty days. They want to control God rather than have him lead them. They prefer to have a golden calf they can manipulate than a living God they have to obey. A lot of us are like that. With an idol, a golden calf, we get our way. With God, we must listen and follow his way. Amazingly, Aaron gives in. He knows better, but he won't stand up to them. As a result, he fashions a golden calf and gives it to the people.

There is tremendous irony in this story. Moses is on the mountaintop receiving the Ten Commandments from God and making a covenant with God. Simultaneously, while that is happening, the "people of the covenant" are down below worshiping an idol and engaging in the kind of sexually abhorrent practices that God was trying to purge from the human race.

LIFE APPLICATION | *Taking Responsibility*

We learn another key lesson from Israel in Exodus 32. It is a lesson about taking responsibility. That's always the struggle for human beings. We have seen this ever since the garden of Eden when God came to Adam and said, "Adam, did you eat the fruit?" And Adam said, "Ask the woman that you gave me."

Here Moses confronts Aaron. Exodus 32:21 says, "Moses said to Aaron, 'What did these people do to you, that you led them into such great sin?'" In other words, there must have been some horrible coercion, some terrible threat, physical pressure, something.

"'Do not be angry, [now notice this phrase] my lord,' Aaron answered." Now remember, Moses is Aaron's brother. Do you ever call your brother, "My lord"? He's laying it on a little thick because he's trying to appease Moses. "'Do not be angry, my lord,' Aaron answered. 'You know how prone these people are to evil.'"

Now look at the follow-up excuse Aaron tries to use. "They said to me, 'Make us gods who will go before us. As for this fellow Moses who brought us up out of Egypt, we don't know what has happened to him.' So I told them, 'Whoever has any gold jewelry, take it off.' Then they gave me the gold, and I threw it into the fire, and out came this calf!"

In other words, "It's unbelievable! You should have been there. I've never seen anything like it. In goes the gold and out pops the calf." It's the same old tendency — an inability or refusal to say, "This is what I did. Here's my part. I am responsible."

As we walk through this series, we will see many examples of people who refuse to take personal responsibility for their sinful actions. We need to learn from their bad example and choose not to respond in the same manner. We need to identify where we have sinned and confess honestly. This is the way to healing and hope.

SIGNIFICANT SCRIPTURE

Numbers 11:26–29

Wilderness Lesson 7: A Lesson about Humility

NARRATIVE ON THE TEXT | *Celebrate*

We need to celebrate God's work in and through others. Two men in the camp of Israel begin to prophesy. Their names are Eldad and Medad. Up to this point Moses was the one who did this. All of a sudden, the Spirit descends on these two men out of the blue, and they begin to speak prophetic words. When this happens, Joshua tells Moses to make them stop. In Joshua's mind, only Moses is supposed to prophesy. It is one of the things that makes Moses special. And since Joshua is Moses' assistant, it makes Joshua special. But if everybody is going to start prophesying, then Moses and Joshua won't be special anymore.

> Nothing sets a person so much out of the devil's reach as humility.
> *Jonathan Edwards (eighteenth century)*

Moses looks at things differently than Joshua. Joshua says, "Moses, my lord, stop them!" Moses, says, "Are you jealous for my sake? I wish that all of the LORD's people were prophets and that the LORD would put his Spirit on them!" The humility of Moses shows through, and we can almost hear him say, "I really don't want to be more special, more unique, or more spiritual than anybody. I wish that God would put his Spirit on everyone."

LIFE APPLICATION | *Time to Celebrate*

We need to get serious and intentional about celebrating the way God works in and through the lives of others. It would be a great practice for every follower of Jesus to make a regular habit of celebrating God's work in the people around them. Speak a word of affirmation, write an encouraging note, or even give a small gift to celebrate a specific way you see God working in the life of another person.

Wilderness Lesson 8: A Lesson about Fear and Faith

NARRATIVE ON THE TEXT | *The Good News and the Bad News*

Moses sends out twelve spies, and they are gone for forty days. They come back and file their report. Look at Numbers 13:27: "They gave Moses this account: 'We went into the land to which you sent us, and it does flow with milk and honey!'" It's a land of abundance. They are clear that the reports of the amazing bounty of this land were not exaggerated!

However, they also point out that the people who live there are big and strong. The cities are fortified. They want Moses and all of the people to know that this is a really dangerous place. Ten of the spies bring a bad report and discourage the people from even trying to go in and take the land.

Now two of the spies, Joshua and Caleb, give a dissenting report. Numbers 13:30 says: "Then Caleb silenced the people before Moses and said, 'We should go up and take possession of the land, for we can certainly do it.'" But the people in the wilderness school don't believe this. They don't believe that God's protection will be enough for them. They refuse to enter.

PAUSE FOR REFLECTION

A Hunger for God's Presence

Moses makes a beautiful request of God in Exodus 33:15: "Then Moses said to him, 'If your Presence does not go with us, do not send us up from here.'" In other words, Moses says, "You know, God, even though you're offering to send us to a promised land that's flowing with milk and honey, and even though you will give us security, peace, and affluence, we need more. Even though you have given us the Ten Commandments and all the moral guidance we could ever need, there is still something we need. We need your Presence with us!" Moses is saying that he would rather live in a desert with God than live in the Promised Land with abundance, affluence, security, and protection, but without God's presence.

Pause for a time of silent reflection and encourage people to consider places in their lives where they haven't welcomed God's presence. Ask God to fill these areas with his presence in fresh and powerful ways.

INTERPRETIVE INSIGHT | *Fear and Faith*

Fear robs us of joy and the potential of walking with God to new and exciting places. *Faith* leads us on an exciting journey of daily trust in God. Numbers 13:32–33 contains a poignant image. The ten spies with the bad report say, "We can't attack those

SIGNIFICANT SCRIPTURE

Numbers 13

PAUSE FOR REFLECTION

I'm No Grasshopper

Some people live with a deep-seated grasshopper complex. If the truth were known, they would say, "I look in the mirror, and all I see is a grasshopper. I'm not adequate. I'm not competent. I'm not strong enough." They live with the daily pain of feeling deeply inferior. But the issue isn't whether we are adequate or competent or strong enough. The question is: Are we willing to trust God one day at a time?

Take time for silent reflection so that people can identify areas of life where they live with fear and feelings of incompetence. Challenge them to meditate on the reality that God's power in them is enough to bring hope and strength to overcome.

people; they are stronger than we are." And they also say, "The land we explored devours those living in it. All the people we saw there are of great size. We saw the Nephilim there (the descendants of Anak come from the Nephilim). We seemed like grasshoppers in our own eyes, and we looked the same to them."

Here's the sentence that reveals the power of fear: "We seemed like grasshoppers in our own eyes." Not only did the spies feel like grasshoppers with no strength. They let the poison of their fear spread through the people of Israel until they all had a grasshopper complex.

> Faith is ... believing what you do not yet see; its reward is to see what you believe.
>
> *Augustine (fifth century)*

Many of these people have never really recovered from the "slave mentality" they learned in their years of bondage in Egypt. As far back as they can remember, all they have ever been is somebody's slave—no dreams, no power. The tragedy is that this generation will never see themselves as anything but grasshoppers. They will not allow hope and joy to fill their hearts. They will not allow themselves to trust God for the great adventure he wants to lead them through.

God wants his children to follow him in faith. He wants us to trust his provision, his power, and his faithfulness. When we do, we will enter a life of joy and a journey of faith beyond our wildest dreams.

LIFE APPLICATION | *Walking in Faith*

But God does not desert his people. He waits with the Israelites in the desert for forty years. He holds them in his arms while a new generation grows up—a generation that will walk by faith into God's plan. He forgives them. He stays with them. He keeps watch over them. He keeps the manna supply going.

What is sad to realize is that the present generation never knows what might have been. They miss the adventure of what it could have been to enter the Promised Land of God. It is their children who will see this dream become a reality.

God wants us to be a generation of risk-taking, faith-filled adventurers. God is asking us to do something new and fresh. Maybe it's an involvement in ministry. Maybe it's leading a small group. Maybe it's a new level of commitment with your family. Maybe it's a financial adventure in giving with a new level of sacrifice and joy. Whatever it is, make the commitment to walk by faith and enter the blessing of being in the center of God's will.

Message 8

What Indiana Jones Was Looking For

Exodus 24–30; Leviticus 16

THE HEART OF THE Message

You can tell a lot about people by where they live. If you get a chance to visit someone's home and do a brief walk-through, you can gain insight into their values, loves, and priorities. For better or for worse, we make pretty strong judgments and decisions about a person based on the environment where they live.

In this message, we will look at the house of God. In the Pentateuch we learn about God's choice to live among his people. His dwelling place, the tabernacle, gives us amazing insight into the heart of God and how he relates with his children.

BRIEF MESSAGE OUTLINE

1. The tabernacle
2. The furnishings in the tabernacle
3. Entering God's presence with confidence

THE HEART OF THE Messenger

As you prepare to bring this message, take time to walk around your home and reflect on what you see. What do you learn about your values, priorities, and passions? Let this experience help shape how you look at the passages in this week's message. The tabernacle, with all its furnishings, points to God's values, priorities, and passions. After you have surveyed your home and God's dwelling place as shown in these passages, think about how you might change the furnishings in your home (literally or spiritually) to line up your life more closely with God's priorities for you.

Introduction

Most of us dream about the kind of place we'd like to live in someday. There are all kinds of magazines, TV shows, websites, and books devoted to home building and improvement. Our homes take up a good amount of our time and finances. Even with all we put into them, most of us still have a list of changes we want to make and things we want to fix. For some of us, this list gets longer and longer as the years pass. If we look at our home and our plans for improvement, we can learn a lot about what matters to us.

SIGNIFICANT SCRIPTURE

Exodus 24 – 27; Leviticus 26:11

1. The Tabernacle

INTERPRETIVE INSIGHT | *God Is with Us*

The instructions for what God's dwelling place should look like begin in Exodus 25. Take a moment to read Exodus 24:17 – 18, "To the Israelites the glory of the LORD looked like a consuming fire on top of the mountain. Then Moses entered the cloud as he went on up the mountain. And he stayed on the mountain forty days and forty nights."

During this specific time when the people of God were at Mount Sinai, they saw God's presence, and it was glorious. It was like a cloud on the mountain. You can be sure they would have loved to see that glory stay in such a powerful and visible way, but it did not.

ON THE LIGHTER SIDE | *In a Van Down by the River*

There was a character on a television show some years ago who had a unique home situation that spoke volumes about him. He was a "wannabe" motivational speaker, but life was not going well. He always ended up reflecting on his problems, plight, and present life situation, and his final line would always be a summary of his housing situation (a metaphor for his whole life): "I live in a van down by the river." Let's be honest, who is going to listen to a motivational speaker who is living in a van down by the river?

CREATIVE MESSAGE IDEA | *A Look at Houses*

Set a table (or a number of tables) in the entry area to your church. Cover these tables with magazines that focus on homes and home repair. You might even invite people to bring these kinds of magazines the week before, but don't tell them why. Just ask them to bring them and place them on the tables as they enter. Set a placard on each table with just one question, "What do you learn about a person's character and priorities by looking at their house?" As people come in, they can browse through a couple of magazines and begin making the connection between houses and the people who live in the house.

You Will Need

- Tables set up near the entry area of your church
- An announcement about bringing magazines (a week early)
- Magazines for the tables
- Placards on the tables

God wanted his people to know he would be with them, even when the mountain was not consumed in fire, so he showed them a new way to know he was with them. In Exodus 25, God begins to give instructions about the building of the tabernacle, his dwelling place. Exodus 25:8 helps us understand the reason God wanted a tabernacle to be built: "Then have them make a sanctuary for me, and I will dwell among them." The key word is "dwell." The tabernacle was a visible sign of the presence of God with his people. When the people of God saw the tabernacle, they could say, "God is with us!"

INTERPRETIVE INSIGHT | *A Meeting Place*

It is as if God is telling Moses that the people need a physical reminder that he is with them. They need a place that will be full of details and activities that will teach them about God's character and will and about how they can relate to him. So God tells Moses to build a tent (tabernacle) in the middle of the camp. Specifically, the people of Israel are to build a courtyard, and in the courtyard a tent, and in the tent a compartment called the Most Holy Place. In that compartment they are to put a box called an ark.

God says, as we will see, "I will come and meet with you on top of that box, and I will provide manna for you every morning, and I will give you water to drink. I will lead you through the desert from one river to another." And the God of the universe says, "I will live in a tent out in the desert just so I can be with my people." All this detail, all the instructions, is given so that the people can have a place to meet with their God.

> The best way to prepare for the coming of Christ is to never forget the presence of Christ.
>
> *William Barclay*

LIFE APPLICATION | *Learning to Dwell with God*

As we study the tabernacle, we are really studying how we can learn to dwell with God. The tabernacle gives powerful insight and instruction that helps us learn to enter a new and rich relationship with our Creator. As we begin to walk through the tabernacle toward the dwelling place of God, we need to realize that our attitude and heart condition influence the process.

God tells Moses in Exodus 25:2: "Tell the Israelites to bring me an offering. You are to receive the offering for me from each man

WORD STUDY

Tabernacle

The word "dwell" (Exodus 25:8) has a specific meaning. In the Hebrew language it is the same word as that used for a tabernacle. It's a little like our modern word "tent." It could be used as a noun or a verb. Literally, Exodus 25:8 could be translated that God is saying, "I will tabernacle with my people." As we see the word "tabernacle," we need to understand that it is not just the word used for the place (the tent) in the middle of the camp of Israel. It is also the word that describes what God was doing. His activity was, and is, to tabernacle (dwell) among his people.

whose heart prompts him to give." Everybody can be part of making a place where they can meet with God, but it will be strictly voluntary. God gives the invitation, but the people must respond. This is true for us today as well. God invites us to places of intimacy with him, but we have to hear his invitation and enter in.

INTERPRETIVE INSIGHT | *Hearts Overflowing*

Exodus 36:3–6 tells us that the hearts of the people were so moved that they just kept bringing offerings day after day. They could not stop themselves; they kept on giving. Finally, it got to the point where Moses had to give a command that the people stop giving. Their hearts were overflowing with love so much that they gave more than was needed!

PAUSE FOR PRAYER

Draw Me Close

Pause to pray that each person present will hunger more for God's presence. Invite each person to quietly ask God to help them draw near. If there are things standing in the way, ask for the Holy Spirit to come and begin a process of removing those things.

LIFE APPLICATION | *Heart Check*

We all need to check our hearts when it comes to the matter of giving. Do we have hearts that are overflowing in response to God's goodness, or has the well run dry? When was the last time you found yourself looking for ways to give toward God's work? When was the last time a pastor stood up in your church and said, "Attention, members of the congregation, please stop giving! The bills are paid, our missionaries are taken care of, the mortgage has been burned, all salaries are paid, and we simply have too much. No more offerings until we find a way to spend what we have saved from all your generous gifts."

ON THE LIGHTER SIDE | *Joyful Extravagance*

The tabernacle was made of the finest materials available, including a lot of gold and silver. We know that God does not need precious metals. They are no more rare to him than tin or bronze. But the use of these had specific significance. To put it in a contemporary context, if you're a man and you've ever had a wife or a girlfriend, you might know what it feels like to buy flowers for her. Why does one person spend a big chunk of cash on a dozen red roses? Is there anything strategic about a rose? Wouldn't it be more practical to get her a minor appliance or something useful?

The reason one person gives another a bouquet of roses is that this gift is a way of honoring the other person. It is a way of communicating value and paying homage. It is this kind of extravagance that cries out, "I love you!" A heart of love longs for the opportunity to pay honor.

ILLUSTRATION | *The Middle of Life*

The placement of the tabernacle gives a visual picture of how God wants to be in the very center of our lives. God had his people arrange their lives, physically and spiritually, around the tabernacle. When they set up camp, the tent of meeting was to be in the very center. Then the priests camped around the tent. Finally, all the tribes of Israel camped surrounding the tabernacle. There were to be three tribes on the north, three on the south, three on the east, and three on the west. The door of each tent was to be facing the tabernacle. The entire community was built around the tabernacle, which represented God's presence in their midst. When they marched, the pieces of the tabernacle were carried in the middle of the congregation. This was a way of physically picturing that they were to be a community centered on God.

NARRATIVE ON LIFE | *On the Road*

The presence of the tabernacle in the middle of the camp was to serve as an ever-present reminder that God was with his people. This spiritual reality should have a transforming impact on how God's people live.

Here is a modern-day example of how this works. Have you ever noticed how people drive differently when they see a police car near? Traffic can be flying along, and all of a sudden brake lights begin to flash. Everyone slows down. What's going on? A police car has been sighted. The presence of this car reminds people that there is a speed limit and it would be wise to follow it.

CREATIVE MESSAGE IDEA | *A Picture of God's Presence*

Show the congregation a picture of how the tabernacle was central in the community of God's people. Have a flip chart and draw the tabernacle, then the tents of the priests, and finally the tribes of Israel all around the tabernacle. Let this visual picture help people see that God was central among his people.

You Will Need

- A flip chart
- Wide-tip markers

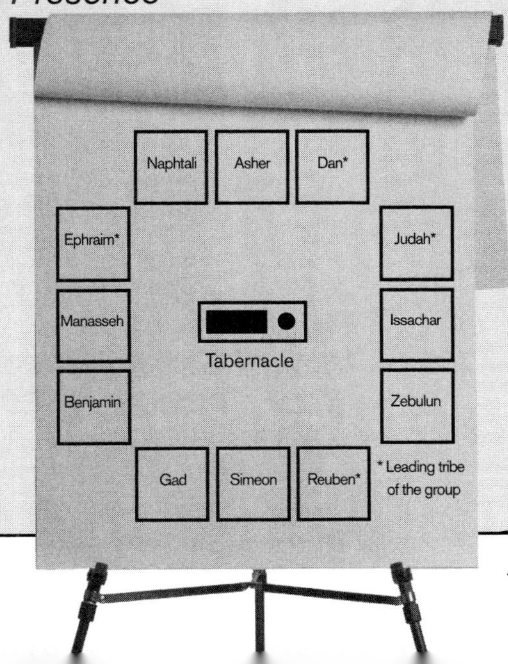

The tabernacle had this same kind of impact on the people. When they saw it, they were reminded that God was with them, leading, guiding, and watching. This impacted the way they related to each other and to God.

LIFE APPLICATION | *What If?*

What if God were watching me in the workplace? What if he were present on my school campus? What if God knew what was happening behind closed doors? What if God were with me every moment of every day?

The tabernacle reminds us that God *is* with us all the time. Through his Holy Spirit he is still present. We need to live each moment with a clear awareness that God is with us, that he still tabernacles among his people. This should have a powerful impact on all we do.

INTERPRETIVE INSIGHT | *The House of God*

The tabernacle was to be the "dwelling place" of God (Leviticus 26:11). It is important to note that the tabernacle and its furnishings were built along the lines of an ancient Near Eastern home. If you could have visited the home of a Near Eastern nomad at that time, you would have noticed that the structure of the average dwelling place was similar to the tabernacle. The objects that were placed in the tabernacle would also have been found in most homes in that day. They would have been made of more common materials, but the basic concept was the same.

The tabernacle had a large outer courtyard that was 75 feet wide and 150 feet long — about half the length of a football field and not as wide. This outer courtyard was enclosed by a structure with wooden frames and brilliant curtains so that it could be torn down and transported. Much like a fenced-in yard in our day, these frames and curtains offered a kind of safe, quiet place for people to gather and meet with God.

SIGNIFICANT SCRIPTURE

Exodus 25; 27:1 – 8; 28:29; 30:1 – 10; Romans 12:1

2. The Furnishings in the Tabernacle

INTERPRETIVE INSIGHT | *The Bronze Altar*

As a person entered the courtyard of the tabernacle, the first object to be noticed would be the altar. In homes in those days there was generally some kind of grill or pit for cooking food. In the tabernacle the bronze altar for sacrifices was the equivalent of the grill in a home. This altar is described in Exodus 27:1 – 8. The bronze altar was about 7½ feet square and about 4½ feet high. There were horns on each side, and animals would be tied to the horns and offered as a sacrifice.

The burnt offering. Sometimes people think that back in those days, animal sacrifices happened all over Israel on a regular basis. As a general rule, sacrifices only happened in the tabernacle. There were five main types of sacrifices, and it is important that we have a basic sense of what they were.

One offering was called the burnt offering. This offering was distinct because the entire animal was consumed by the fire. Most of the other sacrifices were actually part of a meal. A person or the family would go to the tabernacle, and priests would literally butcher the meat and bring it back to the person or family who offered it, and they would have a meal as a part of worship.

But the burnt offering didn't work that way. In the burnt offering, the whole animal was consumed by fire. Nobody could eat any part of it. All of it was offered to God, and it was a picture of total consecration. As the people saw the offering being consumed, they were reminded that Israel was to be *totally devoted* to God.

The grain offering. The grain offering was designated for the poor who couldn't afford an animal for the burnt offering. A lot of people fell into that category. The beauty of this offering or sacrifice was that it revealed the heart of God for all people. God's sacrificial system was designed to teach that everybody — no matter how rich or how poor — has something to offer God.

The fellowship (peace) offering. Peace or fellowship offerings were offered as expressions of intimacy to God. When somebody had received an unexpected blessing, they would bring a fellowship offering to honor God for his goodness. This sacrifice was a tangible way to say thank you to God. At other times someone would make a vow or commitment of something they wanted to do for God. This offering would be a way of declaring that they were serious about their commitment. At other times when somebody just wanted to say, "God, I love you," they would bring what was called a freewill offering. This was another kind of peace offering.

The sin and guilt offerings. There were two other kinds of offerings called sin offerings and guilt offerings. They were very closely related. They were offered as expressions of sorrow or repentance for wrongdoing. When someone was aware of personal sin, he or she would give an offering. When they were dealing with guilt and wanted to express sorrow to God, they brought an offering. These offerings were important in the process of atonement. Guilt offerings often involved an act that required financial restitution if they had wronged someone.

The entire sacrificial system, which was detailed and complex, pointed forward to a final sacrifice that would be offered for sins. One day Jesus would come and would become the perfect sacrifice. Until then, the sacrificial system reminded people of the cost of sin and the hope of cleansing and restored relationship with God.

NEW TESTAMENT CONNECTION

Living Sacrifices

The varoius sacrifices took place every day. They were offered first thing in the morning and last thing in the evening. The priests would offer sacrifices for individuals, for families, and for the nation. This altar is the picture the apostle Paul has in mind in Romans 12:1 when he writes, "Offer your bodies as living sacrifices."

The picture would have been clear in the minds of the Jews. When an animal was to be sacrificed, it was tied to the horns that were on the corners of the altar. It didn't have the option to say, "Well, I think I'm done now. I'm going to get up and leave." It was tied to the altar, and there was no way off the altar except through death. Paul's words in Romans 12 are an expression of utter surrender and submission. Like the animal tied to the altar, we are bound to give our whole lives in sacrifice to the God who sacrificed all for us.

LIFE APPLICATION | *My Sacrifice*

There are many ways we can offer ourselves as living sacrifices. We can offer up a sacrifice of thanksgiving and praise as we cry out, "Thank you." We can offer our hearts in confession as we say, "I want to confess my sin and my sorrow to you. Cleanse me and change my heart and life." We can offer up surrendered lives as we pray, "God, I'll obey you even if it's painful. I will stay on the altar and let you do what you will with my life." The altar may not be sitting in the entrance area of the tabernacle, but it still exists, and we are called to lay down our lives on it every day!

> There is but one king that I know;
> It is he that I love and worship.
> If I were to be killed a thousand times for my loyalty to him,
> I would still be his servant.
> Christ is on my lips,
> Christ is in my heart;
> No amount of suffering will take him from me.
>
> *Genesius of Rome (martyr, third century)*

INTERPRETIVE INSIGHT | *The Basin*

The next thing someone would see upon entering the courtyard of the tabernacle was a large bronze basin. In it the priests cleansed themselves before and after offering the sacrifice. The basin was a common amenity in ancient Near Eastern homes. People entering homes were dusty and dirty and felt a need to clean up. We live in such a clean society that we can't imagine what it would be like to be dirty most of the time. But in those days, when a person entered a dwelling, there was usually a basin for cleansing. In the tabernacle, therefore, there was a similar piece of furniture — the basin.

INTERPRETIVE INSIGHT | *A Clear Conscience*

In Bible times people didn't have the opportunity to get cleaned up very often. When they did, it was an act of gracious hospitality. In the tabernacle a large part of what the priests did was to butcher animals. That's a messy job. In Exodus 30:17 we learn that the basin was placed between the altar and the Tent of Meeting so that when the priests entered God's presence, they could clean themselves first "so that they will not die" (Exodus 30:20).

This is a picture of being clean in the sight of God and what that means. Such cleansing was not just for the body, not just for the clothes, but especially for the conscience. Through this symbolism, people realized that God offered purity. Imagine a heart with no stain, no regret, and no remorse.

LIFE APPLICATION | *Cleanse Me, Lord*

We live in a world that is unclean. We can feel the grit and grime of the world cling to our minds and souls. Yet God still offers cleansing. God offers purity of heart, even for the greatest of sinners. As we look into the water of the bronze basin, we see a reflection — ourselves. We see our sin, our offenses, our hopelessness. But as we plunge beneath the water, we are reminded that God has the power to cleanse. Jesus has offered to make us white as snow, if we will receive his cleansing.

INTERPRETIVE INSIGHT | *The Holy Place (Outer Chamber)*

Inside the tabernacle proper was an outer chamber called the Holy Place. In an ancient Near Eastern home, there was a place where you could receive a guest and perhaps break bread. In the tabernacle there were three main pieces of furniture in the Holy Place, similar to common furnishings in homes at that time: a lampstand, burning incense, and fresh bread.

INTERPRETIVE INSIGHT | *The Lampstand*

The lampstand is described in Exodus 25:31. It was made of pure hammered gold, and the priest's job was to keep it filled with olive oil so that the flame would never go out. It remained lit all through the night.

Why did they do this? This is the one part of the tabernacle that could be seen from the outside. The ever-burning light was a little bit like leaving a porch light on to send a message that somebody's home. Anybody in Israel could come to the courtyard, even at night, when they were alone, when they were worried, and there was a light on in God's house. Somebody was home!

ILLUSTRATION | *Leave the Light On*

In a popular commercial for the motel chain called Motel 6, the spokesperson would always end by saying the same line, "We'll leave the light on for you." The advertising hook was to make possible customers feel they are always welcome. In the same way, God said to his priests, "Don't let the lamp go out. I want all my people to know that when they're confused, when they're afraid, when they're in the dark, I'll leave the light on. I am here. I am available to them all day and all night."

LIFE APPLICATION | *Walking in the Light*

Some of those who gather to hear this message will be living in dark times. They may wonder if God is really there or if they are welcome to enter his presence. They need to know that God has a light burning for them. Remind them of God's light that never goes out. Remind them that God cares so much that his light burns twenty-four hours a day, seven days a week, three hundred and sixty-five days a year. We can enter his presence any time. We don't have to wait until tomorrow. God is available now!

NEW TESTAMENT CONNECTION

The Prayers of God's People

In Revelation 5:8 we read about the golden bowls full of incense. We are told these are the prayers of the saints, a sweet thing to God. Incense is a picture of a sweet aroma ascending to God. As God's people, we must learn that our prayers are sweet to God and that they ascend like fragrant incense.

INTERPRETIVE INSIGHT | *The Altar of Incense*

When you entered the Holy Place, you would see the altar of incense (see the description in Exodus 30:1 – 10). In homes in the ancient Near East at this time in history, people often burned incense to cover up the odor of people who did not bathe often, animals that lived in the house, and the smell of animals that had been slaughtered and cooked for family meals. The tabernacle had incense burning in the entry area of the Holy Place. This would have been a relief, since the smell of slaughtered animals would have been intense throughout the entire tabernacle.

INTERPRETIVE INSIGHT | *The Bread of the Presence*

In the Holy Place was also the table of the Presence. It was built of wood and covered with gold. The serving utensils also were made of gold. The primary purpose of this table was to hold the bread of the Presence. Every week the priests were to bake twelve loaves of bread, one for each of the twelve tribes of Israel.

ILLUSTRATION | *The Smell of Freshly Baked Bread*

Have you ever smelled freshly baked bread? It is one of the most powerful aromas! If you walk into a home and are met by the smell of freshly baked bread, something happens. A feeling of warmth comes over you. A smile finds its way to your lips. You might even begin to salivate a little, as your mouth and body imagine partaking of this simple but wonderful delicacy. This is true today if we visit the home of a friend and smell freshly baked bread, and it was true when priests came into the Holy Place and smelled the fresh baked bread of the Presence.

LIFE APPLICATION | *Seeing the Face of God*

One of the reasons the bread was called "the bread of the Presence" is that it pointed to the warm, fresh, sweet presence of God. Literally, the expression means "the bread of the face." This was the bread that was always before the face of God. It was also bread that reminded the Israelites of the face of God through his daily provision and fresh presence every day.

God is still present today. He shows himself in new and fresh ways. He provides our daily bread and all we need. What we need to do is learn to see his face. We need to look and see the face of God's presence in each loaf of bread, each meal, each friendship, each paycheck, and each gentle breeze of the Holy Sprit that blows into our lives. We need to learn to see, taste, feel, hear, and even smell the presence of God!

INTERPRETIVE INSIGHT | *The Most Holy Place (Holy of Holies)*

After passing through the Holy Place, seeing the light, and smelling the bread, the priests encountered a heavy veil, a blue, purple, and scarlet curtain. These were rich, majestic colors. This curtain was the entrance to the Most Holy Place (the Holy of Holies). This was the room of greatest intimacy, much as a bedroom would be in a home. It was set aside for only the most intimate companion of God, the high priest. Access to it was restricted to once a year.

INTERPRETIVE INSIGHT | *The Ark of the Testimony*

Exodus 25 tells us about the single piece of furnishing in the Most Holy Place: "the ark of the Testimony [covenant]." It was a place where atonement could be made for the sins of the people. This ark was a box made of acacia wood and overlaid with gold—forty-five inches long, about twenty-seven inches high, and twenty-seven inches wide.

God said regarding the ark: "I want you to put poles on that ark so it cannot be touched, because it's holy. It's set apart." Here are God's instructions about the formation of the ark:

> "Make an atonement cover of pure gold—two and a half cubits long and a cubit and a half wide. And make two cherubim out of hammered gold at the ends of the cover. Make one cherub on one end and the second cherub on the other; make the cherubim of one piece with the cover, at the two ends. The cherubim are to have

HISTORICAL CONTEXT | *Table Fellowship*

Breaking bread and sharing table fellowship (a meal) with others was important in Bible times. In our day, we tend to sit down for a meal only with people we know and like. But in those days there was deep meaning in sharing a meal and breaking bread. When you broke bread, you were entering a level of intimate fellowship that was much deeper than what we express through a shared meal in our culture today.

This is why the religious leaders of Jesus' day were so outraged when Jesus, a rabbi, actually broke bread with sinners. He was entering an intimate experience with people who were to be avoided, according to the religious laws of the day. In the days of Moses, everyone knew that breaking bread and sharing table fellowship was a sign of deep intimacy. With that in mind, the idea that God would have bread prepared for his people spoke volumes about God's desire to be close to his people.

their wings spread upward, overshadowing the cover with them. The cherubim are to face each other, looking toward the cover." (Exodus 25:17–20)

People often wonder what these cherubs looked like. Today we tend to think of cherubs as cute, chubby little valentine figures. But that's not accurate at all. These were mighty angelic beings of great power. But even these great forces in the universe humble themselves before the awesome presence of God. They bow down!

In Exodus 25:22 God says, "There, above the cover between the two cherubim that are over the ark of the Testimony, I will meet with you and give you all my commands for the Israelites." It is as if God is saying, "I'll come sit on a box in a tent, and you'll know I'm always with you. I will guide you." What an amazing picture of God's willingness to be present with his people, right where they are.

3. Entering God's Presence with Confidence

INTERPRETIVE INSIGHT | *What's in the Box?*

One way God invited his people to come near to him was through simple reminders. In the ark, God had the people place some objects that would always be there to help them see that they are welcome to come near to him.

The first object was a bowl of manna. This was a reminder that God would always be faithful and provide, one day at a time.

Next was Aaron's rod. The people knew the story (from Numbers 17) about how God miraculously caused Aaron's rod to bud as an expression to all the Israelites that God had chosen Aaron and his descendants to be priests to lead them in worship. This second object was a reminder that God invites his people to come near and worship.

Finally, God told the people to put the two tablets that contained the Ten Commandments into the box. This was the people's copy and God's copy of the covenant. It was God's reminder that they were to draw near to him with obedient hearts.

HISTORICAL CONTEXT | *One Penalty*

There was one specific penalty prescribed for anyone who entered the Most Holy Place without being invited: death! Now, this might seem extreme and excessive, but this was a place of unsurpassed intimacy. You did not just barge into the Most Holy Place. As a matter of fact, only the high priest entered this place, and he only went in once a year!

It is interesting to note that there was also a prescribed penalty for violating the bed chamber in the home of a family in Israel. If a person invaded the bedroom and committed adultery, the penalty was death. There was this similar penalty because adultery involved breaking the most intimate boundary in the home.

Each item in the box taught a lesson and gave a reminder from God for his people:

- Manna—trust me.
- The rod of Aaron—worship me.
- The tablets of the Ten Commandments—obey me.

Trust, worship, and obedience represent the heart of what it means to live with God. The objects in the box became symbols and reminders of God's desire for intimacy with his people.

NEW TESTAMENT CONNECTION

A Holy Priesthood

In 1 Peter 2:9 we read: "But you are a chosen people, a royal priesthood, a holy nation, a people belonging to God, that you may declare the praises of him who called you out of darkness into his wonderful light." Today, every person who is a follower of Jesus is one of his royal priests.

In other words, since the coming of Christ and the sending of the Holy Spirit, we are a priesthood of believers. There are many acts of ministry that we can enter into as God's priests, but here are a few practical areas we can all see to move into priestly ministry: (1) We can declare praises to God. As Peter teaches us, this is a responsibility of a priest. (2) We can lift up others in prayer, interceding on behalf of those in the family of God. Our prayers are part of a priestly ministry. (3) We can carry the names of God's people on our hearts. We might not have a literal ephod to wear, but we can inscribe the names of God's people into our hearts and seek to love them in the name of God.

LIFE APPLICATION | *Life with God*

The entire tabernacle, beginning with the altar, ending with the ark of the covenant, and everything in between, was an invitation to draw near to God. This place was a visible sign that God had open arms extended to his people.

God still has arms open to us today. We need to notice the reminders all around us. God still provides for us—each meal, each paycheck, and each breath of life is a reminder of his love. God still meets us in worship; when we feel his presence and the moving of the Holy Spirit, we are reminded that his arms are open. God's law still leads and guides our lives; we need to hear him speak through his Word. God's invitation for us to draw near to him is being extended over and over, every day.

> To those who are tried by the tempest,
> You are the calm harbor;
> You are the object of all that hope.
> To those who are sick, you are health;
> You guide the blind and give help to those in need.
> To those who face suffering, you always grant mercy,
> You are a light in darkness, a place of rest for the weary.
>
> *Severus of Thrace (third century)*

INTERPRETIVE INSIGHT | *The Ephod*

Skilled workers fashioned an ephod, a kind of vest with twelve precious stones, for the high priest. This article of clothing had powerful symbolism. Each one of the stones was to have the name of one of the twelve tribes of Israel on it. Exodus 28:29 says, "Whenever Aaron enters the Holy

Place, he will bear the names of the sons of Israel over his heart on the breastpiece of decision as a continuing memorial before the LORD." He was to carry all of the people on his heart every time he came before the Lord. This is a beautiful picture of what a priest was to do—carry the people on his heart to God.

INTERPRETIVE INSIGHT | *The Leading of the Holy Spirit*

The priests had something called the Urim and Thummim. These were concrete, tangible objects designed to train the priests to consult God, to pray, to listen, and to submit before making a major decision. There is a lot of speculation as to what they were, but we can be certain they were tools God used to teach them to seek his will in every decision.

Too often we do dumb things and make foolish decisions because we don't seek God's guidance. The priests of God were trained to seek God and to pray for wisdom. Like them, we too can seek God and ask for wisdom. We must pray with confidence that God can still give specific guidance to us. He is perfectly capable and willing to guide us through the Holy Spirit. God calls us to slow down and listen. He wants us to search his Word closely and follow his leading.

NARRATIVE ON THE TEXT | *A Day of Cleansing*

Leviticus 16 records the events of the Day of Atonement. This was a day for cleansing from sin—a time of new beginnings. On this day the whole community came to a stop. Nobody worked. Nobody ate. On this day alone, the Most Holy Place was entered. This was a way of teaching the people that their sins were keeping them from intimacy with God.

Imagine the people of Israel gathered around the courtyard; everybody is watching. Then Aaron, the high priest, begins to offer a sacrifice to atone for his own sin, because he is a sinner just like everybody else.

Next, he prepares to make a sacrifice for all the people. Aaron, the high priest, takes the blood from that sacrifice and goes into the Most Holy Place to sprinkle the blood on the atonement cover on the ark of the covenant. While Aaron is in the Most Holy Place, all the people stand outside waiting. Some of them are praying. Some of them are crying. Some of them are explaining to their children what's happening. All of them are deeply aware of the reason Aaron is in the Most Holy Place. They are sinners, and he is there to deal with their sins. On this day, everybody remembers their sin.

The crowd is filled with people like you and me: greedy people who have cheated others, people whose marriages are falling apart, people who struggle with sexual sin, parents who have short tempers with their children, people with every sin imaginable; they all stand there and wait.

Will the priest come back out soon? Is everything alright? Will God show up? Is God still with them even though they struggle with sin? Can they truly be forgiven? These and countless other questions are swirling through their minds.

There was an ancient teaching that the high priest was not to remain too long in the Most Holy Place lest he put Israel in terror. As the people wait, the tension mounts. Then, finally, he comes out. The people search his face for any expression; they watch his every move.

Next the high priest takes another animal, a goat, chosen by lot, and places his hands on the goat's head and confesses the sins of all the people. This goes on for some time. As Aaron does this, the people think of all their sins and know that in some way Aaron's hands on this animal have to do with them and their sins. Then, as Leviticus 16:22 tells us, the goat is sent away: "The goat will carry on itself all their sins to a solitary place; and the man shall release it in the desert."

NEW TESTAMENT CONNECTION | *The Lamb of God*

The tabernacle was the beginning of God's teaching about the coming of Jesus, Immanuel, God with us. In the gospel of John we read, "In the beginning was the Word, and the Word was with God, and the Word was God" (John 1:1). Later in the same chapter we discover that this Word is Jesus, God in human flesh, "The Word became flesh and made his dwelling among us. We have seen his glory, the glory of the One and Only, who came from the Father, full of grace and truth" (John 1:14).

Any Jewish person in the first century would have recognized the word for "made his dwelling among us" as the word that meant Jesus "camped," "tented," or "tabernacled" with us. The Greek word meant "to tabernacle." When any Jewish person read these words in John's gospel, they saw an immediate connection to the glory and presence of God as experienced in the wilderness tabernacle.

Another New Testament connection with the tabernacle is found in Hebrews 9–10. These two chapters are all about the tabernacle. They reflect on how the tabernacle has been fulfilled by what Jesus did. In Hebrews 10:19–22 we read:

> Therefore, brothers, since we have confidence to enter the Most Holy Place by the blood of Jesus, by a new and living way opened for us through the curtain, that is, his body, and since we have a great priest over the house of God, let us draw near to God with a sincere heart in full assurance of faith, having our hearts sprinkled to cleanse us from a guilty conscience and having our bodies washed with pure water.
>
> We can now enter the Most Holy Place with confidence because of Jesus. Once again God is dwelling with his people. But this time, everyone can have access.

Note too that when Jesus went to the cross and died for our sins, the veil in the tabernacle was torn in two, and the way to the Most Holy Place was opened for all (Matthew 27:51; Mark 15:38).

> **CREATIVE MESSAGE IDEA**
>
> *Meeting God at the Table*
>
> This message could lead very naturally into a communion experience. You may want to close your service by sharing together in the Lord's Supper.

Finally, the people can breathe again. All is well. They have been reminded of their forgiveness for another year. Year after year and decade after decade pass by as over and over again the high priest goes through the same process. Generations of people are born, live, sin, confess, and die. In all of this God is teaching his people about his presence.

INTERPRETIVE INSIGHT | *Narrowing the Focus*

The narrowing of a place. All throughout the building of the tabernacle in the Old Testament, there is a narrowing of focus about God's presence. God says, in effect, "Out of the *whole world* I'm going to come to *one camp*, and I'll come to *one courtyard*, and I'll come to *one tent*, and I'll come to *one box*, and that will be the place where I dwell."

The narrowing of a people. God says, "Out of *all the people* on earth, I'll come to *one nation*, I'll come to *one tribe*—the tribe of Levi. I'll come to a subset of that tribe, *the priests*—Aaron and his descendants. And I'll come to *one man,* to the high priest."

The narrowing of a time. God also says, "Out of the *year* I will choose *one month*, the tenth month. Out of this month I will choose *one week, one day,* and finally, *one moment*." That moment was when the high priest laid his hands on the head of the goat. Similarly, at one climactic moment, Jesus became the final sacrifice for sins.

God says, "One place, one man, one moment; I'll be there." The tabernacle taught people for centuries. It pointed forward to the day of Jesus. Then God said, "Now the Word has become flesh; and the Word has tabernacled among us. We saw his glory, and we saw it most fully on the cross." At that one moment the veil was ripped in two, and the greatest invitation in all human history was extended: Come to God; the way is open.

LIFE APPLICATION | *God's Dwelling Place*

Where is the Most Holy Place today? It is here and now! Any place can be the dwelling of God. Anybody is welcome to come. Any time is fine! In Christ there was a shift in the fabric of eternity from one place, one man, and one moment to the reality in which we live—anybody, anytime, anywhere.

Where is the Most Holy Place? It could be in your living room. It could be at your desk at work tomorrow. It could be on your construction site or on your high school campus. The God who was present in Israel's Most Holy Place can be present in all of his glory as you drive in your car. Right here, right now, you can tabernacle with God!

Message 9

Loving God's Law

The Book of Deuteronomy

THE HEART OF THE Message

Jesus said, "For where your treasure is, there your heart will be also" (Matthew 6:21). We live in a world that invites us to fall in love with something new every day. New products, new hobbies, new culinary sensations, and new entertainments cry out for our attention. Yet, in the midst of this cacophony of voices, God speaks to us and invites us to love his law. God does not scream his invitation; he simply sets before us the richness of his law and invites us to hear, learn, and grow to cherish the words of life and truth that his people have loved for millennia.

This message gives a window into the heart of the law as expressed in the book of Deuteronomy. When we get a clear picture of what God's law truly teaches, we begin to see why it was the prized possession of the nation of Israel. When we taste the goodness of God's law, we start to hunger for more. As we meet God, the Lawgiver, we fall more in love with him and his law.

BRIEF MESSAGE OUTLINE

1. Laws regarding giving and generosity
2. Laws regarding feasts and celebrations
3. "Head-scratching" laws

THE HEART OF THE Messenger

Do you love God's law? Do you meditate on it day and night? Do you find yourself hungering to know God's law in deeper ways? As you prepare to bring this message, meditate on the goodness of God's law. Consider taking time each day of the coming week to read a section of Psalm 119. This psalm celebrates God's law in a way that will draw you in and invite you to see it in new and fresh ways. As you read, reflect on the following questions:

When was a time that I really fell deeper in love with God's Word?

What life experiences draw me deeper into God's Word?

What can I do to make the personal study of Scripture a bigger priority in my life?

SIGNIFICANT SCRIPTURE

Deuteronomy 1:1–2; 4:1–14; 6:4–8

Introduction: Loving the Law

Deuteronomy is quoted more than eighty times in the New Testament. Only Genesis, Isaiah, and the Psalms are quoted this often. It's a very influential and powerful book that turns our heart to the law of God. In Deuteronomy we discover that God sees his people, he knows his people, and he is committed to transform them into a nation that honors him and reflects his righteous heart in a world that is dark and sin-filled. This same God still wants his children to be transformed through the process of growing in knowledge and love of his law.

INTERPRETIVE INSIGHT | *A Beginning and an End*

Imagine the setting for a moment. The people of Israel are about to enter the Promised Land after forty years of waiting. They're excited, they're afraid, they're overwhelmed, and they're curious. But Moses is not going with them. For forty years they've relied on him for all of their spiritual leadership, and now they will be moving forward without him.

For them this is just the start of their adventure, but for Moses this is the end. Moses is going to die. He knows it and they know it. This is a poignant moment in their history. What we read in Deuteronomy are the last words Moses will say to this group of people whom he has led, helped to liberate, struggled with, wrestled with, yelled at, and loved for forty years.

Deuteronomy is structured as the final message that Moses gives to these people. It comes in three sessions, or three talks. What is interesting is that Moses does not do what most people do at retirement events. He does not reminisce about his career or all he has accomplished in his life. Rather, by the inspiration of the Holy Spirit, he

HISTORICAL CONTEXT | *The Cost of a Stubborn Heart!*

In the opening two verses of Deuteronomy we get a brief geography lesson. We are told that "it takes *eleven days* to go from Horeb to Kadesh Barnea by the Mount Seir road."

This information might seem a little random at first, but it is there for a specific reason. This is not just bonus information on travel times on an ancient road. The writer wants every reader to remember that the trip from Mount Sinai, which is also known as Horeb, up to the edge of the Promised Land, *normally* takes only eleven days.

Thus, a trip that usually took a week and a half took Israel forty years to complete. The writer of Deuteronomy is subtly setting the context here: A whole generation of human beings wasted their lives in the desert and lost the opportunity to enter God's Promised Land because of their stubborn refusal to trust God and do what he said. The writer is also saying to all future readers, including us, "Don't make the same mistake. Don't blow forty years of your life on an eleven-day lesson."

gives one more appeal to the people of Israel. He calls them to follow God's plan, God's law for their lives.

In the first three chapters, Moses reviews what God has done and how often the people stumbled and messed up. Then he gives this appeal (Deuteronomy 4:1–2):

> "Hear now, O Israel, the decrees and laws I am about to teach you. Follow them so that you may live and may go in and take possession of the land that the LORD, the God of your fathers, is giving you. Do not add to what I command you and do not subtract from it, but keep the commands of the LORD your God that I give you."

WORD STUDY

The Second Telling of the Law

Deuteronomy is a desperate plea for people to *remember* and *follow* God's law. The name Deuteronomy comes from two Greek words:

- *deuteros*, meaning "second"
- *nomos*, meaning "law"

In other words this book is a second telling or second giving of the law. God knows we all need reminders, and Moses brings the people of God back to the truth they have already heard but need to hear again.

INTERPRETIVE INSIGHT | *A Prized Possession*

The law was Israel's prized possession. In Deuteronomy 4:5–14 we see that the laws of God were to be followed in a way that the world would look on in amazement. God's people knew that following the law would make them wise and discerning. They also knew that the world would look at them and see God's presence and power as they walked in obedience to his laws.

Moses calls the people to reflect deeply on this question: "What other nation is so great as to have such righteous decrees and laws as this body of laws I am setting before you today?" (Deuteronomy 4:8). Their military force, wealth, or position in the eyes of the world did not establish their greatness. Their prized possession was not the tabernacle, Solomon's temple, or even the Promised Land once they entered. The people of Israel identified the law of God as the one thing that set them apart among the nations. It was their most valued treasure.

God's law was so prized that the people were to keep their eyes focused on it. They were to hold tightly to his teachings so they would not slip through their fingers, out of their hearts, and be lost. This is an interesting image in light of the fact that later in their history, the people of Israel lost their focus, let their grasp on the law slip, and actually lost it. Recall that in the days of King Josiah, as the temple was being renovated, a copy of the law was rediscovered (2 Kings 22:1–13). Its contents shocked the king, since he was unaware of what it said.

LIFE APPLICATION | *Remembering God's Law*

In Deuteronomy 6:4–8 we see that God's intent is clear. He wants us to remember his law, and not for just a moment. It is for the next generation, and for those who follow after them. God does not want us to remember his law in the way that a high school student crams for an exam and then forgets everything after the test is done. He wants his law so deep in our hearts that nothing can shake it loose.

WORD STUDY

Shema

In Deuteronomy 6:4 we read these words, "Hear, O Israel: The LORD our God, the LORD is one." This is a declaration, a core statement of faith, that God's people have repeated over and over through the ages. The Hebrew word for this declaration is *shema*. This word means "hear." *Shema* is the first word in Deuteronomy 6:4 in the Hebrew language.

PAUSE FOR REFLECTION

What Do I Love?

The people of God showed their love for his law by spending vast amounts of time studying it, speaking of it often, committing it to memory, and letting it shape their lives. Take time for quiet reflection right in the midst of the message to give people time to think about what they truly love. You might want to suggest that they think in these categories:

- Where do I invest my time?
- What do I talk about?
- What fills my mind?
- What shapes my life and actions?

The picture God paints for us in Deuteronomy is vivid. Teach his law to the next generation and talk about it throughout the day ... any time. Reflect on it and celebrate it everywhere we go. Do whatever it takes to remember God's law. If we need to tie a string around our finger, do it. We can write it on the back of our hand if that's what it takes. Put a Post-It note on the doorway, on the mirror in the bathroom, on the refrigerator, or anywhere else we might see it. For those who are into technology, they can load it into their hand-held computer, set a reminder alarm throughout the day, and have significant Scriptures pop up just to remind them to meditate on God's law.

INTERPRETIVE INSIGHT | *Loving the Law*

The people of Israel did not see the law of God as some whip-cracking taskmaster that ruled over them. They loved the law of God. They saw how it was lifting them out of the chaotic darkness of sin and closer to the heart of God. To get a sense of how the people cherished the law, read these verses:

> [The ordinances of the LORD] are more precious than gold,
> than much pure gold;
> they are sweeter than honey,
> than honey from the comb. (Psalm 19:10)
>
> Oh, how I love your law!
> I meditate on it all day long. (Psalm 119:97)
>
> Your statutes are my heritage forever;
> they are the joy of my heart. (Psalm 119:111)

The wisest people who lived in Israel loved the law with all their hearts. We don't think about the law that much in our day. We certainly don't love and cherish it. It is unlikely that many people meditate on the legal code of their city or state. We don't love our law that way. But the Israelites saw their law as the greatest source of wisdom the world had ever seen.

1. Laws Regarding Giving and Generosity

One of the first words most children learn to say is, "Mine!" By nature we are selfish and seek our own good. Yet God is committed to help us learn the joy of generosity. He wants us to see that giving and sharing are part of his plan for our maturity. The book of Deuteronomy is filled with instruction on how God's people are called to grow in a spirit of giving. As we study Deuteronomy, we will discover that God still calls his children to a life of generosity that grows out of a profound understanding that God has given us more than we can imagine or dream.

SIGNIFICANT SCRIPTURE

Deuteronomy 15:1–8; 24:19–22;
Leviticus 27:30; 25:2, 8–12

NARRATIVE ON THE TEXT | *God's Call to Giving*

The tithe—10 percent. Leviticus 27:30 says, "A tithe of everything from the land, whether grain from the soil or fruit from the trees, belongs to the Lord; it is holy to the Lord." It is common knowledge in the church that followers of Christ are still called to give the first 10 percent of their income (harvest) to God. This was true back then and it is still true now.

The Sabbath year—14 percent. The giving for a faithful Israelite didn't stop with the tithe. In Leviticus 25:2 we read about what was called a Sabbath year. Out of concern for the earth that God had made, God says, "Every seventh year, people are not to plant anything. No sowing, no reaping, let the land rest."

That meant they would give up their income and produce a seventh of the time. Moreover, Deuteronomy 15:1 taught the people to cancel debts on the Sabbath year. The people were to forget debts and celebrate God's goodness and provision. This meant that the people of Israel would give up 14 percent of their income because, in an agricultural economy, these commands meant they would have no income for a full year every seven years!

CREATIVE MESSAGE IDEA | *You Do the Math*

Use a flip chart as you walk through the various Old Testament laws about giving and generosity. Each time you finish a category, write the percentage on the board. Use this as a visual aid to help people see that the people of Israel were called to a level of sacrificial giving that would stretch most Christ-followers today.

As you begin this exercise, do two things. First, ask people to take out a piece of paper and a pen or pencil. Invite them to follow along with you. Next, ask them to write down their guess as to what percentage of his or her income a faithful Israelite would give to God if he or she simply followed the teaching in the law. When you are done, your chart will look like this:

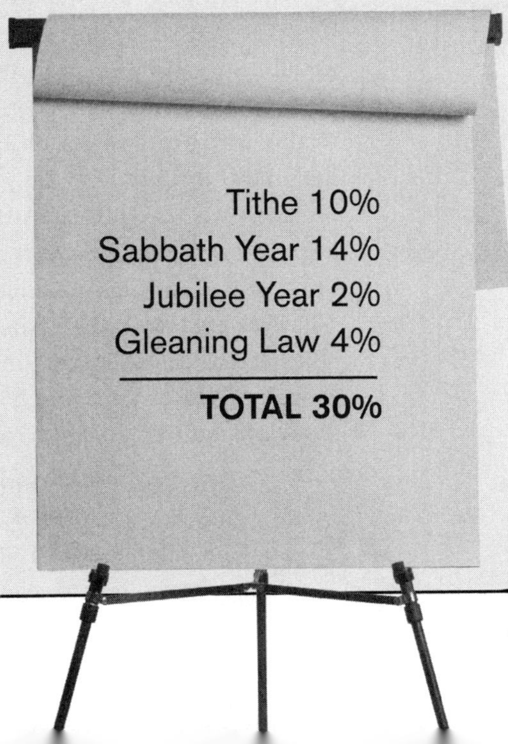

ILLUSTRATION | *A Call You Will Never Get*

Try to imagine this Sabbath spirit in our world today. You are sitting at home one evening doing your bills. You feel tension because the pile of bills is getting larger and your income is not. You are looking at the balance in your checkbook, trying to figure out how you can make ends meet for this month. All of a sudden the phone rings and startles you. You pick it up and swallow hard when you realize it is a representative from your credit card company.

You begin to explain to them that you were just sitting down to do your bills and that the check will be in the mail by the morning. They tell you not to send a check. You worry that this is some kind of a threat and that maybe they are sending over a collection agent to "make you pay." At this point they explain that it is the seventh year since you opened your account with them, so they are going to wipe your account clean. You have a zero balance! You owe them nothing. The debt and all interest are gone.

Can you imagine this happening? Of course not—and it won't. But it did happen back in Moses' day. The people following God's law learned how to live with this level of generosity.

NARRATIVE ON THE TEXT | *God's Call to Giving (continued)*

Jubilee year—2 percent. For a faithful Israelite, the giving did not stop there. Leviticus 25:8–12 teaches us that every forty-nine years God declared a year of Jubilee. Like the Sabbath year, it was a time when the earth rested and there was no planting or harvesting. It was also a time when debts were forgiven and people were set free from bondage.

This is a great picture in the Old Testament. When Jesus came, he used Jubilee language to describe the era he inaugurated. It would be a time when freedom came for all people. To prevent chronic poverty, God said in effect, "Every fifty years, all the land is to go back to its original owner." This was a radical redistribution of the wealth, where everyone got back the family inheritance that had been established in the time of Joshua.

There were two Jubilee years in every century. This meant that the Israelites would lose a full percent of income if they observed the two Jubilee years. In practical terms, this meant the giving of 2 percent of their income to the Lord.

Gleaning laws—4–5 percent. It would seem that Israelites who gave their tithes, observed the Sabbath years, and also celebrated the year of Jubilee, would be doing enough. Think about it, this is 26 percent of their income. But God was calling them to radical and sacrificial generosity. Deuteronomy 24:19–22 says:

> "When you are harvesting in your field and you overlook a sheaf, do not go back to get it. Leave it for the alien, the fatherless and the widow, so that the LORD your God may bless you in all the work of your hands. When you beat the olives from your trees, do not go over the branches a second time. Leave what remains

for the alien, the fatherless and the widow. When you harvest the grapes in your vineyard, do not go over the vines again. Leave what remains for the alien, the fatherless and the widow. Remember that you were slaves in Egypt. That is why I command you to do this."

God is telling his people to be a little sloppy when they farm. They could have gone over the fields twice and beat the olive trees a little harder to be sure everything fell to the ground, and thus they could have made a bigger profit at the market and gotten a better return on their investment. But God called them to be sloppy and always leave some in their fields.

Why? Because something inside the human heart tends to say, "I've got to wring every ounce of profit out of this I can. I've got to make every dime I can grab." To counteract this selfish tendency, God instituted the gleaning laws. These laws moved God's people to show tender compassion for the poor and needy. They were to leave something in the fields and on the trees so the poor could come through and get a little harvest to help meet their needs. It was a sign of the compassion of God extended through the hands of his people. It's hard to estimate what percentage of income the Israelites would give away from these gleaning practices, but it is safe to say it was at least 4 to 5 percent.

Final conclusions—30 percent or more! What's the total amount that would be given by the child of God who faithfully observed the laws of generosity? Faithful Israelites would give an average of 30 percent of their income to God and those in need. This is a pretty amazing thing. People often think Old Testament law calls people to give only 10 percent. The truth is, an Israelite who was devoutly following the law would have given closer to 30 percent. And it would have been higher if you include freewill offerings, which were common in those days.

ILLUSTRATION | *"Mine!" and "Not Mine!"*

Outside of the word "no," what's a two-year-old's favorite word in the whole world? It is "Mine!" Just think about it: "My blanket," "my toys," "my food," "mine, mine, mine!" This propensity to be selfish is deep in the heart of human beings. Yet God says, "I want you to learn how to let go. I want you to provide for somebody else. So, as you're farming, as you're walking through life, as you're doing your work, I want you to look at all you have and occasionally say, 'Not mine.'"

NARRATIVE ON LIFE | *Radical Commitment*

In his book *Dedication and Leadership*, Douglas Hyde tells about the radical sacrifice he had seen prior to his becoming a follower of Jesus. Hyde had been a communist during the 1930s and 1940s but had come to see the truth of the Christian faith. What troubled him, and what he writes about in his book, is how much communists

NEW TESTAMENT CONNECTION

A Dream Comes True

In the book of Acts we see this dream of sacrificial generosity lived out in the early church. The Holy Spirit descended, hearts were changed, and people began to live with an openhanded and giving attitude. "All the believers were together and had everything in common. Selling their possessions and goods, they gave to anyone as he had need" (Acts 2:44–45).

were willing to sacrifice for their cause (which was false) and how little Christians were willing to give up for the sake of Jesus.

Hyde had been a leader in the communist party for over twenty years. During most of this time he worked for the British Communist Party's daily paper, the *London Daily Worker*. He, and many others like him, had taken radical pay cuts to leave their jobs in the marketplace and take posts in the communist party. Hyde writes:

> Some of the workers were earning one-tenth of what had been their salary when they had worked for the "capitalist" press. There were times when, small as our salaries were, these could not be paid at all.
>
> Even when the paper became slightly more prosperous and the staff were technically given the union rate for the job, the sacrifices still continued. We got our packets, opened them and immediately gave eight-fourteenths of their contents to the Party and the paper—before it burned our fingers. Since everyone did this, it became something of a meaningless ritual after a while and so we did not bother even to receive the cash, it just went direct to the cause. And so it continues to this day.

When Hyde came to accept Jesus as the leader of his life, he was staggered by the meager expectations of the church when it came to his finances. He had seen people take a 90-percent pay cut to work for the communist cause. Then these same people (including him for twenty years), who had already given so much, gave over 50 percent of every paycheck to the cause. Now he heard that the church was calling people to give 10 percent to the cause of Christ. He was shocked by the small amount, and even more shocked that so few people responded to this call. Hyde also writes:

> The Communist's appeal to idealism is direct and audacious. They say if you make mean little demands upon people, you will get a mean little response, which is all you deserve, but, if you make big demands on them, you will get an historic response.

Hyde writes these things not to praise the Communist Party but to challenge those who follow Christ. If people can follow a misguided cause with such reckless abandon, why can't Christ's followers learn to sacrifice with a joy-filled surrender? Of all people, it is Christians who should be most generous and willing to sacrifice, because our Savior has sacrificed everything for us!

LIFE APPLICATION | *Tightfisted or Openhanded?*

The goal of the Old Testament laws is never to make us mechanical in our responses. In Deuteronomy 15:7–8 we read, "If there is a poor man among your brothers in any of the towns of the land that the Lord your God is giving you, do not be hardhearted or tightfisted toward your poor brother. Rather be openhanded and freely lend him whatever he needs." Imagine a community where everybody is joyfully openhanded with what they have. Think about what a community of people could be like if they made their resources available to God, to the people of God, and to those in need. We need to ask ourselves how we can grow in generosity and keep our hands open and our resources available.

NARRATIVE ON LIFE | *Put It on the Table*

At church conferences all over this country, there is a sad reality that restaurant staff members have learned to face. It is simply this: Church leaders and evangelical church members are not always famous for being generous tippers. They are often notorious for being stingier than people who don't even know God. When a leadership conference takes a lunch break and the people flood into the local restaurants (often with their name tags still on), many members of the wait staff brace themselves for the worst.

Yet, it should be just the opposite! Followers of Christ, of all people in the world, should live with an openhanded spirit of giving. We have everything! We are rich in God's mercy and goodness. We should be quick to put a great tip on the table and back it up with a joy-filled attitude.

LIFE APPLICATION | *Leave Something in the Bag*

There are many ways we can apply what we learn from the laws of generosity in Leviticus and Deuteronomy. Most churches or communities have some kind of occasional food drive or a food pantry for those who are in a time of need. One simple discipline is to begin practicing a modern application of the ancient gleaning laws. This might mean committing to buy one or two additional items to give away each time you go to the store. When you get home, put these in a separate bag and set this aside. Once the bag is full, give it away.

This practice will be a simple reminder, every time you go to the store, that God calls you to be generous toward those who are in need. You might even want to call the food pantry and ask them what they most need during that particular season of the year. Many such ministries have changing needs through the year, and being aware of specific needs could help you be strategic in your shopping. Who knows, maybe one day God will prompt you to make a shopping trip and give everything to those who are in need.

> Man should not consider his outward possessions as his own, but as common to all, so as to share them without hesitation when others are in need.
>
> *Thomas Aquinas (thirteenth century)*

---

2. Laws Regarding Feasts and Celebrations

SIGNIFICANT SCRIPTURE

Deuteronomy 16

Too often people see God as solemn and angry. They miss the reality that God is filled with passionate joy and that he calls his children to lives of committed celebration. The book of Deuteronomy recounts God's call for his people to gather for festivals and times of joy-filled remembrance. In Deuteronomy we hear the invitation to live as people who regularly celebrate the goodness of our God.

Right in the middle of Deuteronomy we find laws that have to do with feasting and celebration. There were three main feasts required in the Book of the Law. To help us remember them, we will use analogies from our national (American) experience. If you, as a teacher, are using this resource but live outside of the United States, you will need to find parallels in your national calendar to use. For instance, in the United States the Passover could be compared to the Fourth of July (Independence Day); in Mexico the best parallel holiday would be Cinco de Mayo.

PAUSE FOR PRAYER

Count Your Blessings

If we are going to grow in generosity, we will need God's help. When our eyes begin to focus on his goodness and all he has given us, our hearts will desire to give. As followers of Christ, we live with the knowledge that our heavenly Father has given us countless gifts and blessings that we could never have attained on our own. First among these gifts is Jesus, who gave his very life for us. Pause to pray and thank God for the amazing gifts he has given to his children. Pray for each person gathered to grow in their understanding of God's goodness and for hearts that will be ready to be generous toward God and those who are in need.

INTERPRETIVE INSIGHT | *Three Great Times of Celebration*

Passover (Independence Day). In Deuteronomy 16:1–8 we read about God's call for his people to remember and celebrate their independence from Egypt. The Passover marked their deliverance from bondage and the time they became free as a nation. The Fourth of July is the closest equivalent in the United States to this ancient celebration.

Passover celebrated the time when God's people became independent. But the big difference was that their hero was God. They did not fight for their freedom. Rather, God set them free and then called them to celebrate for a whole week once a year. If you look closely at Deuteronomy 16:1, you will notice the word "celebrate." Their job was to eat, rejoice, remember, be thankful, and celebrate what God had done for them. Only a God of joy would command his people to have a week-long festival every year!

The Feast of Weeks (Labor Day). The second great festival of Israel, found in Deuteronomy 16:9–12, is called the Feast of Weeks. This came during the latter part of the growing season, when they had just begun to take in the first crops. In our calendar year the holiday that marks the end of summer, when we honor the work that has been done, is Labor Day. This Israelite feast was a time to celebrate all the work that had been done and God's provision through the harvest. It is important to note that everyone was called to celebrate this festival: family members, servants, the alien, the orphan, and the widow. No one was to be left out.

The Feast of Tabernacles or Booths (Thanksgiving). The third great feast is described in Deuteronomy 16:13–17. It's called the Feast of Tabernacles or the Feast of Booths. During this feast the people would actually live in tents in order to remember when they lived in the wilderness in portable dwellings. In our day, it might be called the Feast of the Minivans or Campers. This celebration came at the end of the harvest, after the entire harvest had been brought in. In our calendar the time we remember our earliest settlers' thanking God for the harvest is Thanksgiving Day. This is the best modern-day equivalent to remind us of the spirit of the Feast of Booths.

INTERPRETIVE INSIGHT | *Celebrate and Rejoice*

There are two words that come up again and again when these feasts and remembrances are commanded in the Pentateuch: *celebrate* and *rejoice*. God is deeply concerned that we grow as people of joy. He wants us, he commands us, to celebrate his great works and amazing provision. In Deuteronomy 16:14 the people are told to "be joyful at your feasts." What a great reminder!

LIFE APPLICATION | *The Issue of Inclusiveness*

Notice God's concern for including everyone in the celebration (Deuteronomy 16:1–12). The religious leaders, who had no land as their possession, were called to be part of the festival. The immigrants, widows, and orphans were also to be included. They were to be invited, and provision was to be made for them.

God still wants his followers to invite others to join in our celebrations. From church services to backyard holiday BBQs, God wants us to invite others to join in the joy. Our joyous celebrations speak volumes to a world that looks on and wonders if our faith is real. Each time we get ready for some kind of celebration, why not ask ourselves, *Are there people I know who need a little joy in their lives? Whom might I invite to a special church event, a party, or some gathering where Christ-followers are going to be celebrating life?* We can learn to include others in our modern-day festivals and watch what happens as they are swept into the joy of God and his people.

INTERPRETIVE INSIGHT | *Set Apart by Joy*

Many people think that the Old Testament is a story of a dark, grim God overseeing a scared and somber people. It is not so. God calls his people to be holy. "Be holy as I am holy" means to "be set apart." One of the ways God's people were to be holy, unique, set apart, was to be joyful. The law commands the feasts as reminders, in a sense a kind of training exercise, for joy. Many people have trouble being joyful, but God is ready to help us grow in joy.

If you want to see how serious God is about our growth in joy, look at Deuteronomy 14:22–27. God tells people who can't make it to the formal celebration to plan their own personal festival. God does not want them to miss out on the party! They were called to take their tithe of produce and trade it for silver. Then they were to buy food and drink and resources and throw a party right where they were. Can you believe that's in the Bible? God calls his people to be set apart, and one of the best ways is when our lives reflect the joyful heart of God.

LIFE APPLICATION | *Feast Days*

How are we doing in the joy category? If we need a little help growing in joy, it might be good to establish a personal feast day once a week. On this day we could eat food we love to eat, listen to music we love to hear, and wear clothes that make us happy. We might even make a point of connecting with people who bring joy to our lives. What a wonderful discipline it would be to establish weekly or monthly days of feasting and joy!

INTERPRETIVE INSIGHT | *God's Desire for His Children*

The laws about feasts are wonderful. They are designed to free us and train us to become joyful people. God says, "Why don't you get together for a week and just celebrate? Remember my goodness and rejoice in it, revel in it, drink it in!" What is amazing is that God calls his people to this level of celebration many times every year. What a truly joyful God we serve! God wants us to commit ourselves to consistent and passionate celebration of his goodness, because if we keep doing it week after week, month after month, and year after year, there's a good chance that we will become convinced that God is good. As this conviction grows, we will become more joyful people.

ON THE LIGHTER SIDE | *Joy-Challenged People*

We all know people who are joy-challenged. These are the folks who have the ability to see the cloud inside every silver lining. They have what might be called the "Eeyore Complex." There might be days we need to tell them, "I can't be with you today. It's my feast day today. You'll suck the joy right out of me. I'll be with you tomorrow, but not today. Today I will be walking in joy."

Of course, we would not say it just like that. We would be a little more diplomatic. But the truth is that there should be days we give ourselves space to walk in joy, and this might mean avoiding those who bring our joy-quotient way down. We can encourage them and help them grow in joy another day.

3. "Head-Scratching" Laws

SIGNIFICANT SCRIPTURE

Exodus 21:22–24; Deuteronomy 24:1–4; Matthew 5

In addition to the laws about generosity and festivals, there are other laws throughout the Pentateuch that can be somewhat confusing. We might call these "head-scratching" laws. These laws seem strange, severe, or sometimes contradictory to the way we envision God.

Through the Pentateuch we read laws that say:

- If you have a rebellious son, you can stone him.
- People can have slaves.
- A husband can write a certificate of divorce to his wife and just send her away if he is displeased with her.
- A woman's vows to God must be cleared through her husband or her father.
- "Eye for eye, tooth for tooth, hand for hand, foot for foot, burn for burn, wound for wound, bruise for bruise" (Exodus 21:24–25).

How do we respond to these laws? In this section we will look at these "head-scratching" laws and put them in a historical context that will help us make sense of them.

ILLUSTRATION | *Eagles, Robins, and Pigeons*

In the early years of grade school there are often three reading groups. The teacher always pretends that these groups are all the same, but everyone knows this is not the case. You can tell which group is which by their names. For instance, you might have the eagles as one group — they are the best readers. Then there might be the robins —

HISTORICAL CONTEXT | *Starting Where We Are*

God has to start where people are. We must remember that at this time in history, the Old Testament had not been written. There were no Scriptures. There was no law of God, and morality was at a rock-bottom level. The world was in relational, spiritual, and moral chaos.

To put it in context, there were all kinds of common practices that would be shocking today. Child sacrifice was practiced and was even part of some religious rituals in pagan worship. Radical revenge and retribution was acceptable. If someone was wronged, they would often take revenge on a whole family rather than just the person who offended them. In some cases, they would take vengeance on a whole city. Cult prostitution existed all over this part of the ancient world, and the people of Israel saw this happening as a normative practice.

As God began to call a community of people to follow him, he started where they were. There was no morality, so he began to introduce beginning steps so they could understand. In a similar way, God still meets each of us where we are and then begins to lead us to where he wants us to be.

these students can read fairly well, but they still need some work. Finally, there are the pigeons — these kids know that they will not be soaring with the eagles.

As we look back at the people of Israel at this time in their history, they are in the pigeon group. Spiritually speaking, they are not eagles or even robins. These are the pigeons. That's what Deuteronomy 1:2 is all about. That is why it took them forty years to take an eleven-day walk. This is not the advance-placement class.

INTERPRETIVE INSIGHT | *Fully Inspired Yet Written by and for Real People*

The Bible is not an example of God dictating heavenly rules for perfect angels. The law was not written by or for angels. Just as Jesus was both fully divine and fully human, the Bible is both fully inspired by God and also written by real human beings. These people had to wrestle, study, and think long and hard about what they wrote.

The Bible was written in a context for real people who had habits, customs, and patterns that were unbelievably destructive. God did not give them everything all at once; they would not have been ready for it. In a sense, God was slowly weaning them away from what was destructive and teaching them the new way of life.

NEW TESTAMENT CONNECTION | *The Issue of Hardheartedness*

A great example of this is found in Mark 10. In this passage Jesus is teaching about the Old Testament law. Mark 10:2–5 says:

> Some Pharisees came and tested him by asking, "Is it lawful for a man to divorce his wife?"
>
> "What did Moses command you?" he replied.
>
> They said, "Moses permitted a man to write a certificate of divorce and send her away."
>
> "It was because your hearts were hard that Moses wrote you this law," Jesus replied.

It is important for us to understand Jesus' interpretation, his understanding, of the Old Testament. He tells them it was because of hardheartedness that Moses permitted divorce. Jesus uses the same word found in those early chapters of Deuteronomy — stubborn, stiff-necked, and hardhearted.

Jesus goes on to teach that God's plan was always for the permanence of marriage. When the Pharisees ask why Moses allowed men to write a certificate of divorce, Jesus basically says, "Because Moses was working with the pigeons. It was a concession to hardheartedness."

You've got to start somewhere, and Moses was taking a first step in getting people to begin taking marriage seriously and to create some accountability. But God's intent was clear in the Old Testament to anybody who looks with an honest, open heart. If we look at Genesis 2, we see that God's plan was for one husband and one wife for an entire lifetime. Jesus was not setting the law aside; he was correctly interpreting it.

INTERPRETIVE INSIGHT | *Restraining Common Practices*

Often, because God was working with the pigeons back in Moses' day, the laws were given to wean people away from unhealthy and ungodly practices. Because the people's hearts were hard, the strategy was to put limits and restraints around these practices and to help them begin to take steps of change.

For instance, slavery already existed when the Old Testament was written. Moses did not eradicate slavery completely, but a limit of six years was established. Moses also taught that a slave was to be regarded as a brother. Slaves were even allowed to worship with the people of God. Moses said that when a slave was released he should be given gifts to help establish him in freedom. In light of where things were at this time, these were huge steps forward. From where we stand today, they might seem like a step backwards, but in that day, this showed forward progression in human rights and the dignity of people.

When we look at Genesis 1–2, we read that human beings were made in the image of God. That's not compatible with slavery. That's not compatible with God's ultimate dream for the human race. So God kept moving people forward until they finally realized that no one should ever be a slave!

NEW TESTAMENT CONNECTION | *An Eye for An Eye*

Another example of this concerns Jesus' statement in the Sermon on the Mount, "You have heard that it was said, 'Eye for eye, and tooth for tooth'" (Matthew 5:38). Jesus is quoting from Deuteronomy 19:21 here (also Exodus 21:24; Leviticus 24:20).

In the ancient world, the world in which Moses lived, people with power took whatever vengeance they wanted on somebody who hurt them. If someone was hurt a little bit, they could hurt back a lot. Not only that, but they would even inflict punishment on the next of kin. If they couldn't get at the perpetrator, they would attack and punish a son, daughter, spouse, or even extended family and friends. This disproportionate punishment was common practice. It was considered acceptable.

In light of this, when Moses wrote, "Eye for an eye, tooth for a tooth," it was not encouraging vengeance; it was *limiting it.* This law was intended to restrain vengeance. It taught that evil must be punished, but the punishment must be proportionate, not disproportionate. In light of where people were at this time in history, the people would have realized that this law was given to discourage violence, not to encourage it.

But then Jesus begins talking about loving enemies and offering grace (Matthew 5:39–48). We might wonder: Is Jesus saying that the Old Testament was wrong? The answer is no! Instead, he is taking the limiting power of the law to the next level. He is saying that the time of pigeon responses to enemies is gone, and it is time to soar like an eagle.

NARRATIVE ON LIFE | *How Jesus Describes God*

Jesus describes the Father in ways that help us know God and love him even more. The God Jesus describes is a God who watches out for sparrows and clothes the lilies of the field. He counts the hairs on our head and searches for a single lost sheep. That's the God Jesus loves, and human beings were so captivated by that picture of God that they sacrificed their lives to follow Jesus.

Many people think there is a gap between the God of the Old Testament and the God Jesus describes. But there is at least one person in history who did not think there was any gap between the God of the Old Testament and the God Jesus knew. That person was Jesus!

We must remember that Jesus is a really smart guy. He read the same Old Testament we read. He was the greatest scholar, interpreter, and teacher of the Old Testament who ever lived. Jesus was convinced that the God he read about in the Old Testament was the same God he describes so beautifully.

PAUSE FOR PRAYER | *Closing the Message*

As you close the message, consider inviting people to begin praying these words, "May I find in the Old Testament the God that Jesus found." What a wonderful prayer to guide each person as they continue forward in their study of the Old Testament.

Part 2

Stepping Out in Faith

Life-Changing Examples from the History of Israel

Message 10

Joshua: The Law of the First Step

The Book of Joshua

THE HEART OF THE Message

If we are going to follow God, we will have to live by faith. There is no other way. To walk with God *is* to walk in faith. The people of Israel had to learn this message over and over, and so do we!

In the book of Joshua God's people are called to take huge steps of faith. In some cases, their human minds cannot make sense of God's way of doing things. But they learn to follow even when his leading is beyond their understanding. What is the law of the first step? *Sometimes God waits to act until we begin to move in faith!* When we step out in faith, God reveals his power and presence. When we take the first step, God shows up and reveals his glorious might. However, if we stand still, paralyzed by fear, and refuse to take the first step, we may miss the faith-building experience of seeing God at work.

BRIEF MESSAGE OUTLINE

1. God's love for every generation
2. The law of the first step
3. Lessons in first-step living

THE HEART OF THE Messenger

As you prepare this message, take time to do a personal inventory of your own heart and life. Are there places God is calling you to step out in faith, but you are not responding? Is there fear in your heart that has caused you to freeze up and miss an opportunity to walk in faith? If you are going to teach about taking risky steps of faith, it may be time for you to walk with a new measure of boldness and confidence in God's power to act. As you prepare to bring this message to God's people, invite the Holy Spirit to infuse you with a boldness and a willingness to take a first step of faith in an area you have been resisting his leading.

SIGNIFICANT SCRIPTURE

Deuteronomy 5:8–10

1. God's Love for Every Generation

The generation of Israelites who left Egypt free from Pharaoh's clutch had died in the desert because of their refusal to trust God. They could not believe that God had the power to overcome the nations on the other side of the Jordan. They did not trust him to enable them to occupy the Promised Land. That lack of faith consigned them for the forty years of wandering in the desert. Now there is a new generation of Israelites, who must decide if they will have greater faith than those who came before them. They must determine whether they believe God can lead them into the Promised Land, even when it seems the odds are against them.

INTERPRETIVE INSIGHT | *Understanding Hebrew Poetry*

The only way we can make sense of Deuteronomy 5:8–10 is by taking some time to do a little background on how to read Hebrew poetry. The Old Testament is filled with examples of poetic structures that must be read in a specific way. Hebrew poetry is primarily characterized by something called *parallelism*. In English, we tend to recognize poems because the words rhyme or have a certain meter. In Hebrew poetry, however, the primary characteristic is how one word or sentence parallels

ILLUSTRATION | *"You Are in Trouble!"*

Some passages in the Bible are hard to understand. Through this series we refer to them as passages that make us say, "What's up with that?" These passages tend to confuse people if they read them quickly and don't take the time to dig in and discover what is actually being said. One such passage is Deuteronomy 5:8. All through the Bible we learn that God loves people. He is passionate about us. Yet, in this verse, it seems as if God is presented as unfair, harsh, and even unloving. Until we dig in and see what this passage is really saying, this misunderstanding will remain in the minds of many people.

Deuteronomy 5:8 can be a little confusing. Imagine a father sitting down with his little girl when she is five years old and saying, "Young lady, I just found out that your grandmother, your mother's mother, has been masterminding an auto theft ring in California. Your grandmother is breaking the law! She is out of control!" Then this little girl's daddy looks at her sternly and says, "Young lady, you are grounded! You can't play with your friends; you will have a very long time-out. If your grandmother does not straighten up, you might not be going to your senior prom in about thirteen years! You better hope your grandmother gets her act together or you're going to be in really deep water!"

This is quite a harsh scenario. The little girl would naturally feel the punishment is unfair and undeserved, and anyone who hears about this father's proposed punishment would probably agree with the little girl!

another word or sentence. In its simplest form, Hebrew parallelism expresses the same thought, in different words, in two successive lines. See Psalm 19:1 as an example:

> The heavens declare the glory of God;
> the skies proclaim the work of his hands.

"The heavens" in the first line is parallel to "the skies" in the second line, "declare" is parallel to "proclaim," and "the glory of God" is parallel to "the work of his hands." Both lines say the same thing with different words.

There are dozens of variations of Hebrew parallel structure in the Bible. One of them involves numbers. Sometimes to emphasize a key point the writer will use what is called numerical parallelism. Examples can be found in Proverbs 6:16 and 30:15b:

> There are six things which the LORD hates,
> seven that are detestable to him. (6:16)
>
> There are three things that are never satisfied,
> four that never say, "Enough!" (30:15b)

In the second line of Proverbs 6:16 the writer is not saying that he just thought of another thing God hates. Rather, it is a way of giving poetic emphasis to a single point. It is meant to draw our attention to all seven things the Lord hates!

Another variation on Hebrew numerical parallelism occurs when the numbers draw out a dramatic contrast. In Genesis 4:24 we read:

> If Cain is avenged seven times,
> then Lamech seventy-seven times.

Lamech says this as a way of pointing out a contrast. "If you think there was danger going after Cain, that's nothing compared to the danger of going after me." The point of these numbers is to draw out the *difference* between them.

Another example of numerical parallelism is found in 1 Samuel 18:8:

> Saul was very angry; this refrain galled him. "They have credited David with tens of thousands," he thought, "but me with only thousands. What more can he get but the kingdom?"

King Saul of Israel is saying, "The people say that I've only slain thousands in battle, but David ten times that many." This song of the people is a form of numerical parallelism, and Saul does not miss the contrast—he gets the point so well that it angers him!

In Deuteronomy 5:9b–10 we read:

> "I, the LORD your God, am a jealous God, punishing the children for the sin of the fathers to the *third and fourth* generation of those who hate me, but showing love to a *thousand* generations of those who love me and keep my commandments."

The numerical contrast captured here is not just ten or eleven times bigger; it's hundreds of times bigger. This is by far the most dramatic example in all of the Old

Testament of Hebrew parallelism that draws out a numerical contrast. The key thing to realize is that this is *not a statement of emphasis*. Rather, it is clearly an expression of *contrast*. Notice in verse 10 God says, "I ... am a jealous God, punishing the children for the sin of the fathers to the third and fourth generation of those who hate me, *but* [here is the contrast] showing love to a thousand generations [or thousands of generations] of those who love me...."

The teaching here is that God is ready to punish sin. We must not be deceived. He will judge evil. He will. But it's not what he longs to do. What he longs to do is show love. God is willing to punish, but he's longing to show love.

Notice the last phrase in verse 9, "punishing the children for the sin of the fathers to the third and fourth generation *of those who hate me*" (or "those who rebel against me"). This phrase is describing the *third* and *fourth* generation. In other words, God is not saying he will punish a future generation of innocent people who haven't done anything wrong, because their ancestors sinned. The punishment will come only if that third or fourth generation hates God. If they rebel against God like their ancestors, they too will be punished for their sin.

INTERPRETIVE INSIGHT | *Identifying Generational Sin*

There is an important warning in this passage about what is sometimes called "generational sin." This occurs when unresolved problems and sins of one generation tend to pop up again and plague the next generation, and the next one, and the one after that. Children who are victims of mismanaged anger or rage are much more likely to have anger problems of their own and pass them on to the next generation. Young people who grow up in a family where deceit is commonly practiced learn it, and they are much more likely to have problems telling the truth. The same is true for children in families where there is divorce or sexual addiction.

When we are growing up, we often look at the previous generation and see patterns of unhealthy behavior and sin and say to ourselves, "I'm never going to be like that." But what happens? We get caught in the same trap until somewhere along the line somebody in some generation makes a courageous decision to change.

LIFE APPLICATION | *Breaking the Chain*

Many people are at a decisive point where they must make a decision to break the generational sin that is plaguing their life and family. What if you have deeply entrenched patterns of sin that go back a generation or two or three? What if you are seeing this same pattern develop in the lives of your children? What can you do when you realize that your sinful attitudes, choices, and actions are poisoning the lives of the next generation?

When we face our sin and realize that it is infecting our children (and it always does), we must make a mammoth decision—to decide what we love more, our sin or our children! We have to ask, "Which one am I willing to sacrifice, my sin or my son? What do I love more, my daughter or my sin?"

It is not enough just to do our best to hide the sin from our kids or to try to manage it. We have to repent and change the way we are living, thinking, and speaking. Such a decision takes a lot of courage. We must get ready to say, "I'm going to break the chain. It stops here. I'll do whatever I have to do. I'll bring this behavior or pattern or habit into the light. I will enter into accountable relationships. I'll go to a Christian counselor and get help if that's what I need to do. I'll do whatever it takes, but the legacy of sin stops here. I will not hand it on to my children. I love them too much."

God has not condemned us to suffer the fate of our ancestors. Our God's desire is to heal and show love. He'll wait a thousand generations if he has to. God cheers for every generation.

SIGNIFICANT SCRIPTURE

Joshua 1:1 – 9

NARRATIVE ON THE TEXT | *A New Generation*

A new generation stands on the banks of the Jordan. God does not want them to experience the pain of forty years in the desert as their parents did. The old generation suffered from a serious case of the grasshopper syndrome. They had said, "We're just grasshoppers in the eyes of our enemies and in our own eyes. We're small and inadequate. We could never occupy the Promised Land" (cf. Numbers 13:33). Although God had promised the previous generation that he would lead them and empower them to take the land, they stayed east of the Jordan and refused to enter into God's plan.

Now their children are looking west and wondering if they will have the faith to do what their parents did not. God speaks to the new generation and assures them that the land is theirs for the taking. He calls them to be "strong and courageous" and go up to take the land. God calls them to hold his law in their hearts and promises

HISTORICAL CONTEXT | *Waiting for Deliverance*

The expression "third day" (see page 164) is used so frequently in the Old Testament that it may have become a technical expression meaning the short time of waiting for God's deliverance. Often a word or term takes on a certain colloquial meaning that goes beyond the simple words. It may well have been that when the people of Israel heard the expression "third day," they began to anticipate some way that God's deliverance and power would be experienced soon. Hosea wrote:

> After two days he will revive us;
> on the third day he will restore us,
> that we may live in his presence.
> (Hosea 6:2)

This verse uses Hebrew numerical parallelism to bring this point home. The third day was a time of restoration and revelation of the presence of God!

NEW TESTAMENT CONNECTION

Third-Day People

The many examples of third-day hope and deliverance in the Old Testament set the groundwork for the ultimate third day. The apostle Paul writes, "For what I received I passed on to you as of first importance: that Christ died for our sins according to the Scriptures, that he was buried, that he was *raised on the third day* according to the Scriptures" (1 Corinthians 15:3–4).

The third day is the greatest day in the history of this world! The third day is when prisoners get set free, mountains shake, rivers get parted, harem girls face down kings, and prophets get dropped off at seaside ports by giant fish. It's the day stones get rolled away and a carpenter opens his eyes and comes back to life. Since Jesus rose on the third day, the world has never been the same.

From that day to this, Jesus' followers have observed that resurrection third day. The apostle John, in Revelation 1:10, called it "the Lord's Day." We are third-day people now. We are betting the farm on this one. The same Jesus who rose on the third day promises us hope of eternal life.

that he will be with them every step of the way. God's command to Joshua and the people is crystal clear: "Be strong, be courageous." Why? "I will be with you. Everywhere you set your foot, I've already gone ahead of you. I'll be right there." God is saying to Joshua and his generation, "Don't live in fear!"

God had given this same message to the parents of these people when Moses was their leader. Yet they were unable to take the step of faith needed to cross the Jordan and enter the land. Once again, God is ready to lead his people forward in victory. The question is, are they ready to follow?

INTERPRETIVE INSIGHT | *The Third Day*

Joshua sends out the word to the Israelites that they will be crossing the Jordan. After forty years in the desert they hear the command: "Get your supplies ready. Three days from now you will cross the Jordan here to go in and take possession of the land the Lord your God is giving you for your own" (Joshua 1:11). The phrase we should notice is "three days from now." Often in the Old Testament, people are told they'll have to wait a short while for divine deliverance. Consistently the waiting period is three days. The three-day time period became a time of anticipation for God's people.

- Joseph says to the cupbearer in prison that in *three days* Pharaoh will free him from prison and restore him to his job (Genesis 40:13).
- Moses asks Pharaoh, "Let us take a three-day journey into the desert" (Exodus 3:18). You may wonder, why three days? That gets explained in Exodus when they get to Mount Sinai. God says, "Consecrate them today and … have them … be ready by the third day, because on that day the Lord will come down" (Exodus 19:10–11).
- Esther says that she will fast for three days and then go to the king to seek deliverance for her people (Esther 4:16).
- Jonah is inside the fish three days and three nights (Jonah 1:17).

NARRATIVE ON THE TEXT | *Betting It All!*

God has something extraordinary in mind for Joshua and Israel on the third day. God tells his people to "get ready." Joshua sends two spies into Jericho. Rahab risks her own life to protect them. When you think about it, that is remarkable. If anybody else in Jericho were

ON THE LIGHTER SIDE *A Strange Prayer*

A pastor once said that Jonah's prayer during those three days in the belly of the great fish may have been, "God, just let me go out the same way I came in." Think about that one, but don't think about it too much!

to find out that she hid spies of the nation that was about to invade their land, her life would have been worthless. They would have killed her. Rahab risks her own life to protect these men because she's betting everything on the God of Israel.

She does what God would want her to do. This is so remarkable because Rahab is a pagan and a prostitute. Yet, she is mentioned in the genealogy in the gospel of Matthew. She becomes a hero in Israel's history. Rahab is listed as an ancestor of Jesus and is honored by being mentioned in Matthew, in the book of Hebrews, and in the book of James.

SIGNIFICANT SCRIPTURE

Joshua 2:1 – 16

2. The Law of the First Step

The people have waited forty years, and now there seems to be no way they can cross the river. Into this seemingly hopeless situation God says, "Not a problem. I'll make a way. My power is sufficient. I'm Lord over all the earth, including the waters of the Jordan." God assures the people that he will make it possible for them to cross the Jordan, even at flood stage. There is just one condition. They have to step into the Jordan River first; then he will part the waters. It won't work the other way around. God won't part the waters first. They must take a step of faith, and then they will see God move in power.

What is the law of the first step? *Sometimes God waits to act until we begin to move in faith!* When we take the step of faith, God parts the waters. He is teaching an important lesson to his people on the banks of the Jordan. It is a lesson God is teaching his people today: "When you face a huge obstacle and you are sure you can't surmount it, my power is sufficient. I will make a way. I will deliver you. But you've got to trust me. You've got to take the first step." He wants us to know that when we walk in faith, we will see his power displayed in amazing ways. But we won't see it until we trust him enough to obey him. We have to take the first step.

INTERPRETIVE INSIGHT *The Significance of the Jordan*

To the people of Israel the Jordan River was always seen as a literal and symbolic barrier. It was something that they had to get across to enter the land God had prepared for them. Moses' final wish expressed in Deuteronomy 3:25 was: "Let me go over and see the good land beyond the Jordan." The only thing between Moses and his dream of entering the Promised Land was the Jordan.

To the people who lived west of the Jordan in the land of Canaan, the Jordan represented protection. This river helped keep their enemies away. Their primary pagan god, Baal, was the god of water (among other things). Often in the ancient world, because water was so prized, the gods were supposed to have power over water.

SIGNIFICANT SCRIPTURE

Joshua 3:1 – 13

That's one of the reasons why many Old Testament miracles involve water. Think about it: God parted the Red Sea, provided miraculous supplies of water several times in the desert, and dried up the Jordan River during the flood season! God is saying to his people and to the nations who were watching, "I really am the Lord of *all* the earth."

INTERPRETIVE INSIGHT | *Geography of the Jordan*

To understand the significance of God's call for the people to cross the Jordan at this time, we must understand more about the river itself. The Jordan started on Mount Hermon at an elevation of about seven thousand feet. There were springs up in the mountain that fed the Jordan and snow that melted in the springtime. The Jordan ended in the Dead Sea, which is the lowest body of water in the world (1,290 feet below sea level). This means the water in the Jordan River moves pretty rapidly. Some scholars think the word "Jordan" comes from a Hebrew word that meant "river that descends rapidly."

Normally the Jordan is not difficult to cross, because it is not a big river. When you picture the Jordan in your mind, you must not think in terms of the Mississippi River. Think much smaller. In Joshua's day, in many places the Jordan was only three to six feet deep. Archaeologists have found about sixty places all along the Jordan River where it used to be forded. If an army held a site along the Jordan where the river could be crossed easily, this spot held strategic significance. Most of the year it was not difficult to find a place to cross the Jordan.

During the flood season, however, it was a whole different story. The waters would surge from the heights of Mount Hermon and overflow the normal river bed. These rushing waters would fill a second and larger area called the Zor. This expanded river-

HISTORICAL CONTEXT | *Rivers in the Ancient World*

God gives careful instructions to the people of Israel. After three days the officers go through the camp giving orders to the people. All the people are to go down to the Jordan River, and the priests will carry the ark of the covenant; they are to lead the way. The people are assured that when the priests (who carry the ark of the Lord) set foot in the Jordan, its waters will be cut off and the people will cross on dry ground.

The Jordan defines the eastern border of Israel. Because water was such a precious thing in the ancient world, it was common for people to consider the primary river of their country sacred. That was true for Egypt (Nile) and India (Ganges). It was never the case for the Jordan River. It was never considered sacred or holy.

bed was about 150 feet wide and 10 to 20 feet deep. At flood stage, this gorge, the Zor, filled all the way up. To make things even more treacherous, the banks of this gorge are essentially perpendicular. This meant, during the flood season, that stepping into the Jordan was much like a death sentence. What we must remember is that the time God called his people to step into the Jordan was right during the most dangerous time to cross the river (Joshua 3:15).

INTERPRETIVE INSIGHT | *Always Remember*

This was a significant moment in the history of God's people. They have waited forty years, and they have finally reached the Jordan. The waters are at flood stage, and guess what happens? The people step into the river and into a whole new chapter of their history and faith. When their feet hit the rushing waters, God parts the river. They all walk across to the other side on dry land in complete safety. This is a landmark moment, so God calls them to set up a memorial so they will never forget the law of the first step.

God tells his people to get twelve men, one from each tribe, and gather twelve stones to pile up as a visual reminder of God's power and presence at this moment of their history. They are to build a memorial to the Lord. This memorial will remain there for their children and their children's children to see. This is such an important moment that God wants to be sure the next generation hears about it. When their children ask, "What do these stones mean?" (Joshua 4:6), their parents can tell the story once again and teach the next generation that sometimes God's people must take a step first in order to see the deliverance of the Lord!

Here's the kicker. The people of Israel are supposed to get the twelve stones for the memorial from the Jordan. It is important to note that they are not only getting them from the Jordan, but from the *middle* of the Jordan (Joshua 4:3). They have just arrived at the other side, and God says, "Go back in. I want you to trust me. If you want to see my power in your life, you'll have to take the risk of trusting me, of obeying me first."

LIFE APPLICATION | *Where Is Your Jordan?*

What's your Jordan River? Where is God asking you to take a step of faith? The truth is, everybody faces the Jordan many times in the course of his or her life. Everybody

CREATIVE MESSAGE IDEA | *Map Time*

You will find a series of maps and visuals of the Jordan (and the Zor) in the PowerPoint presentation on the DVD-ROM resource. Use these to describe the Jordan River at its normal level and flood level. These maps will also illustrate the topography of the Jordan.

faces barriers. If we are not careful, these experiences can prevent us from leading the kind of life God wants. We can be like the first generation in the desert who refused to cross the Jordan and died in the desert. Or we can take that first step into the Jordan, watch the waters part, and enter into God's adventure.

God says, "I've gone ahead of you. I'll be there. I'll occupy the land. But you've got to choose. You have to believe in me enough to take the first step, no matter how much it scares you." God wants us to step into the river! How do you know what your Jordan is? *Your fear will tell you.*

3. Lessons in First-Step Living

INTERPRETIVE INSIGHT | *A Dangerous First Step*

Once the nation has crossed the Jordan, it would seem that the next natural step is to begin their conquest of the land. God promised this entire territory to them, and now it is in their grasp. God surprises Joshua and all the people by calling them to take a different approach to their first few days in the Promised Land. He says that all the men of Israel should be circumcised. Apparently during the desert wanderings they have not upheld the sign of the Abrahamic covenant. This generation has never been circumcised.

Think about this for a moment. The nations are watching and waiting. They are aware of this massive military force lurking on their border. Now they have crossed over. They are a clear and present danger. The people of the land are on high alert!

Now imagine you are a soldier in the army of Israel. You have crossed into enemy territory. You are poised to march in and take the land. You are on the west side of the Jordan River at flood stage, and there is no escape route from your enemies if they

ON THE LIGHTER SIDE | *First in Line*

The priests were supposed to lead the way across the Jordan River. They were leaders who would have the chance to show their faith by stepping into the swollen waters of the flooded river. Think about being the priest on the front end of the ark of the covenant. As you are walking toward the Jordan, you are saying to yourself, "Just one foot in," that's what Joshua says. But you know that when one foot goes into this river, your whole body is going in.

Remember, you are carrying the ark of the covenant. You don't drop the ark! The ark is heavy to start with, and then it is filled with the stone tablets with the Ten Commandments. It is not likely to float with all that gold and stone.

If you or I were the lead priest carrying the ark, we might be tempted to say to the priest behind us, "You know, I think I was in front yesterday. I think it's your turn to go in front."

come after you. This is the moment you have been waiting for. With a willing spirit you await the official word from your commander-in-chief. Finally it comes, but, to your surprise, it is not an order to attack. The word comes from the top: It is time for all the men to be circumcised!

What? Wait a minute! What kind of a military strategy is this? Isn't this a risky move at best and a highly dangerous one at worst? The men of Israel, every able-bodied man and soldier, will be flat on their backs in pain and demanding recovery for a number of days. It seems obvious that Joshua's announcement for all the men to be circumcised is not a real morale booster.

SIGNIFICANT SCRIPTURE

Joshua 5

LIFE APPLICATION | *Do You Really Trust Me?*

In the call for the men to be circumcised we see God reestablishing his covenant with the people. But we also hear God asking the people, "Do you really trust me? Do you believe I can protect you? Are you confident that I am sufficient for you? Will you obey me even when it seems dangerous to do so?"

God is asking the people how much they trust him. Will they take another step of faith? At this same time we discover another trust lesson. We read that "the day after the Passover, that very day, they ate some of the produce of the land: unleavened bread and roasted grain. The manna stopped the day after they ate this food from the land; there was no longer any manna for the Israelites, but that year they ate of the produce of Canaan" (Joshua 5:11 – 12). God proved his trustworthiness day after day, week after week, month after month, decade after decade, by providing the manna. Now that they have the produce of the land, the manna is no longer needed. At that moment, God stops providing. God is showing them that they can trust him in a unique way. He proves his presence by taking away something they don't need! No more manna is needed because they are in the land of milk and honey.

INTERPRETIVE INSIGHT | *God's Way Versus My Way*

From an outward appearance it would seem that Israel can take this city without much effort. A siege by an army their size would lead to a victory and the conquest of Jericho in a short time. It is an opportunity for the army of Israel to flex their muscles. Instead, God says, "Here's your command. I want you to walk around this city, which you can defeat, for seven days. The seventh day, walk around the city seven times and then blow your trumpets."

These soldiers have been thinking about this moment for years. They are ready for battle; this is their first time to march out in force to take their land. You have to believe they are going to feel a little goofy marching in circles and blowing trumpets. This is not what they signed up for. This is not in the "Conquer Canaan" military training manual! This is not your typical soldier's behavior. But God makes it clear why they must take this approach. He will be the one giving them the first city of the land, the first conquest after crossing the Jordan, their first victory in their new home. This is why we read, "Shout! For the LORD has given you the city!" (Joshua 6:16).

God is saying, "Will you trust me enough to do something that feels and looks foolish, even when you can do it in your own strength and look impressive and strong? Will you trust me? Will you take the risk?" This theme goes throughout the book of Joshua. God still wants to know if his people will continue taking first steps of faith.

SIGNIFICANT SCRIPTURE

Joshua 6

INTERPRETIVE INSIGHT | *The Spirit of Caleb*

Caleb is one of twelve spies Moses sent to explore the land so many years earlier. Of those twelve, he and Joshua were the only ones with enough faith to believe God could help them conquer the land. They came back and said, "Let's go for it. We can surely do this thing."

But because of Israel's unbelief, Caleb has to spend forty years of his life in the desert. He was ready to go! He had faith! But his life was impacted by the lack of faith in the hearts of those around him. Think about what that could have done to Caleb's attitude and spirit. Four decades of his life were spent wandering in the desert. The consequences he faced were not because of anything he did wrong but because of what other people have done.

LIFE APPLICATION | *"My Sin"*

Sometimes we forget that "my sin" is never just mine. We don't commit sin in a vacuum. Our sin touches those we love; it always impacts people around us. When we sin, we pay the price. But so do our children, spouse, friends, and others who are connected with us.

Here is a simple but profound exercise anyone can do to help resist sin. Sit down with a blank sheet of paper and do four things.

1. At the top of the sheet, write down the specific sin you are thinking of committing. Be brutally specific ("I am going to gossip about a dear friend and

HISTORICAL CONTEXT | *A Look at Jericho*

Jericho was one of the oldest fortified cities in Canaan and possibly in the entire world. It was also quite small. The story of Jericho reveals how small it is because on the seventh day the whole nation of Israel walks around it seven times.

An archaeologist in the early twentieth century who explored the ruins of Jericho concluded, according to his calculations, that Jericho covered only about four or five acres with double walls around. Whatever the actual size, this walled city is small.

reveal secrets this person has entrusted to me," or "I am going to commit an act of unfaithfulness to my spouse by entering an inappropriate relationship with someone else").

2. Put a line down the middle of the page. At the top of the left column write these words: "Implications of this sin on my life and the lives of those I love."
3. At the top of the right column, write: "What this sin will do to the heart of God and to my relationship with God."
4. Take time to fill in the columns by writing the impact this sin could have on those you love and on God.

Remember the story of Caleb. The lack of faith in the lives of ten other men cost him forty years in the desert. Ask yourself if you really want to risk the things you have listed on that sheet of paper. If you want to take this process one step further, sit down with a close and trusted friend who loves God and share the sheet with him or her. Invite that person to pray for you and to keep you accountable to resist this area of temptation and follow God's plan for your life.

SIGNIFICANT SCRIPTURE

Joshua 14:10–12

The beginning of anxiety is the end of faith, and the beginning of true faith is the end of anxiety.

George Mueller

INTERPRETIVE INSIGHT | *Whom Can God Use?*

Caleb was forty years old when God sent him with eleven other men to spy out the land. By the time the people of Israel cross the Jordan, he is about eighty years old. Now by the time of Joshua 14, five more years have passed. Caleb is eighty-five. Almost all of his peers have died of old age. What do you think this elderly man is going to ask for?

> "Now then, just as the LORD promised, he has kept me alive for forty-five years since the time he said this to Moses, while Israel moved about in the desert. So here I am today, eighty-five years old! I am still as strong today as the day Moses sent me out; I'm just as vigorous to go out to battle now as I was then. Now give me this hill country that the LORD promised me that day. You yourself heard then that the Anakites were there and their cities were large and fortified, but, the LORD helping me, I will drive them out just as he said." (Joshua 14:10–12)

Caleb is eighty-five years old, but he is still ready to join with God in the conquest of the land. This is astounding! Not only does Caleb ask if he can go in and help take the land, but he asks for the hill country. This elderly man asks God for one more chance to stretch his faith.

He wants to face the Anakites—Israel's most formidable opponents. They are the ones mentioned in Numbers 13:33 when the people say, "We saw the Nephilim there (the descendants of Anak come from the Nephilim). We seemed like grasshoppers in our own eyes, and we looked the same to them." Caleb wants to fight for the hilly, rocky land of the Anakites. This guy is eighty-five years old, and we might expect him to be settled into a nice condo at Shalom Acres, but he asks for one more hard assignment—one more chance to see the miraculous power of God, one more step of faith!

LIFE APPLICATION | *When Do We Retire from Serving God?*

Our world often sends the message that as people age, they don't have much left to offer. This is radically different in God's kingdom. In God's plan, as long as we have breath, we are called to serve the Lord. There is no retirement age when it comes to serving the Lord. God is honored by those who are pressing forward in years but continue to say, "I will climb one more hill for the Lord! I will teach one more class! I will reach out to one more person!" Not only does God rejoice when an older person lives with the spirit of Caleb, but God promises to empower them.

For those who have been walking with God for many, many years and are moving toward Caleb's territory, it might be time to say to the Lord, "I am ready for one more assignment." They may want to pray for a spirit like Caleb. They should realize that the church needs their wisdom, strength, and leadership. We need to see people like them still living the adventure, still trusting in God, and still embracing life. What a gift these people are to a community of faith.

> When one door of happiness closes, another opens; but often we look so long at the closed door that we do not see the one which has opened for us.
>
> *Helen Keller*

ON THE LIGHTER SIDE | *Sweaty Palms*

There's a true story about a man who was facing a Jordan he knew he had to cross. There was a choice he knew he had to make, something he knew he had to do. It scared him to death.

He took a long walk with his wife to talk about it. He said, "Every time I think about taking this step of faith and actually doing it, my palms get sweaty." About an hour later, they're still talking about the same subject, and he says, "Every time I think about doing this thing, my mouth gets dry." Then his wife said, "Well, why don't you lick your palms?"

LIFE APPLICATION | *Palm-Licking Time*

God's people need to realize that it's palm-licking time. It's time for spiritual risk-taking. This is the day we need to say, "I will step into the Jordan; I will march around the walls of Jericho; I will enter the land and fight!" God's power generally gets released when somebody trusts him enough to obey.

Some people spend their entire lives standing on the banks of the Jordan in fear. They say to God, "You part the water *first*, then I'll step in. Make it easy for me. Take away the fear. Give me some kind of guarantee." But as we see in the lives of God's people in Israel, God often waits to act until we step out in faith. We all have a Jordan. The key is for us to identify it and learn to step out into God's purposes even when we are fearful.

Some people are tempted to say, "God, give me lots of money, *then* I will be a generous person." Yet God wants us to commit our firstfruits, our tithes, to him no matter what. That is living by the law of the first step. We give to God and trust he will provide.

Others say, "God, give me lots of confidence, and then I'll tell somebody else about you." But we must realize that the call to share the good news of Jesus with others is not based on our confidence quotient. This calling belongs to every follower of Christ, no matter how bold or timid. First-step people are ready to tell others about Jesus even when they are afraid.

Just think about God's call on Moses: "Go talk to Pharaoh, the most powerful man in the world. Tell him, 'Let my people go.' " The worst-case scenario for Moses was that Pharaoh could kill him. God says to Joshua, "I want you to cross the Jordan at flood stage, then circumcise all the men, then go march around Jericho." Worst-cast scenario: Joshua and the people of Israel could have ended up dead. God called the apostle Paul to preach the gospel in the face of Jewish and Roman persecution. Again, the worst-case scenario was death.

God says to us, "Tell a friend about how much I love them." Or, "Invite a coworker to a special church event where they will hear about how much they matter to me." Worst-case scenario is that this person says, "I really don't want to hear," or, "No thanks, not interested."

We are not likely to die for reaching out to someone. But what are the possible benefits of taking this step of faith? They might just hear the message of salvation and become a follower of Jesus! Their life could be changed forever!

Maybe you are tempted to say, "God, give me lots of extra time, then I'll really start to study your Word." The temptation is to say, "I just don't have the time. God, give me the time." In Joshua 10, Israel is fighting at Gibeon, but they are running out of time. What does God do? He makes the sun stand still. God says, "You need more time to do what I'm asking you to do? Not a problem. I made time. I can make more of it."

Here's the challenge. We must all commit to do some spiritual risk-taking. Whatever our Jordan might be, it is time to step in and see what God will do. Maybe it will work out great; maybe we'll fail; maybe we'll get in over our head. It doesn't really matter, because when we obey God, God uses what we do. What we must always remember is that we have to get our feet wet. We must step into the Jordan. Nobody can do that for us.

NARRATIVE ON LIFE | *What If?*

Reflect on one alternative reality for a moment. Imagine God said to Joshua and the children of Israel, "I want you to put your foot in the Jordan" and everybody said, "No." Imagine nobody in Israel was willing to get their feet wet. What if all the people said, "God, you part the water *first.* Then, when it is safe, we will step in."

The entire history of Israel would have been different. No Promised Land, no miracles, no community, no prophets, and no adventure with God. They would be sitting on the banks of the Jordan waiting for something to happen.

It is important to imagine this scenario because many of Christ's followers have been sitting on the banks of the Jordan way too long. They have become comfortable on the bank of the river and have forgotten God's call to step in. But God is still looking for somebody who will trust him enough to say, "I'll get my feet wet." Will we be those people? Will we be the generation who says yes to God's adventure, even when we are facing fear?

Message 11

Joshua: The Old Testament and Holy War

Leviticus 18; Deuteronomy 7:1–16; 20:10–18;
Joshua 6:20–7:26; Zechariah 9:9–10

THE HEART OF THE Message

The Old Testament and holy war might be the hardest subject many Bible teachers ever address. It is a topic many of them prefer to avoid, but there is no way to walk through the Old Testament with integrity and sidestep this topic. In this message, we will face the reality of warfare in the Old Testament head-on. Our goal is *not* to find quick and easy answers but to enter a process of seeing why God called the people of Israel to war, with all of its brutality and pain.

THE HEART OF THE Messenger

The only way to teach on this difficult topic is to help people see what the Bible says and then help them grapple with what God's Word teaches us about these wars. As a teacher, be ready to acknowledge that you do *not* have all the answers on this topic. There are aspects of this subject that we all find hard to understand. This means you must be ready to teach with a heart filled with humility. No easy answers, no quick fixes, just a desire to live with a deep, authentic faith in God and his revealed Word. Take time to measure the condition of your own heart. Can you approach this message with a humble spirit and with the realization that there are some questions we have that may never be fully answered until we meet God face-to-face?

Go into this message knowing there will not be many light moments, humorous stories, or application sections. This is a serious topic, and you need to prepare your heart to teach with a deep measure of sobriety.

BRIEF MESSAGE OUTLINE

1. Understanding the term ***holy war***
2. God's judgment on evil
3. Pure worship of the one God
4. God plays no favorites
5. Looking back and looking forward
6. Ending with hope

Introduction

> **SIGNIFICANT SCRIPTURE**
>
> Deuteronomy 7:1–16; Joshua 6:21

INTERPRETIVE INSIGHT | *Irreconcilable Differences?*

In the second century, a man named Marcion said there was an irreconcilable gap between the loving God Jesus taught about in the New Testament and what he termed the "cruel and violent God" of the Old Testament. His solution to his perceived dilemma was to do a cut-and-paste job and remove the Old Testament from the canon of Scripture. He had such a hard time dealing with the war and bloodshed in the Old Testament that he simply got rid of it! Is that what we ought to do? Should we ignore hard passages? Is the God of the Old Testament consistent in character to the God Jesus preached in the New Testament? These are some of the questions we must address if we are going to look at the topic of God and holy war.

INTERPRETIVE INSIGHT | *A Tough Place to Start*

If we are going to address one of the hardest topics in all the Bible, we might as well start with the hardest passage. In Deuteronomy 7, Moses is talking to the Israelites before they enter the Promised Land. He tells them the rules that will govern their warfare after they cross the Jordan and enter Canaan. These war instructions seem severe and merciless.

Then, after the people of Israel won their victory over the people of Jericho, we read Joshua 6:21, which summarizes the end result of the battle: "They devoted the city to the LORD and destroyed with the sword every living thing in it—men and women, young and old, cattle, sheep and donkeys."

These two passages put the topic clearly on the table for inspection. One clarifies God's call to wage war on the nations in the land with no possibility of treaties and with a call to destroy them completely. The second passage assures us that this is exactly what the people of Israel did. There is no candy coating to make this one go down easy. We need to face the reality of these wars and learn all we can from this period in the history of God's people.

> **PAUSE FOR PRAYER**
>
> *Prayer for Wisdom, Humility, and Grace*
>
> At the very start of this message, even before you read a biblical text, it would be wise to open with a word of prayer. Ask God to grant his wisdom as you look at this topic. Pray for humility in your life as a communicator and ask for God's grace to fill each heart as you seek to gain insight to a biblical reality that is difficult to understand.

NARRATIVE ON LIFE | *These Are Real People*

As we read our Bibles and tell children the great stories of faith, we must remember that we are talking about real people, both in the nation of Israel and the surrounding peoples. Some of our children's songs and Bible storybooks do an injustice to the severity of what is recorded in Scripture.

For instance, when kids sing the "Arky, Arky" song (about the flood), they rarely take time to reflect on the implications of what they are singing. With smiles on their faces they chime out, "The Lord told Noah, there's gonna be a floody, floody. Get those animals out of the muddy,

muddy.... So rise, and shine, and give God the glory, glory, children of the Lord." What children often miss is that real men, women, and children, as well as a lot of animals, died in that flood! In the same way, when they read and sing about Joshua fighting the battle of Jericho and those walls coming tumbling down, they miss the sobering reality that every person in that city, except for the family of Rahab, was slaughtered!

This is not to say these songs can't be used. It is also not to say that we *should* teach preschoolers to sing about the slaughter of women, men, and children. It is certainly not to say that God was wrong in his judgment of the earth and the people of Jericho. However, it is a sobering reminder that when real people come under judgment, God weeps, and so should we. The Bible is clear that God does not take pleasure in the death of the sinful but that he longs for them to repent and come to him (Ezekiel 33:11). As we look closely at the topic of the Old Testament and holy war, we need to move out of the vague realm of generalities and remember that real lives are involved.

WORD STUDY

Holy War

It is important to note that the expression "holy war" is never used in the Bible. It's a phrase that's used a lot in the modern world, but never in the Bible. Throughout the Old Testament the term *holy* describes many things that are set apart for God – but it is never applied to war. There's nothing "holy" about war. Scholars debate where the phrase "holy war" comes from. Many think it has a Greek origin, but it's not found in Scripture. In other words, we may use the expression "holy war," but God does not. War is never his plan and it is not holy. However, there are times God calls his people to go to war. In the days of Joshua, war is necessary to accomplish God's purposes, but it does not delight his heart; rather, it breaks his heart.

1. Understanding the Term *Holy War*

INTERPRETIVE INSIGHT | *Violence in the Old Testament*

The first episode of violence in Scripture does not occur until *after* the Fall. This is quite different from many other religions in the ancient world. In many ancient religious systems the gods themselves were violent by nature. The primary deity had a warlike nature. In many religious systems where there was a whole pantheon of gods, these gods not only waged war on people but also on each other! In the Bible, violence does not occur until after the Fall, when Cain kills Abel. Violence is a reminder of the Fall.

After the first blood was spilled, one of the primary indicators of sin in the world was violence. The Scriptures are clear that violence is displeasing to God. All the way back in Genesis 6:11 – 13 we read that "the earth was corrupt in God's sight and was full of violence.... So God said to Noah, 'I am going to put an end to all people, for the earth is filled with violence because of them.'" Violence is deeply disturbing to the God of the Bible.

2. God's Judgment on Evil

INTERPRETIVE INSIGHT | *When Sin Reaches Its Full Measure*

SIGNIFICANT SCRIPTURE

Genesis 15:16; Leviticus 18

The wars God commanded his people to enter into were, in part, an expression of his judgment on the inexpressible evil of the Canaanite culture. There is an important statement found in Genesis 15:16, "In the fourth generation your descendants will come back here, for the sin of the Amorites has not yet *reached its full measure*." God promises Abraham here that one day the people of God will occupy the Promised Land, but not yet. He gives an important reason why they can't yet take the land.

God is saying in effect, "In Abraham's time the Amorite culture was defiled. It was wicked, but not yet past the point of no return." God is going to offer mercy to the people who live in Canaan and give them time to repent. Later, in Joshua 2, we learn that

HISTORICAL CONTEXT | *To Spiritualize or Not?*

Sometimes teachers and followers of Christ have a way of spiritualizing these difficult texts. They read passages about battles and then talk about how the real message is, "God will strengthen me in my battles against fear or other obstacles in my life." Of course this is true. But there is far more to these passages. To honor Scripture, we have to start with the literal text. These are real battles with real people, and real blood is shed. You could not have gone to the people of Jericho, in the middle of the battle, and tried to comfort them that this was about some spiritual lessons people in the future might glean from their experience.

First and foremost, we must focus on the actual battles and what God was doing among the people of Israel. Then, wherever appropriate, we can draw spiritual lessons for our lives today. In this message, however, the focus should remain on the real battles and on God's motivation for calling his people to these actions. The goal is to understand that the God of the Old Testament is the same God and Father whom Jesus describes in the New Testament. This God is all-powerful, and he is a consuming fire. Yet he is also tender and grace-filled. This God is the one whom Jesus loves so deeply, and so should we.

CREATIVE MESSAGE IDEA | *Tell Your Neighbor*

Pause before talking about the historical context note "A Culture of War" (page 180) and ask everyone gathered to do one thing. Let them know you are going to give one word, and they are invited to do a free association. You will say the word "spring" (specifically, the season of spring) and ask them to tell the person next to them what comes to mind. What word, image, or concept comes to mind when they hear the word "spring"?

Then, ask for a quick show of hands. Use the following questions to see what came to mind for those gathered:

- How many of you associate spring with a certain sport, such as baseball?
- How many of you said something about spring cleaning?
- Were there some who thought of gardening, flowers, or spring activities that involve agriculture?
- Did anyone think about vacation or spring break?

We have many things that come to mind when we think of spring, but for the people of Israel, there was *one thing* that came to everyone's mind when they thought of spring: For them it was time for war!

Rahab herself puts her trust in this God, and when she does, she is spared! However, the Canaanite people in general do not repent, and their sin finally reaches its full measure.

The depth of the Canaanite sins is reflected in many places in the Old Testament. Leviticus 18 is a catalogue of all kinds of twisted practices that were part of the cult of Canaanite religion. One of these practices was the sacrifice of children to a god called Molech. There is evidence that human sacrifice was practiced regularly with firstborn children in the Canaanite religions. God used the people of Israel to bring judgment on a nation that had become so perverse that their sin had reached its full measure. The cup of rebellion and wickedness had become so full that it was overflowing, and God was ready to put a stop to it.

ILLUSTRATION | *God Should Judge Evil*

The ability of the human heart to commit atrocities is evidenced all throughout history. In ancient days we can look at the practices of nations like the Canaanites and be shocked by their brutality. But in more recent history, we can look at the Crusades, the Spanish Inquisition, Stalin's reign of terror, Nazi Germany with its concentration camps, ethnic cleansing in Bosnia, or many other examples to remind us that the human capacity for sin continues to grow.

There is a story called "One Instance, One Child," written by a historian named Philip Friedman. It may be appropriate to tell in some teaching contexts, though you may decide (particularly if you have children in your services) to refrain from using it as an illustration.

This is a contemporary example from a culture that was approaching the full measure of sin—Nazi Germany. This is an eyewitness account of what happened to one Jewish girl in a Warsaw ghetto during the Nazi occupation.

Zosha was a little girl. One of the Germans became aware of her beautiful, diamond-like, dark eyes. "I could make two rings out of them," he said, "one for myself and one for my wife." His colleague was holding the girl. "Let's see whether they really are so beautiful. Better yet, let's examine them in our hands."

ILLUSTRATION | *Some Things Don't Change*

Sometimes the Old Testament times seem barbaric, and we might breathe a prayer of thanks that those times are behind us. But the human propensity for violence is just as great today as it was thousands of years ago. *National Geographic* did a television special where they interviewed a man from Afghanistan. He was holding an axe and with great delight he said, "I have used this to decapitate 1,300 people." And he was laughing as he talked about the blood he had shed with his own hands. With great confidence he declared, "We are called to kill the infidels." Violence was clearly a big part of his world. What a reminder that the more things change, the more they stay the same.

The soldiers began to laugh. One of the wittiest proposed to take the eyes out. Shortly thereafter the fainting child was lying on the floor. Instead of eyes, two bloody wounds were staring. The mother, driven mad, was held by the other women. Soon after, they decided it was necessary to annihilate the blinded child.

It's just one child. But multiply the murder of one child after another after another, generation after generation. Imagine that being done in the name of a god. Think about what it does to the children who survive and are brought up in such a culture. Then you begin to get some sense of what it means for a culture to reach the full measure of sin. God says it has to be stopped. It must end. Such evil demands a clear response from a holy and just God.

Many of the wars in the Old Testament are a response to nations of people who have reached the full measure of their sin. They have passed the point of hope, and it was time for judgment. In some cases, God raised up another nation to be the instrument of his punishment on this sin. Scripture teaches that these wars are part of the expression of God's holy judgment on human evil.

HISTORICAL CONTEXT | *A Culture of War*

For the people of the ancient world, when spring came, it was the time for war. This may be a foreign concept for us, but at that time of history, spring and war went hand-in-hand. In 2 Samuel 11:1 we read, "In the spring, at the time when kings go off to war, David sent Joab out with the king's men and the whole Israelite army. They destroyed the Ammonites and besieged Rabbah." Just as some people today may say, "Every spring I wash my miniblinds and plant my flowers," people back then would say, "In the spring we go to war." It was a part of life.

We will never understand the Old Testament era until we see the extent to which it was dominated by violence and war. The Hebrew word for war is used about three hundred times in the Old Testament. This may be shocking to us, but people in the ancient world took it in stride. In those days they lived in what might be called a "culture of war." What might look like barbarism and cruelty to us was not even surprising to them. It was standard operating procedure.

HISTORICAL CONTEXT | *In Our World but Not of Our World*

There are many practices and institutions in the ancient world that were not pleasing to God. War, polygamy, divorce, and slavery were part of the world into which Israel was born. Because sin permeated the whole human race, many practices became standard operating procedures in the world, but they still broke the heart of God. As God began forming the nation of Israel, he moved them one step at a time toward his vision for humanity.

3. Pure Worship of the One God

INTERPRETIVE INSIGHT | *Worship Only God!*

The wars recorded in the Old Testament do not just express judgment on evil. In addition, the Canaanites have to be removed if Israel's worship of the one, true God is to survive. It is clear to God that Israel's devotion to him is immature and fragile. If the Canaanites remain in the land, the hearts of God's people may be stolen away by their false religion.

History has proved that if the Canaanites were allowed to remain in the land, the Israelites would be seduced into the same kind of evil practices. Deuteronomy 20 records additional instruction for warfare. God tells his people that when they come to a city outside of Canaan, they might begin by offering terms of peace. For the cities in Canaan, however, they are called to destroy their populations utterly. God is clear about his concern that the Canaanites not be allowed to teach the people of Israel to follow all the detestable things they have been doing. God does not want his people to end up sinning against the Lord their God (Deuteronomy 20:10–18). God is ready to do whatever it takes to protect his people and keep them from having their hearts seduced and drawn away from him.

NEW TESTAMENT CONNECTION

Don't Love the World

Jesus understood the human tendency to fall in love with the things of this world. Certainly he warned us about not loving material things, but there is more to the story than just riches. Jesus knew that the very systems of this world could be opposed to the ways of God. As in Old Testament days, those who follow God must be careful to identify commonly accepted practices that are sinful. When these are identified, they must be resisted. In 1 John 2:15 we hear a clear warning: "Do not love the world or anything in the world. If anyone loves the world, the love of the Father is not in him."

NARRATIVE ON LIFE | *This Is Someone's Little Girl*

Think about these Canaanite practices in terms of real people. So many parents in our culture teach their daughters how to say "No!" In an effort to protect the hearts of little girls, their parents teach them to set boundaries, to make wise relational choices, and to walk away from specific temptations. Although we live in a sex-saturated world, most parents seek to give some kind of moral compass to their children.

It is impossible for most parents in our day and age to comprehend a culture where fathers commonly gave their daughters to be used as prostitutes. This was considered commendable because it was part of their family religion. These little girls grew up knowing that this was normative practice.

SIGNIFICANT SCRIPTURE

Deuteronomy 6:4–9; 20:10–18

This is one of the reasons God uses imagery of being "seduced" by other gods. Not only did the Canaanite religion entice the hearts of God's people to stray from fidelity to the one true God, but it literally invited the people of Israel into sexual immorality as a lifestyle. Through the wars on the people of Canaan, God was saying, "This must be stopped!" If worship of the one true God was to survive, Canaanite religion had to be removed from the land—completely. Some scholars have termed the motivation for the extermination of the Canaanites as being more *deicide* (killing of a god) than *homicide* (killing of a human being).

ILLUSTRATION | *God Should Judge Evil*

In the world of medicine, a surgeon does not hesitate to amputate part of the body to save the life of the patient. Amputation causes real pain. It involves enormous loss. But when life is at stake, the doctor will do an amputation because he knows that it is truly the best and wisest course of action.

In a real sense, the spiritual life of Israel and the world was at stake. If the Canaanites' religion won the day and polytheism became the core belief system of the Israelites, God's plan for a community could have come to an end. The beliefs of the Canaanites were a cancer that had to be removed from the land before the people of God could live there with any hope of health. Thus, God ordered surgery for the long-term health and life of his people.

NARRATIVE ON THE TEXT | *Just As God Warned*

There was no way the people of Israel could worship the one true God and also embrace the Canaanite religion of that day. It is simply impossible for someone to be monotheistic and polytheistic at the same time. These two religious systems were diametrically opposed and could not coexist. Yet, throughout the history of the Old Testament, the people of God often tried to embrace both religious systems.

In fact, as history played out, God's concern about Canaanite religion proved to be justified. Wherever Israel allowed Baal worship to continue and Canaanite populations to live and keep growing, Israel was seduced into their pagan worship. In Numbers 25:1–3 we read a heartbreaking example of this:

> While Israel was staying in Shittim, the men began to indulge in sexual immorality with Moabite women, who invited them to the sacrifices to their gods. The people ate and bowed down before these gods. So Israel joined in worshiping the Baal of Peor. And the LORD's anger burned against them.

HISTORICAL CONTEXT | *This Must Be Stopped!*

Tablets excavated from a city called Ugarit near Canaan have shed a lot of light on ancient Canaanite religious practices. These tablets tell about the god Baal, who was the god of fertility (as well as water and the storm). Canaanite religion taught that Baal was killed by another god named Mot, who was said to be the god of barrenness and death. Mot, in turn, was killed by a goddess named Anath. Baal later came back to life and had sexual intercourse with Anath. In Canaanite religious stories, the fertility of the earth came through this union of Baal and Anath.

For the Canaanites, every year when the rains stopped, it was as if Baal had died. So they entered into sexual activity with cultic prostitutes in an effort to induce Baal to make the earth fertile again. One scholar says this: "Sexual intercourse with temple prostitutes was as much a part of the job of a farmer as the actual operations of agriculture." This was one of the main activities of Canaanite worship.

As the Israelites were getting ready to occupy the Promised Land, the men began to indulge in sexual immorality with local women on the east side of the Jordan River. As a result, their hearts began to turn away from God. In a real sense, the coming wars in Canaan were not just about the physical survival of the Israelites, although this was part of the issue at hand. On a deeper level, these wars (with all their severity) were about the survival of the *worship* of the one true God.

WORD STUDY

Monotheism

The people of Israel were taught, with no exception, that there was one, and only one, God. This belief in only one God is called *monotheism*. This is taken from the Greek words *monos*, meaning "one," and *theos*, meaning "God." Perhaps the clearest expression of this is found in this simple declaration, which became a core belief in Judaism: "Hear, O Israel: The LORD our God, the LORD is one" (Deuteronomy 6:4).

The Canaanites were polytheistic, meaning they believed in a pantheon of gods. Yet at the core of biblical faith is an unyielding belief in only one God. Any time throughout the Old Testament, when the hearts of the people wandered toward false gods, there were consequences! God's people are to be thoroughly monotheistic.

4. God Plays No Favorites

INTERPRETIVE INSIGHT | *God Plays No Favorites*

In the Old Testament it is clear that God plays no favorites. Just as he could and did use Israel as an instrument of judgment against other nations, so God could and did use other nations as an instrument of judgment against Israel. His people had to learn that he was not a genie in a bottle, to be their secret weapon anytime they went to war just because they were his people.

God started teaching his people this truth early in their history. He was not on Israel's side, but they existed to serve and glorify him. Their role was to accomplish his purposes on the earth. Even before the battle of Jericho this became crystal clear:

> Now when Joshua was near Jericho, he looked up and saw a man standing in front of him with a drawn sword in his hand. Joshua went up to him and asked, "Are you for us or for our enemies?"
>
> "Neither," he replied, "but as commander of the army of the LORD I have now come." Then Joshua fell facedown to the ground in reverence, and asked him, "What message does my Lord have for his servant?" (Joshua 5:13–14)

Joshua learns here what the people of Israel must be reminded of many times in the years to come. God loves them, but he is not on their side. They are to be on his side.

> My great concern is not whether God is on our side; my great concern is to be on God's side.
>
> *Abraham Lincoln*

SIGNIFICANT SCRIPTURE

Joshua 5:13–14

NARRATIVE ON THE TEXT | *C, None of the Above*

There is a dark kind of humor to Joshua's encounter with the "commander of the army of the LORD." Joshua comes face-to-face with a man who has his sword drawn. That would be just like us facing a person with a loaded gun pointed right in our face. Notice the question Joshua asks: "Whose side are you on? Are you on their side or our side?"

Notice too the response. In effect, he says to Joshua, "No." The problem is that "No" was not one of the choices. This is not a yes/no question; rather, it is an either/or question. But the man here is communicating a profound and critical truth in his response. Look at it closely. In effect, he is saying, "Joshua, the question is *not*, 'Is God on your side?' The question *is*, 'Are you on God's side?' "

God will fight for his people. But if they defy him, he will fight against them. God's righteous judgment is a sword that cuts both ways. Just because the people of Israel are his chosen people does not mean that they will automatically win every battle or will always have God's favor. What a sobering reminder for all who follow Christ. God does not exist to be on our side and to do our bidding. We exist to be on his side and to follow his plan for our lives.

SIGNIFICANT SCRIPTURE

Joshua 7:1–26

NARRATIVE ON THE TEXT | *The Consequences of Sin*

Sometimes in battle, soldiers were allowed to keep the plunder. In many other cases, however, they were not. In the situation of Jericho, it was communicated clearly that no one was to keep any of the plunder; everything was to be devoted to the Lord. Fully aware of this, Achan, one of the soldiers, took some of the devoted things and hid them in his tent.

Achan violated a basic rule. He was trying to profit from the battle. As we read on, we discover that the consequences were far reaching.

The people of Israel were about to attack the city of Ai. Ai was probably not a large city. This name actually means "ruins" in Hebrew. It was probably a settlement not worth a whole lot. It had been settled by some nomadic people. In other words, it should have been a quick and easy victory. After the people saw God's power revealed at Jericho, the invasion and conquest of Ai should have been a cakewalk!

As a matter of fact, those who spied out the city of Ai came back and said it would only take a few thousand men to win the city. Joshua sent out three thousand men—and they were beaten! In the battle, thirty-six soldiers were killed. To top it off, the people of Israel became fearful. How could this small city of people beat them?

Joshua cried out to God and asked, "Why did this happen? How could this happen?" God spoke clearly to Joshua and let him know that their loss in battle was due to Achan's actions. Because of his sin and hardness of heart, the whole nation suffered defeat, and his own family came under severe judgment.

LIFE APPLICATION | *My Sin Is Never Just Mine!*

We like to think we can sin in a vacuum. We want to think that our sin is just ours and no one else will ever know or suffer. The truth is, our sin always has a ripple effect that touches our family members, friends, and everyone who matters to us.

Achan buried the stolen articles and figured no one would ever know. Within a short time, thirty-six soldiers lay dead because of his sin. Later, he paid with his life, and his family suffered the same fate. Yet we should not be surprised. We have all seen how our sin can impact the next generation.

So, before we start that bad habit, before we say yes to that secret sin one more time, or before we pacify ourselves by saying, "No one will ever know," we need to ask about the consequences by asking questions such as these:

- How will this impact my life?
- Who might pay for this sin?
- What will it cost my children?
- How might it impact my spouse?
- In what way will this compromise my testimony as a follower of Christ?

Honest answers to these questions can help us decide not to step into sin but to say "no" and follow God's plan for our life.

INTERPRETIVE INSIGHT | *The Fairness of God*

Just so that we are clear that God is fair and never plays favorites, the first two battles in the book of Joshua make this point in a profound way. Rahab, though she is a Gentile, is saved. She honors God by hiding the spies, and her whole family is saved. Achan, though he is an Israelite, is punished for his sin. These are early indications that God's concern is faith and character, not the proper blood ties.

INTERPRETIVE INSIGHT | *God Will Fight for You*

In the first battle of Ai, Israel sent three thousand men to take the city. To their shock, thirty-six were killed, and the whole force of Israel had to retreat. Normally in warfare, thirty-six casualties out of three thousand soldiers would not be a cause for alarm. But in this case, Joshua and the people fell down on their faces and cried out in distress.

Why? Because when Israel went to war, they had an understanding that God would do the fighting for them. Deuteronomy 20:4 says, "For the LORD your God is the one who goes with you to fight for you against your enemies to give you victory." This is what they expect! In Jericho God brings down the wall and the soldiers mop up afterward. The reason Joshua is so concerned with the loss of thirty-six men at Ai is that he knows the protection of God around the army of Israel is gone. The people realize that if God is not fighting for them, they are doomed.

WORD STUDY

Devoted Things

In Joshua 7:1 one of God's people takes some of the "devoted things" and hides them. This has disastrous consequences. That little phrase "devoted things" is an important phrase in the Old Testament understanding of warfare. It was the Hebrew word *cherem*, which means "things that are under the ban." It is used about eighty times in the Old Testament and refers to things that were to be set apart (generally for destruction). These items belonged to God, and no person was to touch them. In this account, the "devoted things" were taken by a person for his personal gain, and the whole nation paid the price for this act of disobedience.

NARRATIVE ON LIFE | *Old Testament War Versus Jihad*

War in the Old Testament is quite different from the idea of *jihad* that we hear about today. Soldiers fighting in a jihad are taught to covet martyrdom. They are told that death in battle is something to be desired. This is why people who declare jihad will do almost anything and are willing to die if they feel it will further their cause. Many of these people have been told that as soon as they die, they will enter paradise and receive seventy-two virgins as payment for their sacrifice.

In the Old Testament wars there was an understanding that God would fight for his people. If they were obedient and followed God's leading, Israel's soldiers were not supposed to die. They were expected to live. There was not a sense that they were heading off to a bloody death but to a glorious victory! There is no exultation of martyrdom in the Old Testament.

INTERPRETIVE INSIGHT | *Ending Where They Started*

The descent of Israel is a reversal of their rise. Some of them begin to reflect on this and realize that when they rose as a nation, they were used as instruments of God's judgment against other nations. Now, while they are falling, God uses nations like Assyria and Babylon as instruments of judgment on them. When they were rising, the walls of Jericho came down. During their decline, when the Babylonians invade, the walls of Jerusalem come down.

They defeated many kings during their rise, but now their final king, Zedekiah, is captured. The last thing he sees is the execution of his sons; then his eyes are put out and he is led to Babylon, where he dies in exile.

The great crisis for Israel is that they end up in the same situation as when they started. Once again they are subject to a powerful nation. Once again they are in servitude. Once again the people of Israel are on the bottom. At this point they face a spiritual and theological crisis, asking, "Is the covenant gone? Are God's promises wiped out? Is our future hopeless?"

HISTORICAL CONTEXT | *The Danger of Taking Plunder*

In most armies back in the Old Testament days, soldiers were paid by defeating enemies and taking their possessions. This booty or plunder became their reward for risking their lives in battle. Professional soldiers got rich if their army was powerful and took many cities. In a very crude sense, these ancient soldiers were working on a kind of commission. One of the main consequences of this approach was that nations got addicted to war because it increased their wealth. God did not want war to become a norm. Sometimes God told his people not to take any plunder in battle. This could be an indication that God may have been concerned that his people not become reliant on the spoils of war as a primary source of wealth.

5. Looking Back and Looking Forward

CREATIVE MESSAGE IDEA | *Showing Israel's Ascent and Descent*

Take time to draw out this picture of Israel's rise and fall and show how they ended up where they started. Indicate how each step was marked by violence.

You Will Need

- A flip chart or dry erase marker board
- A large tip pen
- If you use projection and can do it, have a video camera focused on the chart and then project the drawing on your screen so everyone can see.

The history of Israel starts in oppression in *Egypt*. God delivers them, and they go into the *desert*. Then, after forty years, they enter the time of *conquest*. After this, they begin a time where they experience a *united kingdom*.

Every step in their ascent is marked by violence. When they leave Egypt, we see the destruction of the firstborn and later the drowning of Pharaoh's armies. They go into the desert and many of their people die. The conquest involves one battle after another. They say, "We want a king," and that united kingdom is formed through violence.

Though many people don't realize it, the first king crowned in Israel was not Saul. He was the first to reign. In Judges we find that the first man crowned king was a son of Gideon. His name is Abimelech, and he has seventy brothers. The first thing he does is to murder his brothers so he can protect his throne.

Later the people demand a king, and Samuel warns them that a king will take their sons and make them soldiers. The people continue to press for a king, so God gives them Saul, David, and then Solomon. Each of these kings reigns over a united Israel. Even during this high point of unity, there is violence between Saul and David. Later, there is war between David and his son Absalom.

Then after Solomon's rule, the kingdom is divided. Never again will there be one people of Israel. The nation is divided into a northern (Israel) and a southern (Judah) kingdom (about 930 BC). That lasts for a couple centuries. Then in 721 BC the northern kingdom is defeated by the Assyrians, and it disappears from the face of the earth. The southern kingdom lasts longer, but they are conquered by the Babylonians in 586 BC. Every step in the ascent and descent of Israel is marked by violence.

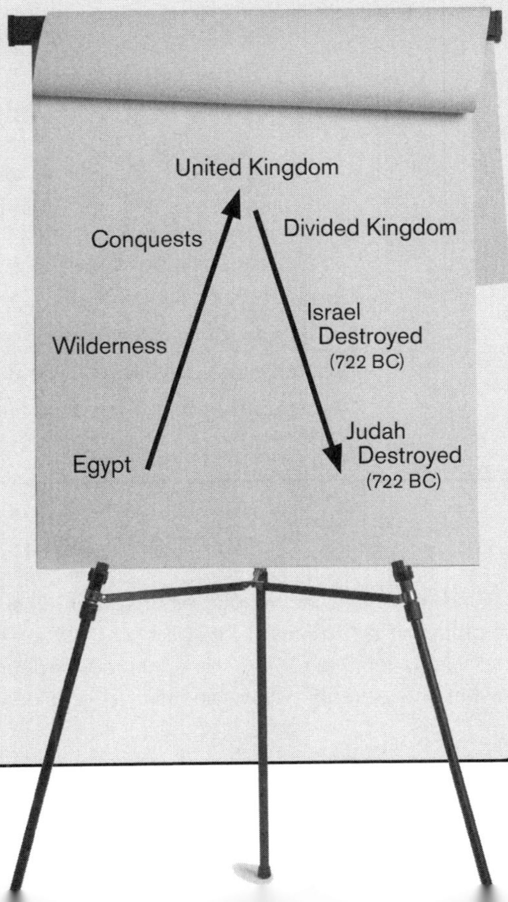

6. Ending with Hope

INTERPRETIVE INSIGHT | *A New Kind of Person*

Among God's inspired prophets at this great crisis time in their history arises a new and better vision. It is something no human being has ever conceived before. The prophet Jeremiah is alive during those days. He calls the people to repent, and they don't. He sees what looks like the end of his people. God's voice through Jeremiah reveals that what is needed is not another shot at the old covenant and not the power to wage war with greater violence. What is needed is a changed vision and transformed hearts.

> The love of God created us, but the humility of God saved us.
> *Hildegaard of Bingen (twelfth century)*

SIGNIFICANT SCRIPTURE

Jeremiah 31:31–34;
Zechariah 9:9–10

Their story is our story. Their sins are our sins. Jeremiah realizes that what God has in mind is a whole new kind of person. Hearts need to change and minds need to transform. The people need a whole new beginning.

INTERPRETIVE INSIGHT | *A New Covenant and a New Beginning*

One of the most striking prophecies to come out of this time in history comes from a prophet named Zechariah (a long time after Judah fell):

> Rejoice greatly, O Daughter of Zion!
> Shout, Daughter of Jerusalem!
> See, your king comes to you,
> righteous and having salvation,
> gentle and riding on a donkey,
> on a colt, the foal of a donkey. (Zechariah 9:9)

In those days, as well as in our day, a king conjured up all kinds of images of military power. But Zechariah turns things upside down and declares that this king will come in humility, riding on a donkey. Kings normally rode in chariots pulled by stallions and war horses. A donkey was a farm animal. This vision is radically different. It is pointing to a new time, a new beginning, and a new covenant.

ON THE LIGHTER SIDE | *Reward and Punishment*

Jihad theology teaches that when a man dies fighting in a "holy war," he will have a group of virgins waiting for him. One has to wonder what the seventy-two virgins did to end up in their situation. Maybe it is paradise for the martyr, but it might be eternal punishment for the virgins.

ILLUSTRATION | *The President on a Tractor*

For us to understand this in contemporary language, it would be like saying, "The Commander-in-Chief is riding into Washington on an old used tractor. No limousine and no fanfare." If you can imagine the President on an old muddy farm tractor, riding into the capital, you start to get the picture.

LIFE APPLICATION | *Let There Be Peace on Earth*

We often look around the world and are shocked by all the violence, wars, and atrocities. We want peace. We pray for peace. Yet we forget that we have to do our part.

NEW TESTAMENT CONNECTION | *A Peaceful King on a Donkey*

One day the King of all kings rode into the capital city humbly on a donkey. His name was Jesus, and he came with a whole new way of seeing life, a whole new covenant! Zechariah 9:10 prophesied of this coming king and his rule of peace:

> I will take away the chariots from
> Ephraim
> and the war-horses from
> Jerusalem,
> and the battle bow will be broken.
> He will proclaim peace to the nations.
> His rule will extend from sea to sea
> and from the River to the ends of
> the earth.

This is fulfilled in the New Testament when Jesus rides into Jerusalem: "The disciples went and did as Jesus had instructed them. They brought the donkey and the colt, placed their cloaks on them, and Jesus sat on them" (Matthew 21:6–7).

It took a long time for the human race to begin understanding that the old way did not work. The violence and force that seemed to be the strongest tool in the world was not nearly strong enough to usher in God's kingdom or to transform the human heart. But when Jesus came, God ushered in a new time in human history. Divinity arrived on a donkey. Even the night that he came to the earth, his arrival was also humble, in a manger. That night the message was clear: "Glory to God in the highest, and on earth peace to men on whom his favor rests" (Luke 2:14).

Jesus brought with him the call to peace and the potential of peace. Not everyone would accept his ways, but Jesus was clear: His kingdom would not be established by violence, but he would rule as the Prince of Peace.

Jesus shocked the people of his day, and he continues to challenge us today by calling his followers away from violence and to peace:

> "You have heard that it was said, 'Eye for eye, and tooth for tooth.' But I tell you, Do not resist an evil person. If someone strikes you on the right cheek, turn to him the other also. And if someone wants to sue you and take your tunic, let him have your cloak as well. If someone forces you to go one mile, go with him two miles. Give to the one who asks you, and do not turn away from the one who wants to borrow from you.
>
> "You have heard that it was said, 'Love your neighbor and hate your enemy.' But I tell you: Love your enemies and pray for those who persecute you" (Matthew 5:38–44).

An old song, which is really a prayer, communicates a simple truth to remember. The words of the chorus speak to the topic of this message: "Let there be peace on earth, *and let it begin with me*!"

We all want peace, but most of the time we want it to begin with someone else. We cry for world peace, but we cannot be reconciled with our spouse. We expect world leaders to work out their differences, but we cannot resolve a conflict with our neighbor. We pray for nations to find a middle ground on complex political issues, but we fight over who gets to hold the remote for the TV. We cry out for peace in a war-torn world, but we refuse to forgive that person who has wronged us. We need to keep seeking peace in the world, but we also need to humble ourselves and seek peace in our spheres of influence.

Jesus made it clear that the peacemakers were the ones called "the children of God." Jesus, the Prince of Peace, taught that his people would not be a political nation armed with swords and chariots ready to inflict suffering on the rest of the world, but a church armed with love and prayer, ready to endure suffering on behalf of the world. This is the vision of Jesus, and it should be the passion of those who follow him.

Be the living expression of God's kindness, in your face, your eyes, your smile, your greeting. Give not only your care but your heart.

Mother Teresa of Calcutta

Message 12

Identifying Spiritual Entropy

The Book of Judges

THE HEART OF THE Message

The book of Judges is one of the saddest books in the Bible. The faith that could have and should have burned so brightly was beginning to wane. Each successive generation of God's people did not effectively pass on the torch of faith. Instead of growing more passionate and committed to the God of Israel, the people found their hearts wandering away time and time again.

One definition for entropy states that "increased entropy results in disorganization." Over time, things tend to move toward disorder in life. If we don't exert energy to fight against it, almost everything tends toward a state of disorganization. What would your yard look like if you never pulled a weed or mowed? How would your house look if you never cleaned up? Even our relationships will come apart if we don't invest time and energy in them. The people of Israel discovered that their relationship with God and their life as a community was at serious risk of entropy. Sadly, too often they failed to exert the energy needed to keep their faith strong and their spiritual fires burning bright.

This message begins a two-week focus on the book of Judges and this process of spiritual entropy. In this message we will identify some signs that spiritual entropy is setting in. In the next message the focus will be on how we can intercept this process and move toward spiritual authenticity and passion.

BRIEF MESSAGE OUTLINE

1. A vicious cycle
2. The causes of spiritual entropy

THE HEART OF THE Messenger

The cycle that occurs over and over again in the book of Judges is one that can happen in the life of every follower of Christ if he or she is not careful. Our spiritual fire can begin to burn down and our passion for God can grow cold. Look at the cycle that recurs in the book of

PAUSE FOR PRAYER

Find God's Plan

Take time to pray for the people gathered to find God's plan and follow his will rather than missing a great opportunity as the people of Israel did in this time of their history. You might want to use the prayer below:

Dear Lord, as the Israelites entered the Promised Land, as they finally took possession of what you promised centuries before, it was a time of such potential. As we look at the book of Judges and reflect on this time of lost potential, open our eyes. We pray, O Lord, that you will spare us from the same kinds of mistakes in our individual lives, our families, our church, our nation, and our world. When we hit these decisive moments, we pray that we will follow your plan. Even today, help us recognize these tendencies in ourselves and to respond to you in greater devotion. We pray this in Jesus' name. Amen.

Judges (you will find it at the beginning of this message). Search your heart and be honest about where you are in this cycle right now. Pray that you will come to a place of peace and intimacy with God and passion in your faith. If you become convicted that you are in a time of complacency or sin, cry out to God and ask him to bring you to a place of trust in him and humble repentance. God has a strong history of responding to that kind of prayer.

Introduction

INTERPRETIVE INSIGHT | *A Critical Crossroad*

We all have moments in our lives where we hit a crossroads. When we come to a critical fork in the road, we can choose to follow God or our own desires. In the book of Judges, God's people stand at a critical crossroad and must decide whether they are going to rely on their own power or on God's power. It is a time when they can move forward into God's purposes for them in new and fresh ways, or they can miss God's plan.

1. A Vicious Cycle

NARRATIVE ON THE TEXT | *Where Do We Go from Here?*

Finally, the long wait is over. In the book of Judges, for the first time in history, we meet a generation of human beings who have the opportunity to live freely, unencumbered, under the direct rule of God. They have the potential to be a community of such love and righteousness that all the peoples of the earth will be blessed by them. But will they take advantage of this decisive time in their history? Will they keep their eyes fixed on the God who gave them the land and formed them into a people?

In Genesis 12:1–3, God told Abraham that he would do two specific things. He would make him into a mighty nation—which would be as numerous as the sands of the seashore and the stars of the heavens—and he would give them a place, a land of their own. Through this process they would become a blessing to all the nations of the earth.

Over the years, this promise began to unfold. During the days of Abraham, Isaac, and Jacob, a nation was being formed. The dream was starting to take shape. In Joseph's life, the people ended up in Egypt for four hundred years. This appeared like a hopeless situation, but God was building a nation of people. Over the centuries, slowly but steadily, a nation was being born in the furnace of Egypt.

When the people of Israel were set free through Moses and left Egypt, there was a sense that they were walking forward into God's destiny for them. They crossed the Red Sea and were only weeks away from the land God promised. Yet they ended up stalling for forty years in the desert. Moses died and Joshua was raised up as their new leader. They crossed the Jordan, came into the land, and for almost a decade they fought to make it their own. God said, "I will give you the land, but you have to take the land." So they did!

More time passes, but finally it happens. In Judges 2:6 we discover that the promise made to Abraham is now a reality. The people of Israel have become a mighty nation. They are now settled in their land. This vision, this dream that has been in their hearts for so long is now a reality.

Try to get the picture in your mind. Joshua dismisses the Israelites, and each tribe goes to take possession of its own inheritance. The moment has finally come. God has made a nation of his people. It is a vast nation. There are twelve tribes, spread all over the land. There are so many that some of the people are even on the other side of the Jordan. God has formed a people and has given them their place, the Promised Land. After centuries of waiting, the promises in Genesis 12:1 – 2 are being fulfilled.

Now comes the question: How is it going to go with God's people? Will they take advantage of this unique moment in their history and love God, love each other, and become a blessing to the nations? It is now their opportunity to show the world what a community of believers can look like. It is their time to live out this life of faithfulness and devotion to the one true God. They are at the decisive crossroad. Will they follow God and seek him only? Will they model to the world the blessings of God? Or will their hearts turn away and they become faithless?

Here is the heartache in the story. At this moment, when there is so much potential, it all falls apart. When they finally have their place and finally have become a nation, they miss God's plan. All that God wants to put in place has finally happened, and yet things go from bad to worse.

NARRATIVE ON THE TEXT | *A Deadly Cycle*

There is a basic cycle that repeats itself twelve times in the book of Judges. Over and over the people of God go through this heartrending process, and it seems as if they do not have the ability to look back and learn from their past. The cycle (which is illustrated on the PowerPoint presentation) follows this basic pattern:

It begins with a time of *peace*. When Joshua and the people come into the land, there is a time of peace and prosperity. Things are going great. The people are seeking God. They are thankful to God. They believe in him and hold fast to his plan.

Then comes a season of *complacency*. The hearts of the people begin to grow cold. They get used to the goodness of what God has given them. They do not have a vision to become a nation for the world, but they have a dream of becoming a nation for themselves. As their hearts grow complacent, their eyes begin to wander away from the one true God and toward the idols and false gods of the nations around them.

In time, their hearts aren't devoted to God alone. They begin to compromise. *Sin* enters in. Their sinful hearts lead to wicked actions, and the people enter into idolatry. In the land where they are living, there are still people they haven't driven out. These people worship false gods, and soon the people of Israel begin to worship them as well. They begin to enter into all kinds of immorality, the same kinds of immorality as the people who lived in that land.

In the next stage, they learn (even as we learn) that sin always brings *pain*. Even the sins that look the most attractive and seem "safe" lead to pain. Most often the people of Israel experience pain when the nations around them invade, attack, and conquer their land. These invading people oppress the people of God and bring untold pain and sorrow into their lives.

Each oppression lasts for years, sometimes up to two decades. But, finally, the people hit such a point of brokenness that they *cry out to God*. They say, "God, save us. Help us. Get us out of this situation. We don't like what we are experiencing anymore."

Then God sends a *judge* to deliver the people. God raises up a leader who helps the people fight off their oppressors. Over time, their enemies flee and the hearts of the people turn back to God—for a time.

WORD STUDY | *Judge*

We must clarify a couple of things as we look at the book of Judges. When most people today think of a judge, they imagine somebody sitting in a courtroom with a gavel and making detailed legal decisions. When we read the word "judge" in the Old Testament, it has a different meaning. In answer to the question, "What is a judge?" we find three primary definitions:

1. A judge is a political leader over the people of Israel. This person is called to give leadership to the nation.
2. A judge is a military deliverer. The judge stands up and helps fight against the oppressive forces of other nations who come in and take over their land. As we read through Judges, we see this again and again. The people turn their hearts from God. God, in a sense, takes his protective arms from around the community of his people, and another nation comes in and oppresses them. When they are finally heartbroken enough to cry out to God, he sends a judge to deliver them. This leader rallies the people, mounts a military attack against their enemies, and drives the enemy out of the land.
3. A judge is an agent of God's power. The power of God flows through the judges in surprising and mighty ways.

Their victory leads to a time of *peace.* As long as the judge is alive, the people seek after God and follow his ways. But, after a time of peace, the judge dies and the hearts of the people become complacent again. Over and over this cycle repeats itself. The people dive back into the same sins their parents have committed, and often to a greater degree! Generation after generation falls into the same pattern. This is the time of the judges.

ILLUSTRATION | *When Will They Learn?*

If a little boy walked over to a stove, reached up, and touched the burner, he would burn his hand. Even if he was not a bright kid, most likely he would not touch it again. The sheer pain would drive him away from the stove. If he was foolish enough to touch the burner again and was burned again, it would seem this little guy would catch on after being burned a couple of times. Can you imagine a kid being so dense or stubborn that he reached up and touched a hot burner over and over and over again? It would be unthinkable!

Yet God's people do exactly that! Over and over they rebel, worship false gods, and experience the pain of military invasion. Yet they do not learn. Each time they cry out to God and are delivered, they reach out one more time and experience the searing pain of judgment.

LIFE APPLICATION | *A Personal Invitation*

Before we are too hard on the people who lived in the days of the judges, we should spend a little time looking in the mirror. The process of spiritual entropy—this moving toward spiritual disorder and this pushing away from God—is something every follower of Christ faces. It seems to happen almost naturally. Unless we identify it and fight against it, it will creep into our own lives.

As we look at the Israelites, lest we judge them too harshly, we must look back at our lives over the past year. Do we see a pattern of falling into the same sinful actions over and over? Have we repented, confessed our sin, and then found that in a short time we are right back to the same sinful lifestyle and attitudes?

We must also look at what lies ahead in our lives and say, "Look at the blessings God has given me. Look at the place he has put me." When we come to those crossroads where we can honor God and live for him, do we do it? Or do we become self-seeking and turn our hearts away from him? God wants us to learn from this cycle in the book of Judges so that we don't have to live in this painful cycle for the rest of our lives.

PAUSE FOR REFLECTION

Am I Ready to Learn?

We will now identify seven different signs that spiritual entropy is setting in. This entropy can impact a nation, a church, individuals, a family, or any community of people. These things can slowly erode our faith and move us away from God instead of toward him. As we identify these seven examples of spiritual entropy, we must ask some serious questions about our own lives. We must also look at our nation and see where we might be wandering. It is also wise to humbly look at our church, the community of God's people of which we are a part, and discern whether we are in a time of spiritual entropy. It is wise for each of us to pause, right now, and make a decision to look with humble honesty and ask God to show us where entropy might be impacting our lives.

2. The Causes of Spiritual Entropy

INTERPRETIVE INSIGHT | *Spiritual Entropy 1*

The first sign of spiritual entropy in the book of Judges is when *we do not passionately and consistently impart faith to the next generation*. Judges 2:10 presents something that, at first glance, seems unthinkable: "After that whole generation had been gathered to their fathers, another generation grew up, who knew neither the LORD nor what he had done for Israel."

SIGNIFICANT SCRIPTURE

Judges 2:10

How could this be? After all the miracles, battles won, heavenly provision, and powerful revelations of God's presence, this generation forgets to tell their children about their faith. How can an entire generation of believers fail to pass the faith on to their sons and daughters? These are the people who were raised on the words of Deuteronomy 6:4–9. They knew God said: "These commandments that I give you today are to be upon your hearts. Impress them on your children. Talk about them when you sit at home and when you walk along the road, when you lie down and when you get up" (verses 6–7).

NARRATIVE ON LIFE | *History Repeats Itself*

How does a whole generation grow and never learn what God has done for the generation before them? It is hard to imagine, but it was true in Israel's history over and over again. It has also been the case throughout history. How does a vast part of the continent of Europe, which was a place of Spirit-filled reformation and revival, grow cold to the gospel? At one time the continent of Europe was covered with churches

HISTORICAL CONTEXT | *Meeting the Judges*

We meet twelve different judges as we walk through the pages of this book. Six of them are called *major judges*, the other six the *minor judges*. The major judges are "major" only because we know more about them; their story is longer and more detailed. The minor judges get less time and space; some have only one or two verses in the Bible.

Here is a brief overview of the judges. You might call it "Judges at a Glance."

Judges	Passages in Judges	Major or minor
Othniel	3:7–11	*major*
Ehud	3:12–30	*major*
Shamgar	3:31	*minor*
Deborah	4:1–5:31	*major*
Gideon	6:1–8:35	*major*
Tola	10:1–2	*minor*
Jair	10:3–5	*minor*
Jephthah	10:6–12:7	*major*
Ibzan	12:8–10	*minor*
Elon	12:11–12	*minor*
Abdon	12:13–15	*minor*
Samson	13:1–16:31	*major*

filled with passionate worshipers who burned with a love for Jesus. Just a few generations later these churches are all but empty. They have become museums and tourist attractions. Thankfully there are pockets of renewal where God is beginning to kindle a new fire and passion for Jesus. Yet thousands of years later this continent reveals the same sickness that existed in the days of the judges. One generation fails to pass on the flame of faith to the next, and the torch is extinguished.

SIGNIFICANT SCRIPTURE

Judges 6:1 – 15

LIFE APPLICATION | *Love God and Speak of His Presence*

Spiritual entropy doesn't begin with a whole generation wandering from God. It begins with a generation who is not passionate enough to inspire their children to seek the face of God. This was true in Israel thousands of years ago, it was true in Europe over the past centuries, and it is true in America today. Spiritual entropy never begins with a generation that refuses to love Jesus. It starts with parents and grandparents who have grown complacent in their faith.

It isn't that followers of Christ do not love God. It isn't that they do not know the stories of faith. It certainly isn't that they have not experienced God's faithfulness. One of the primary problems is this: Many Christians today don't talk with a sense of joy and freedom about who God is and what he has done.

We must learn to pass on our faith to the next generation. We must get on our knees and pray for our children and grandchildren. We must tell the stories of faith again and again. Each generation needs to express the depth of their love for God and tell their own story of how God is real to them. Listen again to what God commands: "Impress them [God's words and instructions] on your children. Talk about them when you sit at home and when you walk along the road, when you lie down and when you get up" (Deuteronomy 6:7).

PAUSE FOR PRAYER

Let Revival Come

We must pray for renewal in the church around the world, including Europe. We must ask God to visit these parts of the world and bring a new reformation and a return of revival fires. We must also pray for our own country. The church must cry out for this generation to tell to the next generation the great stories of faith and give testimony to the presence of God's power today!

INTERPRETIVE INSIGHT | *Spiritual Entropy 2*

Another sign of spiritual entropy is when *we focus on our abilities, strength, and status to accomplish God's purposes*. If we want to see the strength of a spiritual life, a nation, a family, or a church begin to deteriorate, simply commit always to ask this question: "Can *we* do it?" When we begin by asking, "Do we have enough strength to accomplish things on our own?" we are in trouble! Our strength is never enough to accomplish God's purposes.

NARRATIVE ON THE TEXT | *Gideon's Perspective*

Gideon is a great example of a person who measured his ability to serve God by looking at his own strength. In his story, we see the whole cycle of peace, complacency, sin, pain, crying to God, the coming of a judge, and deliverance repeated. In Judges 6:12 an angel of God comes and speaks to Gideon. He tells Gideon that God is with him, and the angel actually calls Gideon a "mighty warrior." Gideon responds: "But sir … if the LORD is with us, why has all this happened to us?" Gideon wants to know why they are in a time of oppression and suffering if God is with them. Gideon goes on to ask: "Where are all his wonders that our fathers told us about when they said, 'Did not the LORD bring us up out of Egypt?' But now the LORD has abandoned us and put us into the hand of Midian."

God then speaks to Gideon and tells him, "Go in the strength you have and save Israel out of Midian's hand. Am I not sending you?" Here is the key. God says, "Am I not sending you?" But we see Gideon's recurring insecurity come through when he says, "But Lord … how can *I* save Israel? My clan is the *weakest* in Manasseh, and I am the *least* in my family."

> Whatever God can do, faith can do; and whatever faith can do, prayer can do when it is offered in faith. An invitation to prayer is, therefore, an invitation to omnipotence, for prayer engages the omnipotent God and brings him into our human affairs. Nothing is impossible to the Christian who prays in faith, just as nothing is impossible with God. This generation is yet to prove all that prayer can do for believing men and women.
>
> *A. W. Tozer*

NARRATIVE ON LIFE | *Looking at Ourselves*

If you want to see a key to spiritual entropy, just look at Gideon. His eyes were only on himself. When God called him to a great task, all he could see were his own inadequacies and his own weakness. He could not see God's power that was available to him.

When we face challenges in life and when God calls us to difficult tasks, we cannot look at ourselves as the source of power to accomplish these things. These are the questions that cause spiritual entropy:

- Do *I* have the strength and power to accomplish this?
- Do *we* have enough money in our budget?
- Can *we* manage it?
- Can *we* handle it?
- Can *we* do it?

If we operate with this mentality, we will never walk in faith. This mind-set has two pitfalls. (1) It leads us to look to ourselves for the source of strength to accomplish God's calling. (2) It shows a lack of faith that God can accomplish far more than we ever can.

LIFE APPLICATION | *Walking by Faith*

In the coming week, we should all take time to reflect deeply on our lives. We need to ask ourselves some honest and revealing questions, such as:

- Do I walk by faith?
- Do I seek to do the things that I could never do in my own strength but that I know I can do in his power?
- Am I saying "No" to God's leading because I am afraid and don't believe I can do it?
- Do I need to learn to place my trust in God's power, not in my own abilities?

SIGNIFICANT SCRIPTURE

Judges 6:36–40

INTERPRETIVE INSIGHT | *Laying Out the Fleece*

As Gideon seeks to muster his confidence to face the Midianite army, he uses a fleece as a test to see if God is really with him. This is a famous episode in his life. Since then, "setting out a fleece" has become a common phrase and is often practiced in Christian circles. It is important that we take a moment to look at this idea of "laying out a fleece" because this passage makes it clear that this is *not* a behavior that followers of Christ should follow.

In verse 36 (we need to look carefully at the grammar) Gideon says to God, "If you will save Israel by my hand as you have promised...." Notice that God has already promised Gideon that he will do it. In a real way, Gideon is telling God that he has already heard the promise, but he wants more evidence. The fact that God answers Gideon in his insecurity and lack of faith does not make this a positive practice.

In other words, the fleece is *not* an expression of trust in God. *It's an expression of weakness and immaturity.* This is important to note because people often misuse this passage and get superstitious. Some people use the fleece idea to try to validate all kinds of things. But this is not the way to learn God's will. Discovering God's plan for your life is all about discernment, being immersed in Scripture, prayer, listening to God speak through others, learning how to discern God's voice, and growing in wisdom. Fleeces are about our lack of faith, manipulating God, and superstition.

INTERPRETIVE INSIGHT | *Spiritual Entropy 3*

A third sign of spiritual entropy is when *we limit ministry to a few elite and trained professionals.* When we get the idea that ministry is reserved for the highly schooled,

ON THE LIGHTER SIDE | *The Bakery*

The Christian comedian Ken Davis tells about the time he was driving and came to a bakery. This was his little prayer: "God, if there's a parking space in front of this bakery, then I'll know you want me to stop and have a doughnut." He was laying out his own little fleece. Ken then goes on with the story, "Sure enough, the fifth time around the block there was a parking space right in front of the bakery."

seminary-educated people who have learned Greek and Hebrew, we are missing God's plan for his church. When we come to believe that only those who have had the "official classes" and who have jumped through all the religious hoops can serve God, we weaken the church and compromise the health of Christ's body.

LIFE APPLICATION | *God Will Use Whom God Will Choose*

Those who believe that God only uses people who have the official pedigree and the framed degree have not spent much time in the book of Judges. God uses whomever he chooses. It was true in the days of the judges, and it is true now. God knows that his church will enter a time of spiritual entropy and weakness the moment we begin to reserve

CREATIVE MESSAGE IDEA | *Seeing the Numbers*

Invite five strong, healthy men in the congregation to stand up. Be sure to remind people that back in Gideon's days only men were in the army, so you aren't being sexist. Ask people to imagine one of these men fighting against the other four. These were the odds when Gideon's troops were first gathered. It is also important to remember that the Israelites did not have any good weapons and that the Midianites had iron weapons. The soldier count was one Israelite against four of their enemies, and on top of this, the Midianites had better weapons! They were not only outnumbered, they were outgunned.

God says to Gideon, "I see that there is a number problem here." Gideon may have thought, "Thank you, Lord. I didn't want to be the one to mention it, but we are outnumbered! I don't like the odds!" Then God clears things up. "Gideon, you have *too many soldiers.*" Gideon is instructed to tell every man who is afraid that he should go home. Gideon makes his announcement, and 22,000 of the soldiers head home!

The new ratio is 13 to 1. *Ask nine more men to stand.* Let everyone see that the one man now represents Israel and the thirteen men represent the Midianite army. Gideon must be thinking, "I don't think I appreciate God's math." God speaks to Gideon again and says, "Gideon, there is still a number problem." Gideon probably thinks, "Lord, don't help me any longer with the number problem!" Of course he doesn't say anything. God then tells Gideon to watch how the men drink at the watering place. Of those left, 21,700 of the men kneel down to drink, and God sends them home! The new ratio is 450 to 1.

To illustrate the unthinkable odds at this point in the story, *ask another 437 people to stand.* If you have less than 450 people in worship, just ask everyone to stand. Then, ask them to imagine the one man fighting all of them at the same time! We look at these odds and tremble. God looks at them and says, "Perfect! These are the kind of odds I love!"

We must remember that Gideon was afraid when the odds were 4 to 1. God does not mind 450 to 1 odds because when it is all done, everyone will know who won the battle! When we look at our strength and abilities, one-to-one odds can be fearful. But when we see things from God's vantage point, anything is possible.

ministry for a special class of people. We need to look in the mirror and say, "If I am a follower of Christ, I am his minister. I have gifts, I have a calling, and God can use me!"

SIGNIFICANT SCRIPTURE

Judges 7:1–8

NARRATIVE ON THE TEXT | *Surprising Example*

If you are not sure whether you believe that God can use whomever he will choose, take a look at a few examples from the book of Judges.

Ehud may have been physically challenged (Judges 3:15). Most Bibles translate the word "left-handed," but there is a good chance that more is going on here. What the text actually says is that he was unable to use his right hand; something was wrong with that hand. We don't know exactly what, but there is a good chance there was some kind of deformity with Ehud's right hand.

Deborah was called to be a leader of Israel (Judges 4:4). In those days a woman in leadership was unheard of. Notice a couple of unusual things about this particular judge. First, Deborah was a prophet. That's not true of any of the other judges. Deborah alone among the judges walked so closely with God that he chose her to be a judge and a prophetess. She was the highest leader of Israel. While she was the judge, Barak was the commander-in-chief of Israel's army. Yet, when it came time to go to battle, Barak said, "If you go with me, I will go; but if you don't go with me, I won't go." The head of the military force of Israel would not go into battle without Deborah at his side. At that time of history, this was a dramatic role shift that would have shocked virtually everyone!

Gideon was the least in his family and had a real problem with fear, yet God used him! Moreover, his family was the smallest in the clan, voted least likely to succeed.

Jephthah was a prostitute's son and an outcast, but he was still called to lead Israel.

Samson had serious issues with anger, lust, and personal pride.

God is not confused in his choices of leaders. God does not make mistakes or poor choices. God knows that he has no perfect people to work with. All of his servants are broken people who are being restored by his grace. He can use whoever he wants.

NEW TESTAMENT CONNECTION

Why Have Pastors?

The spiritual reality that all of God's people are his ministers runs throughout the Bible. God can and will use each of his followers if we will make our lives available to him. This may cause some people to ask the question, "Then why do we need pastors?" The apostle Paul answers this question with great clarity:

> It was he who gave some to be … pastors and teachers, to prepare God's people for works of service, so that the body of Christ may be built up until we all reach unity in the faith and in the knowledge of the Son of God and become mature, attaining to the whole measure of the fullness of Christ. (Ephesians 4:11–13)

The primary role of a pastor is to equip and train all of the ministers (followers of Christ) to fulfill their ministry.

INTERPRETIVE INSIGHT | *Spiritual Entropy 4*

A fourth thing we should identify in terms of spiritual entropy is when *we become so enmeshed in secular culture that we don't even notice when we adopt ungodly practices.* One of the things that happens in Judges again and again is that the people are so immersed in the culture around them that they begin to adopt pagan, ungodly, unhealthy practices. The scary part is that they hardly even notice it is happening.

NARRATIVE ON THE TEXT | *Beware What You Vow*

In Judges 11 we meet Jephthah. Over time, he is called out to be a judge over Israel. When he is preparing to go to battle against the Ammonites, he makes an unthinkably rash vow to God. He promises to make an offering of whatever first comes out of his home when he returns from the battle.

In those days, it was common for animals to live in houses with the people. Jephthah has only one child, his precious daughter. Most likely he expects an animal to come out of his house when he returns. In any case, he makes a vow: "God, if you deliver the Ammonites into my hand, if you set my people free, then when I come home, the first thing that comes out of the door of my house I will give as a sacrifice." Jephthah wins the battle, but when he arrives home his daughter, his only daughter, comes out of the door of the house to greet him. She is singing, rejoicing, and glad to see her father home safe. He mourns because of his vow!

ON THE LIGHTER SIDE | *A Surprising Shift*

There was a story in the paper years ago about a surprising shift in the gender roles of some toys. At a major toy factory somebody switched the voice boxes in some of the dolls. At the factory the voices and statements that were supposed to go in the G.I. Joe's body went into the Barbie dolls and vice versa. Many girls were traumatized when their Barbie dolls barked out, "Show some guts! Let's move out!" In the same way, boys were confused when their G.I. Joe said, "Let's go shopping!"

HISTORICAL CONTEXT | *Too Close to the Culture*

Whether or not Jephthah actually sacrifices his daughter, something has gone very wrong. To get a sense for what is happening here, we must understand the religious climate of the world at this time. In the land where Jephthah lives, some of the people still take part in human sacrifices. It may well be that Jephthah, even though God has forbidden any sacrifice of human beings, has been so immersed in the culture of that day that he does not have a sense of how deeply wrong this is. He may be so much a part of the culture around him that his thinking is corrupted. Perhaps the distinctives of the culture are molding his thinking, choices, and leadership style more than God's truth is.

INTERPRETIVE INSIGHT | *Did He or Didn't He?*

There are two primary schools of thought on what happens next. Some scholars think that what Jephthah does is to have his daughter take a vow of virginity. She goes into the hills for two months and laments her virginity and the fact that she will never marry. Those in this camp believe Jephthah allows her to live but never marry. In a sense, she is set apart for the Lord, a kind of sacrifice.

Other scholars feel, because the passage goes on to say that Jephthah does exactly as he has vowed, that this man takes his daughter and sacrifices her. We don't know for certain, but what we do know is that his vow is rash and should never have been made.

NEW TESTAMENT CONNECTION

Don't Let the World Shape You!

The warning needed in Jephthah's day is also lifted up by the apostle Paul. He puts it this way: "Do not conform any longer to the pattern of this world, but be transformed by the renewing of your mind. Then you will be able to test and approve what God's will is—his good, pleasing and perfect will" (Romans 12:2). God does not want us to be shaped and formed by the thinking of the world. He calls each of his followers to experience a transformed mind that will lead us to the center of his will.

LIFE APPLICATION | *Culture or God's Word?*

Does our thinking ever get molded and shaped by our culture rather than by God's Word? The truth is that for most of us this is a battle. We must enter into this spiritual warfare because spiritual entropy will set in like gangrene the moment we are shaped by our culture rather than God's will.

One of the quickest ways for a church, a nation, a family, or an individual to experience spiritual entropy is to be shaped by culture and not by God's Word. God's call for us is to identify where the world is molding our thinking and resist it.

INTERPRETIVE INSIGHT | *Spiritual Entropy 5*

Another sign that spiritual entropy is setting in is when *we forget and break the covenant commitments we have made before God and others.* Samson is an example of a leader who starts well and ends poorly because he fails to keep the covenant commitments he has made.

SIGNIFICANT SCRIPTURE

Judges 13:4–5; 14:8–10

NARRATIVE ON THE TEXT | *Vow Breaking*

Samson has a good beginning. An angel speaks of his birth. He is born to godly parents. The Spirit of God is upon him from his childhood. He starts so well. Early on Samson makes the vow of a Nazirite, which has three parts: Touch no unclean thing; drink no wine or fermented drink; don't cut your hair. Every indication is that Samson has agreed to these vows. He has made the vow before God that he will be a Nazirite, and he understands what it means. As he goes through his life, he systematically breaks each of the vows.

At one point Samson kills a lion. He leaves the body of the dead animal, but later he comes back. When he does, the dead carcass has become a beehive and is filled with honey. The Bible tells us that Samson uses his hand to remove honey from the body of the lion. The first part of his vow, touch no unclean thing, is broken when he touches the body of a dead animal.

Later in Samson's life we read about a time he throws a party (Judges 14:10). The language in this passage is strong and points to a specific kind of feast or party. It is a drinking party and may be seen as a fairly inappropriate kind of a party. We can't know for sure, but there are indications that Samson not only throws the party but enters into the drinking. If he does, he breaks his Nazirite vow of never drinking.

Later on he tells Delilah that the secret of his power is in his hair. She cuts his hair, and Samson loses his power. Why is the cutting of his hair such a big deal? Because it is the last sign of his vow. Every indication is that he has broken the first part of the vow, the second part of the vow, and now the third part of the vow. He becomes weak not so much because of the length of his hair but because of the condition of his heart.

> All practical power over sin ... depends on maintaining closet communion. Those who abide in the secret place with God show themselves mighty to conquer evil, and strong to work and war for God.
>
> *A. T. Pierson*

SIGNIFICANT SCRIPTURE

Judges 14:1–2; 16:1, 4

LIFE APPLICATION | *Covenant Keepers*

We live in a time when people think nothing of breaking vows. Covenants mean little to most people. The words "I do" become "I don't" more and more quickly, and few people are surprised. When a couple hits a ten-year wedding anniversary, many are amazed. Yet, God calls his people to be promise keepers, not breakers. Spiritual entropy occurs when people take their commitments and covenant promises lightly. This is the way of this generation. Yet we must live in a different way. We must reflect deeply on the promises we have made to our family members, to our God, to our employers, and to our church. We must keep our word with tenacity!

INTERPRETIVE INSIGHT | *Spiritual Entropy 6*

Another sign of spiritual entropy is when *our desires and impulses begin to rule our lives rather than the Holy Spirit of God.*

Samson is a walking impulse machine. If he wants it, he takes it. If he sees it, he gets hold of it. In Judges 14:1–2 we read: "Samson went down to Timnah and saw there a young Philistine woman. When he returned, he said to his father and mother, 'I have seen a Philistine woman in Timnah; now get her for me as my wife.'" Do you get the sense that Samson has gotten to know her, built a deep relationship, and talked a lot about her hopes and dreams for life? The text is clear! Samson sees her and wants her, and that is the end of the story.

As we walk through Samson's life, we discover that this becomes a pattern. In Judges 16:1, Samson sees a prostitute (most likely one of the many temple prostitutes). He spends the night with her in an ungodly sexual union.

In Judges 16:4 we meet another one of Samson's poor romantic choices, Delilah. Again Samson has seen an attractive woman and falls head over heels in lust with her. As we survey his life, we discover that he is driven by his personal passions far more than by the Spirit of God.

PAUSE FOR REFLECTION

A Week of Investigation

Next week we will focus on how to break the cycle of spiritual entropy. Take time through this week to do a thorough investigation of your life. Reflect on the seven signs that spiritual entropy may be setting into your life and see if you recognize any of these in your life. Then, ask the Holy Spirit to prepare you for a process of breaking this cycle as we gather next week to continue our study of Judges.

LIFE APPLICATION | *Check Your Impulses*

Before we judge Samson too quickly, we must realize that we can be driven by our desires and impulses just as he was. Maybe it is the impulse to gossip and speak negatively about others. Perhaps it is the insatiable love for shopping, buying, and acquiring more. It could be anger, lust, greed, or any other sin. The truth is, all of us can be driven by our desires. Samson has the power to fight against a hundred men and conquer them, but he cannot fight off one woman. It becomes a weakness in his life. It is a sign of the spiritual entropy he battles. We need to ask, "Is there an area in my life where I am driven by my impulses? Do I face a besetting sin that keeps getting the best of me?"

NARRATIVE ON LIFE | *Besetting Sins*

Many followers of Christ discover that they struggle with a besetting sin. This is an area of spiritual battle that seems to come up over and over again. These sins plague the life of a believer and bring great discouragement in his or her spiritual life. These sins tend to be very *convenient*. They are right around you. They are easy to get ahold of.

They are also *self-gratifying*. When you enter into this arena of sin, it usually feels good. For instance, if you struggle with gossip, you need to recognize that Proverbs says words of gossip are like tasty morsels. Lust has an immediate gratification. Eating offers instant pleasure. All these things can be besetting sins.

Another common factor of besetting sins is that they are often *culturally normative*. Most of these sins are things that people in our culture say, "It's fine. Go for it! What's the big deal?"

A final aspect of these kinds of sin is that they are *attractive*. They are like a candy apple filled with poison—pleasing to the eyes but in the end, deadly.

INTERPRETIVE INSIGHT | *Spiritual Entropy 7*

A final evidence of spiritual entropy is when *we cry out to God for help because we are facing pain but not because we are truly sorry for our sin*. Over and over the people of

Israel cry out for God's help. Yet as we read Judges, we get the impression that they may have been less than sincere in their repentance. The people of Israel cry out, "God, help us! Help us! We are being oppressed! Help us!" Yet it seems they are crying out of their pain, not out of sorrow for their sins.

We can do the same thing. We can cry out, "Lord, help me. I don't like the situation I am in." But our heart may not have changed. We may be ready to go out and commit the same sin week after week, but we want help right now because we are experiencing pain. We don't want to live with the consequences of our sins, so we ask God to bail us out. However, we have no intention of changing our life patterns. Like the people of Israel, we can offer up a repentance that is all about delivering us and has nothing to do with true sorrow before God. This is a clear sign of spiritual entropy.

Message 13

Intercepting Spiritual Entropy

The Book of Judges

THE HEART OF THE Message

Spiritual entropy means our spiritual lives tend to move toward disorder if we don't put energy into keeping them vibrant and alive. Without investing effort and time we tend to lose our passion, focus, and energy for spiritual things. Spiritual entropy is the reality that if we simply leave things the way they are in our spiritual lives, they won't stay the same. With time they will grow weak and move toward disorder. Like the people of Israel, we will watch as our spiritual lives move toward disarray unless we continually seek to strengthen ourselves spiritually.

In the last message we identified seven different signs and sources of spiritual entropy. In this message we will look at how we can intentionally intercept each of these seven signs. We are not destined to repeat the mistakes of the past. God offers us a way out. We can break the cycle of spiritual entropy and move toward maturity and spiritual health.

BRIEF MESSAGE OUTLINE

1. A vicious cycle
2. Identifying spiritual entropy and intercepting it

THE HEART OF THE Messenger

This message is very practical. We can experience new direction and spiritual health if we are open to what God desires to do in our lives. As you prepare this message, take time to reflect on each of the seven ways to intercept spiritual entropy. Ask the Holy Spirit to show you how this message applies to your life. Invite God to reveal one or two practical ways you can fight against the cycle of sin we learn about in the book of Judges. As you bring this message, seek to come from a place of humility with a clear understanding that every person gathered, including yourself, can be challenged to grow through the message of the book of Judges.

1. A Vicious Cycle

INTERPRETIVE INSIGHT | *Can the Cycle Be Broken?*

Last week we examined the vicious cycle that the people of Israel were experiencing over and over again. It began with a time of peace. A judge led the people, and as long as the judge was alive, the people prospered, followed God, and experienced a fairly tranquil existence. Over time, however, the judge died, and the people became complacent. They became lazy about their spiritual lives and began to slide away. Compromise began to enter their lives, and it grew until full-blown sin took over. Sin poisoned the community life of God's people and their personal spiritual lives. In most cases, it was the sin of idolatry.

Next, pain came crashing in, because pain always follows sin. Even the most hidden and "private" sins can cause deep pain. Finally, the people cried out, "God, help us! We can't take it anymore!" When they did so, God sent a judge, who came and delivered Israel from the hands of their enemies. They were set free from their oppressors and the pain ended as they entered a season of peace. But, after a time of peace, the cycle repeated itself. As we watch God's people go through this cycle over and over, we begin to wonder: Is there any way to break this process of spiritual decay?

NARRATIVE ON LIFE | *Maybe Tomorrow*

Many people live with a *maybe tomorrow syndrome*. This is the habit of saying: I'll get to it tomorrow instead of addressing life issues today. When it comes to breaking the cycle of spiritual entropy, the only time to start is *now*! We have all seen the results of waiting until tomorrow.

The syndrome goes something like this. You say: "I know I need to get some things right in my spiritual life; I'll get to it soon, but not today. I know I need to stop

HISTORICAL CONTEXT | *A Critical Time (Review)*

In the book of Judges we see that the two things God promised Abraham had become a reality. First, God said his people would be such a great nation that they would be like the stars of the heavens and the grains of sand on the seashore—you could not count them! Moreover, he also promised that he was going to give them a place, a land of their own.

For centuries the people were waiting, longing, and praying for the day that they would be a mighty nation in their own land. In the book of Judges, this dream has become a reality. Last week we looked at the sad fact that the people missed this divine moment in time. They could have become a beacon to the nations. Instead of walking closely with God during this time, however, their hearts begin to wander. Spiritual entropy sets in and they fall away!

that bad habit, and I will, tomorrow. I feel a conviction that I need to make space in my day to be with God in prayer. Yet, my schedule is so full, maybe next week." Everything can wait just one more day, but before we know it, a lifetime passes. Time rushes past and our good intentions remain only intentions and never become actions.

We can almost hear the words spoken in self-deceived sincerity: "I may not be serious about my faith right now, but when I graduate from high school I am going to adjust my priorities. This is my time to play and enjoy life." Years later the same person is saying, "I'm in college, I'm single, and I'm having the time of my life. I want to focus on my faith, but it doesn't fit into my lifestyle right now. Maybe I'll get serious about God later in life—when I get married and settle down." More years roll by and we hear the words, "How can I really devote my life to God in this busy season of life? My spouse and children demand too much—maybe I can really focus on my faith when the kids are grown ... maybe when I retire ... maybe when I die!" A lifetime can pass in the snap of a finger, and good intentions are never realized.

INTERPRETIVE INSIGHT | *No Peace*

Four of the first five judges have a season of peace after deliverance comes to the people. After Othniel, there are forty years of peace—a whole generation. After Ehud, there are eighty years of peace. After Shamgar there is no mention of peace at all. After both Deborah and Gideon there are forty years of peace. Since forty years represented a generation, it is clear that each of the judgeships of these leaders leads to a generation who experiences peace, and in Ehud's case, there are two generations of peace. What is shocking is that there is no mention of any time of peace after the next seven judges. In other words, after their judgeship ended, they go right from deliverance back into complacency and sin.

At this point, a part of the sad cycle of judges disappears. Unfortunately, one of the only good parts of the cycle, the time of peace, is gone. Sin is like that. The more we enter into it, the more times we go through that cycle, the less peace we experience. The longer we give in to the same sin, the deeper the claws of that sin dig into our soul. Like the people of Israel, we can cry out to God, "Help me, I'm sorry, I'll never do it again!" Then, when God delivers us and spares us from ourselves, we dive right back into the same sin again.

2. Identifying Spiritual Entropy and Intercepting It

We can learn from the mistakes of Israel during the season of the judges. God wants to say to us, "I can change your life. I have a way to redirect your future. You don't have to live in this heartbreaking cycle of sin any more!" In the rest of this message we will note again each of the signs of spiritual entropy and then discover ways we can end the cycle. We are going to learn how to intercept spiritual entropy.

SIGNIFICANT SCRIPTURE

Judges 2:10

The truth is that one, two, or even three of the examples we are going to study might apply to you as an individual. Perhaps for some of you, all seven examples will bring conviction. What is important is that each one of you says to God, "Lord, please speak to my heart. Challenge me to grow. Show me at least one area I can grow and teach me to break the cycle of spiritual entropy in my life." If you are willing to open your heart today to God's Word, you can hear the Holy Spirit speak and lead you to growth.

INTERPRETIVE INSIGHT | *Interception 1*

Spiritual entropy 1 occurs when we do not passionately and consistently impart the faith to the next generation. To intercept that spiritual entropy, *we must have a deep commitment to pass on the torch of faith to the next generation with grace, consistency, and passion.*

Last week the first area of spiritual entropy we looked at is found in Judges 2:10 — that spiritual entropy comes in when faith is not passionately and consistently imparted to the next generation. When this happens, a generation begins to wander from the Lord. Sadly, this is happening in the church today. We must all ask the question: "Will I pass on the faith to the next generation? Will I take part in the great task of sharing the faith with those who follow me?"

NEW TESTAMENT CONNECTION

The Generations

God celebrates when the faith is entrusted to the next generation. Look at the powerful example found in the life of Timothy. The apostle Paul writes in 2 Timothy 1:3 – 5:

> I thank God, whom I serve, as my forefathers did, with a clear conscience, as night and day I constantly remember you in my prayers. Recalling your tears, I long to see you, so that I may be filled with joy. I have been reminded of your sincere faith, which first lived in your grandmother Lois and in your mother Eunice and, I am persuaded, now lives in you also.

God celebrates when a sincere and authentic faith is passed from one generation to the next. If we want to avoid spiritual entropy, we must get serious about doing all we can to be sure our children and grandchildren are growing in their faith.

LIFE APPLICATION | *Making Spiritual Growth a Priority*

Those who have spiritual responsibility for children should make decisions about what will be a priority in their lives and schedules. Spiritual growth, connecting in the community of the church, and worship experiences need to be priorities in our schedules. As we raise children, we must help them understand that regular worship, Sunday school, youth groups, mission trips, and the many opportunities offered in the church are deeply important for their spiritual formation.

In recent years sports for both boys and girls seem to demand more and more time. Many teams practice three, four, or even five days a week. Parents will drive their children to and from practices and make attending games a priority. At the same time, many of these same parents find it difficult to get their children to church for worship and times of fellowship with other young Christians their age.

When a young person says, "I don't feel like going to my soccer, basketball, or football practice," parents tend to respond, "You made a commitment. It is important, you need to be there." What about when a young person says, "I don't feel like going to church, youth group, Sunday school, or my church choir"? In the same way, those who have been given spiritual responsibilities for these young people need to help them see that consistency and commitment in gathering with God's people is very important.

PAUSE FOR PRAYER

May the Lord Bless You

As your children and youth volunteers are still standing, (see sidebar below) take a moment to lift up a prayer for them. Focus on two specific areas of prayer:

- Thank God for their commitment and faithfulness and for the fruit they are bearing.
- Pray that God's Holy Spirit will fill each of them and lead them forward in their area of ministry to children and youth.

INTERPRETIVE INSIGHT | *Interception 2*

Spiritual entropy 2 is focusing on our own abilities, strength, and status in order to accomplish God's purposes. To intercept that entropy, *we must become profoundly aware that only God has the power to win the victory in the battles we face.*

When Gideon was called to lead the people of Israel, he said, "How can I save Israel? My clan is the weakest in Manasseh, and I am the least in my family." Gideon looked at his own abilities, strength, and power and simply said, "God, I can't do it. I just don't have what it takes." We get into big trouble when we focus on our abilities rather than on God's power.

NARRATIVE ON THE TEXT | *Only God Could Win This Battle*

In Judges 7:2 God tells Gideon he is concerned that if the people of Israel think they have won the battle in their own power, they will boast and act as if their own strength is enough to overcome their enemies. God then establishes odds to make it painfully clear that it is divine deliverance, not human might, that wins battles. The odds for Gideon's battle start out as challenging. They are 4 to 1, and Israel is on the low side of the equation. Then the odds shift to 13 to 1. Finally, Gideon and the people of Israel go to war, when the odds are 450 to 1!

SIGNIFICANT SCRIPTURE

Judges 6:1 – 15

CREATIVE MESSAGE IDEA | *Stand and Be Blessed!*

In every church there are people who have a special call to invest in the lives of children and students. These gifted servants help in the nursery, teach preschoolers, work with grade school children, lead the youth, and facilitate small groups for the youngest church members. These people must be reminded just how important their ministry is to the spiritual future of the church.

Invite all those who are part of your ministry to children from nursery through high school to stand. Take a moment to thank them for their faithfulness to say yes to God's invitation to minister to the next generation. Remind them that only eternity will truly show what a difference their lives and ministry have made.

At this point there is no possible way that Gideon and the people of Israel feel they are going to win the battle with their own abilities, strength, or resources. God is teaching his people that they cannot win on their own. At the same time, they are learning that with God, any odds can be overcome.

SIGNIFICANT SCRIPTURE

Judges 7:1–8

NARRATIVE ON LIFE | *Joni*

Many are aware of the amazing story of Joni Eareckson Tada. On July 30, 1967, a diving accident transformed this active and energetic teenager into a person confined to a wheelchair for the rest of her life, paralyzed from the neck down. No longer did she have the physical ability to do anything for herself. In her long road to recovery, Joni fought physical battles with bedsores and constant pain, and emotional and spiritual battles with anger, helplessness, and depression.

But through reading and reflecting on the Scriptures and other Christian literature, and through the help of friends, Joni turned her life over to dependence on Christ as she faced these many battles. Her incredible paintings, done with a brush in her mouth, are known everywhere, and she now leads a worldwide ministry of hope and encouragement (JAF Ministries) to other people with disabilities and to their families.

INTERPRETIVE INSIGHT | *Interception 3*

In *spiritual entropy 3*, we limit ministry to a few "elite" and trained "professionals." In order to intercept this entropy, *we must invite all of God's people to minister according to their gifts and calling.*

Far too often we are content to limit ministry to a few people whom we see as specially called or having certain training. If we are going to intercept this spiritual entropy, we must turn this mentality around and invite *all of God's people* to minister according to their gifts and calling. We need to say to all God's people, "You are

CREATIVE MESSAGE IDEA | *Remember Your Commitments*

Many church traditions have specific times when vows are given and commitments are made. For some, with newborns there is a dedication or baptism. At these services there are often specific commitments made by the parents. If you have this kind of tradition in your church, consider reading these words of commitment to the congregation. Remind all of the parents what they promised when their child was dedicated or baptized. Ask them to honestly reflect on whether or not they are being intentional about fulfilling their vows. You may even want to go a step further and have copies of your church's dedication/baptism vows available for parents to take with them as they leave the service.

called by God to serve and minister according to your gifts. It doesn't matter what your background is."

Recall that Ehud had a physical disability, Deborah was a woman in a patriarchal society, Gideon was the least in his family and had deep fear, Jephthah was an outcast, and Samson struggled with self-control and lust. Yet God used these unlikely people and endowed them with his grace when they made themselves available.

LIFE APPLICATION | *Excuses, Excuses*

The church will never become all God wants it to be until every follower of Jesus Christ is ministering according to his or her spiritual gifts. Some people are still sitting on the sidelines, refusing to serve. God wants to speak to their hearts and calls them to change their lifestyle. They have plenty of excuses: "I could never do that, I don't have the skills! I am not strong enough. I am not old enough. I am not mature enough. I don't have the education." These and countless other excuses are used every day! Yet God says, "I have a plan for you! I will start with you right where you are, but it is time to start serving." Maybe God needs to start with a heart change. He is going to challenge you, his people, his church, to new places of service to each other, in the community, and around the world. Excuses might work on people but never on God.

Maybe your service will be expressed quietly through intercessory prayer. It may be expressed through calling on shut-ins. God may be calling you to be part of the evangelism and outreach ministry of your church. A year from now you may be teaching children in the church or working with the youth. But if you say, "I am a believer in Jesus Christ," God intends for you to serve in some tangible way. Entering into regular ministry in an area where you are called by God and gifted to serve will help break the cycle of spiritual entropy.

INTERPRETIVE INSIGHT | *Interception 4*

SIGNIFICANT SCRIPTURE

Judges 10:6–10; 11:30–35

In *spiritual entropy 4*, we become so enmeshed in secular culture that we adopt ungodly practices. In order to intercept this entropy, we must keep God's Word and standards as our first and final authority for life and faith.

As we saw last week, Jephthah became so much a part of his world that he didn't even see where he was wandering from God's plan. This also happened with Gideon at the end of his life, when he made an idol and the people began to worship it, leading their hearts away from God. Even Gideon, who started so well, made some really unwise decisions because he was doing things the way people in the world did at that time rather than following God's way.

NARRATIVE ON LIFE | *God's Truth Is Our Authority*

We intercept this kind of entropy and turn it around when we keep God's Word and standards as our first and final authority for life and faith. Too often we make decisions by doing an informal survey of four or five friends. We ask them what they think we should do about a particular life situation rather than seeking God's counsel. Of course the Bible is clear there is wisdom in godly counsel. But simply taking a poll will not necessarily help us determine God's will. If somebody gives us advice that contradicts God's Word, they are wrong. If that which is popular or "common practice" is inconsistent with Scripture, we must follow God's Word every time. Otherwise, spiritual entropy is bound to set in.

ILLUSTRATION | *Flying by the Instruments*

When pilots, especially military pilots, train to fly airplanes, the trainer takes the plane into a variety of loops and moves, designed to confuse the trainee as to which way is up and which way is down. The trainer then turns the controls over to the trainee and tells him or her to straighten the plane out. The *only* way for the trainee to get the plane oriented in a safe direction is *to use the instruments.* If the trainee goes on gut feelings, he or she is bound to send the plane into a tailspin and crash it the ground. The Bible is like that set of instruments. In the confusion of society values and norms, the only way to place life on the straight and safe pathway is to use its principles and guidance for life.

SIGNIFICANT SCRIPTURE

Judges 13:4–5;
14:8–10;
16:17–19

INTERPRETIVE INSIGHT | *Interception 5*

In *spiritual entropy 5,* we forget and break the covenant commitments we have made before God and others. In order to intercept this entropy, *we must remember our covenant commitments and find joy and fullness of life in keeping them.*

Samson broke at least three covenant commitments he had made before God. With each vow he broke, Samson grew weaker and weaker. Finally, when his hair was cut, the mighty and seemingly invincible Samson became utterly weak.

NARRATIVE ON LIFE | *The Importance of Remembering*

We intercept spiritual entropy when we remember our covenant commitments and find pleasure and fullness of life in keeping them. When we joyfully hold to our mar-

CREATIVE MESSAGE IDEA | *This Is My Bible*

There is a short reading that exists in many different forms, which reminds us of what the Bible means to followers of Christ. You may want to use it at this point in the service.

Invite people to hold their Bible in their hands or even up in the air. Then, as the leader, speak each line and invite people to repeat after you:

This is my Bible.
It is the Word of God.
I am who it says I am.
I have what it says I have.
I will live as it calls me to live.

riage vows and seek to live them out each day, we find health and strength in this covenant relationship. When we honor agreements and contracts in the marketplace, our integrity is preserved and people trust what we say and do. Most of all, when we remember the promise we made to love God with all our heart, we overcome spiritual entropy. Each time we go back to the cross of Jesus, where we first experienced grace, we gain power to move forward and keep growing in our faith. God wants us to honor our covenant commitments, both with him and with each other.

INTERPRETIVE INSIGHT | *Interception 6*

In *spiritual entropy 6*, our desires and impulses begin to rule our lives rather than the Holy Spirit of God. To intercept this entropy, *we must look to the Holy Spirit of God to grant us the strength we need to overcome sinful desires and impulses.*

> Sin is to be overcome, not so much by direct opposition to it as by cultivating opposite principles. Would you kill the weeds in your garden, plant it with good seed; if the ground be well occupied, there will be less need of the hoe.
>
> *Abraham Fuller, tenth century*

NARRATIVE ON LIFE | *Inviting the Spirit to Work*

When we cry out to the Spirit of God and say, "O Spirit of God, this temptation is enticing my heart, this struggle is wearing me down, this impulse is driving me where I don't want to go. Please help me!" At this moment, the moment we call out with a sincere heart, the cycle of spiritual entropy begins to break. God is waiting for us to cry out and say, "I know I don't have the strength to deal with this! I am convicted that I will fall if I don't receive your strength. Spirit of God, please give me power to turn away from this sinful enticement. Help me come to a place of humble repentance. I need you. Deliver me!"

SIGNIFICANT SCRIPTURE

Judges 14:1 – 2; 16:1, 4

INTERPRETIVE INSIGHT | *Interception 7*

In *spiritual entropy 7*, we cry out to God for help because we are facing pain but not because we are truly sorry for our sin. To intercept this entropy, *our cry for deliverance must come from a true awareness of our sin, a genuine sorrow for how we have broken God's heart and hurt others, and a commitment to change.*

All too often we are tempted to cry out and say, "God, help me! I don't like the circumstances I am facing and I don't want to experience the pain or consequences of my sinful choices." The problem is that our hearts are not broken over the sin we have committed and how we have dishonored God.

NARRATIVE ON THE TEXT | *Authentic Repentance?*

In the book of Judges, some passages lay bare the true heart condition of the people of Israel. These passages also help us see how God feels about false repentance that is really just lip service to make us feel better. Look at Judges 10:10 – 14:

> Then the Israelites cried out to the LORD, "We have sinned against you, forsaking our God and serving the Baals."
>
> The LORD replied, "When the Egyptians, the Amorites, the Ammonites, the Philistines, the Sidonians, the Amalekites and the Maonites oppressed you and you cried to me for help, did I not save you from their hands? But you have forsaken me and served other gods, so I will no longer save you. Go and cry out to the gods you have chosen. Let them save you when you are in trouble!"

SIGNIFICANT SCRIPTURE

Judges 10:11 – 16

God speaks with cutting clarity here. He reminds the people of the way they called to him and offered confession of sins, but they didn't mean it! The next moment they were out chasing after false gods again. Their actions showed that their confession was not authentic.

INTERPRETIVE INSIGHT | *Does Confession Always Bring Forgiveness?*

This passage seems to draw a picture of God's people crying out for help and forgiveness, but God refuses to help and forgive them. How can this be? We always hear that if we cry out to God and are truly sorry, he will always forgive. This is absolutely true! The problem in this passage is that the people are not truly repentant. Their sorrow is not over their sin; it is over being caught. They are not confessing because they are

CREATIVE MESSAGE IDEA | *Remembering Our Vows*

All throughout the Old Testament we see God's people setting up memorials. They pile up stones or build an altar so that these monuments will stand as a physical reminder of who God is and what he has done, and of the agreement made between God and his people. We should learn how to set up reminders that bring us back to the basics of what God wants for our lives.

If your church has some kind of liturgy that is read when people join the church or some membership agreement or covenant, plan to have copies available as people leave the service. Invite people to pick up a copy and place it where they will see it on a regular basis. They may want to frame it and place it in a prominent place in their home. Some may fold it up and put it in their wallet or purse. Others may feel the best place for this reminder to be posted is on the refrigerator or the bathroom mirror, where they will see it every day. The key is for people to see these words and be reminded, on a regular basis, of God's call for them to hold to their vows.

broken over their sinfulness; rather, they are trying to throw out words of confession with hearts that are not sorry for their sin and lives that have no intention of changing.

We can almost hear the people of Israel, "O Lord, we're sorry. We won't do it again. Get us out of this mess we have gotten ourselves into. Then we will always do everything you want us to do. We really mean it this time. Really!" And God says, "No, I won't. You don't mean it. You have no intention of changing. Your hearts are not broken and your confession is not authentic." God will not reinforce a false confession with deliverance.

NARRATIVE ON THE TEXT | *True Repentance in Action*

What happens next brings hope to our hearts (Judges 10:15–16):

> But the Israelites said to the LORD, "We have sinned. Do with us whatever you think best, but please rescue us now." Then they got rid of the foreign gods among them and served the LORD. And he could bear Israel's misery no longer.

This passage clarifies for us that the first words of confession and cry for help (10:10–14) were not authentic. They had not even gotten rid of their idols. They had no intention of changing. But now they are broken. They confess their sin again, and this time they mean it! They invite God to do whatever he must do to give them a new beginning. They take action and get rid of their idols. True repentance fills their hearts and their lives. What happens next? God's heart grows tender toward them, and he cannot stand to look on their pain and misery. He takes action to deliver them.

LIFE APPLICATION | *True Confession*

True confession is more than the words of our lips; it is hearts that are broken because we have broken the heart of God. It is sincere repentance that flows because we have seen the pain we have caused others. When we come humbly before God, ready to throw out our idols and the sin that clutters our life, God's heart is softened toward us.

It is time that followers of Christ do a heart-check and make sure that our prayers of confession are not just a routine to make us feel better and justify continued sin. When we confess and repent, we must be ready to change. Think about what true repentance looks like:

- A prayer of confession about having lips that gossip should lead to a commitment to no longer slander others with the things we say.

NEW TESTAMENT CONNECTION

Our First Love

In the book of Revelation Jesus speaks to his people in seven churches. After he affirms what they are doing right, he also speaks words of conviction as to where they have strayed from his paths. When speaking to the church in the city of Ephesus, Jesus says: "Yet I hold this against you: You have forsaken your first love. Remember the height from which you have fallen! Repent and do the things you did at first" (Revelation 2:4–5).

Jesus knows the pain we will experience if we give ourselves to false gods, and he is concerned that his children love him first and foremost. When we love him with conviction and passion, we hold to the covenant he has established with us. When we seek to honor our Savior and love him, we grow in our ability to keep the vows and commitments we make to others.

- Asking for forgiveness for cheating at school should be accompanied with a commitment to study harder and never take answers from another student—or give them.
- Crying out for forgiveness for an affair should lead to the severing of the sinful relationship and a new level of accountability to remain pure and faithful to our marriage vows.
- Confessing the sin of gluttony should be followed with new eating patterns and even a commitment to regular exercise.
- Repentance from filling your mind with ungodly images should include removing any lust-producing images that have been stored in some secret hiding place or in a computer file.
- Admitting that the money monster has gotten a grip on your heart and asking for forgiveness for greed should lead a follower of Christ to a new level of generosity and joy-filled giving.

The point is that every time we truly repent and confess our sins, transformation will occur.

NARRATIVE ON LIFE | *The Cycle Can Stop!*

God has good news for all of his followers. The cycle that repeats over and over again in the book of Judges can be broken. His power is great enough. We don't have to live in an endless cycle of falling into sin over and over again. The process of spiritual entropy can be broken, and we can live in freedom.

Message 14

Samuel: Learning to Listen to God

1 Samuel 1–8

THE HEART OF THE Message

Prayer has always been seen as a central element of the Christian life. It is essential for spiritual health. The prayer life of Hannah stands as a profound example of honest and passionate prayer. The story of Samuel also gives us insight to prayer on many levels. Through the example of his life, we learn about listening to God and learning to recognize his voice. Through Hannah's and Samuel's lives, we also learn about honesty, repentance, thankfulness, and the heart of a prayer. In this message we will discover how to grow more intimate with our Maker through a growing life of prayer.

THE HEART OF THE Messenger

God longs to be in close relationship with each of his children. He wants to hear from us even more than we want to talk with him. He also longs to speak to us and give direction to our lives. As you prepare to bring this message, spend time listening for the voice of God. He may speak through the Bible, through another believer, through circumstances, or through the still small voice of his Holy Spirit. Prepare your heart by finding time to be silent before the Lord and listening for his leading and prompting in your life.

BRIEF MESSAGE OUTLINE

1. Lessons from Hannah
2. Lessons from Eli
3. Lessons from Samuel

1. Lessons from Hannah

INTERPRETIVE INSIGHT | *A Look at Polygamy*

Hannah and Peninnah were both married to the same man. These two women were part of a culture where men would often have more than one wife. This institution is called polygamy.

There is no indication in the Bible that polygamy was part of God's plan. Rather, it was part of many pagan cultures, and some of God's people adopted the practice.

As we study through the Old Testament, we discover that there are no examples of happy polygamist families. People in polygamous marriages faced rivalry, bitterness, and ongoing conflict in their homes. Over and over in the Old Testament we see examples of how this kind of arrangement does not work.

Although the Old Testament does not overtly condemn this practice, it is clear that God never intended his people to enter into polygamous relationships. His plan was for one man to be in a covenant relationship with one woman for a lifetime, and they are to become one flesh. We see this in the very beginning when Adam and Eve were placed in the garden (see Genesis 2:23–24). God's intent is monogamy.

SIGNIFICANT SCRIPTURE

1 Samuel 1:1–20

NARRATIVE ON THE TEXT | *Meeting Samuel's Family*

Hannah and Peninnah are not good friends. They go through years of family life filled with conflict. Early on Peninnah gets pregnant and gives birth to a little baby. She is blessed with a child again and again. We can imagine Hannah standing off in the wings just watching and wondering if she will ever hold a child in her arms. First Samuel 1 emphasizes this extended time of waiting twice to help us see how long this painful process goes on for Hannah—year after year.

Hannah goes through the trauma of infertility, which is always painful. In her culture, barrenness carried the added pain of people assuming that if a woman could not bear children, she must have offended God in some way. People would look at Hannah and wonder if she was under some kind of a curse. There was a huge stigma attached to infertility in Bible times.

To make matters worse, Peninnah mocks Hannah's misery, perhaps because she knows Elkanah loves Hannah more than her. When Elkanah and his family go to Shiloh to worship, he gives portions of the meat to Peninnah and her children, but to Hannah he gives a double portion. Why? Because he loves her.

ON THE LIGHTER SIDE | *The Punishment for Having Two Wives*

There is a leader who looked at the practice of polygamy and asked, "Do you know what the biblical punishment was for having two wives?" His answer: "Having two wives." The same would have been true if a woman had two husbands (although this never happened). Polygamy always led to misery. One of the ways the writers in the Old Testament undercut the institution of polygamy was by using narrative material to paint an honest picture of just how painful and conflict-filled polygamous relationships would become.

In other words, Peninnah, though she has children, is not cherished and loved in the same way that Hannah is. She knows this, and it must have eaten away at her soul. Hannah is the woman who possesses what Peninnah wants most in all the world, the love of her husband.

Peninnah is a raving success in the child-bearing department and Hannah a total failure. So, Peninnah seems to rub this in Hannah's face every chance she has. Hannah shows no sign of striking back, but she does get depressed. She weeps and will not eat. Because she has no children, Hannah is living in the depth of despair. On top of her sorrow is the constant provoking of Peninnah.

LIFE APPLICATION | *The Power of a Listening Ear*

When we have no idea what to say to someone in the midst of his or her pain, the best thing to do is to simply listen. Often our presence is the best gift we can give. Elkanah would be better off just sitting with his wife and sharing in her pain. Instead, he opens his mouth wide and puts his foot in it.

SIGNIFICANT SCRIPTURE

Job 2:12–13

In the book of Job we see a similar situation. Job is suffering and experiencing a depth of pain that most of us have a hard time even imagining. When his three friends come to visit him, they show amazing restraint and wisdom. We read this account in Job 2:12–13:

> When they saw him from a distance, they could hardly recognize him; they began to weep aloud, and they tore their robes and sprinkled dust on their heads. Then they sat on the ground with him for seven days and seven nights. No one said a word to him, because they saw how great his suffering was.

ON THE LIGHTER SIDE | *You Got Me, Babe!*

Hannah is miserable. She is hurting. Sorrow fills her heart. Her husband loves her and wants to do something to cheer her up. He is not Mr. Sensitivity. Elkanah has not taken any classes on how to communicate in potentially volatile situations. He comes to his brokenhearted wife and says, "Hannah, why are you weeping? Why don't you eat? Why are you downhearted? Don't I mean more to you than ten sons?" (1 Samuel 1:8).

Can you say, "*Ouch*"?

"How can you be sad? You've got me, babe!" The truth is, she does not even have all of him, for she has to share her husband with another wife! Elkanah does not win the husband of the year award. He gets no prizes for sensitivity and he will not be on the cover of this month's *Tenderhearted Husband* magazine.

Here is one practical suggestion. It is not a wise idea to tell someone they should not be sad just because they have you in their life! It did not work for Elkanah, and there is little chance it will work for you!

These friends express their shared sorrow and sit with their friend. They do not say a word. Unfortunately, after a week of sitting with their broken friend, they open their mouths and start talking. Things go downhill from there.

From these stories we can learn that our presence is often the best gift we can give to people in a time of suffering. Words can be of help, if they are sensitive and chosen with wisdom. But simply being with those who are suffering is often the best thing we can do.

NEW TESTAMENT CONNECTION

Partners in Grief

In the New Testament we receive a strong affirmation of God's desire for his children to care for each other in times of need. In both 1 and 2 Corinthians the apostle Paul gives a clear call for followers of Christ to be willing to enter into the sorrow and pain of others in the family of God. In 1 Corinthians 12:26 we read: "If one part suffers, every part suffers with it." Paul is talking about how the whole church is connected like parts of the body, and we all need to learn to suffer with those who are hurting. In 2 Corinthians 1:3–4 we read:

> Praise be to the God and Father of our Lord Jesus Christ, the Father of compassion and the God of all comfort, who comforts us in all our troubles, so that we can comfort those in any trouble with the comfort we ourselves have received from God.

What a clear affirmation of God's desire for us to walk with others through their times of grief and pain.

INTERPRETIVE INSIGHT | *Honest Prayers*

Hannah has nowhere else to go except to God. Peninnah is far more prone to taunt Hannah than offer compassion. Elkanah loves her, but he is not really tuned in to the need for sensitivity toward his wife. So Hannah turns to God, out of her hurt, pain, and disappointment, and even though we don't have her exact words, her prayer becomes one of the great examples of prayer in all Scripture.

The depth of Hannah's emotional honesty in prayer is an example we can all follow. In bitterness of soul, Hannah comes before the Lord. She comes with tears, brokenness, and lament. She comes with a transparent heart. She comes as she is rather than trying to hide the condition of her heart.

NARRATIVE ON LIFE | *How Honest Should We Be?*

When we experience deep bitterness of soul, confusion, disappointment, and sorrow, we must come to God just as we are. He is not surprised and he is never offended by our honesty. Hannah holds nothing back. Through her tears she speaks to God of her misery, trouble, anguish, and grief. She learns that honesty in prayer is not only permissible it is preferred.

As we watch the example of Hannah, we should make a decision to be honest in our prayers. Holding back the truth from God is foolishness because he already sees our heart. God invites our sorrow, our pain, our struggles, and even our anger.

LIFE APPLICATION | *Being Fully Present*

There are people who have focused a great deal of their time and energy on learning to pray with depth and profound intimacy. Some of them speak of being "fully present" with God. Being fully present with God is about honesty, authenticity, and transparency. When we are fully present, we speak what is on our heart and are confident that God hears and cares.

If you are praying but in your mind are thinking, "I feel really tired right now," or "I'm bored," or "I wish I was doing something else right now," talk to God about how you are feeling. Tell him you are tired, bored, and distracted. The first step to being fully present with God is being a truth-teller in prayer. Hannah is a master at this, and we can be too. Hannah is fully present with God when she cries out, "Look at my misery, I'm brokenhearted, and I'm filled with grief. I am still your servant, God, but I am so sad."

WORD STUDY

Hard in Spirit

Hannah tells Eli that she is "deeply troubled." In the Hebrew this phrase literally means, "I am *hard in spirit*" (1 Samuel 1:15). It can mean deeply troubled, but the sense of this passage goes much deeper. In this setting it means that she is in a persistent, "tough-minded" place of prayer. There is a sense that she is struggling and grappling with God in prayer.

NARRATIVE ON LIFE | *The Pain of Being Misunderstood*

As we look at Hannah, she is clearly misunderstood by so many in her life. She is fully present with God, struggling to pour out her heart in prayer, and the priest accuses her of being drunk! Talk about a moment when a person must have felt misunderstood! Hannah does what she can to communicate honestly with Eli, the priest. It is important to note that authentic prayer leads to honest conversation with people. In the same way, being fully present with God helps us become fully present with our friends and family. Hannah speaks to Eli, and she is just as honest and transparent as she was with God. In a culture where women were often cautious about speaking to men, and religious leaders in particular, Hannah expresses herself with a clarity that is startling. But, in her honesty with God, she is learning to be authentic with people.

Hannah lets Eli know that she is not drunk but is seeking God with a broken heart that has run out of words. She does not want to be seen as a wicked woman but as one who is seeking God. She has learned to live with being misunderstood—by her husband, by Peninnah, and by others—but in this situation, she has to speak.

HISTORICAL CONTEXT | *Praying Out Loud*

Hannah's silent praying catches the attention of Eli the priest. In those days, the Israelites usually prayed out loud. This was true in private prayer and in public prayer. It is still a common practice in the Middle East today. In Psalm 3:4 we read, "To the LORD I cry aloud, and he answers me from his holy hill."

When Eli sees Hannah moving her lips but no sound is coming out of her mouth, it looks unusual. He thinks she must be drunk because her behavior, in light of their culture, looks more like the actions of a drunken person than someone who is praying. So Eli rebukes Hannah for drunkenness, but he soon discovers something more is happening in her heart and life. She tells him that appearances can be deceiving. She is not drunk; rather, she is deeply troubled in soul and is calling out to God from a place of inexpressible grief.

LIFE APPLICATION | *Persistence in Prayer*

Hannah's struggles persist year after year after year. We would not be shocked if her passion for honest prayer began to wane with time. But it does not. Peninnah has child after child, but Hannah keeps praying. Months turn into years, and she persists in prayer. When she runs out of words, her heart cries out, but Hannah never stops praying.

> Pray hard when it is hardest to pray.
> *Charles H. Brent*

What is so encouraging in this story is that Eli assures Hannah that her prayer will be answered. She has continued to seek the face of God with humble tenacity. She has not given up on her dream, and now she gets her answer. It will be months before the child is born, but God, through Eli, gives her a promise that she will be granted what she has asked.

We can learn a great deal from this powerful woman of God. God desires honest prayer. We need to be fully present in prayer and pour out whatever is on our heart. And persistence makes a difference. We should keep on praying, even when our situation might seem hopeless.

INTERPRETIVE INSIGHT | *Believing in Prayer*

When Eli tells Hannah that God will grant her what she asks, she believes in faith. Eli utters just a few words, and Hannah's whole disposition changes. She eats a good meal and her countenance is changed. Her face looks different. Instead of discouragement, she is filled with hope. Just one sentence of hope from Eli and her world transforms. Why? Because Hannah believes in prayer and God's promise through Eli and she is certain that she will have a child!

NEW TESTAMENT CONNECTION

Don't Give Up!

In Luke 18:1–6 Jesus tells a story about persistence in prayer. We know this is the message of the parable because it begins with these words, "Then Jesus told his disciples a parable to show them that they should always pray and not give up." This is a great passage to study for those who want to go deeper into this topic.

LIFE APPLICATION | *Don't Quit!*

In every church there are people who are called to pray and to pray with great persistence. Of course every follower of Christ is called to learn how to be persistent in prayer, but some will have opportunity to pray like Hannah. Many of these people have the spiritual gift for intercessory prayer, and they will have more opportunities to develop persistence.

The local church needs intercessors more than most of us know. Every ministry of the church needs to be supported by prayer. All who feel they may have the gift of intercession should seek to offer support to one or more ministry. They should keep a current prayer list for leaders of a ministry area, for the programs that are in place, for continued vision, and for great fruit to grow out of this ministry. Persistence in praying for the work of the church is a blessing to the heart of God and a gift to the church.

There are people in every church like Hannah. They have some area of great pain that lasts for weeks, months, and sometimes years. In some cases they have been praying for a long time already. They may even be tempted to give up. What a great opportunity for these people to be reminded that God is still with them. Jesus invites these people to keep on praying and never give up. He also wants to draw others near to them to bear their burden in community and join in their prayer efforts.

SIGNIFICANT SCRIPTURE

1 Samuel 1:19; 2:1 – 10

LIFE APPLICATION | *Saying "Thanks!"*

Hannah's response to the good news that God gives through Eli is to worship (1:19). Then, after God's promise is realized, Hannah lifts up a prayer of praise and thanksgiving that is recorded in 1 Samuel 2:1 – 10. God chooses to devote a whole section of Scripture to recording Hannah's prayer of thanks. It is interesting to note that the biblical record of Hannah's thanksgiving prayer is greater than her petition.

God cares about our level of thankfulness. He wants us to be devoted to celebrating the great things he does. We must learn from the example of Hannah and commit to become serious about saying thank you to the One who has given us every good gift we have ever received.

NEW TESTAMENT CONNECTION

One Came Back!

In the gospel of Luke we read the story of ten lepers who experience miraculous healing from Jesus. Jesus promises their healing and then sends them to the priest for inspection so they can be declared clean. As they are going, all ten of them are healed; their leprosy is gone! Nine of them proceed forward, but one turns back to find Jesus and say thank you. With his voice lifted to heaven, he gives praise to God for his healing. He comes and falls at the feet of Jesus, declaring heartfelt thanks.

The response of Jesus speaks volumes: "Were not all ten cleansed? Where are the other nine? Was no one found to return and give praise to God except this foreigner?" (Luke 17:17 – 18).

ILLUSTRATION | *"What Do You Say?"*

Thankfulness is learned. It does not come naturally. If you are not sure you believe this, just picture a little girl and her mother. How does a mother teach her daughter how to express her thankfulness? She asks a question over and over. For weeks, months, and years, her mother asks the same question again and again. It is just four words, but it is a key part of every child's upbringing. Here are the words: "What do you say?" The desired answer, of course, is, "Thank you!"

No child is born with a thankful spirit. No parents have to teach a child to be thankless. It is thankfulness that must be nurtured in the human heart. In the same way, our heavenly Father wants his children to learn to be thankful. He will ask us, "What do you say?" for a season of our life. But there comes a time, as exemplified beautifully by Hannah, when spontaneous thanks should erupt from our hearts.

Only he who gives thanks for little things receives the big things. We prevent God from giving us the great spiritual gifts he has in store for us, because we do not give thanks for daily gifts.

Dietrich Bonhoeffer

---

2. Lessons from Eli

SIGNIFICANT SCRIPTURE

1 Samuel 2:12–36

NARRATIVE ON THE TEXT | *Meeting Eli's Family*

This portion of the Bible does not just focus on Hannah and her prayer life but also on Eli and his family. Eli the priest has two sons, Hophni and Phinehas. As we read through 1 Samuel, we learn quickly that things are not going well in the house of Eli. His boys are wicked and do not honor the Lord. These two boys are about as unattractive figures as we can find in the Old Testament. They serve in God's house, but they extort people's offerings for their own selfish gain. Imagine coming to a place of worship where the clergy steal offerings for themselves and use violence to force people to give even more. These two men also sleep with women who serve in that place.

God is deeply troubled by the hearts and lives of Eli's sons. We read, "This sin of the young men was very great in the LORD's sight, for they were treating the LORD's offering with contempt" (1 Samuel 2:17). The problem is, Eli does not take their sin as seriously as God does. When Eli learns what his sons are doing, he confronts them. What's really striking is the way Eli speaks to his sons and how he responds to this situation. Eli says:

> "Why do you do such things? I hear from all the people about these wicked deeds of yours. No, my sons; it is not a good report that I hear spreading among the LORD's people. If a man sins against another man, God may mediate for him; but if a man sins against the LORD, who will intercede for him?" (1 Samuel 2:23–25)

In light of all they have done and are continuing to do, this seems like a tame response.

NARRATIVE ON LIFE | *Understating Things*

Eli's response to his sons is unbelievable. Just think about it. The poor are being ripped off. The weak are being oppressed. The women are being violated. It is all being done by his sons in God's name, and Eli is the priest responsible over these two wolves in sheep's clothing. It's his job to serve and protect the people and to make sure God is honored.

So, what does he do with his sons? He doesn't punish them. He doesn't remove them from office. He doesn't even force them to make amends. He takes no action at all.

They are guilty of greed, theft, extortion, violence, abuse of power, and sexual misconduct. And Eli says, "It's not a good report I'm hearing here." Isn't that kind of an understatement? We have to wonder what it would take to make it a bad report?

INTERPRETIVE INSIGHT | *Looking the Other Way*

It is tempting at this point to think that Eli is just being a nice guy. Because he is a godly man, we may want to make excuses for him. Maybe Eli is a bit naïve! He's just too nice for his own good. Perhaps he doesn't know how wicked his sons are. It's just that he loves his boys so much. We could give a big long list of excuses for Eli, but the text of Scripture gives us insight as to what is really going on with Eli.

The text seems to indicate that Eli does not want to know the whole truth about his sons. If he knows all the details, he'll have to act to restrain them. If he has to play the heavy and do serious discipline, his boys might not like him anymore. Things could get pretty unpleasant in Eli's family if these things were really uncovered and confronted. Eli doesn't want to face things as they really are, so he buries his head in the sand.

God sends a messenger to confront Eli. This man of God speaks on behalf of the Lord and asks Eli, "Why do you scorn my sacrifice and offering that I prescribed for my dwelling? Why do you honor your sons more than me by fattening yourselves on the choice parts of every offering made by my people Israel?" (1 Samuel 2:29). God knows that Eli prefers avoiding unpleasantness with his sons over doing what is right. His family had become a kind of idol in his life. Eli chooses to keep peace with his sons over honoring his duty to God. For the sake of peace in the family, Eli looks the other way.

LIFE APPLICATION | *A Word for Parents*

If you are a parent with a child heading down the wrong path, don't look the other way and don't make excuses. God calls parents to speak the truth in love. At some point, every child will stray. At this moment, the most loving thing to do is sometimes the hardest.

If you need to confront, confront. If you must declare unpopular consequences, declare them. If you don't take the necessary steps of discipline, if you back down, if you look the other way, the consequences could be bigger than you imagine. Love never hides behind an avoidance of reality. Love always deals with truth. It always honors God.

HISTORICAL CONTEXT | *Like the Other Nations*

An important contextual note about the behavior of Eli's sons is related to the women who serve at the Tent of Meeting. We read that Eli's sons, Hophni and Phinehas, sleep with these women. Most likely what is happening is that the sons of Eli are beginning to lead Israel into the same kind of cultic prostitution that was common in the pagan religions of that region of the world. Although this seems unthinkable, there are clear indications that this is what is happening. It is not just that Hophni and Phinehas are engaging in sexual relations with prostitutes, but they are also leading the whole nation toward spiritual prostitution by including pagan practices in their worship of the true God.

Eli did not speak the truth and did not bring loving discipline into the lives of his sons, and the consequences were disastrous. Even when he was warned that if he did not take action, his sons would fall under God's judgment, he did nothing. We need to learn from his poor example and avoid the same fate in our lives and the lives of those we love.

INTERPRETIVE INSIGHT | *Two Ways to Live*

There is a wonderful weaving of stories in this portion of the Bible. While we are hearing about Eli's sons and their rebellion, we are being introduced to Samuel. He is a young man who is learning to hear the voice of God and faithfully follow it. His heart will be true, and he will speak God's word with boldness. In these opening chapters of 1 Samuel we see that there are two ways we can live. What a dramatic contrast is drawn out for us!

In Psalm 1 we learn that there are two kinds of people. They live very different lives. The story of Hophni and Phinehas gives us a living illustration of how a foolish life is lived and how it can end. In the same way, the account of Samuel helps us see how wisdom forms a life and how a life of faithfulness produces fruit.

SIGNIFICANT SCRIPTURE

1 Samuel 3

3. Lessons from Samuel

INTERPRETIVE INSIGHT | *Hearing the Voice of God*

Samuel learns some critical life lessons early in his spiritual journey. Under the mentoring leadership of Eli, he discovers that God really does speak and that those who follow God can hear his voice. It is possible to live a life in partnership with God and be led by God's Spirit.

NARRATIVE ON THE TEXT | *Speak, Lord!*

Samuel is growing up in God's house in Shiloh. His mom promised, "If you give me a son, I'll give him back to you," and she did. Hannah sees her boy Samuel only once a year when they visit him in Shiloh. She makes him a new garment each year, comes to see how much he has grown, prays for him, hugs him, and goes back home.

Eli and God watch over Samuel. He is raised to serve God all of his life. One night, while he is still a boy, he hears his name called out in the night. Think about what this would be like. It actually happened. He is lying in bed and he hears his name. He figures it must be Eli, so he runs to Eli's room. Eli says, "I didn't call you. Go back to bed."

It happens a second time. He gets up, and Eli says, "I didn't call you. Go back to bed."

A third time the night silence is broken, "Samuel."

There is a clarifying comment that bears inspection: "Now Samuel did not yet know the LORD: The word of the LORD had not yet been revealed to him" (1 Samuel

3:7). Samuel has been around godly people. He lives in the place of worship. His mother is praying for him, but he has never heard God's voice. Samuel does not yet understand how to discern and recognize God's voice. The Maker of heaven and earth is speaking to Samuel, and he doesn't know it.

The third time Samuel wakes up the old prophet, Eli catches on to what is happening. He realizes it is the voice of the Lord calling to Samuel. So Eli says, "Go and lie down, and if he calls you, say, 'Speak, LORD, for your servant is listening' " (1 Samuel 3:9).

LIFE APPLICATION | *"The Ministry of Eli"*

In his book *Hearing God*, Dallas Willard coins a great phrase: "the ministry of Eli." Eli helps Samuel learn to discern when God is speaking to him. This wise man of God walks with Samuel and gives him counsel as he learns to recognize the voice of the Master. Eli knows that Samuel's life will never be the same once he learns to hear and follow the voice of God and work in partnership with his Maker.

God is looking for people today who will practice the ministry of Eli. Those in the family of God who recognize the voice of the Savior need to teach the next generation that God still speaks and his people can still hear his voice. Those who have learned to hear the voice of the Lord and to follow his leading must make their lives available to help others learn to say, "Speak, Lord, for your servant is listening."

NEW TESTAMENT CONNECTION

"My Sheep Know My Voice"

Jesus was emphatic that his people would recognize his voice. He is the great Shepherd, and we are his sheep. Our ability to follow him is directly linked to hearing his voice. Followers of Christ should not be surprised when we hear him call our name. This should be normative. And when he calls, we must listen and obey. Jesus said:

> "The watchman opens the gate for him, and the sheep listen to his voice. He calls his own sheep by name and leads them out. When he has brought out all his own, he goes on ahead of them, and his sheep follow him because they know his voice." (John 10:3–4)

INTERPRETIVE INSIGHT | *Obedience in Prayer*

One of the most critical variables in entering into a life of hearing and following the leading of the Holy Spirit is found in 1 Samuel 3:19, "The LORD was with Samuel as he grew up"—and here's the phrase—"and he let none of his words fall to the ground." In other words, whatever God says, Samuel does. Samuel's response to God is always, "Speak, Lord, for your servant is listening." He lets none of God's words fall to the ground. This is a beautiful phrase.

Today the Holy Spirit has been poured out on all God's people. He is ready, willing, and able to guide us. Our part is to quiet our hearts, listen, and then follow him.

LIFE APPLICATION | *Prayer in Action*

One of the most important things we can do in our spiritual lives is to say, "I will let none of God's words fall to the ground." When a thought comes to our heart and mind and we think it may be the Holy Spirit prompting us, we need to be ready to obey. Of course, we must always test everything with Scripture. If a prompting is consistent with God's Word in the Bible and it leads toward growth of the fruit of the Spirit (Galatians 5:22–23), we must act on it. When a prompting comes to encourage somebody, share the faith, do an act of kindness for somebody, or make a needed confrontation over an important life issue, we must just do it.

In these moments we must act no matter what. We may not feel like doing it. It may feel a little awkward. We may even be afraid. But obedience is an essential in the life of a Christ-follower. God wants us to do everything we can to make sure that not a single word of his falls to the ground.

> Time spent in quiet prostration of soul before the Lord is most invigorating. David "sat before the Lord"; it is a great thing to hold these sacred sittings; the mind being receptive, like an open flower drinking in the sunbeams, or the sensitive photographic plate accepting the image before it. Quietude, which some men cannot abide, because it reveals their inward poverty, is as a palace of cedar to the wise, for along its hallowed courts the King in his beauty deigns to walk.
>
> *Charles Haddon Spurgeon*

Message 15

Saul: Where Is Your Confidence?

1 Samuel 9–28

THE HEART OF THE Message

The world has always offered many places for people to put their confidence. God offers only one—in him! It was this way in Saul's day, and it is no different today. In terms of where we place our confidence, Saul's life is a great example of how *not* to live. He places his confidence everywhere and anywhere except in God. The enticement to place our confidence in anything except God rages on.

Throughout the Bible we see many examples from which we can learn. Sometimes the examples are positive and we see a picture of faith in action. At other times the examples are negative and God uses them to show us how *not* to live! For instance, the counsel of Job's friends was unwise; we would never want to follow it. Also, Samson's exploits were legendary, but so were his anger and lust. He is an anti-example when it comes to how we should pursue a romantic relationship. In many ways, Job's friends, Samson, and others stand as examples of how not to live. In the same way, many of Saul's choices and motives are wrong. As we look at where he puts his confidence, we see an example we should not follow. As we look closely at his negative choices, we can clarify how we should not live and, in particular, where not to place our confidence.

THE HEART OF THE Messenger

Those who are called to open the Bible and teach God's Word have a serious responsibility. In the New Testament, James gives this warning in James 3:1–2:

> Not many of you should presume to be teachers, my brothers, because you know that we who teach will be judged more strictly. We all stumble in many ways. If anyone is never at fault in what he says, he is a perfect man, able to keep his whole body in check.

BRIEF MESSAGE OUTLINE

1. Saying farewell to Samuel
2. Meeting Saul
3. Where do you put your confidence?

When we preach and teach the Bible, our confidence must be in God alone. Through this study you will see some dangerous places you may be tempted to place your trust. Ask God to search your heart and help you place your confidence more and more in him and less and less in your own abilities.

Introduction

Take time as you begin this message to set the historical context of the united kingdom. There is a PowerPoint slide that will help as you do this. Since you are entering a whole new era of the kings, it is important to place this season of Israel's history in its proper context. Use this basic outline to review what has led up to the united kingdom where Saul, David, and Solomon ruled over Israel.

- Creation (Genesis 1–2)
- Sin and the Fall (Genesis 3–11)
- The time of the patriarchs (Genesis 12–50)
- Slavery in Egypt and the Exodus (Exodus)
- Wandering in the desert (Leviticus; Numbers; Deuteronomy)
- Conquest of the Promised Land (Joshua; Judges; Ruth)
- The united kingdom (1–2 Samuel; 1 Kings 1–11; 1 Chronicles–2 Chronicles 9)

God isn't looking for brilliant men and women, nor is he depending upon eloquent men or women, nor is he determined to use only talented Christians in sending his gospel out into the world.

H. A. Ironside

SIGNIFICANT SCRIPTURE

1 Samuel 8

1. Saying Farewell to Samuel

NARRATIVE ON THE TEXT | *Be Careful What You Ask For*

When Samuel is an old man, he appoints his sons to follow him. Sadly, they become greedy and take bribes and pervert justice among God's people. Near the end of Samuel's life the elders of Israel gather to talk with him about who should lead Israel after he dies. They start their conversation with stark bluntness and then really say what is on their minds. After acknowledging Samuel's old age, they remind him that his sons are not following in his footsteps. They know that these sons will not lead the nation in the ways of the Lord. Thus, they make a request that will change the course of the nation: "Appoint a king to lead us."

Samuel is brokenhearted by their request. He longs for the nation to follow God as their king. Yet when Samuel speaks to the Lord about this, God gives clear insight and instructions:

> "Listen to all that the people are saying to you; it is not you they have rejected, but they have rejected me as their king. As they have done from the day I brought them up out of Egypt until this day, forsaking me and serving other gods, so they are doing to you. Now listen to them; but warn them solemnly and let them know what the king who will reign over them will do." (1 Samuel 8:7–9)

God tenderly assures Samuel that it is not him they are rejecting. It is much worse; they are rejecting God as their king. But this is not the first time they have done so. All through their history they have struggled with hearts that tended to reject God and clung to everything else. God also tells Samuel to be clear about the consequences they will face if they have a king to rule them.

> God is looking for broken people, for those who have judged themselves in the light of the cross of Christ. When he wants anything done, he takes up men and women who have come to an end of themselves, and whose trust and confidence is not in themselves but in God.
>
> *H. A. Ironside*

INTERPRETIVE INSIGHT | *God's Dream*

Why is this request for a king such a huge problem? From the beginning of the time of the judges, God was offering Israel the opportunity to occupy the land. This is the most wonderful opportunity that has been given to human beings since the garden of Eden. They could freely live in a community of love under the direct reign of God. This was the desire of God's heart. This was his dream for the people he had created and loves so desperately.

Instead of having to use force, power, and threats of violence to control society (which has been the story of every society since the Fall), God was offering them the chance to live as free and equal subjects under his loving, personal rule. This was all in their grasp.

But, year after year, decade after decade, they rejected this dream. In their actions and with their words they cried out, "We don't want God to be our king. We want to do it by ourselves." Every time they committed idolatry, cheated someone, neglected the poor, oppressed the alien, and ignored the plight of a woman, they were saying to God, "We have something better to do than build your kingdom. We'd rather build our own kingdom. We don't trust you to take care of us."

NARRATIVE ON THE TEXT | *The Cost of a King*

At its heart, the request for a human king is the climax of centuries of stubborn refusal to trust God. God knows exactly what is going to happen if they get what they are asking for, and he calls Samuel to give the people a clear picture of what lies ahead:

> [Samuel] said, "This is what the king who will reign over you will do: He will take your sons and make them serve with his chariots and horses, and they will run in front of his chariots. Some he will assign to be commanders of thousands and commanders of fifties, and others to plow his ground and reap his harvest, and still others to make weapons of war and equipment for his chariots. He will take your daughters to be perfumers and cooks and bakers. He will take the best of your fields and vineyards and olive groves and give them to his attendants. He will take a tenth of your grain and of your vintage and give it to his officials and attendants. Your menservants and maidservants and the best of your cattle and donkeys he will take for his own use. He will take a tenth of your flocks, and you yourselves will become his slaves. When that day comes, you will cry out for relief from the king you have chosen, and the LORD will not answer you in that day." (1 Samuel 8:11 – 18)

All of this becomes a reality. All these warnings will become the life experience of the whole nation. With time, they cry out and complain.

WORD STUDY

The End of the Story

At the end of 1 Samuel 8 we find a small phrase, "Then Samuel said to the men of Israel, 'Everyone go back to his town'" (1 Samuel 8:22b). This is a stock phrase in the Old Testament that simply means, "We've come to the end of the story."

If you listen to a fairy tale, you always know you're at the end when you hear the words, "And they lived happily ever after." At that point, the book is closed, the story is over, and you have hit "The End."

In the Old Testament we come across the phrase, "Everyone went to his own town" (or some variation), a number of times. This means that the story is over. Something new is beginning. In this case, the new thing is the story of the first king of Israel – Saul.

INTERPRETIVE INSIGHT | *Real Need, Wrong Solution*

God's whole mission for Israel has been that they are *not* to be like the other nations. He wants them to be different, distinct, and better, to be a light and a hope to all the other nations.

When the people of Israel make their request for a king, it comes out of a time of real need and genuine pain. There is chaos and disorder all over the place. Samuel's sons are not living in a way that they could give proper leadership to the nation. But the people pursue a foolish solution. The right solution is to turn their hearts back to the God who has made them, called them, provided for them, protected them, and led them each step of the way. Instead, they take the easy way and ask for a human king.

HISTORICAL CONTEXT | *A Dangerous Passage*

In the Middle Ages, 1 Samuel 8:11–18 was seen as dangerous because it showed the inevitable implications of being under a human king. It stands as one of the strongest warnings *against* having a human being on the throne of a nation. Because this warning is so severe, kings in the Middle Ages did not like this passage. Some of them even forbade its being read in the churches because they thought it could incite the people to rebel.

LIFE APPLICATION | *Remember to Pray*

When the people of Israel cry out for a human king, this reveals a fundamental lack of trust in God. They have legitimate pain, but they pursue a foolish solution. When Samuel speaks wise counsel, they should listen, but they do not.

They could have prayed, "Help us, God, we're in pain. We're in chaos and disorder. We can't manage ourselves. What do you want for us? What do you want us to do? Not our will but yours be done. We don't need a human king; we place our trust in you." Instead, they refuse to turn back to God and live with all the painful realities God tells them will come.

Every follower of Christ will stand at this same crossroad. Throughout our lives we will be tempted to look to a human solution to a problem that only God can resolve. Over and over we will be tempted to follow a person rather than God. At these decisive moments we will have to decide if we are going to put our trust in God or in our own wisdom. Will I keep God on the throne of my life, or will I ask him to step aside so I can enthrone someone else? As with Israel, God will not demand the throne. We need to look at our lives and make absolutely certain that no one or nothing except for God has taken the place of supremacy in our own lives.

SIGNIFICANT SCRIPTURE

1 Samuel 9:1–6, 14–17

2. Meeting Saul

NARRATIVE ON THE TEXT | *Going on a Donkey Hunt*

Kish was a man of wealth and prominence in his community. He was a man of standing, and those from his family had a good pedigree. His son Saul was an impressive young man who stood out in any crowd because of his height. When we first meet Saul, he is being sent on a mundane and routine task. His father's donkeys have wandered away, and Saul sets out to find them.

ON THE LIGHTER SIDE | *"Everyone Else Is Doing It!"*

"But Dad, but Mom, everyone else is doing it!" Have you ever heard a kid try to pull that one? "All the other parents let their kids rent a limo and have a hotel room to celebrate sixth grade graduation. All the other parents think it's fine. Why do you have to be the only fuddy-duddy? I want to be like all the other kids."

Sadly, this is about the maturity level of the people of Israel. They cry out for a king, and one of the main reasons is that they want to be like the other nations. They are afraid they will get teased on the playground. The other nations will make fun of them and taunt them, "We have a king and you don't. Our king is bigger than your king. You can see our king on the throne; where is your king?"

What is unique about Saul's story is that the writer is setting us up for a major contrast. Saul thinks he's going out on a donkey hunt, but God has something else in mind. Saul is heading out to do a domestic chore, but God is planning to make him king. That's one of the amazing and exciting things about how God is revealed in the Old Testament. You never know what he is up to.

Saul looks for the donkeys in all kinds of places, but he can't find them. Finally he says, "Let's go back home." His servant responds, "No, let's go ask Samuel. Samuel is a prophet and he should be able to help if he's a really good prophet."

Meanwhile, behind the scenes, God is at work. In 1 Samuel 9:15–16 we read, "Now the day before Saul came, the LORD had revealed this to Samuel: 'About this time tomorrow I will send you a man from the land of Benjamin. Anoint him leader over my people Israel; he will deliver my people from the hand of the Philistines. I have looked upon my people, for their cry has reached me.'" When Samuel catches sight of Saul, God assures him that this is the one who will be Israel's first king.

NARRATIVE ON LIFE | *If You Were in Saul's Shoes*

Try to put yourself in Saul's place for a moment. Imagine what it would be like to be out on a donkey hunt and have your whole life turned upside down. All you are doing is trying to find lost donkeys. In the course of doing your chore, you end up going to a religious leader for advice. Before you know what's happening, you are seated at a banquet table and served a special portion of food, and everyone is looking at you wondering what this all means. The next thing you know, this great religious leader pours oil over your head and declares that you will be the king over God's people.

This is what happens to Saul. He goes out looking for donkeys and he comes home trying to understand what has happened to him. His head is spinning, his stomach is full, the oil is still on his scalp, and his whole life's direction has been radically altered.

LIFE APPLICATION | *When God Interrupts Your Life*

What do you do when God interrupts your life and assigns you a task you never dreamed of? What do you do when you are out looking for donkeys and God says, "I want you to be king"? How do you respond when God says, "I have a job for you," and the concept has never entered your mind? In a sense, the story of Saul is one man's response to these questions.

We all need to ask ourselves: Am I ready to follow God on a new adventure? Am I ready to move in a new direction? Will I live life with an ever-present willingness to readjust my life as God surprises me with new direction?

SIGNIFICANT SCRIPTURE

1 Samuel 10:2–14

NARRATIVE ON THE TEXT | *Three Signs for Saul*

Because Saul is going to need a lot of reassurance, Samuel gives him three signs to confirm that he is God's chosen leader for Israel. The first sign is that he will be told the donkeys have been found. The second is that three men will bring food. The third is that he will meet a group of prophets and the Spirit of the Lord will lead Saul to prophesy. Samuel tells Saul, "Once these signs are fulfilled, do whatever your hand finds to do, for God is with you" (1 Samuel 10:7).

This is an unbelievable task, an unbelievable promise, and an unbelievable interruption in an ordinary life. Saul's response to these amazing happenings in his life is intriguing, but also a little ambiguous. When he gets home, his uncle asks him where he has been. Saul tells the truth but misses a lot of the details. He simply says that he was out looking for the donkeys and that he also dropped in on Samuel for some prophetic help. When his uncle inquires about what Samuel has said to him, Saul mentions nothing except that the donkeys were home safe. With all that Saul has experienced, this seems like an incomplete answer.

SIGNIFICANT SCRIPTURE

1 Samuel 9:17–21; 10:17–22

3. Where Do You Put Your Confidence?

We now come to a unit in our study of Israel's history that challenges us to put our confidence only in God and not in other things. The life of Saul instructs us on this issue, and we will see several other options that God's people have had of where to place their confidence.

INTERPRETIVE INSIGHT | *First Signs of a Problem*

1. Do you put your confidence in your abilities, your family name, or your status in the eyes of others — that is, human pedigree?

Saul has mentioned nothing about a special seat at the banquet, a choice portion of food, his anointing, or Samuel's words about his future kingship. There are indications, from the very outset, that Saul is really going to struggle with trusting God for the task assigned to him.

When Samuel first approaches Saul, he lets him know that the hearts of the people are turning toward him, but Saul resists by declaring he is just a Benjamite and that his tribe and clan are of no consequence.

ON THE LIGHTER SIDE | *A Question for the Women*

Ask this question just of women in the room. *Have you ever asked a man, "How did your day go?" and have him leave out something important?* You may even want to ask for a show of hands in response to this question.

Saul seems to be setting a new record on giving a brief answer that leaves out significant details. We might expect Saul to say something like, "Samuel said to me, 'You'll find the donkeys.' Oh, he also took out a flask of oil, poured it over my head, and mentioned something about becoming the king of Israel! So I've got that going for me, which is nice."

Another indication that Saul is trust-challenged comes at his inaugural ceremony. Saul has already been chosen king. That's been settled. But his public inauguration becomes somewhat of a comic scene. Samuel goes through a formal process of having all the tribes and clans and families come by, and Saul is chosen as the new king. Everyone is there and they all know the results. Yet when they go to look for Saul, they cannot find him. Finally they do find him hiding in the baggage. This is certainly not a good sign that Saul is entering his new post with confidence.

SIGNIFICANT SCRIPTURE

1 Samuel 13:1–7, 19–22

ILLUSTRATION | *Where Is the President?*

Imagine a presidential inauguration with all of its pomp and formal ceremony. It is televised and the world is watching. When the time comes for the soon-to-be president to step forward, there is an awkward silence. He can't be found. Finally, someone opens a closet and he is cowering on the floor under a pile of coats. This would not be the best indication that we are dealing with a man who has a healthy sense of confidence.

NARRATIVE ON LIFE | *Trusting in Yourself Is Shaky Ground*

Saul was tall! Real tall! Others look up to him, literally and also as a leader. In this story we learn that the people cry out, "Long live the king!" Yet Saul's confidence is not bolstered! Even though God has called him, Saul is still insecure.

Saul could have wrongly placed his confidence in his own physical stature or abilities, but he did not. What he should have done is place his confidence in the God who called him, gave several signs to confirm his call, and then came upon him in the power of the Spirit. But, Saul's insecurities run so deep that he has a hard time believing God can work through him.

NARRATIVE ON THE TEXT | *An Unfair Fight*

2. Do you put your confidence in physical strength, military might, or national power—that is, human might?

Early in their history, the people of Israel had to learn to place their confidence in God and not their own might. The truth is that many of the nations around them had a better weapons program, a larger army, and a longer history of fighting and winning wars. Among all of their neighbors, none was as fierce and feared as the Philistines. To get a sense of what a battle between Israel and the Philistines would look like, the book of Samuel gives a sketch of each group's assets and liabilities. Here are two passages that will put things in perspective:

> The Philistines assembled to fight Israel, with three thousand chariots, six thousand charioteers, and soldiers as numerous as the sand on the seashore. They went up and camped at Micmash, east of Beth Aven. When the men of Israel saw that

> their situation was critical and that their army was hard pressed, they hid in caves and thickets, among the rocks, and in pits and cisterns. (1 Samuel 13:5–6)
>
> Not a blacksmith could be found in the whole land of Israel, because the Philistines had said, "Otherwise the Hebrews will make swords or spears!" So all Israel went down to the Philistines to have their plowshares, mattocks, axes and sickles sharpened. The price was two thirds of a shekel for sharpening plowshares and mattocks, and a third of a shekel for sharpening forks and axes and for repointing goads.
>
> So on the day of the battle not a soldier with Saul and Jonathan had a sword or spear in his hand; only Saul and his son Jonathan had them. (1 Samuel 13:19–22)

These passages are not setting up a hypothetical battle. They speak of the reality Israel faces as they prepare to fight the mighty Philistine army. The Philistines clearly have the advantage in the arms race and a profound technological edge over Israel. The Philistines control iron technology, and the Israelites have to go down to the Philistines to get their tools sharpened. When it comes time to fight, Israel has two swords, one for the king and one for his son. On the other hand, the Philistines have three thousand chariots as well as soldiers numerous as sand on the seashore. To make matters worse, the Philistines have pressed so far into Israel's territory that they have almost cut the forces of Israel in two.

SIGNIFICANT SCRIPTURE

1 Samuel 13:7b–14; 15:7–29

NARRATIVE ON THE TEXT | *Clear Instructions*

3. Do you put your confidence in your ability to figure things out and make decisions—that is, human intelligence?

When the Israelites see the invading Philistine army, they are filled with terror. Their response, in light of the odds on their winning, is understandable: "When the men of Israel saw that their situation was critical and that their army was hard pressed, they hid in caves and thickets, among the rocks, and in pits and cisterns" (1 Samuel 13:6). They begin to run away, knowing they will be slaughtered.

While the Philistine army is invading, there is another level to the story that is unfolding. Saul is waiting to make any military move until Samuel, the prophet, comes and offers sacrifices. Samuel has promised that he will come within seven days, but Saul is getting tired of waiting. The people are losing heart and beginning to scatter. Saul feels pressed to do something.

At this seemingly hopeless moment, the only option available to Israel is to trust in the God who has delivered them in the past. There is no way they are going to win this battle on their own, and everybody knows that. Samuel was crystal clear with Saul about God's instructions: "Go down ahead of me to Gilgal. I will surely come

PAUSE FOR REFLECTION

When the Odds Are Against You

What do you do when the odds are against you? How do you respond when you are certain you *can't* accomplish the things God has called you to do? To whom do you look when your strength fails? As followers of Christ we must learn that *we* may not have the power to win every victory, but if the battle is the Lord's, he will provide all the strength we need.

> **NEW TESTAMENT CONNECTION**
>
> *Strength in Weakness*
>
> God's ways are radically different from our ways. His kingdom is upside-down and backwards according to the thinking of the world. Yet, we must learn that our weakness can bring about the greatest moments of faith, when we look to God for strength. Only God can turn weakness into strength. The apostle Paul experienced this over and over again:
>
> > To keep me from becoming conceited because of these surpassingly great revelations, there was given me a thorn in my flesh, a messenger of Satan, to torment me. Three times I pleaded with the Lord to take it away from me. But he said to me, "My grace is sufficient for you, for my power is made perfect in weakness." Therefore I will boast all the more gladly about my weaknesses, so that Christ's power may rest on me. That is why, for Christ's sake, I delight in weaknesses, in insults, in hardships, in persecutions, in difficulties. For when I am weak, then I am strong. (2 Corinthians 12:7–10)

down to you to sacrifice burnt offerings and fellowship offerings, but you must wait seven days until I come to you and tell you what you are to do" (1 Samuel 10:8). It seems so clear, so simple, so easy to follow. Can you hear the conversation?

Samuel: Listen carefully, Saul. I want you to go to Gilgal and wait seven days. Got it? Seven days.
Saul: Got it! Seven days.
Samuel: Once you have waited seven days, I will come and offer a sacrifice and instruct you on what God wants you to do. Does that make sense?
Saul: Yes. I wait seven days. You show up. You do the sacrifices. Then you give me instructions.
Samuel: Perfect. That's it. That's all. You just go to Gilgal and wait.
Saul: I wait. I can do that!
Samuel: One more time so we are clear. Where do you go?
Saul: To Gilgal.
Samuel: What do you do?
Saul: I wait.
Samuel: How long do you need to wait?
Saul: Seven days.

INTERPRETIVE INSIGHT | *Option 2*

Let's just say that Samuel is very clear about the instructions and Saul understands exactly what he is to do. However, the days pass slowly. The troops get restless, and Saul comes up with his own plan—option 2.

Saul decides Samuel is taking too long. He does not want to wait the full seven days. He looks at the troops and the condition of their hearts and makes an executive decision. Saul decides to offer the sacrifice on his own rather than waiting for Samuel to arrive. Saul's sin in this passage is impatience. He won't wait for God's timetable. God will deliver his people, but it needs to be in his way. Saul decides that he has a better plan. In a sense, this is intellectual arrogance. God has a plan, the prophet Samuel has laid out the plan, but Saul decides he has a better idea!

LIFE APPLICATION | *Thy Will or My Will?*

Before we get too judgmental with Saul about his impatience and intellectual pride, we need to ask ourselves a few questions. Do I ever get impatient? Do I like to do things my way instead of God's way? Do I ever have clear instructions from God's Word or a prompting of his Spirit and say, "Thanks anyway, but I'll do things my way"? The truth is, every follower of Christ can struggle with the same sin Saul did. We can decide that our way of doing things is better than God's way.

NARRATIVE ON THE TEXT | *New Situation, Same Sin*

We see a recurring theme develop early in Saul's kingship. He is called to attack the Amalekites, and the Lord speaks through Samuel and makes the instructions very clear. The people of Israel are to devote everything to God and to take no plunder. Yet again, Saul decides he has a better plan. After the battle, we read these words: "But Saul and the army spared Agag and the best of the sheep and cattle, the fat calves and lambs—everything that was good. These they were unwilling to destroy completely, but everything that was despised and weak they totally destroyed" (1 Samuel 15:9). Again, Saul decides he has a better way to do things than God commanded.

> Stop considering your emotions and simply regard your will, which is the real king in your being. Is your will open to God? Does your will decide to believe? Does your will choose to obey? If this is the case, then you are in the Lord's hands.
>
> *Hannah Whitall Smith*

INTERPRETIVE INSIGHT | *When God Says, "Stop!"*

SIGNIFICANT SCRIPTURE

1 Samuel 15

Along with this sin Saul adds the sin of spiritual evasiveness. When he is caught by Samuel, he lies, spins, and makes excuses. He won't come clean and acknowledge the true intent of his heart and sinfulness of his actions. When he does finally admit some wrong, he pairs his admission with excuses and blaming. Samuel does all he can to give Saul a chance to truly come clean, but he won't. Finally, Samuel speaks a powerful word: Stop!

Samuel cries out, "Stop!" (1 Samuel 15:16). As you read this passage, you can feel the heart of Samuel breaking because Saul doesn't get it. He has no idea what is at stake. We can almost hear the thoughts racing through Samuel's mind and heart.

> Saul, don't you understand what's at stake here? Don't you see what you're doing? You're just trying to spin the truth. And with every word you speak, you're doing damage to your own mind, soul, and conscience. Don't you remember when God sent his Spirit to come upon you? But now you are choking the Spirit's presence and influence right out of your life. Your choices and denials are damaging God's community. All of the soldiers you're supposed to be leading toward God's plan and obedience are moving toward disobedience because of your poor example. With every inauthentic word, you wander farther away from God. Just stop!

But Saul won't stop. His heart remains hard. "But I did obey the LORD.... I went on the mission the LORD assigned me" (1 Samuel 15:20). To this, Samuel speaks these great words in 1 Samuel 15:22:

> "Does the LORD delight in burnt offerings and sacrifices
> as much as in obeying the voice of the LORD?
> To obey is better than sacrifice,
> and to heed is better than the fat of rams."

All of the other religions get it wrong. There is one God, and he cannot be manipulated by human actions. He is concerned with our heart, character, and ethics. He wants obedience most of all. More than sacrifices such as church attendance, memorizing a whole bunch of the Bible, or some money in the offering plate, he wants an obedient heart. God knows that when he has our heart, he has all of us!

In Saul's case, he does give a halfhearted attempt to repent by saying, "I have sinned. I violated the LORD's command and your instructions" (1 Samuel 15:24). At first glance this seems sincere, but we have to read the rest of the verse, "I was afraid of the people and so I gave in to them." His admission comes with an excuse and some blame on the people. The truth is, he was afraid of the people, but he also wanted the plunder for himself. To the very end Saul is still trying to spin things a little bit so he will not have to look as dark as he really is.

LIFE APPLICATION | *Coming Clean*

Saul's refusal to take the blame for his poor leadership and intellectual pride leads to the sin of spiritual evasiveness. But again, before we are too hard on Saul, we need to look at our hearts. When we are forced to own up to our sins, we also can resist coming into the light.

INTERPRETIVE INSIGHT | *Stubborn to the End*

Finally, Samuel tells Saul that God has rejected him as king and that his kingship is over. Saul's response is staggering. He grabs onto Samuel's robe and won't let go. It almost seems that Saul believes that if he can hold onto that robe, he can cling to the power, glory, and crown. But Samuel's robe tears, and Saul is left with just a piece in his hand. This snapshot of Saul becomes an image of the spiritual reality that is taking place in his life.

SIGNIFICANT SCRIPTURE

1 Samuel 16:17, 23

There is a heartbreaking irony in Saul's life. God calls him to be king, and he hides in the baggage. He does not come joyfully or willingly. Now God calls him to let go of the crown and his kingship. But, stubbornly, Saul holds on and won't let go. From the beginning to the end, Saul never really gives God a submitted heart.

INTERPRETIVE INSIGHT | *Masking the Pain*

4. Do you put your confidence in activities and habits that mask pain and cover sin—human entertainments?

Saul goes through psychological and emotional collapse in the time that follows the loss of his kingship. It's painful to read this portion of the Bible. Saul literally experiences the disintegration of his personality. He goes into a deep depression with violent mood swings. As time passes Saul deals with defiant, erratic behavior, homicidal anger, and constant paranoia.

In the midst of his growing madness, Saul discovers that when David plays his harp, it soothes his restless spirit. The music makes Saul feel better. First Samuel 16:23 says, "Whenever the spirit from God came upon Saul, David would take his harp and play. Then relief would come to Saul; he would feel better, and the evil spirit would leave him." The key words here are "relief" and "feel better."

Saul is not looking for healing. He is not looking for repentance. He is not looking to set things right. He doesn't want to do the hard work of examining his soul. He just wants to feel better. He just wants relief. He finds a form of entertainment that masks his pain and helps him make it through. But he does not change. He is distracted and relieved, but not transformed.

WORD STUDY

An Evil Spirit

In 1 Samuel 16:14 we read, "Now the Spirit of the LORD had departed from Saul, and an evil spirit from the LORD tormented him." When Saul was anointed, God's Spirit came on him in a very powerful way. Now we are told that the Spirit of God leaves and an evil spirit comes. What could it mean when we read about an evil spirit from the Lord coming to torment Saul?

There are a couple of options as to how we can define the concept of an "evil spirit from the LORD." It could mean that God sent a demon to oppress Saul, and some people argue that Saul was demon-possessed. This does not seem consistent with how God works in the rest of Scripture. Another option that seems much more likely is that the word "evil" here can also be translated a "distressing spirit" or a "troubling spirit." If this is the case, the idea of this passage is that God is allowing, even causing, Saul to experience deep pain in the hopes that the pain will do what nothing else could do – cause Saul to turn and repent.

LIFE APPLICATION | *No More Hiding*

Through history many people have played the same game Saul played centuries earlier. When they face pain and struggle, they simply try to mask it with some kind of entertainment, substance, or distraction. Rather than really looking at the source of their pain and getting to the root of it, they are happy to simply cover it up for a time.

Some people need to do some character work, but they would rather have a few more drinks and forget the mess they are making of their life. Others need to look at their soul and ask God to do some renovation, but they are happy to sit in front of the TV night after night and shift into couch potato mode. There are all kinds of distractions people use to avoid facing the real issues in their lives. Some people bury themselves in an insane work schedule; others turn to drugs; still others plunge themselves into destructive relationships, time-consuming hobbies, or anything else they can find to keep their mind off the real issues they need to face.

What they learn, with time, is that no amount of distractions can cover the pain of rebellion against God. The only path to true peace is honest confession and repentance that leads to a transformed life. This was true for Saul, and it is just as true for every follower of Christ today. If we are hiding from God and trying to cover up our pain with mind-numbing activities, it is time to stop and enter a time of humble repentance.

SIGNIFICANT SCRIPTURE

1 Samuel 28:3 – 20

NARRATIVE ON THE TEXT | *Breaking His Own Law*

5. Do you put your confidence in false religion or the stars and heavens — deceitful spirits?

Saul's final descent begins in chapter 28. Samuel has died and Saul is still rebelling against God. We read an important background sentence in 1 Samuel 28:3: "Saul had expelled the mediums and spiritists from the land." Yet, when the Philistines come to fight against Israel, Saul is desperate to get advice on what to do. God will not answer Saul because of his rebellion, so Saul does the unthinkable; he asks for a medium.

Saul himself has outlawed this practice. But the Philistines have proceeded north, almost all the way up to Mount Carmel. They are within fifteen miles of the Jordan River. He is terrified, and he wants a crystal ball. So his advisors find a medium in Endor.

LIFE APPLICATION | *Never Put Confidence in Deceitful Spirits*

People today are looking for somewhere to put their confidence. Sadly, many of them look to the stars, tele-psychics, horoscopes, and other occult practices. As we study through the Old Testament and also the New Testament, it becomes clear that the spiritual world is very real. Satan and a host of demons are seeking to deceive and mislead anyone who will follow. There are also all kinds of charlatans out there glad to take the money of anyone who will pay for their deceptive services.

In any case, God is clear that dabbling in these things is nothing a follower of Christ should ever entertain: "Let no one be found among you who ... practices divination or sorcery, interprets omens, engages in witchcraft, or casts spells, or who is a medium or spiritist or who consults the dead" (Deuteronomy 18:10 – 11).

ON THE LIGHTER SIDE | *Surprise!*

A sad irony runs throughout this story. Saul disguises himself when he comes to the medium. She says to him, "No, I can't do this. King Saul has outlawed this behavior." What irony that Saul is breaking his own law. He says, "The king will never find out." She says, "Who do you want to see?" Saul says, "I want to see the prophet, Samuel." She says, "OK. I'll call him up for you."

The next part of the story is actually comical. It is implied in the story that this woman is a fake. She is like the people on late night TV infomercials who give vague generalities about people's lives like, "I sense you have faced conflict in your life with someone you care about," and people are stunned by this amazing insight. It was just a sham and a moneymaker.

This woman asks, "Whom do you want to see?" Saul (still in disguise) says, "Bring up Samuel." Well, to the woman's utter amazement, Samuel actually shows up! She screams at the top of her voice. You get the sense that nothing like this has ever happened before. She plans to look into a hole in the ground, squint her eyes, and pretend she sees Samuel. She about jumps out of her skin when she looks – and Samuel is there!

INTERPRETIVE INSIGHT | *The Tears of Samuel or the Tears of Saul?*

In 1 Samuel 25:1, we are told that when Samuel dies, all Israel weeps. This is a poignant verse. The whole country weeps. They weep because of all that Samuel became — because of his fiery courage, his boundless love for all the people, and his passion for God. They weep because of how much they will miss those things. They weep tears of gratitude that Samuel had lived among them. They weep tears of thanksgiving for who they have become because Samuel has been in their midst.

When Saul dies, we are told that David *commands* Israel to weep (2 Samuel 1:17–18). This time the people weep because of all that Saul had not become. They remember what he had once been. He was thirty years old when he became king, and he was tall, strong, humble, and full of promise. So many things might have been possible if Saul would have only followed God with all his heart. The people undoubtedly think of what Saul might have been but never became, and they weep.

SIGNIFICANT SCRIPTURE

1 Samuel 25:1; 28:3;
2 Samuel 1:17–18

LIFE APPLICATION | *Following God with Our Whole Heart*

It's a funny thing about Saul. He didn't set out to be bad. He wasn't a Goliath. He just never got around to giving God his full devotion. We need to be careful that we don't make that same mistake.

- If God is setting a task before you, don't hide in the baggage.
- When God calls you to do something, do it his way, not your way.
- If you've been disobedient to God, don't try to spin it, hide it, or blame it on someone else. Just fall to your knees and confess it.
- If envy is choking your heart, let God do surgery and change you.
- If God tells you the time has come for you to let go of something, don't clutch it tightly, but let it go.

We need to commit ourselves to give our full devotion to God. We need to follow God with such humility and passion that when we come to the end of our lives, people will cry the tears of Samuel for us and not the tears of Saul.

HISTORICAL CONTEXT | *In the Pits*

In the Hebrew, when Saul says he wants a woman who is a medium, he is saying, "a woman with a pit." This is how the medium business worked in those days. Some people had access to a cave or a fissure in the ground. They would set themselves up in a business claiming that they had access to spirits in the underworld. Most of these people were charlatans who were out to make a buck.

Message 16

Finding Jesus in the Old Testament

Selected Texts from the Old Testament

THE HEART OF THE Message

From Genesis to Malachi, Jesus is present in the Old Testament. It is clear that the Father wanted the world to know that his Son, the Messiah, would be coming to this earth. Thus, throughout the Old Testament we get glimpses and pictures of what this anointed Savior will look like. The character of Jesus begins to shine through the Old Testament, and his mission starts to take shape. Hope begins to grow in the hearts of those who read the Old Testament and hear the promise of the coming Savior of the world, Jesus Christ.

In a sense, the Old Testament is inviting us to open our eyes to see the Messiah before he actually arrives. As these messianic passages unfold, we hear the call to get ready for his coming. The Old Testament passages we will study in this message are designed to get us ready to see Jesus. They call us to open our eyes, tune in with our ears, and prepare our hearts for Jesus.

(If you are near the Christmas season, this session will fit in particularly well. But, any time of the year is a great time to focus on the person of Christ and how he is unveiled in the Old Testament.)

BRIEF MESSAGE OUTLINE

1. First sin and first grace (Genesis 3:15)
2. A Messiah from the sticks (Micah 5:2)
3. A virgin will be with child (Isaiah 7:14)
4. A messenger will come (Malachi 3:1)
5. Our shepherd (Ezekiel 37:24–25)
6. The stump of Jesse (Isaiah 11:1–2)
7. The coming of the Holy Spirit (Isaiah 61:1–2)
8. One Jesus, many names (Isaiah 9:6–7)
9. Nothing attractive (Isaiah 53:2–3)
10. Coming to suffer for us (Isaiah 53:4–6)
11. On the clouds of heaven (Daniel 7:13–14)

THE HEART OF THE Messenger

Some people in Old Testament times heard the prophecies of the coming Savior and believed. Their hearts raced fast as they began to dream of how the world would change when the Messiah finally came. Others heard the same words and missed the message. Their hearts did not skip a beat, their anticipation levels stayed flat, and there was no sense of hope filling their hearts.

For followers of Christ today, we have a similar situation. Although we are on the other side of Christ's coming to earth that first Christmas, we now await his second coming. We can choose to live with joy-filled anticipation that Jesus is coming soon. As you prepare to share in this message with your congregation, pray for a renewed sense of anticipation and excitement about the return of Jesus. Ask for the Holy Spirit to ignite your heart with a burning desire for Jesus to come. As your heart is filled with this desire, you will begin to get a sense for how the ancient Jews felt as they awaited the first coming of the Christ.

Introduction

NARRATIVE ON LIFE | *The Power of Hearing*

There is something powerful about hearing voices raised together in worship. In this service, everyone will be invited to join together as they read God's Word in unison. We will be giving each other the gift of reading and hearing the Scriptures. Each time an Old Testament passage is read, invite those who read to stand. After they read, they will be seated as the service continues. Some of the passages will be followed with some teaching or a few brief comments about the meaning of the Scripture. At other times, there will be movement directly into worship in song. You may even give time

CREATIVE MESSAGE IDEA | *Say It Out Loud!*

This message will be different from any other in the series. It is unique on two levels. (1) This message will focus on Jesus every step of the way. Jesus appears in the Old Testament, and in this message we will see him unveiled. (2) Everyone will be invited to participate in this message through a united voice in reading Scripture and song.

Each prophetic passage can be read by all those who are gathered. You can project the words of the Old Testament readings or you can have them printed and distributed as people gather. You can have all the passages read in unison by everyone, by sections of people in your worship center, or in any way you feel will best engage your congregation. You will find suggested songs at various points in the message. These songs follow the themes of the readings. You can use these or choose your own.

You Will Need

- Partnership with those who lead music in your services and those who handle the technical aspects of worship (if you will be using the PowerPoint presentation).
- The PowerPoint on the DVD-ROM with all of the Scripture readings. It will be important to keep the passage on the screen when the teacher is speaking about it. It will be helpful for those gathered to look back at the words of the passage over and over.
- A worship leader and team that is ready to stay through the full service. They will share in leading worship throughout the readings and message.

for quiet reflection and waiting on the Holy Spirit to bring the message of the Word to our hearts.

NEW TESTAMENT CONNECTION

Sharing in the Victory

The apostle Paul unpacks this truth and helps us see that we will actually share with Jesus in this victory. He writes, "The God of peace will soon crush Satan under your feet" (Romans 16:20). Jesus will be the ultimate victor, but we will win the battle with him.

1. First Sin and First Grace (Genesis 3:15)

"And I will put enmity
between you and the woman,
and between your offspring and hers;
he will crush your head,
and you will strike his heel."

NARRATIVE ON THE TEXT | *Sin and Grace*

In Genesis 3 sin enters history. The first sin is committed, and immediately the grace of God is seen. God's perfect creation has been marred, but God speaks words of judgment on the serpent. This creature is the embodiment of evil and darkness and the origin of the temptation that led to human rebellion.

God says to the evil one, "Your days are numbered! Take a good look at this man and this woman. They may have fallen for your line, they may seem like easy marks, and their children may battle with the same weaknesses, but one day one of their offspring will come along and it will be a different story. A Son of Man, one of the descendants of Adam and Eve, will undo all you have done."

God lets Satan know, right at the outset of history, that while it may look as if he has the upper hand, he does not. He may have succeeded in destroying God's plan for community, but looks can be deceiving. One day a real flesh-and-blood descendant of Adam and Eve will do battle with the ancient serpent and strike him with a crushing blow of his heel.

INTERPRETIVE INSIGHT | *Hope from the Start*

What heart-lifting hope comes from God in this verse! The world hears that the evil one will not win, no matter what our eyes see. His reign of terror will have an end. He will be crushed by the descendant of Adam and Eve who will rise up and throw him down. Before the echoes of the first sin have faded away, God has given us a glimpse of Jesus, the Mighty Warrior who will redeem human beings from the enemy.

LIFE APPLICATION | *The Battle Begins Now*

When Jesus died on the cross, Satan was defeated. The curse of sin and power of death were destroyed, and life was offered to all who believe in Jesus by faith. When Jesus comes again, the final destruction of the enemy will happen, and he will be cast down forever. But even today we can enter into the victory. Every time we resist temptation in the name of Jesus, a heel comes crashing down on the head of the serpent. Each time we say no to sin, another blow is dealt. When we repent with humble hearts and walk in God's grace, heaven sees the victory.

We can live each day with absolute confidence that we share in the messianic promise in the third chapter of the Bible. God promised that a deliverer would come — and he has. His name is Jesus. When the dissonant sounds of the first sin were still ringing in his ears, God spoke words of hope.

NEW TESTAMENT CONNECTION

The First Shall Be Last

This prophetic passage points to the Savior of the world, the Christ, coming from a place of no consequence. This is a foreshadowing of the law of the kingdom. All through the New Testament we see what Dallas Willard calls "the law of inversion." This is seen clearly in the New Testament: "But many who are first will be last, and many who are last will be first" (Matthew 19:30). And again: "The greatest among you will be your servant. For whoever exalts himself will be humbled, and whoever humbles himself will be exalted" (Matthew 23:11 – 12).

In our world, things work a certain way. The weak are weak; the last are last; the exalted are exalted. In God's kingdom things are inverted. The weak are strong, the last are first, and it is the humble who are exalted. In God's economy, the Messiah who comes to save the world can come from a small, unknown, backwater town – and he does.

2. A Messiah from the Sticks (Micah 5:2)

Teaching note: Before having people read this passage, you might want to pronounce the word "Ephrathah" so they know how to say it. Phonetically, it is pronounced EF-re-theh.

"But you, Bethlehem Ephrathah,
    though you are small among the clans of Judah,
out of you will come for me
    one who will be ruler over Israel,
whose origins are from of old,
    from ancient times."

INTERPRETIVE INSIGHT | *Time to Bow*

The traditional site of the birthplace of Jesus is a small cave that is now enclosed in the Church of the Nativity in Bethlehem. We often think of Jesus being born in a stable, but there is a good chance he was born in a cave. In AD 150 Justin Martyr identified a cave in Bethlehem as the birthplace of Jesus.

William Barclay, a biblical scholar and commentator, notes that when you come to the Church of the Nativity, there is a great wall with a door that is so low that you have to stoop down to enter the cave. Barclay writes, "There is something beautiful in the symbolism that the church where the cave is has a door so low that all must stoop to enter. It is supremely fitting that every man [and woman] should approach the infant Jesus on his knees."

LIFE APPLICATION | *An Invitation to an Inverted Lifestyle*

God came to set up an upside-down kingdom. His followers are invited to enter willingly into a humble life of serving others. If the last are to be first, the servants to be the greatest, and the weak to be strong, we would be wise to begin living with a passionate commitment to lifting up others and serving with a humble and sacrificial heart.

NEW TESTAMENT CONNECTION

Pointing to Jesus

John the Baptist exemplified humility. His singular passion was that people would know Jesus, the Savior. He saw himself as a sign pointing down the road that leads to heaven. He knew the only road was Jesus.

> John replied in the words of Isaiah the prophet, "I am the voice of one calling in the desert, 'Make straight the way for the Lord.'" (John 1:23)

> The next day John saw Jesus coming toward him and said, "Look, the Lamb of God, who takes away the sin of the world!" (John 1:29)

3. A Virgin Will Be with Child (Isaiah 7:14)

> Therefore the Lord himself will give you a sign: The virgin will be with child and will give birth to a son, and will call him Immanuel.

Move directly into a time of worship in song. You can have a soloist or a group sing and then invite the congregation to join. Or the congregation can join in for the entire time. You may want to create some visuals of the infant Jesus to project on a screen.

Here are some suggested songs:

- "O Come, O Come, Emmanuel"
- "O Come, Let Us Adore Him"
- "O Come, All Ye Faithful"

4. A Messenger Will Come (Malachi 3:1)

> "See, I will send my messenger, who will prepare the way before me. Then suddenly the Lord you are seeking will come to his temple; the messenger of the covenant, whom you desire, will come," says the Lord Almighty.

NARRATIVE ON THE TEXT | *A Messenger Will Come*

God was promising that before the Messiah came, he would send a messenger to prepare the way for his arrival. This forerunner was John the Baptist. His role was to

HISTORICAL CONTEXT | *Ephrathah and Bethlehem*

Ephrathah was an older settlement that was of so little consequence that it was absorbed into Bethlehem. Keep in mind, of course, Bethlehem itself was no cosmopolitan metropolis. No one was looking for a Savior to come from an insignificant town like Bethlehem. Most expected the Messiah to come from Jerusalem or some place that mattered, not a little place out in the sticks called Bethlehem.

call people to a place of readiness for the coming Savior. When Jesus arrived, John pointed people to Jesus and let them know that he was the long-awaited Messiah that the Old Testament Scriptures pointed to so clearly.

LIFE APPLICATION | *Prepare the Way*

The ministry of John the Baptist was to point lost people to the Savior, the Lamb of God, the Messiah. We are invited into the same ministry. Every follower of Christ is called to point people toward Jesus. We can do this through our actions, our words, and our lifestyle. We can invite people to events, informal gatherings, or worship services where they will hear about how much they matter to God. The New Testament is filled with clear teaching that every Christian is part of God's plan to reach out to the world with his love.

> "You are the salt of the earth.... You are the light of the world." (Matthew 5:13–14)

> "But you will receive power when the Holy Spirit comes on you; and you will be my witnesses in Jerusalem, and in all Judea and Samaria, and to the ends of the earth." (Acts 1:8)

5. Our Shepherd (Ezekiel 37:24–25)

INTERPRETIVE INSIGHT | *Our Shepherd*

Ezekiel prophesies of the character of the Messiah. He will be a good shepherd over his people. What a comfort to know that the coming Savior will have the heart of a shepherd. It is important to remember that David was a shepherd, and his descendant

ON THE LIGHTER SIDE | *A Surprise Reading*

Explain that the Ezekiel passage is deep and rich, but that it is best understood in the original Hebrew. Assure those gathered that there are nuances that could be missed without a look at the Hebrew. So, let everyone know that the next reading will be in the original language. Project the passage on the screen in Hebrew.

If the reading does not go off well (and there is a good chance it will not!), then offer the English as a second option.

"My servant David will be king over them, and they will all have one shepherd. They will follow my laws and be careful to keep my decrees. They will live in the land I gave to my servant Jacob, the land where your fathers lived. They and their children and their children's children will live there forever, and David my servant will be their prince forever." (Ezekiel 37:24–25) who will rule over God's people will also have a shepherding heart. In this passage, Ezekiel refers to Jesus, the coming Messiah, as David because he is from the Davidic bloodline.

ILLUSTRATION | *Two Sticks*

Earlier in this chapter Ezekiel writes:

> The word of the LORD came to me: "Son of man, take a stick of wood and write on it, 'Belonging to Judah and the Israelites associated with him.' Then take another stick of wood, and write on it, 'Ephraim's stick, belonging to Joseph and all the house of Israel associated with him.' Join them together into one stick so that they will become one in your hand." (Ezekiel 37:15–17)

Have two thick sticks, about two feet long ready to use as an illustration. Also have two feet of twine or rope. As you teach briefly on this passage, begin binding the two sticks together and hold them firmly in your hand.

These two sticks represent the painful division among God's people between the northern and southern kingdoms. Yet God says he can bind them together and unite his people. The two sticks show us a picture of division and brokenness of community. The sticks bound tightly together and held in the hand show that God has the power to heal, restore, and rebuild his community.

LIFE APPLICATION | *Restore Us*

Of all the people in the world, Christians should be the most united and conscious of the need to build community. Of all the places in the world, the church should be the beacon of unity. In every church you can find story after story of marriages that seemed hopeless but were healed. There are friendships that were tattered and torn but have been restored. We can find story after story of family members who were estranged, but the power of Jesus' shepherding love brought them back together again.

If you are living with a broken relationship, it is time to seek healing again. It is time to remember that the same Good Shepherd has power to bind together broken relationships today. The one who could get Jews and Gentiles to sit down and share table fellowship can heal our relationships. The same Jesus who could overcome the gap between men and women in the first century can certainly help us relate with love and grace today.

NEW TESTAMENT CONNECTION

One in Christ

Jesus, the Shepherd of his people, is the one who can bind back together what has been divided. All throughout the New Testament we see that Jesus has power to build community even where it seems hopeless. The apostle Paul writes:

> You are all sons of God through faith in Christ Jesus, for all of you who were baptized into Christ have clothed yourselves with Christ. There is neither Jew nor Greek, slave nor free, male nor female, for you are all one in Christ Jesus. If you belong to Christ, then you are Abraham's seed, and heirs according to the promise. (Galatians 3:26–29)

It is hard for people today to imagine the chasm that existed between Jews and Greeks, slaves and free people, and men and women in the first-century world. But Paul affirms what Ezekiel prophesies, that Jesus Christ, the Messiah, is the one who can bind them together in harmonious community.

6. The Stump of Jesse (Isaiah 11:1 – 2)

A shoot will come up from the stump of Jesse;
from his roots a Branch will bear fruit.
The Spirit of the LORD will rest on him —
the Spirit of wisdom and of understanding,
the Spirit of counsel and of power,
the Spirit of knowledge and of the fear of the LORD.

INTERPRETIVE INSIGHT | *The Stump of Jesse*

This passage has a striking image. In the Near East there were not many trees, and the ones that grew were highly valued. They gave shade, offered a place for birds to live, and were a sign of water and life. In that region it was a sad sight to see a tree cut down. When a thriving, growing, fruitful tree was cut down and only a stump was left, it left an impression.

Isaiah uses this image of a stump to paint a picture of the kingdom of Israel. When it was governed by David, Jesse's son, it was a thriving and life-giving nation. Now it had been cut down. It was divided in two. The kingdom was a mere shadow of what it used to be.

But again hope flows from the pages of the Old Testament. Jesus is portrayed as a branch that will start growing. Life will return. Out of what appears to be a dead stump, a fruitful branch begins to reach out. Life comes from death. This picture of Jesus assures us that he will come with wisdom, understanding, and power.

NEW TESTAMENT CONNECTION

It Has Been Fulfilled

When Jesus came and began his ministry, he went to a synagogue and read this Scripture from Isaiah. When he had finished reading, he rolled up the scroll and proceeded to tell everyone that today this Scripture had just been fulfilled in their hearing (see Luke 4:16 – 21).

The anointing of the Holy Spirit was on Jesus, but he also made it available to all who follow him. It was John the Baptist who said, "I baptize you with water for repentance. But after me will come one who is more powerful than I, whose sandals I am not fit to carry. He will baptize you with the Holy Spirit and with fire" (Matthew 3:11).

7. The Coming of the Holy Spirit (Isaiah 61:1 – 2)

The Spirit of the Sovereign LORD is on me,
because the LORD has anointed me
to preach good news to the poor.
He has sent me to bind up the brokenhearted,
to proclaim freedom for the captives
and release from darkness for the prisoners,
to proclaim the year of the LORD's favor. . . .

INTERPRETIVE INSIGHT | *The Coming of the Holy Spirit*

This is one of the most beautiful passages in Scripture. In those days, a king was identified by being anointed. The phrase "the anointed one" was a way of referring to the king. The terms *meshiach* (Messiah) in Hebrew or *christos* (Christ) in Greek simply mean "the anointed one."

This text is saying that one is coming who will be anointed, not with oil, but with the Spirit of God. Isaiah is prophesying that one day a Savior will enter human history and that one of the distinct signs that this Messiah has arrived will be the anointing on him.

8. One Jesus, Many Names (Isaiah 9:6–7)

For to us a child is born,
to us a son is given,
and the government will be on his shoulders.
And he will be called
Wonderful Counselor, Mighty God,
Everlasting Father, Prince of Peace.
Of the increase of his government and peace
there will be no end.
He will reign on David's throne
and over his kingdom,
establishing and upholding it
with justice and righteousness
from that time on and forever.
The zeal of the LORD Almighty
will accomplish this.

PAUSE FOR PRAYER

What a Wonderful Savior

Close your time of reflection with a prayer thanking Jesus for who he is and what he means to his children. Celebrate his wonder and majesty.

Allow time for those gathered to quietly meditate on the names of Jesus unveiled in this passage. Have quiet music playing as people reflect on the names of Jesus. You may simply want to say nothing and let the Spirit speak to the hearts of his people. But you may also want to give brief direction as people reflect. If you want to do this, consider asking a few brief questions and then allowing a few moments for people to quietly reflect:

Wonderful Counselor. *Do you need wisdom today?* He will give it to you. He will be your counselor.

CREATIVE MESSAGE IDEA *Worship*

Move directly into a time of worship in song. You may want to receive your offering at this time. You can have a soloist or a group sing and then invite the congregation to join. Or, the congregation can join in for the entire time. Here are some suggested songs:

- "Jesus, What a Beautiful Name" (by Tanya Riches)
- "Holy and Anointed One" (by John Barnett)

Mighty God. *Do you need power in your life?* He is not limited to human power. He can accomplish all things.

Everlasting Father. *Do you need love? Does your heart hunger for acceptance and mercy?* He loves you as his child and opens his arms to you.

Prince of Peace. *Do you need some peace? Are you afraid, anxious, or angry?* He loves to bring peace where there is turmoil.

9. Nothing Attractive (Isaiah 53:2 – 3)

He grew up before him like a tender shoot,
  and like a root out of dry ground.
He had no beauty or majesty to attract us to him,
  nothing in his appearance that we should desire him.
He was despised and rejected by men,
  a man of sorrows, and familiar with suffering.
Like one from whom men hide their faces
  he was despised, and we esteemed him not.

NARRATIVE ON THE TEXT | *Nothing Attractive*

The Bible does not say much about what Jesus looked like. Most of us have seen drawings and paintings, but it is up to our imagination to paint our own picture. One thing we can know is that he had no special physical beauty or majesty to attract people to him. Pause and think about what Isaiah says about Jesus in this prophetic passage, "He had *no beauty or majesty* to attract us to him, *nothing in his appearance* that we should desire him." This does not sound like one of the "pretty people" our world loves to love. What we can know for certain is that Jesus was not numbered among the attractive elite of his day.

ILLUSTRATION | *Blessed Are the Beautiful*

We live in a world that is obsessed with appearance. The beatitude of our age is, "Blessed are the beautiful!" In an effort to address our societal mania over beauty, Karen Thorp writes:

> Studies confirm that parents and day-care workers smile, coo, kiss, and hold pretty babies more than plain ones.
>
> Children's stories reinforce this impression that attractiveness is the secret to love. The prince wasn't enraptured with Cinderella's intelligent conversation. Snow White and Sleeping Beauty netted their men while comatose. Rapunzel had great hair. What child would *not* conclude that beauty is the key to people's hearts?

INTERPRETIVE INSIGHT | *He Knows How We Feel*

Jesus experienced rejection and suffering. Have you ever felt rejected? Have you ever been outcast? Have you ever had a sobering moment when you realized that you might not end up on the top ten list of this year's most beautiful people?

Jesus knew what it felt like to be rejected. He experienced abandonment greater than we ever will. He knew betrayal and watched as his closest friends denied him and ran away. He was despised, rejected, and a man of sorrows. He knows how we feel in our moments of rejection and pain.

Yet Jesus embraced suffering voluntarily. He lived and taught in such a way that he knew he would be shunned. This leads to the deepest and most surprising teaching about the Messiah: *He did not come to conquer but to suffer.*

What comes next in Isaiah 53 is staggering. We learn about the doctrine of the atonement. Isaiah teaches us that the price would be paid for sin. But it would not come through the endless sacrifice of animals; rather, it would be through the perfect and final sacrifice of a supremely willing and indescribably good person.

10. Coming to Suffer for Us (Isaiah 53:4–6)

Surely he took up our infirmities
  and carried our sorrows,
yet we considered him stricken by God,
  smitten by him, and afflicted.
But he was pierced for our transgressions,
  he was crushed for our iniquities;
the punishment that brought us peace was upon him,
  and by his wounds we are healed.
We all, like sheep, have gone astray,

CREATIVE MESSAGE IDEA | *Come to the Table*

This passage brings us to the sacrifice of the Messiah–his body broken and his blood poured out for the forgiveness of our sins. You may want to celebrate communion at this time in the service. If you incorporate the Lord's Supper, plan to celebrate it according to your own church tradition.

As people receive the elements, speak of God's invitation to open their hearts to receive grace. No matter how far away we might feel from him, he is ready to receive us. In this moment we can abandon ourselves to his infinite mercy. The death of Jesus, his shed blood, is enough to wash us clean.

As a possible song to sing, try "My Jesus, I Love You," by William Featherson and Adoniram Gordon.

each of us has turned to his own way;
and the LORD has laid on him
the iniquity of us all.

NARRATIVE ON LIFE | *Never Too Far Away*

If you have a story to tell about someone who wandered far away from God and discovered that the arms of the Father are always open, consider sharing it now. Let this story be a reminder that no one can wander so far away that God's grace can't reach him or her.

11. On the Clouds of Heaven (Daniel 7:13 – 14)

Through the service you may have had various groups read passages. Now, be sure that everyone stands together for the final Scripture reading. Have the whole congregation join their voices in unison as they read Daniel 7:13 – 14:

> In my vision at night I looked, and there before me was one like a son of man, coming with the clouds of heaven. He approached the Ancient of Days and was led into his presence. He was given authority, glory and sovereign power; all peoples, nations and men of every language worshiped him. His dominion is an everlasting dominion that will not pass away, and his kingdom is one that will never be destroyed.

HISTORICAL CONTEXT | *The Already and the Not Yet*

All the passages that have been read up to this time were clearly pointing to the Messiah, Jesus. Each of them is quoted or referred to in the New Testament. This final passage primarily looks forward to something that will still come. In the same way that people in the Old Testament days looked ahead to the fulfillment of the passages we have already read, we can look forward to the fulfillment of this passage. We can read it with bold, confident hope!

As a possible song, try "The Lord's Prayer," by Matt Shepardson.

Part 3

Developing a Heart for God

Life-Changing Lessons from the Wisdom Books

Message 17

David: Developing a Heart for God

2 Samuel 5, 6, 9, 11, 12; Psalm 51

THE HEART OF THE Message

This message is about the heart of God's people. God is deeply concerned about our hearts. He wants the throne of our heart to be his dwelling place. The problem is, there are many other things that are battling for the place of supremacy in our lives.

In this message we look at King David and discover that he had the same struggles we all face. He loved God with all his heart, but he faced many temptations to let other things push God off the throne. As we look at David's lifelong struggle to yield his heart fully to God, we will discover that we too can develop a heart that beats passionately for God.

THE HEART OF THE Messenger

Like David, every follower of Christ faces the lifelong challenge to keep God firmly on the throne of his or her heart. As a teacher, you will bring this message to your congregation, class, or small group. Your preparation and communication will be a journey of self-examination.

For you to communicate God's message with clarity and integrity, you will need to invite the Holy Spirit to search your own heart. Is God fully enthroned in your life? Does he rule in your heart? Are there people, habits, life patterns, fears, or anything else that have begun to take a place of supremacy in your life? Come before God with deep humility and ask him to reveal any idol, any alternative to God, that may be alive in your heart. You may want to meditate on Psalm 51 as you prepare this message.

BRIEF MESSAGE OUTLINE

1. David's story
2. Learning from David: Worship
3. Learning from David: Relationships
4. Learning from David: Temptation
5. Learning from David: Confession

1. David's Story

SIGNIFICANT SCRIPTURE

2 Samuel 5

NARRATIVE ON LIFE | *The Furnace of the Desert*

It is in the desert that David is really at his best. That's where his life gets shaped and defined by God. In his life, David has many victories in battle. He has accomplishments, wealth, and the praise of people. But when it is all said and done, David seems to be at his best when he is in the furnace of the desert. The dry air cracks his lips; the heat drains his energy. But in this arid place of desolate silence, David meets with God. In the desert he wrote many of the Psalms, he speaks to God, and he learns.

Rarely do God's people ask to be placed in the furnace of the desert. It would seem masochistic to ask for such an experience. Yet, God often leads his people to this place of training, discipline, refining, and preparation. Moses spent time in the desert, and so did the nation of Israel. David was trained in the desert school. Even Jesus, who never sinned, was led by the Spirit into the desert for forty days.

Sometimes God leads those he loves through a season of desert wandering. But when he does this, it is always with a purpose. When we find ourselves in the desert, we must look to God and ask, "What can I learn in this place?" We must avoid the natural reaction of running away. We must learn, as David did, that God does some of his best work in us when we are in the desert.

ILLUSTRATION | *Martyrdom of Polycarp*

Called upon to curse Christ, Polycarp, in the second century, spoke these words before he was martyred for his faith: "Eighty and six years have I served him, and he has done me no wrong; how then can I blaspheme my King who saved me?"

HISTORICAL CONTEXT | *David's Story, Part 1*

More is written about David (and by David) than any other character in the Old Testament. Hundreds and hundreds of books have been written about his life. In this study, we will focus primarily on the years of David's kingship.

Many are familiar with the stories of David. They may have grown up seeing his life as a shepherd boy, his battle with Goliath, and his ascension to the throne played out on the two-dimensional world of a flannelgraph in Sunday school classes. Prior to 2 Samuel, David was a shepherd tending his father's flocks around Bethlehem. Samuel, the prophet of Israel, was led to the home of Jesse and was called by God to anoint David as the new king.

Soon David fights the giant, Goliath. He defeats him and becomes famous in the land. Over time, King Saul becomes incredibly jealous of David and threatens his life so much that David has to flee from Saul. He then finds himself in the desert, wandering for years, separated from his family and the kingdom. In 2 Samuel 5, David finally steps into the role of Israel's king. He conquers Jerusalem, defeats the Philistine army, and begins his kingship.

And then, at the stake in the sports arena at Smyrna, right before the end, Polycarp said: "Make me a true athlete of Jesus Christ, to suffer and to conquer; an anvil, Lord, let me be an anvil, smitten but standing firm."

2. Learning from David: Worship

SIGNIFICANT SCRIPTURE

2 Samuel 6

NARRATIVE ON THE TEXT | *Celebrating God!*

The ark of the covenant was the closest thing Israel had to a throne for God. Over the atonement cover on the ark, the presence of God was said to dwell. It was a sacred reminder to Israel that God was with them. And David knows that the ark must be back in Jerusalem.

Thus, David gets a group together, and they go down to get the ark from the house of Abinadab. Just to give you a sense of how important this is to David, he chooses thirty thousand men to accompany him to retrieve the ark. After a long journey getting the ark back to Jerusalem, an incredible party breaks out.

We may picture Mardi Gras or the Rose Parade and think they are a big deal, but the celebration that accompanies the return of the ark is huge! The ark of the covenant is back in Jerusalem. God's presence can be felt and seen. A party erupts and rolls through Jerusalem. "David, wearing a linen ephod, danced before the LORD with all his might, while he and the entire house of Israel brought up the ark of the LORD with shouts and the sound of trumpets" (2 Samuel 6:14–15).

In this public setting, David is swept into worship. With all his might he begins to express his praise and thanks to God. This is full body, full contact, no-holds-barred worship. He is letting it loose for God.

HISTORICAL CONTEXT | *David's Story, Part 2*

The nations around Israel had kings. For many years, Israel did not. However, at their own insistence they got a king. Their first king was Saul. He had many flaws and his story ended sadly. But when David took the throne, there was a chance for a new beginning. As David's kingship began, it appeared that he would be an A+ monarch.

Israel was excited about their new ruler. Yet we must always remember as we look at the history of Israel that God had made himself available to be their one and only King. The tragedy of their story, and often ours, is that God isn't enough. They, and we, want a person on a throne to rule.

In 2 Samuel 5 we see David experience a time of great success. He has incredible success at taking back Jerusalem—this chief city of Israel. Next he defeats the Philistines, their prime enemy. As part of his victorious campaign, David decides he will bring back the ark of the covenant to Jerusalem.

NARRATIVE ON THE TEXT | *Not Everyone Will Understand*

The king of Israel is dancing with all his might . . . in his underwear. David worships the Lord with complete abandon and disregard for what anyone else may think. This includes his wife, Michal, who is the daughter of Saul. Michal is quite disgusted and offended to see her husband, the king, dancing around the kingdom in his ephod. She is sure this will not be good for public relations. It is certainly going to make the next morning's paper. She is incredibly distressed. But David doesn't care; he is worshiping God with all his might. His attention is fixed and focused and lost in the glory of God.

CREATIVE VIDEO ELEMENT

What's Up with That?

"The Diner" (4:50 min.).

This feature, hosted by Jarrett Stevens, answers tough questions from the Old Testament in an entertaining way. It can be used with any session.

ILLUSTRATION | *Wild in Worship*

On the included DVD-ROM, Jarrett tells about his wife and the wild worship sessions she has as she drives. You may want to tell a story about someone you know who is an authentic and passionate worshiper.

NARRATIVE ON LIFE | *Freedom in Worship*

Imagine what it may look like to be free in your worship of God. What impact would it have on you as a worshiper if you had no concern for what the person next to you sounded like or what you sounded like to them? What if you did not worry about what other people may think of you if you were truly free in worship? How would it feel to be so lost in the glory and wonder of God that you stopped thinking about what others were doing or thinking?

In 2 Samuel 6:22 David tells his wife Michal, "I will become even more undignified than this, and I will be humiliated in my own eyes." It is as if David is telling his

ON THE LIGHTER SIDE | *A Linen Ephod*

Right in the middle of this scene of celebration there is a side-note that can be easily missed. David is wearing a linen ephod. What is an ephod? Why is that important? Why are we given information about a linen ephod? An ephod was sort of a sleeveless undergarment that came down to about hip length. Essentially, it was really nothing more than his underwear. Of course, this has implications for how David appears and how people perceive him.

If you listen to Jarrett's message, you will notice that he has fun with this idea. He says, "In fact, to be honest with you, I'm wearing a linen ephod right now and they are incredibly comfortable. They breathe and they move so nice." You can decide if your congregation will appreciate a comment like this.

wife, "You think this is bad? Just wait until I get going. Wait until I start worshiping God with all my might."

The truth is that many people have grown up in a church where worship of God was seen as a "dignified" thing. Everyone stood properly with their nice clip-on ties or neatly pressed dresses. They sang from their hymnals, knew when to stand and sit, and followed a clearly printed order of worship. It was all done in a proper manner.

This is not the picture we have of King David. He is passionate, reckless, invested, and even undignified. David's example can become God's invitation for us to enter a deeper, richer, messier kind of worship.

NEW TESTAMENT CONNECTION

Please God, Not People

In Galatians 1:10 Paul writes, "Am I now trying to win the approval of men, or of God? Or am I trying to please men? If I were still trying to please men, I would not be a servant of Christ." When we tailor what we do and say just to please people, we fail to please God. Paul understood what David was learning. Sometimes pleasing God means that people won't be impressed. The question is, who do we most want to please, God or people?

LIFE APPLICATION | *Getting Undignified*

David is lost in the glory of God, worshiping God with all his might. What would it look like if we learned to worship with all our might? How might our worship services change? What risks would we learn to take?

We may ask the Holy Spirit to fill our hearts and our churches in new and fresh ways. We may also begin taking risks as his worshipers. The key is that our outward expressions of worship be consistent with what is really happening in our hearts. Expressiveness and passion in worship are not some preplanned action that appears to be spiritual. They are a natural and free outward expression of the work that the Holy Spirit is doing inside of us. There is a consistency between our outward expression and our inward experience of God.

You may want to begin by singing praise with all your might when you are driving down the road, in the shower, or with God's people. Maybe you have wanted to lift your hands in worship for a long time, but you always resist because you fear what others may think. The next time you sense the Spirit prompting you to lift your hands, begin by simply turning them upward in your lap or right in front of you. Let your outward posture match what is happening in the depth of your heart. The key is to begin taking steps of responsiveness to God's leading in worship.

NARRATIVE ON LIFE | *The Reality of Community*

Our worship can be full and expressive. However, we should remember that when we worship in community with others, they are also seeking to worship. In other words, if our freedom to worship consistently keeps our brothers and sisters from worshiping, we must limit our freedom.

Oliver Wendell Holmes, a past U.S. Supreme Court judge, is quoted as saying, "Our freedom of speech ends when someone yells 'fire' in a crowded theater." Another quote attributed to him is, "Our freedom to extend our arm ends where the nose of the person standing next to us begins." In short, our freedoms, in every area of life, are limited when we are with other people. This includes worship.

If I am worshiping in a church where (to use the example from David's life) dancing in the aisles is normative, I can express my worship in dance and no one will notice — except God! However, if I am attending a church service where this kind of expressiveness is totally foreign, I may choose to limit my dancing activities. If I am sure that my freedom will cause every person gathered to stare at me, I can also be confident that they will no longer be worshiping God, but will be focusing all their attention on me. In this case, I can choose to limit my freedom for the sake of community and the worship of all those gathered.

The apostle Paul addresses this issue of believers choosing to limit their freedom for the sake of community in 1 Corinthians 8. It is a powerful reminder of both our freedom as Christ followers and the wisdom of limiting our freedom for the sake of building community.

LIFE APPLICATION | *Worship – Who Is on the Throne?*

Throughout this message you will ask the same question as a refrain: "Who is on the throne?" The primary focus of this message will answer the question, "Who is on the throne of David's heart?" This is quickly applied to the hearts of all those gathered.

When David is dancing through the streets, worshiping God with all his might, who do you think is on the throne of his heart at that moment? Is it God or David? It seems obvious that God is on the throne of David's heart. That's all David sees as he worships God with all his might.

When you gather with other followers of Christ to worship or when you worship God throughout the week, who is on the throne of your heart? Are you more concerned about what people may think or say, or is God on the throne of your worship? Is your worship more about how you feel and the experiences you have, or what God receives as you exalt him and lift him up?

CREATIVE MESSAGE IDEA | *See the Throne*

There is a refrain that runs through this message. We will be asking the question, *Who is on the throne?* It would be helpful to have a throne or large throne-looking chair on the stage area. This can be used as a focal point and visual reminder that someone or something will be on the throne of each person's life.

You Will Need

- One large chair or throne-like area on the stage area where you will be preaching or teaching. Be as creative as you like. You could even have a few people who have skills in decorations help set this up.

David gives us a model of fully abandoned worship. God is before his eyes. God is on the throne of his heart. David is lost in worship. We can worship in a similar way, with God fully on the throne of our hearts.

SIGNIFICANT SCRIPTURE

2 Samuel 9

3. Learning from David: Relationships

NARRATIVE ON THE TEXT | *Actions of Grace*

Mephibosheth is brought before David, the most powerful man in the land, and he bows down to him. What might have been going through Mephibosheth's mind? He knows that his grandfather tried to kill David and that new kings often slaughtered the family members of old kings. When he bows his head before David, there is a chance it will be the last thing he ever does. All his life, he has lived in exile. Now, he is brought before his grandfather's successor.

The words David speaks undoubtedly shock him and many of those gathered. David says, "Don't be afraid ... for I will surely show you kindness for the sake of your father Jonathan. I will restore to you all the land that belonged to your grandfather Saul, and you will always eat at my table" (2 Samuel 9:7). David takes what has

HISTORICAL CONTEXT | *Looking for Family*

In 2 Samuel 9 David does something that was not uncommon for kings to do in those days. He goes out hunting for any of Saul's blood relatives. In those days, when a new king took the throne, he would scour the land to find any living relatives of the previous monarch. Then, he would gather all of these people together and kill them! These people represented a challenge, or threat, to the throne. Running through the veins of these relatives was the blood of the previous king, and killing them was a form of job security.

When David becomes king and asks for an inventory of any living relatives of Saul, it seems clear what is coming next. But what David does will be remembered forever! What he does can only happen when God is dwelling on the throne of someone's heart. David is seeking the relatives of Saul (the king who vowed to kill him and who tried to pin David to the wall with a spear) so that he can honor and bless them!

David is not searching for Saul's relatives to exact vengeance but to extend mercy and grace. Second Samuel 9:3 says, "The king asked, 'Is there no one still left of the house of Saul to whom I can show God's kindness?' Ziba answered the king, 'There is still a son of Jonathan; he is crippled in both feet.'" David desires to show mercy to a relative of the man who has chased him like a criminal through the desert.

"'Where is he?' the king asked. Ziba answered, 'He is at the house of Makir son of Ammiel in Lo Debar.' So King David had him brought from Lo Debar, from the house of Makir son of Ammiel" (9:4–5). In verse 6, we find the last existing relative of Saul. His name is Mephibosheth.

rightfully become his, and he gives it to this outcast man who could have easily been seen as an enemy. David extends grace and gives gifts to this man. David even goes so far as to invite Mephibosheth to dine at the royal table for the rest of his life!

SIGNIFICANT SCRIPTURE

2 Samuel 11

INTERPRETIVE INSIGHT | *Extending Mercy*

Does David's compassion and care for Mephibosheth remind you of anyone? Isn't that what God does for you and me? He invites us into his home. Though we are strangers and aliens to God, he invites us in to be a part of his family, to share in his wealth, and to sit at his table. What an incredible image of God we have in David. When David extends mercy to Mephibosheth at every meal, when he looks across the table and sees Saul's grandson, who do you think is on the throne of David's heart?

LIFE APPLICATION | *Relationships – Who Is on the Throne?*

When you see David extending amazing grace and mercy to Mephibosheth, who is on the throne of his heart? God is clearly on the throne and ruling David's life at this time. Only God's mercy and only God's kindness can do that.

The heart of God can beat within us too. When God is on the throne of our heart, we can extend compassion, grace, and generous kindness. Each of us needs to learn to look at our relationships through the eyes of the God whose name is compassion, becoming like Jesus who blessed and prayed for those who nailed him to the cross.

Who in your life does not deserve mercy but needs it? How may God call you to treat this person? What can you do to show that God is on the throne of your relational life?

NEW TESTAMENT CONNECTION

Loving Enemies

In Matthew 5:43–48 Jesus is calling his followers to love their enemies and pray for their persecutors. Sometimes we want to pass over a section of the Bible that seems radical. But as we look at the life of David, we discover that God does have the power to help ordinary people live out this kind of radical relational grace.

4. Learning from David: Temptation

NARRATIVE ON THE TEXT | *Temptation*

Up to this point in David's career, everything is going incredibly well. The kingdom is expanding. He is known as one of the greatest kings ever. But in 2 Samuel 11 things begin to shift. This story is familiar to many, but it may be new to some. We begin to see the downfall of King David. Although he is a man after God's own heart and God's chosen one to lead Israel, David is also susceptible to the pitfalls of temptation.

Things have begun to change in David's heart. This throne is up for grabs. David, the king of Israel, the most powerful man in all of the region, the one who has been blessed with everything he's ever wanted, begins to desire more. Despite all he has been given, he wants what is not his — what he should never have.

David notices Bathsheba, a beautiful woman, bathing a couple of rooftops over from the palace. He sends his servants to bring her to the palace. David is clearly warned that she is the wife of Uriah the Hittite. It is important to know that Uriah is one of David's most faithful warriors. He is named among David's legendary thirty mighty men (1 Chronicles 11:41). He was with David during his desert years and had served the king and fought at his side.

> It is not temptation itself that grieves God; he is displeased when we give in to temptation.
>
> *Charles Stanley*

Knowing all of this, David still brings her to the palace and sleeps with her. It is hard to imagine how incredibly unromantic this scene is. The king sees what he wants and treats her like a food item on a menu or some trinket he sees in the marketplace. He simply says, "I want her. Bring her to me." Then, in one moment of temptation and weakness, David changes the course of his life. He has sexual relations with Bathsheba and sends her home. He dishonors God, shames Bathsheba, and breaks relationship with Uriah, one of his most faithful servants.

Soon Bathsheba realizes she is pregnant and that David is the father. Uriah cannot be the father because he is off fighting in David's war. In response to the news of Bathsheba's pregnancy David concocts a plan to cover his tracks. He tries to convince Uriah to come home and sleep with his wife. But because of Uriah's noble character, he won't do it. Although he comes back to Jerusalem at David's request, he will not go home and enjoy his wife because he is too loyal to his men that are in battle. He will not enjoy a pleasure that they cannot. What painful irony! Uriah has too much integrity to sleep with his own wife while the armies of Israel are at battle, but David had no qualms about sleeping with Uriah's wife and committing adultery.

Since Uriah does not go for David's plan, the king has Uriah killed to cover up his own sin. David actually sends the note that will condemn Uriah to death on the battlefield in Uriah's hand, to be delivered to the commander of Israel's army.

CREATIVE MESSAGE IDEA *Say It Loud!*

The only relative of Saul that David can find is Mephibosheth. This is a son of David's dear friend Jonathan. We are also told that Mephibosheth is crippled in both of his feet. Now, just so you will remember this important biblical name, you are all going to say "Mephibosheth" together.

As a leader, first pronounce the name for everyone. Be sure you get it right. If you are not sure of the pronunciation, it is on the copy of the message included in the supplemental materials.

If you want to have a little fun, ask everyone to say "Mephibosheth" on the count of three. Count: one, two, three … and then when everyone says Mephibosheth, you respond by saying, "God bless you!"

Once Uriah is dead, it seems as if David has gotten away with murder and adultery. In a matter of weeks David, the man after God's own heart, has Bathsheba move in with him as his own wife. David seems to have convinced himself that nothing happened and everything is fine.

LIFE APPLICATION | *Temptation – Who Is on the Throne?*

Now comes the question again: Who do you think is on the throne at this moment of David's life? It is clear that David is ready to take whatever he wants. Temptation comes and he falls for it, hook, line, and sinker! Not only does David fall into this sin, but he spirals downward deeper into deception by trying to cover his tracks. His sin of adultery and cover-up, followed by murder, and the subsequent actions will end up costing David more than he ever dreamed.

When you face temptation, as we all do, who is on the throne? Do you yield to the enticement, or does God's power fill you and allow you to resist? Are you giving in to the same sin over and over? Are you expending large amounts of energy covering your tracks and trying to hide your sin?

When you look at the temptations you face right now, who is on the throne of your life? What causes you to lust and want what is not yours? It is important that we look at the story of David and learn from his experience. He was not satisfied by his sin. It did not end with the one act. David's surrender to temptation began a landslide of sin, deceit, and pain. What a powerful reminder for us to resist the enticement to sin and cling to God's plan for our lives.

NEW TESTAMENT CONNECTION

Paradigmatic Laws

The New Testament speaks often about temptation and God's power for us to resist the enticements of the devil. Here are a few passages that speak to this topic:

> No temptation has seized you except what is common to man. And God is faithful; he will not let you be tempted beyond what you can bear. But when you are tempted, he will also provide a way out so that you can stand up under it. (1 Corinthians 10:13)
>
> Submit yourselves, then, to God. Resist the devil, and he will flee from you. (James 4:7)
>
> For we do not have a high priest who is unable to sympathize with our weaknesses, but we have one who has been tempted in every way, just as we are – yet was without sin. (Hebrews 4:15)

Sin will always take you farther than you want to go, cost you more than you want to pay, and keep you longer than you want to stay.

Author Unknown

---

5. Learning from David: Confession

INTERPRETIVE INSIGHT | *How God Feels about Sin*

God is outraged by David's sin. Sometimes we can rationalize our sin and convince ourselves that it is not a big deal. God, however, never looks the other way. He sees David's sin and is ready to deal with it. God sends Nathan to confront the wayward king. Nathan tells David a story about a selfish wealthy man. When David hears how this rich man took a neighbor's pet lamb and slaughtered it to serve a visitor instead of taking a lamb from his own vast flock, he is outraged!

In a shocking twist, Nathan looks at David and says, "You are the man." The prophet then goes on to say:

> "This is what the Lord, the God of Israel, says: 'I anointed you king over Israel, and I delivered you from the hand of Saul. I gave your master's house to you, and your master's wives into your arms. I gave you the house of Israel and Judah. And if all this had been too little, I would have given you even more. Why did you despise the word of the Lord by doing what is evil in his eyes? You struck down Uriah the Hittite with the sword and took his wife to be your own. You killed him with the sword of the Ammonites. Now, therefore, the sword will never depart from your house, because you despised me and took the wife of Uriah the Hittite to be your own.'" (2 Samuel 12:7 – 10)

NEW TESTAMENT CONNECTION

We think of confession of sins as something private. God sees things differently. Through James, God calls his people to take a posture of mutual confession. The more private we keep our sins, the more likely we are to repeat them! "Therefore confess your sins to each other and pray for each other so that you may be healed. The prayer of a righteous man is powerful and effective" (James 5:16).

INTERPRETIVE INSIGHT | *The Ministry of Nathan*

Aren't you thankful that God had someone in the kingdom who had enough courage to speak the truth? As king, David could have spoken one word and had Nathan executed. Nathan's willingness to go face-to-face with the king and confront him with his sin is no small task. This is bold and risky.

Nathan is ready to call sin exactly what it is. He does this because he speaks for God and God never sugarcoats sin. Nathan's job is to call David to a higher standard — God's standard. Because of his ministry, David's heart finally breaks over his sin. He comes to a place of humble confession and repentance.

The ministry of Nathan is the call to speak the truth with loving boldness. It is a hard ministry because it puts relationships at risk. Still, it is a ministry we all must be ready to receive. What will you do when God sends a Nathan to call you to repentance and humble confession?

SIGNIFICANT SCRIPTURE

2 Samuel 12

LIFE APPLICATION | *Extending and Receiving the Ministry of Nathan*

Most of us like to be a Nathan more than we like to hear from a Nathan. We don't mind speaking for God when someone is not living right. We may even have radar that picks up sin in others with great accuracy. If this is the case, we must beware. The ministry of Nathan should be extended with a humble heart and often with tears. We should never take joy in bearing bad news. But if God calls us to speak to another follower of Christ about their sin, we should do this in love and with deep humility.

We also must be ready to receive the ministry of Nathan in our lives. When God sends another believer into our life to raise an issue or uncover a sin, we must be ready to receive this ministry. They have taken a risk by raising an issue in our life. We must be willing to hear their words and then seek God to see if this is his word for us. If it is, repentance is in order.

Is there any place right now, in your life, where someone may be trying to extend the ministry of Nathan and you are stubbornly resistant? Maybe there's somebody you know who needs to hear you speak God's truth into their life. God has put this person on your heart and you are avoiding them like taxes because you don't want to say anything. Just imagine what David's life would have been like if Nathan had said nothing.

SIGNIFICANT SCRIPTURE

Psalm 51

ILLUSTRATION | *An Approachable Spirit*

In the message included with the DVD-ROM materials, Jarrett tells about a time when someone came to him with a concern. They spoke truth that he needed to hear but did not want to face. However, after they extended the ministry of Nathan, he felt that God had spoken to him in a way that would help him grow as a Christ-follower. If you have a story of someone who came to you with the ministry of Nathan, you may want to share it at this time.

INTERPRETIVE INSIGHT | *Confession – Who Is on the Throne?*

When Nathan confronted David, David could have resisted and run. He did not have to confess and repent, but he did. In response to the conviction God brought into David's heart, he wrote Psalm 51. This psalm captures the heart of confession as well as any passage in the entire Bible. In this prayer we hear David admit his sin, face his own weakness, ask for God's forgiveness, and even begin to express hope for how God may still use him to be a blessing to others in the future. Confession gave birth to forgiveness, and forgiveness brought hope alive. Like David, we must learn that confession is often the beginning of a healed and restored relationship with God.

When David finally confesses his sin, when he stops running, when he repents, who is on the throne? Who is on the throne every time we confess from the heart? Who is on the throne when tears of brokenness flow and our heart is bowed before God? The answer is clear: These are the moments that God is on the throne.

PAUSE FOR PRAYER

A Prayer for Nathans

God wants us to extend and receive the ministry of Nathan far more than we do. Take time to pray in two distinct directions:

- Pray for hearts that are humble and receptive to those who may come and speak the truth into our lives.
- Pray for courage and humility as God leads you to speak his truth to other followers of Christ.

LIFE APPLICATION | *Time to Confess*

All of us have times when confession is exactly what we need. Maybe this is a moment that we need to pray, "Have mercy on me, God, have mercy on me. I've been putting myself on the throne. I have been resistant to you. Have mercy on me."

David desperately needed the ministry of Nathan to wake him up, to get him off of the throne. All of us need the ministry of Nathan in our lives—people who are willing to speak truth to us. Maybe God is using this message to call you to a point of confession and repentance.

INTERPRETIVE INSIGHT | *Who Is Jedidiah?*

The truth is, anyone who is in a relationship with God is Jedidiah. You're Jedidiah. I'm Jedidiah. That is our true name. You are the one whom God loves. These are the most precious words we can ever hear. God speaks these words to his own son, Jesus, "This is my Son, whom I love; with him I am well pleased" (Matthew 17:5). All who are followers of Christ can live with this assurance that we are loved by God. Our name is Jedidiah!

LIFE APPLICATION | *Write it Down*

It may be helpful to write that name down in your Bible. Put it in bold letters: Jedidiah.

Write it on the mirror so that when you wake up, you will see it and be reminded that you are the beloved of the Lord. You may want to put a message on your screen saver at home or work: My name is Jedidiah! If someone asks what it means, let them know that you are the beloved of God, and they can be too, through Jesus Christ.

> "Justification by grace through faith" is the theologian's learned phrase for what Chesterton once called "the furious love of God." He is not moody or capricious; he knows no seasons of change. He has a single relentless stance toward us: he loves us.
>
> *Brennan Manning*

INTERPRETIVE INSIGHT | *Back in the Desert*

Later in David's life he ends up in the desert again. His son Absalom mounts a political coup (2 Samuel 15), and David leaves Jerusalem. He flees from his kingdom and from his failure as a father. Once more, David finds himself wandering through the desert, alone again with God. He finds himself right back where God had done some of the most formative and important work in David's heart and life many years before.

PAUSE FOR REFLECTION

Hidden Sin

Sin is deceitful and our hearts are skilled at ignoring it. Yet, God wants to lead us to a place of seeing, admitting, and confessing our sin. This process cannot begin until we identify the places of hidden sin in our lives. Take time for private reflection. Read Psalm 139:23–24 below and allow a time of silence as people invite the Lord to search their heart and reveal any area of sin that is still covered or hidden.

> Search me, O God, and know my heart;
> test me and know my anxious thoughts.
> See if there is any offensive way in me,
> and lead me in the way everlasting.

PAUSE FOR PRAYER

Come and Rule

As a community of believers, take time to invite God back into your hearts. Be honest. Confess where other things have taken God's place on the throne and invite God to rule and reign in every area of your lives.

WORD STUDY

Jedidiah

The child Bathsheba is carrying dies shortly after birth. But God allows her to become pregnant again, and this time she bears a son. David and Bathsheba name this boy Solomon. He later becomes the king of Israel. But Nathan the prophet comes to them and informs them that God has a special name for this child: Jedidiah. This name means, "Loved by the LORD." What a powerful reminder that God is still with this family. With all they have faced, God chooses to remind them of his love, day after day, by giving this baby boy the name Jedidiah.

Again it is in the desert that God does some of his best work. It is also in the desert David is at his best. As he is refined in the furnace of the desert, David is taught humility and dependence on God, and his priorities come back in line. In the desert, God is put back on the throne of David's life.

LIFE APPLICATION | *Don't Run from the Desert*

There are a lot of people who are in the desert right now. For some people it took all the strength they have just to gather with God's people to hear this message. You don't have to imagine what it would be like to enter the furnace of the desert because you are living there! Your desert may be the loss of a job, the loss of a spouse, brokenness in a significant relationship, financial turmoil, or some other painful situation. The temptation is to try to run out of the desert as quickly as possible. The desert feels scary, it can hurt, and sometimes you wonder if God is really with you in the desert. What you must realize is that you are never alone in the desert. God is with you. In fact, sometimes God leads us into the desert, because it's in the desert that he does some of his greatest work in us. Today God may be asking you to linger in the desert and invite him to do a new and transforming work in your life.

PAUSE FOR REFLECTION | *Is God on the Throne of My Life?*

As you draw near the end of this message, give people a couple of minutes for reflection to consider honestly what it would look like for them to put God fully on the throne.

He is the only one who is worthy, the only one who is capable, the only one who has ever been able to rule our hearts. He alone can lead with justice and mercy, freedom and love, truth and grace. He is the King of kings and Lord of lords who deserves to be on the throne.

Invite people to identify any place in their lives where they must put God back on the throne. Encourage them to confess if they have been on the throne in their work life, their relationships, their worship, their response to temptation, their family, or any other area. Finally, take time to invite God back onto the throne in any area where he has been removed.

Message 18

The Heights and Depths of Prayer

Psalms 22, 42, 103, 136, 137

THE HEART OF THE Message

For over 2,500 years, the book of Psalms has been the prayer book of God's people. There is no greater collection of prayers in the history of humanity. The psalms were the prayer book of Jesus. They have guided the prayers of his followers since the church was formed. The church today needs to continue the rich tradition of letting the psalms form and guide our prayer life.

There are many kinds of psalms, and we will survey these over the next two sessions. In this session we will focus specifically on the heights and depths of prayer. The psalms lead us to the heights of celebration, praise, and worship. They also lead us to prayers of honest lament. In this session we will discover the full range of prayer that God invites and encourages. We will also seek to enter into this full spectrum of prayer.

BRIEF MESSAGE OUTLINE

1. Understanding the psalms
2. A look at Hebrew poetry
3. Psalms of praise
4. Psalms of lament

THE HEART OF THE Messenger

In this session we ask God to help make Psalms our prayer book. We will seek to express joy-filled praise as well as the sorrowful depths of lament. To lead a group (large or small) through this process will only happen if you, as the leader, are ready to express your heart to God on both levels.

Take time to prepare your heart by meditating on some of the psalms of praise (Psalms 99, 103, and 104) and the psalms of lament (Psalms 22, 42, and 69). Ask God to free you to express the heights of praise and depths of sorrow to him in prayer as you prepare to bring this message.

CREATIVE VIDEO ELEMENT

Street Comments on Prayer (2:50 min.). This montage of street interviews asks the questions: Do you pray? Why do you pray? Why do you think people pray? It then integrates Scripture from the Psalms with on-screen text. These are real-life answers from real people.

1. Understanding the Psalms

INTERPRETIVE INSIGHT | *Not a Happy Little Devotional Book*

The book of Psalms is not a happy little devotional book filled with uplifting thoughts and inspiring words. It is not given so we can read one page quickly every morning to help us start the day with a positive attitude. Many people turn to Psalms hoping to have this kind of experience. They hope every psalm will be a piece of uplifting, inspirational, and devotional literature. About half the time they get what they are looking for. The other half of the time they just might end up disappointed or even confused. If you are looking for a daily devotion that is guaranteed to make you smile, Psalms just might throw you a curve ball!

NARRATIVE ON LIFE | *From the Heights and the Depths*

The book of Psalms does contain some of the most uplifting and encouraging words ever penned. At the same time, it contains some of the most honest and tearful prayers ever lifted up. The psalms range from the heights of joy to the depths of sorrow and contain every emotion in between.

Suppose you wake up one morning and decide to read Psalm 136:1–4. Here is what will greet you:

> Give thanks to the LORD, for he is good.
> *His love endures forever.*
> Give thanks to the God of gods.
> *His love endures forever.*
> Give thanks to the Lord of lords:
> *His love endures forever.*
> to him who alone does great wonders,
> *His love endures forever.*

CREATIVE MESSAGE IDEA | *Experiencing the Heights and Depths of Prayer*

In this session you will take time to sing and pray in the midst of the message. There will be suggestions offered for specific songs, Scripture, and prayer direction, but you can structure this in any way that fits your context. If you have instrumentalists and vocalists who lead the worship time, be sure they are prepared to stay the entire time, especially if you have more than one worship service.

If you want to have a good start to your day, this psalm is the ticket! It brings a positive feeling of celebration, victory, and joy. This is a psalm that will breathe life into your soul.

Suppose the next day you continue your reading and turn to Psalm 137:1–4. This is how your reading will begin:

> By the rivers of Babylon we sat and wept
>   when we remembered Zion.
> There on the poplars
>   we hung our harps,
> for there our captors asked us for songs,
>   our tormentors demanded songs of joy;
>   they said, "Sing us one of the songs of Zion!"
> How can we sing the songs of the LORD
>   while in a foreign land?

This psalm is sung in a minor key by people who are in exile. These are prisoners of war. Their hearts are broken and they are weeping. As you read this psalm you may find yourself saying, "Well, that's not very happy. That doesn't make me feel very good."

But here is the truth of the matter: It is not meant to make you feel good. It is there for you to learn to express your sorrow when you feel oppressed, abandoned, and alone. The beauty of the psalms is that they help us express our hearts no matter where we are in our journey of faith and no matter how we are feeling.

LIFE APPLICATION | *I Will Learn to Pray the Psalms*

Why are the psalms so broad in their perspective? Why do these prayers embrace so much joy and yet so much pain? Because this is how we experience life. Each day can bring moments of incredible satisfaction, joy, passion, and fulfillment. Then, right next to these moments, we can feel inexpressible heartache and sorrow.

We can wake up one morning feeling happy and peaceful. We are sure it is going to be a wonderful day. By the end of the day, something has happened and our heart is broken. We feel sorrow and must face the reality of the pain in this life.

There are other days we wake up and feel down. We are sure there is no reason to get out of bed. But by the end of the day, God has surprised us with joy. God has shown up in some way and amazed us with his goodness and his grace.

What could possibly prepare us for this kind of expansive life experience? The book of Psalms! This is why your reading plan includes reading psalms on a regular basis. We want all those who walk through this series to learn to love and pray the psalms. Perhaps commit to read a chapter of Psalms each day. However, when you read them, don't expect a daily dose of happy medicine; just let the psalms speak to your heart, from the heights as well as from the depths, and learn to pray authentically as they teach you.

ILLUSTRATION | *Never an Unexpressed Thought*

Most of us have experienced the innocent words of a child who has blurted out something and shocked everyone within earshot. Children often speak their mind with no filters at all. Only as they grow older and learn to censor themselves (usually at the prompting of concerned parents) do children adjust what they say. The psalms in the Bible have this same unfiltered, uncensored feeling. It is as if every thought is expressed with no concern for the consequences.

If you have a humorous personal story of a child who expressed some thought or information that should have remained censored, you may want to share it.

NARRATIVE ON LIFE | *Sometimes Things Get Messy*

Some people who have high administration gifts might wonder, "Why didn't they organize the psalms better? Why didn't they put all the happy ones together, the sad ones together, the mad ones together, and so on?" The psalms are kind of messy because life is messy. A happy day and a sad day sometimes come right next to each other. There are even times we experience a great breadth of emotions on the same day.

The psalms teach us to bring our lives in all their fullness before God in all of his fullness. They teach us to bring our lives with all their messiness, ups and downs, before God. Let's face it, our lives are not always tidy. The good news, however, is that God understands.

SIGNIFICANT SCRIPTURE

Psalm 103

2. A Look at Hebrew Poetry

NARRATIVE ON THE TEXT | *Poetry in the Old Testament*

It is important to have some background on the psalms and the structure of Hebrew poetry. All of the psalms are poems and were used as songs in worship, so understanding how Hebrew poetry works is helpful.

HISTORICAL CONTEXT | *A Specific Kind of Literature*

The Bible is filled with many types of literature. Some passages are parables, others are allegory, and still others are letters (or epistles). Some are historical narrative, and others are poetry. It is critical that we identify the kind of literature we are reading in the Bible and understand it accordingly.

Reading Psalms is like reading somebody's personal spiritual journal. That's really the kind of literature this book is. If you have ever kept a personal prayer journal, this will make more sense. The book of Psalms is uncensored, unfiltered, raw expressions of the heart. None of the highs or the lows get flattened out. It takes a poetic form, but the words come from the core of the heart.

In English we recognize much of the poetry that has been written by rhyme. For example, if someone says, "Twinkle, twinkle little **star**," you may finish the poem with the words: "How I wonder what you **are**." We all recognize how the words rhyme and identify this as a poem.

Hebrew poetry is not characterized primarily by rhyme or by meter. It is identified by something called *parallelism*. This is when ideas or concepts get expressed in pairs. There are three primary variations of Hebrew parallelism. These can be seen over and over in the psalms and other poetic literature in the Old Testament.

The most basic type is called *synonymous parallelism*. This occurs when two thoughts express the same idea. The second line reinforces and reiterates the message of the first. One great example is found in Psalm 103:1:

Praise the LORD, O my soul;
all my inmost being, praise his holy name.

This is synonymous parallelism. "O my soul" is parallel to "all my inmost being." It's another way of saying the same thing. "Praise his holy name" is another way of saying, "praise the Lord." It's emphasizing the absolute importance of praise.

The second kind of parallelism is called *synthetic parallelism*. That occurs when the second phrase elaborates on or explains the first phrase. Psalm 103:2–5 reads:

Praise the LORD, O my soul,
and forget not all his benefits —
who forgives all your sins
and heals all your diseases,

PAUSE FOR PRAYER

Inviting God into the Mess

God sees us, right where we are, and he loves us. If you have a hard time accepting this truth, remember the words of Romans 5:8, "But God demonstrates his own love for us in this: While we were still sinners, Christ died for us." Sometimes we try to hide the truth about our lives from God. As ridiculous as this may sound, we actually try to keep God from seeing the mess in our lives. What we must do is to invite God into the mess. He invites us to tell him about the fears we hold in our hearts, the anger we nurse, our hidden desires, and all the things we would rather not talk about.

ON THE LIGHTER SIDE

Major and Minor Keys

At the most basic level we can divide the psalms into two different groups. There are hymns (psalms that praise God for his great goodness), and there are laments (psalms that ask God for help in times of difficulty, desperation, or need). You might think of them as psalms in major keys and psalms in minor keys.

At this point you may want to have someone ready to play some minor chords on a keyboard, guitar, or some other instrument. As they play these chords, read a few verses from a psalm of lament. Then, have them play a few major chords and read from a psalm of praise.

> who redeems your life from the pit
> and crowns you with love and compassion,
> who satisfies your desires with good things
> so that your youth is renewed like the eagle's.

As you read this part of the psalm, you can see how David, the author of this psalm, declares that God should be praised for all of his benefits, and then he goes on to list many of them: who forgives sins, heals diseases, and so much more. The first line sets the stage and the following lines build on it.

The third type of Hebrew parallelism that is common is called *antithetical parallelism*. This occurs when thought one and thought two express opposite ideas or feelings. This type appears quite a bit in the book of Proverbs, but also in the book of Psalms. Here is an example from Proverbs 12:15:

> The way of a fool seems right to him,
> but a wise man listens to advice.

There is a clear contrast here. A foolish person sees his or her own way as the only way. It seems right to him or her all the time. By contrast, a wise person listens to the advice of others. This type of Hebrew poetic structure gives one perspective and then the opposite. The second line is in contrast to the first.

WORD STUDY

The Psalms Declare What Is in Our Hearts

In New Testament times the people used the psalms to express what was on their heart. These people knew the psalms well, and when they wanted to express themselves, they would often simply recite the words of Psalms.

In possibly the greatest day in the history of the human race, when Jesus rode into Jerusalem, the people could only express their joy by reciting a psalm. During the triumphal entry, as the people got a little taste of what it would be like to live in the kingdom of God, they grabbed on to the Psalms to help them communicate what they were feeling: "Blessed is the king who comes in the name of the Lord!" (Luke 19:38 from Psalm 118:26).

In the darkest moment of human history, when Jesus hung on the cross and felt utterly abandoned and alone, he used one of the psalms to express his heart. At the only time in all eternity when the Son was estranged from the Father and the fellowship of the Trinity was broken, the only words that could do justice to his pain came from the book of Psalms: "About the ninth hour Jesus cried out in a loud voice, *'Eloi, Eloi, lama sabachthani?'* – which means, 'My God, my God, why have you forsaken me?'" (Matthew 27:46 from Psalm 22:1).

The entire Bible is *God's Word to us.* Part of what is so wonderful about the psalms is that they were written to *become our words to God.* They tell the story of our lives – not just the happy parts. The book of Psalms includes the highs, the lows, and everything in between.

> The coordination of "bless" and "don't forget" expresses a profound truth. Only those who praise do not forget. Forgetting God and turning away from God begins when praise has been silenced.
>
> *Claus Westermann*

3. Psalms of Praise

NARRATIVE ON LIFE | *Made to Praise*

Praise of God is different from praise that humans may look for. God deserves our worship and adoration. He is worthy of all our praise—and even more than we can give. Heaping praise on God is never wrong because he is God!

Furthermore, we were made to praise him. We are most content and happy when we are doing what we were made to do. Birds fly; it is natural for them. Otters frolic. Plants grow and produce fruit. These things are not shocking; it is the natural order of things. People were made to praise God and give him worship.

ILLUSTRATION | *Praise Is Natural*

If you have ever stood at the edge of Niagara Falls or seen the Grand Tetons, you understand how natural praise can be. Nobody has to tell you to say, "Ohhh!" and "Ahhh!" It just comes out. If you have ever watched a professional or Olympic athlete break a record or make a game-winning shot, no one had to tell you to cheer or clap; it just happens. We burst into celebration and praise when we see, hear, or even taste something that is praiseworthy.

If we cannot express our wonder and affirmation, we feel cheated. It leaves us feeling empty. There is something God has placed within us that makes us erupt in praise.

ON THE LIGHTER SIDE | *Seeking Praise*

John Ortberg tells the story of when his daughters were young. Sometimes when he was tucking them in at night, he would sit on the side of the bed and ask them, "Who's the smartest, strongest, handsomest, most charming, most wonderful man in the whole world?" They would pause and finally smile and say, "Santa Claus," or, "the Easter Bunny," or some handsome movie star. They would laugh about it because little children understand that you don't pander to somebody's ego needs. It is just not right to heap praise on someone who is out looking for it.

> There's something about life and human nature that when you see something that's praiseworthy or admirable, our instinct is to express adoration.
>
> *C. S. Lewis*

ILLUSTRATION | *Love Expresses Itself*

Imagine a single man who meets a beautiful single woman. They notice each other. They begin to build a relationship. They fall in love. He is filled with admiration for her character and beauty. Do you think he wants to express it? Do you think she wants him to express it? If he is going to put his feeling of admiration and celebration into words, who should hear them first?

The answer is her!

It is natural for this man to express his feelings of love. In the same way, it would be right for her to express what she feels in her heart. When it comes to human relationships, we don't want to express our praise in some general sense. We want to express it to the right person. If that person receives the praise and takes joy in it, that's the best! When this happens, we know what it means. The relationship is reciprocal, and we can begin giving and receiving love and joy together.

INTERPRETIVE INSIGHT | *Praise Completes Us!*

When we as human beings encounter God, we must express praise, in the same way as a young couple in love express admiration for each other. When we see that God is all-wise, infinitely powerful, eternal, utterly holy, all-loving, completely merciful, inexhaustibly patient, ceaselessly creative, beautiful, and joy-filled, adoration erupts. It is the natural response. Our experience with God will never be complete until we express the praise, wonder, and adoration that is in our hearts. Moreover, it can't be some general expression to whoever is listening; it must be lifted to God directly.

When we express our love to God and when we know he receives and delights in our praise, nothing compares. It just doesn't get any better. That is when we know we're in a relationship with him of reciprocal joy, giving and receiving honor and delight. That is why praise is so important in the life of a follower of Christ.

NARRATIVE ON THE TEXT | *Called to Worship*

Psalms of praise have two basic parts. The first part—and it is in most of the praise psalms—is the call to worship. This is the invitation for God's people to enter into his presence and to express their praise to him. Psalm 103 begins:

> Praise the Lord, O my soul;
> all my inmost being, praise his holy name.
> Praise the Lord, O my soul,
> and forget not all his benefits —

In a sense the psalmist is calling himself to worship. Before he invites anyone else to worship, he invites himself. Listen to the words, "Praise the LORD, O *my* soul." At the end of Psalm 103 he calls others to worship:

SIGNIFICANT SCRIPTURE

Psalm 103

Praise the LORD, you his angels,
you mighty ones who do his bidding,
who obey his word.
Praise the LORD, all his heavenly hosts,
you his servants who do his will.
Praise the LORD, all his works
everywhere in his dominion.

David throws open the doors and starts inviting angels, the heavenly host, and everyone and everything in creation to come praise the Lord. Then, at the very end of the psalm, in one final phrase, he comes back to himself with a final invitation to his own soul ("Praise the LORD, O my soul"). The call to worship is a critical and important part of worship.

LIFE APPLICATION | *Calling Yourself to Worship*

Like David, we need to call ourselves to worship. In the morning we can echo David's prayer and say:

CREATIVE MESSAGE IDEA | *Say It Out Loud*

At this point in the message it might make sense to pause and make time for people to respond in praise. You can have people do this silently, but you can also invite corporate expressions of praise.

- First, ask people to write down two or three words that express their praise to God.
- Second, invite them to lift up silent prayers of praise to God.
- Third, ask if there are a few people who would like to stand and express a short word of adoration to God. Encourage others to agree in their heart as members of the family give word to their praise.

If you want to give a little more direction, you could read the following words:

Take a moment and write down two or three words that express who God is to you. The focus is not what he has done for you but on who God is ... his character. Maybe you find yourself focusing on his holiness, forgiveness, power, or tender mercy. Take a moment quietly before the Lord and write down two or three words that express who God is. Then tell him how you feel. Express these words to God just between you and him. Take a moment to praise him for his qualities, for his attributes.

If you feel it will be appropriate in your worship context, invite a few different people to say a word or sentence prayer out loud to express who God is to them.

> Praise the LORD, O my soul;
>   all my inmost being, praise his holy name.
> Praise the LORD, O my soul,
>   and forget not all his benefits.

Then we can do exactly that, all day long.

We also must take seriously the need to call ourselves to worship when we are getting ready to gather with God's people. It used to be that people came early to church; they entered the place of worship in advance of the service so they could prepare their hearts and souls to meet with God among his people. Now we tend to rush into church at the last minute. For some people, their only real consistent preparation is getting a cup of coffee into their system before the service starts.

Why not get a good night of rest the day before worship as part of your personal preparation? You might want to make a point of arriving early so you can pray and prepare. You can use the drive time to pray silently or even out loud with others in the car. If you know the passage you will be studying as a congregation, you might want to read it in advance. Get creative in finding ways to call yourself to worship and prepare to meet with God.

NARRATIVE ON THE TEXT | *Reasons for Worshiping God*

In addition to a call to worship, psalms of praise simply list and expound reasons God is worthy of praise. Some psalms will focus on one attribute and develop it. Others will give a number of qualities of God. There's an interesting example of this in Psalm 103:15–17:

> As for man, his days are like grass,
>   he flourishes like a flower of the field;
> the wind blows over it and it is gone,
>   and its place remembers it no more.
> But from everlasting to everlasting
>   the LORD's love is with those who fear him,
>   and his righteousness with their children's children.

This is also an example of antithetic parallelism. There is a contrast of human beings, whose days are numbered, and God, who is everlasting. Human beings are finite; God is eternal.

ON THE LIGHTER SIDE | *Time Flies*

The psalmist notices that the years of a person are like the flower of the field. In other words, time flies. Our life begins, and before we know it so many years have passed. Have you ever noticed how fast life goes? Have you ever noticed how fast you are aging? If not, just ask the person next you. They have noticed!

There is an interesting variation in this passage. We are reminded that the days of people are like grass; they are limited. We would then expect the psalmist to say, "As for God, his days are eternal, from everlasting to everlasting." But he doesn't. What the psalmist says is, God's *love* is everlasting.

David is overwhelmed by both the eternal existence of God and God's everlasting love. It never ends. You never get to the bottom of it. How can you not want to worship a God like that? The reality of God's love moves David to express praise and delight. This is the heart of worship.

NARRATIVE ON LIFE | *Worship and Music*

There is an important distinction that we all need to understand. The essence of worship is *not* great music. Sometimes people talk about worship as if it's synonymous with music. It's not. Worship is not primarily about getting to hear music that I like. Worship is not about having an emotional experience. It is also not simply about showing up at a church and making it through the service. Sometimes people go to a service of worship, a corporate gathering of Christ followers, and their focus is on, "Can I feel what I want to feel?" That's not the heart of worship. Sometimes God gives gifts of great joy or great emotion in worship, but that is not the heart of it. Worship is so much more than any of this.

> To worship is to quicken the conscience by the holiness of God, to feed the mind with the truth of God, to purge the imagination by the beauty of God, to open the heart to the love of God, to devote the will to the purpose of God.
>
> *William Temple*

INTERPRETIVE INSIGHT | *The Heart of Worship*

The heart of worship is to delight in the goodness, greatness, and glory of God. It is to reflect deeply on his character and attributes and then to respond in natural praise and adoration. We then express this directly to him, and we know he receives it. Worship is to reflect on God with our mind, our will, and our heart in a way that moves us to delight in him and then to be overwhelmed when we realize that he also delights in us, far more than we ever dreamed.

NARRATIVE ON LIFE | *Unmanaged Faces*

Dallas Willard says, "One of the things that we love about children is they have not learned to manage their faces. Whatever is going on in a child's heart is just right there on their face. There's joy on the face of a child when there's joy in their heart."

As we grow up we learn to manage our faces carefully. Yet, God wants us to praise him with an unmanaged face. We can learn to express our praise to God with our words and faces. It may be helpful for many of us to rediscover the free expressions of childhood when it comes to our worship.

SIGNIFICANT SCRIPTURE

Psalm 42

4. Psalms of Lament

INTERPRETIVE INSIGHT | *Prayers from the Depths*

The psalms of lament are a much different psalm from the praise psalm. These are recorded in the Bible to help us learn how to pray this way also. Just as God invites and gladly receives our prayers of praise, he also welcomes and blesses us for our prayers of lament.

Many people might say, "I don't think I know how to lament. I am not sure what a lament really is." Well, here are some questions:

- Do you know how to complain?
- If your body is aching, do you know how to groan?
- When hard times come, do you ever shed tears of sorrow?
- When people treat you unfairly, do you ever tell God that you don't understand?

If you answered yes to any of these questions, you already know something about laments.

CREATIVE MESSAGE IDEA | *Worship Together*

Note: Watch the video supplied with the DVD-ROM materials here.

Before you begin looking at the psalms of lament, plan to have a time of praise and celebration. Invite people to meet with God and express their praise and adoration in a number of ways.

Small Groups

You can have people get into small groups of three or four and offer up short prayers of praise. Those who feel more comfortable praying on their own should feel free to do this. This particular kind of expression in praise fits best in a context where most of the people gathered are already believers.

Corporate Worship

Plan a time of singing together. Have a praise team ready to lead. Some possible songs might be:

- "Shout the Name of Jesus," by Matt Shepardson
- "Sweet Presence of Jesus," by Tommy Walker
- "All Creatures of Our God and King," by Francis of Assisi
- "Doxology," by Thomas Ken
- "Holy, Holy, Holy," by Reginald Heber

A lament psalm is basically a complaint. It is an honest and heartfelt expression of pain, sadness, and brokenness. Interestingly, the psalms of lament are the largest single category in the whole book of Psalms.

> **NEW TESTAMENT CONNECTION**
>
> *The Hope of Resurrection*
>
> When we come to a place where we have to face the reality of death, it is critical that we remember that death is not the end for followers of Christ. We need to be free to lament and express our fear, anger, and sense of loss. At the same time, we must keep in mind the truth that those who die in Christ have an eternal inheritance that nothing, including death, can ever take away. Read 1 Corinthians 15 to see what Paul says about the assurance we can have if we are followers of Christ.

NARRATIVE ON THE TEXT | *Tears and a Broken Heart*

As we read Psalm 42, we begin to understand the heartbeat of a lament. Listen to these words and see if you can identify with this kind of psalm. Read Psalm 42:1–6, 9. Can you feel the pain? Can you hear the despair? Can you sense honest complaint coming through? The psalmist holds nothing back:

- My only food, day and night, is my tears.
- Other people are taunting me because it seems God will not deliver.
- I used to gather with God's people for worship; now I can't. My joy and thanksgiving are gone.
- My soul is downcast and disturbed.
- I feel forgotten by God.
- I am oppressed by my enemies.

These are not the statements of someone at the top of his spiritual game. This is a far cry from the celebration of Psalm 103. Yet this is a prayer that is pleasing to God. When was the last time you dared pray with this kind of bold honesty?

NARRATIVE ON LIFE | *The Laments Are for Us*

The psalms of lament deal with a number of areas of struggle, though they tend to be somewhat general. There are few details in Psalms, and this is intentional on the part of the psalmists. The psalms were written to be all-purpose prayers. They can be used by people in many various situations. The beauty of these psalms is that we can adapt them to our unique needs. We can use them to give voice to what's happening in our lives and hearts.

NARRATIVE ON THE TEXT | *The Content of Laments*

The laments can help us when we face any kind of pain or time of struggle. However, there are four primary topics that are addressed in the laments.

The fear of enemies. In the laments we hear people crying out to God because they are being attacked by an enemy. Enemies can take many shapes and forms. Usually in the psalms they were people attacking the psalmist physically or perhaps emotionally. The psalmist was seeking relief or deliverance from such individual(s).

PAUSE FOR REFLECTION

Identifying My Pain

Provide time for everyone gathered to take a few moments, privately between themselves and God, to lift up prayers of lament. We all have some area where we have a deep need for God's help. Encourage each person to think through the four topics that come up often in prayers of lament and identify where they are feeling pain, hurt, fear, or just a sense of being stuck.

For you, an enemy could be your boss, a neighbor, a coworker, or everybody on the freeway. It could even be somebody you usually love but are facing conflict with at this time. It could be somebody you are sitting near in church, even the person next to you. Your enemy could be depression, loneliness, fear, or sin. It's whatever or whoever you need deliverance from. God invites you to come to him and cry out for strength to resist the attack you are under today.

The battle with illness. A second category in the laments is the problem of sickness. This can be a physical problem or even the stress you feel due to the burdens of life. Anything that creates stress and pain in your body is included in this kind of lament.

Here's the truth about us: We carry things in our bodies all day. We can be anxious about a test in school, fearful about a work review coming up, or tense about a broken relationship. These things impact our bodies. Maybe we are facing financial pressures or are worried about a child who is making poor choices. We might be walking around with churning stomachs, stiff necks, aching heads, sweaty palms, and boiling blood. We all know exactly what the psalmist means when he says, "My bones suffer."

In a sense, God is using your body to tell you to pray. Laments are a way to tell God how you are feeling and to cry out for help. Life in this fallen world brings so much more than we were ever intended to handle on our own. Thus, our physical sickness, pain in our bodies, and emotional turmoil are all opportunities to pray.

The reality of death. The sense of pressure or trouble is often so severe in the psalms of lament that the psalmist speaks of being at the point of death. When the psalmists talk about Sheol (NIV "grave"), one idea behind this term is that they don't

PAUSE FOR PRAYER

Seeking God's Comfort

Take a moment to pray for all of those gathered. You may want to prepare your own prayer or use the one provided below:

> Heavenly Father, you hear every prayer. You know every heart. You count every tear. You know, God, that we have a desperate need for you. You know, Father, the stories of all of the men and the women in this room who will not make it if you don't help them. In this moment, because you ask us to, as your people have done for thousands of years, we place before you our heaviest burdens, our biggest worries, and our darkest fears. We cry out to you and seek you for the help that only you can offer. We do this trusting that you are the God who listens and cares for his people. In Jesus' name we pray. Amen.

see any way out. Death becomes a picture of a life that feels hopeless and a soul that is in mortal agony.

Of course, there are also times when a lament is about more than fear of death or a sense of utter hopelessness. There were times when the psalmist was under attack and genuinely fearful for his life. Sometimes a prayer of lament will be lifted up by a person who is on the edge of death because of an illness or even old age. The reality of death can bring us to a place of honest prayer.

The anxiety of being trapped. The fourth and final category in the laments is the anxiety of being trapped. Through the psalms of lament we find images like drowning or being stuck in a pit. The idea is that we all know how it feels to be stuck in a situation we can't seem to get out of. In our prayer of lament we might cry out to God and say, "I'm stuck in a financial pit and I can't get out." We might call out to God because we feel trapped in a painful marriage, habitual sin, destructive relational patterns, or some kind of addiction. In a lament we call to God, admit that we are stuck, and ask him to help get us out of our situation.

INTERPRETIVE INSIGHT | *Affirmation of Praise*

Although the laments do have the feeling of a complaint, they are unique in that they almost always have a feeling of hope. Even in the deepest pits of despair, the psalmist seems to have an unquenchable spirit of hope. Bernhard W. Anderson, in his classic book, *Out of the Depths (The Psalms Speak for Us Today)*, writes:

> The term "lament" is not an altogether satisfactory label for these psalms. The word may suggest a pessimistic view of life, a "bemoaning of a tragedy which cannot be reversed." But this is not the mood of the psalmists. What characterizes these psalms, with very few exceptions, is the confidence that the situation can be changed if Yahweh wills to intervene.

What a great reminder that even in the most painful and difficult times, God's people can cling to hope.

Message 19

The Greatest Prayers of All Times

Psalms 19, 30, 51, 58, 96, 103, 119, 137

THE HEART OF THE Message

In this message we will look at five different kinds of psalms. Each of these categories helps us speak our heart to God in new and powerful ways. We will practice making the psalms our prayer to God. God longs for us to learn to pray in deeper and richer ways, and one of the best tools we have for developing our prayer life is the book of Psalms.

As we learn from the psalms and as they become part of our very hearts, we will grow. The psalms will enable us to give voice to our thanks, sorrow, anger, fear, praise, and so much more. The psalms have been an indispensable tool in the spiritual lives and growth of God's people for thousands of years. We need to let them become ours.

BRIEF MESSAGE OUTLINE

1. Thanksgiving psalms
2. Penitential psalms
3. Wisdom psalms
4. Imprecatory psalms
5. Enthronement psalms

THE HEART OF THE Messenger

Each section of this message holds the key to unlock a part of our heart and express it to God. From the heights of thanksgiving to the raw edge of anger, the psalms help us tell God what we are feeling. From the depths of rebellious shame to the heights of the throne room of God, the psalms will instruct us if we let them. As a leader, take time to let the psalms speak to your heart and prepare you to speak to God. Meditate on the following psalms as you prepare your heart to bring this message to God's people (Psalms 30, 51, 19, and 58).

NARRATIVE ON LIFE *How Do We Teach Prayer?*

How do you teach someone to pray? Jesus' disciples came to him and said, "Lord, teach us to pray." All followers of Christ have a desire to learn how to pray in authentic ways. Where do we look to find tools to develop our prayer lives?

Many parents have grappled with this question and have developed standardized ways to teach their children to pray. Often it looks something like this. You learn to pray by talking to God each night before bed. Kneel next to the bed, fold your hands, close your eyes, and say:

> Now I lay me down to sleep,
> I pray thee, Lord, my soul to keep.
> If I should die before I wake,
> I pray thee, Lord, my soul to take.
> God bless.... [At this point you list as many people as come to mind.]
> [Then you finish with a declarative] Amen!

Is there anything wrong with this approach to teaching prayer? No. It is a great starting point for children. It is also helpful to teach some basic prayers that can be offered before a meal or at a time of need. But, if a follower of Christ gets to be twenty, thirty, or fifty and that is the entire sum of his or her prayer life, he or she has missed the breadth, beauty, and power of prayer. There is so much more, and the book of Psalms is the best guide to help us navigate the rich and varied landscape of prayer.

SIGNIFICANT SCRIPTURE

Psalm 30

1. Thanksgiving Psalms

INTERPRETIVE INSIGHT | *Thanksgiving Psalms*

Psalm 30 is one of the greatest psalms of thanksgiving in the Bible. Invite those gathered to read the first five verses with you.

Psalms of thanksgiving explode with celebration for what God has done. In the last session we looked at psalms of praise that focus on who God is. The direction of those psalms was God's character and attributes. Psalms of thanksgiving shift our attention to the mighty acts of God and all he does for his children. God has been good, beyond description. The psalms of praise help release the thanks that are locked up in our heart. They remind us that God is worthy of being thanked for all of his mighty deeds.

ILLUSTRATION | *What Do You Say?*

It is a short sentence, only two words. The entire declaration is only two syllables, but it is so hard to learn. The sentence is, "Thank you!" Why is it so hard to learn these two words?

Every parent discovers that part of their job is to ask each child, over and over again, "What do you say?" When a meal is served, they ask their daughter, "Honey, what do you say?" When a gift is received from grandparents, they prompt their son, "What do you say?" When a neighbor has given them a ride home from school, they ask them, "What do you say?" Over and over, year after year, parents ask their children this question countless times in a variety of ways.

Why do parents do this? Because thanksgiving is an appropriate response to someone's kindness. Parents ask this question again and again, longing for the day when their son or daughter will say it on their own. What joy fills a mother's heart when her son gives a smile and says, "Thanks, Mom!" all on his own.

> Worship – the only gift we can bring to God that he himself has not first given to us.
>
> *Isobel Ralston*

NARRATIVE ON LIFE | *Remember God's Goodness*

We need to learn to remember how good God has been to us. We have admitted our need and cried out to him on many occasions. In response, God has heard our cry and responded in powerful ways. Now we need to respond with heartfelt thanks.

- How have you cried to God and seen him work on your behalf?
- Maybe you needed healing and God came and touched you.
- Maybe you had financial needs at some point and God was generous.
- Maybe you were sad, or you were in deep pain, and God gave you comfort.
- Maybe you felt useless and God showed you that you have distinct gifts that he wants to use for his glory.
- Maybe you felt alone and God sent you a friend.
- Maybe you were anxious and God gave you hope.

Whatever God has done, the appropriate response is thanksgiving.

HISTORICAL CONTEXT | *Ancient Covenants*

There is a basic structure or movement in the psalms of thanksgiving. They follow this basic format:

1. **An admission of need.** The psalmist will declare an awareness that he was in a time of need. This can be a specific need or something general, but there is an expression of need lifted up to God.
2. **A cry to God.** Next, the psalmist declares that he cried out to God in his time of need. He made his need known and trusted in God to protect, provide, deliver, or meet his need in some other way.
3. **An expression of thanks for God's work.** Finally, the psalmist identifies the way that God heard his prayer and acted. Then, a natural and joy-filled expression of thanksgiving follows. This prayer of thanks is always rooted in what God has done and how his mighty power has been revealed.

NARRATIVE ON LIFE | *Giving a Joyful Offering*

During your time of singing you may want to receive the offering. If you do, take a moment and talk about how the giving of offerings is really a response of thankfulness. When we give with joy in our hearts, we are acknowledging that God has been so good to us, he has provided all we have, and we are glad to give back to him. The offering is not an interruption in our worship service. It is an act of worship, and especially it is an act of thanksgiving. It's a way of saying to God, "Thank you that you've blessed me with so much. I want to give this to you as an expression of my gratitude."

LIFE APPLICATION | *Remember to Say Thank You!*

Just as children need to hear parents ask them, "What do you say?" we also need to be reminded to be thankful. The truth is, sometimes we forget. We get busy, we become

CREATIVE MESSAGE IDEA | *Put It on Paper*

Take time as a group to write a short psalm or prayer of thanksgiving. Use the basic structure we find in the psalms of thanksgiving. Invite all those gathered to experience what it feels like to be a psalmist. Even those who are not fond of writing should be encouraged to participate.

After a short time for writing, you may want to invite a few people to stand and read their psalm of thanksgiving.

You Will Need

- Half sheets of paper that have the basic structure of thanksgiving psalms (admission of need, cry to God, response of thanksgiving) printed on them.
- If you meet in a large room, you may need some microphones set up so people can use them to read their psalms of thanksgiving.

CREATIVE MESSAGE IDEA | *Lifting Up Our Thanks*

After people have written their psalms of thanks and some have read them, plan to lift your voices together in songs of thanks. There are many songs of thanks that are appropriate. Some possible songs you could use are:

- "For the Beauty of the Earth," by Folliott Pierpoint
- "Now Thank We All Our God," by Martin Rinkart
- "For All That You've Done, I Will Thank You," by Dennis L. Jernigan
- "Give Thanks," by Henry Smith
- "I'm Forever Grateful," by Mark Altrogge
- "Better Is One Day," by Matt Redman
- "I Could Sing of Your Love Forever," by Martin Smith
- "Mourning into Dancing," by Tommy Walker

selfish, or we just get used to God's goodness and don't notice how much he does for us.

Commit to grow as a person of thankfulness. Remember to say thank you. Here are two ideas for growing in thankfulness:

Daily reminders. Use the things that come up every day as thanksgiving prompters. Here are some ideas of things that can remind you to pause and lift up thanks to God:

- when you wake up in the morning
- each time you have a meal
- whenever you hear someone complain (including yourself!)
- each time you hear a bird chirp, a dog bark, or a cat meow
- when a baby cries
- when you hit a green light (and when you hit a red light)
- when someone smiles at you (and when someone scowls)
- when you lay your head on the pillow at the end of the day

Identify specific things that happen regularly in your day and use these as thanksgiving prompters.

Do a life inventory. Plan a time when you will get thirty or more minutes free of interruptions. Start from your childhood and begin identifying times you have seen a need in your life, cried to God, and watched him answer. Each time you identify a life situation where God moved on your behalf, write it down. Write just a few words to remind you what God did and when he did it. Then spend a few moments saying thank you.

Some of the things you will remember may have evoked great thanks in your life back when they happened. In other cases you may realize that you never really thanked God for his goodness and provision at that time of your life. In either case, use this as an opportunity to express the depth of thanks you feel.

Then, move on in your life and continue the same process. Here is a helpful way to walk through your life:

- my birth to my toddler years (you probably don't remember, but others may have told you stories of God's goodness to you, even before you were born)
- my childhood
- my teenage years (think of all the potential dangers God saved you from — sometimes without your even asking!)
- my young adult years
- my middle age years
- my elderly years

NEW TESTAMENT CONNECTION

A Cheerful Giver

In 2 Corinthians 9:6 – 8 we read:

> Remember this: Whoever sows sparingly will also reap sparingly, and whoever sows generously will also reap generously. Each man should give what he has decided in his heart to give, not reluctantly or under compulsion, for God loves a cheerful giver. And God is able to make all grace abound to you, so that in all things at all times, having all that you need, you will abound in every good work.

Our attitude in giving should be one of cheer and joy. Our giving should be generous and willing. How can this be? In hard economic times, when we work so hard for what we have, when giving to God means that we have less, how can we be joyful? Because giving is a great way we express thankfulness. God is the one who is able to give us grace and all the resources we need. Our generous and thankful offerings are a declaration that we understand that every good thing we have in this life is a gift from God's hand (James 1:17).

2. Penitential Psalms

INTERPRETIVE INSIGHT | *Penitential Psalms*

SIGNIFICANT SCRIPTURE

Psalms 51 and 103

Another category of psalms are called penitential psalms. They help us to learn how to do self-examination and how to express confession to God. They are open and honest prayers where we say, "Lord, in the light of your goodness, in the light of your glory, I see myself as I really am. I have got to say, I am sorry. I have sinned. I have wronged you. I have broken your heart." These psalms give voice to our sorrow over sin, and they also move us to a place of repentance and transformed lives.

ILLUSTRATION | *The Value of Examination*

In a sense, the penitential psalms are like X rays that look into us and show where we are broken and where the sickness of sin is hidden. We need these psalms for our souls in the same way we need a regular physical to be sure we are physically healthy.

There is a true story about a couple with a five-year-old daughter. The little girl fell out of a tree and dropped about ten feet to the ground. They rushed her to the hospital to make sure she was not injured. The doctors did X rays and CAT scans to see if there were any broken bones or any internal damage. The good news is that she wasn't damaged by the fall. But, to the surprise of everyone, the tests revealed a brain tumor.

The tumor was benign, but it was growing. The doctors did surgery as soon as they could, and it went very well. As a matter of fact, she asked for a cheeseburger the day after surgery! Her life may well have been saved because she fell out of a tree and had unplanned X rays. Those tests revealed what would not have been found otherwise.

On a lighter note, the little girl's mom talks about how she can picture two guardian angels looking over that little girl when she was up in the tree. One of them says to the other one, "You push her." The other one replies, "No, I'm not going to push her. You push her."

CREATIVE MESSAGE IDEA | *Songs of Confession*

After a time of silent prayer and reflection, respond together by singing a song of confession. Here are a few ideas:

- "Cleanse Me," by J. Edwin Orr
- "Just As I Am," by Charlotte Elliott
- "Whiter Than Snow," by James Nicholson
- "Come, Let Us Worship and Bow Down," by Dave Doherty
- "You Are Merciful to Me," by Ian White
- "Create in Me–Psalm 51," by Matt Shepardson and Greg Ferguson

NARRATIVE ON LIFE | *Examining Our Hearts*

We don't have to fall out of a tree to get X rays of our heart and soul. God has given us the penitential psalms to help in this process. It is as if the psalmist is saying, "How can I find out about something that's toxic to my body, that could destroy my soul, paralyze my heart, sear my conscience, and separate me from God, but I can't see it? How do I examine my heart?"

Each time we read these psalms and make them our own, God helps us see where we need to confess and repent. Sometimes we see the sickness growing in our soul. At other times we are blind to it. But always God is ready to reveal it, if we ask, and deal with our sin.

> **PAUSE FOR REFLECTION**
>
> ### *Words of Assurance*
>
> You may want to give these words of assurance as you close this session of the message:
>
> Regret doesn't get the last word. Sin doesn't get the last word. Guilt does not get the last word. *You are forgiven.* As far as the east is from the west, that's how far God has removed your transgressions from you. If you have received the forgiveness that comes through a relationship with Jesus Christ, you can be filled with joy right now. This is the good news God has for you. All your sins are gone, and you are loved by God with an everlasting love!

LIFE APPLICATION | *Doing Moral Inventory*

Pause in the message and invite people to a time of moral inventory. Read some selected verses from Psalms 51 and 103 that you feel will be helpful for those gathered. Then, allow silent time for private reflection and confession.

First, invite God to help in the process of searching our hearts. If we do this on our own, we are likely to miss things and go through the process too fast. Or we can become neurotic and get into all kinds of unhealthy guilt. Self-examination is only safe and right when we do it with God's help.

Question 1: God, please show me my hidden faults! Maybe it's a bad habit; maybe it's an attitude; maybe it's something I've done today or even something that has been hidden for years. It could be a failure to love someone, or perhaps I have avoided speaking the truth. Maybe you have been choosing pain avoidance rather than courage. Whatever it is, ask God to show you.

Question 2: God, send me a Nathan! That is a courageous prayer. When we pray this, we are admitting that there are some areas of darkness in our hearts and lives that we know we can't deal with on our own. Maybe we can't see the sin. Or perhaps we see it and feel God's conviction, but can't seem to stop. It could be that we need a brother or sister to come alongside of us and help us in the process of turning from our sin.

Second, invite people to come before God humbly in these moments with no defensiveness or no stiff necks, but with soft and open hearts. Pray for the convicting ministry of the Holy Spirit to take place in each heart. Acknowledge God's great desire to heal and forgive.

NEW TESTAMENT CONNECTION

Forgive Us Our Debts

Jesus taught his followers to pray: "Forgive us our debts, as we also have forgiven our debtors" (Matthew 6:12).

It is clear through both the Old and New Testaments that we are to respond with a spirit of forgiveness toward those who have wronged us. There is a relationship between the ways we offer forgiveness and how we will receive it.

LIFE APPLICATION | *Extending Forgiveness*

Think about David for a moment. After he committed murder, adultery, and a number of other sins, his heart was broken, and he came back to the Lord. He asked God for mercy and compassion. David pleaded with God to blot out his transgressions and wash away all his sin. David realized there was great brokenness in him and that he could not get himself out of the pit he had fallen into. Only God could save him. David also committed to help extend grace to others and to help them turn back to God.

Like David, when we have become aware of the greatness of God's grace toward us, we want to help others know that his grace is available to them as well. We can begin by seeking to have a forgiving heart toward those who have wronged us. The more we understand and accept the forgiveness God offers, the more freely we extend grace to those who have wronged us.

CREATIVE MESSAGE IDEA | *Receiving Forgiveness*

Invite everyone to stand before God to receive a reminder of his promise to forgive and cleanse. You may want to ask them to take a posture of receiving in the following way.

Ask them to imagine that they love M&M candies. Ask them how they would put their hands if they knew you were going to pour out as many M&Ms as they could hold. How would they cup their hands together to get the maximum volume of candy? Invite them to hold out their hands in that kind of receiving posture. If they are not a fan of M&Ms, they can imagine you are going to give them as many fresh blueberries (or some other favorite food) as they can hold.

As they stand with hands and hearts ready to receive a reminder of God's grace and power to forgive, read the following passages with bold confidence:

> The Lord is compassionate and
> gracious,
> slow to anger, abounding in love.
> He will not always accuse,
> nor will he harbor his anger forever;
> he does not treat us as our sins deserve
> or repay us according to our iniquities.
> For as high as the heavens are above
> the earth,
> so great is his love for those who
> fear him;
> as far as the east is from the west,
> so far has he removed our
> transgressions from us.
> As a father has compassion on his
> children,
> so the Lord has compassion on
> those who fear him. (Psalm
> 103:8–13)

> If we confess our sins, he is faithful and just and will forgive us our sins and purify us from all unrighteousness. (1 John 1:9)

Whom do you have in your life that needs to experience the fullness of God's forgiveness? How might God want to use you as an ambassador of his grace in the life of this person? Are there people you need to forgive as you grow in your understanding of how much God has forgiven you?

3. Wisdom Psalms

SIGNIFICANT SCRIPTURE

Psalms 19 and 119

INTERPRETIVE INSIGHT | *Wisdom Psalms*

The wisdom psalms give instruction and guidance to God's people. They praise and celebrate God's law. They rejoice in the pure beauty of the words God has given us in the Scriptures. These psalms are intended to motivate and help us desire to follow the teachings of God's law with all our heart. The most remarkable one of these wisdom psalms is Psalm 119. It has 176 verses, every one of which calls us to delight in God's law.

INTERPRETIVE INSIGHT | *The Arrangement of Psalms*

There are many ways the psalms were structured by the authors. We already looked at Hebrew poetry, but Psalm 119 introduces a new structure. It is a praise of God's wisdom from the beginning to the end. For this reason, the entire psalm, all twenty-two

ON THE LIGHTER SIDE | *Let's Read It Together*

Using the PowerPoint slides provided on the DVD-ROM, invite those gathered to read the portion of Psalm 119 as it is printed on the screen (it will be in a very small font—too small to read). Remind people that this is only a portion of the psalm (which is 176 verses long).

CREATIVE MESSAGE IDEA | *In Praise of God's Wisdom*

Encourage each person present to open a Bible to Psalm 119 and begin reading anywhere in the psalm. After they have read four to five verses, invite them to do the following:

- Begin circling (if they have their own Bible) all of the varied words that are used as references to God's law (precepts, statutes, teachings, word, decrees, and more).
- Have them see how far they read before they run into something about the power and goodness of God's law.
- Invite them to tell the person next to them one thing they learn about God's law from the verses they read.

stanzas, is based on the Hebrew alphabet. Each verse in the first section begins with the first letter of the Hebrew alphabet, Aleph. Each verse in the final section begins with the last letter, Taw. This is the author's way of saying that the law of God, his wisdom, is all we need for life; it is all-inclusive!

> Trouble and perplexity drive me to prayer; and prayer drives away perplexity and trouble.
>
> *Philipp Melanchthon (sixteenth century)*

NARRATIVE ON LIFE | *The Power of God's Word*

Read the words of Psalm 19:9–11 in unison with those gathered:

The fear of the LORD is pure,
  enduring forever.
The ordinances of the LORD are sure
  and altogether righteous.
They are more precious than gold,
  than much pure gold;
they are sweeter than honey,
  than honey from the comb.
By them is your servant warned;
  in keeping them there is great reward.

This passage, and others in the wisdom psalms, put life into perspective. God's wisdom is more valuable than anything else in the entire world. We don't often see it this way, but it is true. The Hebrews prized the wisdom of God more than any other possession. God's wisdom warns us and keeps us from stumbling. It is the source of truth and blessing.

God longs for us to come to a place where we love his Word and hunger for it. Reading the Word of God and growing in his wisdom is not a chore but a privilege. It is not a burden we bear but a source of amazing strength in the life of a follower of Christ.

SIGNIFICANT SCRIPTURE

Psalms 58 and 137

LIFE APPLICATION | *Making Space for God's Word*

If we went for two weeks without eating any food, our bodies would become weak. We would notice it! If we go too long without the food of God's Word and the filling of his wisdom, we become spiritually malnourished. It is critical for God's people to make space in their day to read, study, and meditate on God's Word. This can be first thing in the morning, at a lunch break, in the evening, or at the close of the day. The timing is not as important as the condition of our hearts.

God longs to meet with us and speak into our lives. One of the most powerful ways he does this is through the wisdom of his Word. Each of us should find a time and place where we can spend some uninterrupted moments with God and feed on his truth.

ILLUSTRATION | *Holy Space*

One man found that the best time and place for him to meet with God was over his lunch break. Every day he would go out to his red pickup truck and climb into the cab. He kept his Bible on the dashboard, and he used these moments to meet with God. With a praise tape playing quietly, he would pray and read the Bible. The cab of his truck became a holy space, a sacred meeting place where God met with this follower of Christ.

4. Imprecatory Songs

INTERPRETIVE INSIGHT | *Imprecatory Psalms*

In the last session of this study we focused on psalms of lament. Imprecatory psalms are actually a specific kind of lament. These are prayers that deal with the issue of vindication. We might call them, "Get-My-Enemies Laments." In these prayers we hear the psalmist expressing harsh words that sound something like this, "Lord, I feel oppressed by this person, and I would really like you to break all their teeth. Okay?" Some of them get even more graphic. In some of these prayers the psalmist is saying, "God, I am under attack and I am asking you to rain down judgment upon my enemy!"

To get a sense for how severe these psalms could be, listen to these words from Psalm 58:6–8:

> Break the teeth in their mouths, O God;
> tear out, O LORD, the fangs of the lions!
> Let them vanish like water that flows away;
> when they draw the bow, let their arrows be blunted.
> Like a slug melting away as it moves along,
> like a stillborn child, may they not see the sun.

These are harsh words. Nevertheless, they are spoken from an honest and broken heart. Most important, they are expressed to God. Rather than go out and get revenge, the psalmist cries out to God and leaves judgment where it belongs, in the hands of a just God.

NARRATIVE ON LIFE | *Where Do I Take My Anger?*

There is a strange beauty to this kind of prayer. We come to God with a lament of vindication and say, "God, this person has made me so mad, they have hurt me so deeply, all I want to do is get them back. But I won't, Lord. I won't strike out. I leave judgment to you." Do you

NEW TESTAMENT CONNECTION

Praying for Our Enemies

For Christ's followers, when we come to words like this, it causes us to stop and wonder: How can I reconcile these words with what Jesus teaches? Jesus said things like Luke 6:27–29:

> But I tell you who hear me: Love your enemies, do good to those who hate you, bless those who curse you, pray for those who mistreat you. If someone strikes you on one cheek, turn to him the other also. If someone takes your cloak, do not stop him from taking your tunic.

How does this kind of teaching fit with these psalms? Although scholars debate exactly how to understand the imprecatory psalms, there is a sense that God wants us to bring all of our feelings, including our deepest anger, to him. By bringing it to him, we are deterred from taking it out on those who have made us angry. Also, in his presence, as we pour out all that is in our hearts, he can begin a work of changing our hearts and teaching us how to respond in a manner that honors him.

begin to see the importance of this kind of prayer? As harsh as it sounds, it is a powerful prayer because in an imprecatory prayer we are saying, "I won't strike back. I won't raise my hand. I won't return evil for evil. I put it in your hands, Lord. By the way, if you would like to get them for me, that would be just fine!" What a great reminder that we can, and should, come to God with all of our feelings, even anger!

> Rage belongs before God.
> *Myris Lowhof*

LIFE APPLICATION | *Where Do I Go with My Anger?*

Where do you go with your anger? There are lots of places we can take our rage, and most of them are terribly destructive. What happens when you take your anger to your spouse or your children? What consequences might this have? Some take their rage out on the road, or they put a fist through a wall. Again, how does this help? Still others carry their anger into the workplace or they take it out on the family pet. Take time to identify where you tend to take out your anger and identify some of the possible repercussions if you continue with this practice. Then try bringing your anger, in all of its messiness, right to the throne of God. He knows you, he loves you, and he understands.

> Worship renews the spirit as sleep renews the body.
> *Richard Clarke Cabot*

CREATIVE MESSAGE IDEA | *Say It, Read It, Pray It, Sing It!*

As you finish this message, consider doing one or more of the following things to help people focus on the God who is enthroned in power and glory:

Say it! Invite people to turn to the person next to them and say, "Our God reigns." Then have everyone say it together, as loud as they can!

Read it! Have everyone read selected verses of Psalm 96 in unison.

Pray it! Lead the congregation in a prayer expressing confidence and certainty that God is on the throne and that he is able to take care of his children.

Sing it! Close with a song expressing awareness and confidence that God rules and reigns.

Possible song ideas:

- "Bless His Holy Name," by Andrae Crouch
- "Come, Thou Almighty King," author unknown
- "Hosanna," by Carl Tuttle
- "How Excellent Is Your Name," by Michael W. Smith
- "Our God Is an Awesome God," by Rich Mullins
- "We Bow Down," by Twila Paris
- "What a Mighty God We Serve," author unknown
- "Be the Center," by Michael Frye
- "Shout to the North," by Martin Smith
- "Only a God Like You," by Tommy Walker

NARRATIVE ON LIFE | *A Changed Heart*

Think of David and his relationship with Saul. Saul committed so much injustice against him, yet David refused to raise his hand against Saul because he was the Lord's anointed. Yet, in some of David's psalms, you can hear him saying, "I won't touch Saul, but Lord, if you want to deal with him, it would be fine with me."

Like David, we can take our wrath, anger, and vengeance to God. God says, "Bring it to me. I will help you walk through this." Then, at the footstool of God, our anger and wrath begin to dissipate. Slowly, God changes our hearts. At the throne we discover that God can do what we can't. He can change our hearts. He can take a heart filled with anger and bitterness and begin to transform it. With his power, we can even learn to love our enemies.

SIGNIFICANT SCRIPTURE

Psalm 96

5. Enthronement Psalms

INTERPRETIVE INSIGHT | *Enthronement Psalms*

The final category of psalms we will learn about are enthronement psalms. These are psalms that recognize that this world may have troubles and that earthly leaders may not always be fair, but God is on the throne. These prayers turn our eyes upward, toward the very throne room of God, and remind us that no matter what we face, God is still enthroned.

NARRATIVE ON LIFE | *Remember Who Is on the Throne*

We need to learn from the example of God's people in the Old Testament. When times were hard, they kept their eyes on the one who rules and reigns. In the midst of sickness and in scarcity, when they were in exile, when they were under the oppression of the Assyrians or Babylonians, or when Jerusalem and the temple and all they loved was a distant memory, they would turn to these psalms. Every time they read Psalm 96 and other enthronement psalms, they remembered, "Our God reigns."

When we go through the trials this life brings, when we are hurting and feeling powerless, we need to look to the throne of God and remember that he rules. Also, when we talk with other Christ followers who have lost their focus, we might need to point them back to the throne and remind them who is in charge of this universe.

NEW TESTAMENT CONNECTION

Where Do You Look?

In the New Testament we find a similar example in the book of Hebrews. The author writes in Hebrews 12:1–3:

> Therefore, since we are surrounded by such a great cloud of witnesses, let us throw off everything that hinders and the sin that so easily entangles, and let us run with perseverance the race marked out for us. Let us fix our eyes on Jesus, the author and perfecter of our faith, who for the joy set before him endured the cross, scorning its shame, and sat down at the right hand of the throne of God. Consider him who endured such opposition from sinful men, so that you will not grow weary and lose heart.

As followers of Jesus, we need to keep our eyes fixed on Jesus. He is on the throne, and when we remember this, everything takes on a different tone. We see life through the eyes of eternity.

ON THE LIGHTER SIDE | *A Psalm for April 15*

As we have already seen, there are both psalms of praise and psalms of lament. Different ones were used on different occasions. Think, for a moment, what kind of psalm would you use on April 15, a praise or lament? (Give time for those gathered to respond.) The answer is obvious, a lament! People have always complained about government and, particularly, taxes! But the psalms acknowledge that no matter how bad human government might get, God is still on the throne.

Message 20

Enter the Romance

Song of Songs

THE HEART OF THE Message

When God created human beings, he made men and women. His perfect plan was a man and woman together in covenant love and community. In Eden, before the Fall, God said, "Be fruitful and multiply." It is clear that human romance and sexual intimacy were part of God's perfect plan. Even in Paradise, before sin entered in, God saw his creation of a man and woman in intimate relationship and declared it "Very good!"

The Song of Songs is a celebration of God's plan for romantic and sexual intimacy in the covenant of a marriage relationship. It is a bold reminder that God made us male and female and that his plan is still good. No matter how the world misuses God's good gifts, he always has the power and desire to restore them to his original plan.

THE HEART OF THE Messenger

Get ready to blush! Teaching from Song of Songs is a roller-coaster ride of passion, excitement, and intimacy. There is no way to teach this book with integrity and avoid the presence of honest expressions of romantic love and clear longings for sexual fulfillment. If you feel uncomfortable addressing these topics, it is time to pray for God's strength and leading. God celebrates the goodness of human romance, and so should we. If you are married but your relationship is not healthy and filled with romance, let this be a time to seek the Lord for a new flame to begin burning in your marriage.

BRIEF MESSAGE OUTLINE

1. Setting the scene
2. Movement 1: Anticipation (1:1 – 3:5)
3. Movement 2: The wedding and the honeymoon (3:6 – 5:1)
4. Movement 3: Romance and relationship (5:2 – 8:14)

1. Setting the Scene

NARRATIVE ON THE TEXT | *An Allegory of the Church or a Love Story?*

There are those who teach that the Song of Songs is really an allegory of God's love for the church. Generally people who hold this position have not read this book very closely. There is no indication of that anywhere in the text.

Song of Songs starts right in with kissing in the very first section and then it really gets going! It is a raw, unabashed, uninhibited celebration of romance and sexual attraction and passion between a man and a woman. Every indication, from looking at the text of this book, is that it is not an allegory about the church but an honest expression of love between two people.

CREATIVE VIDEO ELEMENT

Solomon's Courtyard (4:50 min.) In this humorous dramatic sketch, Solomon uses his gift of poetic writing to help a friend romance a woman.

NARRATIVE ON THE TEXT | *Meeting the Characters*

There are three main characters in the Song of Songs:

The woman: She is often called "the beloved." This woman is deeply in love and longs for her lover (the man). She is bold in her expressions of praise for the man's character. She also freely expresses her longing for intimacy and the depth of love she has for the man.

The man: He is called "the lover." This man is a common shepherd, but the woman sees him like a king. He is also bold in his declaration of love and is quick to praise his beloved. He celebrates her beauty and rejoices in her love.

The friends of the woman: They speak in concert together. Their combined voice celebrates the relationship of the man and woman and cheers them on in their relationship.

As you read the Song of Songs in most Bibles today, you will find captions that tell who is speaking. These headings are not in the Hebrew text. They have been supplied by interpreters to help us understand who is speaking at each point in the story. Because this is a poetic book, these title headings help us stay in touch with the drama and movement of the book.

NARRATIVE ON THE TEXT | *Scenes in the Drama*

There are three primary movements in the Song of Songs, which help us follow the plotline of the book. They are:

Movement 1: Anticipation (1:1–3:5). As you read this section, you meet a couple who is crazy in love. They can't wait to be together. They long for each other. But they are not married yet, so they dream, wait, and prepare for that day.

Movement 2: The wedding and honeymoon (3:6–5:1). This section is a poetic, highly stylized description of a wedding. It's a picture of commitment and covenant.

Movement 3: Their relationship after the wedding (romance and relationship) (5:2–8:14). The rest of the book is a celebration of love, romance, and the joy of covenantal sexual intimacy. It is a great reminder that true romantic fulfillment begins on the wedding day but does not end there.

NARRATIVE ON LIFE | *How to Hear This Message*

Some of those who are hearing this message are in marriages that are terrific. Others feel trapped in marriages that may be quite painful. There are also people who are married, but their spouse is not a believer. Almost every possible marital situation is represented in most churches.

No matter what your situation, God has something to say to you through the Song of Songs. Even those who are not married have a great deal to learn from this book. Every person who is gathered should be asking the question: "God, what do you have to say to me through this book of the Bible?" We must try to refrain from the temptation to think about what we wish someone else (even a spouse) would learn from these words. God wants us to ask, "God, what do you want to say *to me*?"

For those who are *married*, it is helpful to remember when your heart was the most tender toward your spouse. It may be when you first met and fell in love. Perhaps it was at your wedding, or else at some other point in your relationship. No matter when it was, even if it has been a long time since you have felt this way, try to remember what it felt like when your heart was tender toward your spouse.

Some of those gathered are *single*. Marriage may still be on the horizon. It could be something you are longing to experience. You can ask God, "What do you have to teach me about marriage and the kind of marriage that would honor you and bring joy?" Or, perhaps the question you need to ask is, "How could I support a married couple that I care about?"

ON THE LIGHTER SIDE | *What a Place to Start!*

The books of the Bible start in many different ways. Genesis begins with creation. Matthew starts with a record of the ancestral line of Jesus. Only Song of Songs begins with kissing! Just listen to the opening words of this book. Or better yet, read them together:

Let him kiss me with the kisses of
his mouth—
for your love is more delightful
than wine.

This book begins with the woman expressing her longing for the man to kiss her! No other book of the Bible opens with kissing (first base) and then goes on to hit a home run!

This is not Leviticus! It is a book unlike anything else in the Old or New Testament.

Some of those gathered have *lost a spouse*. You were married and your spouse died. Maybe part of what God wants to do is to help you experience some moments of thankful remembering. God may engage you in a combination of both grief and comfort.

For those who have walked through the painful experience of *divorce*, it may be that God wants to remind them of the tenderness and love that can exist between a man and a woman. God made this relationship to be "good" and wants us to remember the beauty of his perfect plan, even if our experiences have not mirrored what God has in mind.

SIGNIFICANT SCRIPTURE

Song of Songs 1:1–3:5

2. Movement 1: Anticipation

ILLUSTRATION | *My Big Fat Greek Wedding*

In the box office smash *My Big Fat Greek Wedding*, there is a scene where the mother takes her daughter aside and passes on an important piece of information. It is just before the wedding and the honeymoon. The mother lets her know that Greek women are not passive in the romance department. Her advice to her daughter is this: "Greek women might be lambs in the kitchen, but they are lions in the bedroom."

ON THE LIGHTER SIDE | *Confession Time*

To this day people are still fascinated with names. When a woman is going to be married, she will often practice writing her new name. Now it is confession time. By a showing of hands, how many of the women here spent time practicing writing their new name before you were married? Are there any men who want to admit that they practiced writing their wife's new name?

HISTORICAL CONTEXT | *Your Name*

In Song of Songs 1:3 the woman says, "Your name is like perfume." She's captivated by his name. This often happens with deep attraction. We can become fascinated by the name of a person we love.

But there is more happening here than just a mere fascination with a name. A name in the Scriptures generally refers to someone's *identity*, *reputation*, or *character*. This is why God's people were always careful to honor his name and never misuse it. God's name was equivalent to his character. Thus, when the woman is saying that her lover's name is like a pleasing fragrance, she is speaking of who he is as a person. She is deeply drawn to the character of this man. He is a man of deep integrity, honesty, and loyalty; he can be trusted.

INTERPRETIVE INSIGHT | *The Need for Balance*

Throughout the Bible we find many warnings, cautions, and safeguards concerning the potential dangers of human sexuality when it is expressed outside a covenant relationship between a man and a woman. The Bible has many examples of what happens when people mishandle sexuality. Those are all important, and they bring a much needed balance to our understanding of sexuality. We do not, however, find those warnings in the Song of Songs. This book is a celebration of the goodness of covenantal romance.

HISTORICAL CONTEXT

Beware . . . Song of Songs

Jewish parents in ancient days actually had an age restriction on the Song of Songs. Young boys were not to read this book until they were old enough. Some books of the Bible were rated G, but Song of Songs was rated R and was restricted until parents felt it was the right time for their children to read it.

LIFE APPLICATION | *A Word of Caution*

This is a word for every young person and every single person—whatever age. Be careful about to whom you give your heart. Be sure to examine their character closely and thoroughly. Be sure their name has a fragrance like perfume and not manure. Some of the saddest stories you will ever hear involve people who develop a passionate attachment to somebody with an untrustworthy character. Get to know their name, their character, their reputation, before you make any lasting commitments.

LIFE APPLICATION | *A Call to Celebrate*

If you are married to someone with a good name, tell them how grateful you are. Let them know how much it means to you. Express the depth of your appreciation for their name in a letter, a poem, a song, a piece of art, in any way you can. Make sure you tell them how much it means to you that they are a person of character and integrity. Make a point of celebrating their name any chance you get. Also, freely tell others how much you appreciate the integrity and character of your spouse.

HISTORICAL CONTEXT | *Women in the Ancient World*

Notice that the woman is the first to speak in the Song of Songs. She is honest, bold, and clear in what she is longing to have–kisses! We often think of women in the Middle East (especially the ancient Middle East) as being modest and even prudish. We think about the veils and long robes, and we can forget that they were women with the same desires and longing women have today. As we walk through this song, it becomes clear that the woman has a level of desire and passion every bit as powerful as the man's. It also becomes apparent that God is so pleased with her desires (and the man's longing) that he includes all of it in Scripture.

NARRATIVE ON THE TEXT | *He Said, She Said*

In the Song of Songs 1 we hear the man and woman speaking to each other. We need to realize that they use words and images that might seem strange to us, but their passion shows through. The woman speaks and declares her desire for her lover, she celebrates his name, and then she calls out for him. In 1:7 she says:

> Tell me, you whom I love, where you graze your flock
> and where you rest your sheep at midday.
> Why should I be like a veiled woman
> beside the flocks of your friends?

We find out a little bit more about the identity of the groom here. He is a common shepherd. He may not be wealthy, but he is like the king to her. Her words reveal that she longs to be with him.

Next, the man goes on to speak to her in these words (1:9):

> I liken you, my darling, to a mare
> harnessed to one of the chariots of Pharaoh.

INTERPRETIVE INSIGHT | *"The Delight Factor"*

There is a striking feature that runs through this book. It might be called "the delight factor" in the conversation of a man and a woman who love each other. Behind their words is a deep desire to build each other up. They get creative in how they do this and in the words they use. Their words pour out of a generous heart. Each has a deep longing to build up the other and celebrate who they are.

ON THE LIGHTER SIDE | *You Look Like a Horse!*

Imagine a wife taking her husband to a mall to help her pick out a dress for a wedding they will be attending. She gathers a few options and heads into the dressing room. He sits in the special "husband-chair," strategically positioned just outside of the dressing room area. There he waits for the moment she reappears. He knows what the question will be, for he has sat in this chair before.

"How do I look?"

He pauses, reflects, and then he says, *"You look like a horse!"*

Let's be honest, this would not go over very well! In our day, calling a woman a horse is not a complimentary thing. Even if he clarified by saying she looked like she was harnessed to a chariot, this would not help. Some images just don't transfer over from the Song of Songs to the Nordstrom changing room.

In those days, Pharaoh's horses were prized above all others. The woman would have taken these words as a flattering compliment. All through this book we need to realize that the images that seem strange to us were understood in a positive light.

LIFE APPLICATION | *A Time to Praise*

Husbands and wives today need to learn to praise the good they see in each other. Maybe we need to discover the dove-like beauty that is in the eyes of our spouse. If we have not looked deeply into our spouse's eyes in a long time, it is time to start gazing.

A loving husband should find things about his wife that he celebrates and tell her on a regular basis. In turn, his wife should receive these words of celebration. She should not say, "No. It's not true. I'm not that pretty." She needs to receive his words of praise and drink in his love.

In the same way, a wife should compliment and affirm the good attributes she sees in her husband. When she sees something in his appearance or character that is praiseworthy, she should let him know. He also needs to learn to receive her words of blessing.

NARRATIVE ON THE TEXT | *Playful Interactions*

There's a playful aspect to the banter that's going on with the woman and the man. She is saying that she feels ordinary and plain, but she is also giving him an opportunity to say that he sees her in a different light. When it's overdone, it can be manipulative, like fishing for compliments. But when it is honest, it can open the door for mutual expressions of blessing and affirmation.

This can be a playful way of saying, "I'm open to your expressions of love. I really am. I'll receive them. I'm interested." The lover responds by saying: "Like a lily among thorns"—because every other woman in the world is a thorn, it causes pain even to look at them compared to you—"is my darling among the young women."

NARRATIVE ON LIFE | *A Culture of Two*

Throughout the Song of Songs both the man and woman use pet names for the other. The man uses the name "my darling" nine times in the book. The woman also has

HISTORICAL CONTEXT | *A Rose and a Lily*

In Song of Songs 2:1 the woman says, "I am a rose of Sharon, a lily of the valleys." That sounds a little boastful at first. "I'm a rose, I'm a lily—look at me!" But Old Testament scholars say that a rose in ancient times was not like what we think of in our day. It was not something you would get from a florist's shop. It was a common, not a valuable flower. It was a type of crocus and was not noted for its beauty or expense.

When the woman calls herself a "lily of the valley," she is speaking of a plain, everyday blossom. It was the kind of flower that would be picked up, smelled, and then tossed aside by any shepherd. In reality, these are modest words. She is saying, "I'm not that attractive. I'm just kind of average."

her pet names for the man. This practice is still common today. One contemporary psychologist notes that strong marriage relationships actually create what he calls a "culture of two."

This is expressed by things like special nicknames. He notes that the nicknames couples have for each other tend to come from one of three categories: food, animals, and body parts. Some examples are: sugar, honey, teddy bear, and that kind of thing. Sometimes we combine them and come up with real creative options like: sugar lips, honey bear, muffin ears, and other combinations.

ON THE LIGHTER SIDE

Just Kidding!

Some people use baby talk when they relate to their dogs. Most of us have heard this. C. S. Lewis says this is really stupid. No, he didn't actually say that. Just kidding!

ILLUSTRATION | *The Most Tender Language*

Some people even create a private love language that seems almost like baby talk. They would be embarrassed if others heard the way they communicate with each other in intimate moments. C. S. Lewis writes about this in a book called *The Four Loves*. He makes note of a certain scientist who discovered that certain animals (including specific species of birds) do a similar thing. They make infantile sounds normally made only by young birds of their species when courting another bird. Lewis says the reason for this is that it is the most tender language. Among animals and people, it expresses a tender heart.

LIFE APPLICATION | *A Generous Heart*

Here's a question for those who are married: Do you relate to your spouse with a generous heart or a stingy heart? Do you give sincere, authentic praise? Do you speak words that honor and value your spouse? Do you treasure secrets together—things that only the two of you hold and share? Do you build rituals into your lives? Do you go on dates with each other? Do you create memories? Do you guard your culture of two?

NARRATIVE ON THE TEXT | *Belong to Each Other*

There is a classic phrase from the Song of Songs in 2:16. The woman says, "My lover is mine and I am his." This is such an important declaration that it gets repeated almost verbatim in 6:3 and again in 7:10. To this day it is often used by Jewish brides at weddings. It's a statement of possession: We belong to each other. This is not an unhealthy, controlling, or jealous sense of belonging. Rather, this is an expression of the deep meaning of covenant.

Through the Old Testament we learn that God is deeply concerned about covenants. God's covenant is, "I will be your God, and you will be my people." In a similar way, the marital covenant is, "My lover is mine and I am his." When these words are promised between two human beings in marriage, they are saying, "There's not much you can count on in this world. Your health may go south, your pension fund may collapse, your career may never look like what you hoped it would look like, and your appearance may change over the years, but you can count on one thing: As long as this heart is beating, it's yours. I will not give my heart and body to anybody else in the way that I give it to you."

CREATIVE MESSAGE IDEA

A Blessed Arrangement

You may want to use the brief wedding scene from the movie *The Princess Bride*. (Be sure to get permission.)

LIFE APPLICATION | *I'm Not Going Anywhere*

Sometimes when a relationship is going through hard times, the best you can say is, "I'm not going anywhere." In a world where everything seems dispensable, we need to commit that our covenants mean something. When times are hard and we feel like giving up, we remember the promise we made to our spouse and God and we declare, "No matter how hard things get, I will never even entertain the idea of giving up. We are in this marriage together and with God's help, we will make it!"

3. Movement 2: The Wedding and the Honeymoon

NARRATIVE ON THE TEXT | *A Wedding Scene*

SIGNIFICANT SCRIPTURE

Song of Songs 3:6–5:1

The next section in Song of Songs begins in 3:6. The anticipation is over, and the wedding day has come. There are disagreements among scholars about how to interpret this scene. Some people think Solomon is the literal bridegroom being described. This is unlikely for at least two reasons: (1) This man is a shepherd (1:7) while Solomon was not. (2) The major theme of this book is the mutual exclusiveness of the man and the woman ("My lover is mine and I am his"), while Solomon had seven hundred wives and three hundred concubines. He was not a model of exclusive love.

It is likely that "Solomon" in 3:7, 9, and 11 is kind of a code name for the groom. Poetry often works that way. The pageantry and the court imagery used here express something important. When the woman looks at this man, he may be just a shepherd, but in the eyes of the one who loves him, he's a king.

LIFE APPLICATION | *How Do You See People?*

In God's eyes, the world is not divided up into important people like Solomon and CEOs, and then unimportant people like shepherds. In God's eyes, everybody bears his image. In God's eyes, everybody is made to reign with him. True love enables us to see just a little bit of what God sees when he looks at us through the eyes of Christ. When we love somebody, we can see the ragged shepherd, but we can also see a king or queen.

HISTORICAL CONTEXT | *Understanding the Images*

Look at Song of Songs 4:1 – 5. Again, the man is praising his beloved's beauty. Notice the various images he uses (some are highlighted below):

> How beautiful you are, my darling!
> Oh, how beautiful!
> Your eyes behind your veil are
> *doves.*
> Your hair is like a *flock of goats*
> descending from Mount Gilead.
> Your teeth are like a *flock of sheep*
> just shorn,
> coming up from the washing.
> Each has its twin;
> not one of them is alone.
> Your lips are like a scarlet ribbon;
> your mouth is lovely.
> Your temples behind your veil
> are like the halves of a
> *pomegranate.*
> Your neck is like the *tower of David,*
> built with elegance;
> on it hang a thousand shields,
> all of them shields of warriors.
> Your two breasts are like two fawns,
> like twin fawns of a gazelle
> that browse among the lilies.

This is the kind of imagery that tends to bog some people down when they read through the Song of Songs. Here are some quick insights that may help make sense of this imagery.

"Your eyes ... are doves." Doves in that culture were prized, especially for their color. In the sun, they were kind of a translucent gray. This is the man's way of saying he sees her eyes and they are beautiful.

When you look into somebody's eyes, it's a very intimate thing. It is a soul gaze. Their eyes will tell you if they're happy, if they're sad, or if they're beaten down by life. If you are deeply attached to someone, you know the color of their eyes because you have looked into them many times. This man has looked deeply into this pair of eyes.

"Your hair is like a flock of goats." This is not a common compliment in our day, but in biblical culture it made sense. When a large herd of goats came down a hill, they would wind around it in a way that looked quite striking and attractive from a distance. This was the lover's way of saying, "Your hair is thick and wavy. I like how it curls. It looks wonderful."

"Your temples ... are like the halves of a pomegranate." The idea here is that her head is symmetrical. Today we talk about somebody having good bone structure. He is appreciating the shape and size of her head.

"Your neck is like the tower of David." The neck was a symbol of strength. Even in our day we have a similar phrase: "Her head will not be easily turned by someone who comes along." This is about elegant strength. Also, the tower of David was covered with shields that shone in the sun. He is admiring her neck for its beauty.

This is an ecstatic celebration of the worth of the one the man loves. He is using images that would be deeply compelling to the Middle Eastern heart. He's going on record to say, "This is how much I want you. This is how deeply I love you. This is how firmly I devote myself to you. I notice your beauty, and I have to express it!"

So many people in our world are good at seeing faults. Those who are married are always tempted to focus on the shortcomings of their spouses. What we need to learn to see, in all of our relationships, are the good qualities. We need to learn to see people as God does. If you tend to be quick to judge and find yourself seeing the weaknesses in everyone you meet, it may be time to ask God to give you new eyes.

NARRATIVE ON THE TEXT | *The Wedding Unfolds*

Now the groom speaks. His anticipation has mounted to this point, and their wedding day has come (4:9–11):

> You have stolen my heart, my sister, my bride;
>   you have stolen my heart
> with one glance of your eyes,
>   with one jewel of your necklace.
> How delightful is your love, my sister, my bride!
>   How much more pleasing is your love than wine,
>   and the fragrance of your perfume than any spice!
> Your lips drop sweetness as the honeycomb, my bride;
>   milk and honey are under your tongue.
>   The fragrance of your garments is like that of Lebanon.

Notice that in this section the title "bride" is used for the first time. Most likely the use of this word here is to be understood as the place in the wedding where the man is making his vows.

LIFE APPLICATION | *Remember Your Vows*

If you are married, take out a copy of your wedding vows and read through them together. How are you doing at keeping this covenant? How can you be more faith-

ON THE LIGHTER SIDE | *A Bad Tooth Millennium*

"Your teeth are like a flock of sheep just shorn, coming up from the washing. Each has its twin." Let's be honest, that just sounds bizarre! But in those days it made sense–it really did. Remember, those were days when there were no dentists, orthodontists, toothpaste, toothbrushes, braces, fluoride in the water supply, or flossing. It was a bad millennium for teeth. Everybody had missing teeth. But, the beloved's teeth are lovely. They are white. They look like sheep that have just been shorn and washed.

When the lover says that each of her teeth has a twin, it is his way of affirming the fact that she is not missing any teeth. There was a lower tooth for every upper tooth. He is noting that it is more attractive than if she had a few teeth missing.

ful to live out the promises you made on that important day? You may even want to have a copy of your wedding vows framed and place it somewhere you will see it on a regular basis.

NARRATIVE ON THE TEXT | *The Honeymoon*

Right in the context of the wedding and the honeymoon, we read some intimate words (4:16–5:1). Notice that each of the three primary parties in this drama speaks:

> *The Beloved (the bride)*
> Awake, north wind,
> and come, south wind!
> Blow on my garden,
> that its fragrance may spread abroad.
> Let my lover come into his garden
> and taste its choice fruits.
>
> *The Lover (the groom)*
> I have come into my garden, my sister, my bride;
> I have gathered my myrrh with my spice.
> I have eaten my honeycomb and my honey;
> I have drunk my wine and my milk.
>
> *The Friends*
> Eat, O friends, and drink;
> drink your fill, O lovers.

Again we see many word pictures intended to communicate what is happening here. It is not hard to decipher what these images mean. This is their wedding night. They are to enjoy the fullness and wonder of sexual expression within a covenantal relationship.

When the man and woman speak of a garden, they are not talking about a literal garden with sunflowers and rutabagas. This is a metaphorical way of saying, "Whew! Whee!" They are rejoicing in the intimacy God has given them. It is important to recognize that the man, the woman, and the friends all see the romantic and sexual

HISTORICAL CONTEXT | *"My Sister, My Bride"*

The groom uses the phrase "my sister, my bride" a number of times in this book. This may seem strange to us, but in that culture family ties were the most binding ties of all. Blood was definitely thicker than water. He is saying, "My tie to you will be the most binding of all. All of the loyalties that would go into any relationship with a member of my birth family, I now give to you." When he calls her his sister, it is a high compliment and a sign of deep devotion.

expression of a married couple as something to be celebrated. The fact that this is all recorded in Scripture teaches us that God rejoices in this also.

LIFE APPLICATION | *The Role of Friends*

The friends in this scene are giving a toast to the bride and groom and cheering for their intimacy and closeness. There is a specific role that the friends play in this book of the Bible. They cheer, bless, and give positive direction to the couple. This is still the role of those who have friends who are married.

Marriages don't occur in vacuums. When we think about friends who are married, we should ask the question, "Is their marriage stronger and better because of me?" We can all learn more about how we can encourage and bless those who are married.

Praying faithfully for married couples is a great place to start. God also invites us to cheer and affirm when a marriage is strong and heading in the right direction. We can encourage our married friends, listen to them, and respond in ways that build hope. If a marriage is in trouble, we can encourage our friends to talk with a pastor or see a good Christian counselor. When a marriage is doing well, we can make specific observations about the good parts of the relationship we see and rejoice with our friends. Every marriage needs a cheering section, and it is an honor when we can be part of a chorus of voices that celebrate a good marriage.

PAUSE FOR PRAYER

Lifting Up Marriages

Take time as a group to pray for marriages. As a leader you might want to give some brief words to prompt those gathered as they pray:

- Pray for healing and restoration in marriages that are strained.
- Cry out to God on behalf of those who are widows and widowers. Pray for the comfort and strength of God to fill their hearts.
- Lift up words of thanksgiving for marriages that are strong and healthy.

4. Movement 3: Romance and Relationship

NARRATIVE ON THE TEXT | *The Story Goes On*

The wedding day is not the end; it is the beginning. Too many couples focus on the wedding day and the honeymoon and spend all of their time getting ready for this one short period of time. They forget that the marriage will last a lifetime. Song of Songs does not miss this reality. The rest of the book deals with the need to build a relationship and maintain a romantic and growing life of intimacy in marriage.

SIGNIFICANT SCRIPTURE

Song of Songs 5:2–8:14

When we come to 5:2, we discover that the wedding and the honeymoon are over. We don't know how much time has passed, but the couple is now into their married life. This is kind of a dream sequence. The wife says, "I slept but my heart was awake" (5:2). The husband comes home from work. He has been out in the fields tending the sheep and is covered with dew. He has something specific on his mind.

As he comes to the door, you can almost hear him say, "I had to work late, dear. My head is covered with dew, but I'm home now." Then notice all of the pet names he throws in: "my sister, my darling, my dove, my flawless one." Can you guess what he has in mind?

Her response is found in verse 3, "I have taken off my robe — must I put it on again? I have washed my feet — must I soil them again?" In other words, "Do I have to get up and let you in?" This is a Middle Eastern way of saying, "Not tonight, I've got a headache." Even in the Song of Songs marriage is not idealized to the point of being unrealistic.

CREATIVE MESSAGE IDEA

A Closing Song and Prayer

Have someone sing a closing song that is often used in weddings. Let these words strike a chord in the hearts of those who are married. Then, close with a prayer for God's power and blessing to be released in the marriages of those gathered.

NARRATIVE ON LIFE | *Tough Times Will Come*

Even in the strongest, most passionate marriages there will be tough times. Every couple needs to be ready for this. If you get married expecting perfect harmony, endless romance, and no conflict, you will be disappointed. The issue is not if we will face difficult days, but how we will respond when these times come. These are the days when we need to receive God's power and grace when ours is in short supply. These are the times we need our chorus of friends to support and encourage us. These are the moments that we might need to seek the help of a professional Christian counselor to help us get perspective and tools that will help us move forward and build a marriage that honors God and brings blessing to our hearts.

LIFE APPLICATION | *Unquenchable Love*

As Song of Songs continues, there are more expressions of joy, celebrations of beauty, and expressions of commitment to make this relationship last. Then we come to one of the most beautiful sections of the entire book (8:6–7):

> Place me like a seal over your heart,
> like a seal on your arm;
> for love is as strong as death,
> its jealousy unyielding as the grave.
> It burns like blazing fire,
> like a mighty flame.
> Many waters cannot quench love;
> rivers cannot wash it away.
> If one were to give
> all the wealth of his house for love,
> it would be utterly scorned.

There is a closing declaration that their love will be unquenchable. In a world where intimacy, romance, and relationships seem to get snuffed out by busyness, apathy, unresolved conflict, financial stresses, poor communication, and selfishness, we need to hear these words. Love seems to get quenched each day, but it does not have to. If you are married, let this be the moment you say that your love will not be quenched. Commit to sit with your spouse and talk about how you can fan the flames of your marriage. What will it take to rekindle the spark of romance? What habits need to start? What needs to end? Who will keep you accountable to build a healthy relationship? How will you celebrate when you take steps forward on this journey?

CREATIVE MESSAGE IDEA *Live/Video Testimony*

If you have a couple who has worked through a time of struggle but are now deeply committed to their marriage and growing in a very healthy direction, you may want to have them share a brief testimony at this time.

Message 21

Solomon: Extreme Wisdom

1 Kings 3:7 – 28; Proverbs

THE HEART OF THE Message

God desires for us to walk and live in his wisdom. Although we may see wisdom as the ability to answer trivia questions or do well on tests, God sees it differently. Wisdom is the ability to make right decisions that honor him and move us toward his purposes for life. In this message each person will be challenged to find a proverb that they can carry in their heart in a way that will transform their lives. This message is about growing to understand and love God's wisdom so much that we long to see it grow in our lives.

BRIEF MESSAGE OUTLINE

1. Meeting Solomon
2. Understanding proverbs
3. Adopting a proverb

THE HEART OF THE Messenger

As you prepare to bring this message, be sure to adopt a proverb from the six key verses in this message. Once you have chosen your proverb, commit it to memory. Spend a week meditating on this verse and let God's wisdom sink deeply into your heart. Ask God to shape your thoughts and actions around the message of this proverb. As you begin to see a transformed life, you will know that you are growing in wisdom.

1. Meeting Solomon

NARRATIVE ON LIFE *Important Questions*

This may seem like a harsh question to ask at the beginning of a message, but it is an important one. Ask those gathered: "Have you ever done anything really stupid?"

The truth is that we have all done more stupid things than we want to remember. When we identify the reality of our poor decisions, we become profoundly aware of our need for God's wisdom.

Here are a couple of other questions that might be helpful for us to answer:

- Do you do stupid (unwise) things that you end up regretting on a fairly regular basis?
- Would you like for it to stop, or would you like to cut down on the number of stupid things you do?

SIGNIFICANT SCRIPTURE

1 Kings 3:7–28

The book of Proverbs was given by God to help us do exactly that: It teaches us to do less stupid things and to grow in our ability to live wisely.

NARRATIVE ON THE TEXT | *Encounter with Solomon*

At the beginning of 1 Kings, David is dying. This leads to a lot of intrigue and jockeying for the throne. The first few chapters describe a political mess, but God is still at work.

In chapter 3 God comes to Solomon in a dream. God says to him, "Ask me for whatever you want—anything." This is an interesting test. If God were to offer you or me anything in the world, we have to wonder what we would ask for. Solomon's response is amazing! He prays:

> "Now, O Lord my God, you have made your servant king in place of my father David. But I am only a little child and do not know how to carry out my duties. Your servant is here among the people you have chosen, a great people, too numerous to count or number. *So give your servant a discerning heart to govern your people and to distinguish between right and wrong.* For who is able to govern this great people of yours?" (1 Kings 3:7–9)

The text goes on to say God is pleased that Solomon asks for wisdom, for it shows that he is viewing himself as a servant. He could have asked for anything for himself, but he asks for a gift that will benefit the people that he is called to serve.

NEW TESTAMENT CONNECTION

The Ultimate Servant

In the gospel of Mark we hear Jesus declare why he came to this earth. When we know who he was, this is astounding. Jesus said, "For even the Son of Man did not come to be served, but to serve, and to give his life as a ransom for many" (Mark 10:45). In John 13:1–17, Jesus washes the feet of his disciples, an act of incredible service. And in all four of the Gospels, we watch as Jesus extends the ultimate act of service by laying down his life to pay for our sins. His example is one that should be duplicated in the lives of all who are his followers.

LIFE APPLICATION | *Am I Passionate about Serving?*

As we look at Solomon's desire to serve the people and as we are reminded of Jesus' example of service (and call for us to serve), we should take time to evaluate how much we serve. Do we tend to like people waiting on us and serving us more than us serving them? Is the natural disposition of our heart to serve others? Have we found practical ways to serve in our home, on our campus, at our workplace, and in the church? God calls us to a posture of service, and we need to learn that the wise person follows this call.

ILLUSTRATION | *Amazing Wisdom*

Right after Solomon's prayer, we read a famous story that shows how his wisdom is put to the test in a dramatic way. Two prostitutes come before Solomon. One of their sons has died in the night. Both claim that the living boy is theirs.

"Bring me a sword," Solomon says. "We'll just cut the remaining baby in half and you can each have a portion." Then the real mother reveals herself. Rather than have her son killed, she is willing to give him up. Solomon identifies this woman as the true mother and returns her son to her arms.

What a powerful picture of wisdom in action!

INTERPRETIVE INSIGHT | *Justice for All*

In the story of the two women and their babies there is mention of their occupation. Did you notice what it was? They were prostitutes. In the ancient world prostitutes were generally slaves because they had been sold by their own parents at a very young age. In that culture they were despised. They were the lowest of the low. In those days people with wealth could get a hearing and justice, but often the poor and outcasts were not able to get justice. The writer is showing us that Solomon is committed to making sure *everybody* in the kingdom receives justice, even the outcast and marginalized.

NARRATIVE ON THE TEXT | *How Wise Was This Guy?*

First Kings 4:29–34 gives us this description of Solomon:

> God gave Solomon wisdom and very great insight, and a breadth of understanding as measureless as the sand on the seashore. Solomon's wisdom was greater than the wisdom of all the men of the East, and greater than all the wisdom of Egypt. He

HISTORICAL CONTEXT | *Good Times*

In 1 Kings 4:20 we get a picture of life at the beginning of Solomon's reign. We read that "Judah and Israel were as numerous as the sand on the seashore; they ate, they drank and they were happy." What a pleasant description of life. This was a good time.

Solomon was sovereign over all the kingdoms from the Euphrates River to the land of the Philistines and all the way down to the border of Egypt. People brought tribute and gifts to him from all over the known world. We go on to read of the vast wealth of Solomon and how peace prevailed and the kingdom expanded. From an external perspective, Solomon had military success, economic prosperity, peace in the land, and everything the people ever dreamed and hoped for. These verses show us the highest point Israel will ever achieve. For Israel this is their one, brief, shining moment as a people. It was a golden era in the history of Israel.

NEW TESTAMENT CONNECTION

Who Could Be Greater than Solomon?

Solomon led the people to a time of unparalleled prosperity, peace, and hope. Yet one day there would come a leader even greater than Solomon. In Matthew 12:42 Jesus makes a remarkable statement about himself: "Now one greater than Solomon is here." We tend to skim over those words, but to the listeners in Jesus' day this bold statement would put them on tilt. In their minds Solomon was one of the greatest and most glorious people in their history. How could an obscure, impoverished, and homeless carpenter's son says he is greater than Solomon? Jesus is declaring that God's kingdom was never really about land, armies, wealth, and power. It was always intended to be a kingdom of changed hearts. This was a great message in Jesus' day, when the people of Israel were still looking for a military and economic kingdom. It is also an important reminder in our day because we can fall into the trap of believing that God's ultimate plan is economic and political power for his people. But there is so much more to God's kingdom.

was wiser than any other man, including Ethan the Ezrahite — wiser than Heman, Calcol and Darda, the sons of Mahol. And his fame spread to all the surrounding nations. He spoke three thousand proverbs and his songs numbered a thousand and five. He described plant life, from the cedar of Lebanon to the hyssop that grows out of walls. He also taught about animals and birds, reptiles and fish. Men of all nations came to listen to Solomon's wisdom, sent by all the kings of the world, who had heard of his wisdom.

It was a tradition in the ancient Near East to have wise men who dispensed wisdom. Kings were also expected to be wise and to surround themselves with counselors who understood wisdom.

ILLUSTRATION | *The Best of the Best*

If you follow distance running at all, you know that Africa produces many of the best long-distance runners in the world. If you plan to win a marathon or an Olympic event in distance running, you had better be ready to compete against some great runners from Kenya. You can count on it!

In the same way, in Solomon's day the people of the Near East were the long-distance runners when it came to wisdom. They were famed. They were legendary. Yet we are told that the wisdom of Solomon lapped them all!

INTERPRETIVE INSIGHT | *All People Are Welcome!*

At the dedication of the temple Solomon prays one of the greatest prayers in all Scripture. Here is a part of his prayer:

> "As for the foreigner who does not belong to your people Israel but has come from a distant land because of your name — for men will hear of your great name and your mighty hand and your outstretched arm — when he comes and prays toward this temple, then hear from heaven, your dwelling place, and do whatever the foreigner asks of you, so that all the peoples of the earth may know your name and fear you, as do your own people Israel, and may know that this house I have built bears your Name." (1 Kings 8:41 – 43)

God said to Abraham many centuries earlier, "And all peoples on earth will be blessed through you" (Genesis 12:3). Even in the Old Testament, Israel was never chosen just for their own sake, but for the sake of the world. God's heart has always been to bless the whole earth and all people, never just one group.

INTERPRETIVE INSIGHT | *Solomon's Greatest Legacy*

What was Solomon's greatest legacy and contribution to God's people? Certainly he brought a time of unparalleled fame and prosperity. His building of the temple ranks

CREATIVE MESSAGE IDEA | *Map Time*

Look at a map that shows the breadth and expanse of the kingdom under Solomon. You may also want to remind people that in Solomon's day, the people were realizing the promise made to Abraham so many years before. Their descendants were as numerous as the sands of the seashore and were safe in the land of Canaan.

NEW TESTAMENT CONNECTION | *God's Call to Us*

Jesus reinforced what God taught his people through Abraham, Solomon, and so many others in the Old Testament. Even though the Old Testament is filled with clear calls for God's people to reach out to those who were not a part of them, many still missed it. This is why Jesus was so emphatic about this. Some of the last words Jesus spoke reinforce this calling:

> Then Jesus came to them and said, "All authority in heaven and on earth has been given to me. Therefore go and make disciples of all nations, baptizing them in the name of the Father and of the Son and of the Holy Spirit, and teaching them to obey everything I have commanded you. And surely I am with you always, to the very end of the age." (Matthew 28:18–20)

> But you will receive power when the Holy Spirit comes on you; and you will be my witnesses in Jerusalem, and in all Judea and Samaria, and to the ends of the earth. (Acts 1:8)

HISTORICAL CONTEXT | *The Importance of the Temple*

One of the high points of Solomon's reign was the building of God's temple. This achievement meant more to Israel than almost anything else. Solomon spent seven years and countless amounts of wealth on this project. That temple is described in great detail (much like the tabernacle was) because it was extremely important to the Israelites. The temple was supposed to be a glorified, permanent tabernacle to house the ark of the covenant. This became the central place of worship for God's people.

HISTORICAL CONTEXT

A Curriculum for Wisdom

The proverbs Solomon wrote were collected, most likely, as a part of an effort to train and develop a whole new generation of leaders that would serve under Solomon. The purpose of this book was to impart wisdom to all who were willing to receive it. It is likely that the book of Proverbs was gathered into a formal collection so that it could be used in the tutoring and developing of leaders for Israel.

near the top of the list. He expanded the borders of Israel. All of these things are noteworthy. But they are not his greatest legacy.

The proverbs are Solomon's greatest contribution to the people of God. All through his life Solomon reminded the people that wisdom is a path they must walk every day. More important than Solomon's building projects, expansion of the kingdom, or the time of peace he ushered in is the book of Proverbs and the wisdom that continues to speak to each new generation.

2. Understanding Proverbs

INTERPRETIVE INSIGHT | *Wisdom Defined*

In the Old Testament, wisdom is fundamentally the ability to make right decisions. In ancient times, wisdom was not primarily about how high your IQ was or how educated you were. It was not primarily about information. In our day, we tend to confuse information with wisdom. Do you ever feel overloaded with information? That's not wisdom. Wisdom is practical. It is the ability to discern what the noble, constructive, God-honoring course of action will be in actual, real-life situations. And then, wisdom is making the choice to do it! That's wisdom.

A fool, on the other hand, is not primarily an ignorant person—not primarily someone with a low IQ. Folly in the Old Testament is a problem of the will, not the mind. At its heart, folly is rebellion against God, moral depravity, spiritual blindness, and social irresponsibility toward others. A fool may know all the answers, but his problem is that he cannot seem to do the wise thing.

Proverbs is an urgently important book for followers of Christ today. It is not just a casual collection of affirmations that we can take or leave as we see fit. It has been written and given to us to save us from folly, which leads to death. The stakes are high when it comes to this book. If we read it, understand it, and live it out, we are on the path to life. If we ignore Proverbs, we do so at our own peril!

SIGNIFICANT SCRIPTURE

Proverbs 1:1–7

ILLUSTRATION | *A Gold Ring in a Pig's Snout*

Proverbs were deliberately written to be catchy. They were often visual. Sometimes there was even a comic visual element to the proverbs. Try Proverbs 11:22 on for size:

> Like a gold ring in a pig's snout
> is a beautiful woman who shows no discretion.

What a memorable mental image. What a great warning for people who might get married one day. You can almost hear Proverbs crying out: "If you get hooked up with somebody who has poor judgment and a defective character just because they're physically attractive—beware! If you value looks over integrity, you are not the brightest bulb on the chandelier."

INTERPRETIVE INSIGHT | *A Classic Example*

A classic example of a proverb that some people try to make a law is Proverbs 22:6: "Train a child in the way he should go, and when he is old he will not turn from it." This proverb was never intended to be taken as an ironclad guarantee, but many people try to read it this way.

CREATIVE MESSAGE IDEA | *Who and Why?*

Take time to read the first seven verses of Proverbs. These verses hold the key to who this book was written for and why it was written. Ask everyone who has their own Bible to circle each person this book is written for and then to underline any clues as to why it was written.

The proverbs of Solomon son of David, king of Israel:

for attaining wisdom and discipline;
for understanding words of insight;
for acquiring a disciplined and prudent life,
doing what is right and just and fair;
for giving prudence to the **simple**,
knowledge and discretion to the **young**—
let the **wise** listen and add to their learning,
and let the **discerning** get guidance—
for understanding proverbs and parables,
the sayings and riddles of the wise.
The fear of the LORD is the beginning of knowledge,
but fools despise wisdom and discipline.

ON THE LIGHTER SIDE | *Writing a Proverb*

Writing an effective proverb takes a brilliant mind. A good proverb has to be brief and pithy, have deep insight into human nature, and get expressed in a few unforgettable words that you just cannot get out of your brain. They stick with you. Every culture produces a few minds capable of this kind of writing. In our day, many of them live in Nashville and write country and western music.

Here are a few titles of country and western songs that are proverb-like in their brevity and brilliance.

- "How Can I Miss You If You Won't Go Away?"
- "I've Got You on My Conscience, but at Least You're Off My Back"
- "I Would Have Wrote You a Letter, But I Couldn't Spell … Yuck!"
- "I Bought the Shoes That Just Walked Out on Me"

These are all short, sweet, to the point, and certainly memorable. That's the way a proverb works.

This proverb does not guarantee that if you raise a little girl in the church, teach her the Bible, and do your best, you can be assured that she will become a devoted follower of Jesus. It also doesn't mean that if your children go down a destructive or rebellious path that you did a bad job and didn't train them right. Adam and Eve went down the wrong path, but that doesn't mean God (their heavenly Father) did something wrong.

Proverbs 22:6 is simply wisdom for parents. Our children grow up, to a large extent, as we shape them, for better or for worse. They are likely to go in the direction and pursue the trajectory that we trained them for. So, if we train up a son or daughter to know and love Jesus, there is a good chance they will. But this is not a guarantee.

NARRATIVE ON THE TEXT | *Read Slowly and Reflect Deeply*

Another important feature of Proverbs is they are designed to force us to think about them slowly and ponder them over time. It does not benefit us to skim this book. Proverbs may not make sense right away, but a day, week, or month after we have read them, as we ponder their meaning, we just may have a moment of enlightenment. All of a sudden we stop and say, "I get it!" The meaning unfolds over time. Then, when it makes sense, we begin the process of letting its wisdom shape our lives.

Here is a great example from Proverbs 24:27:

Finish your outdoor work
  and get your fields ready;
  after that, build your house.

HISTORICAL CONTEXT | *Understanding the Type of Literature You Are Reading*

If we are going to benefit from Proverbs, it is crucial that we understand the kind of teaching Proverbs is meant to give us. If we don't get this right, we will become frustrated along the way. It is important that we clarify the nature of a proverb, as we have other kinds of literature in the Old Testament. A proverb is a specific genre and must be read in light of this.

Three specific kinds of literature in the Old Testament are as follows:

Laws: A law is a command you must always obey.

Promises: A promise is a guarantee that is always true.

Proverbs: A proverb is a catchy observation about the way things generally are.

Proverbs are designed to give helpful guidance in real-life situations. But they are not absolutes, nor are they promises.

What does this mean? Does it mean that if a husband doesn't mow the grass, he is supposed to sleep in a tent? Is that the idea? Well, in that culture outdoor work (farming) was income-producing. It was the primary way of making a living and providing for a family. Building a house was income-draining. This proverb is telling us, "It is unwise to spend money you don't have." If we were going to write this proverb in our day it might be, "Get a job before you get a Jaguar."

> As effective as the Proverbs are as a guide to success, they will always be misleading if used as magical sayings, which would always automatically bring results.
>
> *David Hubbard*

CREATIVE MESSAGE IDEA *Laws, Promises, and Proverbs*

Read specific passages (listed below) and project them on a screen if you can. Then ask everyone present to whisper to the person next to them if it is a law, promise, or proverb.

- *Example 1*: "Love the LORD your God with all your heart and with all your soul and with all your strength." (Deuteronomy 6:5)

This is a law. There are never any exceptions. We are always to love God with all we are and have.

- *Example 2*: "No, in all these things we are more than conquerors through him who loved us. For I am convinced that neither death nor life, neither angels nor demons, neither the present nor the future, nor any powers, neither height nor depth, nor anything else in all creation, will be able to separate us from the love of God that is in Christ Jesus our Lord." (Romans 8:37–39)

This is a promise. Again, there are no exceptions. Nothing can separate us from God's love.

- *Example 3*: "Lazy hands make a man poor, but diligent hands bring wealth." (Proverbs 10:4)

This is a proverb. Ask yourself this question: Are there ever any exceptions to this proverb? The answer is ... yes, absolutely. Sometimes lazy people win the lottery or have a rich relative that dies and they inherit money. There are exceptions to this proverb. But as a general rule, that's the way that life works. That's the nature of a proverb. If you don't understand how a proverb works and you want to make it into a law, you will get very frustrated by this book.

Here are a few more examples if you want to expand on this exercise:

- *Example 4*: "If we confess our sins, he is faithful and just and will forgive us our sins and purify us from all unrighteousness." (1 John 1:9) **Promise**
- *Example 5*: "You shall not murder." (Exodus 20:13) **Law**
- *Example 6*: "Do not answer a fool according to his folly, or you will be like him yourself." (Proverbs 26:4) **Proverb**

NARRATIVE ON THE TEXT | *Take Care*

The biblical proverbs themselves warn to take care with how we handle and use them. Proverbs 26:9 says, "Like a thornbush in a drunkard's hand is a proverb in the mouth of a fool." Just think about what happens when an inebriated, unsteady person grabs a plant full of thorns. Such a person is going to get hurt. The same thing happens when a fool starts using a proverb. He is going to get hurt. She is going to misuse it. And others may get hurt as well.

The book of Proverbs invites us to take care and use discernment. The Israelites devoted themselves to this, and so should we. They studied, meditated on, practiced, and committed the Proverbs to memory. They celebrated these proverbs because they found the proverbs changed their lives.

NEW TESTAMENT CONNECTION

Paul Understood

The apostle Paul understood the battle of the soul and expressed his own struggle with sin and folly. He wrote: "I do not understand what I do. For what I want to do I do not do, but what I hate I do" (Romans 7:15).

NARRATIVE ON LIFE | *We Can't Seem to Stop*

Ask a gambler: "Do you think your chronic gambling is a good, long-term bet to produce a worthwhile life?" There is no doubt that this person will say, "No!"

Ask a hot-tempered person: "Is your strategy of bursting out in anger helping you pursue the kind of relational intimacy you most long for?" They will tell you it does not.

Ask an overcommitted person in our crazy society: "Is your hurried, frenzied, exhausting, self-preoccupied lifestyle producing in you the rivers of living water that Jesus promised would well up in the hearts of his followers?" They will admit that their insane lifestyle is robbing them of all they want most.

We keep doing things that we know are going to destroy us, but we can't seem to stop. Even when we identify the problem and resolve to change, we can find ourselves repeating the same sin over and over.

ILLUSTRATION | *A Great Hymn*

Many people grew up singing some of the great hymns of the church. One of them is entitled "My Jesus I Love Thee," which has a message we need to remember today. The hymn begins, "My Jesus, I love Thee. I know Thou art mine. For Thee *all the folly of sin I resign*." What an inspired phrase! What a great reminder! The proverbs were written to help us resign from the folly of sin.

3. Adopting a Proverb

As we conclude this message we are going to think practically about how proverbs can help shape and transform our lives. Proverbs cover many areas of life, but we are going to look at six specific proverbs and the life-transformation they call us to experience. The challenge will be for everybody gathered to adopt a proverb for the week.

After you pick a proverb, it would be wise to tell somebody else what your proverb of the week is. Invite them to pray for you as you seek to develop a wise lifestyle in this specific area. Also, commit to write your proverb down and put it someplace where you will see it often through the week. In addition, plan to memorize your proverb, as the early Jews did. Make this statement of wisdom your own and watch how it impacts your life.

SIGNIFICANT SCRIPTURE

Proverbs 10:19
When words are many, sin is
not absent,
but he who holds his
tongue is wise.

NARRATIVE ON THE TEXT | *A Proverb about Our Words*

Proverbs 10:19 is pretty straightforward. The more you talk, the more you sin. So, one of the simplest ways to cut down on sin is to stop talking so much. A wise person will refrain from speaking in many situations. Sometimes holding our tongue is the best way to show that we are growing in wisdom. Note, of course, that for a person given to silence (or who uses the "silent treatment"), this is not a text to hide behind, nor is this the text for such a one to choose to work on for this week.

LIFE APPLICATION | *A Time for Silence*

Henry Nouwen writes about the value of silence and learning to hold our tongue in a wonderful little book called *The Way of the Heart*. He tells about the early Christian wisdom figures who recommended that followers of Christ engage in the practice of silence. This is valuable for many reasons, but one of the most important is that it is hard to talk without sinning.

ON THE LIGHTER SIDE | *Why Do We Need Proverbs?*

In ancient Israel the proverbs were an essential curriculum for everyday life. They helped people learn how to honor God. Young people memorized these words by the chapter. Not just a verse but a whole chapter! Why do you think God devoted an entire book of the Bible to words of wisdom? Here is the answer, and it has deep theological significance. It may not sound theological, but if you reflect on this truth, it will begin to make sense: *People are stupid!*

If you take nothing else away from this message, be sure to remember this truth. Let's say it out loud together: *"People are stupid."* It is important to remember that this is not the whole truth about us, but it is an important part of the truth.

Consider taking a vow of silence for an hour or set aside a whole day for silence. If your schedule does not allow you to take a full day, then try going a day where you only say what you must. Let your words be as few as possible. When you practice this discipline of silence, you will discover many amazing things. Here are some of the lessons learned in silence:

- You can live without getting in the last word in every situation.
- You can survive without trying to make sure you control how everybody else thinks about you.
- You don't have to win every argument.
- Other people have great ideas and insights and can figure things out without your input.
- You can go for days without drawing attention to yourself.

As you learn the wisdom of silence, you may discover that there is a new and better way to live. Of course the goal is not to stop talking. The discipline of silence is a tool to help you listen more, choose your words more carefully, and to lower the sin level in your life.

ON THE LIGHTER SIDE *What about Contradictory Proverbs?*

Another aspect of Proverbs that can confuse people is that sometimes they sound as if they contradict each other. Since proverbs are not absolute laws, this should not bother us too much. But, to help make sense of this, let's think about how modern proverbs also often seem to contradict each other, and this does not seem to bother us. Think about these pairings of contemporary proverbs:

"Look before you leap," *and* "He who hesitates is lost."
"Opposites attract," *and* "Birds of a feather flock together."
"Absence makes the heart grow fonder," *and* "Out of sight, out of mind."
"Many hands make light work," *and* "Too many cooks spoil the soup."
"You have to keep your eye on the ball," *and* "A watched pot never boils."

What's going on here? The fact is, every proverb addresses one limited slice of reality. They are written to help people avoid folly, and people often err in opposite extremes. The proverb we need to focus on depends on our own tendencies and weaknesses.

For example, think about "Look before you leap," *and* "He who hesitates is lost." People who tend to be impulsive need to heed the first of these two, while those who can never seem to make up their mind need to hear the second one.

NARRATIVE ON THE TEXT | *A Proverb about Laziness*

Proverbs 19:24 depicts a caricature of a person who is lazy. He puts his hand in the nacho bowl and decides it's not worth the energy it will take to transport the food to his mouth. He thinks, "It's too much work. I'll just leave my hand right there. Maybe the wind will blow one of the nachos my way." The point is that no one is ever nurtured by laziness. Lack of action always leads to loss of life. God wants us to use our energy, strength, and abilities for his glory.

SIGNIFICANT SCRIPTURE

Proverbs 19:24
The sluggard buries his hand
in the dish;
he will not even bring it
back to his mouth!

LIFE APPLICATION | *Battling Laziness*

For those who wrestle with passivity, procrastination, inertia, or apathy, Proverbs 19:24 may be one they want to adopt. If this strikes a chord for you, then identify one area of life where you are struggling with procrastination. What will it take for you to move into action in this area? Who can keep you accountable? What can you do to battle laziness and begin to take specific steps forward toward transformation?

NARRATIVE ON THE TEXT | *A Proverb about Enduring*

Proverbs 10:25 acknowledges the fact that storms do come in life. The question is not if, but when! Yet, at the end of the day, God helps the righteous stand strong. Even in the toughest of times, we can rest assured that God will be with his people. For those who are facing times that demand endurance, faith, and a steadfast spirit, this is a great proverb for them.

SIGNIFICANT SCRIPTURE

Proverbs 10:25
When the storm has swept by,
the wicked are gone,
but the righteous stand
firm forever.

LIFE APPLICATION | *Stand Strong*

Some of you who are listening to this message are right in the middle of a storm. You are in desperate need of a word of encouragement that gives hope that when the storm passes, your house will still be standing. Maybe you have been abandoned or betrayed. You're going through a divorce. You have been wiped out by a financial disaster. You've lost your job. Somebody you love has died. You have a child you're so worried about that you can't sleep at night. You are battling depression and can't seem to pull yourself out of it. Some days you even wonder if you can make it.

If this describes you, Proverbs 10:25 may be your proverb. It does not give an easy answer or even a guarantee that everything will be better by tomorrow morning. What it does give is hope that when the storm passes, those who cling to God will still be standing. As you meditate on this proverb, you will be encouraged to say, "I'm not going to let go. I don't care how bad the storm is. It will be over one day in this life or the next, and I will still be standing."

NEW TESTAMENT CONNECTION

A House Built on a Rock

Which of Jesus' parables does Proverbs 10:25 remind you of? Do you remember the parable about the house built on the rock and the house built on the sand in Matthew 7:24–27? When a storm came, the house on the sand was blown away, but the house on the rock stood firm. The parable in Matthew is an elaborated version of this proverb.

NARRATIVE ON THE TEXT | *A Proverb about Discipline*

We all need to hear the unvarnished truth from people who love us. A wise person listens and learns from these words of discipline. A fool ignores and resists loving correction. If we are going to become the people God wants us to be, we need to become humble enough to accept and even invite discipline. If we only surround ourselves with people who agree with us and affirm everything we do, we will never grow. Proverbs gives this powerful word of wisdom: "Wounds from a friend can be trusted, but an enemy multiplies kisses" (Proverbs 27:6).

SIGNIFICANT SCRIPTURE

Proverbs 12:1
Whoever loves discipline loves
knowledge,
but he who hates correction
is stupid.

ILLUSTRATION | *Who Can I Learn From?*

In Numbers 22 we read the story of Balaam and his donkey. Balaam was instructed and corrected by his donkey. What a lesson for all of us. If Balaam could learn from a donkey, then God can certainly teach us through all kinds of people. If we are humble and listen, God wants to instruct us through the most surprising of people.

LIFE APPLICATION | *A Listening Ear and Receptive Heart*

This may seem like a strange thing to say, but one sign that you are growing in spiritual maturity is that you humbly receive criticism. This does not mean every criticism is right or that you have to agree with it. However, a listening ear and a receptive heart honors God. It might be time for you to ask God to soften your heart and help you receive correction. You may even be able to identify specific people God has been using to speak correction into your life, but you have been resisting. Let this be the time you begin accepting, or even inviting, their words.

SIGNIFICANT SCRIPTURE

Proverbs 30:15
The leech has two daughters.
"Give! Give!" they cry.
There are three things that
are never satisfied,
four that never say,
"Enough!"

NARRATIVE ON THE TEXT | *A Proverb about Selfishness*

Have you ever seen a leech? They are natural-born bloodsuckers. They attach onto a host body with both ends of their little bodies; that's where the idea of "two daughters" comes from. These two daughters both say, "Give! Give!" Because the leech is a taker, it is never expected to give anything back. A leech never hooks onto you and says, "I have a gift I'd like to give to you." Leeches only make withdrawals, never deposits. Proverbs 30:15 is pointing to people who take and take and never learn to give. Clearly, they are not walking in the way of wisdom.

LIFE APPLICATION | *Taming the Leech in Us*

It is possible for the human spirit to become leech-like in its selfishness. So much in our culture dictates in this direction. Television commercials and magazine ads encourage self-centered living. A lot of bright folks stay up at night figuring out ways to grow in leech-like living. Jesus also gave many warnings about the power of things and the human propensity for always wanting more. If Proverbs 10:15 connects for you, it may be time to begin identifying behavior in your life that has a "give-me, feed-me" feeling to it. As God begins to show you areas of life where you are always wanting and demanding more, submit these to him and pray for a content and generous spirit.

SIGNIFICANT SCRIPTURE

Proverbs 19:17
He who is kind to the poor
lends to the LORD,
and he will reward him for
what he has done.

LIFE APPLICATION | *A Proverb about Generosity*

If you are kind to the poor, it's like lending to God. Maybe the generosity factor in your life needs to be turned up a notch. What better thing can you do with your resources than share with the poor and be generous toward God? Maybe Proverbs 19:17 is the proverb you need to take with you as you ask God to help you develop a generous spirit.

CREATIVE MESSAGE IDEA | *Share It*

Invite everyone to turn to someone around them and reveal which proverb they have adopted. First, tell them which proverb hit home for you. Second, share how you feel God wants to impact your life through this proverb. Finally, let them know how they can pray for you as you seek to adopt this proverb and see it impact your life.

Message 22

Solomon: Extreme Folly

Deuteronomy 17:14–20; 1 Kings 3; 9:1–9; 10:14–29; 11:1–13

THE HEART OF THE Message

How does a person go from being the wisest man on the earth to a man buried neck deep in folly? How does a person move from being sensitive toward God to living a life of radical disobedience?

The truth is, nobody sets out to experience this kind of fall—least of all Solomon. If you asked him early in his life and kingship, "Solomon, do you think you will stray from the path of wisdom and end up living like a fool?" he would have been shocked. But that is exactly what happened.

In this session we will focus on how a person can move from wisdom to folly, and we will seek to identify ways to stop this process before we go too far. There are decisions that get made all along the way that can help or hinder us. There are steps we can take in our journey of faith that have the potential to ruin even the best of people and lead them into the depths of folly.

BRIEF MESSAGE OUTLINE

1. The road from extreme wisdom to extreme folly
2. Step 1: Allowing a little wiggle room
3. Step 2: Assuming you are the exception
4. Step 3: Failing to deal with predisposed weaknesses
5. Step 4: Ignoring correction

THE HEART OF THE Messenger

Solomon's life is a road map we might call, "The way to disaster"! In this session we will see four detours he took that led him from wisdom to folly. As a leader, you have the opportunity to study this lesson in advance and see if you have begun walking on the road to foolishness. Take time to reflect on each of the four detours Solomon took and ask God to help you see if you are headed toward wisdom or folly. If you see areas where wisdom is growing in your life, thank God for this and pray for the power to stay on the right path. If the Holy Spirit alerts you to ways you are walking the path of foolishness, seek to repent and turn from these ways. Even the wisest of people can be enticed to walk in the way of fools. Let this be an opportunity for you to make sure your feet are on the right path.

1. The Road from Extreme Wisdom to Extreme Folly

ILLUSTRATION | *From the Height of a Wedding to the Depth of Divorce*

In his message (on the included DVD-ROM), Tim Schroeder tells about his experience of seeing the joy of a wedding and the deep pain of divorce. His story is recorded below and can be used as a message illustration. If you have your own story about the dramatic contrast you have seen between a happy marriage and a tragic divorce, you may want to tell it at the start of this message.

Some years ago a pastor stood at the front of his church and was able to share in one of the most special moments a young man and woman can experience. There the couple stood, wearing the nicest clothes they might ever put on. They stood and faced each other, joined hands, and looked deeply into each other's eyes. They spoke vows with absolute sincerity. They said, "In the presence of God and before all of these people, I promise my love to you. I commit to love, cherish, and honor you. I'll be faithful to you. As long as my heart beats, I give it to you." In that sacred moment, they were married in the sight of God.

When the pastor got home, his wife asked, "How was the wedding?" He said, "You know, there's that one moment in all weddings that is just so special. It's so sacred. What a highlight in life. What an unforgettable moment!"

This pastor was bivocational and also worked as a police officer. Later that same evening he changed into his police uniform and went on duty. At about ten o'clock that evening he was called to a domestic dispute. When he arrived, there were already a couple of squad cars on the scene. Several policemen were in the kitchen restraining the husband and the wife who were screaming and shouting obscenities at each other.

They clearly didn't need any more officers in there, so he went into the living room and looked around. As he was surveying the scene, he noticed that the wall unit had been pulled over and smashed. The television and stereo were on the floor. Plants were uprooted and there was dirt from one end of the room to the other. As he stood there surveying the damage, something caught his attention out of the corner of his eye—something moved.

A little girl and boy were coming out from behind the sofa where they had been hiding. The girl was three years old and her little brother was about eighteen months old. They walked right up to this pastor-policeman and the little boy just put up his arms as if to invite the officer to pick him up. The little girl said, "Mister, can you hold my brother? He's scared."

As the officer picked that little guy up and held him close, he turned his face so that no one would walk in and see him. At that moment tears began to stream down his face as he held this brokenhearted little boy and looked down into the scared face of his sister. He stood there bawling and wondering, *How does that happen?* How does anybody go from a vibrant, wonderful declaration of love, where all marriages begin, to a nightmare of disillusionment and sorrow?

SIGNIFICANT SCRIPTURE

1 Kings 3

NARRATIVE ON THE TEXT | *A Quick Review*

In 1 Kings 3 we see Solomon at his best. God appeared to him and asked him to request anything he wanted. As we learned in the last session, Solomon asked for wisdom — and he got it in spades! God poured amazing wisdom into Solomon's heart and also blessed him with riches, honor, and military victories. It seemed as if Solomon had everything.

Later in this chapter we read of Solomon's most famous display of wisdom. Two prostitutes were sleeping, and one of their babies was smothered during the night. In the morning, the woman whose child had died switched the babies. When they brought the one baby to Solomon, each one claimed it was hers. Solomon gave that wisest of all decisions and ended up placing the baby in the arms of the true mother. In response, the people were in awe of his wisdom.

HISTORICAL CONTEXT | *Ashtoreth and Molech*

In 1 Kings 11 we see Solomon at the end of his life. Rather than a celebration of his wisdom, we read a chronicle of his foolish choices and how these choices impacted those around him. Some of the most chilling words about Solomon are found in 1 Kings 11:4 – 6:

> As Solomon grew old, his wives turned his heart after other gods, and his heart was not fully devoted to the LORD his God, as the heart of David his father had been. He followed Ashtoreth the goddess of the Sidonians, and Molech the detestable god of the Ammonites. So Solomon did evil in the eyes of the LORD; he did not follow the LORD completely, as David his father had done.

How did Solomon go from extreme wisdom to such blatant disobedience in a few brief chapters? In these verses we learn that Solomon followed Ashtoreth. She was a Canaanite fertility goddess. This false deity was closely connected to cultic temple prostitution that degraded people and greatly offended God. We also read that Solomon followed Molech, the "detestable" god of the Ammonite people. Molech was another false god, but there was a particularly hideous aspect to Molech worship: He was given human sacrifices. The Ammonites and others who followed Molech were expected to sacrifice their infants to him on his altar.

From there Solomon went on to a season of great wisdom, fame, accomplishments, and approval. God celebrated his choices and wisdom, and so did the people. Sadly, the story did not end there. Solomon, who began as an amazing example of wisdom, ended up falling into a bottomless pit of foolishness.

SIGNIFICANT SCRIPTURE

1 Kings 11:1 – 13

INTERPRETIVE INSIGHT | *A Chilling Irony*

We cannot miss the chilling irony of what's being said here. Solomon began his career with a wise decision that became legendary. That decision restored a live baby to its mother. He ended his career by worshiping a god to whom child sacrifices were made by their own parents.

WORD STUDY

"Except"

In 1 Kings 3:3 we read: "Solomon showed his love for the LORD by walking according to the statutes of his father David, *except* that he offered sacrifices and burned incense on the high places." What's the key word in this verse? "Except"! When we read the word "except," we know Solomon is in trouble. Once we hear this word, we don't even need to know what comes next. This word is a clear indicator that Solomon has decided to leave some wiggle room in his devotion. He will try to love God and be devoted, except for a few areas.

2.The Downward Spiral: Step 1 – Allowing a Little Wiggle Room

The first step in Solomon's downward spiral was to leave a little wiggle room in his commitment. It all began with areas of compromise that many people may have thought were not that important. Of course, a little wiggle room became a lot of wiggle room in a short time.

NARRATIVE ON LIFE | *The Problem with Partial Obedience*

Israel was commanded to have nothing to do with the high places except to destroy them. However, with some regularity, instead of demolishing them, especially before the temple was constructed, the Israelites converted some of them to shrines and began worshiping God there.

They tried to fit in with the religious culture of that day. People from the nation of Israel would go to these pagan high places but instead of worshiping idols, they attempted to worship the one true God. They meant well. They had good intentions. And God didn't strike them down. In fact, sometimes, confusing as it may be, in his mercy, God even met them there.

It is important that all followers of Christ understand what was happening when the people of Israel tried to adopt these pagan places of worship. Even though they had good intentions, even though God didn't punish them immediately, they were *still not fully obedient.* Good intentions are never a substitute for obedience. The people were not separating themselves totally from pagan idolatry. God had commanded them to have nothing to do with these high places, but they decided to dabble a little bit. They allowed just a little wiggle room, and it cost them dearly. This was exactly how Solomon got his start.

He followed what God commanded, except . . .

He had good intentions, except . . .

Like Solomon, we can be tempted to cover up disobedience with good intentions. But we must learn the lesson Solomon faced: Leaving a little wiggle room is one of the most dangerous steps in the downward spiral from wisdom to folly. Leaving a little wiggle room in our commitment to God almost always leads to a little more wiggle room.

LIFE APPLICATION | *95 Percent Devotion Is 5 Percent Short!*

There is no such thing as partial commitment. When you begin with an exception clause, you never arrive at full devotion. A good life lesson for all followers of Christ is that 95 percent devotion to God is 5 percent short. God calls us to a complete

HISTORICAL CONTEXT | *Destroy the High Places*

Solomon's area of wiggle room was this, "except that he offered sacrifices and burned incense on the high places." There's a lot of confusion surrounding these high places in the Old Testament. For one thing, they were almost always associated with pagan worship and idolatry. Numerous times Israel was told that they were supposed to demolish and utterly destroy the high places. In Numbers 33:51 – 52 this issue is addressed with clarity:

> Speak to the Israelites and say to them: "When you cross the Jordan into Canaan, drive out all the inhabitants of the land before you. Destroy all their carved images and their cast idols, and demolish all their high places."

In Deuteronomy 33:29 the people are blessed because they will trample down the "high places."

> Blessed are you, O Israel!
> Who is like you,
> a people saved by the LORD?
> He is your shield and helper
> and your glorious sword.
> Your enemies will cower before you,
> and you will trample down their
> high places.

Clearly God did not want any vestige of false pagan worship to remain in the land. The people were to get rid of it and avoid all practices related to what God had declared an abomination.

ON THE LIGHTER SIDE | *Don't Try This at Home*

Don't try this one at home; it will never fly! Can you imagine a husband coming to his wife and saying, "Honey, I love you and I promise to be faithful to you, except. . . ." What can he say after that that is going to make any difference at all? The simple fact that he says "except" is a guarantee that he will be in deep water.

surrender to his leading in our lives. He does not do this to take away our fun or limit our freedom. He calls us to full devotion because he knows we will find fullness of joy and true freedom when we are 100 percent devoted to him.

We need to look honestly at our lives and ask some hard questions:

- Where am I allowing wiggle room in my devotion to God?
- How am I being tempted to wander from God because of the areas where I am allowing wiggle room?
- What are some of the consequences I might face if I keep allowing this wiggle room in my life?
- What is it going to take for me to be 100 percent devoted in this area of my life?

When we leave any wiggle room in our commitment to God, we are leaving the door open for disaster. If we leave it open just a crack, sooner or later the wind will blow it all the way. Solomon got started with a little wiggle room and ended up in radical disobedience. If we are not careful, we can see history repeat itself in our lives.

3. The Downward Spiral: Step 2 – Assuming You Are the Exception to the Rule

Step 2 in the downward spiral from wisdom to folly is to assume that you are the exception to the rule. You are above God's rules. At this point in the spiral, you don't dispute the rules. You don't disagree with them. In fact, you agree that they're fine for most people. But you just think that you're a little more mature and a little more sophisticated than others. You can handle it. You don't have to follow God's rules as closely as everybody else does.

The problem with anything less than total obedience is that you're the one who then gets to choose what you will submit to and what "really doesn't matter." In a sense, when this happens, you have become your own king. You have become your own god.

HISTORICAL CONTEXT | *Stay Away from Egypt*

As we read more of 1 Kings 3, we see that Solomon made a few more exceptions. Solomon actually had a military and political alliance with Pharaoh, the king of Egypt, and Solomon married Pharaoh's daughter. We might be baffled by this. Why would the king of Israel make this kind of pact with the king of Egypt?

The people of Israel had been specifically commanded *not* to intermarry with people who worshiped foreign gods. Moreover, God had warned them to stay away from Egypt and any alliance with the Egyptians. He had delivered his people from Egypt and wanted them to avoid the Egyptians at all costs.

NARRATIVE ON THE TEXT | *Three Strikes for Solomon*

Solomon began with a little wiggle room. Before too long, he was rewriting the rule book! Take note of how many ways Solomon began to break God's clear commands. In each of these areas Solomon may have felt that God's rules were good and should be obeyed, but somehow they just did not apply to him and his situation.

SIGNIFICANT SCRIPTURE

Deuteronomy 17:14–20; 1 Kings 10:14–29

Look closely at some of the detailed and specific commands God gave to those who would rule over his people. Look at Deuteronomy 17:16–17 (italics added):

> The king, moreover, must *not acquire great numbers of horses* for himself or make the people return to *Egypt* to get more of them, for the LORD has told you, "You are not to go back that way again." He must *not take many wives*, or his heart will be led astray. He *must not accumulate large amounts of silver and gold.*

This seems pretty clear:

- no horses from Egypt
- not too many wives
- no large amounts of wealth

But, Solomon did not think all of these commands applied to him. Just look at what transpired in his life. It is important to note that the specific commands given three centuries earlier were all broken by Solomon. When these are listed in 1 Kings 10, they show up in essentially the same order as they were given in Deuteronomy. What an indictment of Solomon's rebellious heart in 1 Kings 10:26–11:3!

> Solomon accumulated chariots and horses; *he had fourteen hundred chariots and twelve thousand horses*, which he kept in the chariot cities and also with him in Jerusalem. The king *made silver as common in Jerusalem as stones*, and cedar as

ON THE LIGHTER SIDE | *In the G.I. Lab*

Have you ever heard of a G.I. nurse? This is a nurse who works in a specialized discipline of medicine. If you don't know what a gastrointestinal nurse is, you should go home, get on your knees, and say a prayer of thanks to God!

The G.I. lab in a hospital is not a nice place. One of the jobs of a G.I. nurse is to sterilize all of the scopes and instruments. What would happen if a nurse decided that the scopes did not need to be fully sterile? This would be a disaster! There is no such thing as a partially sterile scope. It's either sterile or it's not. If there's one germ alive, it's contaminated.

In Solomon's life he let a couple germs live, and they infected his whole life. In a G.I. lab, every germ needs to be destroyed. In our spiritual lives, we need to be sure that we are 100 percent devoted.

> plentiful as sycamore-fig trees in the foothills. Solomon's horses were *imported from Egypt*. . . .
>
> King Solomon, however, loved many foreign women besides Pharaoh's daughter. . . . They were from nations about which the LORD had told the Israelites, "You must not intermarry with them, because they will surely turn your hearts after their gods." Nevertheless, Solomon held fast to them in love. He had *seven hundred wives of royal birth and three hundred concubines*, and his wives led him astray.

God commanded the kings of Israel to stay away from any arms build-up that would give them the tendency to rely on their own power and not on God. One of the first things Solomon did was strike a treaty with the king of Egypt by marrying an Egyptian wife, and he bought twelve thousand horses, most of which were from Egypt. Strike one! God told the kings to avoid amassing wealth. He wanted them to rely on his provision and not their own stockpile. But Solomon made silver as common as rocks in the street. Strike two! God said to avoid having too many wives, and Solomon went on to set a world record with seven hundred. A big strike three!

NARRATIVE ON LIFE | *From Blessing to Greed*

One thing we must remember is that God did promise he would bless Solomon with riches. But Solomon did what so many people do: He turned blessing into greed. He was consumed by the blessing. He got more and more and more and more, but he was never satisfied. He never had enough. Instead of growing in contentment, he wanted more, and along the way he started to violate every law that God had given for the kings.

ON THE LIGHTER SIDE | *98 Percent to Jesus I Surrender*

There is an old hymn of the church that many people sang as they grew up. The title of this song is "I Surrender All." The chorus goes like this:

> I surrender all,
> I surrender all,
> All to Thee, my blessed Savior,
> I surrender all.

Do you get the message? Is it clear? This is a declaration of absolute, complete, uncompromising devotion. Can you imagine a congregation of Christians gathered and singing this song but lowering the bar just a little? What might they sing? How might they rewrite the song?

- Most to Jesus, I Surrender
- Some to Jesus, I Surrender
- 98 Percent to Jesus, I Surrender

The only thing that makes sense and fits with God's call on our lives is full devotion. We need to declare, "*All* to Jesus, I surrender." Then, we need to do it!

Solomon started out by saying, "I don't know what I'm doing. I need your wisdom," though he left just a little bit of wiggle room. Then, once he got up and was flying high, he started to think, "I can get horses from Egypt. I can get more money. I can marry whomever I want." God's blessings became Solomon's license for greed, and it took over his life.

ILLUSTRATION | *The One Thing the Church Can't Handle*

Tony Campolo, a Christian speaker and author, was once asked, "What do you see as the biggest challenge facing the church today?" His response might surprise you:

> When I look at the church today, especially in America, I see that the church is doing quite well. The church is flourishing. The church has power in a lot of areas. It has a lot of wealth. It's doing really well! And, it terrifies me because throughout history, there is one thing the church has never been able to handle ... success!

He went on to say:

> The church has always thrived in times of persecution. It's done really well when it had hardship placed upon it. But, the church has failed every time it's had power and wealth—every time. The church seems to handle everything except success.

LIFE APPLICATION | *The Humility Quotient*

Solomon started out asking God for help. He saw his need and weaknesses and relied on God. As soon as he got a few things going his way, he got too big for his britches. He started thinking he could choose what he would obey and what he would not.

How's your humility quotient? Are you growing more humble as the years pass? Do you pray for humility and seek to keep pride out of your heart? One of the purposes behind humility is that it is difficult to obey if you are arrogant. It is difficult to submit if you think you know better. So how are you doing on the humility side—step two of the equation?

HISTORICAL CONTEXT | *Lots of Gold!*

We are told that Solomon received 666 talents of gold as a regular payment (1 Kings 10:14). This was just from one source of his income. Did you ever wonder how much gold that was? The basic conversion is that a talent was seventy-five pounds. If you do the math, you will discover that he was approaching eight hundred thousand ounces of gold from just one income stream. The value of gold changes, but it can float around $290 an ounce. At this rate the value of this one income source was about 232 million dollars a year. That's a lot of money.

4. The Downward Spiral: Step 3 – Failing to Deal with Predisposed Weaknesses

SIGNIFICANT SCRIPTURE

1 Kings 11:1 – 8

Step 3 in the downward spiral from wisdom to folly is failing to deal with predisposed weaknesses. We all have them. But when we refuse to look at them and resist turning away from them, we are headed for trouble.

NARRATIVE ON THE TEXT | *He Loved Women*

In 1 Kings 11:1 – 2 we read that Solomon had an insatiable love for women:

> King Solomon, however, loved many foreign women besides Pharaoh's daughter—Moabites, Ammonites, Edomites, Sidonians and Hittites. They were from nations about which the LORD had told the Israelites, "You must not intermarry with them, because they will surely turn your hearts after their gods."

Clearly Solomon was crossing the line. These were women whom God had forbidden the Israelites to marry. The reason for his command to avoid these women is also explicit. They would turn the heart of their husband toward false gods and idols.

NEW TESTAMENT CONNECTION

God Loves Humility!

Throughout the New Testament we are reminded that God loves for his children to walk in humility. He also has a real problem with those who are ruled by pride! This truth, which is expressed so clearly in the Old Testament, is reinforced again and again in the New Testament:

> God opposes the proud but gives grace to the humble. (This is from Proverbs 3:34 and is quoted in both James 4:6 and 1 Peter 5:5.)
>
> Do not be proud, but be willing to associate with people of low position. Do not be conceited. (Romans 12:16)
>
> Be completely humble and gentle; be patient, bearing with one another in love. (Ephesians 4:2)

LIFE APPLICATION | *Nevertheless Moments*

Solomon said, "Nevertheless ..." even when he knew what he was doing was wrong. He just went on and did it anyway. It was as if he could not help himself. His attraction to women was a battle he would fight his entire life.

Have you ever known someone who could not seem to help himself or herself when it came to a certain sin? Have you ever been that person? Are you in that situation right now? Sometimes sin gets a grip on our life and it feels as if we can't get away. We feel enticed or tempted, we know it is wrong, but we end up saying, "Nevertheless."

When this happens, God wants us to look to him for strength. Even if we feel that there is no way we can resist, God wants us to know that there is. Remember the reminder in 1 Corinthians 10:13, "No temptation has seized you except what is common to man. And God is faithful; he will not let you be tempted beyond what you can bear. But when you are tempted, he will also provide a way out so that you can stand up under it."

There is one other life application note that should be made here. Followers of Christ today still need to hear God's warning about marrying someone who is not a committed believer. Many Christians today still say, "Nevertheless" and go on to marry a man or woman who is not a devoted follower of Jesus. This can bring many heartaches and struggles in life. We need to make sure, before we go too far in a relationship, that the other person is deeply committed to Jesus.

NARRATIVE ON THE TEXT | *Deep in the Family System*

Solomon was not particularly discriminating when it came to women. He seemed to love them all! Even when God gave clear commands about this, he kept right on marrying women who were forbidden. We have to stop and wonder why he struggled so much in this area of his life.

When we look back through Solomon's personal history, some clues begin to rise to the surface. Let's ask a few questions. Who was Solomon's dad? David. Who was his mother? Bathsheba. Does anything jump to mind about why Solomon might have had a problem with sexual control when you think of his parents? It is clear that David struggled with sexual temptation, and his choices and lifestyle seem to have impacted his son.

Solomon had been exposed to sexual struggles through his whole life. If you read through the Old Testament, you discover that David's family had one of the most dysfunctional households around. There is a very good chance that Solomon's problems stretched all the way to David's bedroom. The sins and weaknesses of his father infected his life and impacted him for a lifetime!

WORD STUDY | *"Nevertheless"*

When we read the end of 1 Kings 11:2, we come across one of the saddest words recorded about Solomon's life. It is the word "nevertheless." This word jumps off the page as we read it and see what follows. Solomon's "nevertheless" attitude and actions led to his downfall.

> *Nevertheless*, Solomon held fast to them in love. He had seven hundred wives of royal birth and three hundred concubines, and his wives led him astray. As Solomon grew old, his wives turned his heart after other gods, and his heart was not fully devoted to the LORD his God, as the heart of David his father had been. He followed Ashtoreth the goddess of the Sidonians, and Molech the detestable god of the Ammonites. So Solomon did evil in the eyes of the LORD; he did not follow the LORD completely, as David his father had done. (1 Kings 11:2–6)

Solomon knew that what he was doing was wrong. This wasn't just a little rule about some gold and horses from Egypt. God had made it crystal clear that his people were to avoid those who worshiped false gods and idols. God warned them that unbelieving spouses could become a snare to them. Sadly, that is exactly what happened in Solomon's life.

LIFE APPLICATION | *Shaping Our Children's Future*

Parents, do you have any idea of the die you are casting for your children? You are shaping and building habits into their lives that will impact them more than you dream. Their outlooks, strengths, weaknesses, and attitudes will be shaped by your life. If you have kids in your home, they are watching you. They are learning. They are being shaped. For better or for worse, you are forming their lives.

With this in mind, we must do a serious evaluation of our own attitudes and actions. There are lots of questions we need to ask. Here are a few to get us started:

- What are the hidden attitudes in you that you do not want passed on to your children and grandchildren?
- What habits do you have that you hope and pray your children will not adopt as their own?
- What are the secret and hidden sins that you work to keep your children from knowing about?

Too often we live with a level of self-deceit. We think our attitudes, actions, and hidden sins go unnoticed by our children. But we are wrong. They do know. They can see it, smell it, and feel it! Our sins do impact them, no matter how much we try to avoid it.

Do you really think your children and grandchildren don't know about that stuff you've got stashed away in the basement, attic, garage, or some corner at home? You can't even hide their Christmas presents where they can't find them. And kids know how to check the history of computer searches and files better than you do.

With the Spirit of God as your guide, take time for self-examination today! Ask yourself, what am I passing on to my kids? What are the areas of weakness in my own life, the predisposed weaknesses that I'm handing on to another generation?

Then, commit, with all of God's strength, to make the cycle of sin end with your generation! If you need to get a strong Christian accountability partner, do it! If you need to meet with a church leader, do it! If you need to get help from a Christian counselor, take action immediately. But whatever you do, don't pass your sin on to the next generation.

PAUSE FOR PRAYER

An Honest Look at My History

Before moving on to the final portion of this message, pause to pray. This third part of the spiritual spiral downward hits some very tender nerves. Pray for the Holy Spirit to illuminate and reveal areas of sin. Ask for power for God's people to change their life attitudes and patterns. Offer confession for how their lives may have damaged the next generation, and lift up thanks for those in the previous generation who have passed on the blessing of a godly heritage.

ILLUSTRATION | *For Better and For Worse*

One piece of good news is that our good habits and attitudes also get passed on to the next generation. In his message for this session (on the included DVD-ROM), Tim tells a story of his father's godly example and how it impacted his life. If you have a story about someone who passed on a healthy and positive spiritual legacy, you may want to tell it at this time.

5. The Downward Spiral: Step 4 – Ignoring Correction

SIGNIFICANT SCRIPTURE

1 Kings 9:1 – 9

The final step on this downward spiral is to ignore or to silence corrective words. This is one of the surest signs of disaster. When a person is sliding down into sin and rebellion and he or she refuses to listen to anyone who comes with wise and loving correction, disaster is ready to strike. When a person has already gone through steps one, two, and three, sin has a way of deafening one's ears so he or she has a difficult time hearing God's voice.

NARRATIVE ON THE TEXT | *A Loving Warning*

In 1 Kings 9:1 – 2 Solomon had completed one of the high points in his life and career. He had finished and dedicated the temple. We read that God appeared to him again: "When Solomon had finished building the temple of the Lord and the royal palace, and had achieved all he had desired to do, the Lord appeared to him a second time, *as he had appeared to him at Gibeon*." It was at Gibeon (1 Kings 3:5) that God had appeared to Solomon and invited him to ask for whatever he wanted. Do you remember what Solomon asked of God? For wisdom! That was all. Since then, Solomon had become a very different man.

This time when God appears to Solomon at Gibeon, he comes with a warning. In effect, God says, "If you follow me, I will bless you. But if you refuse to follow me, I will cut you off!" God knows the condition of Solomon's life and heart, and it is time for a firm warning. Solomon is on a crash-course to disaster, so God steps in with a warning.

PAUSE FOR PRAYER

Need Your Grace!

Take time to pray for God to break the downward spiral from wisdom to folly. If Solomon could fall into this pattern, none of us is exempt! Pray for the power of God's Holy Spirit to fill each person as we learn to break the cycle of pride and sin and grow in humble obedience.

NARRATIVE ON THE TEXT | *Two Men … Two Responses*

As time passed, Solomon wandered farther and farther from God. He did not listen to warnings but did things his own way. God continued to call Solomon to a place of repentance, but he refused to respond. God raised up Jeroboam, a trusted servant of Solomon who knew the hearts of the people and was aware that the nation could end up being divided if things did not change. But Solomon remained hardhearted. We read words that are shocking: "Solomon tried to kill Jeroboam, but Jeroboam fled to Egypt, to Shishak the king, and stayed there until Solomon's death" (1 Kings 11:40).

This is the difference between David and Solomon. When Nathan came and corrected David for his sin with Bathsheba, David got on his face, repented, and cried out to God, "How could I? Create in me a clean heart." Solomon tried to kill the messenger.

Our hearts should be open to correction. We need to humbly listen when God speaks and calls us to change. Our defense mechanisms can be turned up so high that we have a hard time hearing corrective words from God or his servants. But we must resist this tendency and learn to soften our hearts and open our ears.

Message 23

Job: Where Is God When It Hurts?

The Book of Job

THE HEART OF THE Message

Many people think the book of Job is all about Job. The reality is, it is all about God! In this powerful drama, God reveals much about himself. Along the way we learn a lot about ourselves, but the center of this book is God. He is in control, he made everything, he delights in the creation, and he can be trusted. This book addresses the reality of suffering in life, but most of all, it gives us a window into the heart and character of God.

BRIEF MESSAGE OUTLINE

1. Setting the scene
2. The drama unfolds
3. The characters speak
4. The epilogue

THE HEART OF THE Messenger

Job is a remarkable book. Studying it invariably involves a steep learning curve for anyone who really digs and wants to learn. As you prepare to bring this message, get ready to meet with God. Specifically, take time to read Job 38–41 and reflect on the questions God asks Job. Listen to these words as if they were written to you. Then, prepare your message with a heart saturated with the reality of who God is and what he has done.

1. Setting the Scene

NARRATIVE ON LIFE *Job's Story Is Our Story*

The problems in the book of Job are the problems of the human race. They're the problems we all face. We can all see ourselves in the story of Job.

In the beginning, everything is as we think it should be. Job is a pious man. He is so cautious that he even offers sacrifices for his children just in case they have done something wrong that he does not know about. He wonders if God might be easily offended, and he takes no chances.

God has given him a wonderful life. He is the richest man in the east, the greatest man in his land. The amount of blessing he experiences seems to be directly proportional to the amount of obedience he offers toward God.

SIGNIFICANT SCRIPTURE

Job 1:1 – 5

INTERPRETIVE INSIGHT | *A Place of Unplanned Suffering*

Trouble is coming to the land of Uz. Job does not know it, he is not expecting it, but it is coming like a tsunami. Uz will be a place where very bad things happen to a very good man. Uz will be a place where suffering comes with no warning and with no explanation. This suffering will create confusion and despair beyond words.

The hard truth is that everybody will spend some time in the land of Uz. And some people are there right now. Others have just traveled through and still feel the aftermath. Others don't know it, but the land of Uz is directly ahead.

CREATIVE VIDEO ELEMENT

Personal Interview: "The Reality of Suffering" (3:55 min.). This one-on-one interview offers a brief look inside a mother's ongoing struggle with suffering. Integrates verses from the book of Job.

ILLUSTRATION | *A Play on Two Levels*

As we study Job, it may help to compare it to a play. It is written that way. Think of a play in which there are two stages. There is an upper stage that is built high on risers and is near the ceiling of the theater. On that stage is the activity that takes place in heaven. The people on the upper stage can look down and see what is happening on the stage below. But there is also a lower stage, which features the activity taking place on earth. Those on the lower stage can't see what is happening above them on the upper stage.

INTERPRETIVE INSIGHT | *A Limited Perspective*

We, as the readers (those watching the drama unfold), are able to see what's happening on both stages — upper and lower. This is crucial to the story. We know what's going on in both settings. We must remember, however, that the characters on earth (the lower stage) do not have our vantage point. They are aware of the activity around them but not above them. They know nothing about what's happening on the higher stage. They have a limited perspective, but we see everything as it unfolds.

HISTORICAL CONTEXT | *Where Was Uz?*

The story of Job begins in the land of Uz. What we have to do is try to figure out where Uz was. We know that it was east, but east of what? The answer is, east of Israel. The point of this is that Job was not from Israel. He wasn't one of God's special nation. This is quite a unique book in that it does not involve the history of Israel.

2. The Drama Unfolds

NARRATIVE ON THE TEXT | *How Do You Respond to Deep Loss?*

SIGNIFICANT SCRIPTURE

Job 1:6–12, 20–22

In this portion of Job, Satan appears on the upper stage, in heaven, but then he moves to the lower stage. When he does, Job loses everything. He is pummeled with loss, pain, and heartache. Job's livestock, wealth, servants, and children are all swept away! When this happens, we see Job's response (Job 1:20–22):

> At this, Job got up and tore his robe and shaved his head. Then he fell to the ground in worship and said:
>
> "Naked I came from my mother's womb,
> and naked I will depart.
> The LORD gave and the LORD has taken away;
> may the name of the LORD be praised."
>
> In all this, Job did not sin by charging God with wrongdoing.

We learn that Job grieves and expresses it in outward ways that were common in his day. He tore his clothing and shaved his head. These were clear signs of mourning. We also see Job as he falls to the ground in worship. He speaks words of blessing and praise. Job's response is both sorrow and worship.

INTERPRETIVE INSIGHT | *Does Job Fear God for Nothing?*

SIGNIFICANT SCRIPTURE

Job 2:1–10

In Job 2 we switch back to the upper stage. God says to Satan (Job 2:3):

> Have you considered my servant Job? There is no one on earth like him; he is blameless and upright, a man who fears God and shuns evil. And he still maintains his integrity, though you incited me against him to ruin him without any reason.

Satan tells God that the only reason Job maintains his integrity is that God has treated him well. If God allowed his body to be touched with pain, he would certainly curse God.

From this point on, the action of this drama takes place on the lower stage. It is critical that we clarify what is going on in heaven. At first glance, the action in heaven looks strange and confusing. It appears as if a cosmic wager between God and Satan is taking place. It can seem as if God is using Job and his family as pawns to win a bet or prove a point to Satan.

But this is not what is going on at all. The key question on the upper stage and in the whole book is, "Does Job fear God for nothing?" Satan insists: "Job is devoted to you, God, and worships you because it's in his self-interest to do it. You scratch his back. He scratches yours. It's a quid pro quo." Satan is charging God with being naïve.

ILLUSTRATION | *Why Is Job Devoted to God?*

Satan, the accuser, is insisting that Job's devotion is strictly based on what he is getting from God. Satan is saying that Job loves God the way children love the ice cream

WORD STUDY

Quid Pro Quo

The *Webster's New Universal Unabridged Dictionary* gives this primary definition of "quid pro quo": "Latin. One thing in return for another." The idea of quid pro quo is that one person will do something only as a response for what he or she has received. In the book of Job, the idea is that Job is only honoring God because God has been good to him. Satan argues that once Job stops receiving things from God, he will stop honoring God.

man. He loves God the way a drug addict loves a drug dealer. It is all quid pro quo.

Satan is arguing that if you turn off the faucet of blessing, watch how fast Job turns off the faucet of devotion. If Job is the best man on earth and the rest are worse than him, his response will speak volumes for the human family. Satan is saying that the whole idea of a covenant of self-giving love between God and people is a farce. It's all a joke.

NARRATIVE ON LIFE | *Evolutionary Biology*

The reality of the universe is that everybody's looking out for number one—quid pro quo. This philosophy is extremely current. One dominant view of human nature in the secular culture of our day is called evolutionary biology. The idea is that human beings are simply gene carriers programmed to engage in whatever behavior will maximize the odds that their genes will survive. This same idea was expressed long ago.

INTERPRETIVE INSIGHT | *Who Is on Trial?*

The writer of Job makes masterful use of irony through this book. The ultimate irony is this: We think this is a book where God is on trial. With all the suffering in the world, can God be truly good? On the lower stage, that is the primary question in this book. But, we can also see the action on the upper stage. We can see that there is a God in heaven. This is really a book where the human race is on trial. Satan (the accuser) is the prosecuting attorney who is pointing a finger at us.

Satan is saying, "People are nothing more than slaves to their own self-interest. The whole thing is a farce; people will only love God if he gives them what they want."

God says, "No. Satan has it all wrong!" He makes it clear that the view presented by Satan is cynical, warped, misguided, and wrong. "At the core of this universe is self-giving, self-sacrificing love. Human beings were made to receive and give that kind of love. They are capable of it, when they are experiencing pleasure, and even when they face days of pain."

SIGNIFICANT SCRIPTURE

Job 2:7–10

NARRATIVE ON LIFE | *Responding to Pain*

After losing all his possessions and his children, Job gets hit with a second wave of suffering. His body is afflicted with pain most of us can't even imagine. This time his response is different. He does *not* fall to the ground and worship. He does *not* say, "May the name of the Lord be praised."

This time Job sits on an ash heap. Maybe he's grieving. Maybe he's isolated since people are afraid he has leprosy. His wife speaks for the first and last time in this drama. She simply says: "Are you still holding on to your integrity? Curse God and die!" (Job 2:9).

NARRATIVE ON THE TEXT | *Meeting Mrs. Job*

Mrs. Job gets criticized a lot by preachers and teachers. She seems like an easy target. Job's first response is a measured expression of sorrow and enduring worship. Her first recorded response is a suggestion that Job curse God and die. But before we judge her too harshly, we must remember what she is experiencing. Job and his wife were real people with real feelings.

She too has lost all that she had. She has lost all her children. Her husband is covered with sores and is experiencing indescribable pain. She sees him and must be wondering what it will mean to care for a horribly diseased husband until he recovers or dies. A short time ago she was part of the wealthiest family in the East. Now she and her husband are utterly alone and destitute. Before we judge her too harshly, we should ask how we might react in a similar situation.

NARRATIVE ON LIFE | *Struggling to Understand God*

Job's response (Job 2:10) shows that he is struggling to understand God: "You are talking like a foolish woman. Shall we accept good from God, and not trouble?" The words "and not trouble" can be translated "and not evil." Job is struggling to understand if God is the kind of person who sends evil. Is God really good? That is the question on the lower stage.

Then the text says: "In all this, Job did not sin in what he said." This is a little hint of what is going on inside Job. After the first wave of suffering Job faced, we are told that "in all this, Job did not sin by charging God with wrongdoing." Now, after this second wave of suffering, there's a little qualification: "Job did not sin in what he said." Job has begun to struggle in his heart, but he is not expressing it in words—yet.

NARRATIVE ON THE TEXT | *Support in a Time of Grief*

Job's friends plan to sit next to him and take on his anguish. When they see Job, they can hardly recognize him. They heard it was bad, but nothing could prepare them for what they see when they meet Job.

Usually when we visit somebody who is sick or in a bad condition, we try to cheer them up. Have you ever been so sick that when someone comes to visit you, they take one look and burst into tears? That's

WORD STUDY

Nud

Job was famous because of his great wealth. Today he is famous because of his great suffering. We read that his friends "met … to … sympathize with him." The word for "sympathize" here is the Hebrew verb *nud*. This word means to rock back and forth. It was used to describe a specific body movement where a person rocked back and forth after a time of pain or trauma.

Sometimes when people go through a tremendous trauma and are in shock, they begin rocking. It is almost uncontrollable – automatic. They rock themselves back and forth like a mother comforting a baby. The word *nud* describes this motion of maternal comforting.

> **NEW TESTAMENT CONNECTION**
>
> *Identifying with Those in Pain*
>
> In the New Testament followers of Christ are called to identify with each other in times of loss, sorrow, and pain. This theme occurs again and again. In 1 Corinthians 12:26 we read: "If one part suffers, every part suffers with it; if one part is honored, every part rejoices with it." The apostle Paul is comparing the church to a physical body. We are told that just as every body part is connected in pleasure and pain, so are the members of God's spiritual body, the church.
>
> In his second letter to the church at Corinth, Paul calls us to actively extend care and mercy to those who are hurting. He writes in 2 Corinthians 1:3–4:
>
> > Praise be to the God and Father of our Lord Jesus Christ, the Father of compassion and the God of all comfort, who comforts us in all our troubles, so that we can comfort those in any trouble with the comfort we ourselves have received from God.

what happens to Job. It is so awful that all they can do is weep. Then, they do something remarkable. They just sit with him for seven days and seven nights and do not say a word. They are with him in silence.

LIFE APPLICATION | *Mourning Times Two*

When we mourn with those who mourn and sit with those who are hurting, we are not trying to fix them. We don't come to give some clever advice that will make everything better. One of the greatest gifts we give is our presence. It is interesting to note that the silence of Job's friends was brilliant. It was a gift. Their words later became torment.

Do you have friends who would sit with you through a time of suffering? Do you have people who would sit quietly with you just for the sake of offering support? If so, give thanks to God! If not, think seriously about connecting with a small group of Christ followers who can support and comfort you.

Also, ask yourself who would be comforted by your presence if they were hurting. Do you have people you can sit with when they are in need of a friend? If not, commit to deepen your relationships and be sure to make yourself available to those who are in need.

3. The Characters Speak

NARRATIVE ON THE TEXT | *Job Speaks*

Finally, after seven days of silence, Job speaks. This is a remarkable thing. Imagine the tension that has built up. Seven days have passed, and his friends are still waiting to hear what Job will say. Will he repeat what he said in chapter 1: "The LORD gave and the LORD has taken away; may the name of the LORD be praised." If he could just repeat those words again, the whole test is over. This would be a tiny book.

We don't wait long before we realize that Job's words will not echo what he said in chapter 1.

After this, Job opened his mouth and cursed the day of his birth. He said:

> May the day of my birth perish,
> and the night it was said, "A boy is born!"
> That day—may it turn to darkness;
> may God above not care about it;
> may no light shine upon it. (Job 3:1–4)

This is the kind of thing that keeps Job off the motivational speaker circuit. Things get pretty dark as he goes on to curse his birthday. Job will not curse God, but he does curse the day God made him. This seems like a sneaky way of getting at the same thing. For the rest of the book, Job pours out a level of bitterness, confusion, sorrow, and anger toward God that is staggering.

SIGNIFICANT SCRIPTURE

Job 2:11–15; 3

NARRATIVE ON THE TEXT | *Job's Friends Speak*

Job spews so much venom that his three friends can't stand it. They can't listen to it. Finally they respond—and most of the book of Job is a series of speeches given by Job and his friends' responses. We can't look at all of the speeches, but we can identify the key theme each of Job's friends brings forth.

ON THE LIGHTER SIDE | *An Extra Friend*

Job's friends hear all about the troubles that have come on him. They want to see him and help him through this painful time. They meet together and go to find Job so they can sympathize with him and give him comfort in his time of pain. His friends are: Eliphaz the Temanite, Bildad the Shuhite, Zophar the Naamathite, and Dadgum the Termite. OK, the last one, Dadgum the Termite is not in the text. That is just thrown in to make sure everyone is paying attention.

CREATIVE MESSAGE IDEA | *Silence*

Consider taking a short time of silence with all those who are gathered. Ask everyone to sit in silence, not to say a word. How long is it before the silence becomes uncomfortable? Is it a few seconds, a few minutes, maybe an hour? For the friends of Job, all they can do at this point is to be silent and be with him–for seven entire days.

HISTORICAL CONTEXT | *Sitting Sevens*

The example of Job's friends sitting with him for seven days in silence was such a powerful act that it became a part of Jewish life even to this day. In the Jewish tradition, they will speak of "sitting Shiva." Literally this means "sitting sevens." Friends will come to sit with one who mourns over a period of a week.

Eliphaz argues that the innocent don't perish and the upright are not destroyed. In effect, he is saying that the innocent don't suffer.

> Consider now: Who, being innocent, has ever perished?
> Where were the upright ever destroyed? (Job 4:7)

Bildad gets a little more direct. He says that Job's children died because of their sin. They had it coming! His theory is that our suffering is a result of personal sin and rebellion.

> When your children sinned against him,
> he gave them over to the penalty of their sin. (Job 8:4)

Zophar suggests that Job's suffering is a result of his personal sin. He calls Job to repent and turn from his sin.

> Yet if you devote your heart to him
> and stretch out your hands to him,
> if you put away the sin that is in your hand
> and allow no evil to dwell in your tent,
> then you will lift up your face without shame;
> you will stand firm and without fear. (Job 11:13–15)

In each case, when Job's friends put forth their theory, Job counters with his argument and defense. At one point Job gets testy and somewhat sarcastic: "Doubtless you are the people, and wisdom will die with you!" (Job 12:2). It is important that we hear Job's three friends giving voice to one central idea. Their view is that pain, suffering, and sorrow in this life are a direct consequence for personal sin.

NARRATIVE ON LIFE | *Some Things Never Change*

Philip Yancey notes that the arguments voiced by Job's friends are still repeated in Christian churches today. Yancey writes that suffering people have told him that those who make their suffering worse are often well-meaning Christians who are confused about this very issue. These are some of the lines that well-intentioned but confused Christians might use:

HISTORICAL CONTEXT | *The Doctrine of Retribution*

The view of Job's friends expressed in this book was the primary theology of suffering in Job's day. In Israel and the surrounding area, this was the conventional wisdom. It's written about in what scholars call the "Mesopotamian Wisdom Literature." It is sometimes called the doctrine of retribution. The idea of this theology is simple. Goodness results in prosperity and blessing, and wickedness results in suffering.

- "The reason that you're in the hospital is spiritual warfare. If you were just standing strong and walking in the power of Jesus, Satan would be defeated. You'd be delivered."
- "God promises to heal if we have enough faith. If you will pray with enough faith, you will be healed." (Implication—if you're not healed, you're not praying with enough faith.)
- "God has handpicked you to suffer to bring him greater glory. You just need to thank him for the pain you're suffering, because it's glorifying him."
- "Your suffering is a wake-up call. It's a punishment for sin. You need to figure out what you've done wrong and repent."

LIFE APPLICATION | *Sincere, But Sincerely Wrong*

This doctrine of retribution goes all the way back to the book of Job. It's that old. Eliphaz, one of Job's friends, even claims he has divine insight. He says, "A word was secretly brought to me, my ears caught a whisper of it" (Job 4:12). We need to be careful about telling people that God has given us a word of knowledge for them. Eliphaz is sincere, but he's wrong. He did not speak a word from God for Job. Before we speak such a word or receive such a word, we had better be sure it is really from God.

INTERPRETIVE INSIGHT | *The Implications*

The doctrine of retribution inevitably turns God into a means for pursuing good circumstances—the blessed life. Pretty soon we are not trying to pursue God. Rather, we are trying to use God. When Christians buy into this system of belief, they become smug, self-righteous, and judgmental when things are going well. When things are going badly, they fall into despair. This is why God teaches us that this way of seeing things is absolutely wrong!

NARRATIVE ON LIFE | *The Value of True Friends*

Job suffers under the judgmental words of his friends. Along the way he responds with these words:

> A despairing man should have the devotion of his friends,
> even though he forsakes the fear of the Almighty. (Job 6:14)

Right in the midst of a battle of words, Job makes this remarkable statement about friendship. In other words, a real friend doesn't give up on you no matter what; even when it looks like your faith is on the ash heap.

NARRATIVE ON LIFE | *All Over the Map*

People in anguish often contradict themselves. They seem to move all over the emotional map. In Job 19 Job goes through all kinds of emotions. Everything he feels and says does not make sense, but he pours it all out. What a great reminder for us that God knows all that is inside us and he allows us to express it honestly.

NARRATIVE ON THE TEXT | *Taking God to Court*

SIGNIFICANT SCRIPTURE

Job 19
Job 23:1–10

As Job goes on, he questions God, he clings to God, he hollers at God, and he hollers for God. Mostly, he challenges God. Job's boldness is staggering:

> If only I knew where to find him;
> if only I could go to his dwelling!
> I would state my case before him
> and fill my mouth with arguments. (Job 23:3–4)

It is as if Job wants to take God to court. He wants to sue him. Job is challenging God to show up so they can fight man to man.

NARRATIVE ON THE TEXT | *God Speaks*

In chapter 38, Job gets his wish. God answers Job out of the storm! What do you think that moment was like? Do you think there was a little drama? Do you think the atmosphere changed when God showed up in a storm?

God says, "OK, Job, let's have a face-off!" Then, for the next four chapters, God speaks! Job and his friends remain quiet. God has now come from the upper stage to the lower stage. Moreover, he has some questions for Job! Over and over God asks Job about how the creation came into being. He asks him about specific animals. He puts Job on the witness stand, but Job has little to say!

INTERPRETIVE INSIGHT | *A Finite Mind*

Part of what's happening is that God is reminding Job that he has a finite mind and a limited point of view. Only God can see the whole story. An Old Testament scholar by the name of Ellen Davis notices that God's questions actually give great insight into the kind of person he is. He is the kind of God who creates in such a way that the morning stars sing together and the angels shout for joy! In this portion of Job, God's creative beauty shines through, and his delight in creation is clear to see.

SIGNIFICANT SCRIPTURE

Job 38–41

INTERPRETIVE INSIGHT | *God Delights in His Creation*

All through this section we see God delighting in his creation. Even creatures that are of no apparent and no strategic value are a joy to God. There is no quid pro quo about it. God doesn't get anything from them, but he still loves them. A quick survey will make this very clear.

- *The ostrich* (Job 39:13–18): This is just a wonderful, fun passage. The ostrich is a goofy-looking animal. God says that she flaps her wings joyfully—as if she thinks that's going to get her somewhere. She's not a great mom. She lays her eggs but can't even remember where she left them.

- *The hippo* (40:15–19): In the ancient world, the behemoth was considered what they called the chaos monster. Some people wrote that it had to be eliminated for the earth to be habitable for human beings. But that's not God's opinion. God ranks this strange creature as a great success among his works.
- *The wild ox, the donkey,* and other animals are listed. You can't miss God's joy and celebration of his creation.

LIFE APPLICATION | *So Should We!*

If God delights in his creation, so should we. We need to slow down and look around us. There are colorful birds, strange insects, and animals all over the place. The stars shine, the oceans crash, and the trees lift their hands. We need to be like God in our appreciation of his wondrous creative work. It is time for us to notice and celebrate.

ILLUSTRATION | *The Creator Loves His World*

Why would God make and love a world like ours? Annie Dillard writes: "Because the Creator loves pizzazz. Because he revels in the beauty and delight and joy of the least strategic creature that will never do him any good. He just loves to give."

The God of the upper stage is a God who is endlessly good, uncontrollably generous, and irrationally loving! He gives no reason for this, nor does he have to! It is his nature.

NARRATIVE ON THE TEXT | *I Can Trust You!*

By the end of the story, Job finds out the kind of person God is, and that's enough for him. The hinge—the resolution of this whole book—is in 42:5–6. Job is speaking to God:

> My ears had heard of you
>   but now my eyes have seen you.
> Therefore I despise myself
>   and repent in dust and ashes.

This is enough for Job. He has heard; he has seen; he is satisfied! When Job says that he repents in dust and ashes, he is not saying, "I will now live with low self-esteem." This is a Hebrew way of saying he is entering into a new strategy for living. He is saying to God, "I can trust you." We can almost hear Job declare, "I can trust you with my children; I know that they are better off in your hands now. I can trust you with my pain; I know that you will redeem every bit of it. You are the kind of God who treasures and cares for everything. I place my full trust in you."

4. The Epilogue

The book of Job ends with restoration and blessing (Job 42:12 – 17):

> The LORD blessed the latter part of Job's life more than the first. He had fourteen thousand sheep, six thousand camels, a thousand yoke of oxen and a thousand donkeys. And he also had seven sons and three daughters. The first daughter he named Jemimah, the second Keziah and the third Keren-Happuch. Nowhere in all the land were there found women as beautiful as Job's daughters, and their father granted them an inheritance along with their brothers.
>
> After this, Job lived a hundred and forty years; he saw his children and their children to the fourth generation. And so he died, old and full of years.

INTERPRETIVE INSIGHT | *The Truth about God and Us*

Why does the writer include all these strange details? It seems these things are there to reflect what is happening in the heart of Job. He is now delighting in those who are seen as the least strategic of creatures. Job is becoming gratuitously good, uncontrollably generous, and irrationally loving. In short, he is being shaped into the image of the God he has met and learned to trust.

Satan was dead wrong about Job. He was also wrong about the human race. He was wrong about the universe. And he was dead wrong about God. The book of Job is *not* about some odd, cosmic wager. It was written so you and I could know what the truth is about us and God.

SIGNIFICANT SCRIPTURE

Job 42:12 – 17

NARRATIVE ON LIFE | *A Word to Those Living in Uz*

Job never got to look on the upper stage. He never realized that his faithfulness had meaning beyond his own life. He did not know that something cosmic and eternal was at stake in his little life. When he was sitting on an ash heap, scraping boils off his skin with shards of broken pots, he did not know what was happening on the upper stage. Even though he was broken, sick, mocked, confused, and hopeless, Job's faithfulness was used by God to vindicate God's whole wild adventure in covenant love.

Job's honesty, courage, tenacity, and perseverance have inspired billions of people who have lived in the land of Uz. Job still speaks out and says, "Hang on. Keep going. Don't let go. Don't give up. Don't quit now."

PAUSE FOR PRAYER

Give a short time for prayer, both silent and out loud. Then, close the time with a prayer for each person who is living in the land of Uz to meet God in a new and powerful way. Pray for strength for them to make it through. Pray that God will bring friends alongside of them who will sit with them, love them, and see them through.

LIFE APPLICATION | *Living in the Land of Uz*

Some of those gathered and hearing this message are in a time of pain, sorrow, and suffering. This is the land of Uz.

Why are you there? I don't know.
How long will it last? I don't know.
Does your response matter? Does what you do and how you live make any difference at all? More than you could ever dream.

The eyes of heaven are on our little lives as we travel through the land of Uz. What we do is of eternal and cosmic significance to God.

HISTORICAL CONTEXT | *Blessing the Daughters*

There are some details in Job 42:12–17 that we might miss, but they would have jumped out at ancient readers. In the first place, the writer gives us the names of Job's daughters but not of his sons. This was unheard of in ancient Hebrew genealogies. This was unprecedented because the sons were the ones, in the ancient world, whose names got mentioned.

Usually, Hebrew names are serious, especially the ones that make it into the Bible. They express character, virtue, or theological truth. The three names given for Job's daughters are all about the beauty of creation.

- *Jemimah* is the name for a dove – a bird that was prized for its beauty.
- *Keziah* means cinnamon. It was a prized spice.
- *Keren-Happuch* was the oddest one. It means "horn of eye shadow." She was named after make-up. This would be like naming your daughter Estée Lauder or Maybelline.

Not only did Job give them strange names, he also gave them an inheritance. In an ancient, male-dominated world, a father with seven sons would never dream of leaving something to a daughter.

CREATIVE MESSAGE IDEA | *Offering Support*

Invite those gathered to take a moment and ask a person sitting near them how they can support them in prayer. Allow a time for people to talk. Then, encourage people to pray together. They can do this out loud or silently. This is not a time to give answers to each other or try to solve problems. It is a time to pray for God's comfort, presence, and love to flow into the lives of all those who are living in the land of Uz.

Message 24

The Divided Kingdom: What Puts Community at Risk?

1 Kings 12–15

THE HEART OF THE Message

First Kings 12–15 is one of the saddest sections in the Old Testament. What began as the magic kingdom under David became the tragic kingdom under David's successors. What started out as Camelot under Solomon deteriorated into chaos upon Solomon's death. The unity and community that had been enjoyed for over a hundred years was soon to be shattered by civil war!

In this session we will be learning from the demise of the community of ancient Israel. We will look at their mistakes so that we can avoid taking those same paths. One of the reasons we study the Old Testament is to learn from the past so that we will not repeat the same mistakes and enter into the same folly. Historians tell us that those who do not remember the past are condemned to repeat it. Thus, in this session we want to discover those factors that contributed to the downfall of the community of ancient Israel so that we can discover what puts biblical community at risk. Once these things have been identified, we can seek to avoid them and build a biblically functioning community that is marked by an enduring spirit of unity.

BRIEF MESSAGE OUTLINE

1. Understanding the times
2. Risk factor 1: Failing to be a servant leader
3. Risk factor 2: Using spiritual language for selfish motives
4. Risk factor 3: Following God halfheartedly
5. Risk factor 4: Turning away from God

THE HEART OF THE Messenger

In this session we will identify four factors that put community at risk. Take time before you teach this session to examine your heart and life. Do any of these community-breaking patterns exist in your life? Do you need to change a life pattern or attitude for the sake of becoming more of a community builder? Take time to ask God to shape you into a follower of Christ who blesses and builds community.

1. Understanding the Times

INTERPRETIVE INSIGHT | *All We Need to Know*

As you read through the history of Israel, you will discover that events are not always recorded chronologically. Some people get concerned about this. In modern history books, we tend to list things in a clear chronology. The Bible is historically reliable. But we must remember that it is not primarily given as a history book. It has not been given to us to satisfy our historical curiosities. The Bible is primarily given to us to reveal the character of God, to change our lives, and to help us become the people he wants us to be. The Bible does not always tell us everything we want to know. However, it does tell us everything we need to know for building a living relationship with God and for developing community with other people.

NARRATIVE ON THE TEXT | *The Measure of a King*

As we study the books of Kings and Chronicles, we are introduced to thirty-nine kings of Israel and Judah. This message focuses on the Divided Kingdom Period. There is a formula that's followed for almost every one of the kings from both the

HISTORICAL CONTEXT | *A Basic Timeline*

Before we look at the community risk factors, we should look at some introductory information about this section of the Bible. It's important, first of all, to understand that the kingdom period of ancient Israel lasted about five hundred years—from 1050 to 586 BC. This period of history can be broken into four distinct phases.

(1) The first phase was the *United Kingdom Period* under Kings Saul, David, and Solomon. This lasted 120 years.

(2) Next was the *Divided Kingdom Period.* This is when civil war broke out between Israel and Judah. During this time, ten tribes of Israel formed the northern kingdom with Samaria as its capital and Jeroboam as its king. The two tribes of Judah and Benjamin formed the southern kingdom with Jerusalem as its capital and Rehoboam as its king. This phase lasted about two hundred years.

(3) In 722 BC the northern kingdom (Israel) was attacked, destroyed, and dispersed to the four corners of the ancient world. This marked the beginning of phase three—the *Surviving Kingdom Period* of the south (Judah). For about 136 years Judah survived, but then the Babylonians came and invaded. They destroyed Jerusalem and took many of the people to Babylonia as exiles for seventy years.

(4) This exile marks the fourth phase of the kingdom: the *Dissolved Kingdom Period.* Israel, the northern kingdom, had been gone for generations. Now Judah, the southern kingdom, was exiled to a foreign land. They were prisoners of war. At this point, the kingdom was dissolved. Although a remnant came back to the land under the leadership of Zerubbabel and later Ezra and Nehemiah, the history of God's people as a nation with a human king from their midst was over.

north and south. It goes like this: Each king is introduced by stating the length of his reign. His reign is then synchronized with the reign of the corresponding king in the other kingdom. Each king is compared to his immediate predecessor as either being better or worse. And all of the kings are evaluated against the benchmark of King David as either being good or evil in comparison to him. We see this formula, for example, in 1 Kings 15:1–3:

> In the eighteenth year of the reign of Jeroboam son of Nebat, Abijah became king of Judah, and he reigned in Jerusalem three years. His mother's name was Maacah daughter of Abishalom.
>
> He committed all the sins his father had done before him; his heart was not fully devoted to the LORD his God, as the heart of David his forefather had been.

NARRATIVE ON LIFE | *How God Sees Us*

We tend to evaluate greatness by a leader's achievements, but God evaluates greatness by a person's character. In the life of every one of the kings of Israel and Judah a simple and divine evaluation is given. God declares an epitaph for each one. He either says, "He was good," or "He was evil." Of the twenty kings of Israel, all of them "did evil" in God's sight. Only eight of the kings of Judah "did good." The truth is that even kings and presidents answer to a higher authority. They may think they are sovereign and the last word, but they are not. And neither are we! We should all ask the question: "What will God say about my life when it's all over?"

2. Risk Factor 1: Failing to Be a Servant Leader

The rest of this message will focus on four community risk factors we find in the books of Kings and Chronicles. God wants unity and health in the community of his followers, but often this is not the reality we experience. By learning from some of the mistakes made in the time of the kings, we can discover how to build community and avoid the pitfalls they experienced.

ON THE LIGHTER SIDE | *A Look at Presidents*

Most nations and cultures evaluate their leaders in some way. In the United States most people have an idea of who they think is the greatest president ever. Invite those gathered to lean over to the person next to them and say who they think was voted as the best president ever.

According to an ABC news poll conducted on Presidents' Day weekend every year, the largest group of people said Abraham Lincoln was the greatest president in U.S. history. In 2002, this poll showed the top three presidents as: Abraham Lincoln, John F. Kennedy, and George W. Bush.

Nothing puts community at risk more than a leader who takes advantage of people for selfish gain. Those who never learn the principle of being a servant leader will watch the erosion of community all around them. By contrast, when a leader uses his or her position and power to serve others, this generates loyalty and strengthens community.

SIGNIFICANT SCRIPTURE

1 Kings 12:1 – 17

NARRATIVE ON THE TEXT | *Lighten the Load!*

One of the defining moments for the community of ancient Israel came when Rehoboam succeeded Solomon, his father, as king. At his inauguration, when the leaders of the twelve tribes of Israel came to crown their new king, he had an opportunity to build community — to strengthen community — and instead he blew it up.

The elders of the twelve tribes came with one request to Rehoboam: "Your father put a heavy yoke on us, but now lighten the harsh labor and the heavy yoke he put on us, and we will serve you" (1 Kings 12:4). Rehoboam responded by asking for three days to think about it.

During those days he sought counsel from the elders who had served his father, Solomon. Here is what they said: "If today you will be a servant to these people and serve them and give them a favorable answer, they will always be your servants" (1 Kings 12:7).

Then Rehoboam consulted the young men he had grown up with. Their advice was different (see 1 Kings 12:10 – 11):

> "Tell these people who have said to you, 'Your father put a heavy yoke on us, but make our yoke lighter' — tell them, 'My little finger is thicker than my father's waist. My father laid on you a heavy yoke; I will make it even heavier. My father scourged you with whips; I will scourge you with scorpions.' "

After listening to both sides of advice, Rehoboam refused the path of service. Instead, he decided to rule with an iron fist, and it cost him the unity of the kingdom. Over a century of the twelve tribes being united ended when Rehoboam declared that he would not be a servant leader.

HISTORICAL CONTEXT | *The Twelve Tribes*

When we talk about the division of the kingdom and the fracturing of the twelve tribes of Israel, we need to remember their history. These were the descendants of Abraham, Isaac, and Jacob, the great patriarchs of Israel. Jacob had twelve sons, who became the heads of the tribes of Israel. These tribes were all family. Many years and generations had passed, but the tribes of Israel who were part of the united kingdom were all related to each other. When this division came and civil war ensued, this was a division of God's covenantal people – and blood relatives.

NARRATIVE ON THE TEXT | *A Divided Kingdom*

How do you think the people responded to Rehoboam's decision to reject the path of being a servant to the people? How do you think they reacted to his declaration that their load would be even heavier and that he would be scourging them with scorpions?

The answer is, they responded very predictably. They cried out:

> When all Israel saw that the king refused to listen to them, they answered the king:
>
> "What share do we have in David,
> what part in Jesse's son?
> To your tents, O Israel!
> Look after your own house, O David!" (1 Kings 12:16)

In other words, they said, "Forget you! We don't need you. We'll choose our own king." And that's exactly what they did. They appointed Jeroboam as king over the ten tribes of the north and set his throne in Samaria. Rehoboam's foolish, self-serving decision caused the people to rebel, and it divided the kingdom and birthed a civil war that lasted for over two centuries.

NARRATIVE ON LIFE | *Defining Moments*

Rehoboam failed to be a servant leader. He abused his position. He did not listen to wise counsel. He was more concerned about himself than his people, and he put the

NEW TESTAMENT CONNECTION | *The Greatest Example*

In all of history, the greatest example of a servant leader is Jesus Christ. To the surprise of his followers, Jesus Christ, the Son of God, declared that he came as a servant. His words are as staggering today as they were when he first said, "For even the Son of Man did not come to be served, but to serve, and to give his life as a ransom for many" (Mark 10:45).

Later, before he went to the cross, Jesus again affirmed his commitment to live as a servant. He washed the feet of his followers. This was one of the most humble and menial tasks a servant could do in those days. After he offered this profound act of servant leadership, he said:

> "Do you understand what I have done for you?... You call me 'Teacher' and 'Lord,' and rightly so, for that is what I am. Now that I, your Lord and Teacher, have washed your feet, you also should wash one another's feet. I have set you an example that you should do as I have done for you. I tell you the truth, no servant is greater than his master, nor is a messenger greater than the one who sent him. Now that you know these things, you will be blessed if you do them." (John 13:12–17)

PAUSE FOR PRAYER

Make Me a Servant

You may want to pause and pray for all those gathered to grow a heart that longs to serve. Pray for humility and for an expanded understanding of how Jesus has served us as well as how he calls us to serve each other.

community of Israel into a tailspin from which they never recovered. It was a defining moment in his life and in the history of Israel.

In the same way, leaders today consign their churches, businesses, families, and any group of people to disunity when they refuse to be servant leaders. Every leader faces the same defining moment Rehoboam encountered. *Will I serve or demand that I be served? Will I build community or destroy it?*

LIFE APPLICATION | *An A-WICS Attitude*

At a church in Grand Rapids, Michigan, the staff members talk about having an A-WICS attitude. This came from one staff member who was often heard saying, "Any way I can serve!" Over and over as opportunities to serve presented themselves, she kept saying, "Any way I can serve." Even when a task or project was not in her area of ministry or under her job description, she kept looking for ways to serve and support others.

At some point along the way, the pastor coined the phrase, "An A-WICS Attitude." This term describes a person who is ready to say:

Any Way I Can Serve!

Consider adopting an A-WICS attitude in your home, church, workplace, and wherever else God leads you. You may even want to write this word somewhere you will see it on a regular basis as a reminder of Jesus' call for us to serve each other. If someone sees it and asks you what it means, let them know how you have been served by Jesus and how you are called to a life of serving others.

Your attitude should be the same as that of Christ Jesus:

Who, being in very nature God,
did not consider equality with God something to be grasped,
but made himself nothing,
taking the very nature of a servant,
being made in human likeness.
And being found in appearance as a man,
he humbled himself
and became obedient to death – even death on a cross!
Therefore God exalted him to the highest place
and gave him the name that is above every name,
that at the name of Jesus every knee should bow,
in heaven and on earth and under the earth,
and every tongue confess that Jesus Christ is Lord,
to the glory of God the Father.

The apostle Paul in Philippians 2:6 – 11

---

3. Risk Factor 2: Using Spiritual Language for Selfish Motives

Community is at risk when people seek to manipulate others by using spiritual language to accomplish selfish purposes. This happened in the days of the kings, and it still happens today. Every time someone seeks to leverage another person with hyperspiritual language, we need to be cautious and make sure we know their motives.

NARRATIVE ON THE TEXT | *Don't Strain Yourselves*

SIGNIFICANT SCRIPTURE

1 Kings 12:25–33

Although the kingdom was divided politically, with Rehoboam as the king in the south and Jeroboam as the king in the north, they were still united spiritually. All of the Israelites in both kingdoms were still expected to make a pilgrimage several times a year to Jerusalem to worship God. Jerusalem was still the location of the temple and the center of the religious life of all Israelites. It also happened to be the capital of the southern kingdom and the place where Rehoboam ruled! This caused a problem for Jeroboam, the king of Israel. He articulated his concern in 1 Kings 12:26–27:

> Jeroboam thought to himself, "The kingdom will now likely revert to the house of David. If these people go up to offer sacrifices at the temple of the Lord in Jerusalem, they will again give their allegiance to their lord, Rehoboam king of Judah. They will kill me and return to King Rehoboam."

Jeroboam was filled with fear because he knew his kingship would always be in jeopardy as long as the people under his rule went to the capital of the southern kingdom to worship. Thus, he came up with a solution. He made two golden calves and set up his own places of worship. Jeroboam established a formal system of idolatry, which was clearly forbidden! Then, in an effort to sway the people of Israel away from Jerusalem and toward his new places of worship, he said: "It is too much for you to go up to Jerusalem. Here are your gods, O Israel, who brought you up out of Egypt" (1 Kings 12:28).

Nothing can get a biblically functioning community going down the wrong path faster than individuals who manipulate spiritual language for personal agendas. That was the sin of Jeroboam. He made idols for his own political agenda, and then he manipulated people into following his false gods. We must be careful when people use spiritual language in dogmatic tones. It could put a community at risk.

NARRATIVE ON LIFE | *"God Told Me!"*

There is a word for people who do what Jeroboam did: *manipulation*! Community is at risk when people use spiritual language for selfish motives. Jeroboam manipulated people by using religious language for his personal, political agenda. Clearly he was not concerned about the people truly worshiping God. He just wanted to be sure their hearts did not turn back to Jerusalem and the king who ruled there.

This still happens in churches today. When people use God-talk in dogmatic terms and in demanding tones so that they can get what they want, that's spiritual manipulation. Every time someone uses spiritual language to advance his or her personal agenda, it is a recipe for broken community. We must learn to have our antennas up so that we can identify when this is happening—specifically, when people come to us saying things like:

- "God spoke to me and told me you should . . ."
- "God told me his plan for you is . . ."
- "God showed me that our church has to . . ."
- "Pastor, I have a word for you from God! He said . . ."

We must approach this topic with a double caution. First, let's admit that God does speak and we must listen when others have received a word from God. We must take care not to miss when God is speaking to us or his church. Yet the second caution, and one that applies to the passage we are studying, is that we must be careful when people are using spiritual language to forward their own selfish agendas. This happened in Jeroboam's day, and it still happens today.

ILLUSTRATION | *"I Was Wrong!"*

If you have your own story of someone who used spiritual language to manipulate you or someone you know, you may want to use it at this time. You can also use the story Jim Tomberlin told in his message.

A pastor tells of how he now lives with a real sensitivity to the issue of spiritual language being used to manipulate someone. You see, he was a victim! When Jim was a college student, he was a young and naïve Christian. He got involved with a Christian organization on campus. In that organization was a really cute girl who caught his eye. To his joyful surprise, it seemed he caught her eye as well!

One day she came up to Jim and said, "God told me you're the one." He thought to himself, "Who am I to question God? If God told her I am the one, how can I argue with that?" He was smitten. He was head over heels in love—or maybe infatuation, but it felt like love.

Three months later, she dumped Jim, and it broke his heart.

Jim asked her, "What happened? I thought God spoke to you and told you I was the one." Her answer staggered him: "I was wrong."

Jim learned a lesson that day that we would all be wise to learn. Whenever someone uses superspiritual language, has a dogmatic tone, and is insistent that they know God's will for you and everyone else, it is wise to be cautious! This does not mean that we refuse to let God speak to us through others. What it does mean is that we need to use discernment and wisdom and to take great care with those who are quick to declare God's will for our lives.

PAUSE FOR REFLECTION

Heart Check

Invite those gathered to quietly reflect on their own lives. Encourage them to identify if they are being manipulated or if they are manipulating others with spiritual language. Give time for each person to identify if community is being broken because of a misuse of spiritual language.

LIFE APPLICATION | *Be Careful*

God still speaks! There is no question about this. However, we must live with two cautions that will prove helpful in our effort to become the people God wants us to be.

(1) We must be wise in how we listen to others. When you bump into people who are emphatic and dogmatic about knowing God's will for your life, be cautious. You should seek the wisdom of the Holy Spirit and godly counsel from people you trust. In other words, if someone comes up to you and says, "God told me you are the one!" you had better be sure he or she did in fact hear it from God before you dive into the relationship.

(2) You must also be careful that you are not guilty of using spiritual language to manipulate others. If you have gotten into the habit of declaring what God wants others to do, you should humbly look at your motives. If God is giving you divine promptings that will help others, great! You can humbly share what is on your heart and let God move people as he will. But, if you tend to be dogmatic and demanding, if your language is heavily spiritualized, and if you sense you may be seeking to manipulate people, it is time to stop. This is sin — and God wants us to repent!

SIGNIFICANT SCRIPTURE

1 Kings 15:1 – 3

4. Risk Factor 3: Following God Halfheartedly

God calls us to be fully devoted followers. He wants 100 percent from us. When we follow him with a halfhearted devotion, we will see community erode all around us. This is a huge risk factor!

NARRATIVE ON THE TEXT | *A Heart Not Fully Devoted*

Abijah became the king of Judah after Rehoboam. When we read of his life and how God evaluated him, we are struck by these words: "He committed all the sins his father had done before him; his heart was not fully devoted to the LORD his God, as the heart of David his forefather had been" (1 Kings 15:3).

The sin of halfheartedness repeats itself over and over again during the history of the kings. Abijah was a king who did not follow God with his whole heart. He soon discovered that following God halfheartedly is not only foolish; it's dangerous. The problem with a heart that is only half full of God is that it is half empty! This leaves room for other affections to move in and crowd God out. It opens the door for idolatry, which is exactly what crept into Abijah's heart, just as it had entered the heart of his father. When our hearts are only half full of God, we become vulnerable to temptation, sin, and all kinds of evil. A heart that is not fully devoted to God quickly becomes a heart that wanders away.

NARRATIVE ON LIFE | *Two Kinds of People*

There are really two kinds of Christians when it comes to the matter of devotion.

(1) There are those Christians who are fully devoted followers of Christ. These are people who live with a deep level of surrender and commitment before God. When

God leads, they follow. They understand that their whole life is under the lordship of Jesus Christ, not just a few selected areas they want to devote.

(2) There are those who are half-devoted Christians. They give God some of their heart, some obedience, and some devotion. They want God, but they also want to cling to the things of the world. These people are half full of God, but they are also filled with all kinds of things that poison their heart and destroy the community God longs to build.

ILLUSTRATION | *Dogs and Cats*

Again, you can insert your own cat and dog story, or you can use the one below. This is not meant to exalt dogs over cats; it is simply an observation of how these two animals are wired differently.

A man tells his story of his initiation into the world of cats and dogs. This is his story:

> Several years ago my wife's parents came for a visit. On the way over they found a half-dead kitten on the side of the road. It was a cute, black-and-white kitten on the edge of death. They brought it to us, and we nursed it back to health.
>
> But when that little kitten was back to full strength, was it grateful? No! When we called its name, did it come? No! When it saw us, did it wag its tail and show that it was happy to see us? No! All we were to that cat was food and shelter. We could see that it had divided affections. It cared little about us and a lot about many other things.

The same man tells about another animal experience. He says:

> Several years ago, I brought home a twelve-week-old Golden Lab puppy. That puppy, when it was full-grown, was as devoted as you can imagine. When we called her name, she came running. When she saw us, she smiled and wagged her tail. She stayed at our feet everywhere we went. Sometimes she would wander off, but when we disciplined her, it was clear that even then, her devotion never wavered. There's a reason why dogs are man's best friend.

SIGNIFICANT SCRIPTURE

1 Kings 15:9–24

LIFE APPLICATION | *Growing in Devotion*

What kind of Christian are you—fully devoted or halfhearted? The amazing thing is that just as it's the nature of a dog to be loyal and devoted to its master, fully devoted followers are tenaciously committed to the master of their souls. Moreover, it is also in the nature of God to love us with unwavering passion. He longs to be our best friend.

We need to look intensely into our own hearts and see if we are fully devoted to God. If we have divided attentions, we need to set aside those things that are taking us away from full devotion and intimacy with God. Maybe we have not made time in our daily schedule to meet with our Savior. We should be sure that he gets prime time in our day. This is not some legalistic process of setting aside a mandatory devotional time. It should be the longing of our heart to be with the one who loves us so deeply. God wants us to desire to be with him and look forward to the time we can pull aside and sit at his feet, building relationship and growing in love with him.

> The cross is laid on every Christian. The first Christ-suffering which every man must experience is the call to abandon the attachments of this world.... We surrender ourselves to Christ in union with his death – we give over our lives to death.... When Christ calls a man, he bids him come and die.
>
> *Dietrich Bonhoeffer*

NEW TESTAMENT CONNECTION

Taking Up the Cross

Jesus was clear that he called his followers to full devotion. He said:

> "If anyone would come after me, he must deny himself and take up his cross and follow me. For whoever wants to save his life will lose it, but whoever loses his life for me will find it." (Matthew 16:24 – 25)

The cross is a sign of absolute surrender. To take up one's cross is to lay down one's life. This is the pathway of the fully devoted follower of Christ.

5. Risk Factor 4: Turning Away from God

A fourth factor that puts community at risk is to turn our hearts away from God. Sometimes a follower of God does not understand something that happens in his or her life and lets his or her heart become cold toward God. Every time we turn from God, we open the door for conflict and division in community.

NARRATIVE ON THE TEXT | *Starting Well and Finishing Poorly*

Asa, one of the kings of Judah, ruled for forty-one years. He started out well. In 1 Kings 15:11 we read, "Asa did what was right in the eyes of the Lord, as his father David had done." When a superior army from Ethiopia came and invaded Judah, he

PAUSE FOR PRAYER | *With All My Heart!*

One of the most amazing verses in all the Bible is found in 2 Chronicles 16:9: "For the eyes of the Lord range throughout the earth to strengthen those whose hearts are fully committed to him." God is searching all across the world, looking into the hearts of each one of us. What does he see? A heart full of God or a heart half full? He strengthens those whose hearts are fully devoted, fully committed to him.

What keeps a community of Christ followers strong? People whose hearts are fully devoted. God strengthens those people. God strengthens that congregation. Following God with half a heart puts community and individuals at great risk.

called on God for help. God answered his prayer and gave him a great victory against overwhelming odds.

For thirty-five years, Asa trusted and relied on God, and he experienced peace on his borders. But there was no peace within the divided kingdom because Asa and Baasha (king of Israel) were at war throughout their reigns.

Then something happened in the thirty-sixth year of Asa's reign. The king of Israel took one of the border towns between Israel and Judah. When this happened, Asa stopped trusting in God. He turned away from God. Instead of relying on God to overcome his enemies, Asa turned to Ben-Hadad, king of Aram, for assistance. He actually robbed the gold and silver from the treasury of the temple in Jerusalem to pay this pagan king to help protect him against his own kinsmen.

Then, when a prophet came and rebuked him for turning away from God and for making an unholy alliance with a foreign king, Asa responded in anger. The Bible says he was so enraged that he put the prophet in prison and brutally oppressed some of the people. Asa's heart had departed so far from God that he would not hear or receive godly counsel. Within a couple years, Asa died a broken and defeated man. Even in his illness he did not seek help from the Lord.

NARRATIVE ON LIFE | *Could It Happen to Me?*

What happened to Asa? What caused his heart to change? For so many years he had followed the path God set before him and had made many wise decisions. Then, he stopped trusting God and began placing his trust in his own wisdom and ability to figure things out.

That's a dangerous thing to do. We must realize that we are not exempt from such a change in life's direction. Maybe you even have to admit that Asa's story is your story. Maybe, like Asa, you went through a time in your life when you knew God's presence and power. You saw God work mightily in and through you. You trusted him and things happened — supernatural things, dramatic things — and you knew God was at work in your life.

Then, something changed. You faced a hard time, suffered an intense loss, made an unwise choice, or fell into a pattern of sin. Whatever happened, you slowly discovered that your heart had turned away from the God you used to love so intensely. Perhaps this is where you are today.

LIFE APPLICATION | *Guarding Our Path*

If something has gotten between you and God, it is time to deal with it. If you are no longer trusting in him, it is time for a change. If you have turned away from him, let this be the day you turn back. Let this be the day you say, "I will not end up like Asa. I want to be strong to the end!"

It may be helpful to reflect on the words of Proverbs 3:5 – 8:

> Trust in the LORD with all your heart
>   and lean not on your own understanding;
> in all your ways acknowledge him,
>   and he will make your paths straight.
> Do not be wise in your own eyes;
>   fear the LORD and shun evil.
> This will bring health to your body
>   and nourishment to your bones.

If you identify ways you are placing your trust in yourself and not in God, it is time for a change. Ask God for forgiveness. Then, place your trust in his power and wisdom, not your own.

Each of us needs to carefully examine our attitudes and actions in the days to come. Do we build community or tear it down? Are we living lives that strengthen the congregation we are part of or tear it apart? We need to learn to pray:

> Search me, O God, and know my heart;
>   test me and know my anxious thoughts.
> See if there is any offensive way in me,
>   and lead me in the way everlasting. (Psalm 139:23–24)

ILLUSTRATION | *A Lesson from Lincoln*

Abraham Lincoln is a dramatic contrast to Asa. Lincoln was president in the United States of America during a time of national crisis. The nation was divided. More Americans died during the Civil War than all the Americans in all the other wars. It was a time that would test the faith of any leader.

But, during that time, Lincoln relied on God. He also led the nation to rely on God. He wrote: "I have been driven, many times, to my knees by the overwhelming conviction that I had nowhere else to go."

He was a great leader. As the Civil War was coming to an end and it was clear that the North would be victorious, Lincoln was reelected for a second term as president. He delivered his second inaugural address in March of 1865.

Many of the scholars think it was his greatest speech. Sadly, it was his last speech. A month later, he was assassinated. If we read his last speech closely, we see words of healing, reconciliation, and trust in God. He concluded his speech with these words:

> With malice toward none; with charity for all; with firmness in the right, as God gives us to see the right, let us strive on to finish the

NEW TESTAMENT CONNECTION

Learning from the Past

In this message we have focused on four factors that put community at risk. Each of these contributed to the demise and downfall of the community of Israel. We need to remember that God records these events in the history of Israel to serve as examples for us. In 1 Corinthians 10:11 the apostle Paul assures us that "these things happened to them as examples and were written down as warnings for us, on whom the fulfillment of the ages has come." May God give us all the wisdom to learn from these examples.

> work we are in; to bind up the nation's wounds; to care for him who shall have borne the battle, and for his widow, and his orphan — to do all which may achieve and cherish a just and lasting peace, among ourselves, and with all nations.

What a great leader! Many said that Abraham Lincoln was the best friend the South ever had. Unfortunately, he didn't live long enough to bring about the healing that needed to come to the country at that time.

Part 4

Pursuing Spiritual Authenticity

Life-Changing Words from the Prophets

Message 25

Elijah: Holding Steady in a Roller-Coaster World

1 Kings 15:25–19:18

THE HEART OF THE Message

In this life, we will have moments of great joy and intense sorrow. We will experience times of deep faith when God feels close and we see his power. We will also walk through the valley—times of confusion and darkness when God seems distant and removed. No matter what we face in this roller-coaster life, we can hold steady because God is always with us, even when our eyes can't see him and our hearts can't feel him.

THE HEART OF THE Messenger

Elijah is an amazing example of holding steady in a roller-coaster world. He had times of astounding victory in his life when he saw the power of God pour down from heaven. He also had times of deep fear, insecurity, and even depression! He rode the roller coaster of life and faith and held on with all his might.

As you prepare to bring this message, take time to reflect on where you are in your life. Maybe you are in a season of joy, peace, and confident faith. Maybe you are discouraged and feel as if you are holding on for dear life. Maybe you are in the depths of depression and sadness. Wherever you are, God wants to speak to your heart and teach you about holding steady in your faith through this amazing ride we call life. God used Elijah to accomplish his purposes when he felt weak and when he felt strong, and God can use you to communicate this life-changing message right where you are today.

BRIEF MESSAGE OUTLINE

1. Elijah: Setting the context
2. Elijah: Experiencing God's power and victory
3. Elijah: Meeting God in the depths of despair
4. Elijah: A fresh beginning

1. Elijah: Setting the Context

SIGNIFICANT SCRIPTURE

1 Kings
15:25–16:28
16:29–34

NARRATIVE ON THE TEXT | *From Bad to Worse!*

There is no question that Jeroboam was an evil king. At his death, God clearly declared that Jeroboam had done evil in the sight of God. He was so evil that other kings in the future were compared to him as a measuring rod in regard to how displeasing they were to God.

After Jeroboam died, his son Nadab takes the throne. He is as evil as his father. He is hated so much that he is killed by a man named Baasha. In short order, Baasha murders every single surviving member of Jeroboam's family to solidify his power and protect his throne.

Baasha is also an evil king, who misleads the people of Israel and pushes them away from God. His son Elah follows him and reigns for two years; he also is corrupt and evil. He is hated so much that he is killed by a man named Zimri.

Zimri reigns for only seven days. He can see that his reign will never last so he burns down the palace while he is inside of it. When Zimri dies, there is a civil war in the northern kingdom between Tibni and Omri. These two men battle to see who has the goofier name. Actually, they fight for the throne, and Omri wins. The text says that he is the worst king up to this point in Israel's history. Just imagine the climate in Israel at this time. King after king ascends to the throne, and each one is worse than the one before. Israel is spiraling deeper and deeper into sin. When things seem like they just can't get any worse, we are surprised!

HISTORICAL CONTEXT | *A Divided Kingdom*

If we think there is unrest in the Middle East in our day, we need to take a close look at the political climate that existed during the ministry of Elijah. God's people had been split in two through an intense civil war, never again to be a united nation. The northern kingdom of Israel and the southern kingdom of Judah are blood relatives who are now enemies as two distinct political entities. The northern kingdom's first king is Jeroboam. He is afraid that if the people of Israel who live in the north go down to Jerusalem to worship, he will lose control and their hearts will turn back to Jerusalem and Rehoboam, the king of the southern kingdom.

To keep the people from traveling to Jerusalem to worship God, Jeroboam sets up idols in in the cities of Dan and Bethel. He says to the people, "It's too much for you to go down to Jerusalem. That's too inconvenient. So here are your gods." Jeroboam has two golden calves made and set up as formal idols for the people to worship. The kingdom has been divided politically and geographically, but now Jeroboam makes sure that religious division is absolutely clear. In doing this, he leads the people into idolatry.

NARRATIVE ON THE TEXT | *Meet the King and Queen*

When Omri dies, his son Ahab becomes king. As hard as it might be to believe, Ahab takes evil to new heights and the people of Israel to new depths of sin. The writer of Kings puts it this way:

> Ahab son of Omri did more evil in the eyes of the LORD than any of those before him. He not only considered it trivial to commit the sins of Jeroboam son of Nebat, but he also married Jezebel daughter of Ethbaal king of the Sidonians, and began to serve Baal and worship him. He set up an altar for Baal in the temple of Baal that he built in Samaria. Ahab also made an Asherah pole and did more to provoke the LORD, the God of Israel, to anger than did all the kings of Israel before him. (1 Kings 16:30–33)

CREATIVE VIDEO ELEMENT

What's Up with That? The Village Hall (4:50 min.) This feature, hosted by Jarrett Stevens, answers tough questions from the Old Testament in an entertaining way. It can be used with any session.

Ahab marries a pagan wife from Sidon named Jezebel. She becomes famous for her hatred of God and his prophets. Ahab puts her in charge of religion, and her express agenda is to destroy the worship of Yahweh in all the land of Israel and to replace the one true God with her god, Baal. Up to this time, the people in the northern kingdom were at least attempting to worship Yahweh, though they used the golden calves to engage that worship rather than going to the temple in Jerusalem. But Jezebel sets her heart on replacing Israel's God with her idol god, Baal. Among other things, she seeks to systematically kill all of God's prophets. This is unprecedented. Past kings, even when they hated the prophets, wouldn't dare touch them. Not Jezebel—she has them killed with no indication that this bothers her at all.

This background is very important because Elijah's ministry begins when Ahab and Jezebel are leading Israel. This is clearly not a popular time to go into the ministry in the northern kingdom. Elijah is called by God and steps into ministry in a time of unparalleled tension, apostasy, and danger. This roller-coaster time demands a prophet who can hold on and follow God through the highs and lows of doing ministry in such a climate.

2. Elijah: Experiencing God's Power and Victory

SIGNIFICANT SCRIPTURE

1 Kings 17:1–6

INTERPRETIVE INSIGHT | *A Man of Courage*

In these opening verses of 1 Kings 17 we see Elijah square off with King Ahab. Elijah says, "As the LORD, the God of Israel, lives, whom I serve, there will be neither dew nor rain in the next few years except at my word." Elijah is announcing a drought that is going to come as a judgment on Ahab. It is important to note that God chooses a drought as the sign of his judgment because Baal was said to be the god of the weather. God will soon be defining for everyone exactly who is the true God!

Imagine the courage it takes for Elijah to speak these words. This is the king who is the culmination of evil from a whole line of kings that just got worse and worse.

This is the king who marries a pagan woman and allows her to kill the prophets. In the face of this fearless and hateful king, Elijah speaks a word of coming judgment. In a place where water and rainfall mean life and death, these words cause inexpressible anger and rage in Ahab. But when God calls Elijah to speak, he speaks!

SIGNIFICANT SCRIPTURE

1 Kings 17:7–24

INTERPRETIVE INSIGHT | *God Provides in Surprising Ways*

Not only is this woman a poor widow, but she is also from Sidon. This is Jezebel's hometown, which means the woman is most likely a pagan. But God sees and God cares for this pagan widow and for his prophet Elijah.

The story is powerful and dramatic because when Elijah meets this woman and asks if she will feed him, she informs him that her situation is so desperate that her plan for that day is to make one final meal for her and her son and then to die of starvation! Just think about it. She has two items to check off her "To Do" list for the day:

- Fix a meal
- Die

Yet Elijah gives her hope. He assures her that if she takes what she has left and prepares a meal for him, she will still have enough for her and her son. Beyond that, Elijah lets her know that God will provide miraculous resources for them every day until the drought is over. What Elijah promised comes to pass. Every time she uses the flour and oil, there is more in the containers.

Their hopeless situation is turned upside down by God's surprising provision. Who would have dreamed that a pagan widow on the edge of poverty and starvation will be the one to have enough faith to give her final meal to a traveling prophet? Who would have dreamed that each day the jars will remain full of oil and flour? But this is just like God—his provision is often a mystery, but always enough.

INTERPRETIVE INSIGHT | *"But First"*

The key phrase in the story of Elijah and the widow is when Elijah says, "But first." God's question of this widow is, "Will you trust me now with what you have?" Here

ON THE LIGHTER SIDE | *The First Fast Food*

God tells Elijah to head east and hide in the Kerith Ravine that is to the east of the Jordan. This makes sense because Ahab is ready to kill Elijah after the words he has spoken. But with no rain in the forecast, how will Elijah eat and drink out in the desert? God tells Elijah that ravens will fly in and drop off bread and meat twice a day. This is the original fast food!

is a lesson about human nature: *If you won't trust God now with what you have, you won't trust him when you get more.*

In verse 15 we read an amazing statement, "She went away and did as Elijah had told her." Think about the drama of this episode. This is a widow who is desperate. She is going to die. She takes the flour and oil — all that she has left — and prepares a meal for a man she just has met. Most of us would be tempted to make Elijah a very, very, very small loaf of bread — maybe a cracker-size loaf.

She does not do this. Before she prepares a funeral meal for herself and her son, she makes a cake of bread for Elijah. She makes a whole meal for Elijah, and she has nothing left. If God doesn't act, she and her son will die, and die without a final meal. But then, she looks into her oil and flour jars, and they are full! She and her son have enough to eat that day, and the next, and the next. One day at a time God meets the need of somebody who has no idea that there really is a God who sees and cares. She follows the "but first" invitation and never regrets it! She gives to Elijah first and never lacks for food again.

Give all he asks; take all he gives.
Thomas R. Kelly

PAUSE FOR PRAYER

Praise for Surprising Provision

You may want to pause right here in the message and lift up a prayer of thanks to God for his wonderful and surprising provision. If your congregation has experienced God's provision in recent days, lift up praise. Maybe there has been a time in the recent or distant past where God has poured out resources needed in your church; give him praise!

LIFE APPLICATION | *Reckless Generosity*

We should all pause occasionally and ask if we are living with the kind of reckless generosity we see in the life of the widow in this story. Maybe we have a whole lot of oil and flour in our jar. Maybe we only have a little. Maybe we have a large flour jar, or maybe a very small one. No matter what we have, we can still learn to live with a generous spirit.

Take time to ask some questions that will help people reflect on their own patterns of giving and generosity:

- Are you being faithful with your tithe to God?
- Are you being responsive to the needs of the poor?

HISTORICAL CONTEXT | *Widows in the Old Testament Days*

When the drought gets bad and the stream dries up, God sends Elijah to a widow to be fed. At first glance, this may not seem strange, but in those days widows were the poorest and most vulnerable members of society. Because of the place of women in general and widows in particular, these are usually very poor people who are often outcasts. Yet, God chooses to use a poor widow to provide for his prophet.

NEW TESTAMENT CONNECTION

From the Lips of Jesus

Jesus had a great deal to say about how we use the resources in our care. The lessons from Elijah's life are reinforced by these words of Jesus: "Give, and it will be given to you. A good measure, pressed down, shaken together and running over, will be poured into your lap. For with the measure you use, it will be measured to you" (Luke 6:38).

- Are you learning to take risks in giving that stretches your faith?
- Are you giving in a way that is becoming a natural part of how you live?
- Are you noticing God's generous provision in your life and responding by growing more generous toward others?

Dallas Willard says the law of the kingdom is the law of inversion, where the last are first, and the servants are the greatest. This is modeled in a striking way in the life of this widow. The weakest, most vulnerable person, an impoverished, pagan, Gentile widow, becomes the one whose generosity keeps the prophet Elijah alive.

INTERPRETIVE INSIGHT | *Miracles*

Later in the story the woman's son dies. But Elijah prays, God sees and cares, and her son is restored. This woman comes to believe in the true God.

As you read through the lives of Elijah and Elisha, you will quickly notice that many miracles take place. In the Old Testament the miracles are not evenly distributed. They tend to come in bursts.

- At the time of the *Exodus* and the conquest of the land, there are the ten plagues, the parting of the Red Sea, the manna and the quail given in the desert, water from a rock, the parting of the Jordan, the walls of Jericho falling

CREATIVE MESSAGE IDEA | *Clusters of Miracles*

Use a flip chart or overhead to draw a graph like you see here. Show the high points and peaks where there are many miracles. Note three of the times when many miracles are clustered together. Also show the valleys, where there is not much miraculous activity.

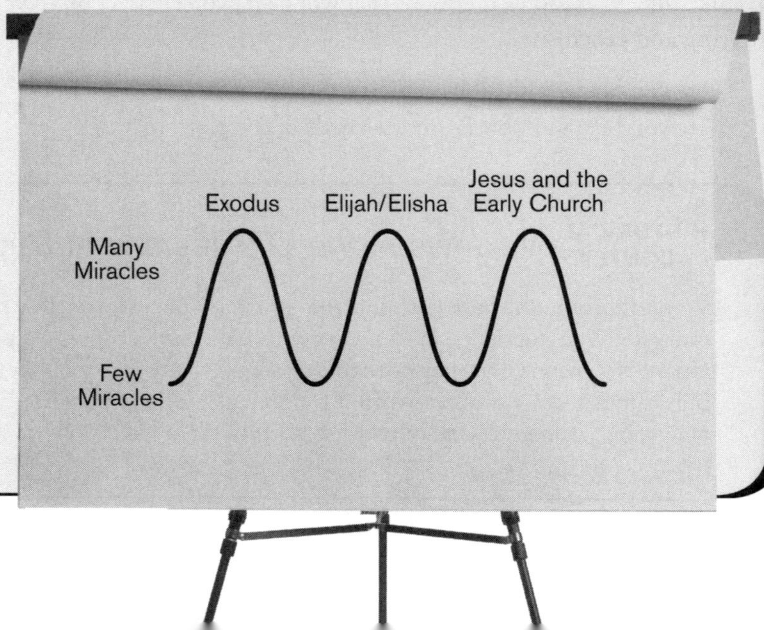

down, and many other miracles. At this time there are many miracles.

- In the era of *the judges and the kings* there are fewer miracles.
- When we come to the time of *Elijah and Elisha*, once again there is another amazing burst of miracles. Elijah prophesies that a drought is coming, and that is exactly what happens. Elijah is fed by ravens. There is the miracle of the widow's flour and oil and also her son being restored to life. Elijah predicts the coming of rain, and it starts to pour. He also foretells about the death of Ahab. Later, Elijah will be swept up into heaven by chariots of fire. Elisha's ministry, which follows Elijah's, is filled with as many miracles.
- The biblical record of miracles shows a drop-off during the *Exile* time of Israel's history.
- At the coming of *Jesus and Pentecost* in the early church, there was another huge burst of miracles—healings, deliverance from demons, and resurrections, to name just a few.

In the Old Testament miracles come at certain crucial moments in bursts of many astounding signs and wonders. This is important to note because sometimes people think that if they have strong faith, they will always be experiencing a string of spectacular, supernatural events. In the Scripture this is not the case. Miracles come in larger numbers at certain points, and we don't always know exactly why this is. Miracles come at key moments in the process of revelation. In the days of Elijah and Elisha God is seeking to build up and solidify his covenant people, and the miracles are part of that process.

WORD STUDY

Syncretism

Syncretism is the effort to embrace various religious systems at the same time. In the Old Testament, this practice occurs when God's people try to retain the practice of worshiping Yahweh, the God who has revealed himself to Abraham, Isaac, and Jacob, but they also try to adopt the religions of the nations around them. In many cases, it appears as if the people really believe they can hold onto worship of Yahweh with one hand and Baal with the other. Through time they have tried to adopt the religious practices and worship the idols of the Canaanites and other nations and still maintain their distinct worship of Yahweh.

HISTORICAL CONTEXT

A Critical Moment

It is crucial that we understand that in the era of Elijah and Elisha, worship of God is being threatened by the worship of Baal. The threat of idolatry, which has troubled Israel from the very beginning, has come to a crisis point. God is going to use Elijah to force Israel to choose between the false god Baal and the one true God of Israel. There is no room for holding on to this false pagan god and also embracing Yahweh, the true and living God.

The people don't yet know it, but they are racing full speed into a moment where they will decide their whole future as a nation. It is a moment of forced decision. Worship of idols is going to stop in Israel, or Israel will hit the end of the road. The whole issue of syncretism and God's people will be dealt with on Mount Carmel. This is a crucial moment in Israel's history.

PAUSE FOR REFLECTION

Has Syncretism Crept In?

You may want to pause for a brief time of reflection. Invite people to search their hearts and identify where idols have been set up or false gods are being worshiped. You may want to have someone play a few moments of quiet music during this time or simply leave things silent. Allow time for the Holy Spirit to search and identify places where syncretism has settled into the lives of God's people.

This is important because of the message that follows. In Elijah's confrontation with the prophets of Baal and his call to the people of Israel to make a choice whom they will follow, we all learn that God will not allow us to have our heart's devotion divided.

LIFE APPLICATION | *Syncretism Is Alive and Well*

Many people still try to make room in their hearts for God and other religious systems. There are people who follow Jesus but also look to horoscopes or the stars to guide their lives. Others embrace the Christian faith with one hand and try to scoop up all they can from other world religions with the other.

There are many expressions of syncretism in our world today, and God opposes them all. He is clear that our arms are not big enough to hold onto him and other false gods. If we are trying to keep a place in our heart for other "gods," we are living a syncretistic life and God has strong feelings about this that will be revealed as we continue looking at the life of Elijah. For now, we need to invite the Holy Spirit to search our hearts and see if we are seeking to embrace the one true God and some false god or idol.

NARRATIVE ON THE TEXT | *You Troublemaker!*

Elijah is commanded by God, after several years of drought, to go to Ahab. At this time, Ahab and particularly his wife Jezebel are systematically killing the prophets devoted to the God of Israel. God tells Elijah, "Go confront Ahab." When Ahab meets Elijah, he says to him, "Is that you, you troubler of Israel?" Ahab treats Elijah as if he is the one causing problems in Israel.

Elijah does not stand for this, and he turns the tables. In the face of the evil and murderous King Ahab, Elijah replies, "I have not made trouble for Israel ... but you and your father's family have. You have abandoned the Lord's commands and have followed the Baals." Ahab points a finger at Elijah, and Elijah points right back at him.

NARRATIVE ON THE TEXT | *The Battle Lines Are Drawn*

SIGNIFICANT SCRIPTURE

1 Kings 18

Elijah tells Ahab what to do. He has him gather the people from all over Israel to meet on Mount Carmel so that they can settle this issue of religious syncretism once and for all. Elijah tells the king to bring all of the false prophets that Jezebel has set up in places of authority all over the land. This includes 450 prophets of Baal and 400 prophets of Asherah. All of these 850 are sponsored and supported by Jezebel. And Ahab does exactly as Elijah commands.

We must picture this scene on Mount Carmel. People from all over Israel have gathered. The 850 false prophets are there, and Elijah shows up. The whole country is gathered for this moment. On one side stand all the false prophets, the king, and all the power of his government and his army. On Ahab's side is the absolute license for the people to do whatever they feel like. There are no Ten Commandments there. There is no law about caring for orphans, widows, and aliens. There's no call for devotion to love God and neighbor. It's just idolatry that promises sexual pleasure as part of the cult worship and material abundance for all who bow down to Baal.

On the other side stands one man, one solitary prophet who emerges from years of hiding to confront a king and a country. But with that one man is God—Israel's God—the God who made them a people. The God of Abraham, Isaac, Jacob, and Joseph is with Elijah. Standing with Elijah is the God who delivers meals by ravens and who fills the oil and flour jars of widows. To the naked eye, it seems as if Elijah is outnumbered 850 to 1. To the spiritual eye, Elijah is far from alone!

Standing in the middle are the people of Israel. They are at their critical deciding point. They have tried holding on to Yahweh and Baal. They have been living syncretistic lives, but now a line is being drawn.

INTERPRETIVE INSIGHT | *The True Source of Authority*

There is something striking in this story. Elijah is a runaway, fugitive preacher whom Jezebel is trying to kill. Ahab is the king of Israel who sits on the throne and has all authority in the nation of Israel. But notice who is giving the orders in this story: Elijah is! He has no office, no crown, no throne, but he says, "Do this," and the king does it. Where does he get such authority? This is the authority of one human being who is utterly yielded to God. It's a remarkable thing.

Ahab wears the crown. But Ahab is a man without a single serious conviction. It's a miserable way to live. Ahab seems to become passive in the face of any strong character or conviction—whether it's Jezebel and evil, or Elijah and God. In this confrontation we see that Ahab has the official authority of the throne but no personal authority. Elijah has no human political authority, but God's presence in his life gives a greater strength and authority than Ahab will ever know.

INTERPRETIVE INSIGHT | *Limping Along*

In an act of immense courage, Elijah challenges a whole nation. He cries out the question that has been burning in the heart of God: "How long will you waver between two opinions? If the Lord is God, follow him; but if Baal is God, follow him."

Here is why Elijah is saying the people are wavering between two opinions: They don't think they have rejected Yahweh. They still pray to him if nothing else works. They just think they have added Baal to their religious portfolio. They have decided they will worship both. The word translated "waver" here literally means "to hobble" or "to limp."

The Hebrews would often use "walking" as a metaphor for life. Elijah is saying, "You are just limping through life. You have chosen a miserable way to live. You are being torn between two gods, and one of them is false." This image of limping speaks as loudly today as it did in the days of Elijah. When people try to follow the one true God and still embrace false gods, they will never walk securely, and they will certainly never run; they will limp along!

LIFE APPLICATION | *Where Is Baal Today?*

At this point it would be easy to dismiss this issue of syncretism and limping along as something that ended way back when people stopped bowing down to stone idols and when making sacrifices to the storm god ceased. But Baal is still alive and well. Anything we let take the place of God in our lives is idolatry. Often the things we try to embrace while we still hold on to God can become idolatrous and can cause us to limp along.

Take time to identify some of the ways that idolatry is still alive and well in the lives of Christ-followers today. Invite people to examine their hearts, with the help of the Holy Spirit, so that this will become a day when a line is drawn and each follower of Jesus declares that they will follow the one true God alone!

A Baal is *anything* that can tempt us away from full devotion to God. In other words, a Baal can be:

- a *relationship* that dishonors God
- a *lifestyle* that keeps you from being generous to the poor
- a *habit* or an *addiction* that you know God wants you to give up
- a *grudge* against someone who has really hurt you
- a struggle with *pride* and the power it has over you—perhaps the stubborn will to say, "I want to be in control of my own life. I want to call the shots."
- *anything that is diverting your devotion* from God

Maybe you've been telling yourself that you can hang onto your little Baal and hang onto God too. What God wants us to understand is that we can't. It is impossible! The process of trying to hold onto God and to Baal will make our lives miserable.

INTERPRETIVE INSIGHT | *The People Say Nothing*

When Elijah calls the people to a point of decision, we can almost feel the tension. They have grown used to embracing Yahweh and Baal. They like the freedom of options. They have become comfortable with the cultic prostitution and the open-minded posture of accepting every religious option on their spiritual horizons. Now they are being called to decide, to make a choice, to stand on one side of the line or the other.

This is an extraordinary moment. Hear the words again: "How long will you waver between two opinions? If the LORD is God, follow him; but if Baal is God, follow him" (1 Kings 18:21).

What follows is staggering. We read the words: "But the people said nothing." No one knows how long this silence lasts, but it must have been deafening to Elijah and heartbreaking to God.

Can you imagine that moment? Some of the people are sullen. Some of them are defiant. Some are confused. Some are thinking, "Why should I have to choose? This life is working for me. Baal lets me do whatever I want. I can call on Yahweh anytime I really feel the need. Why should I change? I can follow my own agenda." No one says a word.

How sad that silence must have been for God. After all the centuries of his care and love for this people, nobody stands up for him. Nobody says a word. It's just dead silence. After parting seas, raining down manna, leading with a pillar of fire, breaking down walls, working mighty miracles for his people, they all stand in silence.

ILLUSTRATION | *The Pain of Silence*

Imagine a man and woman who have been dating for years. They have taken all the normal steps toward a growing and maturing relationship. They began as friends, and every indication is that they have fallen in love and are progressing forward. The man is certain she is the one. He is head over heals, punch-drunk, crazy in love with her. He shops and buys a beautiful diamond ring. He takes her to their favorite restaurant. He waits for the perfect moment. He slips out of his chair and takes a knee next to her. As he opens the jewelry box to reveal the ring, he says, "I love you, I want you to be my wife, will you marry me?"

Now imagine that she sits there in silence. She says nothing. For ten seconds, twenty, thirty, and a full sixty seconds, she says nothing. It feels like an eternity! Sometimes silence can be the loudest message of all.

NARRATIVE ON THE TEXT | *850 Voices Lifted with No Answer*

Elijah and the prophets of Baal each build an altar, sacrifice a bull, and place it on a pile of wood on the altar. At this point in the sacrificial process, the normal next step is to set the wood on fire and let the flames consume the sacrifice. But, the agreement is that neither will be allowed to set the wood on fire. This will be the job of their respective deity. Elijah will pray to Yahweh and ask him to reveal his presence and might through sending fire from heaven and igniting

NEW TESTAMENT CONNECTION

You Can't Serve Two Masters

Elijah is expressing a fundamental spiritual truth. The human heart is only capable of giving its ultimate allegiance and devotion to one master. God has hard-wired us in such a way that we can't serve God and Baal and still remain healthy and thriving people. Jesus said it this way: "No one can serve two masters. Either he will hate the one and love the other, or he will be devoted to the one and despise the other. You cannot serve both God and Money" (Matthew 6:24).

Jesus is emphatic that his followers cannot love material things with their whole hearts and still have room to love him with full devotion. They have to choose. This is the same message on the heart of God as he speaks through Elijah to the people. "No man can serve two masters," Elijah says. "If it's going to be Baal, at least be honest about it. Don't add hypocrisy to disobedience. Just be truthful. But if it's going to be God, then get right with God. Fall on your knees, confess, repent, and follow him. But one way or another, you must choose. It's decision time!"

the wood. The 850 prophets will do the same as they call out to Baal to manifest his might through heavenly fire. Once the rules of engagement are established, all the people say, "What you say is good." They all agree that the one who answers with fire from heaven will be declared the true God!

The prophets of Baal call on him from morning until noon, but he does not respond. They cry out, "O Baal, answer us!" but there is silence. No one answers. They dance around the altar and unite their 850 voices, but the heavens remain silent.

NARRATIVE ON THE TEXT | *They Just Don't Get It!*

We learn quickly that the prophets of Baal don't have much of a sense of humor, or maybe they just don't catch the tone of subtle sarcasm. They take Elijah seriously and decide, "Yeah, Elijah is right. We've got to work harder to try to get Baal's attention."

HISTORICAL CONTEXT | *The "Nature God"*

Baal was said to be the god of nature. He is pictured in ancient etchings with lightning bolts in his hand. The ancient writings say that Baal rode the thunderstorm as his chariot. In other words, a little fire from heaven should have been a piece of cake for Baal. If he really did exist, sending fire from heaven would have been in his job description! Since Baal was known as the "Nature God," the people would have seen this challenge as an easy task for him.

ON THE LIGHTER SIDE | *Where Is Your God?*

At this point in the drama Elijah wants to make sure that everybody understands the absolute absurdity of putting trust in Baal—a nonexistent god. In 1 Kings 18:27 Elijah engages in a little prophetic trash talk. Listen to Elijah's words:

> "Shout louder!" he said. "Surely he is a god! Perhaps he is deep in thought, or busy, or traveling. Maybe he is sleeping and must be awakened." (1 Kings 18:27)

This passage is a little hard to translate, but clearly Elijah is intending to use mockery, humor, and sarcasm to show how ridiculous it is to pray to a god who isn't there. Elijah lays it on quite thick. *The Living Bible* (with good indication from the sense of the Hebrew in this passage) translates the passage like this:

> "You'll have to shout louder than that to catch the attention of your god. Maybe he's talking to someone or out sitting on the toilet."

Elijah is going full throttle. He's trying anything to show the people how crazy this is. You can almost hear Elijah taunt, "Maybe your god suffers from irregularity."

They shout louder and slash themselves with swords and spears. They try to get Baal's attention by making themselves bleed. What a sad testimony to the utter emptiness of this false religious system.

Midday passes, and they are exhausted and bleeding! Yet, they continue their frantic prophesying until the time for the evening sacrifice. With all their yelling and signs of religious devotion, there is no response. No one answers. No one pays attention.

INTERPRETIVE INSIGHT | *A Decisive Turning Point*

This is a magnificently written account. The prophets of Baal go on for hours until it is the official time for the evening sacrifice that would normally be made to the God of Israel. Elijah finally just puts an end to the craziness. He calls the people over to him and carefully prepares the altar. He pours water over the sacrifice three times to make it even harder for the wood to ignite and to make sure everyone knows that only God could light this fire. Then he prays. But his prayer is an absolute contrast to the wild excesses of the behavior of the prophets of Baal.

He simply prays:

> "O Lord, God of Abraham, Isaac and Israel, let it be known today that you are God in Israel and that I am your servant and have done all these things at your command. Answer me, O Lord, answer me, so these people will know that you, O Lord, are God, and that you are turning their hearts back again." (1 Kings 18:36–37)

God sees and cares, and fire comes down from heaven and consumes the offering, the wood, the water, the soil, and the stones! God wins the battle, hands down!

This is a decisive turning point in the history of Israel. All the people who stand in muted silence up to this point now begin to cry out, "The Lord—he is God! The Lord—he is God!" The prophets of Baal are defeated and the nation returns to Yahweh.

LIFE APPLICATION | *How Do We Pray?*

It is helpful to pause for a moment and observe the vivid contrast between the way the prophets of Baal prayed and the way Elijah prayed. The 850 false prophets yelled, screamed, acted out, and put on a show. Elijah simply spoke and watched God manifest his power.

This is important to note because sometimes Christians pray more like the prophets of Baal than like Elijah. They pray as if they think that they have to get God's attention by doing something dramatic. Some followers of Christ believe they must pray loud enough, long enough, with the right formula, with enough boldness, or with some kind of radical and special behavior if God is going to hear. This is simply not true. Elijah talks to God calmly and expects God to take care of the results.

3. Elijah: Meeting God in the Depths of Despair

SIGNIFICANT SCRIPTURE

1 Kings 19:1–9

INTERPRETIVE INSIGHT | *From the Mountain to the Valley*

How many people in the history of the human race have ever experienced manifestations of the power of God as Elijah did? He saw God work in ways most of us could never even dream possible. Yet, right after seeing God pour fire from heaven and defeat the prophets of Baal, things take a dramatic turn for Elijah.

When Jezebel hears of Elijah's triumph over her prophets, she vows to see him dead. Elijah, who defied a king, defeated 850 prophets, and confronted an entire nation single-handedly, runs in fear at the threat of one queen. This turnabout is so sudden and so dramatic that some Old Testament scholars are convinced that this part of the story is out of place. However, there is nothing in the text, or in life, that supports this idea.

Elijah experiences what many followers of Christ have gone through. After a mountaintop experience of intense intimacy with God and awareness of God's presence, Elijah hits a low point in his spiritual life. He seems to enter a time of fear and even depression. Elijah goes from the mountain to the valley in a very short time.

ON THE LIGHTER SIDE | *Time for a Run*

Now Elijah gives Ahab another command. He says, "Go, eat and drink, for there is the sound of a heavy rain." Remember, there hasn't been rain for years and there's not a cloud in the sky. But Elijah says, "It's going to rain." Next Elijah sends his servant to give the king instructions. This time Elijah does not even bother going to the king, but he has a servant give a secondhand command to the ruler of Israel. Ahab is told to ride in his chariot to the palace in Jezreel.

Elijah decides he's going to jog back to Jezreel. In 1 Kings 18:46 we read, "And the power of the LORD came upon Elijah and, tucking his cloak into his belt, he ran ahead of Ahab all the way to Jezreel."

Here's the kicker: The run from Mount Carmel to Jezreel is about sixteen miles. Can you imagine trying to outrun a chariot in a sixteen-mile race?

Now, you have to imagine Ahab sitting in his chariot. All he can think of is Elijah. Elijah who called for a drought that could ruin him; Elijah who eluded him for years; Elijah who goes around giving him orders; Elijah who had single-handedly challenged all the prophets of Baal and destroyed them. Certainly Ahab is also thinking about how he will tell Jezebel that all of her 850 prophets are now dead and her whole religious takeover of Israel has been crushed by one man – Elijah.

You can almost see Ahab in his chariot riding along and thinking, "At least in my chariot I get a break from Elijah. I'll have a few hours when I get to Jezreel, before Elijah arrives, to get a break from this guy!" Then Ahab looks and sees something approaching. There is Elijah, running faster than his horse-drawn chariot. Elijah waves at him as he's running by: "See you at the palace."

Elijah has outfoxed Ahab's soldiers and outprayed Ahab's prophets, and now he's outrunning Ahab's horses!

NARRATIVE ON LIFE | *We All Visit the Valley*

Nobody stays on top of the mountain forever—nobody. We will all have spiritual peaks and valleys as long as we live. Sometimes, after an unbelievable, adrenaline-filled, record-setting run of achievement and spiritual victory, we can find ourselves in the most vulnerable times of doubt, fear, or depression. The question is not, "Will I ever visit the valley?" The real issue is, "How will I respond when I visit the valley?"

NARRATIVE ON THE TEXT | *Praying from the Depths*

Elijah is about to snap. The same Elijah who prayed and fire came down from heaven to consume a sacrifice, who prayed for rain and a drought ended, who received the strength to outrun a chariot, prays for one more thing: "Let me die." How much lower can a person go!

But the good news is that God loves a person so much that sometimes he answers that prayer in the way it is asked. Elijah is so down that he does not know how he can press on, yet God still has a plan for Elijah. God hears Elijah's honest and passionate prayer. He is down, he is discouraged, and he feels he can't go on, so he tells God just how he feels. Elijah prays from the depths, God hears from the heights, and God prepares to lift Elijah out of the pit.

CREATIVE MESSAGE IDEA | *Map Time*

Elijah goes on quite a journey. You may want to use the PowerPoint slide provided with the supplemental resources to show where God leads him. Elijah goes from Jezreel to Beersheba (in the southern kingdom), to the Negev, and into the desert, which is outside the boundaries of Israel.

ON THE LIGHTER SIDE | *Snack Time*

It is wonderful to see what happens after Elijah's despairing prayer. He falls asleep, and while he gets some much needed rest, God sends an angel to help him. The angel brings a cake and some water. When Elijah wakes up, the angel has him eat, drink, and then take another nap!

God treats Elijah the way you treat a cranky two-year-old. "Here are some Twinkies and some juice. Have a snack and take a nap." Elijah does as he is told, and when he wakes up, he feels a lot better—so much better that he is ready to travel for forty days and nights.

> Extraordinary afflictions are not always the punishment of extraordinary sins, but sometimes the trial of extraordinary graces. Sanctified afflictions are spiritual promotions.
>
> *Matthew Henry*

4. Elijah: A Fresh Beginning

SIGNIFICANT SCRIPTURE

1 Kings 19:10–18

INTERPRETIVE INSIGHT | *A Time of Depression*

When Elijah reaches the Negev, at least geographically, he has left the people of Israel. He is far from God's people. In a sense, he has left his post. That's why God says, "What are you doing here?" Elijah is running away from what God has for him to do. He has classic signs of depression: suicidal thoughts, loss of appetite, and a distorted perspective on reality.

And you can bet that inside of his mind a little voice is saying things like, "You call yourself a prophet? You have more doubt and fear than the people you preach to. You ran out on God after all he did for you. You left the people just when they started turning from Baal and needed you most. There's no way God could ever use somebody like you."

Elijah must have felt like we all do on some days. He must have had a sense that he was not real useful for God's purposes and that his future was pretty bleak.

NARRATIVE ON THE TEXT | *A Whole New Start*

But God sees and God cares. God does an amazing thing. Elijah pours out his heart, and God begins a process of giving him a whole new beginning. God calls him out of a cave and into the light. On the mountain Elijah stands and waits for the Lord

CREATIVE MESSAGE IDEA | *Communion*

At the table of Jesus we find one of the best reminders that God offers a new beginning to all who ask. You might want to consider having communion together at the end of this message. In Exodus, and scattered throughout the whole rest of the Pentateuch, we find every one of these features. God is all about covenant.

What we have to keep in the forefront of our minds is that the laws were never intended to be a list of rules that somebody had to keep to earn salvation. These laws were given after God had redeemed his people from Egypt and called them his beloved children. They were intended to describe *what a covenant relationship with God was supposed to look like*. What would it look like to be a kingdom of priests and a holy nation?

to pass by. First, there is a powerful wind, then an earthquake, and finally a fire. But God is not in these things. Finally, there is a gentle whisper and God is there, with Elijah, showing him that he still sees and cares.

At this time, God lets Elijah know that he can have a whole new start. He reminds him that he is not alone and that there are many who still follow Yahweh. And, best of all, God begins to reveal his plan to bring a new friend into Elijah's life, a man named Elisha, who will follow in his steps as a prophet. God is not even close to being done with working in Elijah's life.

> The lament is an appeal to God's compassion to intervene and change a desperate situation ... they raise a cry out of the depths in the confidence that God has the power to lift a person out of the "miry bog" and set one's feet upon a rock. Hence the laments are really expressions of praise—praise offered in a minor key in the confidence that Yahweh is faithful and in anticipation of a new lease on life.
>
> *Bernhard W. Anderson*

LIFE APPLICATION | *The God of New Beginnings*

Sometimes when people are hurting, what they need most of all is a sense of purpose. God often brings renewal by giving new meaning and life direction. That is the gift God gives to Elijah. Elijah goes back down the mountain and begins a whole new chapter in his adventure with God.

This may be the gift God wants to give to many people who hear this message. There may be people who feel discouraged, depressed, and even useless to God. But every follower of Christ can be confident that honest expression in prayer, even in the hardest times, can lead to a new beginning and even fresh life direction.

Elisha: Receiving a Spiritual Legacy

1 Kings 19:15–21; 2 Kings 2:1–15; 4:1–7; 6:8–23

THE HEART OF THE Message

It has often been said that the Christian faith is always one generation away from extinction. If we don't pass the flame of faith to the next generation, it will not continue. Of course God is always active in accomplishing his purposes, but he invites us to be part of his plan in the world.

In this session we will look at how God calls Elijah to pass on the flame of faith to the next generation. His flame is given to Elisha, and he, in turn, continues to pass it on. In a similar way, followers of Christ today are invited into the joy-filled experience of investing their lives and faith in another generation of believers. It may be a class of children taught during a Sunday school hour. It could be high school students in a youth group that receive the flame. For many it will be their sons and daughters and grandchildren. There are also those who will become spiritual sons and daughters, much like Elisha becomes a spiritual son to Elijah. Whoever it is, God calls us to be ready to invest our lives in passing the torch of faith to the next generation and so leave a spiritual legacy.

THE HEART OF THE Messenger

Take time to reflect in two different directions as you prepare to bring this message. First, think about those who have passed on the flame of faith to you over the years. Thank God for their lives and faithfulness. Next, think about those whom God has placed in your life and to whom you are called to pass the torch. Pray for boldness, consistency, and wisdom as you continue to follow God's leading in passing on a spiritual legacy to others.

BRIEF MESSAGE OUTLINE

1. A call to bear the torch
2. Elijah passes the torch to Elisha
3. Elisha carries the flame

1. A Call to Bear the Torch

ILLUSTRATION | *Passing the Torch*

In ancient Greece when it was time for the Olympic games, athletes from around the country would be handed a torch with a special flame. Every one of them would run their leg of the race and then hand off their torch to the next runner. Eventually the torch would make it to an altar in Olympia and remain there. Other flames came and went but this one was never to be extinguished.

This was a sacred matter to the Greek people. The flame symbolized the light of spirit and knowledge and life that gets passed down from one generation to another. These people considered themselves keepers of the flame. They were passers of the torch.

LIFE APPLICATION | *Looking Back and Looking Forward*

Every follower of Christ is where he or she is because somebody passed on the torch of faith. Maybe it was parents, grandparents, a teacher, a Sunday school teacher, a schoolteacher, a pastor, or someone else, but somebody nurtured our faith. Someone

CREATIVE MESSAGE IDEA | *Lighting the Torch*

If you want to use a visual reminder of what's at stake in this call to pass on a spiritual legacy, you might look into lighting a torch that you will keep burning throughout the entire message. If you have issues of fire code, be sure to get the right permissions and have a fire extinguisher handy. You may even want to invite someone from the local fire department to be on hand and ensure everything stays safe and sane!

HISTORICAL CONTEXT | *The Flame from the Beginning*

God lit the flame and passed it on from the beginning. It really started with Adam and Eve. Later, Abraham passed the torch to Isaac, and he handed it to Jacob, who in turn passed the torch to Joseph. In the Bible we learn that passing the flame does not just happen between parents and children. Moses passed the torch on to Joshua. Eli did the same with young Samuel. Jesus passed the torch to his apostles. The apostle Paul, as an old man, celebrated as he saw the flame of faith ignite in Timothy's life.

From the beginning, it was God's plan that his followers be torchbearers. If we fail to rise up to this calling, each new generation is at risk! The question God is asking is clear: "Will somebody guard the flame? Will we continue the legacy and pass on the torch to the next generation?"

prayed, invested, loved, and let the flame burn bright in his or her life. It is terribly important that we all understand that in every generation, from Abraham's to ours, somebody passed the torch to somebody else and then to somebody else. Not a single generation was skipped. That's why we are where we are today.

Take a moment to reflect on these questions:

- Whom did God use to pass on the flame of faith to me?
- Who has prayed for me, loved me, and let their light shine for me?
- Who has been a torchbearer in my life?
- How can I thank or bless those who have passed on the torch in my life?

Next, take a moment to reflect on these questions:

- Do I have people in my life to whom I am passing the torch?
- In whom am I investing myself?
- Am I keeping the flame bright in my life so that the torch gets passed on to others?
- Who are specific people God has placed in my life so that I can pass the flame to them?
- What are some of the steps I can take to be a torchbearer more intentionally in the lives of others?

2. Elijah Passes the Torch to Elisha

SIGNIFICANT SCRIPTURE

1 Kings 19:15–16

NARRATIVE ON THE TEXT | *Grooming the Replacement*

When Elijah was on the mountain, God spoke to him. Elijah was in despair and was pouring his heart out to God. In the middle of this low point in his life, God lets him

CREATIVE MESSAGE IDEA | *Putting It on Paper*

Invite everyone to write down the names of two kinds of people in their lives. First, have those gathered write down the names of those who have passed on the torch of faith to them. Second, have them write down at least one or two names of people to whom they feel God wants them to pass the flame in the coming weeks and months. It would be helpful if you had a card that you gave each person as they entered the worship service or class where this message will be communicated. There is an example of a simple card you can create printed below. After each person has written down a few names, encourage them to put this card somewhere where they will see it on a regular basis.

Receiving and Giving a Spiritual Legacy

People who have passed on the torch of faith to me:	People to whom God wants me to pass the flame:
•	•
•	•

know that he is not done passing on his flame. There is a man named Elisha who needs the leadership Elijah has to offer. God lets Elijah know that he will be grooming Elisha to be the new prophet in Israel.

NARRATIVE ON LIFE | *You Won't Always Be Israel's Prophet!*

In 1 Kings 19:15–16 God is telling Elijah that he will be anointing two kings. Then God just slips this in: "And, by the way, you will also be anointing your replacement." How do you think Elijah feels when he hears those words? It takes a certain kind of humility to do what Elijah is called to do.

Up to this point, Elijah has been the key prophet for God in Israel. When you are a prophet, you tend to get a certain amount of attention, and your role carries a certain measure of power. Elijah is informed that he will be giving up his place as the number one prophet in the land. Elijah is going to have to acknowledge that a younger man will take over for him. He must face the reality that a new prophet will replace him and that Elisha may even go further than Elijah did.

SIGNIFICANT SCRIPTURE

1 Kings 19:19–21

CREATIVE MESSAGE IDEA | *Torch-Bearing Testimonies*

You may want to consider having one or two pairs of people share a brief testimony about how they have passed and received the torch of faith. This can be a parent and child, a youth and an adult, or any pair of people who have a story to tell about how one of them has invested in the life of the other and passed on the flame. Allow one to tell the story from the perspective of passing on a spiritual legacy and the other to tell about what it means to them to have received a spiritual legacy. This can be done live or on video.

HISTORICAL CONTEXT | *A Rich Kid*

When Elijah comes to Elisha and invites him to follow in the steps of the prophet, it will involve great commitment and sacrifice on the part of Elisha. Take note of the number of oxen Elisha is plowing with. In that day, most families were poor enough that they might own a few chickens. For a family to own one ox was quite rare and a sign of wealth. They'd be fairly well off. To have twelve teams of oxen (twenty-four) was almost unheard of. This is an indication that Elisha's family are people of immense wealth. In contemporary terms, they had a huge house in the most wealthy neighborhood in town and a condo in Maui. Elisha is a rich kid, no question about it!

NARRATIVE ON THE TEXT | *The "Mantle"*

Elijah does exactly what God asks. He is ready to pass the flame, and Elisha is the one God has chosen. Elijah comes down the mountain and sees Elisha plowing in the field. All the people there know who Elijah is, and here is Elisha out doing his work and he sees Elijah, Israel's prophet, coming right toward him. When he reaches Elisha, Elijah takes off his cloak and drapes it around Elisha's shoulders. There is no report that he says a word. He simply places the cloak over his shoulders, turns, and walks away.

In the King James Version, this cloak is called a "mantle." Today, when we talk about a mantle of responsibility or a mantle of leadership getting passed on, it comes from this story. In a visible way, Elijah is saying to Elisha, "I am inviting you to follow me and learn from me. I want to walk with you and teach you. I want to have you watch what I do and then see how God can also work in and through your life." In a real sense, Elijah is saying, "I want to pass the flame to you. I want to give you the spiritual legacy God has given to me. I want your flame to burn brighter and brighter, and one day you will lead as the prophet in Israel without me even being at your side."

PAUSE FOR PRAYER

Praise and Power

Take time to pray for God to move followers of Christ in two different directions. First, ask for a sense of praise and thankfulness to overflow for those who have passed on the torch of faith to us. Celebrate how God has used family members, friends, Sunday school teachers, youth leaders, pastors, and others to pass on the flame. Second, ask for the power of the Holy Spirit to fill each Christ-follower with the strength and boldness they need to be a bearer of the torch and a keeper of the flame. Ask God to help us pass the flame to a new generation.

Also, pray for those attending who are still spiritual seekers. Give thanks to God that they have people in their life who love them enough to want to pass on the flame of faith. Pray for them to find joy as they continue their journey. Pray that if they come to a place when they receive Christ as their personal forgiver and leader, they will one day become passers of the torch of faith.

ILLUSTRATION | *The Role of Mentors*

In our world today there is often talk of mentors. These are people who pass on a legacy in the business world, athletics, or some other area of life. Many people see the value of going through an internship or mentoring relationship before they step out on their own. If this is important in the world of business or athletics, how much more important when it comes to the eternal issues of life.

NARRATIVE ON LIFE | *Making Sacrifices*

What Elijah is asking Elisha to do involves enormous sacrifice. The Bible says nothing about Elijah's background. He may very well have been from a poor family. He may not have had too many career options. But Elisha is another story. Elisha's got it made. He will inherit a way of life that will keep him comfortable for the rest of his days.

But God has called Elijah to ask Elisha to walk away from his secure and wealthy lifestyle and follow him on a path that may very well lead to poverty, rejection, and the opposition of stubborn kings who want him dead. From the beginning, Elisha must have realized that following God's plan for his life would mean making significant sacrifices.

NEW TESTAMENT CONNECTION

The Example of Jesus

Jesus knew the absolute importance of passing on a spiritual legacy. He had many groups of people who followed him and learned from his example. There was a group of seventy-two people who had access to Jesus and who learned from him (Luke 10). He also had a group of twelve (Matthew 10:1 – 2), and finally, there were Peter, James, and John (Matthew 17:1). These last three received close instruction and were invited to learn from Jesus at the most critical moments of his life and ministry. Jesus' example of passing on a spiritual legacy and the flame of faith should inspire each of us to do the same.

At the same time, Elijah knows, from personal experience, that he is calling Elisha to give up more than he could dream, in terms of earthly things. It would have been so easy for Elijah to say, "God, you made a mistake. Elisha is not going to walk away from a great future like that to follow a prophet like me. He's got too many attractive options. You've got the wrong guy. He would never do something like this. I'm not even going to ask."

LIFE APPLICATION | *Never Say "No" for Someone Else*

It would have been so easy for Elijah to walk right past Elisha and look for someone who seemed more likely to say yes. But, that is not what he does. Elijah makes the big ask. He places the mantle over Elisha's shoulders and invites him into a whole new life!

What happens next is a joy to see. Elisha takes the challenge, receives the invitation, and begins a whole new life. Because of Elijah's courage to ask and Elisha's willingness to follow, Israel is changed and the world is changed.

What a powerful reminder for each of us that it is never our place to say "no" for someone else. We must never assume that somebody doesn't want to get involved, learn, grow, and serve just because it might not make sense to us. Never assume that anybody has too many options that are more attractive to them than living and serving in the kingdom of God. God knows that so many people are one conversation away from being a keeper of the flame and a carrier of his message.

HISTORICAL CONTEXT | *What They Said and What They Meant*

When Elijah places his cloak over Elisha and extends the invitation to follow him, Elisha's response is, "Let me kiss my father and mother good-bye, then I'll come with you." This may seem a little ambiguous to us, but it would not have seemed strange back in the Old Testament days. In Middle Eastern culture it was extremely rude to say an outright "no" to somebody. That would be very impolite.

Thus, when Elisha gives this response, it could be just what it looks like on the surface, but it could also be his way of asking for more time to think about it. It could be a polite way of trying to say, "I'm not sure, or I am not ready to commit, but give me time."

Notice Elijah's response, "Go back to your parents," he says. "What have I done to you?" In other words, Elijah is saying is, "I'm not going to use any guilt. I'm not going to use any pressure. I want you to be free in this decision. It is your call."

LIFE APPLICATION | *The Important Place of Celebration*

When Elisha volunteers and decides to follow Elijah, this is a significant event in his life. It needs to be acknowledged and even celebrated. So, they have a big party. What is recorded here is a brief account of something that would have taken a considerable amount of time to plan. It may well be that Elijah and Elisha plan the celebration together.

> Never insult anybody by asking them to do an easy job.
>
> *Max Depree*

They decide the appropriate celebration will be a huge barbecue. The word "huge" might not really hit the mark. Look at it this way: Have you ever seen a side of beef? Can you imagine how many people you can feed with two oxen? Oxen are big animals. Elijah and Elisha put on an enormous feast to celebrate this step in Elisha's life. Friends and family affirm his decision.

We need to learn from this example in our homes, relationships, and churches. When people say yes to a volunteer place of ministry, it is a big deal! When somebody volunteers and says, "Yes, I will! I don't have to do it, I have other options, but I'm going to devote myself to the task God has placed before me," this deserves celebration.

It is important in the life of the church to make time to rejoice over those who are serving God as volunteers. We need to have a barbecue, throw a party, publicly bless and pray for people, and do all we can to celebrate those who follow God's example of being a volunteer.

> When volunteers are asked how they happened to get involved in their particular activity, the most common answer is, "Somebody asked me." Conversely, when people are asked why they did not volunteer or donate, they say, "Nobody asked."
>
> *Robert Putnam*

NARRATIVE ON LIFE | *Leaving the Past Behind*

Once Elisha has made the decision to become a volunteer and follow Elijah, he does something dramatic. If you read too quickly, you might miss it. As part of the big barbecue celebration party, Elisha uses his plowing equipment to set the fire and roast his oxen. In other words, his primary past occupation and source of wealth all go up in smoke. He is not leaving an easy door open to return to his past life. He knows God is calling and he is ready to follow, so he closes the door on his past through a dramatic gesture of burning his plowing equipment and serving his oxen up for a community feast.

WORD STUDY

Volunteer

Elijah shows tremendous respect and honor toward Elisha. If Elisha follows, it will be his choice, and he will never be able to say that Elijah has forced him. Elisha is really a volunteer. Our word "volunteer" comes from a Latin word, which means "will" or "choice." We sometimes think of a volunteer as somebody who is not getting paid. But at its core, volunteer means something much more. A volunteer is someone who freely embraces a task, even though he or she doesn't have to, even though he or she has other options. A volunteer willingly chooses to devote oneself to a task he or she doesn't have to do.

NARRATIVE ON LIFE | *A Humble Spirit*

Once the party is over, we read that Elisha "set out to follow Elijah and became his attendant." The idea of Elisha's following is not just geographical. It is a matter of submission. He's going to become a follower of Elijah. Specifically, he becomes his "attendant." We see the humility of Elisha from the very beginning. He gives up a privileged position as a wealthy heir—a man who's got it made—to become a learner, a student, a follower, a servant, of Elijah.

When we look for somebody to pass the torch on to, we need to look for somebody who has a coachable spirit and a humble heart. Elisha is so eager to learn that he becomes an attendant to Elijah. Part of what makes the relationship between Elijah and Elisha work is the humility on both sides. Elijah doesn't claim to be the only prophet. Elisha doesn't demand to be the star. They become passers of the torch together.

NARRATIVE ON THE TEXT | *A Strange Journey*

Elijah and Elisha begin their journey in *Gilgal*, which is close to the Jordan River. Elijah tells Elisha to stay there while he goes on to Bethel. But Elisha said, "As surely as the LORD lives and as you live, I will not leave you." This is a strong response from Elisha. He lets Elijah know, "Nothing doing. I'm going to stick with you." So Elijah moves on, and Elisha goes with him.

Next they go to *Bethel*, which is inland almost halfway to the Mediterranean Sea. Once they are in Bethel, they go through the same set of speeches. Elijah tells him to wait there, and Elisha is emphatic that he is not leaving Elijah's side.

They travel on to *Jericho*. In Jericho they echo the same conversation and move on. Finally, they end up at the *Jordan River*. This seems

CREATIVE MESSAGE IDEA | *Guilt in the Church?*

Have you ever heard of a church using guilt or pressure to try to get someone to volunteer to do something? There is a powerful little clip of Bill Hybels telling about how a pastor tried to manipulate members of his congregation into volunteering to be Sunday school teachers by talking about how little fourth grade kids end up on drugs if they don't have a good Sunday school class. This story can be found at the start of the Network video curriculum in the materials published by Zondervan and Willow Creek.

like a strange journey, and the recurring conversation between these two prophets can seem quite odd. But, the issue at hand seems to be a test to see if Elisha is fully committed to following Elijah, and ultimately, following God.

SIGNIFICANT SCRIPTURE

2 Kings 2:1 – 15

INTERPRETIVE INSIGHT | *Unshakable Loyalty*

We don't know exactly why Elijah keeps telling Elisha to stay behind. Maybe Elijah wants to face the end alone. Maybe he's afraid what he is going to experience will be too much for Elisha to handle. Maybe it is a test to see if Elisha proves to be a follower of unshakable loyalty. No matter what the reason, the result is clear to see. Elisha is so committed to following his leader that he proves a level of loyalty that is tenacious and unshakable. Like a bulldog with his teeth locked onto a steak, Elisha will not let go of his mentor and friend.

Not only is there no jealousy or rivalry between these men, there is deep affection and God-honoring friendship. When the torch is passed the right way, it can create extraordinary oneness and community.

NARRATIVE ON THE TEXT | *A Wonderful Gift*

Finally the two of them come to the Jordan River. They know their time together is short. Elijah takes off his mantle — the same one he spread over Elisha so long ago — wraps it up, and strikes the River Jordan. Just as the water separated a long time ago for Moses and for Joshua, now it separates for Elijah.

The two of them cross over together on dry ground. They leave the Promised Land, the ordinary world, for an extraordinary event. At this decisive moment Elijah does a wonderful thing. He is about to leave this world and Elisha's side. But he doesn't give a lot of advice, instructions, or commands. Elijah simply asks Elisha one last question.

Like all great questions, this one is a little bit of a test. It's a little like the question God asked Solomon, "What do you want if I could give you anything?" Specifically, Elijah asks Elisha, "What can I do for you before I am taken from you?" What a great

ON THE LIGHTER SIDE | *A Teachable Spirit*

A father was sitting in church with his three-year-old son. The message was being given and the boy was really paying attention. But, the little boy was also wiggling and it looked as if he might have to go to the bathroom. Finally the little boy expressed the problem to his dad. He said, "Dad, I gotta go potty, but I don't want to miss this point."

That is a teachable spirit! That is a little boy who will learn much, because his heart longs to learn, even beyond the capacity of his little bladder.

NEW TESTAMENT CONNECTION

The Volunteering Heart of God

A scholar named Brackley notices the fundamental heart of a volunteer is much like the heart of God. He says, "This is moving to us, because it flows out of the nature of a God who voluntarily gives himself to his people." In John 10:17–18 we read:

> "The reason my Father loves me is that I lay down my life – only to take it up again. No one takes it from me, but I lay it down of my own accord. I have authority to lay it down and authority to take it up again. This command I received from my Father."

Jesus reveals the heart of a volunteer. His life declares this message: "I volunteered to leave heavenly glory; I volunteered to be born in a stable; I volunteered to suffer and die on a cross. I willingly chose this assignment. I didn't have to do it, but I gladly volunteered!"

The Father loves to see a volunteer stand up and say, "I will do it!" That's why the church has always been, and always will be, fundamentally a volunteer-based organization.

question! This is a question that every torch-passer should learn to ask, "What can I do for you?"

LIFE APPLICATION | *How Can I Help You Become All God Wants You to Be?*

Before we look at Elisha's response, think of those to whom you are called to pass the torch. How often do you say, "What can I do for you?" How often do you ask them how God might use you to help them become more of what he wants? How can you begin asking the kind of questions that will help you learn how God can use you more effectively as a bearer of the torch and passer of the flame?

NARRATIVE ON THE TEXT | *The Flame Is Passed*

Elisha asks for exactly the right thing. Elijah lets him know that what he has asked for is difficult, but not impossible. When it comes to choosing his successor, in the final view, no mere human being can do that. Elijah can help, shape, and encourage, but ultimately Elisha's work is between him and God.

But Elijah says, "If you see me when I'm taken from you, it will be yours." Tension is now introduced to the story. Not only is Elisha going to lose Elijah, but he doesn't know if his own ministry is just beginning or about to end.

As they wait to see what God is going to do, they walk together. This is a beautiful picture of two friends walking along the Jordan side by side. We can only imagine what is going through their minds. They have traveled so many miles together. God has used them to do amazing things. They have forged a friendship. Soon, Elisha will be alone. What will his future look like?

Suddenly, out of nowhere, a chariot of fire and horses of fire appear, and Elijah and Elisha are separated from each other. Elijah is swept up into the arms of God, and Elisha is left behind. Elisha cries out, "My father! My father!" He sees the whole thing. His friend, mentor, and leader is gone so he tears his garments — a sign of grief and loss.

Elisha looks down on the ground and sees Elijah's cloak. It's his reminder of the torch that's been passed to him. He picks up the mantle, walks back, and stands on the bank of the Jordan. What a pivotal moment in Elisha's life. He takes the cloak and rolls it up, just as he had seen Elijah do. He lifts his arm, just as he had seen Elijah do. Then, he swallows hard and gets ready, and he strikes the water of the Jordan.

The water parts, and Elisha crosses on dry ground. The mantle has been passed, the Spirit is alive in Elisha, and he is ready to be a torchbearer for God.

NARRATIVE ON LIFE | *God's Work through Elisha*

The God of Elijah has become the God of Elisha. This prophet goes on to have an extraordinary life that parallels Elijah's in many ways. He dictates battle strategies to the kings of Israel and Judah. He challenges the most powerful people in society with utter fearlessness. He helps a powerless, impoverished widow in a time of need. These are all things Elijah has done. Elisha has learned well at the feet of the master prophet, and along the way, he became a great prophet as well.

CREATIVE MESSAGE IDEA | *Map Time*

You may want to show the route Elijah and Elisha take as they walk together on their final journey. There are slides in the PowerPoint presentation on the included DVD-ROM that show where they travel.

HISTORICAL CONTEXT | *A Double Portion*

Elisha's answer to Elijah's question can be confusing if we don't understand the historical context behind it. Elisha says, "Let me inherit a double portion of your spirit." This can sound a little greedy. It can almost sound as if he is saying, "Elijah, however much of the Holy Spirit you have, I want twice as much. I want twice as much power as you and I want to do twice as many miracles."

Sometimes people have taken this to mean that the Spirit can come in different percentages in different people. For example, "You might be filled with 23 percent of the Spirit, I'm 46 percent filled up, and Billy Graham is probably 99 percent filled with the Spirit." Is that what Elisha is communicating? It does not seem so.

Elisha is using classic inheritance language. Back in Deuteronomy 21:17 God said that the heir – the firstborn – is to receive a double portion of the inheritance. To ask for the double portion is to ask to be someone's heir. That's what it means here. The double portion is that which goes to the heir. Elisha even uses this explicit word: "Let me inherit it."

Elisha is not asking for two helpings of the Spirit. He's saying, "Elijah, I've watched your life and I've seen your ministry. I've witnessed your devotion and the difference you've made. I've seen how Israel is a different place because of your ministry. The power of Baal worship has been broken because of your devotion and courage. I want to continue following in your steps, even after you are gone."

3. Elisha Carries the Flame

SIGNIFICANT SCRIPTURE

2 Kings 4:1–7

NARRATIVE ON THE TEXT | *Don't Ask for Just a Few*

Elisha encounters a woman who is in dire straits. Her sons are about to be sold into slavery. She is deeply in debt and has nowhere to go and no one to help her. So, she runs to Elisha. This woman is sure she has nothing of any value. But, Elisha poses a provocative question. He asks the woman if she has *anything at all* in her house. Her response is, "Your servant has nothing there at all except a little oil."

Elisha tells her that God will miraculously give all the oil she needs so she can sell it and pay off all her debts. His words bring hope that she and her sons will have all they need to live. But, Elisha asks her to do something specific. He has her gather as many jars as she can find. She is to go around to all of her neighbors and ask for every container they can spare. Elisha speaks these words: "Don't ask for just a few."

> I have learned to place myself before God every day as a vessel to be filled with his Holy Spirit. He has filled me with the blessed assurance that he, as the everlasting God, has guaranteed his own work in me.
>
> *Andrew Murray*

LIFE APPLICATION | *A Big-Jar God!*

God gives this widow, her sons, all of Israel, and all who read the Bible an unforgettable lesson. "Don't ask for just a few. If you give God a few jars; he'll fill a few. When we give him a lot of jars, he'll fill a lot." In this story we learn the lesson that our God is a big-jar God! He has the resources to fill every jar we bring to him.

God comes to us today and asks, "What do you have?" We may look and say, "Nothing!" But God says, "Look closer." If all we have is a little oil, God can multiply it and provide all we need. The same God who gave manna in the desert, who delivered meat special delivery by ravens, who sent angels to bring cake in the desert, can fill our jars also. We need to look at the little we have, place it in the hands of our big-jar God, and watch what he can do with it!

SIGNIFICANT SCRIPTURE

2 Kings 6:8–23

NARRATIVE ON THE TEXT | *Who's the Mole?*

Another amazing story about Elisha's ministry and character occurs when the king of Aram is trying to kill the king of Israel. He makes many attempts to assassinate Joram, king of Israel, but every time he makes a plan, God tells Elisha, who in turn passes the information on to the king of Israel. So, every time the king of Aram advances, Joram escapes.

The king of Aram starts to get angry. He can't figure out why the king of Israel is always one step ahead of him. So, the king of Aram starts to ask some questions,

"Who's the mole? Where's the leak? How can Joram know my plans before I execute them?" He is sure there is someone in his camp that is working as a double agent.

His leaders assure him that there is not a mole. They tell him that Elisha has the power to know the very words the king speaks in the privacy of his own bedroom. The king of Aram thus decides that the only way he will ever get to Joram, king of Israel, is to take out Elisha first. So, again, a prophet of God finds out what it is like to be on the death list of a king.

The king of Aram finds out that Elisha has gone to the city of Dothan, so he brings in his army and surrounds the city. They are there for one reason—to capture and assassinate Elisha. Just think about it, one man demands the attack of a whole army.

The next morning Elisha's servant gets up and looks outside of the city. There is a human wall surrounding the city on every side. There are soldiers, chariots, and a military machine that would send fear into the heart of any ordinary man. But Elisha is not an ordinary man, because he serves an extraordinary God. When Elisha's servant looks and sees their situation, all he can see is the apparent power and impenetrable position of the army surrounding the city. When Elisha looks, he sees something very different, so he says to his servant: "Don't be afraid.... Those who are with us are more than those who are with them" (2 Kings 6:16).

INTERPRETIVE INSIGHT | *Spiritual Realities Beyond the Physical*

How do you think Elisha's words sound to his servant as he looks and sees the army surrounding the city? You can almost hear him saying, "How many are with us? Two." And then looking outside the city again, he says, "How many are with them? I can't count that high!" He must have wondered what Elisha is talking about. How can Elisha say that those who are with them are more than the ones who surround the city?

But then, Elisha prays for God to open his servant's eyes and help him see beyond the physical world to the spiritual reality. When God opens the eyes of Elijah's servant, he sees a radically different reality. The hills all around Dothan are full of horses and chariots of fire. The army of God surrounds the army of Aram, and the angels also surround Elisha. Human eyes showed that the odds were in favor of the king of Aram. Spiritual eyes reveal that the King of heaven is with Elisha—and the victory always goes to God!

LIFE APPLICATION | *Open My Eyes!*

Many followers of Christ need to hear the words: "Don't be afraid. Those who are with us are more than those who are with them." Whatever we face—problems, challenges, difficulties, fears, or worries—we all have times we need to shift our eyes from earthly to heavenly realities. Sometimes we need to ask God to show us what is happening in the heavenly realms so that we can walk with courage in this life.

PAUSE FOR PRAYER

As you close in prayer, ask God to make each person a passer of the torch. Thank God for those who serve as volunteers with humble and committed hearts. Pray for your church to be deeply committed to pass on the spiritual legacy God has given you from those who have gone before you.

At other times, we need to pray for faith to believe what our eyes can't see. Like the servant of Elisha, we need to learn that those who are with us, when we stand with the Lord, are always more than those who are with them.

NARRATIVE ON THE TEXT | *Shocking Compassion*

There is a postscript to the story of Elisha's servant learning that "those who are with us are more than those who are with them." Elisha prays for God to blind the entire army. Once they are blind, Elisha leads them into the capital city of Israel. This is the home city of King Joram, who the king of Aram has been plotting to kill. Once they are in the city and surrounded by the army of Israel, God opens their eyes and they realize that they are in big trouble.

The king of Israel asks Elisha if he should execute the entire army. Elisha says, "I have a better idea! Let's have them sit down and let's serve them a feast!" And that is exactly what they do. Elisha exercises shocking compassion and grace. The postscript to the postscript is that the army of Aram stops raiding and harassing the people of Israel. Is that any surprise?

NEW TESTAMENT CONNECTION | *He Who Is in You*

The lesson learned by Elisha's servant is reinforced many times and in many ways in the New Testament. Two passages that hit this theme hard are:

> You, dear children, are from God and have overcome them, because the one who is in you is greater than the one who is in the world. (1 John 4:4)

> Finally, be strong in the Lord and in his mighty power. Put on the full armor of God so that you can take your stand against the devil's schemes. For our struggle is not against flesh and blood, but against the rulers, against the authorities, against the powers of this dark world and against the spiritual forces of evil in the heavenly realms. Therefore put on the full armor of God, so that when the day of evil comes, you may be able to stand your ground, and after you have done everything, to stand. (Ephesians 6:10–13)

Over and over the Scriptures remind us that there is a spiritual reality beyond the physical world we see day in and day out. But in the battles we face, God is always able to bring the victory.

LIFE APPLICATION | *Growing in Compassion*

Elisha shocks the people of Israel, the king of Israel, and certainly the army of Aram. When is the last time someone was shocked by the compassion they saw exhibited in your life? When is the last time you exercised radical compassion that revealed the deep love of God for people who don't deserve forgiveness and grace? Why not take time to think of someone who could use a dose of compassion and then ask God to help you be the one to deliver it.

CREATIVE MESSAGE IDEA | *A Time to Bless!*

You may want to close this message by taking time to bless and affirm those in your church who have committed themselves to humble volunteer service. There are countless ways this happens in the church, but identify some of the examples of this and celebrate those people who have heard the call and followed God into a life of serving. Remind them that the heart of Jesus beats loudly through their example no matter where they serve:

- in the nursery
- as a children's teacher
- in youth ministry
- in prayer ministry
- in counseling and visitation
- on a church board
- in women's or men's ministry
- as a missionary at home or abroad
- and the list goes on and on!

Message 27

Amos: How to Measure a Life

Deuteronomy 24:12–22; Amos 1:1–4:3; 5:21–24; 7:1–9

THE HEART OF THE Message

In a critical time of Israel's history, God spoke through Amos to give the people a serious wake-up call. The time of Amos's ministry was one of great affluence and peace. Not since the days of Solomon could the people remember a time when things were going so well in their nation. The economy was strong, and those who were rich just seemed to be getting richer! It seemed everyone was reaping the benefits of this season of God's blessing—except those who were poor.

BRIEF MESSAGE OUTLINE

1. Meeting Amos
2. Hearing Amos
3. The message of Amos
4. The warning and challenge of Amos

As we read the book of Amos, it quickly becomes apparent that the rich were indeed getting richer. At the same time, however, the poor were getting poorer and, in some ways, the wealth of the rich was being amassed at the expense of the poor and through unjust practices.

God intervenes and calls Amos to speak to the nation. He calls them to justice, righteousness, and compassion. God is deeply concerned for the plight of all those who are marginalized and calls his people to adopt a new attitude and lifestyle that reflect his care for the poor and oppressed.

This message has a great deal to say to those who live in affluence. The warnings and exhortations from Amos echo throughout the millennia and speak to the church and followers of Christ in our day. If we listen closely, we can hear the call from complacency to acts of justice and compassion.

THE HEART OF THE Messenger

Anyone who lives in an affluent society can be tempted to consume more and express less compassion with each passing year. Followers of Jesus need to do a close lifestyle examination to be sure that they are living with a generous spirit, a heart of compassion, and eyes that are always open to the needs of the poor and the outcast. As a leader, take time to do a personal life examination. Invite the Holy Spirit to show you areas of your life and behaviors that might lead to injustice. Take all you have, and all you are, and place it before the Lord. Ask him to use these resources to bring glory to him and blessing to others.

SIGNIFICANT SCRIPTURE

Amos 1–3

1. Meeting Amos

NARRATIVE ON THE TEXT | *Meeting Amos*

Amos lived and ministered around 750 BC. He was *not* a professional prophet. Rather, he was a farmer. He took care of a few sheep and tended some fig trees. He was from

CREATIVE MESSAGE IDEA | *Bold Words*

What's the boldest thing you have ever said to somebody? What's the one statement you made that took more guts than you knew you had? What was it that moved you to a place of speaking with this level of boldness?

The Bible is filled with examples of people who spoke words of amazing boldness. Here are just a few examples.

(1) When David faced Goliath and this human tank threatened to give his flesh to the birds and animals of the field (and he meant this literally), this was David's response:

> "You come against me with sword and spear and javelin, but I come against you in the name of the LORD Almighty, the God of the armies of Israel, whom you have defied. This day the LORD will hand you over to me, and I'll strike you down and cut off your head. Today I will give the carcasses of the Philistine army to the birds of the air and the beasts of the earth, and the whole world will know that there is a God in Israel." (1 Samuel 17:45–46)

(2) When John the Baptist met the religious leaders of his day, this was his greeting:

> "You brood of vipers! Who warned you to flee from the coming wrath? Produce fruit in keeping with repentance. And do not think you can say to yourselves, 'We have Abraham as our father.' I tell you that out of these stones God can raise up children for Abraham. The ax is already at the root of the trees, and every tree that does not produce good fruit will be cut down and thrown into the fire." (Matthew 3:7–10)

(3) When the apostle Paul stood before King Agrippa and boldly presented the gospel, Agrippa asked this question:"Do you think that in such a short time you can persuade me to be a Christian?" Paul's response is heartfelt and incredibly bold:

> "Short time or long–I pray God that not only you but all who are listening to me today may become what I am, except for these chains." (Acts 26:29)

If you have someone in your church who can help you develop a short video, it might be fun to collect a number of short accounts of people telling about the most bold thing they ever said. These statements might be serious or humorous. You could show this brief video at the start of this section of the message.

a little town near Bethlehem called Tekoa, in the southern kingdom (Judah). One day, God called this man to leave his sheep and go proclaim God's word. God did not call Amos to preach in Judah, his hometown, but to go up to the northern kingdom (Israel) and preach there.

ON THE LIGHTER SIDE

Finding Amos

Invite people to turn to the book of Amos. If they seem to have a hard time finding this brief prophetic book tucked away in the Minor Prophets of the Old Testament, tell them that it is right before Obadiah. All they have to do is find Obadiah (a one-chapter book) and go back a book.

2. Hearing Amos

INTERPRETIVE INSIGHT | *When Things Are Going Great!*

At the time that Amos is called to prophesy, the northern kingdom (Israel) is enjoying political success and economic prosperity unknown since the days of Solomon. The people in the northern kingdom who have wealth are real happy with the way their lives are going. Investments are paying great interest and the market is strong, to put things in modern terms. If you have money to invest, you are sure to become even richer! God sends Amos to Samaria, the capital city of the northern kingdom. Samaria is the center of wealth and power in Israel—New York City and Washington, D.C., combined.

NARRATIVE ON THE TEXT | *A Brilliant Set-Up!*

When Amos shows up in Samaria and begins to preach, we can be confident that the people are wondering what the new prophet from Judah (the southern kingdom) will say. When they hear his opening words about judgment on Damascus, the capital city of the Aramean state, they are thrilled. The Arameans are a bitter enemy and a constant threat to Israel. All who hear will undoubtedly stop and wait to hear more. Their initial response would be, "I like this prophet! He must be from God because he is speaking against our enemies! I want to hear more from this new prophetic voice." In the Creative Message Idea (see page 418), however, you can see how Amos is setting up this people for some shocking news.

3. The Message of Amos

INTERPRETIVE INSIGHT | *How You Treat the Poor Really Matters*

When we listen to the words Amos speaks about Israel, it almost sounds as if God sees them as one of his enemies. God appears to lump Israel together with the Arameans, Philistines, Edomites, and the other nations of the world. And that is exactly what God is doing through the words of Amos. He is charging Israel with living as though they were God's enemies.

What's the last straw?

What is the act that sets God's teeth on edge?

What is the third and fourth sin that pushes God over the limit?

Amos is crystal clear on this issue. The sin of Israel is the way they are treating the poor. God has given them abundance and plenty of resources. But instead of helping the poor and oppressed, they are hoarding it all for themselves. They are living in luxury while poverty exists all around them, and they don't even care!

This is amazing. Amos charges Ammon with ripping open the wombs of pregnant women (Amos 1:13) and the Philistines with taking whole communities captive and

CREATIVE MESSAGE IDEA | *Make Some Noise*

In Old Testament days, when a prophet or preacher spoke, the people would often respond out loud to what was said. In other words, if they liked what they were hearing, they would cheer. If they were offended, they might hiss, boo, or even grind their teeth in anger. The message was interactive.

In each of the eight prophetic words to the nations, there are three movements.

1. It begins with the announcement of a nation that has pushed God too far. The people have placed the final straw on the camel's back and have crossed the line. So, God announces that judgment will be coming. At this point, the people may have responded with a gasp of amazement, a sigh of awe, or a cheer of affirmation.
2. Next is an unveiling of what the nation did that has pushed God over the edge. A specific sin, or list of sins, is recorded. At this point the people may have hissed, given a boo, or expressed great shock at the sins of the pagan nations around them.
3. Finally, there was a declaration of judgment on the nation. Amos expresses what God is going to do to this nation for their sin. At this, the people of Israel would be cheering, celebrating, giving high fives, and outwardly expressing their joy that their enemies are finally getting what they deserve!

As you read Amos 1:3 – 2:3, invite people to imagine they are the Israelites hearing these words for the first time. You may even want to have everyone stand as they listen. Invite them to respond, out loud, in a way they think reflects how the people of Israel would feel about what they are hearing. Their bitter enemies, who have persecuted, attacked, and oppressed them for years, are now getting judged by God. You may want to use the visual prompters provided in the PowerPoint on the included DVD-ROM.

When you get to 2:4 – 5, the judgment on Judah (the southern kingdom), pause for a moment. Remind those gathered that Amos is from Judah, and now he is prophesying against his own people. Remind them that Judah and Israel are in a time of regular conflict and war. Then, read Amos 2:4 – 5 and invite people to respond as they feel Israel would respond.

At this point the people of Israel would be applauding and cheering, and if those hearing the message get the point of this exercise, they will be applauding and cheering too! Israel is sure that they are righteous and loved by God and that every other nation is evil and deserves God's judgment. They are thrilled to hear that God is finally going to step in and punish the nations for their sin. This was all good news to Israel.

But, what comes next shocks them all!

Ask for complete silence. Ask everyone to imagine what is going through the minds and hearts of the people of Israel as they hear these words – the words of Amos 2:6 – 16.

selling them to Edom (1:6). But these sins are not nearly as bad in God's eyes as what his own people are doing — trampling the heads of the poor among them and denying justice to the oppressed (2:6–7).

SIGNIFICANT SCRIPTURE

Deuteronomy 24:17–22

LIFE APPLICATION | *Seeking Balance*

God does not say that the people of Israel don't worship enough. He doesn't say that they don't know the Scriptures. He doesn't say a whole lot of things we might have expected him to say. He says, "My heart is broken over the way my people hoard their resources and neglect the poor while they claim to follow and know me."

God is deeply concerned about our worship. He cares very much that we know the teaching of Scripture. God wants us to attend church services and share in life-giving fellowship among his people. But this is not the whole story! When we truly worship God, our hearts are captured by the things that matter to God, and God cares about the poor, the oppressed, and the outcast. When we study the Bible, we should follow what it teaches. This means we must learn from Amos and begin to act in ways that will bring justice for those who are marginalized. God longs to see a balance in the lives of his followers. Spirit-led worship should lead to passionate service and compassionate acts of justice.

Many years earlier, God had spoken through Moses to teach the people the importance of compassion and justice. He said:

> "Do not deprive the alien or the fatherless of justice, or take the cloak of the widow as a pledge. Remember that you were slaves in Egypt and the LORD your God redeemed you from there. That is why I command you to do this." (Deuteronomy 24:17–18)

The people of Israel were always to look back and remember that God had shown them compassion when they were oppressed in Egypt, and they were to live with care for those who were oppressed, outcast, and needy. The community established by God should be marked by compassion and justice.

INTERPRETIVE INSIGHT | *The Heart of God for the Needy*

In Deuteronomy 24:17 we see three groups of people specifically listed. They are the:

- alien
- fatherless
- widow

WORD STUDY

"For Three Sins and for Four"

When Amos begins preaching, he uses a specific formula as he speaks words of judgment on eight different nations. Each time he speaks about a nation, he begins with these words:

> This is what the LORD says:
> "*For three sins* of [city/territory name], *even for four*, I will not turn back my wrath." (Amos 1:3, 6, 9, 11, 13; 2:1, 4, 6)

Then Amos goes on to tell how each nation has offended God and pushed his patience to a breaking point. The phraseology used here, "For three sins and for four," has specific meaning. This is a formal pronouncement of judgment!

In English we might say something like, "That was the straw that broke the camel's back." The words "For three sins and for four" is the Hebrew way of saying, "The camel is in a full-body cast. The people have gone too far. Judgment is coming!"

Since Israel experienced oppression in Egypt, they should be particularly sensitive to those who were in a similar situation. And, since they knew the heart of God, they should extend the same kind of grace and justice that God gives. But just to make sure, God made it explicit.

> "When you are harvesting in your field and you overlook a sheaf, do not go back to get it. Leave it for the *alien*, the *fatherless* and the *widow*, so that the LORD your God may bless you in all the work of your hands. When you beat the olives from

HISTORICAL CONTEXT | *The Writing Prophets*

All through the Bible we see bold words expressed. Amos is no exception. He speaks some of the boldest words in the Bible. In these chapters Amos speaks to the enemies of Israel, to Judah, and then to his own people!

Amos is probably the earliest of what were called the "writing prophets." These are the prophets who have books in their names that contain the story of their lives or the messages God called them to speak. There were other prophets before them, like Elijah and Elisha, but they were not writing prophets. Their stories are recorded by others in the flow of the Old Testament narrative. But Amos, as well as many other prophets, wrote down their messages, which are recorded in the latter part of the Old Testament.

HISTORICAL CONTEXT | *Garment Taken in Pledge*

One of the accusations God levels at the people through the words of Amos is this: "They lie down beside every altar on garments taken in pledge" (2:8). In those days garments were often taken as collateral from the poor. For those who lived on the ragged edge of poverty, sometimes their only possession was a cloak or garment that they wore during the day and used as a blanket at night. If they needed a small loan or if they owed something to another person, this garment could be taken until they paid back what was owed. God strictly commanded, however, that any garment taken in pledge had to be given back at nightfall so the poor person would not freeze.

In Deuteronomy 24:12–13 we read:

> If the man is poor, do not go to sleep with his pledge in your possession. Return his cloak to him by sunset so that he may sleep in it. Then he will thank you, and it will be regarded as a righteous act in the sight of the LORD your God.

But the wealthy people of Israel were taking garments in pledge and failing to give them back at nightfall. On top of that, they were taking these garments into pagan temples, drinking wine, and laying down on them as part of their idolatrous revelry.

Amos points these out as glaring acts of injustice, so that the judgment of God is coming, and you can be sure the people of Israel are not cheering anymore.

CREATIVE VIDEO ELEMENT

Personal Story: St. Charles Place (4:40 min.) This interview segment shows the impact we can have on the world when people reach out to the needy.

your trees, do not go over the branches a second time. Leave what remains for the *alien*, the *fatherless* and the *widow*. When you harvest the grapes in your vineyard, do not go over the vines again. Leave what remains for the *alien*, the *fatherless* and the *widow*. Remember that you were slaves in Egypt. That is why I command you to do this." (Deuteronomy 24:19–22)

There is no way to miss the refrain in this passage. Moreover, this same concern is found throughout the Old Testament. God cares about those who cannot care for themselves, and he expects his followers to care too.

> We choose to be poor for the love of God. In the service of the poorest of the poor, we are feeding the hungry Christ, clothing the naked Christ, and giving shelter to the homeless Christ.
>
> *Mother Teresa of Calcutta*

LIFE APPLICATION | *The Marginalized of Our Day*

Every society and generation must face the reality that there are groups that can be easily marginalized. In the days of Amos, as we have seen, it was the alien, the fatherless, and the widow. Our responsibility is to discern where these groups exist in our society and then seek to extend the compassion and tender love of God toward these people. We need to seek justice for those who are treated with injustice. The particular groups of people may change with varied contexts, but there will always be marginalized people groups, and God will always expect his children to seek them out and extend justice and mercy toward them.

The marginalized could be persons of color, immigrants, senior citizens, teenagers, people with physical or mental disabilities, or some minority group, but every society that has ever existed has them. It is so important that we understand the heart of God toward these people and take actions that communicate God's love for the outcasts.

PAUSE FOR PRAYER

Search Our Hearts, O God!

You can use the prayer below, or your own prayer, to invite the Holy Spirit to speak to each heart through the words of Amos.

> Holy Spirit of God, search our hearts today. Spare us from the folly of listening to your Word and judging others by what we hear. Please help each of us see where injustice rules in our heart and life. Help us see where we are in need of conviction, challenge, and change.
>
> We confess that we can be quick to judge others while we absolve ourselves of any responsibility for our choices and actions. Teach us justice and change our hearts and lives to reflect what you want for us and the world we live in. Spirit of God, speak to us in power and open our ears to hear, our hearts to receive, and our lives to be transformed!
>
> We pray this in the name of Jesus. Amen.

SIGNIFICANT SCRIPTURE

Deuteronomy 24:12–13

NARRATIVE ON LIFE | *How God Sees a Society*

God says he will judge a society by the way it treats marginalized people. God makes it unmistakably clear that he takes it on himself to be the protector of the weak and outcast in a society. Anybody who neglects them neglects him. Anybody who oppresses them oppresses him.

SIGNIFICANT SCRIPTURE

Amos 2:6 and 3:15

> He who is kind to the poor lends to the LORD, and he will reward him for what he has done. (Proverbs 19:17)
>
> A father to the fatherless, a defender of widows, is God in his holy dwelling. (Psalm 68:5)

Throughout the Old Testament God expresses his heart toward the marginalized and invites us to join in his commitment to bring love and justice to those who often don't receive it.

God, being who he is, cannot cease to be what he is. He cannot act out of character with himself. Because he is faithful, he is faithful in all his actions.

Millie Stamm

ILLUSTRATION | *The Feet of Mother Teresa*

A story is told of a man who spent time serving with Mother Teresa in Calcutta. Once, while working at her side, he noticed that her feet were badly misshapen. This troubled him, though he did not ask her about it. Later on, he asked somebody in the community about her feet.

HISTORICAL CONTEXT | *The Alien, the Fatherless, and the Widow*

Why was God so concerned for these three groups of people?

Aliens were those people who immigrated into the land of Israel. They were not ethnic Israelites, so they did not have the same rights and privileges as the people of Israel. The *fatherless* were those who had been orphaned and had no one to provide for them or to look out for them. The *widows* were women who had lost their husbands; in the patriarchal society in which they lived, these people were without legal and political power or economic means.

In our day these are called marginalized people. They are the groups that will most likely be forgotten, mistreated, oppressed, and broken if someone does not speak up. God is concerned for them because they need someone to help them, to speak for them, to love them.

He was told that among the poor there are never enough shoes. Mother Teresa always insisted that when shoes were donated, the best pairs always be given away to the most poor. She always took the worst for herself—whatever was left over. As the years passed, her feet became badly deformed. For Mother Teresa, consistent acts of compassion for the poor cost her something. Compassion always does.

NEW TESTAMENT CONNECTION

The Least of These

Jesus affirms the heart of God for those who are outcast. He too speaks of the hungry, imprisoned, sick, and marginalized and is emphatic that how we treat these people reflects how we see God. Listen to his words: "I tell you the truth, whatever you did for one of the least of these brothers of mine, you did for me" (Matthew 25:40). A close study of Matthew 25:31–46 will affirm that he has the same heart toward the outcast and the needy as God the Father expresses throughout the Old Testament.

INTERPRETIVE INSIGHT | *A Look at What Is Really of Worth*

Amos hits the people of Israel right where they live. He lets them know that God sees their greed and devaluation of human life. To many of these people a human life was worth as much as a pair of sandals. In many cases, people valued a pair of their shoes more than a person.

Over time, many of the people became so wealthy that they built winter and summer homes. They invested all their money in creating luxurious places to live and had nothing left to give the poor. God lets the people know that their opulent lifestyle and hard hearts will lead to their downfall. God speaks through Amos and says, "I will tear down the winter house along with the summer house; the houses adorned with ivory will be destroyed and the mansions will be demolished."

ILLUSTRATION | *Getting a Little Justice*

The first Mayor Daley of Chicago was famous for many things. One of them was his great self-confidence and brashness. He was approached once by one of his speechwriters who said, "Mayor Daley, I'm not making enough money." Daley's response was, "I'm not going to give you any more money. It ought to be enough that you work for a great American hero like me." That was the end of the discussion, or so he thought.

Several weeks later, Daley was on his way to give a speech. He was famous for never reading his speeches before he got up to deliver them. In this case, he got up to

HISTORICAL CONTEXT | *Archaeological Evidence*

In the days of Amos there was a shocking disparity between the rich and the poor. Archaeologists have confirmed this through various finds over the years. Back when Canaan was first populated, God gave equal property to all the tribes. Everybody lived at a fairly modest level. Archaeological evidence shows that houses from the tenth century BC are all fairly similar. But by the time we reach Amos's day (the eighth century BC), archaeologists find evidence of enormous mansions for the rich and miserable hovels for the poor.

give a speech to a large group of veterans on a Veterans Day celebration. It was getting national press coverage.

Daley began the speech, and as he delivered it, he was quite impressed with how eloquent and passionate it was. He talked about how everybody had forgotten the veterans. Then he assured them, "I remember and I care." He said, "Today I am proposing a seventeen-point program — national, state, and citywide — to take care of the veterans of our country."

By this time everyone was on the edge of their seat. They wanted to find out what he was going to say next. They were excited to hear about this elaborate and expansive plan to care for the veterans. The truth is, at this point Mayor Daley was pretty interested himself. He couldn't wait to find out what he was going to say next. So, he turned the page over and all it said was, "You're on your own now, you great American hero."

This story has been floating around for years. It might be true or it might be apocryphal, but it is a great example of someone getting the justice he deserved. We all love a story when wrongs are made right and injustice is stamped out.

INTERPRETIVE INSIGHT | *Do You Think God Fails to Notice?*

The people of Israel knew the words of Deuteronomy that called them to justice and compassion. They had simply decided they did not want to follow this teaching. It almost seems as if they believed God had forgotten or failed to notice what they were doing. They had reached a point where they felt they were entitled to all the money and power they could gather. In their blindness they betrayed God's vision for a just, compassionate society.

So Amos says to them, "Do you think God was just joking when he gave his law? Do you think God doesn't see what's going on? Do you think God doesn't care about these people he has defended for so long? Do you really think that you can take all of your resources, which all come from God's hand, and use them in whatever way you choose to just enrich yourself?" The people had become so blind to the plight of the poor and so numb to the cry of the oppressed that they actually were getting mad at God for not giving them even more.

SIGNIFICANT SCRIPTURE

Amos 4:1 – 3

NARRATIVE ON THE TEXT | *A Word to the Women of Israel*

Amos uses any tool he can to try to wake up people from their complacency. He gives a specific word to the women who are living in opulent wealth:

> Hear this word, you cows of Bashan on Mount Samaria, you women who oppress the poor and crush the needy and say to your husbands, "Bring us some drinks!" (Amos 4:1)

Ouch!

Amos is calling the wives of the wealthy and powerful "cows of Bashan." Do you think they feel complimented by this? Bashan was a fertile area. The cows there were famous for being well fed and large! That's why he calls the women "cows of Bashan."

This is not just random name-calling. Think about the nature of a cow. Cows are not notable for their good works. Cows are just a walking appetite. They actually have four stomachs and are eating machines. They consume — it's what they do best! The only question they ask is, "Where can I get more?"

NARRATIVE ON LIFE | *The "Cows of Bashan Syndrome"*

We live in a society that often encourages us to live like cows of Bashan. Our media culture wants us to become walking appetites for money, food, and pleasure. The questions many of us ask are:

How can I get a bigger house?

How can I get a larger income?

How can I drive a newer car?

How can I have greater sexual pleasure?

How can I be more attractive?

Our culture has become effective in producing cows of Bashan. This reality should cause every follower of Jesus to evaluate his or her life and motives closely.

The deeper problem for the people of Israel was that they made no connection between their treatment of the poor and their relationship with God. We can fall into this same pattern. We can worship, give our offerings, and feel pretty good about ourselves, but our hearts might still be hard toward those who are poor and outcast. God wants to get into our hearts and help us feel as he does for the poor. Then, he wants to transform our lifestyle and teach us to be generous toward the marginalized and needy.

ILLUSTRATION | *The Games We Play*

There are many board games that children play as they are growing up. Think for a moment about Monopoly. The goal of this game is to gain all of the property and wealth possible. In doing so, it demands that a player take money from others, and if necessary, send them to the poorhouse. Another classic game is Risk, a game whose goal is a little broader than Monopoly. In Risk, the goal is to conquer the whole world. To win, a player must go to war and defeat every other player until their players cover the face of the earth.

This is not meant to be a criticism of these board games. It is simply an observation. The games we play growing up can reinforce the idea that gaining wealth and power is the goal of life. God has a very different vision for us to see.

4. The Warning and Challenge of Amos

SIGNIFICANT SCRIPTURE

Amos 5:21 – 24

INTERPRETIVE INSIGHT | *When Injustice Meets Worship*

Imagine the shock waves going through the crowd when they hear Amos claiming that God says he hates their worship and religious observance. They have never heard such a thing. What can this mean? Amos cries out:

> "I hate, I despise your religious feasts;
> I cannot stand your assemblies.
> Even though you bring me burnt offerings and grain offerings,
> I will not accept them.
> Though you bring choice fellowship offerings,
> I will have no regard for them.
> Away with the noise of your songs!
> I will not listen to the music of your harps." (Amos 5:21 – 23)

God is saying to the people, "Your worship and your lives can't be separated!" They want to hoard wealth, trample on the poor, oppress the weak, and then show up for church as if God doesn't notice any of their behavior. God is clear that life does not work this way. Injustice and authentic worship cannot coexist in the life of someone who follows Jesus.

LIFE APPLICATION | *A Call to Justice*

In one of the great statements in all the Bible, Amos unveils the heart of God:

> "But let justice roll on like a river, righteousness like a never-failing stream!" (Amos 5:24)

God is saying, "Let justice and compassion flow out of your lives. Don't sit there eating vast amounts of food at your religious feasts while the poor are starving to death outside your door, and don't congratulate yourselves on how much you love me.

ON THE LIGHTER SIDE | *Plumb Is Plumb*

A wall is either true to plumb or it is not. Carpenters, if you notice, are not really into relativism. They never say things like, "You know, you have your plumb and I have my plumb. We all have our own plumbs really, and if our plumbs should meet, that's a beautiful thing, but if they don't, that's beautiful too." Or, "Don't complain to me if you think your house isn't in plumb, because maybe it's not in plumb for you, but it's in plumb for me." Or, "Don't inflict your plumb on my plumb. We all have our own plumbs." Plumb doesn't work that way.

It is time for the earth to be covered with rivers of righteousness and justice, and my people are the ones I will use to make this dream a reality."

As followers of Jesus we need to identify the ways God can use us to let justice and righteousness flow across this earth. Local churches need to be places where the marginalized know they are welcomed and loved. We even need to go a step further and go out to find those who are outcast and extend the loving mercy of God to them.

If your church has ministries that reach out to the poor, the oppressed, and the marginalized, you may want to introduce these at this time.

SIGNIFICANT SCRIPTURE

Amos 7:1–9

NARRATIVE ON THE TEXT | *Three Pictures of Judgment*

God gives Amos three images, three pictures, of coming judgment. First, God threatens to send locusts. In an agricultural society, a locust swarm meant devastation to the economy and the ecology. Amos cries out, "God, don't do it! Your people can't survive," and God relents. Next, God says he is going to send fire on the land. Again Amos pleads for the nation and says, "Don't do it! It will destroy your people." Once again, God relents. Finally, God gives Amos a third image of judgment. This picture seems less threatening, but it is still shocking. God gives him a vision of a wall and a plumb line.

WORD STUDY

Plumb Line

In ancient days, a plumb line was a standard tool for a builder. It was a very simple tool that was used to be sure a wall was built straight up and down. All it took to make a plumb line was a piece of string, a rock, and gravity.

A builder would hold a string, tie a stone to the end, and let the weight of a stone pull it straight toward the ground. This string would be exactly straight. It could be held up against a wall to see if it was built with integrity. If the wall was straight, or plumb, it could stand. If the plumb line showed that the wall was leaning one way or the other, it would often be torn down and rebuilt.

LIFE APPLICATION | *How Do We Measure Our Lives?*

We don't live in a plumb-line society. In our world, we like to measure ourselves by comparing ourselves to others. We don't like unchanging standards. We can always find somebody who is worse than us, greedier, and further away from God's standards. It's tempting to try to evade God's Word and standards by comparing ourselves to other people or to society as a whole. We can do this in many areas of life:

- *Generosity*: We can say, "My heart's generous. I want to be generous. I just don't have very much money right now. Things are kind of tight. Someday, I'll have more money and then I'll help take care of people who are in need." But for now, we go on spending every dime we have on ourselves.
- *Serving*: We can say, "I'm really busy right now. I'd love to serve people who are in need, but I can't fit it into my schedule. Maybe when I have more time and get on top of things, then I will serve those in need." But, our schedule never seems to open up, and serving never fits into our day planner.
- *Reaching out*: We can say, "I'd love to form a relationship with somebody of a different ethnicity or in a different culture. I'd love to do that. I really want to be part of God's solution to

> breaking down the walls that divide us, but it involves taking risks, and I am not up for that. I will wait for someone else to reach out to me, then maybe I can respond instead of initiate." But time passes and the walls grow higher and higher.

We can measure our lives by comparing ourselves, but God does not. He sets a standard that is radically different than the constantly changing world in which we live. We need to look to his Word, discover his standard, and then ask him for the strength to grow in our devotion to live with the justice, righteousness, and compassion that marks the heart of God.

God says, "I will measure my people by the one standard that counts. And it's a real simple standard. Are there hungry people? Feed them. Are there sick people? Help them. Are there oppressed people? Stick up for them. Are there lonely widows? Visit them. Are there uneducated children? Teach them. Are there people who get rejected because of the color of their skin? Befriend them."

ILLUSTRATION | *When Theory Meets Real Need*

This is a story about a real person who encountered real need. His name was Frank. He was a lawyer in Miami. His wife talked him into going on a mission trip to the

CREATIVE MESSAGE IDEA | *A Wall and a Plumb Line*

To illustrate the concept of a wall being plumb or straight, you may want to have a small section of a wall built where you will be teaching. Also have some twine and a stone (about the size of a fist). While you are talking about a plumb line you can make one. Then, as you talk about how it is used, you can show it. You may want the section of wall to be out of plumb so you can illustrate how God saw the people of Israel. They were an unstable and dangerous wall; they would have to be knocked over before they could be rebuilt.

CREATIVE MESSAGE IDEA | *Project Child Help*

The PowerPoint presentation on the included DVD-ROM has some pictures of Project Child Help. As the pictures are showing, read these words:

God said, "I'm a father to the fatherless."

What do you think seeing this does to the heart of God?

Jesus said, "As you have done it to the least of these, you have done it to me."

Dominican Republic, and he reluctantly agreed. He really thought he would do some scuba diving and get some R & R. What happened was different than he ever dreamed.

One afternoon Frank and his wife found themselves with a doctor friend of theirs. They were on the third floor of a five-story building totally unprepared for what they were about to see. The building was supposed to be a kind of an orphanage. They walked into a room, and immediately they began reeling from the stench of human waste. In that one room they saw dozens of children. Some had cerebral palsy. Others had Down's syndrome. Their doctor friend told them that most of these children had been thrown out like garbage. They were the ones Amos called the "aliens, widows, and orphans." They were society's outcasts.

Frank saw a boy about eight years old kept in a cage three feet tall, three feet long, and three feet wide. He asked why this boy was kept in a cage. He was told the boy was hyperactive and he was in there because it was the only way to control him. No one knew his name. He was like a nameless animal in a cage. He lived among seventy-five naked, deformed, dehydrated, starving orphans.

This place had no running water, no air conditioning, no working toilets, broken windows, decaying walls, and exposed electrical wiring. That was the only world these seventy-five children knew.

PAUSE FOR PRAYER

How Can This Be?

Pray for those who have been swept up into the "cows of Bashan" frenzy of our culture. Ask God to help each person see a new vision of what life can really mean. Pray for those who are seeking to do justice and let righteousness flow like a river. Ask God to bring them joy and strength to continue moving forward. Finally, pray for the local church to grow in a commitment to accomplish God's justice in a world that so desperately needs to see God's love modeled in our actions.

Frank said that when they first got involved, the children would take turns eating. One child would eat on Monday. And then, because there wasn't enough food to go around, that child wouldn't eat again until Wednesday. On the weekends no one received anything to eat at all. A bath consisted of pouring a cup of water on the child. Most of the children lay on the floor, chained to the beds or huddled in cages. They were trapped inside their bodies, unable to communicate, untouched by the outside world, craving for someone to see them, for someone to hold them, for someone to love them.

Frank and his wife, Lori, prayed and felt led to start a venture called Project Child Help. They run it out of their garage. They recruit doctors and nurses — everybody they can — to visit the Dominican Republic with them to help the children who are in need. They collect everything they can. Every time Frank has a vacation, he spends it taking 5,000 pounds of medicine, food, and clothes to the orphanage. American Airlines found out what he was doing, and they ship all the supplies there for free. And now, three years later, there's a little group of children who eat three times a day and who get bathed every day, because Frank and Lori have hired caretakers to be with them.

The lives of these children have dramatically changed because this couple took God's Word seriously. They were willing to go someplace for a couple of days and have their heart broken open by things that break the heart of God. Then, this couple had the courage to take their resources and place them in the hands of God.

NARRATIVE ON LIFE | *The Difference God Can Make Through One Person*

You never know the difference one human being can make. One man—a shepherd named Amos, a collector of figs—had a huge impact on his generation. One couple, who let God get inside of their hearts, is now being used by God to touch the lives of hundreds of children. You never know the difference one person can make. But God does.

Message 28

Isaiah: Pursuing Spiritual Authenticity

Exodus 3:5; 2 Chronicles 26; Isaiah 6; 49:6; Matthew 5:8; Acts 8:26–39

THE HEART OF THE Message

God invites Isaiah into a staggering place of worship. Isaiah sees God, and he is never the same. He learns that true and authentic worship has a price tag. It will cost us all we have and all we are. When we see God in the glory of his holiness, we enter worship as it was meant to be.

No more halfhearted songs, sleepy prayers, and leftovers in the offering plate. The radiance of God's holiness invites us to place our hearts and lives on the altar and to echo the words of Isaiah, "Here am I. Send me."

BRIEF MESSAGE OUTLINE

1. The context: Uzziah's death
2. The confrontation: Seeing God
3. The conversion: Changed by God
4. The call: Led by God

THE HEART OF THE Messenger

We will never learn spiritual authenticity until we come to the throne of God. In the light of his holiness all pretense, facades, and playacting melt away. We learn to be authentic, who we really are, before God's throne.

As you prepare your heart to bring this message, spend time at the throne of God. Speak with him in prayer. Sing to him. Meditate on his Word. Meet with God and ask the Holy Spirit to remove any attitudes or actions that are inauthentic. Ask God to help you see his holiness and to transform you through his presence.

1. The Context: Uzziah's Death

SIGNIFICANT SCRIPTURE

Isaiah 6:1–8

NARRATIVE ON LIFE | *Cost Free or Costly?*

There are actually people who take the time to study things like channel surfing. There really are! Their studies tell us that habitual channel surfing has some negative effects:

- It decreases our attention span.
- It decreases our ability to pay sustained attention — to learn.
- It increases our sense of isolation and passivity.

The obvious question is, if channel surfing sucks away so many hours of our life and gives so little back, why do we do it? The answer, of course, is because it doesn't cost us anything. It's easy to do. There's no effort involved.

In a world where channel surfing has become a national pastime, followers of Jesus need to be careful that we don't take a channel-surfing attitude into our worship experiences. In Isaiah 6 we see a model of worship that is anything but passive! In this passage of the Bible we discover that worship is active and costly. Authentic worship always demands an investment.

ILLUSTRATION | *You Are Here*

Every person who is gathered to hear this message on Isaiah has paid a price already. It takes a commitment to come to a worship service. Some people drove a long distance. Others exerted great energy motivating children to get ready for church. Still others felt emotionally depleted and spent every ounce of their emotional energy reserve just to get dressed and show up. On some level, every person gathered has already made an investment to gather with God's people for worship. The simple fact that you are here and are listening to the message is a reminder that worship costs something — every time.

INTERPRETIVE INSIGHT | *Sustained Attention*

The costly nature of worship goes beyond the investment we make to be sure we can show up and gather with others for a worship service. There is a deeper cost when we

CREATIVE MESSAGE IDEA | *An Interactive Message*

In this message it will be helpful if you can weave in some worship experiences with the teaching. There are worship suggestions at two points during the message, including songs, Scriptures, prayers, and silence. Let people know, from the beginning of the message, that this will be an active and participatory worship experience. Invite them to engage and be active in worship.

decide to worship God. In worship we give the gift of concentrating sustained attention on God. We seek to authentically bring the fullness of our emotional life before God as we worship. We submit to follow the leading and prompting he gives through worship experience. Worship always costs something.

SIGNIFICANT SCRIPTURE

Isaiah 6:1 and 2 Chronicles 26

ILLUSTRATION | *A Long-Term Leader*

Uzziah reigned for a long time. If you do a study of the kings of Israel and Judah, you quickly discover that some of them had short runs as king. But Uzziah ruled in Jerusalem for fifty-two years. Try to get your mind around what it would feel like for an American to have a leader in office for fifty-two years.

To put this into context, think about how many men have held the office of president over the past fifty-two years. To illustrate this there is a PowerPoint slide that lists the following presidents:

- George W. Bush
- Bill Clinton
- George Bush Sr.
- Ronald Reagan
- Jimmy Carter
- Gerald Ford
- Richard Nixon
- Lyndon Johnson
- John F. Kennedy
- Dwight Eisenhower
- Harry Truman

Uzziah's reign spanned the time that all of these men served as president.

HISTORICAL CONTEXT | *The Year Uzziah Died*

Isaiah 6 begins with these words: "In the year that King Uzziah died." The prophet begins this way for some specific reasons. Uzziah became king of Israel when he was only sixteen years old. He was a remarkable leader. Many of his accomplishments are listed in 2 Chronicles 26.

Uzziah was a military genius. He built an army of more than 300,000 soldiers. The Bible says that he built machines designed by skillful men that could shoot arrows and sling large rocks. Under him, the Philistines were finally defeated. Other enemies, like the Ammonites, brought tribute to him.

He was a builder. He fortified the walls of Jerusalem. Under him, Jerusalem was finally safe. He was a technological innovator. He was an economic wizard. He developed a widespread system of cisterns for gathering water and developed Israel's agricultural economy.

Uzziah was also a spiritual leader. He was instructed and trained to follow God by a prophet named Zechariah (not the one who wrote the second to the last book of the Old Testament). The Bible says that he did what was right in the eyes of the Lord.

His fame spread as far as Egypt. With the possible exception of David and Solomon, he was remembered as the most powerful king Israel ever had.

LIFE APPLICATION | *What Do You Do When Uzziah Dies?*

Most of the people of Judah could only remember one leader ruling in Jerusalem. For their whole life, Uzziah had been on the throne. He was their anchor. He was a source of strength and confidence for the nation. He was their king.

Now Uzziah was dead. And Assyria, an emerging superpower, was gobbling up little nations like Judah. The people were getting nervous. If Uzziah was on the throne, he would know what to do. But the king was dead.

What do you do when Uzziah dies?

What do you do when your anchor breaks loose and you feel like you are cut afloat? How do you respond when the very thing you count on falls away? What do you do when:

- you lose your job?
- your tenacity wanes?
- your money runs out?
- your rock-solid relationship begins to shake?
- everything you were counting on begins to unravel and there's no more safety net?

This was the question being asked by the people of Judah in the days of Isaiah. What do you do when Uzziah dies?

Every follower of Jesus has to ask the question: What will I do when the things I place my trust in fall apart and let me down? Where will I look?

ON THE LIGHTER SIDE | *Channel Surfing*

Channel surfing is the exercise of sitting riveted to a TV set and going from channel to channel, often at a fairly rapid pace. Some people can spend a whole evening, a Saturday, or even an entire weekend surfing from channel to channel.

Invite those gathered to a moment of true confessions. Ask the following questions:

- How many of you have ever engaged in an activity known as channel surfing? (Invite people to raise their hands.)
- How many of you found out that channel surfing changed your life for the better?
- When was the last time you heard somebody say, "Last night I channel surfed all night long, from dinner until midnight, and I'm so glad I did. It was such a great experience. I feel like a new person today."

The truth of the matter is that most time spent channel surfing ends up being wasted time. It is the time we unplug our brains, put everything in neutral, and "veg out."

INTERPRETIVE INSIGHT | *The King Is Dead . . . The King Lives!*

Isaiah learned what to do when Uzziah dies. He turns his eyes from the temporary, earthly throne of a man to the eternal throne of God! Uzziah is dead, but God is alive. The throne of Judah is empty, but the throne of heaven is occupied. The king of Judah is gone, but God will never leave. Isaiah needs to remember what we all need to learn, that there is One seated on the throne of heaven and he reigns over the affairs of human beings.

2. The Confrontation: Seeing God

SIGNIFICANT SCRIPTURE

Isaiah 6:2–3;
Exodus 3:5;
Matthew 5:8

INTERPRETIVE INSIGHT | *Heavenly Beings*

As Isaiah sees the glory of the King of heaven, he also sees that God is surrounded by angelic beings. Isaiah tries to use words to communicate this spiritual reality. He points out that the seraphs used two wings to cover their faces. They are covering their faces because of the unspeakable holiness of God. We are told that no one can see God's face and live, and these beings seem to get the point. They are not fallen, but even they don't dare look directly on the glory of God.

HISTORICAL CONTEXT | *Understanding the Hebrew*

Isaiah sees these heavenly beings flying with wings covering their faces and feet. They are crying out, "Holy, holy, holy is the LORD Almighty." We may wonder why the angelic beings declare God's holiness three times. R. C. Sproul helps to clarify by pointing out that in English, we have many ways to emphasize something. If we want to get somebody's attention when we're writing, we can put the words in capital letters, italicize, or use an exclamation!

In the Hebrew language they did not have these options. In ancient Hebrew there were no vowels and little punctuation. There were also no lowercase letters. Hebrew was just a run of consonants with little dots (or else spaces) between words. In other words, the beginning of Isaiah 6 would have read:

N TH YR THT KING WZZH DD

Or, since they read from right to left, it would have been:

DD HZZW GNK THT RY HT N

Isaiah 6:3, then, would look something like this (going left to right):

ND TH WR CLLNG T N NTHR
HL HL HL S TH LRD
LMGHT TH WHL RTH S
FLL F HS GLR

To help those gathered see the complexity of emphasizing something in Hebrew, you can use the slides provided in the PowerPoint presentation.

The main way in the Hebrew language to emphasize something was repetition, repetition, repetition. When the ancient scribes repeated something, it tended to stand out more. The repetition of the word "holy" stands out in Isaiah 6:3. This was the Hebrew way of adding emphasis.

Isaiah also points out that these heavenly beings are covering their feet with another set of wings. Back in those days, feet were a sign of earthliness. They were what connected people to the ground, so covering them was a sign of honor and respect. We see this in Exodus, when God revealed himself to Moses through the burning bush and said: "Take off your sandals, for the place where you are standing is holy ground" (Exodus 3:5).

NEW TESTAMENT CONNECTION

Who Will See God?

We begin to get a sense for the greatness of God's holiness when we see heavenly beings actually covering their faces in his presence. In light of this, we should be amazed at what Jesus says in the Sermon on the Mount. Jesus tells the people: "Blessed are the pure in heart, for they will see God" (Matthew 5:8).

What a staggering reality. Through Jesus Christ we can experience cleansing from sin and a new heart. Through Jesus our hearts are made so pure that we can be confident that one day we will see God face-to-face. We won't have to hide our face, wear a veil, or cover it with anything. We will see the holy God of heaven face-to-face because of the purity that is imparted to us through Jesus.

INTERPRETIVE INSIGHT

The Holiness of God

Sometimes in the Bible a word gets mentioned twice. This was only used when something was very important and needed emphasis. Jesus often would say, "Truly, truly." (The words he used in Greek were actually "Amen, amen.") It was his way of getting the attention of those who were listening, helping them realize that what he was about to say was of the utmost importance.

On a handful of occasions a word gets repeated three times in the Bible. This elevates it to a matter of ultimate importance. But only once in the Old Testament (Isaiah 6:3) and once in the New Testament (Revelation 4:8) is an attribute of God elevated to this level. It is interesting to note that God is never called, "Loving, loving, loving." He is never addressed as, "Just, just, just." Nowhere in all the Bible do we read, "Compassionate, compassionate, compassionate." Although God is absolutely loving, just, and compassionate, these attributes are never repeated three times. Only the holiness of God gets the x3 symbol next to it. Holiness gets to the core of who our God is.

LIFE APPLICATION

Setting Aside Distractions

True worship is always costly. It is the opposite of casual. It involves an investment of self. When we understand the nature of worship, we no longer make casual commitments. We don't say, "If I have time ...," "If it's

ON THE LIGHTER SIDE

"Marcia, Marcia, Marcia!"

Even in English we sometimes use repetition to emphasize what we are saying. One very unsophisticated example can be found in a classic episode of *The Brady Bunch*. Jan, the middle sister in the family, is trying to communicate her frustration about how her older sister, Marcia, seems to get all the attention and that everything always seems to go Marcia's way. What does she say to express her heartfelt frustration?

"Marcia, Marcia, Marcia."

convenient . . . ," "If I like the style . . . ," "When I can get around to it . . ." We don't worship God with a casual spirit. We don't drift in and out of attention as if we are channel surfing.

As we grow in worship, we no longer have an attitude that says, "If something tickles my fancy, then I'll pay attention." We don't worship with a casual attitude. We can't stomach the idea of singing songs about devotion and then go and live the same old self-centered way.

True worship means that we learn to do what the angels did. We come with our whole person before God. We carefully focus our thoughts and our emotions on him. We sing with all our heart, even when we don't really like the tune, because God deserves our undivided praise. We listen intently to the preached word even if the teaching style is not what we like, because we know that God wants to speak each time his Word is opened.

We set aside everything that could distract us, and we strain, with all our strength, to see the Lord seated on his throne. We do all we can to enter the presence of God, who is high and exalted. We stand in awe of his majestic glory, and we respond to him with our voices, bodies, hearts, lives, and all that is in us. When we commit to worship, we purpose in our hearts to take every possible distraction and set it aside because we are going to do the most important thing of all. We are going to worship the God who made us and loves us.

WORD STUDY

Qadosh

It is a challenge to define precisely what "holiness" is. Most people think of moral purity when they try to define holiness. That's an important part of it. But it is not at the core of how we should understand holiness.

The Hebrew word *qadosh* meant separate or set apart. It is something or someone that was wholly other. Imagine the most awe-inspiring moment in your life, where you were so amazed by what you saw, heard, or felt. Take that sense of wonder, mystery, and awe and multiply it by infinity. Only then can you begin to get a glimpse of the effect that God's holiness has on a human being. God is wholly other. There is nothing, no one, like him in all creation. God is an eternally self-sufficient, burning, transcendent, brilliant, perfect being. He is "Holy, holy, holy."

That is why the heavenly beings cry out, "The whole earth is full of his glory." The whole earth can no more contain all of God's glory than a thimble can contain Niagara Falls. This is the God, this holy God, we are called to worship.

3. The Conversion: Changed by God

ILLUSTRATION | *"A Little Crease"*

Isaiah saw himself as he was, and he spoke the truth about his own condition. This is rare indeed! More often, we look at ourselves and downplay our sin and weaknesses. We suffer from something called a self-serving bias. This occurs when we minimize the reality of our sin, the cost of our wrong choices, and the damage we have done to ourselves and others.

Imagine a teenage son who borrows his father's car for the first time. He has permission, and his father has given very detailed instructions on the use of this particular automobile. While pulling into a parking space, the teenage son catches the side of the car on a light post. When he gets out of the car and looks at the damage, he sees a long scrape in the paint and a crease in the body of the car. He calls his father and tries to explain what happened.

"I was being very careful. I didn't see the light post there. It's really just a little scrape and a small crease in the body of the car. I don't think it will cost much to fix it." When the teenage son gives this information,

PAUSE FOR PRAYER

In the Presence of the Holy God

"Holy! Holy! Holy! You are the Lord God Almighty! You love us with a holy love. You forgive us with a holy mercy. We are filled with wonder and amazement at the eternal fellowship of the Trinity. We stand in awe of who you are—one God in three persons: Father, Son, and Holy Spirit. We thank you that you notice us, care for us, and love us with a passion that is beyond our comprehension. We honor you. We offer you our reverence as we lift our worship and praise. We do this all in Jesus' name. Amen."

he really means it. It is dark out. He is not looking really closely. He hopes that it is no big deal. His own self-serving bias leads him to believe it is not a problem and that someone can probably pound the crease out with relative ease.

> We literally could not survive God's holiness. Emotionally, psychologically, we literally could not survive it.
>
> *Dallas Willard*

The next day, in broad daylight, the man at the body shop has a whole different understanding of the extent of the damage. He sees things the way they really are. He knows the real damage, and he knows the cost involved in repairing it. This is not going to be an easy pound-it-out deal. It will be a whole new part deal!

When Isaiah steps into the light of God's holiness, he says, "Woe to me!... I am ruined," because he sees the true condition of his soul. His self-serving bias is gone, and he realizes that only God can remake him.

NARRATIVE ON THE TEXT | *"I Am Ruined!"*

At the throne of God, Isaiah sees the full extent of his ruin and darkness. The sight almost destroys him. Apart from God's grace, Isaiah would be completely destroyed. He is undone when he sees himself in the light of God's holiness. Then, the angel takes a live coal from the altar and brings it to Isaiah. Isaiah stands there and allows it to touch his lips, one of the most sensitive parts of the human body.

Can you imagine what it would be like to have someone approach your mouth with a live coal? Do you think you'd just stand there? Through Isaiah we learn that there is real pain, a real sting, to the process of confession and repentance. Some people think that experiencing grace means they will never feel pain. Isaiah learned that deep grace can often mean feeling deep pain.

INTERPRETIVE INSIGHT | *Redeemed Character*

The goal of God's grace is *not* primarily to spare us from pain. It is to redeem our character. Experiencing remorse and sorrow over our sin is an important part of this process. If you were to ask a judge or parole board whether genuine remorse matters in their decision to let a criminal go free, they will tell you that it is extremely important.

ILLUSTRATION | *When Words Cut Like a Knife*

In his message (found on the included DVD-ROM), John Ortberg tells a story about a time that his words hurt another person very deeply. He also tells about the pain he felt when he realized how deeply he had wounded another person. You might want to tell a story from your own experience about a time you learned how dangerous our unclean lips can be.

ILLUSTRATION | *Hitting Bottom*

Those who have walked through the pain of loving someone who battles alcoholism have heard the term "hitting bottom." This is when a person finally hits a place where he or she sees what alcoholism has done. They see the wasted years, the trashed relationships, the costly lies, the utter selfishness, and the low place they have ended up. In short, they see themselves as they really are.

In a spiritual sense, Isaiah has hit bottom. He sees himself as he really is, and he does not like what he sees. When Isaiah says, "Woe to me!... I am ruined," it is not a matter of neurotic, false guilt. It is the beginning of healing. It is his first step toward grace. When he hits bottom, he begins to look upward!

LIFE APPLICATION | *A Desire to Be Clean*

When we see ourselves as we really are, in the light of God's holiness, we become strongly motivated to be cleansed and made right. Like Isaiah, we are ready to pay whatever price we need to so that we might experience God's healing. Rather than running from the reality of our sinfulness, we are ready to confess it, acknowledge the pain we have caused God and others, and repent.

Christians used to speak of the gift of tears. They would even ask God to give them tears and a broken heart. They would seek the face of God and ask for his light to penetrate their souls and reveal the presence of sin. Their deep desire was that they would be led to a place of authentic repentance that led to cleansing.

CREATIVE MESSAGE IDEA | *An Invitation to Worship*

Consider stopping at this point in the message to spend some time in worship as a congregation. Invite those gathered to seek to be authentic before God during this time. Here are some ideas you can incorporate into worship:

Read: (These can be read in unison or by someone on your worship team.)

- Psalm 99
- Revelation 5:6–14
- Revelation 7:9–17

Sing

- "Holy, Holy, Holy," Reginald Heber/John Dykes
- "Holy, Holy," Jimmy Owens
- "Open the Eyes of My Heart," Paul Baloche
- "We All Bow Down," Lenny LeBlanc

Pray, celebrating the majesty and holiness of God

- If it would fit into your service, invite people to offer short prayers out loud (be sure to provide a microphone if needed).
- If it would fit into your style of worship, invite people to gather in clusters of three and four people and offer up short prayers.
- You may want to use the prayer supplied on page 438.

Invite those gathered to enter a time of private confession and repentance. Ask God to show each person what they need to see in themselves. As people are in this time of quiet prayer and reflection, you might want to share a few prompting thoughts:

- Maybe there is an attitude of jealousy, judgment, or anger God wants to speak to you about.
- Maybe you are driven by the wrong things.
- Maybe there is something you did that has hurt another person and it needs to be set right.
- Maybe you battle with a mouth that lies, slanders, or gossips.
- Maybe you struggle with pride in your heart.
- Maybe God wants you to see that you have a heart that is cold and loveless.

Take a quiet time of confession and ask God for healing.

PAUSE FOR PRAYER

Ask God to tear down division in your city and to build unity among all people. Ask God to build strong churches in every neighborhood. Pray for unity among churches that serve Jesus. Ask God to help each person gathered to offer their life to him in a new way, saying, "Here I am, Lord, send me!"

4. The Call: Led by God

INTERPRETIVE INSIGHT | *Moving into Action*

God doesn't cleanse Isaiah just for his own sake. God has a calling for him. He says, "Whom shall I send? And who will go for us?" Of course, God is not perplexed about this. He asks the question so that Isaiah can freely choose to go.

WORD STUDY | *Woe*

When Isaiah sees the living, holy God, his first response is not excitement. He does not celebrate that he's been singled out for something special. He doesn't start thinking about how he can impress other people with his amazing spiritual experience. He says, "Woe ..." That's a very important, prophetic word. It was the word the prophets used to pronounce judgment. All through the Prophets, the word "woe" is a flag that indicates words of judgment will follow. Likewise, when Jesus spoke of God's judgment on the religious leaders of his day, he said, "Woe to you, teachers of the law and Pharisees, you hypocrites!" (Matthew 23:23, 25, 27, 29).

What is unique and unprecedented about Isaiah is that when he says "Woe," he is getting ready to pronounce judgment *on himself*. He says, "Woe to me!... I am ruined!" The prophets often said "Woe" as they spoke of God's judgment on nations, but Isaiah alone declares a "Woe" on himself. When Isaiah sees the holiness of God, it causes him to see the full extent of the darkness in his own being. He is shattered. The true condition of the depths of his soul – his real thoughts, motives, desires, petty cruelty, and the unrelenting selfishness – becomes visible to him for the first time, and he is horrified. Only one word makes sense at a moment like that: "Woe!"

Isaiah says, "Here am I. Send me!" Spiritually authentic worship always ends with a heart that is willing to follow God. Worship is never just about having an intense emotional experience. It's never simply about how I feel when I am done. Authentic worship always costs something. It costs us a submitted life.

SIGNIFICANT SCRIPTURE

Isaiah 6:8–9; 49:6;
Acts 8:26–39

LIFE APPLICATION | *Radical Reconciliation*

Close with a challenge for those gathered to seek healing and restoration wherever there are broken relationships. If your church has ministries that are seeking God's

NEW TESTAMENT CONNECTION | *A New Day*

In Acts 8:26–39 we read about Philip's encounter with an Ethiopian eunuch. This man was excluded from Israel on multiple levels, but again we see God's arms wide open. Here we see that everyone is welcome, if they will only come through faith in Jesus.

In this story Philip was led by the Holy Spirit to encounter a man who was a foreigner and a eunuch. God tells Philip, "I want this man included in my people."

Here is a bonus question: When Philip met this man, he was reading from a book in the Old Testament. Which one was it? Right! It was Isaiah!

After a conversation and a time of teaching, the Holy Spirit inspired Philip to offer baptism to this man. In that moment, through faith in Jesus, this foreign eunuch became part of God's family.

Jesus also addressed this issue of the open arms of the Father. He said: "My house will be called a house of prayer for all nations" (Mark 11:17).

NEW TESTAMENT CONNECTION | *Time to Mourn*

For true repentance to take place, we must set aside denial, rationalization, and excuses. We must reflect on what we have done from the perspective of those we have hurt. We must be willing to see ourselves as we truly are and allow our hearts to be broken when we see the depth and costliness of our sin. This is why James says:

> Come near to God and he will come near to you. Wash your hands, you sinners, and purify your hearts, you double-minded. Grieve, mourn and wail. Change your laughter to mourning and your joy to gloom. Humble yourselves before the Lord, and he will lift you up. (James 4:8–10)

Notice the verbs in the middle of that text—*grieve, mourn and wail*. This is a command. James is not talking about wallowing in neurotic guilt. He is talking about entering deeply into God's sorrow over sin.

reconciliation with those who have been outsiders, highlight these ministries and encourage involvement.

> My soul is like a mirror in which the glory of God is reflected, but sin, however insignificant, covers the mirror with smoke.
>
> *Saint Theresa*

HISTORICAL CONTEXT | *Who Is Welcome?*

Later in the book of Isaiah we get more insight into the call of Isaiah. We read these words spoken by God:

> "It is too small a thing for you to be
> my servant
> to restore the tribes of Jacob
> and bring back those of Israel I
> have kept.
> I will also make you a light for the
> Gentiles,
> that you may bring my salvation to
> the ends of the earth." (Isaiah
> 49:6)

This idea of God being a light for all the Gentiles is radical and new. Up to this point, God's people considered those who belonged to the nations as excluded from God's love and plan. Foreigners were not thought to be welcome, eunuchs were excluded, and many others were not invited. But now, everything is going to change. Everyone will be welcome!

CREATIVE MESSAGE IDEA | *Confession and Forgiveness*

Songs

- "Just as I Am," Charlotte Elliott/William Bradbury
- "Whiter than Snow," James Nicholson/William Fischer
- "Create in Me a Clean Heart," Norman Johnson

Scriptures

- Isaiah 6:7
- Psalm 51
- Psalm 103:8–12
- 1 John 1:8–9

Prayer

Pray for each person to experience the freedom that comes with forgiveness for all who confess their sins through Jesus Christ. Ask the Holy Spirit to grant the power needed to resist sin and walk in holiness.

Sharing

When we confess and repent, we don't stop there. We need to hear God's promise of forgiveness. Since we are a priesthood of believers (1 Peter 2:9), we can remind each other of the truth that true confession always leads to forgiveness and a new beginning.

Invite those gathered to turn to someone and say something like, "Through Jesus, your sins are forgiven."

Message 29

Hezekiah: Radical Trust

2 Kings 16:7–8; Isaiah 7:1–8:18; 36:1–37:38

THE HEART OF THE Message

The history of the Old Testament records the stories of two radically different kings of Judah. Ahaz is an example of a life driven by fear. Rather than placing his trust in God, he trusts in military might and political alliances. In contrast, King Hezekiah stands as an example of radical trust in God. Rather than take the easy route of establishing strategic military and political alliances, he looks to God as his source of strength.

God invites us into a relationship based on trust. Though we live in a world that can cause great fear and anxiety, God offers another path. Radical trust is God's plan for all followers of Jesus. Through the example of Ahaz we learn of the folly of fear, and through the life of Hezekiah, the pathway of trust.

THE HEART OF THE Messenger

Many devoted followers of Jesus face ongoing battles with fear and anxiety, but it really is possible to live with a deep level of trust in God. The apostle Paul gives this exhortation:

> Do not be anxious about anything, but in everything, by prayer and petition, with thanksgiving, present your requests to God. And the peace of God, which transcends all understanding, will guard your hearts and your minds in Christ Jesus. (Philippians 4:6–7)

BRIEF MESSAGE OUTLINE

1. Understanding the times
2. The example of Ahaz: Fear and folding
3. The example of Hezekiah: Radical trust

As you prepare to bring this message, take time to examine your heart and life. Are there places where anxiety and fear have control? Maybe you have faced a conflict with someone in your church and it is causing you to worry. Possibly your ministry is facing financial pressures and you are dealing with anxiety over this. Lay any area of anxiety you are facing before God in prayer and ask him to help you learn to walk in deeper levels of trust.

1. Understanding the Times

NARRATIVE ON THE TEXT | *Empire-Building*

As we read the Old Testament, it becomes apparent that the nations all around Canaan had a hard time getting along with each other. They were all trying to build their own empire. In most cases the process of empire-building was not about national honor; rather, it was about economic prosperity and survival.

All nations have to face the reality of debt and economic problems at some point in their history. In those days the kings wanted to build palaces, roads, and other national projects. They also had to maintain a military for the protection of their cities. There was no banking system, no loans to be negotiated for all they had to do. Thus, the kings of these nations would invade and take over a neighboring country.

HISTORICAL CONTEXT | *Map Time*

God calls Abraham out of *Mesopotamia*. God says to him, "Leave your country, your people and your father's household and go to the land I will show you" (Genesis 12:1).

Abraham's response is staggering. He simply packs up his family and possessions and heads out. They travel to the region of *Canaan*. Abraham and his descendants – Isaac, Jacob, and Joseph – live in Canaan until a famine drives them to *Egypt*.

While in Egypt the Israelites multiply rapidly. They become Pharaoh's slaves and his source of manpower for many of his massive building projects. God later calls Moses to lead the people out of Egypt. They end up taking the long way on their journey from Egypt to the Promised Land. They spend forty years in the *Sinai Desert*. Then, they enter the *Promised Land of Canaan* and become a nation.

Once the nation is settled in the land and after the time of the Judges, Israel has a succession of kings: Saul, then David, and then Solomon. These three leaders rule over the united kingdom. After Solomon, the nation is split into two countries through a time of civil war.

When the dust settles, there are two nations rather than one. The *northern kingdom*, commonly called Israel, is made up of ten tribes; their capital is Samaria. Jeroboam is their king. The *southern kingdom*, most often called Judah, is made up of two tribes; they have their capital in Jerusalem, with Rehoboam as their ruler.

These two nations are surrounded by many other small countries who are their enemies. Over on the coast are the *Philistines*. Down to the south is *Edom*. Over to the east is *Moab*. A little further north is *Ammon*. These are, in many cases, barbaric, backward, primitive people. To understand what is happening during the reign of the kings of Judah, the geography is important.

This was instant income! At the same time, they would take some of the best people of the country and force them to be slaves for their projects.

In addition, invasion provided an ongoing source of revenue for years to come. Once they ruled a nation, they forced them to pay annual tribute. The process of empire-building and expansion was motivated by the need for wealth more than anything else.

2. The Example of Ahaz: Fear and Folding

SIGNIFICANT SCRIPTURE

Isaiah 7:1 – 25

NARRATIVE ON THE TEXT | *Where Will You Turn?*

In Isaiah 7 we read that Assyria is on the march. The Assyrians are in a process of empire-building and are swallowing up small countries all around Canaan. These small countries realize that they are vulnerable, so some of them begin to look for possible military alliances. Israel (the northern kingdom) and Aram form an alliance. They decide to join forces to try to resist the Assyrian army. They come to Ahaz king of Judah and invite him to join their alliance.

For the sake of self-preservation, it seems like Ahaz would say yes. But Ahaz says, "No." He wants nothing to do with a battle against Assyria.

Thus, the kings of Israel and Aram decide to go to war against Ahaz (and Judah). Their hope is to conquer Judah and force them to stand with them against the imminent Assyrian invasion. When Ahaz hears that Israel and Aram have formed an alliance and are coming against his nation, we read these words: "The hearts of Ahaz

HISTORICAL CONTEXT | *The Rise of Assyria*

One of the reasons Israel was able to exist as a nation for many centuries was that there were no dominant superpowers in their region for much of their history. There were superpowers in the ancient world, such as Egypt, Babylonia, Assyria, and Persia. But for several centuries, all of them were dormant. Then, around 700 BC Assyria began its ascendancy. It started taking over smaller countries all around Israel. As the army took over a country, they sought to leave behind the smallest occupational force possible. The goal was to retain control of the region but not weaken their own military force by spreading them out too thinly. They wanted the core of their army to be able to fight new battles and conquer other countries.

What Assyria (and other ancient nations) learned was that if they conquered a country and left a small force occupying the land, with time the people would revolt. As a result, they started sending thousands of people into exile and replacing them with people from other nations. When this was done, it took a much smaller occupational army to maintain control of a region because the people had lost their sense of national identity. This is exactly what happened to Israel (the northern kingdom) in 712 BC.

NEW TESTAMENT CONNECTION

The Samaritans

After the northern kingdom was defeated, Israel ceased to exist as a distinct nation. But many Israelites were still living in the land along with many imported non-Israelites. Since Samaria had been the capital of Israel, these people were later called the Samaritans. They were a mixture of Israelite blood but also foreign blood. These people had the books of Moses from the Old Testament, but they did not have the prophetic books. They were syncretistic in their religious beliefs and worshiped the God of Israel, but also other gods.

That's why the Samaritans were shunned by the Jewish people in Jesus' day. They were seen as half-Jews at best, and enemies at worst. This is why, in the gospel of John, we read about the kind of tension that existed between Jews and Samaritans. Jesus once engaged a Samaritan woman in conversation, and she was shocked. In John 4:9 we read: "The Samaritan woman said to him, 'You are a Jew and I am a Samaritan woman. How can you ask me for a drink?' (For Jews do not associate with Samaritans.)"

and his people were shaken, as the trees of the forest are shaken by the wind" (Isaiah 7:2).

What a vivid picture! Ahaz and the people of Judah feel trapped. Not only is Assyria on the march, but Israel and Aram are plotting against them. The people of Judah are trembling like trees of the forest when the winds blow! They are shaking in their boots. Isaiah paints a colorful picture of the anxiety and fear that has gripped the heart of Ahaz and Judah.

The question of the hour becomes, *Where will Ahaz and Judah turn in this desperate hour?* They don't want to throw their lot in with Israel and Aram. They know Assyria is too powerful for them to handle. Where will they turn?

Isaiah knows what temptation will face Ahaz—that Ahaz is contemplating an unthinkable option. Ahaz is considering an alliance with Assyria. Since the Assyrians are the rising superpower, an alliance with them will grant Judah protection from invasion and a guarantee that Israel and Aram will back off!

INTERPRETIVE INSIGHT | *The Company You Keep*

To Ahaz, forming an alliance seems like a good idea. But this was not God's plan for the nation of Judah. God is about to use Assyria to bring judgment on the northern kingdom—on Israel—because of their unfaithfulness and their treatment of the poor. But Assyria will also be coming under judgment because of their idolatry, corruption, violence, and paganism. God does not want Judah in partnership with *either* of these nations. Their company is bad company! To partner with them is to enter into their rebellion and sin. It also means taking the possible risk of coming under God's judgment of them.

What God wants is for his people to place their trust in him. Rather than running to the new superpower or bowing to the pressure of neighboring nations, God longs for his people to place their trust in his ability to save them.

NARRATIVE ON THE TEXT | *Ask for a Sign*

God knows that Ahaz is fearful and weak. Thus, he sends Isaiah to bring a word of encouragement:

> "Say to him, 'Be careful, keep calm and don't be afraid. Do not lose heart because of these two smoldering stubs of firewood—because of the fierce anger of Rezin and Aram and of the son of Remaliah.

Aram, Ephraim and Remaliah's son have plotted your ruin, saying, "Let us invade Judah; let us tear it apart and divide it among ourselves, and make the son of Tabeel king over it." Yet this is what the Sovereign LORD says:

> " 'It will not take place,
> it will not happen.' " (Isaiah 7:4–7)

ON THE LIGHTER SIDE

Thank Heaven for 7–11

Listen to the words of Isaiah 7:11: "Ask the LORD your God for a sign, whether in the deepest depths or in the highest heights."

You can almost hear Ahaz saying, "Thank heaven for 7–11!"

God wants Ahaz to take heart. The two kings who are threatening him are like smoldering stubs of firewood. They can make all the threats they want, but God says that their words are idle threats. Their bark is bigger than their bite. No matter what they may threaten, God says it will not happen.

Then, God speaks these words to Ahaz:

> "If you do not stand firm in your faith,
> you will not stand at all." (Isaiah 7:9)

God is speaking to Ahaz and doing everything possible to strengthen and fortify him. First, God assures Ahaz that Israel will not conquer Judah. Second, God calls him to stand strong in faith. Then, in a shocking manner, God invites Ahaz to ask for a sign. This is unusual in the Old Testament. But because Ahaz has such weak faith, God offers to give him a sign. This is not meant to be a normative practice. It is a concession God offers because Ahaz is faltering.

INTERPRETIVE INSIGHT | *Keeping Your Options Open*

We might think that Ahaz would be thrilled with the offer of a sign from God. It seems as if he would love some kind of sign to buttress his faith and guarantee that the nation of Judah would be safe. But his response is surprising and strange. Ahaz says: "I will not ask; I will not put the LORD to the test" (Isaiah 7:12).

HISTORICAL CONTEXT | *Sources of National Income: Taxes, Tolls, and Tribute*

There were three primary ways an empire would gain wealth in the Old Testament times. The first way was by *taxing their own people*. This was a common practice. It is fair to say that taxes were as popular then as they are now. A second source of revenue for a nation was *road tolls*. They charged people to use their roads and travel through their territory. Third, wealth was increased by forcing a conquered nation to pay *tribute*. The conquered nation was looted of much of its treasures and then required to pay an annual tribute to their rulers.

NEW TESTAMENT CONNECTION

Immanuel

Although Ahaz may have been driven by wrong motives, God did give a sign. In the gospel of Matthew we read: "All this took place to fulfill what the Lord had said through the prophet: 'The virgin will be with child and will give birth to a son, and they will call him Immanuel' – which means, 'God with us.'" The final sign that God gives to fulfill this prophecy is Jesus, God with us.

At first glance it may seem as if Ahaz is being reverent by refusing a sign, as if he is doing the honorable thing. But this is not the case. Ahaz is covering his real intentions with a thin veneer of piety and spirituality. The real reason Ahaz won't ask God for a sign is that he wants to keep his options open. He wants to be able to jump in and follow God, or else to go the other way and disobey God if that seems like the better option.

Ahaz knows if he asks for a sign, God will give it and then his options will be limited. If he enters a conversation with God and agrees to submit to him, he will slam the door on the Assyrian option. In other words, when Ahaz says he does not want a sign, he is saying that he wants to keep his options open more than he wants to obey God.

NARRATIVE ON LIFE | *The Truth about Human Nature*

Ahaz reveals something that is deeply rooted in human nature. We like to do what is right, but we also want to keep our options open. We often try to keep an escape route, even though we may know God will not approve of it. We would like to be honest, but if we find ourselves in a desperate situation, we are ready to lie if we have to.

ON THE LIGHTER SIDE | *Tolls Are No Fun*

In some parts of the United States and other places in the world there are toll roads. Nobody really likes to stop and pay tolls, but it is a reality that many people live with on a daily basis. In recent years many of these toll roads have tried to speed things up by developing a technology where a person can buy a pass that pays for many tolls. These people don't have to stop and toss in a handful of change; they drive right through a special lane and a scanner deducts the toll from their pass. It is a real time saver!

In the Chicago area there are many toll roads. A gentleman had borrowed a friend's BMW and was using it as he drove on the toll roads. This car was set up so that it could drive right through the hi-speed lane and not have to stop. His first time through the toll area he slowed down to about five miles per hour to make sure he heard the beep and knew the toll was paid. The second time he came to a toll area he went through the special lane at fifteen miles an hour, and it beeped again.

So, the third time he came to a toll area, he was pretty confident that the technology was working. Everyone else had to slow down and toss their change in the machine, or worse, stop and hand money over to an attendant. He cruised through at fifty miles an hour. The only problem was that this time he forgot to go through the special passing lane. He went right through one of the regular tollbooth lanes at fifty miles an hour and the wooden arm was down. He hit the arm and it exploded. It shook him up so bad that he drove for several miles before he could make himself stop the car.

God wants to reveal his presence and power and invite us into a life of full devotion. We tend to prefer convenient and limited levels of devotion that allow us to keep a few options on the back burner just in case.

LIFE APPLICATION | *Limiting Our Options*

It's scary to say, "I'm going to cut myself off from my sinful options. I'm only going to speak truth. I'm not going to spin or manipulate or hype anyone." Such an intentional limiting of options will be new territory for many people. Too many followers of Christ practice exactly what Ahaz does. Because of fear and anxiety, we leave our options open and we dishonor God in the process.

SIGNIFICANT SCRIPTURE

Isaiah 8:1 – 18; 2 Kings 16:7 – 8

Isaiah goes to incredible lengths to help Ahaz turn from fear and to learn how to trust in God. Ahaz has every opportunity to limit his options and surrender to God's will. In the same way, God invites us to willingly limit our options. Taking this step can look very different for each person who is seeking to be fully devoted to God.

NARRATIVE ON THE TEXT | *What's in a Name?*

God speaks to Isaiah, his prophet and says:

> "Take a large scroll and write on it with an ordinary pen: Maher-Shalal-Hash-Baz. And I will call in Uriah the priest and Zechariah son of Jeberekiah as reliable witnesses for me."
>
> Then I went to the prophetess, and she conceived and gave birth to a son. And the Lord said to me, "Name him Maher-Shalal-Hash-Baz. Before the boy knows how to say 'My father' or 'My mother,' the wealth of Damascus and the plunder of Samaria will be carried off by the king of Assyria." (Isaiah 8:1 – 4)

We discover that Isaiah is married and that both he and his wife are prophets. God is saying that Aram and Israel are about to be plundered by Assyria. Before the child (named Maher-Shalal-Hash-Baz) knows how to say the most basic words, "My father,"

ON THE LIGHTER SIDE | *A Sunday School Lesson*

There's an old story about a girl in a Sunday school class who got her Bible verses a little bit mixed up. One Sunday morning her teacher asked the class to explain what a lie is. She said, "A lie is an abomination under the Lord and a very present help in time of trouble."

Sadly there are a lot of people who live as if they are confident that verse must be in the Bible somewhere. They say, "I'd like to tell the truth. I'd like to put away deceit, falsehood, hype, and spinning. But if push comes to shove, a little lie can be a very present help in a time of need."

ON THE LIGHTER SIDE

A Mouthful

Aren't you glad you were not one of Isaiah's children? Wouldn't you hate going around with the name Maher-Shalal-Hash-Baz? You wouldn't just take a spelling test. You'd be the spelling test!

or "My mother," Assyria is going to swallow up the two nations who have been threatening Judah and Ahaz.

The name Maher-Shalal-Hash-Baz has deep significance. It means "quick to the plunder." The name of this child points to the ruin that will be coming on Israel and Aram in a short time.

INTERPRETIVE INSIGHT | *The Cost of Compromise*

God assures Ahaz that Judah will be safe. He does all he can to calm the fears that drive Ahaz. Sadly, Ahaz will not trust God. He will not hear the warnings of the prophet. He will not trust the promise that Judah will be safe from any invasion of Israel and Aram. Ahaz goes on to make a deal with Assyria. He gets into bed with a nation that is far from God. He sells his soul because he is driven by fear. This decision ends up ruining his life.

In 2 Kings 16:7–8 we read:

> Ahaz sent messengers to say to Tiglath-Pileser king of Assyria, "I am your servant and vassal. Come up and save me out of the hand of the king of Aram and of the king of Israel, who are attacking me." And Ahaz took the silver and gold found in the temple of the LORD and in the treasuries of the royal palace and sent it as a gift to the king of Assyria.

Ahaz willingly becomes a puppet on the strings of the king of Assyria. He figures that in the political climate of his day, he will have to put his trust in somebody, so he goes with the biggest kid on the block, Assyria. He even takes the silver and gold that the people have given for the temple of God and sends it to the pagan ruler of Assyria.

Ahaz begins on a long slide deeper and deeper into sin. By the end of his life he has altars in Israel built to Assyrian gods. He leads the Israelites into idolatry. He places the body of his son in a fire and watches him burn to death as a sacrifice to pagan gods. When it was all said and done, Ahaz compromises in ways that cost him more than he ever dreamed.

Do you think Ahaz planned for his life to end up like this? Do you think he set out to murder his child, sacrifice his freedom, mislead his people, and betray his God? No one plans to shipwreck his or her life. But for Ahaz, and for many of us, fear can be a deciding factor. Fear leads Ahaz to begin a process of compromise that costs him pain and loss beyond description.

NARRATIVE ON LIFE | *The Fear Factor*

Fear makes people selfish, impulsive, foolish, untrusting, and desperate. It dries up our ability for compassion and honesty. Once a human being is afraid, we never know what they can do. Sometimes we hear a voice inside our head that says, "You can't handle this. Even with God's help you will never be strong enough to make it." When we hear a voice speaking in our heart or head that says things like this, we can be confident it is not from God.

The Bible never says, "God panicked." In the entire Bible you will never read, "And then God said, 'What will I do now?' " God never panics and he never leads his people into panic. Ahaz leads a fear-based life, and it ends in disaster. Thankfully, we don't have to live like this. There is a better way.

SIGNIFICANT SCRIPTURE

Isaiah 36 and 37

3. The Example of Hezekiah: Radical Trust

NARRATIVE ON THE TEXT | *A View from the Wall*

The king of Assyria sends officials to intimidate the people and leaders of Judah. The field commander of Assyria enters a conversation with Hezekiah's officials in front of the walls of Jerusalem. All the people of Jerusalem are on the wall, listening to find out what's going to happen. They know that their king is standing in defiance of the king of Assyria. They know that Assyria is on the march.

The general of Assyria speaks to the leaders of Judah. He asks, "On what are you basing this confidence of yours?" He cannot imagine why Judah is willing to stand up against Assyrian might. He assumes that Hezekiah must be looking to Egypt to rescue them. But he is not.

Then this leader from Assyria takes a real shot at Hezekiah and Israel:

> "And if you say to me, 'We are depending on the LORD our God'—isn't he the one whose high places and altars Hezekiah removed, saying to Judah and Jerusalem, 'You must worship before this altar'?" (Isaiah 36:7)

The field commander from Assyria is taunting the people of Israel. He is questioning whether God is even on their side. He is seeking to undermine Hezekiah's spiritual leadership of the nation.

INTERPRETIVE INSIGHT | *Quality Control*

The leader of Assyria's army has it all wrong. He has heard that Hezekiah has torn down altars and destroyed places of worship. He assumes this is a bad thing and that Hezekiah has angered the God of Judah. What he does not know is that Hezekiah has torn down *pagan*

NEW TESTAMENT CONNECTION

No Fear

Certainly there is healthy fear and reverence of God. Proverbs teaches us that the fear of the Lord is the starting place of true wisdom. However, the kind of fear that paralyzes us, drives us from God, and causes us to compromise is never honoring to God. John writes and reminds us that we do not have to live in fear:

> In this way, love is made complete among us so that we will have confidence on the day of judgment, because in this world we are like him. There is no fear in love. But perfect love drives out fear, because fear has to do with punishment. The one who fears is not made perfect in love. (1 John 4:17–18)

HISTORICAL CONTEXT | *A New Time and a New King*

In Isaiah 36 we meet a new king of Judah and discover another way to live. This story takes place several decades after Ahaz was king of Judah. The northern kingdom – Israel – no longer existed, since Assyria swallowed it up in 712 BC. But one thing remains the same. There is political turmoil and the same superpower, Assyria, is threatening to conquer Judah.

The nation of Judah is standing strong, and much of their resolve comes from the courage of their king, a man named Hezekiah. The current king of Assyria, Sennacherib, is prepared to squash Judah like a bug. But he prefers to have Judah surrender so he wouldn't have to lose any soldiers. The time of Hezekiah is much like that of Ahaz, but he responds in a very different way.

altars. He is seeking to drive the people back to the heart of God. It is a kind of quality control. Rather than have the people scattered all over the land worshiping at pagan altars, he wants them to come back to Jerusalem again. His actions are not offensive to God; rather, they honor God.

NARRATIVE ON THE TEXT | *An Issue of Language*

Next, the commander of Assyria's army shouts out words that would have sent shivers down the spines of all the people on the wall: "Furthermore, have I come to attack and destroy this land without the LORD? The LORD himself told me to march against this country and destroy it" (Isaiah 36:10).

This is too much for the leaders of Judah to take. Hezekiah's officials ask the leader of Assyria's army to speak in Aramaic, not in Hebrew: "Please speak to your servants in Aramaic, since we understand it. Don't speak to us in Hebrew in the hearing of the people on the wall" (Isaiah 36:11).

What they are actually saying is, "Let's make these negotiations private." In those days, Aramaic was the language of diplomacy. Many of the people would have understood Hebrew but not Aramaic. The leaders of Judah are asking the commander of Assyria to stop trying to humiliate the king in front of his people.

The response of the Assyrian commander is emphatic: "Was it only to your master and you that my master sent me to say these things, and not to the men sitting on the wall—who, like you, will have to eat their own filth and drink their own urine?" (Isaiah 36:12). The field commander wants the people to know, in their own language, what lies ahead if they try to defy the king and army of Assyria. The comment about eating their own filth and drinking their own urine is not meant to be some kind of disgusting word picture. It is a threat of siege.

INTERPRETIVE INSIGHT | *The Power of Fear*

It is called psychological warfare! The commander of Assyria is intentionally speaking to all the people on the wall. He wants the word spread through Jerusalem. He knows that in a matter of hours rumors will be spreading all over the city. Rumors such as, "Hezekiah is deceiving us; God can't get us out of this situation." "We will all die of starvation when Assyria lays siege to the city." "There is no way we can resist the army of Assyria; we are as good as defeated already." That is what the commander of Assyria wants—it is what he expects!

The Assyrians know that once the people are gripped by fear, their faith, loyalty, and unity will be gone. They know that fear will destroy confidence, paralyze the people, and turn them against each other. What was true about the power of fear then is still true today.

Fear is the great enemy of spiritual community. Every time we choose fear over self-disclosure or being known, we paralyze community. Each time we choose fear over a needed confrontation, we weaken the fabric of Christian community. Every time we bow to fear and refuse to speak the truth in love, community dies a little.

NARRATIVE ON LIFE | *Standing Firm*

Building a healthy community does require boldness and fearlessness. In Isaiah 37, the prophet comes to Hezekiah to encourage him to respond in a God-honoring way to the threats he is facing. Isaiah has seen kings come and go. He saw Ahaz give in to fear and live with staggering consequences. But he tells Hezekiah the same thing he told Ahaz. "Trust God. Be brave. Stand in your faith."

The good news is, Hezekiah listens and follows the wise counsel of Isaiah. He doesn't surrender to Assyria. He stands firm in his faith. No matter what the odds, threats, or possible repercussions, Hezekiah commits to follow God and not human inclinations.

HISTORICAL CONTEXT | *The Threat of a Siege*

In those days, one form of warfare was to surround a city and simply wait until the people were starving to death. At some point, when the conditions became bad enough, the people in the city would surrender. Throughout ancient history the people trapped in a city during a siege were driven to a point of desperation where they even considered cannibalism to stay alive. The commander of the Assyrian army is telling the people, "You had better hear what I say because you will come to a place of utter starvation if you refuse to obey the king of Assyria."

NARRATIVE ON THE TEXT | *You Don't Have a Chance*

Word of Hezekiah's bold refusal to bow to the might of Assyria gets back to the king of Assyria, Sennacherib. He hears that Judah is defying him and Hezekiah is trusting in God rather than him. We can be confident that Sennacherib, king of Assyria, is outraged!

He sits down and writes Hezekiah a letter. We need to remember that there were no telegrams or emails in those days. When communication happened, it could take days or weeks. Hezekiah, and the people of Israel, have undoubtedly been waiting to hear how Sennacherib will respond to Hezekiah's defiance.

They wait, and wait, and wait some more. And then, all of a sudden, Hezekiah gets a letter signed by the king of Assyria:

> "Say to Hezekiah king of Judah: Do not let the god you depend on deceive you when he says, 'Jerusalem will not be handed over to the king of Assyria.' Surely you have heard what the kings of Assyria have done to all the countries, destroying them completely. And will you be delivered? Did the gods of the nations that were destroyed by my forefathers deliver them?" (Isaiah 37:10–12)

The king of Assyria then runs through a laundry list of other countries defeated by his army. This is the worst news possible for Judah and Hezekiah. Sennacherib is saying, "I will completely destroy you and your puny little nation. I've done it before. I will do it again."

Humanly speaking, Sennacherib is absolutely right. The battle between Judah and the might of Assyria is no contest.

INTERPRETIVE INSIGHT | *When the Pressure Is On ... Pray!*

What do you do when you get a letter from the most powerful and bloodthirsty ruler in the world and he wants you to know that he will be dropping in for a personal visit? How do you respond when you get the worst news of your life? Where do you turn when fear comes pounding on your front door?

> Prayer is not overcoming God's reluctance; it is laying hold of his highest willingness.
>
> *Richard Chenevix Trench*

The example of Hezekiah at this moment stands as a beacon for all who want to learn how to follow God. In Isaiah 37:15–20 we read:

> And Hezekiah prayed to the LORD: "O LORD Almighty, God of Israel, enthroned between the cherubim, you alone are God over all the kingdoms of the earth. You have made heaven and earth. Give ear, O LORD, and hear; open your eyes, O LORD, and see; listen to all the words Sennacherib has sent to insult the living God.
>
> "It is true, O LORD, that the Assyrian kings have laid waste all these peoples and their lands. They have thrown their gods into the fire and destroyed them, for

> they were not gods but only wood and stone, fashioned by human hands. Now, O LORD our God, deliver us from his hand, so that all kingdoms on earth may know that you alone, O LORD, are God."

Hezekiah goes to the one place where answers are found, courage is gathered, and hope is restored. He goes to prayer—the throne of God!

LIFE APPLICATION | *What Do You Need to Bring to God?*

Hezekiah takes the letter from Sennacherib and spreads it out before the Lord. He seeks the face of God in prayer, and God hears him. In response, Isaiah sends a message from God to Hezekiah. He assures him that his prayers have been heard and that the threats of Sennacherib will not come to pass.

Here is the question each person must to ask: *What do I need to spread out before the Lord?*

Each of us gets letters from Assyria. A letter from Sennacherib can take many forms. It is anything that tempts us to be driven by fear. It is a piece of bad news that makes us so anxious we can't live for God. It is a threat from a person that robs us of a sense of trust and confidence that God can deliver. It is anything that unleashes fear in our lives:

- Maybe it's a piece of paper from work that says your services are no longer required.
- Maybe it's an assignment that seems too hard, or a performance review that has you worried, or an expectation that you're not sure you can fulfill.
- Maybe it's a test at school.
- Maybe it's a note from your bank with bad news.
- Maybe it's a bill you don't think you can pay.
- Maybe it's a looming black cloud of financial concerns.
- Maybe it's a word from a doctor or a diagnosis that's real bad.
- Maybe it's a letter from a teacher about one of your children.
- Maybe it's a word of rejection from someone you love.

ON THE LIGHTER SIDE | *Bambi Versus Godzilla*

Back in the late 1960s a very short film named "Bambi Meets Godzilla" came out. It opened up with some credits and then a little deer grazing in a field. Then this giant foot came down and squashed Bambi. That was the end of the movie. Then the credits rolled. In the mind of Assyria and Judah, their battle would be a lot like "Bambi Meets Godzilla."

If you can find a copy of this short film, you might even want to show it.

NEW TESTAMENT CONNECTION

Meeting the God of Peace

God does not want his children living as captives to fear. He offers another path, and prayer is the starting point of our journey from fear to faith.

> Do not be anxious about anything, but in everything, by prayer and petition, with thanksgiving, present your requests to God. And the peace of God, which transcends all understanding, will guard your hearts and your minds in Christ Jesus. (Philippians 4:6–7)

- Maybe it's an email that cut you deeply.
- Maybe it's a painful letter from a lawyer's office.
- Maybe it's a deep-rooted anxiety that rules your heart.

Hezekiah takes the worst letter with the worst news he's ever gotten in his life and spreads it out before the Lord. In response, God hears and answers. Like Hezekiah, we can bring our fear-producing, anxiety-building concerns before God in prayer. We can lay them down. We can place our trust in God rather than be ruled and driven by fear.

Prayer is the key that unlocks all the storehouses of God's infinite grace and power. All that God is, and all that God has, is at the disposal of prayer.

R. A. Torrey

NARRATIVE ON THE TEXT | *The Rest of the Story*

The angel of God comes and completely routs the Assyrian army, and they go home. From this point on in history, Assyria goes into a decline from which it never recovers.

As we look back on this biblical account, we realize that Hezekiah was never really alone. He faced hard times and his faith was tested, but God was with him every step of the way. Just as God was with Hezekiah, he wants to be with us.

CREATIVE MESSAGE IDEA | *Lay It Out*

When we face times of anxiety and fear, the single most important activity that we can engage in is prayer. Like Hezekiah, we can come to God and spread out our needs and fears before him. We can admit our anxiety, confusion, and need for him to deliver us.

At this time you can ask everyone to take out the card you gave them as they entered the room. (If you are going to use this creative message idea, you will need to have a card or a blank piece of paper for everyone who is gathered. They will also need a writing utensil.) Invite them to write down a word or sentence that represents a fear that has been gripping and controlling their life. Then, allow a time of silence for each person to bring this fear before God. If your tradition encourages kneeling and if you have space to do so, consider inviting people to take a posture of spreading out before the Lord. After a time of silence, lift up a prayer asking for those gathered to experience freedom and release from the fears that have kept them captive.

God wants us to avoid the pitfalls of Ahaz. We don't have to live under the tyranny of fear and anxiety. We are called to lives of trust and faith.

All of us have ups and downs. No matter how much we love God and walk with Jesus, we still have moments when anxiety slips in. But through the power of God's Holy Spirit, we can have lives that are predominantly characterized by the peace and freedom that come from God's presence in our lives. That's how God wants us to live.

Message 30

Micah: Doing Justice

Isaiah 1:13; Amos 4:1; Micah 2:11; 3:1; 6:6–8; 7:16–19

THE HEART OF THE Message

The prophets call us to hear, see, and feel what we would miss on our own. It is easy for our hearts to become calloused and our eyes blinded to the sin in our lives, churches, and culture. The prophets strip away all of the facades and help us see ourselves as we really are.

Micah calls us to a deep level of self-examination and then to transformation. Three words ring out loud and clear: justice, kindness, and humility. God wants more than offerings and religious observance. He wants our hearts to beat in unison with his heart. He wants our lives to reflect the justice he desires to see on this earth. When we hear the voice of God speaking through the prophets and when we respond to his call, we will see our lives, the church, and the world transformed.

BRIEF MESSAGE OUTLINE

1. Why read the prophets?
2. The call of Micah

THE HEART OF THE Messenger

The prophets have a deep concern that followers of God not fall into the trap of "being religious" but failing to have a heart that reflects the heart of God. As you prepare to bring this message, take time for self-examination. How can you live in a way that brings God's justice alive in this world? Is your heart tender toward others, and do you show kindness freely? How can you grow in humility? Also, take time to think about your habits as a worshiper. Are you just going through the motions, or are you truly meeting God in worship? Does worship bring transforming power into your life?

NARRATIVE ON THE TEXT *Examples of Harsh Prophetic Words*

Throughout the Old Testament we get a window into the heart of the prophets. From some of their words, it would be easy to get the feeling that the prophets got up on the wrong side of the bed. Here are just a few samples of why people might see the prophets as a bit cranky:

> Hear this word, you cows of Bashan on Mount Samaria,
> you women who oppress the poor and crush the needy
> and say to your husbands, "Bring us some drinks!" (Amos 4:1)

SIGNIFICANT SCRIPTURE

Isaiah 1:13;
Amos 4:1;
Micah 3:1

Amos is calling the women of Israel cows! He is saying that they are more concerned about where they will get their next drink than they are about the poor and the needy.

> Stop bringing meaningless offerings!
> Your incense is detestable to me.
> New Moons, Sabbaths and convocations—
> I cannot bear your evil assemblies. (Isaiah 1:13)

Isaiah is telling the people that God is fed up with their offerings, gatherings, and their whole religious lives.

> Listen, you leaders of Jacob,
> you rulers of the house of Israel.
> Should you not know justice,
> you who hate good and love evil;
> who tear the skin from my people
> and the flesh from their bones;
> who eat my people's flesh,
> strip off their skin
> and break their bones in pieces;
> who chop them up like meat for the pan,
> like flesh for the pot? (Micah 3:1–3)

Micah is speaking in metaphor, but the message is loud and clear. The people are filled with injustice and the consequences are grave.

CREATIVE MESSAGE IDEA *The Emotions of the Prophets*

Think for a moment about basic human emotions. We all have feelings. Sometimes we are filled with joy; at other times sadness fills our heart. We feel compassion, anger, fear, happiness, and many other emotions. This is just part of being human.

We also tend to associate certain emotions with different groups of people. Invite those gathered to identify what emotion they most often associate with the different groups of people you are going to list. Have everyone tell someone sitting near them two emotions that come to mind when they think of:

- clowns
- police officers
- school principals
- nurses
- prophets

We often begin to characterize a whole group of people and assign a certain emotional state to this group. When it comes to the prophets, it would be easy to see them as stern, angry, and even a little depressive.

If we simply skim through the words of the prophets, we can get the sense that they were a pretty surly and angry bunch.

NARRATIVE ON THE TEXT | *Examples of Strange Behavior*

Not only did the prophets speak harsh and angry words, but their behavior often looked downright bizarre! Here are a few examples:

- *Hosea* marries a prostitute to reveal the broken heart of God over his people who have wandered away from him. Imagine a seminary student or young single pastor announcing to friends and family that he was getting married to a common hooker who was known by everyone in town.
- *Ezekiel* eats food cooked over excrement to create a picture of just how unclean the people have become and to point to how bad the conditions will become for God's people if they do not repent.
- *Jeremiah* digs up a filthy pair of underwear to show people the disgusting nature of their behavior.

Although all of these men were doing exactly what God called them to do, the casual observer would have seen these choices and behaviors as bizarre.

1. Why Read the Prophets?

There are basically three reasons why believers should read what the prophets have written:

- because they are in the Bible
- because they help us hear what we would never hear on our own
- because we need their message to pierce our hearts

We will examine these three reasons in more detail.

NARRATIVE ON LIFE | *Easy to Avoid*

First, we read the prophets because they are in the Bible. Let's be honest, it would be easy to avoid reading the prophets. As a matter of fact, many people do exactly that. The prophets hold a mirror up to our soul and show us where we have become marred, scarred, and ugly. They are not really happy books. They tell us things we don't want to hear. They convict us of sin. They remind us that there are serious consequences for rebelling against God. It would be easy to relegate these books of the Old Testament to some kind of secondary status.

If we fall for the temptation to avoid reading the prophets, we do so to our own peril. We need the message the prophets bring. We even need the manner in which they communicate. Sometimes a gentle reminder does not get our attention and it takes a spiritual two-by-four to wake us up!

NARRATIVE ON LIFE | *Our Hearts Have Become Numb*

Second, we read the prophets because they help us hear what we would never hear on our own. There are many things God wants us to see, but our eyes can be blind. There are truths the Holy Spirit is speaking to us, but we are often spiritually hard-of-hearing. Our hearts have become numb, and we don't always get the subtle promptings of the Holy Spirit. The prophets speak with such conviction and clarity and at such a volume that they break through numb hearts.

NEW TESTAMENT CONNECTION

It Is All from God

Avoiding any part of the Bible is a mistake. The apostle Paul emphasized that the entire Old Testament is God's Word when he wrote to Timothy: "All Scripture is God-breathed and is useful for teaching, rebuking, correcting and training in righteousness, so that the man of God may be thoroughly equipped for every good work" (2 Timothy 3:16–17).

ILLUSTRATION | *Singing Off-Key*

Imagine you are listening to someone sing, but that person is singing off-key—not just a little off-key, way off! Moreover, he or she is doing so at the full volume.

If you are musically insensitive, such off-key singing won't bother you much. You might notice, but you can live with it. If you have perfect pitch and are a trained musician, however, it's a different story. You notice each note and how it does not fit. You realize how far off pitch this person is. It can be almost painful!

A person with perfect pitch agonizes over the singing not just because it sounds so bad but because he or she realizes how good and beautiful the song could sound. This is the experience of the prophets. God has given them a vision of what could be, and they hear how human beings have gone so far out of tune with God's plan. The prophets see, hear, and feel with God. They know the heart of God and call us to get our lives back in tune.

NARRATIVE ON LIFE | *What's the Big Deal?*

We tend to look at the world through our own personal filters. If we feel happy and have our needs met, we think the world is a pretty good place. When things are going

ON THE LIGHTER SIDE | *What Will You Say to Malachi?*

Just imagine that when you get to heaven, you meet Malachi. This great prophet of Israel asks you, "So, how did you like my book?"

You don't want to have to say, "Oops! I never got around to it. It was in a bad location–you know, way at the end of the Old Testament. It was only four chapters long and didn't seem that significant. I started reading the Old Testament, but I got stuck back somewhere in Leviticus and never got to the end of the story."

well for us, we can walk right past things that break the heart of God and not even notice them.

- We look at the world and our society and think that things aren't that bad.
- We hear about violence on the news, but if it does not touch us or those close to us, it does not seem that important.
- We lie a little bit, but we comfort ourselves by thinking that this is common and everyone does it.
- We are unfaithful in thought or action, but we echo the old saying, "What he/she doesn't know won't hurt him/her."
- We cheat in business or school and justify it by saying that everyone does it.
- Eight thousand children and young people are infected with AIDS every single day in sub-Saharan Africa; it is now the leading cause of death in that part of the world, but because it is so far away, we hardly feel a thing.
- People in our country live on the streets and go to sleep with empty stomachs, and we learn to walk past them and look the other way. We convince ourselves that it is probably their own fault and they deserve the plight they are in.
- Someone shades the truth to close a business deal and make a few more bucks and we say, "That's just how business goes!"
- We get a little wrapped up in our own comfort, focus more and more on our needs, and quickly forget the needs of the poor and outcast.
- We get the paycheck we worked so hard for and don't even think to give back to the God who has provided all that we have.

These things happen every day, every moment, and we say, "What's the big deal? That's life!"

The prophets, on the other hand, act as if the world is falling apart. They get all stressed out and seem to think that these things are a much bigger deal than we ever thought. The prophets echo the heart of God, who sees and cares about all of these things. The prophets wake us up to the fact that all of these things are a bigger deal than we would have ever guessed!

CREATIVE MESSAGE IDEA *Until It Hurts*

Plan to have a trio (of voices or instruments) do a short musical number at this point in the message. Have two of the voices or instruments in tune and together. Have a third that is intentionally, clearly, and loudly out of tune. The number does not have to be long, even one full minute should be enough, but it will feel like eternity! Have them play or sing until it hurts!

NEW TESTAMENT CONNECTION

The Voice of Jesus

The voice of Jesus enters in with the voices of the prophets. He also reminds us that God is very concerned about justice and righteousness. Jesus says:

> "Then the King will say to those on his right, 'Come, you who are blessed by my Father; take your inheritance, the kingdom prepared for you since the creation of the world. For I was hungry and you gave me something to eat, I was thirsty and you gave me something to drink, I was a stranger and you invited me in, I needed clothes and you clothed me, I was sick and you looked after me, I was in prison and you came to visit me.'" (Matthew 25:34–36)

If we ever wonder whether the prophets are overstating their case, all we have to do is read these words of Jesus from the gospel of Matthew. Jesus is clear that justice and righteousness matter more than we dream.

INTERPRETIVE INSIGHT | *The Burden of the Prophets*

The prophets bear the crushing burden of feeling what God feels, seeing what God sees, and hearing what God hears. Their passion is the natural extension of God's call on their lives. Their seemingly bizarre behavior begins to make sense when we understand the depth of their pain over sin. They are giving a human voice to the divine cry of a God who is broken over the depth of sin in our world and the life-crushing injustices that happen every day but no one seems to notice.

The rich get richer and the poor get poorer. Lies are spoken and no one seems to notice or care. Dishonest business practices have become normative and we look the other way, as if it does not matter. Prisoners sit day after day in jail and no one visits them. Children go to bed hungry while their neighbors feast and feel no sorrow for the poor around them. God sees all of this, God feels, and he shares his heart through the words of the prophets.

NARRATIVE ON LIFE | *The Battle of the Prophets*

Third, we read the prophets because we need their message to pierce our hearts. Prophet after prophet learned that people don't really want to know the truth about sin and what it has done to our lives, society, and world. Hearing the voice of the prophets and seeing the broken heart of God make us uncomfortable. It is easier to live with blind eyes, deaf ears, and hard hearts.

Time and time again throughout the Old Testament the prophets come with stern warnings from God. They come to help the people see, hear, and feel with God. Over and over the people reject them. Sometimes the people laugh, at other times they mock, and at still other times they simply walk away. Sadly, there are also times when the people lash out in anger. Prophets are beaten, imprisoned, and even killed!

Today the response to the prophets tends to be a little tamer. Most people simply avoid them. The voices of the prophets still cry out. They still help to pierce our hearts with the truth of God. The question is: Will we fight and resist, or will we receive the words of the prophets with humility?

NARRATIVE ON THE TEXT | *The Effect of Beer or Wine*

Here is a question to ask everyone gathered: What is the effect of drinking beer or wine? Does it make a person more alert and sharp, or does it make them more comfortable and relaxed? (Ask people to respond out loud.)

In general, drinking alcohol causes people to become mellow, relaxed, and less focused. In Micah 2:11 the prophet is making a powerful statement about the condition of the human heart. He says that people prefer to live in a state of spiritual inebriation. We don't want to notice, we prefer not to feel, and we would rather not hear about all the pain in the world. If a prophet came who brought words that made us feel comfortable, mellow, and relaxed, we would love this prophet.

SIGNIFICANT SCRIPTURE

Micah 2:11

The problem is, prophets speak the words of God. The truth of God often convicts and makes us feel uncomfortable. God's truth challenges us and moves us to action.

> The shallowness of our moral comprehension, the incapacity to sense the depth of misery caused by our own failures, is a simple fact of fallen humanity which no explanation can cover up.
>
> *Abraham Heschel*

ILLUSTRATION | *Just Turn on the TV*

Imagine it is seven o'clock in the evening and you are about to sit down in front of the TV to unwind. You figure you will channel surf around the hundred-plus options you have as a result of your new satellite system. Then, there is a knock on the front door. You open the door and are shocked to find Micah, Amos, and Isaiah standing there! You invite them in and you all sit down together for an evening of prime-time channel surfing. Over the next five hours these three prophets watch as you view short clips from some of the following categories:

- talk shows (from Oprah to Jerry Springer)
- reality TV shows
- HBO and Showtime special programming
- sporting events
- situation comedies (from reruns of *Leave It to Beaver* to *Will and Grace*)
- dramas (police, drama, hospital)
- infomercials and TV shopping malls
- news programs
- late night shows

You even give them a sample of some of the special adult pay-to-view channels.

How might these prophets respond to the smorgasbord of viewing options that are commonplace in our world today? If they were sitting with you and interacting about these shows, how might your perspective on these shows change?

NARRATIVE ON LIFE | *Becoming Too Comfortable*

Events that horrified the prophets have become everyday occurrences in our world. Things that the prophets condemned in the name of God have become standard business

PAUSE FOR REFLECTION

Pause for Reflection – Hearing the Prophets

The prophets really do speak for God. They see what he sees. They feel what he feels. They express the heart of God with a human voice and help us see what we often want to avoid. We omit them from our reading of Scripture at great cost and risk to our own souls!

Take a brief time of silence and ask the Holy Spirit to soften your heart to hear the words of the prophets. Also, invite the Spirit to reveal areas in your life where you have become numb to sin. Spend a few moments reflecting on your own life and the transformation God wants to bring.

practice and normal operating procedure in the marketplace today. Attitudes that brought condemnation from the prophets are tolerated in our society and often in our local churches. We have become so comfortable and complacent that we hardly notice the presence of sin all around us.

It is like a necklace or ring that feels strange when we first put it on. After a short time, we don't even notice it. Or, it is like a broken item around the house. It bugs us at first, but with time, it just blends in. We don't even see it anymore. With time, things that should bother us and break our hearts can become part of our landscape of life. The job of the prophets is to get our attention and help us notice what we have forgotten.

> The prophet is a man who feels fiercely. God has thrust a burden upon his soul, and he is bowed and stunned at man's fierce greed. Prophecy is the voice God has lent to the silent agony.... God is raging in the prophet's words.
>
> *Abraham Heschel*

ILLUSTRATION | *Welcome to the Hog Farm*

Have you ever driven by a hog farm? If you have, you know it! As you get close to the farm, you are hit with a wall of stench that is distinct to this kind of animal. If it happens to be a warm and damp day, it can be even more intense. You may find yourself wondering, "How can anyone live close to a hog farm? How can they tolerate the smell?" But, if you actually stay near the hog farm for a few hours, something amazing happens. The smell goes away!

Well, it does not really go away, but you stop noticing it. Somehow, your mind and senses make adjustments. With time, the smell is not nearly as intense. Then, if you stay long enough, it seems to disappear. If you were to leave for a time and come back, you would notice the smell again, but you would also adjust again.

Sin functions in a similar way. With time, if we stay in close proximity to certain sinful practices, we don't notice the smell, we don't see the consequences, and we can't see what the big deal is anyway. It is the job of the prophets to shake us, wake us, and help us realize that something stinks!

SIGNIFICANT SCRIPTURE

Micah 6:6 – 8

2. The Call of Micah

NARRATIVE ON THE TEXT | *Notice the Escalation*

In Micah 6:6 – 8, the prophet begins by asking a fundamental question: What can I bring to God? What does he really want from me? He then forms a list of possible answers to this question. Notice how Micah begins small and then escalates.

- "Shall I come … with burnt offerings?" Micah begins small. A burnt offering could be a dove or a pigeon, which anyone could afford.
- "Shall I come … with calves a year old?" A calf was an expensive gift. Many families could not afford this kind of an offering. This would have been very generous.
- "Will the Lord be pleased with thousands of rams?" This was an offering that only a king could give. The wealthiest person in all the land might be able to muster up this kind of an offering, but it was almost beyond imagination.
- "Will the Lord be pleased … with ten thousand rivers of oil?" This was simply impossible. Micah has now escalated the discussion to the point of being ridiculous. No person could offer God even one river of oil, much less ten thousand.
- "Shall I offer my firstborn for my transgression?" Micah knows that human sacrifice is forbidden by God. He is not advocating human sacrifice in any way, shape, or form. He is simply escalating the discussion. He is saying, "Would God want me to give my child, that which is most precious to me in this world?" Micah is pushing the discussion as far as he can.

PAUSE FOR PRAYER

Soften My Heart

Pray for each person to hear the words God speaks through the prophets. Pray in three specific directions:

- *Open our eyes*: Ask the Spirit to open our eyes to see where sin has crept in and gone unnoticed.
- *Open our ears*: Ask God to sensitize the hearing of each person to receive what God wants to say through his prophets.
- *Soften our hearts*: Pray for hearts that are consistently tender and ready for transformation.

The central message of this part of the passage is that none of these things is really what God wants us to offer to him. What God wants is *us*! He wants our hearts and lives fully yielded to him. What God asks for is something anyone can give. He wants us to act in ways that reflect his justice. He invites us to love what is merciful. And God wants us to walk in authentic humility with him. If we are humble before God, we will follow him, and our whole life will be his. This is what God wants from each of his children.

NARRATIVE ON THE TEXT | *Do Justice*

The prophet Micah continues:

> He has showed you, O man, what is good.
> And what does the Lord require of you?
> To *act justly* and to love mercy
> and to walk humbly with your God. (Micah 6:8)

Justice is a strange thing. We all want it when it comes to us. We long for justice when we have been wronged. We cry "unfair" and expect justice to prevail.

CREATIVE VIDEO ELEMENT

Music video, *Doing Justice* (1:30 min.). Shows imagery of a man sitting alone on a busy street as people walk by.

NARRATIVE ON LIFE | *Beware of the Double Standard*

We all hate it when someone treats us unfairly. If we are wronged, we expect, we even demand, justice. The problem is that most of us live with a double standard. We want justice when it comes to us, but we forget to extend justice to others. We need to ask God to help us be just as concerned and get just as energized over the injustices others suffer. In particular, we need to learn to be concerned over the specific injustices we might be most likely to overlook. God calls us to be his agents of justice in this world.

LIFE APPLICATION | *What Can One Person Do?*

We cannot correct all of the injustice in the world, but we can all do something. There are some first steps that will move a follower of Christ toward a deeper life of justice. Consider taking a step forward in one of the following ways:

Notice: Ask God to help you tune in and notice injustice around you. This can be painful and cause discomfort, but it is critical for all who want to do justice. We must first learn to take note of where injustice exists. Part of this process is learning to notice where we are part of the injustice problem. When we see this, we need to come before God and humbly seek his power to change.

Pray: Every follower of Christ needs to learn the importance of praying for justice and against injustice. There is amazing power in prayer, and this is a critical starting point for Christ-followers.

Changed behavior: God can help us learn to treat others fairly. Before we go seeking world justice, we need to be sure we are treating the people around us with equity

ON THE LIGHTER SIDE | *Swing at Everything!*

A story is told by a former referee and umpire. His story is a great reminder of how we all want moments where we can experience justice. This is how he tells the story:

I was driving too fast in the snow in Boulder, Colorado. A policeman pulled me over and gave me a speeding ticket. I tried to talk him out of it. I told him that I was worried about my insurance costs. I tried to explain what a good and careful driver I am. He told me that if I didn't like it, I could go to court.

The first game of the next baseball season I showed up to umpire. As I stood behind home plate, the first batter walked up. I was surprised to see it was the same policeman who gave me the ticket that winter. Our eyes met. He recognized me, and I recognized him. There was an awkward pause.

He asked me, "How did that thing with the ticket go?"

I paused, looked at him, and said, "Swing at everything!"

and justice. If God shows you an area where you are being unjust in your treatment of another person, it is time to make some behavior and attitude adjustments.

Courage: We can begin to live with courage in how we relate to others. When we see injustice, we can begin to say something and do something about it. If there are patterns of injustice in our home, at our school, in our workplace, or in our neighborhood, we can learn to enter in and make a difference. This takes courage because we know how people responded to the biblical prophets. We have to be ready for people to resist what we say if we begin calling for justice and righteousness.

Generosity: If we have more than we need—and most of us do—we can begin to share with those who have needs. We can do it on our own as we become aware of needs around us. We can also give through our church or other Christian organizations that provide for the basic needs of the poor.

PAUSE FOR REFLECTION

Learning to Notice

Take time to reflect on where there might be injustice in specific areas of life. Invite people to think honestly and deeply about the possible presence of injustice in their sphere of influence. Can you identify any injustice:

- in how you treat members of your family?
- in your local community?
- in the larger community where you live?
- in your workplace?
- in your local church?
- in how you relate to your neighbors?

ILLUSTRATION | *Can I Give It Away?*

A mother and son were walking down a city street on a cold winter night. The little boy noticed a man huddled in an alley with only an old blanket to shelter him from the cold. He had never seen this sort of thing before. The mother was concerned for her son and began to pull him away from the situation. He resisted and asked if they could stop. The mother was anxious, but willing to pause for just a moment. Her son motioned for her to lean over so he could say something. He whispered, "I have three more jackets at home; can I give that man my jacket?" His mother looked at him with surprise and concern. She paused and said ...

How would you finish this story? How do you think it should be finished? What would you have said if you were the mother?

The little boy knew he had three more jackets at home, and he wanted to share. He wanted to help someone who was cold. He had the means to do it. The way we respond in situations like this teaches the next generation about justice.

> If our goods are not available to the community they are stolen goods.
>
> *Martin Luther*

ILLUSTRATION | *An Example of Lavish Loving-Kindness*

In a town called Paradise, California, lives a young man named John Gilbert. When he was five years old, John was diagnosed with Duchenne's Muscular Dystrophy. It was genetic, progressive, and cruel. He was told that it would eventually destroy every muscle in his body. In about ten years this dreadful disease would take his life.

WORD STUDY

Hesed

The second phrase that Micah talks about in Micah 6:8 is to "love mercy." The Hebrew word used here is *hesed*. *Hesed* is the word most closely associated with God's loving-kindness expressed in covenant relationship. It is a love that always seeks to express itself in action toward another individual.

Each year John lost something. One year it was his ability to run; he could no longer play games or sports with other kids. Another year he could no longer walk straight. All he could do was watch other kids play.

John writes that junior high was perhaps the hardest time of his life because other children teased him mercilessly. He was bullied and humiliated until he was afraid to go to school. No one ever stood up for him; maybe they were afraid for themselves and the possible repercussions.

One year John was named the ambassador for Muscular Dystrophy in California. A fund-raising auction was to be held at a big dinner, and John was invited to be a guest for this gathering. It was a highlight for this boy who had experienced so many low-lights in his life. There were actually some NFL stars there who let John hold their massive Superbowl rings.

When the auction began, one item particularly caught John's attention. It was a basketball signed by the players of the NBA Sacramento Kings. John got a little carried away and raised his hand to bid on the ball. He didn't have any money and could never have afforded it, but he was so excited that he bid anyway. When his mom saw his hand go up, she reacted with lightning quickness and pulled his hand down. John later said, "Astronauts never felt as many G's as my wrist did that night!"

> There is a loftier ambition than merely to stand high in the world. It is to stoop down and lift mankind higher.
>
> *Henry Van Dyke*

The bidding for that basketball went on and on, and the price went up and up! Eventually one man offered an amount that shocked the whole room. No one else could match it. He walked to the front and collected his prize. But instead of returning to his seat, he walked across the room and placed the ball in John's frail, thin hands.

That man placed the very expensive ball into hands that would never dribble a ball down a basketball court, never throw a ball to a teammate for a fast break, and never fire a three-point shot at the buzzer in the hopes of winning a big game.

Have you bought a basketball for anybody lately?

LIFE APPLICATION | *First Steps*

Living in a way that expresses loving mercy begins with first steps. There are many starting points, but here are a few ideas to get the wheels turning. Maybe you could:

- Sign up to help in the church nursery and give care to a little one who can't say thanks but who needs the tender love you can give while the family is off to worship.
- Serve at a soup kitchen once a month.

- Volunteer to help in the youth ministry of the church. Some of the young people who have experienced the same sort of merciless teasing as John did could use the kind words and sensitivity you could bring to their life.
- Give an unexpected love gift to your spouse.
- Show up for a blood drive and give the gift of blood to a person you will never meet—even if you are terrified of needles.
- Slow down on your high school campus long enough to notice that new kid whom everybody is walking right past. It could be a warm smile and an invitation for him or her to sit with you at lunch.
- Become part of the calling team at church and commit to visit the shut-ins, who can't gather for worship with the community of God's people.
- Offer to help a neighbor who just had a baby and doesn't have a church family to help through the transition time.

Whatever the first step might be, God wants us to take it. Then, he invites us to a whole lifetime of taking steps that express his tender love and mercy.

PAUSE FOR PRAYER

May God's Will Be Done

In the Lord's Prayer Jesus teaches his followers to pray:

"... your kingdom come,
your will be done
on earth as it is in heaven."
(Matthew 6:10)

Followers of Christ often pray for God's will to be done. Micah helps us see what such a lifestyle will look like. His will is done when we do justice, love mercy, and walk humbly with God. Close by praying for these three things to become realities in the lives of all who follow Jesus.

NARRATIVE ON THE TEXT | *A Fine Line*

The final phrase of Micah in Micah 6:8 is to "walk humbly with your God." It is hard to be a prophet and not get a little self-righteous. There is an important theological distinction between being a prophet and being a jerk. As we study the Old Testament, we discover that what burns most deeply in the heart of a true prophet is not anger; it is love. That is because the prophets' hearts beat with the heart of God, and his heart beats with love. The prophets always remember that they too are sinful people. They too need the grace of God. They have to live with humility, even as they call people to beware of their pride and to be humble before God.

SIGNIFICANT SCRIPTURE

Micah 7:16–19

NARRATIVE ON THE TEXT | *God's Grace*

At the close of the book of Micah, we see the grace of God come shining through. Micah declares who God is and unveils the loving heart of the Father:

> Who is a God like you,
> who pardons sin and forgives the transgression
> of the remnant of his inheritance?
> You do not stay angry forever
> but delight to show mercy.

You will again have compassion on us;
you will tread our sins underfoot
and hurl all our iniquities into the depths of the sea.

NEW TESTAMENT CONNECTION | *The Call to Humility*

All through the Bible, followers of Christ are called to live humbly. In most cases, there is also a warning about the danger of pride. This theme is strong and clear in the New Testament:

> All of you, clothe yourselves with humility toward one another, because,
>
> "God opposes the proud
> but gives grace to the humble."
>
> Humble yourselves, therefore, under God's mighty hand, that he may lift you up in due time. Cast all your anxiety on him because he cares for you. (1 Peter 5:5 – 7)

But he gives us more grace. That is why Scripture says:

> "God opposes the proud
> but gives grace to the humble."
>
> Submit yourselves, then, to God. Resist the devil, and he will flee from you. Come near to God and he will come near to you.... Humble yourselves before the Lord, and he will lift you up. (James 4:6 – 10)

Be completely humble and gentle; be patient, bearing with one another in love. (Ephesians 4:2)

Message 31

Jeremiah: When God Gives a Hard Assignment

Jeremiah 1 – 37; Lamentations 3:21 – 26

THE HEART OF THE Message

Some people teach that following God leads to a safe, painless life. They tell us that if we are faithful to God's call, we will have protection from suffering and things will go our way. These folks have never met a prophet named Jeremiah.

Jeremiah lived with a heart that was humbly yielded to God. He heard the voice of the Father call him to proclaim the word of the Lord, and he lived with a tenacious obedience to this calling. But his faithfulness was met with resistance. His preaching was discarded and ignored. As he humbly followed God, he was mocked, rejected, beaten, imprisoned, and left to rot in a hole in the ground.

In the life of Jeremiah we learn that sometimes God calls his children to a hard assignment. Our responsibility is to follow, even through pain and tears.

BRIEF MESSAGE OUTLINE

1. The beginning of Jeremiah's ministry – a strong start
2. Jeremiah faces reality – pain sets in
3. Jeremiah's enduring spirit – hanging in there
4. A word for those who don't walk Jeremiah's road – seek balance

THE HEART OF THE Messenger

Every follower of Christ will experience moments of struggle and pain. We can be right in the center of God's will knowing it is the right place to be, but it may be a hard place. Take time to reflect on your past. How have you experienced God's presence, care, and strength revealed in the midst of a hard time? When have you been obedient to God's call and discovered that it was a hard place to be? You might even be in such a place right now.

Ask God to help you communicate with humble honesty. Many of those gathered will be in the midst of a painful time of their life. They may be walking the road that Jeremiah walked. Ask God to prepare your heart as you bring this sobering message that being in God's will does not always mean a painless existence. Also pray that God will use you to help people see that hard assignments can bring them closer to God more than almost anything else.

1. The Beginning of Jeremiah's Ministry – A Strong Start

SIGNIFICANT SCRIPTURE

Jeremiah 1:4 – 10, 17 – 19

NARRATIVE ON THE TEXT | *The Call of Jeremiah*

God's call to Jeremiah is loud and clear. Anyone who wonders if Jeremiah is on the right track has failed to read his story. God lets Jeremiah know that his call came from the first moment of his conception:

> "Before I formed you in the womb I knew you,
> before you were born I set you apart;
> I appointed you as a prophet to the nations." (Jeremiah 1:5)

Jeremiah, like many of us, feels as if he is not up to the task. He has a healthy understanding of his own frailness and wonders if he can fulfill God's plan for his life. He cries out, "Ah, Sovereign LORD. . . . I do not know how to speak; I am only a child" (Jeremiah 1:6).

God reassures Jeremiah and lets him know that his abilities and strength are not the primary issue. His job is to follow God's leading and speak the words God has called him to proclaim. God says to Jeremiah: "Do not say, 'I am only a child.' You must go to everyone I send you to and say whatever I command you. Do not be afraid of them, for I am with you and will rescue you" (Jeremiah 1:7 – 8).

Finally, God gives Jeremiah a hint of what lies ahead in his ministry. When we read these words, we get a sense that Jeremiah is not heading out on a journey that will be smooth and easy. God tells him:

> "Get yourself ready! Stand up and say to them whatever I command you. Do not be terrified by them, or I will terrify you before them. Today I have made you a fortified city, an iron pillar and a bronze wall to stand against the whole land — against the kings of Judah, its officials, its priests and the people of the land. They will fight against you but will not overcome you, for I am with you and will rescue you." (Jeremiah 1:17 – 19)

NARRATIVE ON LIFE | *And They're Off!*

When we move into Jeremiah 2 and the chapters that follow, we watch him bolt from the starting blocks. He starts the race with passion and intensity. He is a young man, full of energy and optimism. He loves having a mission and a purpose for his life. Every indication is that Jeremiah leaves the gate running full speed ahead!

We can almost hear him saying to himself, "I'm going to speak the words of God to whoever he tells me to speak them to. No matter how much it costs me, I will fulfill my calling." Jeremiah is deeply committed to the call God has placed on his life. He is ready to run the race with all the strength he has.

SIGNIFICANT SCRIPTURE

Jeremiah 2–19

Most followers of Christ can point back to some point in their spiritual life where they felt as Jeremiah at the start of his ministry. There was a time when God got hold of us and gave us a mission—a calling. It may have been during a camp experience as a young person. We felt God's call and said, "Wherever you lead, I will follow." Maybe it happened in a church service where the Holy Spirit spoke in power and we said, "Take my life; it is yours—100 percent!" Maybe it was in a quiet moment of personal devotional study. We opened the Word and God spoke in a clear way. We were moved to say, "From this day on, I will serve you and use my gifts to further the work of your kingdom."

At some point along the way in our journey of faith we had a clear sense that the transcendent God was inviting us into his grand redemptive drama. We realized that God was orchestrating our involvement in plans for redeeming our fallen world. Like Jeremiah, we were overwhelmed that God would call us. But we were willing to say "Yes."

With deep conviction and commitment we charged out of the starting blocks to run the race that God set before us. We purposed in our hearts to run hard and to run fast. We committed ourselves to run faithfully all the way to the end and to run for the glory of the One whose name we bear.

SIGNIFICANT SCRIPTURE

Jeremiah 20–37

2. Jeremiah Faces Reality – Pain Sets In

NARRATIVE ON THE TEXT | *A Tough Start*

From Jeremiah 2 through 19, the prophet is speaking the words of God. He is being faithful. He's doing the work. Sadly, the people don't respond the way Jeremiah hopes. The people are not responsive to any of his messages. They are clearly resistant. Like any communicator, Jeremiah longs that people will hear, be touched, and respond. But it seems as if Jeremiah's words are hitting deaf ears and hard hearts.

So, in chapter 19, God calls Jeremiah to turn up the heat. He gives him an illustration, a picture to help the people get the point.

> This is what the LORD says: "Go and buy a clay jar from a potter. Take along some of the elders of the people and of the priests … and say, 'Hear the word of the LORD, O kings of Judah and people of Jerusalem. This is what the LORD Almighty, the God of Israel, says: Listen! I am going to bring a disaster on this place that will make the ears of everyone who hears of it tingle. For they have forsaken me and made this a place of foreign gods; they have burned sacrifices in it to gods that neither they nor their fathers nor the kings of Judah ever knew, and they have filled this place with the blood of the innocent.…'

> "Then break the jar while those who go with you are watching, and say to them, 'This is what the LORD Almighty says: I will smash this nation and this city just as this potter's jar is smashed and cannot be repaired. They will bury the dead in Topheth until there is no more room.'" (Jeremiah 19:1 – 4, 10 – 11)

CREATIVE VIDEO ELEMENT

When God Gives a Hard Assignment (4:30 min.)
This interview helps illustrate Jeremiah's life as we see how someone continues to follow God's call even though the assignment is hard.

Jeremiah buys a jar, under the direction of God, and uses it to show the people of Judah what is coming if they do not repent and turn from their wicked ways. He stands in front of all the leaders of the nation of Judah and says, "I'm telling you one last time, 'Humble yourself before God. Stop worshiping foreign gods. Reduce your pride. Open your hearts to his leading and prompting.' And if you don't, watch closely now!" Then Jeremiah smashes the jar.

NARRATIVE ON THE TEXT | *A Bad Day in Ministry*

We don't have to wait long to discover how people feel about Jeremiah's preaching and his "broken jar" illustration. In Jeremiah 20:1 – 2 we read, "When the priest ... heard Jeremiah prophesying these things, he had Jeremiah the prophet beaten and put in the stocks at the Upper Gate of Benjamin at the LORD's temple." He is left there, right by the temple for everyone to see and mock. He is not released until the next morning. It is safe to say that his ministry is not well received.

This is a very bad day in Jeremiah's ministry. It's one thing when your ministry doesn't go along very well — people aren't responsive, there aren't breakthroughs, and there aren't miraculous answers to prayer. It is entirely another thing when you take a physical beating and face public shame just for doing what God has called you to do.

CREATIVE MESSAGE IDEA | *A Shattered Jar*

God is seeking to communicate, through Jeremiah, that the people are in a dangerous place. If you read Jeremiah 19:1 – 15 closely, you will discover that their sins have become so detestable that God is saying, "It is decision time. It's now or never!" The jar becomes a picture of a level of brokenness that cannot be repaired.

The look and sound of the jar being smashed would have shocked the people of Judah. To help create the same kind of feeling, find a large clay pot and have it displayed prominently as people are entering for worship. While you are talking about a clay jar, hold it in your hands. People will begin wondering if you are actually going to smash it.

When you talk about Jeremiah smashing the jar, drop it, or hit it with a hammer. Let the sight and sound sink in before you say anything. Then talk about how this would have made the people of Judah feel. Jeremiah is clear that the jar represents their nation. He smashes it and tells them that this is the future of Judah if things do not change. Imagine how they feel toward him at that moment.

Jeremiah never thought this would happen to him. God promised: "I will be with you. I will protect you. I will rescue you." But Jeremiah doesn't feel the presence of God at this moment. He feels abandoned. He has been beaten mercilessly and then is spread out and put in the stocks for the night. Can you imagine what is going through the prophet's mind as the night wears on, his wounds bleed, his body aches, and the people continue to taunt him?

NARRATIVE ON LIFE | *There Will Be Hard Days*

Like Jeremiah, all who follow Jesus and seek to obey his calling will discover that there are hard days along the way. Some may face only a few days of pain, sorrow, and rejection related to their commitment to follow the Savior. Others may experience far more times of rejection and sorrow. But for all who hear the call and follow, there will be hard times to face.

Many of us start out strong and run the race with excitement. Then, with time, we discover that ministry has its own particular demands, people are not always appreciative, and the seeds we sow don't always spring up into a harvest overnight. We learn that patience and long-suffering are part of doing God's will in this world. With time, we hit a point where we have to decide to keep running the race, even when it gets hard.

NARRATIVE ON THE TEXT | *Commitment through the Pain*

Jeremiah is not afraid to tell God how he feels about all he is facing. He feels tricked, deceived, discouraged, and beaten up. We look at Jeremiah, and the fresh-faced young buck who ran so hard at the start of his ministry appears ragged and tired:

> "O Lord, you deceived me, and I was deceived;
> you overpowered me and prevailed.
> I am ridiculed all day long;
> everyone mocks me.
> Whenever I speak, I cry out
> proclaiming violence and destruction.
> So the word of the Lord has brought me
> insult and reproach all day long." (Jeremiah 20:7–8)

NEW TESTAMENT CONNECTION

Paul's Words to His Friend Timothy

The apostle Paul wrote to his good friend Timothy. Timothy was a young pastor who had started out strong and excited but had become somewhat disillusioned along the way. Some people did not respect him because he was young. Others just outright resisted his ministry. But in the midst of it all, Paul reminded Timothy of the lesson Jeremiah had learned so many years before:

> "You, however, know all about my teaching, my way of life, my purpose, faith, *patience*, love, *endurance*, *persecutions*, *sufferings*—what kinds of things happened to me in Antioch, Iconium and Lystra, the *persecutions I endured*. Yet the Lord rescued me from all of them. In fact, *everyone who wants to live a godly life in Christ Jesus will be persecuted*." (2 Timothy 3:10–12, italics added)

Yet, from the depths of his pain and sorrow, Jeremiah's heart shows through. Although he has been beaten, rejected, mocked, scorned, and openly humiliated, he is still ready to follow the God who formed him in his mother's womb and called him from his childhood. In the midst of unspeakable rejection and back-breaking discouragement, Jeremiah cries out:

> "But if I say, 'I will not mention him
> or speak any more in his name,'
> his word is in my heart like a fire,
> a fire shut up in my bones.
> I am weary of holding it in;
> indeed, I cannot." (Jeremiah 20:9)

In other words, Jeremiah says, "Even if I wanted to stop speaking for God, I can't! His truth is like a fire burning in my soul. I must speak for God! I must do my ministry. I will press on." What an example of tenacious faithfulness in the furnace of life.

> Be not miserable about what may happen tomorrow. The same everlasting Father, who cares for you today, will care for you tomorrow and every day. Either he will shield you from suffering or he will give you unfailing strength to bear it.
>
> *Francis de Sales*

NARRATIVE ON THE TEXT | *When Things Go from Bad to Worse*

As we read Jeremiah 20 – 37, we see the faithful prophet going out and speaking God's words again and again. The fire that burns in him propels him through beatings, rejection, and discouragement out into ministry again. We may find ourselves hoping that this time the people will respond. Maybe they will see Jeremiah's cour-

ON THE LIGHTER SIDE | *Shocking Irony*

One day, Jeremiah is brought from the filth of the dungeon to the king's palace. He faces Zedekiah, king of Judah, and is asked one question. It is almost humorous, in light of all Jeremiah has gone through. The king asks him, "Is there any word from the LORD?"

Jeremiah must have stood there in shock. He has been speaking God's word for years now. He has been proclaiming it over and over. But no one has wanted to hear it. Now the king wants a private meeting with the least popular man in all of Jerusalem. The king wants to know if Jeremiah has a word from God.

Zedekiah is certainly looking for good news, something encouraging. But Jeremiah waits on the Lord, hears him speak, and passes the message on to the king. Here it is: "You will be handed over to the king of Babylon" (Jeremiah 37:17). Jeremiah may have hoped that he could give one piece of good news at this moment. But God calls Jeremiah to inform the king that he will be handed over to the ruler of the nation they fear the most. What a shocking irony!

age and listen to the words God is speaking through him. Maybe this time they will get the message. Maybe the lesson of the broken clay jar will sink in and they will respond.

> Nothing is really lost by a life of sacrifice; everything is lost by a failure to obey God's call.
>
> *Henry Parry Lidden*

Sadly, the exact opposite happens. Jeremiah is beaten again and is then thrown into a dungeon for a long time (Jeremiah 37:15–16). This ministry to which God has called Jeremiah is hard and getting harder. Jeremiah cannot figure out why things are turning out this way. This is not what he signed up for. This is not how he thought it was going to turn out. He actually comes to the point that he feels if he stays imprisoned, he will die (Jeremiah 37:20).

NARRATIVE ON THE TEXT | *Things Can't Get Any Worse, Can They?*

Jeremiah, remarkably, continues to speak the words of God after two beatings, being put in stocks, and being thrown in a dungeon. In response to his continued ministry and preaching, Jeremiah is thrown into a cistern. We read that he is lowered with a rope into a cistern filled with mud and that his enemies are going to leave him there until he dies (Jeremiah 38:7–9).

Later, Jeremiah's friends find out that he's been put in that cistern and bargain for his release. With time, they are able to pull him out with ropes, clean him up, and set him free. Take a wild guess at what Jeremiah does when he is released from his death sentence in the cistern. He goes out yet again and declares the words of God to the people who have resisted and rejected him!

HISTORICAL CONTEXT | *A Little Information about Cisterns*

In ancient days in Israel, water was life. This was a desert land with little water available. If a home or city ran out of water, it was a major crisis. Thus, the people built cisterns. These were different from wells. Wells were a natural source of underground water. Cisterns were a man-made means of catching and saving rainwater.

When a storm came, the rains would fall hard and then wash away or be assimilated into the ground. The people discovered that they could dig down and make large cisterns to capture the water and keep it for long periods of time.

When cisterns were abandoned, they were smelly, awful places, teeming with insects and leeches and often dead animals. They could become a breeding place for all kinds of disease. We don't know the exact condition of the cistern Jeremiah was lowered into, but we can be sure it was not a pleasant place.

3. Jeremiah's Enduring Spirit – Hanging in There

NARRATIVE ON LIFE | *Forty Years Down the Drain?*

Jeremiah's relentless preaching seems to make no impact on the people of Judah. They refuse to listen to his warnings, and just as Jeremiah prophesied, the Babylonian army comes and conquers Jerusalem. They destroy the city, break down the walls, and desecrate the temple. The people of Judah are taken into captivity, as prisoners of war, to Babylon.

Shortly after the fall of Jerusalem, Jeremiah realizes that what he has spent the last forty years of his life trying to avert has just happened. He could have looked at all he suffered—the humiliations, beatings, intimidation, prison time, and the whole cistern ordeal—and feel as if it is all for nothing. He also could have looked at all the hours of preaching, waiting on the Lord, and interacting with the nation of Judah as a waste.

In the same way, we can get discouraged when we try to accomplish God's purposes and face resistance. We can feel as if our devotion and faithfulness have yielded nothing. We can look back and think that all our prayers, effort, and ministry have made no difference at all.

But, like Jeremiah, we must learn that God does not measure success the same way we do. Our faithfulness in following his leading matters to God, even if we don't see the fruit of our work. We also need to have confidence that God sees the impact of our lives with a wide-angle lens. God saw the impact of Jeremiah's life in his day, and he sees the impact Jeremiah is still having today! Jeremiah could not see the big picture. In the same way, we can trust that God will use our ministry even when we cannot see the results immediately.

LIFE APPLICATION | *A Time to Weep*

In the book of Ecclesiastes we are told that there is a time for everything. The writer says, among other things, that there is:

> a time to weep and a time to laugh,
> a time to mourn and a time to dance. (Ecclesiastes 3:4)

HISTORICAL CONTEXT | *The Birthplace of Lamentations*

When you know the story of Jeremiah, you begin to understand why he has been nicknamed "The Weeping Prophet." Later in his life, after the fall of Jerusalem, Jeremiah writes the book of Lamentations. This book is a reflection on how God feels about what happened to Jerusalem and his people. It also seems to express the heart of Jeremiah, the man who did all he could to call the people to a place of repentance so that they would not have to face the invasion of Babylon and the destruction of the holy city.

Jeremiah learns that tears are often appropriate. In particular, when the heart of God is broken, our hearts should break as well. When we see people who resist God and run from his grace, we should be sad, even as God is sad. When we see sin in our lives, tears are appropriate — and these tears should lead to change! Jeremiah teaches us that there are times when tears and mourning are the right response.

Those who have received a difficult assignment from God need to pull up a chair at the feet of Jeremiah. From the vantage point of the casual observer, Jeremiah's whole ministry can look like a total bust. He preached his heart out for four decades, and nobody ever responded. He warned, pleaded, prayed, and smashed jars, and no one repented. Jeremiah's ministry never went the way he envisioned. Yet he wept, looked back to God, and continued on.

INTERPRETIVE INSIGHT | *Messy Prayer*

SIGNIFICANT SCRIPTURE

Jeremiah 20

Jeremiah is disillusioned, frustrated, and angry. He doesn't know what to do with all of his disillusionment. Like the rest of us, he is certainly tempted to stuff it down inside and ignore it. He may have been tempted to put on a happy face, pretend it doesn't bother him, or even quit. Rather than these more common responses, Jeremiah does something few God-fearing people have the courage to do: he spills his guts out to God.

In the midst of his pain, Jeremiah lifts up one of the messiest prayers recorded in all of Scripture. We looked at the basic content of this prayer earlier, but now we need to dig into the heart of it.

- *Jeremiah accuses God of tricking him.* He says, "You deceived me" (Jeremiah 20:7). The root word here means that Jeremiah feels seduced under false pretenses. He is saying to God, "You pulled a bait-and-switch. You indicated to me that my ministry was going to be exciting, that you were going to accompany me on this adventure, and that you were going to protect me. That's not the way it's turning out." Jeremiah pours out honest frustration.
- *Jeremiah tells God that his life and ministry don't make sense.* He says, "I've had it about up to here with speaking your words and getting no results. The end result that I see is only more negative responses from people" (Jeremiah 20:7 – 8).
- *Jeremiah curses the day he was born* (Jeremiah 20:14 – 15). Just as Job did many years before, Jeremiah curses the fact that he was even born. He's saying, "I hate my birthday!" He even goes so far as to say, "I not only hate my birthday, I hate the guy who burst out of the room with cigars saying, 'It's a boy!' I don't like him either."

This is a sloppy prayer. This is the kind of prayer that few people have the courage to pray before a holy God. But Jeremiah lifts it up, and note that it has been recorded in Scripture for our sake. God is not afraid of our honesty. He can handle authentic

NEW TESTAMENT CONNECTION

Hang in There

The apostle Paul addresses the reality of facing suffering and hanging in there. He puts it this way:

> But we have this treasure in jars of clay to show that this all-surpassing power is from God and not from us. We are hard pressed on every side, but not crushed; perplexed, but not in despair; persecuted, but not abandoned; struck down, but not destroyed. We always carry around in our body the death of Jesus, so that the life of Jesus may also be revealed in our body. (2 Corinthians 4:7–10)

prayers lifted from the depth of our pain. As a matter of fact, he welcomes these prayers.

ILLUSTRATION | *The Stories of Ordinary People*

Jeremiah does what all of us can do. He hangs in there! He is bruised, battered, and discouraged, but he keeps his eyes on God. He expresses his sorrow and confusion, but he keeps on preaching. He is knocked down, but he gets up again.

Ordinary people can stand strong, even when it hurts. If you were to talk with a dozen followers of Christ who have stood fast during a hard time, through tears and suffering, you would find a common theme. Each one would tell you that they are glad they hung in there. They are thankful that they did not throw in the towel and quit. In the same way, if you ask those who have faced hard times in their faith and have caved in to pressure, they would tell you how much they regret it.

If you have stories of people you know, even members of your church, who have stood strong through hard times, you may want to tell their story—or perhaps better, let them tell their own story.

INTERPRETIVE INSIGHT | *Hope in the Midst of Pain*

Jeremiah teaches us another lesson as we look at his life. In his prayer recorded in chapter 20, he expresses deep pain and frustration. Yet, right in the middle of his prayer, we are surprised with these words:

> Sing to the Lord!
> Give praise to the Lord!
> He rescues the life of the needy
> from the hands of the wicked. (Jeremiah 20:13)

Where do these words come from? Jeremiah is experiencing the worst time of his life. He is pouring his heart out in a messy prayer, yet he starts praising God. What's up with that?

If we recall Jeremiah's call, we can hear God's promise expressed again. God had said to Jeremiah: "You must go to everyone I send you to and say whatever I command you. Do not be afraid of them, for I am with you and will rescue you" (Jeremiah 1:7–8). It seems as if Jeremiah is starting to understand that God has been with him, even in the hard times. We can almost hear Jeremiah say, "I guess God does rescue the life of the needy from the hands of the wicked." Jeremiah is saying, "I guess he has been with me. I'm still breathing. I'm still alive. I haven't been killed. Maybe it could have been worse." We get the sense that Jeremiah looks up from his pain and realizes that God has been with him. As a result, he lifts up words of praise.

INTERPRETIVE INSIGHT | *Guarding Your Spirit*

It's one thing to stay faithful to a hard assignment. It's another thing to stay sweet-spirited. When we are facing painful times, it is easy to become bitter and hard-hearted. Jeremiah is able to maintain a soft heart, even in hard times. After forty years of faithfulness, with no fruit to show for his efforts, he writes the book of Lamentations. He has warned the people for four decades, and now they are in exile. Jerusalem has been conquered, and the people are prisoners of war. Nevertheless, we hear Jeremiah lift up these words:

SIGNIFICANT SCRIPTURE

Lamentations 3:21–26

> "Yet this I call to mind
> and therefore I have hope:
> Because of the Lord's great love we are not consumed,
> for his compassions never fail.
> They are new every morning;
> great is your faithfulness." (Lamentations 3:21–23)

Jeremiah's heart is still sensitive to God. He still sees beauty; he still sees grace. He still feels the tender hand of God. And he says, "Great is *your* faithfulness to *me*." It is one thing to see the grace and power of God when things are going well. But when a person has spent decades facing pain and struggle and that person can still celebrate the faithfulness and compassion of God, he or she is a true hero of faith.

NARRATIVE ON LIFE | *Thankful for the Harvest*

Jesus talks about how different people will see different harvests for the ministry they do. Some will see a harvest that is a hundred times what was sown, others a harvest that is sixty times, and others a harvest that is thirty times. We will never know why some people do their ministry and seem to have amazing harvests and others are just as faithful and they see very little results. This side of heaven we won't understand why. But what we can all do is enter into the joy of thankfulness whenever we see God bringing in a harvest.

All followers of Jesus should celebrate when they hear about a church where God is on the move. We should be thankful when ministries are growing and expanding. There is no room in the heart of a Christ-follower for petty competition with other churches or believers. The harvest God brings in is for his glory, and we need to be thankful for the harvest, even if it is happening across town or the world.

NARRATIVE ON LIFE | *Ministry Even When It's Tough*

There are some ministries that are especially challenging. These places of service demand a certain kind of person. Often, those who serve in these ministries do so

PAUSE FOR REFLECTION

Self-Examination Time

Some of those listening to this message will be feeling discouraged because they have made a terrible mistake somewhere along the way and quit on God's calling for their life. They need to be reminded that God's grace is big enough for them. They can make this moment a turning point.

Remind those gathered that God will graciously forgive them for any way they have failed to follow his plan for their life. Invite them to grab hold of the calling they once heard and to get back into the game. Assure them that the greatest joy they will ever know in the Christian life is to be rightly related to God through Jesus Christ and to be following the calling he has put on them, however painful. Allow a brief time of silence for people to reflect on their lives and to determine whether they are obeying God's call.

with little praise or affirmation. Use this time to affirm those in your ministry and community who serve in these challenging places.

In his message (found on the included DVD-ROM), Bill Hybels talks about some of the ministries connected to Willow Creek that demand an enduring and faithful spirit:

- Special Friends (ministry to the mentally and physically challenged)
- funeral ministry (ministries of compassion)
- set-up and take-down of chairs (people with the ministry of helps)
- parking attendants
- nursery caregivers
- children's ministry
- work with the homeless
- and the list goes on

Identify some of the ministries connected to your church that demand hard work and get few praises. Then take some time to bless these people and let them know that God sees, God celebrates, and God will continue to empower them.

NARRATIVE ON LIFE | *Hard Assignments Still Exist*

God expects all of his followers to be ready to take hard assignments and to be faithful all the way to the end. In his message (found on the included DVD-ROM), Bill Hybels tells stories of churches in Belfast, Northern Ireland, and the Dominican Republic. These places face challenges that most congregations can't even dream of. You may want to use these stories, or you may use stories of your own about churches that are staying faithful in situations that seem hopeless. Their example of steadfastness can call us to live with greater faith and commitment to God, even when hard times come.

LIFE APPLICATION | *Take Heart and Stand Strong*

God has his reasons for giving certain people hard assignments. He doesn't do it capriciously. He doesn't do it in a cavalier fashion. He figures out who has strong shoulders and a steadfast heart, and he calls them to this needed ministry. He figures out who has the strength that is needed and then entrusts them with a hard assignment. When he does, he still says, "I will be with you and will help you."

> It isn't what you wish to do, it's what you will do for God that transforms your life.
>
> *Henrietta C. Mears*

If we are chosen for a hard assignment, we must remember that we are not the first to face this. Many Jeremiahs have gone before us. The Son of God is the ultimate example of someone who took a hard assignment given by the Father. It was painful, but he did it willingly.

If you find yourself walking the same path that has been traveled by Jeremiah, Jesus, and many others, stand strong. Pray a messy prayer. Share your grief with God. But don't bail out! Stay the course and know that one day you are going to meet the One who had the hardest assignment of all, and he finished it for your sake. Then, he will take your hand in his nail-scarred hands and bring you home. On that day, it will all be worth it.

PAUSE FOR PRAYER

Meet Us Where We Are

Pray for people right where they are. Some possible prayer directions are:

- For those who are standing strong as they complete a hard assignment, lift up prayer for strength and for a sense of God's pleasure over their faithfulness.
- For those who have bailed out and are not fulfilling God's call, pray for grace and a renewed commitment to get back in the game.
- For those who are in a time of joy-filled harvest in ministry, pray to keep balance in their lives and for continued fruitful ministry.

4. A Word for Those Who Don't Walk Jeremiah's Road – Seek Balance

NARRATIVE ON LIFE | *A Word to Those Who Are Seeing a Harvest*

Just as most followers of Christ will have times when they experience what it feels like to have a hard assignment, we will also have times when we see great results in ministry. There will be times when the harvest is coming in, God is moving in visible ways, and joy is flowing freely. In these times we need to give praise to God, but we must also be careful to maintain balance in our lives.

When we get an exciting, adrenaline-producing assignment, we need to be sure we don't let it push us out of balance. Ministry can become an addiction and wreck our lives if we let it get out of control. The key is to thank God for the work he is doing and enter into the ministry with all our strength, but be sure that we still take walks with a spouse, play with our kids, hang out with friends, have time for an occasional nap, and make space to be with God one-on-one.

PAUSE FOR PRAYER

A Prayer for Those with Tough Assignments

Pause and take time to pray for those who are walking the road of Jeremiah. Pray for strength to stand strong. Pray also for them to have eyes to see that God is with them, even when the road is hard.

LIFE APPLICATION | *Slowing and Growing Your Soul*

There is an inverse relationship between speed and the care of your soul. We can't nurture our souls and go deeper when our hair is on fire and we are living life with the speedometer pegged in the red. No one admires the scenery along the Autobahn when they are in the passing lane, shifting into fifth gear and driving 125 miles per hour.

No matter how much fruit we are seeing grow in our lives and ministries, we still need to take time to slow down and grow our soul.

CREATIVE MESSAGE IDEA

I Have Decided

You may want to close your message with the singing of the great hymn, "I Have Decided to Follow Jesus."

This means we must develop a discipline of pulling away from the crowd and the busyness of life and make space to meet with God. We need to pray, listen to God, and feed on his Word. Maybe we need to start keeping a journal of prayers and personal reflections. No matter what we do in this time, we need to be consistent and intentional about unplugging on a regular basis and growing our soul.

Message 32

The Life-Giving Power of Hope

2 Kings 25:1 – 12; Ezra 1:1 – 4; Jeremiah 29:1 – 23

THE HEART OF THE Message

The term "hitting bottom" has become popularized when speaking of individuals who have come to their lowest point in life (often because of addictions) and finally have nowhere to look but up. The people of Israel hit their bottom when the Babylonians invaded and the nation went into exile. Earlier in 722 BC the northern kingdom had been invaded by Assyria and was conquered. In 586 BC Jerusalem, the capital of the southern kingdom, fell. Everything seemed hopeless.

Yet, out of the ashes of judgment, hope began to arise. Even as the exiles were being sent to Babylon, a message of hope was being proclaimed. God's judgment was not just punitive, it was meant to be redemptive. God's plan was to gather a faithful remnant and restore his people, after seventy years of exile.

Since this is the final in this series of messages on the Old Testament, we will take a whirlwind review of some of the key themes found in this entire course.

THE HEART OF THE Messenger

God breathes hope. All through the Old Testament, even in the most painful and darkest moments of Israel's history, God loves and leads his people. From the harshest moments of judgment, we can hear the message of hope come through.

BRIEF MESSAGE OUTLINE

1. The life-giving power of hope
2. Celebrating central Old Testament lessons
    - Lesson 1: There is a God
    - Lesson 2: Sin leads to death
    - Lesson 3: God longs for covenant relationship with his children
    - Lesson 4: God has the power and desire to deliver his children
    - Lesson 5: God is never in a hurry; he is more concerned who we are becoming than when we get there
    - Lesson 6: God will use whom God will use
    - Lesson 7: God is holy and calls his children to grow in holiness
    - Lesson 8: The cycle of sin is vicious
    - Lesson 9: God cares for the suffering
    - Lesson 10: God's wisdom will transform our lives if we let it
    - Lesson 11: God continues to call us back to himself

WORD STUDY

Exile

Exile means forced relocation. It means you will leave your home forever. A superpower conquers a country and gives most of the population a choice: Move or die. This is how ancient superpowers made sure that people would not try to rebel and recapture their homeland. This happened to the northern kingdom in 722 BC and to the southern kingdom in 586 BC.

For nations in those days, exile was the end. Humanly speaking, the idea of coming back to their homeland after a time of exile wasn't even an option. People who went into exile knew what to expect. They would eventually blend in with the other peoples of the ancient world, and their story, their culture, their language, and their faith would all disappear.

Take time as a leader to think through your own reading of the Old Testament. How have you seen God show up among his people and bring hope? How have you experienced God's hope filling your own life over these past weeks? How has a new hope in God and love for his Word grown in the life of your congregation? As you reflect on these hope-filled moments, celebrate God's goodness and let this spirit of confidence in God's power and love guide your teaching of this final session.

Also, since you will conclude with a review of some key lessons and messages from the entire series, be sure to review what God has said to you over these past thirty-two weeks. You can be confident that God has spoken to his people in powerful ways, and the review of these lessons will propel each person forward in a desire to grow in their relationship with God and with the community he has established among his people.

1. The Life-Giving Power of Hope

ILLUSTRATION | *The Borg*

In *Star Trek, the Next Generation*, there is a powerful image that parallels this concept of exile and assimilation into another culture. It is called "The Borg." The Borg is a huge spaceship that travels from culture to culture and takes over entire planets. When the people from the planet are conquered, they are plugged into the Borg, and their minds and any sense of individuality are snuffed out. They become part of a collective mind; they are assimilated.

This picture is similar to what happened when a nation went into exile. The goal of exile was not just to relocate the people; it was to remove all sense of national pride, love for a homeland, language, culture, or anything that would cause the people to long for home. The goal was to assimilate a whole culture and make it disappear.

NARRATIVE ON LIFE | *What If It Happened to You?*

Imagine, for a moment, that you were forced to leave everything familiar. You have to leave your home and your country, and you must go live in a place that you don't know. You lose your job. You don't know the local language but are forced to learn it to survive. You don't know the customs. Everything is different.

Once you arrive as a prisoner of war in your new country, you realize that you will never have power in this place. You will never have influence. You have no resources, no wealth, and no means of attaining them. You are a stranger in a strange land. You will never belong. Your children will grow up with no connectedness to their national or religious roots except what you try to pass on to them. That's what it meant for Israel to live in exile. It looked like the end of the dream.

If this happened to us, how would we respond? Could we press on? How would our lives and our faith be challenged?

SIGNIFICANT SCRIPTURE

2 Kings 25:1 – 12

NARRATIVE ON THE TEXT | *The Beginning of the End*

In 2 Kings 25 we get a picture of how bad things got near the end of Judah's history. Babylon had become the dominant world power. Jeremiah, a prophet at that time, kept saying to people, "Exile is coming. Babylon will invade and conquer Jerusalem." But the people would not believe him. They were sure God would never let the holy city of Jerusalem fall under the sword of a foreign army.

HISTORICAL CONTEXT | *The Saddest Day in Israel's History*

We all have certain moments in our personal history that are low points. This is also true of nations. For the people of God, one of the saddest moments came in 586 BC, when Nebuchadnezzar and the armies of Babylon invaded Jerusalem and conquered it. They had come before and placed the people of Judah under their control, but they had always left the nation intact and someone on the throne. In 586 BC the Babylonians exiled the vast majority of people and destroyed the city. It was the saddest day in the history of Israel.

Earlier in 722 BC the Assyrians had conquered the northern kingdom. At that time, ten of the twelve tribes of God's people had ceased to exist. Then, in 586 BC the southern kingdom fell. This marked the end of Israel as a nation. They were no longer a united nation or a divided nation. They were no longer a political entity at all. They were dispersed among the Gentiles.

CREATIVE MESSAGE IDEA | *A Picture of Exile*

As an object lesson, have a portion of the people gathered with you for worship taken out of the place you are meeting. One or two rows of people should be enough to make the point. You will need to have ushers ready to take this group to a preassigned place. It would be ideal if those who are exiled can still see and hear the worship service while they are gone. Have someone ready to play some quiet, sad music as these people leave. Let these people know that they will be coming back, but for now they are exiled and will be escorted out.

Ask everyone who is staying to wave good-bye! Let everyone know that this should be a sad occasion.

Sadly, everything Jeremiah predicted came true. Zedekiah, one of the final kings of Judah, rebelled against the king of Babylon. As a punishment, Zedekiah's sons were murdered in front of him, and then his own eyes were gouged out so that this would be the last thing he ever saw. Nebuchadnezzar set the temple of God on fire, destroyed the palace and every important building in Jerusalem, and finally broke down the wall of the city. It was a complete and utter demolition of the capital of the nation of Judah and subjugation of all those with any political power.

Those not killed were exiled to Babylon. A handful of the poorest of the land were left to tend whatever part of the land that could be productive. Even this handful of people was under the hand of Babylon and had to pay tribute to the king.

SIGNIFICANT SCRIPTURE

Jeremiah 29:1–23

NARRATIVE ON LIFE | *The Heart of Jeremiah*

Jeremiah writes a letter to the exiles in Babylon. These are the very people he had warned year after year. They are the ones to whom he had come with God's call to repentance over and over. These are the people who had refused to listen to anything Jeremiah said.

Imagine for a moment that you are Jeremiah. You have preached the truth and your audience has turned on you. They laugh at you. They mock you. They don't believe you. They throw you into prison. They cart you off to Egypt. Then, exactly what you warned them about comes true. Now, you write a letter to the very people who mocked you all those years. What tone would your letter have? What would be the condition of your heart?

For most of us, we would be filled with anger and perhaps even righteous indignation. For Jeremiah, his heart is still tender. Although he deals with the reality of judgment and exile, he also speaks of hope and restoration, and he gives practical advice about how to live in their new land. Jeremiah shows a level of tenderness that most of us would find unthinkable in this setting.

NARRATIVE ON THE TEXT | *Praying for Babylon*

In his letter to the exiles in Babylon, Jeremiah calls them to settle in. They should try to establish a normal life there. He wants them to build homes, plant gardens, get married, have children, and establish themselves in the new land. Beyond that, Jeremiah says:

> This is what the LORD Almighty, the God of Israel, says to all those I carried into exile from Jerusalem to Babylon: "Build houses and settle down; plant gardens and eat what they produce. Marry and have sons and daughters; find wives for your sons and give your daughters in marriage, so that they too may have sons and daughters. Increase in number there; do not decrease. Also, seek the peace and prosperity of the city to which I have carried you into exile. Pray to the LORD for it, because if it prospers, you too will prosper." (Jeremiah 29:4–7)

The whole idea seems counterintuitive. Why pray for Babylon? This is the nation who has conquered them. These are the people who have destroyed Jerusalem, their holy city. Babylon is the ever-present reminder that they are strangers in a strange land. But God calls them, through the prophet Jeremiah, to pray for the prosperity of Babylon!

Again, God is concerned about his people and who they are becoming. At the beginning of this series, when we studied the desert wanderings of Israel, we learned that God cared more about who his people were becoming than he did about how long it took them to arrive in the Promised Land. Now again we see that God is shaping his people. He intends to bring them back home, but he wants them to experience growth in their seventy years of captivity. Jeremiah lets the people know that this captivity will not mean the end of their people, culture, and faith. In seventy years they will have another chance to realize God's dream of building a new community of people who love and follow him.

SIGNIFICANT SCRIPTURE

Jeremiah 29:1–23; Ezra 1:1–4

CREATIVE MESSAGE IDEA

Checking In on the Exiles

At this point, check in with your exiles. If you have the capability, project them on a screen so everyone who is gathered can see them. If you don't have the ability to do this, at least pause to remind those gathered that those who were exiled are still off somewhere else in the building.

NARRATIVE ON THE TEXT | *God's Hand in History*

By every known law of human history, the people of Israel should have ceased to exist after 586 BC. There is no way on earth the people of Israel should have survived, except for one thing: God chose that they would. God chose it.

Nebuchadnezzar died in 562 BC, and Babylon went into rapid decline. It is invaded and defeated by a new kingdom — Persia. Cyrus, the king of Persia, decided on a new way to handle exiled people. Under the hand of God, he released the people and allowed them to go back to their homeland. In Ezra 1:1–4 we read:

> In the first year of Cyrus king of Persia, in order to fulfill the word of the Lord spoken by Jeremiah, the Lord moved the heart of Cyrus king of Persia to make a proclamation throughout his realm and to put it in writing:

ON THE LIGHTER SIDE | *"I Told You So!"*

If we were in Jeremiah's shoes, what phrase do you think we might be tempted to use at the beginning of the letter to the people in exile? Jeremiah had been giving warnings for years, but they had ignored him! They had been given countless chances to repent and turn around, but they refused! Jeremiah spoke the truth again and again, only to be met with resistance, beatings, and rejection. After all of this, when judgment finally came and everything Jeremiah prophesied came to pass, what four words could Jeremiah have used to start his letter? Here is a little hint: The four words start with "I" and end with "so."

It would have been easy for Jeremiah to say, "I told you so!" But he did not.

> "This is what Cyrus king of Persia says: 'The LORD, the God of heaven, has given me all the kingdoms of the earth and he has appointed me to build a temple for him at Jerusalem in Judah. Anyone of his people among you—may his God be with him, and let him go up to Jerusalem in Judah and build the temple of the LORD, the God of Israel, the God who is in Jerusalem. And the people of any place where survivors may now be living are to provide him with silver and gold, with goods and livestock, and with freewill offerings for the temple of God in Jerusalem.'"

The behavior of Cyrus was unprecedented in the ancient world. His choice came because "the LORD moved [his] heart." What a reminder that God's hand is always active in human history. We don't know if Cyrus had any idea that God was working in his heart, but through his decisions, God spared his people and brought them home. On top of it all, Cyrus even did some fund-raising and helped gather resources so that the people of God could go back to Jerusalem and begin reconstruction of the city and the temple.

NARRATIVE ON THE TEXT | *The Years of Rebuilding*

When Israel comes home, they begin to rebuild the city. The rebuilding process takes a long time. The books of Ezra and Nehemiah cover more than a century and chronicle the rebuilding of the city, the temple, and the national and religious life of Israel.

But what gets rebuilt is not precisely what many of the people were hoping to see. Israel used to be a nation with millions of people. According to Ezra 2, only about 43,000 people come back. The city is not the grand and impressive place it was before. The temple never takes on the same majestic beauty it had in the days of Solomon. There is an excitement about being home, but there is a sense that something is missing.

All the old things the returned exiles had used to create a sense of identity are gone. They never have a son of David on a throne. They cannot govern themselves.

ON THE LIGHTER SIDE | *Some Things We Have Never Heard Of*

It is important to note that Jeremiah's promise that the people of Judah will one day be set free and return to Jerusalem would have seemed like a complete fantasy to the people. In those days, when a country was conquered and taken into captivity, they never returned. They ceased to exist as a nation. Think about all of the small countries that were once around Israel. What do you hear about them these days? How many of you have a neighbor who's a Moabite? Do you have a favorite Hittite restaurant in your neighborhood where you go occasionally to get some home-style Hittite cooking? Where was the last time you went to a concert and heard vintage music by the Three Edomite Tenors?

They have no army. The walls of Jerusalem are in shambles. They are now an obscure, tiny group of people on a small piece of land somewhere in the massive Persian empire.

NARRATIVE ON LIFE | *A New Time and a New Dream*

At one time Israel had dreams of impacting the world. Now they were a ragtag bunch of refugees who have been released from almost two generations of exile. What can they offer? What impact can they make? What difference can this tiny group of people really have?

Long ago Israel had hoped to become a superpower like Babylon or Assyria. By this time it has become painfully apparent that this dream will never happen. Israel will never see a mighty king lead them to win great battles, possess enormous wealth, and conquer new lands. These dreams are dead, and the people finally realize that these are the wrong dreams. They are foolish dreams. They aren't God's dreams for his people, and they never have been.

A few among them begin to dream a new dream. God births in them a new vision. They realize that what looks like the end could be a beginning. Maybe they can finally become a community that will be great in the sight of God. Some begin to believe and understand that the greatness God wants to birth in them is not about armies, power, wealth, or things that make them look impressive in the eyes of the world. Greatness is to be based on turning their hearts toward God and humbly following him.

From the beginning God had a dream of building a new community of people who loved him, each other, and the world. Finally, it seems as if this dream is beginning to come alive in the hearts of God's people.

NEW TESTAMENT CONNECTION

Pray for Those Who Persecute You

When God calls the people to pray for God's blessing on Babylon, this should be a familiar theme to followers of Christ. It was Jesus who said:

> "You have heard that it was said, 'Love your neighbor and hate your enemy.' But I tell you: Love your enemies and pray for those who persecute you, that you may be sons of your Father in heaven. He causes his sun to rise on the evil and the good, and sends rain on the righteous and the unrighteous." (Matthew 5:43–45)

The heart of God, in both the Old and New Testaments, beats with love. He wants us, as his children, to operate with compassion and mercy, even toward those who have wronged us.

CREATIVE MESSAGE IDEA | *Welcoming the Exiles Home*

The exiles come home after being away for decades. It is hard to imagine the emotion after such a long time lived in forced captivity. Against all odds, God acts and the exiles come home again. Imagine the joy.

At this time, invite the exiles from your congregation to come back. Play music that is joy-filled and energetic—something that fits the excitement of the moment. Use this moment to emphasize what a high point this is in the history of God's people.

INTERPRETIVE INSIGHT *"Not My Will, But Yours Be Done"*

From the very beginning of God's interaction with human beings, he was waiting for a little group of people who would be willing to form a community and say, "God, not our will but yours be done." He longed to see his followers live lives that declared, "We will die to all the stupid, foolish dreams of our lives. We will not long for and invest our lives in the pursuit of wealth, power, and success. We will long for your will, and your will alone."

The irony with Israel is that when they had a place of authority and power, they never used it to expand God's kingdom. When they had kings on the throne and military might, they seemed to become weaker and weaker. Now, with no formal government, no army, no wealth, most of their population gone, and no human authority at all, they have finally come to a place where God can use them. They are finally ready to say, "Not our will but yours be done!"

2. Celebrating Central Old Testament Lessons

With the time you have left, do a brief review of some of the key lessons learned in this series. Touch on these lessons, and other ones you feel your congregation should remember as you bring this journey to a close.

Lesson 1: There Is a God

We started our study of the Old Testament with a fundamental lesson. There is a God. God exists eternally in trinitarian fellowship as Father, Son, and Holy Spirit. Out of this community, this trinitarian joy and delight, God creates. He does not do this because he is bored or because he is lonely. God does not create us so that he will have little servants to do the chores he does not want to do. Rather, out of the magnificent richness of the eternal community experienced by the Trinity, God decides to broaden the circle. He longs to invite us to live in his love. This invitation is not for us to become little gods, but it is for us to bask in the glorious fellowship of the Trinity. God truly exists, and he invites us to enter into a relationship with him.

HISTORICAL CONTEXT *Map Time*

If you look at a map we have of the Persian empire at this time in history, you will see that it went from India all the way to Greece and from central Russia all the way down south to Libya. Within this expansive kingdom, the land now occupied by Israel was almost unnoticeable. It would have been easy for Israel to believe that they had nothing left to offer the world.

You will want to review Message 1 as you focus on the lesson about who God is and his plan for us to live in community.

Lesson 2: Sin Leads to Death

God created men and women to live in community. But when the Fall came, sin entered the picture and community died. God's plan was for community. His desire was for human beings to live in harmonious and loving relationship with him and with each other. God did his part. He made us and gave us a wonderful place to meet with him and enter into rich and life-giving relationship with each other.

Sometimes the best of plans go bad. In chapters 3–11 of Genesis we see the downward spiral of sin. In this section of the Bible we see four distinct scenes: Adam and Eve, the story of Cain and Abel, the Flood, and the Tower of Babel. As we watch the drama unfold, we see things go from bad to worse. In these scenes we see sin go deep and spread wider. We also learn from God's response to the sinful choices made by his children.

You will want to review Message 2 as you focus on the lesson about the impact of sin.

Lesson 3: God Longs for Covenant Relationship with His Children

In our study of the Old Testament we learned that God doesn't give up on his children. The primary expression of the faithful love of God is revealed in covenant. God is a covenant-making God, and he is the one who says, "I'll be with you."

NEW TESTAMENT CONNECTION

The Heart of Jesus

God wants all of his children to live with humble hearts. The more we yield to him, the more he can use us. Jesus is an example of complete humility and submission to the Father. It was Jesus who said: "My Father, if it is possible, may this cup be taken from me. Yet not as I will, but as you will" (Matthew 26:39).

As Jesus faced the cross, he affirmed his full submission to the Father by saying three times that he would not seek his own will but his Father's will. This same spirit must come alive in the lives of Christ's followers today if we are going to realize God's dream for our lives.

CREATIVE MESSAGE IDEA

Time to Celebrate

Pause at this point and take time to celebrate what God has been teaching your congregation through this series. Ask God to help you be a people that dream his dreams and experience his joy in deeper ways. Respond by doing one or more of the following:

- Sing a song that expresses praise to God for his power and presence.
- Have someone share a testimony about how their dreams and longing for life have changed as you have gone through this series.
- Lift up a prayer asking God to help you as individuals and as a group to yield yourselves fully to his dreams and plans.

In the ancient world there were two kinds of covenants. There were *bilateral* covenants between two equal partners, and there were *unilateral* covenants between a stronger and a weaker partner. The covenant between God and Abraham was clearly unilateral.

Generally speaking, in unilateral covenants, the stronger partner always had an agenda. The covenant was based on the idea that there was something the stronger partner could gain from the weaker partner. In Abraham's day, the stronger partner in a covenant was usually after water rights, land to graze his herds on, or something else that would benefit the stronger party in the agreement. Here is the key question we need to ask, "What does God get out of this relationship?" He knows the human race. He knows he will be facing heartache, ingratitude, folly, and sin. So what does he gain from this covenant? He gets someone to bless!

God gets someone on whom he can pour out all of the affection and warmth and mercy and love of his heart, even though it's going to break his heart. This is why the Old Testament writers are staggered by the fact that the God who created the heavens and the earth would choose to enter into a covenant with fallen human beings.

We also learned that God always had a sign that went with a covenant. The sign of Abraham's covenant was circumcision. This sign of the covenant was available to people who were not Hebrews. They too could be a part of the circumcised covenant people. Note that when God called Abraham to institute circumcision, Abraham obeyed that very day.

You will want to review Message 3 as you focus on the lesson about God and how he established covenant relationships with his people.

Lesson 4: God Has the Power and Desire to Deliver His Children

The people of Israel ended up in Egypt and were enslaved by Pharaoh. Out of this situation we learned another important lesson about God: He is a deliverer. He saw their oppression, came down, and called Moses to lead the people out of captivity. Moses was not excited about this assignment. He gave five objections, but God still called him. So, with trembling knees, Moses went to be part of God's delivering plan.

God did amazing things to deliver his people. He sends the many plagues, but Pharaoh remains stubborn. One of the shocking statements of Pharaoh came after the frog plague. There were frogs everywhere, but when Pharaoh asked Moses to get rid of them, Moses asked, "When do you want me to pray for God to send the frogs away?" Pharaoh's answer was almost comical: "Tomorrow. I think I can tolerate one more night with the frogs. I'd rather not have to do what God wants me to do. I think I can put it off another day."

Later God provides manna for the people. He shows that not only is he their deliverer, but he will provide for them, one day at a time. Then they come to the Jordan

River at flood stage and they learn the lesson of the first step. Sometimes God waits to act until we take a step of faith. All through this time in their history we learn that God has the power and the desire to deliver his people.

You will want to review Messages 5, 7, and 10 as you focus on the lesson about God as deliverer.

Lesson 5: God Is Never in a Hurry; He Is More Concerned Who We Are Becoming than When We Get There

There is a huge spiritual lesson in the travel plans God had for Israel: God is not in a hurry! God's primary concern is not speed. Ours usually is. But God knew that *where* the people of Israel were going was not nearly as important as *who* they were becoming. God knew that possessing a land flowing with milk and honey was not nearly as important as having a heart flowing with love, justice, courage, and faith. God's first concern was not how fast his people got to the Promised Land. His deepest concern was that they would be the right kind of people once they arrived. If it took forty years to prepare their hearts, then so be it!

You will want to review Message 7 as you focus on the lesson about God's timing.

Lesson 6: God Will Use Whom God Will Use

All through the Old Testament we discovered that God used surprising people to accomplish his purposes. God used humble midwives, Shiphrah and Puah, to protect the children of Israel. He called Gideon, Deborah, and other surprising people to lead as judges. David was the youngest in his family, but he became king. Elisha was a rich kid who gave it all up to follow Elijah and become a prophet. Amos was a farmer whom God called to preach to kings. Over and over through the Old Testament we see God using whomever he chooses to do his will.

There are examples of this lesson throughout the various messages. Choose one or two to illustrate this lesson.

Lesson 7: God Is Holy and Calls His Children to Grow in Holiness

God is perfectly holy. We are not. We are an unholy people desperately seeking a way to grow in holiness! How do impure people learn to walk in holiness? The answer is, we walk with a God who is holy, and he transforms us. First, he *makes us holy* through his cleansing power and grace. Second, he teaches us to *grow in holiness* as we learn to walk in his ways. The people of Israel learn that growing in holiness is a process that takes a lifetime. As a nation, they learn that the journey toward holiness carries over many generations and centuries.

You will want to review Messages 6 and 9, as well as the words of the prophets from Messages 25–31 as you focus on the lesson about God's holiness.

Lesson 8: The Cycle of Sin Is Vicious

There is a basic cycle that repeats itself twelve times in the book of Judges, and it shows up other places in the Old Testament. Over and over again the people of God went through this heartrending process, and it seems as if they did not have the ability to look back and learn from their past.

It began with a time of *peace*. The people experienced a time of peace and prosperity. Things were going great. People were seeking God. They held fast to God's plan.

Then came a season of *complacency* when the hearts of the people began to grow cold. They got used to the goodness of what God had given them. As their hearts grew complacent, their eyes began to wander away from the one true God and toward the idols and false gods of the nations around them.

Eventually they began to compromise and *sin* entered in. Their sinful hearts led them to wicked actions and the people entered into idolatry. They began to enter into all kinds of immorality, the same kinds of immorality as the people who lived in that land.

Sin gave birth to *pain*. Most often the people of Israel experienced pain when the nations around them came in and invaded, attacked, and conquered their land. These invading people oppressed God's people and brought untold pain and sorrow into their lives.

This oppression could last for years or even decades. When the people hit a point of brokenness, they *cried out to God*, saying, "God, save us. Help us. Get us out of this situation."

Then God sent a *judge* to deliver his people. He raised up a leader who helped them fight off their oppressors. Over time, their enemies fled and the hearts of the people turned back to God—for a time.

Their victory led to a time of *peace*. But, after a time of peace the hearts of the people became complacent again. Over and over this cycle repeated itself.

You will want to review Messages 12 and 13 as you focus on the lesson of the downward spiral of sin.

Lesson 9: God Cares for the Suffering

In the book of Job we learned how God cares about those who suffer. Job's friends said what a lot of people still say, "If you're suffering, you deserve it. If you do good things, God will reward you. If you do bad things, you suffer." God was not pleased with their theology, and he still resists those who misrepresent him with this kind of teaching.

The real question in Job is, "Will Job still love God even if he doesn't shower him with good things?" Are human beings actually capable of love, or are we just reinforcement machines responding to God because he gives us stuff? There is a magnificent statement in Job that answers this question: "Though he slay me, yet will I hope in him" (Job 13:15).

Finally, at the end of the book, God appears. God asks Job all sorts of questions. God is not trying to show Job how ignorant he is. God is reminding Job how he loves all kinds of creatures, such as the wild ox and the ostrich, even though she is a forgetful mother. God loves them all even though they don't seem to be of any strategic value. It is simply God's nature to be gratuitous and loving.

By the end of the book Job cries out, "My ears had heard of you, but now my eyes have seen you [and that's enough]" (Job 42:5). God is seen to be a being of unspeakable goodness who notices and cares for the suffering of every human being. The suffering of Job and every other person matters more to God than we can imagine.

You will want to review Message 23 as you focus on the lesson about suffering.

Lesson 10: God's Wisdom Will Transform Our Lives If We Let It

One rich area of learning came from studying Proverbs. Proverbs aren't laws, and they aren't promises; rather, there are catchy observations about the way things are most of the time.

Wisdom, which is such a key theme in the Old Testament, is not mostly about IQ; it's about the ability to make right decisions. God longs for us to grow in wisdom and flee from folly.

You will want to review Messages 21 and 22 as you focus on the lesson about wisdom.

Lesson 11: God Continues to Call Us Back to Himself

The prophets of Israel became a voice for God—a conscience—that's unparalleled in human history. It is amazing to realize that the Bible makes so much space for all these prophets who were so strongly critical of God's people and their practices. We might think they would have tossed these books out, but they did not.

Elijah confronted a king, a queen, and a nation, and God revealed his power. Elisha left everything to take on the mantle of ministry and continued to be a voice of truth in a dark time of Israel's history. Amos held out a plumb line to show the people that their lives were not straight and true. He called God's people to feed the hungry, to care for the hurting, and to extend the love of God. Isaiah spoke to a generation who practiced religion but had hearts far from God, and he called them to a new and authentic faith. Hezekiah faced fear but chose to follow God even when his eyes could not see how God could deliver him. Micah called a whole generation to justice and righteousness. And, Jeremiah, through tears, beatings, and sorrow, continued to proclaim the word of the Lord. Through each of the prophets God is calling to his people, over and over. They remind us that the arms of God are always open, when we are ready to come home again.

You will want to review Messages 25–31 as you focus on the lessons from the prophets.

Wrap-Up

These are just a handful of the lessons you may want to review as you conclude your study of the Old Testament. You may also want to close with a challenge for each person to begin a personal reading of the New Testament as a follow-up. It would be wonderful to have each person take a next step in their personal Bible study as they conclude this study.

Share Your Thoughts

With the Author: Your comments will be forwarded to the author when you send them to *zauthor@zondervan.com.*

With Zondervan: Submit your review of this book by writing to *zreview@zondervan.com.*

Free Online Resources at www.zondervan.com

Zondervan AuthorTracker: Be notified whenever your favorite authors publish new books, go on tour, or post an update about what's happening in their lives at www.zondervan.com/authortracker.

Daily Bible Verses and Devotions: Enrich your life with daily Bible verses or devotions that help you start every morning focused on God. Visit www.zondervan.com/newsletters.

Free Email Publications: Sign up for newsletters on Christian living, academic resources, church ministry, fiction, children's resources, and more. Visit www.zondervan.com/newsletters.

Zondervan Bible Search: Find and compare Bible passages in a variety of translations at www.zondervanbiblesearch.com.

Other Benefits: Register yourself to receive online benefits like coupons and special offers, or to participate in research.